ADOLESCENT DEVELOPMENT

A LIFE-SPAN PERSPECTIVE

ADOLESCENT DEVELOPMENT

A LIFE-SPAN PERSPECTIVE

RICHARD M. LERNER
GRAHAM B. SPANIER

The Pennsylvania State University

McGRAW-HILL BOOK COMPANY

New York • St. Louis • San Francisco • Auckland • Bogotá • Hamburg
Johannesburg • London • Madrid • Mexico • Montreal • New Delhi
Panama • Paris • São Paulo • Singapore • Sydney • Tokyo • Toronto

ADOLESCENT DEVELOPMENT
A Life-Span Perspective

1 2 3 4 5 6 7 8 9 0 DODO 8 9 8 7 6 5 4 3 2 1 0

This book was set in Melior by Black Dot, Inc. (ECU).
The editors were Richard R. Wright, Janis M. Yates, and James R. Belser;
the designer was Anne Canevari Green:
the production supervisor was Dominick Petrellese.
Portraits and chapter-opening illustrations were done by Cathy Gendron;
all other drawings were done by J & R Services, Inc.
Research for literary selections by Linda Gutierrez and James Spicer.
R. R. Donnelley & Sons Company was printer and binder.

Library of Congress Cataloging in Publication Data

Lerner, Richard M
  Adolescent development.

  Bibliography: p.
  Includes index.
  1. Adolescence. 2. Adolescent psychology.
I. Spanier, Graham B., joint author. II. Title.
HQ796.L38   301.43′15   79-21210
ISBN 0-07-037186-5

To Jacqueline Verdirame Lerner
and Sandra Whipple Spanier

CONTENTS

Texts on adolescence tend to fall into three more-or-less distinct categories. One category encompasses what might be called "avant garde" approaches. These are usually compilations of literary and impressionistic writings that provide an immediate and sentient sense of the adolescent experience. On the other hand, books in this category tend to be light on the scientific literature on adolescence. They leave the reader with the taste of adolescence but not with the recipe. They provide an empathic understanding of adolescence but leave one wishing for more factual information.

A second category of adolescent texts is at the other extreme. Books in this group are avowedly scientific. Whatever is said about adolescence is said cautiously and is supported with abundant references to the literature. Since a good deal of the research on adolescence is far from consistent, a cautious approach involves considerable fence sitting. The experience of reading one of these texts is the opposite of reading an avant garde tome. One has all the recipes and the ingredients, but somehow the finished product, the actual dish, never appears. We have the conception, not the taste, of adolescence.

A third group of adolescent texts tries to take a somewhat middle ground, to provide both recipe and taste. While they pay their respects to research, they are willing to take chances, to take positions, and to give some literary impressions as well. To my mind, the present text fits within the third category and is one of the best examples I know of that genre. It is faithful to the known facts of adolescence, but it also provides, particularly in the splendid "insights," the taste of adolescence. These vignettes give one intense glimpses of the feelings and thoughts of young people as they struggle to maturity.

This book has much else going for it. First of all, the authors view adolescence broadly and place it in the flow of the entire life cycle as well as in a social, cultural, political, and historical context. And it is a delight to see topics, such as education and socialization, incorporated throughout the book rather than isolated into separate chapters. Presented in this way, education and socialization are seen as important to all aspects of adolescent life.

Adolescence as a discipline is still underresearched compared to its brethern, infancy and childhood. But adolescent psychology is rich in theory and the work of Freud, Erikson, and Kohlberg are presented at length. Research investigations are, by and large, nicely integrated within a conceptual framework and are seldom presented as isolated studies. And, finally, the authors, while clearly sympathetic to a humanistic perspective, maintain a critical orientation and present evidence both for and against particular viewpoints.

All in all, this is a splendid text on adolescence. It is solid and up to date with respect to research; broad in its theoretical, social, and historical perspectives; well written; well organized; and abundantly illustrated. In my opinion, it provides not only the facts of this age period, but also a hearty impressionistic sense of that incredible stage in the life cycle that is adolescence.

David Elkind
Eliot-Pearson Department
of Child Study
Tufts University

PREFACE

Of life's transitions, perhaps none has generated more attention, concern, controversy, and confusion than adolescence—the transition from childhood to adulthood. This should not be surprising, since adolescence typically is characterized by some profound changes.

Rapid physical growth and maturation, the capability to reproduce, the beginnings of emancipation from parents, the initiation of work for wages, the right to vote, the development of a new class of consumers, and dozens of other significant life changes all occur during this relatively brief period. Thus, in generation after generation, adolescents become a powerful force in society. Adolescence may be a challenging time for families and a sometimes difficult part of the life cycle for adolescents themselves. This book attempts to discuss adolescents in a unique way.

Multidisciplinary. The first unique feature of this book is its multidisciplinary approach. The book is written by a psychologist and a sociologist. But our goal has been to highlight the contributions of other disciplines as well. The contributions of biology, medicine, anthropology, history, law, and education also are considered. Thus, this book would feel at home on the shelves of students of psychology, sociology, education, child or human development, or multidisciplinary programs.

Life span. Adolescence can be viewed in part as a product of child development and as a precursor to adult development. This book has a life-span approach. In other words, we have tried to present adolescence not as an isolated period of life, but rather as one important part of a continuous life cycle which is very much related to the other parts. Thus, the reader will find some background information on infancy, childhood, and adulthood with attention to how these periods are related to adolescence.

Developmental. "Development" is as much a part of the title of this book as is "adolescent." We have tried to emphasize changes that occur during adolescence, and how these changes influence events in the lives of adolescents and those who come in contact with them. We reject a narrow definition of development in favor of a more general one which refers to individual, familial, and societal changes.

Instructors will notice that our chapter titles may not always correspond to those in many other textbooks on this topic. Our plan is a product of our commitment to a multidisciplinary, life-span, developmental approach. However, it is important to know that our approach also has resulted in coverage of all the topics generally taught in courses on adolescence. For example, although there is no one special chapter on adolescents and the educational system, this topic receives much attention in Chapters 3, 11, and 14. Similarly, although there is no separate chapter on peer groups, this topic is discussed in parts of Chapters 3, 11, and 15. The adolescent and his or her social context, including the family, are considered throughout relevant parts of the book. And topics such as delinquency, drug use, cultural variations, puberty, cognitive development, and moral development are detailed as well.

This book has paid considerable attention to topics we believe are of special interest to adolescents and youth who might be readers of this book: the social context of the adolescent, physical and physiological changes during adolescence, adolescent sexuality, problems in adolescent development, the family, and social problems and social change. In addition, we have included throughout the book a number of "Insights into Adolescence"—excerpts from literature which highlight the experience of adolescents and which complement the more "academic" material the instructor expects the student to master.

This book has profited greatly from the help and advice of many. Thus, our debts are numerous, and we apologize to those whom we may have forgotten. We would like to thank several of our students for their impressive service in helping us to complete this book and the accompanying instructor's manual: Gwendolyn Sorell, Lydia Eato, Harry Olbetter, Linda Thompson, Judy Shea, Frances Hoffman, Marion Palermo, Susan Golbeck, Myra R. Block, Sandra I. Campbell, Francine J. Ceaser, Michele M. Duffy, James P. Fitzgerald, Harold Neal Goodman, John J. Miezejewski, Linda Moran, Joan H. Zeidman, Susan M. Zeidman, and Joan Speicher.

We have been fortunate to have the critical but helpful advice of several reviewers: Gerald Adams, Marc Baranowski, Henry Biller, Karen Dinsmore, Terry Faw, Joseph Fitzgerald, Rita Heberer, Patricia Self, Leighton Stamps, and J. Allen Watson. What flaws remain in the text undoubtedly were pointed out by our reviewers but were too great a challenge for the present.

Several colleagues, especially Lynn Liben, reviewed some of the more specialized material in the text, and made sure we adequately treated some controversial topics. Richard Wright, Janis Yates, and James Belser are McGraw-Hill's superb editors, to whom we are grateful. Linda Gutierrez and Jacqueline Unch helped us select the "Insights into Adolescence" which appear throughout the book. Kathie Hooven typed countless hundreds of manuscript pages, and we are most appreciative of her perseverance and excellent work.

Finally, we would like to acknowledge the willingness of other collaborators and publishers who have permitted us to incorporate from previous works some material which we found useful to include in this book.

Richard M. Lerner
Graham B. Spanier

1
ADOLESCENCE IN THE LIFE SPAN

CHAPTER

The student beginning a course on adolescence might wonder how one approaches such a complex topic. This chapter presents the attributes of the "life-span" approach, which is the one mostly used in this book. The chapter focuses on how the life-span view of human development is an especially useful framework for studying adolescence. There are other approaches to the study of adolescence, and these are also discussed in this first chapter.

THE LIFE-SPAN PERSPECTIVE
ALTERNATIVE VIEWS OF ADOLESCENCE

The Adolescent Psychological View
The Adolescent Developmental View

CHARACTERISTICS OF A LIFE-SPAN VIEW OF ADOLESCENT DEVELOPMENT

A Definition of the Life-Span View
The Multidisciplinary Emphasis

CONCEPTUAL APPROACHES TO THE STUDY OF DEVELOPMENT

World Views of Human Development
The Conflict of World Views
The Need for Multidisciplinary Research

DYNAMIC INTERACTIONS OF DEVELOPMENT

TO CONSIDER

What are the major distinctions between the life-span view, the psychological view, and the developmental view of adolescent development?

What evidence is there that change occurs across the life span?

Why do life-span developmentalists focus on changes within a person over time, as well as differences between people?

What are the descriptive, explanatory, and optimization goals of life-span developmental study?

Why is a multidisciplinary emphasis a necessary component of the life-span approach?

What are the mechanistic, organismic, and dialectic world views of human development?

How is dynamic interactionism consistent with a life-span, multidisciplinary view of adolescent development?

dolescent development is part of the circle of life. Adolescence is one of the most fascinating periods of life. It is a period of development which for some people is volatile or traumatic. Some have family problems which seem endless. Others find adolescence a time of personal and emotional stress. And still others always seem to be in a web of passion and romance. But it can also be a pretty easygoing time of life. Some persons look back on this period of life with fond memories. For most of us, it is the time when we learn what romantic love is all about, when we stop being boys and girls and start being men and women. And it is a time when our social and intellectual growth changes our lives dramatically.

What happens in adolescence, though, is in large part determined by what happened before it. Similarly, much of what happens in adulthood will depend on the adolescent years. Many books present adolescence as an isolated subject, with no concern with what came before or what will come after. This book is different.

The 13-year-old differs from the 16-year-old, and the 20-year-old differs from both. We will see that in order to understand why the 13-year-old behaves as he or she does, one has to understand developments that precede this age. One should know how events in infancy and childhood contribute to making the 13-year-old the way he or she is. Furthermore, what people do as adults does not begin at age 21. The events and developments that occur during the life period labeled "adolescence" shape and texture adulthood—the longest period of our lives.

Thus, although we are most interested in that period of life known as adolescence, in this book we will always try to keep in mind the importance of the years which precede and which follow this period. This general approach to studying human development is known as a *life-span* view.

A life-span approach to human development, and to adolescence in particular, has several characteristics. One of the most important ones is that adolescence is seen as just one part of the entire life span. Another is that the knowledge from many academic disciplines is used to study adolescence. Much of what is presented in this book is contributed by the disciplines of psychology and sociology. But information is taken also from history, biology, anthropology, law, and medicine. This is a very realistic approach to a period such as adolescence, since what happens in our lives during this time is inherently *multidisciplinary* (involving many disciplines).

THE LIFE-SPAN PERSPECTIVE

Let us begin by considering a 15-year-old girl who wants to become a psychologist "when she grows up." If she is able enough to succeed, and does not change her mind in between, the rest of her life will be affected by that decision. How many people in their twenties would agree to make a decision, one affecting their whole life, on the basis of the advice of some 15-year-old? Would you turn to a 15-year-old to decide how to spend the rest of your life? Probably not. But in effect that is what we all do.

The point is that during the adolescent period choices are made. Certain behaviors, and not others, develop. All of us, whether it is at 15, 18, or 21, make decisions and take steps that will carry us into our thirties, fifties, and probably seventies. We initiate plans on the basis of the behaviors of some 15-year-old, someone who has not done very much in his or her life. Yet we do this because the 15-year-old is us!

People change continuously throughout the period of life labeled "adolescence," but the events before adolescence contribute to adolescent changes, and in turn, the events of adolescence contribute to the rest of life. To understand adolescence, one has to see it, then, in the context of the entire life span.

However, the life-span perspective is not the only way to view adolescence. To highlight better the life-span perspective followed in this book, it will be contrasted with other approaches.

ALTERNATIVE VIEWS OF ADOLESCENCE

There are many different approaches to understanding a person at various portions of the life span. Currently, there are three major perspectives. Consistent with discussions in the psychological and developmental literatures devoted to childhood (Gollin, 1965), these approaches may be labeled the "adolescent psychological view," the "adolescent developmental view," and the "life-span view." The third view, the one to which we subscribe in this book, has been mentioned above. Let us briefly describe the others.

The adolescent psychological view

The adolescent psychological approach emphasizes how people of a particular age group perform on a specific task (Gollin, 1965). For instance, in this approach a researcher might ask how a 17-year-old performs on a learning task.

However, with this view no attention is given to how learning in childhood and early adolescence contributed to learning in middle adolescence. And there would be a corresponding lack of concern with the way learning in adolescence influenced learning in later life. Instead, in the adolescent psychological approach the main focus is on the task, and therefore there is little, if any, concern with the history of changes in the person that contributed to task performance over time.

The adolescent developmental view

This approach emphasizes the history of the person. It focuses on the relation between person and task as that relation changes across the history of the person, across the person's age levels. Thus, the adolescent developmental view is one which considers how people of different age groups perform on a given task (Gollin, 1965). This approach goes beyond a primary focus on the task. It considers the changes associated with the person over time. Thus, here there would be an interest in learning that occurs before and after adolescence.

There is a qualification, however. As with child developmental views of child behavior (as in Flavell, 1970), long-term outcomes of developments in adolescence are not typically a focus of the adolescent developmental view of adolescence (for example, Hurlock, 1973). As suggested later in this chapter, as well as at other points in the text, a major reason for this exclusion appears to be theoretical in nature. There are some who believe that the important changes that characterize development emerge sometime prior to or during adolescence. Consequently, anyone who follows such a perspective would not likely be very concerned with the period of life after adolescence.

Piaget (1970), for instance, has an important theory of the development of knowledge. However, in his theory he stresses the view that after some point in adolescence, no new components (or, in his terms, "structures") of thought develop (Piaget, 1972). Thus, although those following Piaget's ideas in their research work would certainly look at the childhood (and even the early adolescent) antecedents of adolescent cognition (knowledge), they would not especially be concerned with how adolescent cognition influences changes in adult life. This lack of concern would occur because of their theoretical view that there is no major structural change in cognition in adulthood (Flavell, 1970).

Thus, the adolescent developmental view of adolescence takes a historical view of the person. However, it is often limited in the *amount* of the person's history considered. In addition, there are other limitations with the adolescent developmental view. To see all these most clearly it will be useful to turn to a discussion of the characteristics of a life-span view of adolescence.

CHARACTERISTICS OF A LIFE-SPAN VIEW OF ADOLESCENT DEVELOPMENT

A life-span view moves beyond the limitations imposed by exclusive commitment to a single theory. A reason for rejecting looking at development from only one viewpoint is a conceptual one. Life-span developmentalists argue that theories are never true or false, but rather are derived from essentially untestable philosophies about human existence. Thus, any single theory can represent no more than just one of an infinite number of ways of looking at development. Attention to any one theory, then, is likely to exclude aspects of numerous other views of development. This key point—the relation between philosophy and scientific theory—will be examined later in the chapter. Here, however, it may be noted that there are also empirical reasons for rejecting a *singular* theoretical approach to development (and for adopting a *pluralistic* one—an orientation which stresses the use of many theoretical approaches).

There are abundant data indicating that people *do* change after adolescence, and that they change in ways that cannot readily be predicted from knowledge of their development in childhood or adolescence. In fact, research in cognitive development shows (1) that people develop well into their adult and aged years; (2) that as people develop, increasingly greater differences emerge between them; and (3) that these increasingly greater differences cannot be understood merely by knowing how people were when they were children or adolescents.

Exhibit 1.1 shows the results of a study by Schaie, Labouvie, and Buech (1973), which demonstrates these points. In this study, people who were born at different times in history were given intelligence tests when they were of different ages. Because they were born at different times, these persons were in different *birth cohorts*. A birth cohort consists of all persons born in a given year.

The changes that people went through clearly were not the same in this study. Some people's scores increased, others' scores decreased, and still others' remained the same over times of measurement. Yet it is clear that (1) people from all cohorts changed, both the young *and* the old; (2) people were more dissimilar in older cohorts than in younger ones in terms of the directions of changes they went through; and (3) it was not really age that related most to how people changed, but rather membership in a particular birth cohort. People from different cohorts are likely to have experienced different events since they developed in different historical years; and it seems that such historical differences—at least insofar as the data in Exhibit 1.1 are concerned—are related more to change than are age-related factors.

We will return in a moment to the intriguing point that history, rather than age, may be most important for understanding change. It is appropriate first to summarize

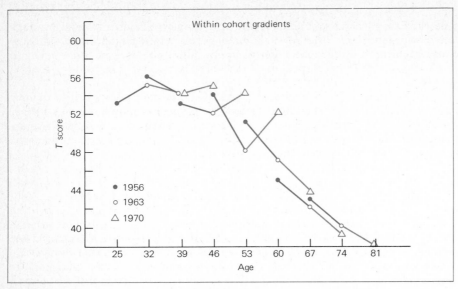

Exhibit 1.1
**Results of a study by Schaie, Labouvie, and Buech (1973): Age changes
in intellectual ability are related to the time in history in which people are
born.** (*Source:* Schaie, Labouvie, and Buech, 1973. Copyright 1973 by the
American Psychological Association. Reprinted by permission.)

a major point of difference between the life-span view and the adolescent developmental view of adolescence. Simply, in the life-span view, developmental change is
considered possible across the entire life span. As such, a complete historical
analysis of a person's change is seen as essential, and adolescent development
becomes a life-span phenomenon.

Moreover, as seen in Exhibit 1.1, life-span change may be related to more than
just age alone. People may change for many reasons, reasons other than those that are
associated with each and every person's *individual life span*. A given group of
people may develop in a certain way because they were born at a particular time in
history. Because of membership in this specific generation (or birth cohort) they
experienced certain events that were unlike those of people born in other generations. Those who went through adolescence during the Vietnam war or during the
time of the Watergate political scandals in the United States may have been
influenced by events unlike those of adolescents existing in times of peace and/or of
political stability. In fact, there is evidence (to be considered in Chapter 7) that such
"cohort effects" do influence adolescents more than do factors associated just with
age (Nesselroade & Baltes, 1974).

Additionally, events other than those associated with birth cohort can influence
adolescent development. For example, critical life events such as marriage, death of a
parent, or leaving home may be influential. Many such additional factors will be
considered in this text. All those events and variables which may influence change
across the life span are of interest. However, at this point it should be clear that the
life-span approach involves more than just consideration of change at all age levels.
In addition to considering characteristics (such as physical growth) which *may be*

common to all people, the life-span view considers influences (such as loss of both parents) which may be special to some people (or even to just one person). In short, all ways that people may change across all of life are of interest. This recognition provides the basis for defining the life-span view of human development.

A definition of the life-span view

A person's individual history is clearly a major focus in the life-span view. Such an approach means looking at how a person changes from "time 1" to "time 2." In short, one compares the person with himself or herself over time. One studies *changes within the person* over time. Such within-person changes are termed *intraindividual* changes. Thus, the life-span view is concerned with intraindividual change across the life span.

But there is more. There may be differences *between* people. These differences are called *interindividual differences*. Thus, the life-span view is concerned with interindividual differences across the life span.

Much more can be said. Baltes (1973) has noted that there are three aspects to a life-span view of development. First, the changes which characterize development must be *described*. We must be able to depict how people change. Second, the changes characterizing development must be *explained*. One must be able to show how previous or current events make behavior take the form that it does over time. Third, once development has been explained, and it is learned what variables influence it, attempts should be made to *optimize* development. One must try to prevent unhealthy development, and to foster change as helpfully as possible.

For instance, during adolescence males and females choose roles—socially defined forms of behavior—that will influence much, if not all, of their later life. As presented in later chapters, male and female adolescents typically do not enter into roles of equal status in areas such as vocational activities. Males typically enter higher-status vocations, while females traditionally enter lower-status ones (Tangri, 1972). The life-span developmentalist would be concerned with describing the patterns of role choice in adolescence, their relation to childhood role-related behavior, and their relation to consequent adult role behavior. In addition, however, the life-span developmentalist would want to explain why the antecedent (previous) and current events led people to behave as they did in adolescence, and then how such adolescent behavior shapes adult life. Moreover, the life-span developmentalist might, through his or her explanatory attempts, come up with accounts of why male and female adolescents differ in the described ways. If so, the developmentalist might next attempt to intervene into the developmental process in order to foster different role-choice behavior. The developmentalist might attempt to promote higher-status role choices in females and thus enhance, or optimize, their development.

In sum, the following definition of the life-span view of human development may be offered: *The life-span view of human development attempts to describe, explain, and optimize intraindividual change, and interindividual differences in such change, across the life span.*

This definition of the life-span view raises two issues. Both illustrate the second major aspect of this approach to development, its multidisciplinary emphasis. First, in contrasting intraindividual change with interindividual differences in such change, researchers following the life-span view must study the group as well as the individual. And to understand interindividual differences in change, researchers must compare the individual with others. Such study requires merging ideas from those disciplines that focus primarily on the individual (biology, genetics, and psychology) with those that focus primarily on the group (social psychology, sociology, and anthropology).

Second, those taking a life-span view relate change to processes in addition to variables associated with age. In order to do this they again must use ideas from many disciplines. Events associated with different birth cohorts, such as wars, politics, economic upheavels, and urbanization, may require understanding the works of historians, economists, political scientists, lawyers, and urban planners. Similarly, understanding how critical life events, such as marriage and breaking parental ties, influence personal change may necessitate integrating the ideas of family sociology with those other disciplines. The life-span nature of development suggests that the most useful route to understanding change lies along multidisciplinary paths.

The multidisciplinary emphasis

A life-span view of any particular period of development, then, involves much more than *just* considering antecedent and consequent events. To illustrate, consider a psychologist interested in studying cognitive change during the adolescent period. He or she may notice that the person moves from being concrete to being abstract in his or her thinking. But the sociologist may view adolescence as a period of change in roles and social relationships, and the economist may view adolescence as a period of transition from having few financial resources to having the potential for many. The lawyer may consider the new legal rights of the person reaching the "age of majority" (18 years of age in most of the United States) during adolescence. In turn, the physiologist and the physician may be concerned with the changing hormonal balance and muscle and fat constitution of the person before, during, and after puberty, and with the diseases or physical problems associated with such physiological and physical alterations (examples are acne and difficult or painful menstruation, known as *dysmenorrhea*). Finally, both the cultural anthropologist and the historian also would be interested in changes involved with adolescence. The cultural anthropologist might study issues relating to cross-cultural differences in the meaning, or even mere presence, of adolescence. The historian might be concerned with time-related changes in the meaning of the period of adolescence.

These examples indicate that although one may tend to think of adolescence in terms of only one discipline, such as psychology, such an orientation is limited. Said another way, the events and phenomena of adolescence involve changes along several dimensions. These dimensions range from the biological to the psychological and from the social to the historical. Consequently, to understand adolescent development adequately one should understand *all* changes and transitions involved; one should have a multidisciplinary orientation. Of course, all portions of the life-span ought to be studied this way.

A life-span approach to understanding adolescent development means more than just looking at all dimensions of change prior to, during, and after adolescence. It means considering the potentially interrelated influence of these changes. In other words, the many dimensions of change the person goes through across the life span do not necessarily occur independently. For example, one's biology may affect one's psychological and social functioning, and one's psychological and social functioning may affect one's biological functioning.

Differences in likelihood of disease and quality of nutrition, for instance, are associated both with social-class differences and with ability to perform intellectual tasks. People who are sick and/or hungry will function differently psychologically (for example, in regard to mood, attentional behavior, and cognitive behavior) than will healthy and/or well-fed people. Moreover, such biological-psychological linkages are not as likely to occur with equal probability at all levels of society. Poor children are likely to be underfed and more disease-prone. They are more likely to suffer the damaging psychological affects of illness and malnutrition than are children of the affluent. Accordingly, children suffering the negative psychological impact of poor health and low social status are not as likely to profit from educational programs necessary for higher-status roles in society as are children not suffering these negative psychological impacts.

Thus, different role behaviors in adolescence would result from the merger of biological, social, and psychological differences prior to adolescence. These adolescent differences will lead to adult-role differences, for instance in regard to status, and hence the economic return for playing one's role. These adult status and economic differences will feed back on the person's other (for example, biological, psychological) dimensions as well. People with different incomes can afford different degrees of health care and recreation time, for instance.

Moreover, although this illustration indicates that biological, social, and psychological dimensions merge across the life span, the illustration can be extended to include the cultural and historical influences that also always exist. Different cultures have different distributions of poor and affluent because of differences in economic, political, and natural resources. The contrasting distributions have implications for the importance attached in society to the relationship of biological, psychological, and social factors. A country with very few poor probably does not need to revise social institutions or functions in order to attend to problems relating nutrition and psychological functioning. However, a country with a significant number of poor people might declare a "War on Poverty" and might institute a "Project Head Start" to help prevent such problems. People in the society might also institute a "Youth Job Corps" to combat chronic adolescent and young adult underemployment among poor, undereducated, disadvantaged youth. Of course, all these latter events happened in the United States in the 1960s and 1970s.

Moreover, these changes in the United States occurred in relation to evolving economic and political events such as the civil rights movement and the 1965 Voting Rights Act. To understand even the effect of nutrition on school performance among children of a certain social class, it is useful to conceptualize all these changes as being embedded in a changing historical context.

In sum, not only do many of the biological, psychological, and social characteristics of the person come together to shape the adolescent's behavior, but also, such adolescent behavior contributes to the joint influence of biological, psychological, and sociological factors across the rest of the life span. Moreover, the nature of these interactions among all these dimensions of change is textured by the changing historical context.

In conclusion, the life-span view, with its multidisciplinary perspective about change, leads to the idea that all dimensions of change are interrelated. Changes in one dimension are related to changes in all others; change in one aspect of development provides a basis of change in all others. Furthermore, change in a given dimension (for example, biology or history) feeds back on itself; it provides a basis of its own change by changing its context, the other dimensions it is embedded within. Development thus involves a series of "feedback loops," an interrelated network of circles. In other words, the adolescent is *both a product* of his or her biological, sociological, psychological, and historical world—*and a producer* of it! This conceptualization of the nature of adolescent development is a complex one, involving a dynamic interaction among all dimensions of development across the entire life span.

CONCEPTUAL APPROACHES TO THE STUDY OF DEVELOPMENT

Conceptual tools for integrating information about development are needed. Concepts and theories from a variety of theoretical perspectives are seen as potentially useful from a life-span approach. To integrate concepts and theories from the various disciplines relevant to life-span development, several writers (for example, Baltes, 1979; Riegel, 1976a) have argued for drawing from all disciplines, and from all orientations within a discipline, those ideas and data sets which jointly may be used to aid in understanding developmental change.

Relatively recently, two trends have emerged in social science. The first deals with the relation of philosophy to science. The second, derived from the first, involves relations among the events and phenomena studied by different sciences. Together, these two trends have combined to deemphasize debates between "competing" theoretical positions. The issues of truth versus falsity or superiority versus inferiority are considered irrelevant. However, at the same time, *uncritical* acceptance of conceptual diversity is considered inappropriate and counterproductive. Instead it is appropriate to draw on many perspectives, with alternative theories being evaluated according to how useful they are. Furthermore, these trends suggest that the utility of a theory must be judged in terms of the quality of a work's contribution to the understanding of life-span human development.

World views of human development

Scientists have come to reemphasize the view that all aspects of scientific work (theory, research methodology, data analysis techniques) are based ultimately on philosophy. Different scientists have different philosophies about the nature of the universe. The set of philosophical views a scientist holds that pertains to his or her ideas about human nature and/or about how the world is constructed is termed a *world view*. There are various world views, and the differences among them provide the general basis for why scientists differ in regard to the theories they follow, what research methods they employ, and how data are analyzed (Lerner, 1976; Overton & Reese, 1973; Reese & Overton, 1970). Several world views are presented below.

Some scientists adhere to the world view that humans are not qualitatively different from other phenomena that exist in the natural world. They believe that humans are controlled by the same forces that control all natural phenomena. All such phenomena are, at their most basic level, composed of the same empirical units—atoms and molecules. Thus, the laws which govern these basic units—the laws of chemistry and physics—should provide information about all phenomena in the natural world, including humans. Humans can be reduced to atoms and molecules, and all that is seen as necessary for the attainment of knowledge is to learn the mechanical workings of chemistry and physics. In sum, scientists who hold this view of the nature of humans—of the place of human existence in the world—are said to follow a *mechanistic* world view (Bertalanffy, 1933; Harris, 1957; Lerner, 1976; Overton & Reese, 1973; Reese & Overton, 1970).

Other world views exist. For example, there is an *organismic* world view. This view proposes that knowledge of humans cannot be gained by reducing events to the atoms and molecules studed by physicists and chemists. Such reduction is inappropriate because, although atoms and molecules certainly exist within humans, when they combine to form the whole organism, something special emerges. When all the parts combine they produce *in their combination* characteristics that did not exist in the parts in isolation. Hence, because of the belief that something new emerges through combination and interaction, reduction to atoms and molecules is seen as inappropriate. Knowledge of the emerging, human level would be lost if the parts were studied in isolation. Thus, people who follow an organismic world view see humans as appropriate to study at their "own level." This is the case because of the unique, emergent characteristics that define the human level, the "whole" (Bertalanffy, 1933; Reese & Overton, 1970).

Additionally, although several other world views exist, one that has recently gained prominence in social science (Adams, 1977) is the *dialectic* world view, sometimes termed the contextual-dialectic world view (Hultsch & Hickey, 1978; Pepper, 1942; Riegel, 1975, 1976a, 1976b). This view considers more than the interaction of the parts that compose the human organism. Human development is seen as emerging from the continuous interaction among all the *different* levels of organization existing in the world. That is, from this view one should not only look at inner-physical or inner-biological phenomena (for example, atoms and molecules, or tissues and organs), or individual phenomena characterizing the whole person (for example, his or her psychological functioning). One also should consider outer-physical phenomena (weather, environmental pollution) and cultural and historical events (wars, political movements) in order to understand human development fully (Pepper, 1942; Riegel, 1976a).

Reduction of one of these dimensions to a molecular level is not appropriate because each level is seen as different. Alternatively, the type of interaction involved in organismic conceptions is not seen as appropriate. The interaction of constituent parts to produce the whole organism, emphasized in organismic conceptions, is quite different from the type of interaction depicted in a dialectical conception (Lerner & Spanier, 1978b).

First, in the dialectic view, all levels of analysis are constantly changing, and this is not necessarily the case in the organismic conception. Once the parts combine to produce the whole, the parts are not necessarily involved in further changes. Second, in the dialectic view, all levels from the atom to the organism are related reciprocally. In other words, rather than being able to speak of one atom as separate from another, or of the person as separate from his or her environment, the adherent of this view sees each level of analysis as actually providing a basis for and actually being part of the other levels with which that level interacts.

For instance, inner-biological phenomena (for example, a beating heart) could not exist without the total functioning of the higher level (the individual). Similarly, the individual could not exist without the liver. Neither is ever independent of the other. Each is a part of the other, and changes in one will always produce changes in the other. A buildup of bile in the liver will affect the person, and too much drinking of alcohol by the person will damage the liver.

Of course, similar examples could be drawn between the individual and the physical environment, the individual and history, the physical environment and inner biology, or any combination of the four levels noted above. The key point is that the constituent levels are never independent, and the parts interact reciprocally. Each provides a basis of its opposite, of the very thing with which it constantly and continually interacts. Thus, the world is seen as a place of constant change, and humans are viewed as products of the reciprocal interactions. Such continuous and reciprocal interactions might appropriately be described as *dynamic interactions*.

Having just seen that there are at least three different philosophical views of human functioning and development, one may ask how they relate to theories and research about human development? How does this relation shape the current trend in social science—to consider the relation between philosophy and science—that was noted above?

The conflict of world views

As even a brief overview of social science shows, those scientists who have been interested in human development have not agreed about the meaning, or interpretation, of behavior development. In fact, it will be argued that the *basic* contrasts to be drawn in science are in regard to how scientists differ about how to interpret a fact, and not, for instance, about what is or is not a fact. Thus, very emininent scientists have differed quite significantly in regard to the interpretations they have advanced about human development.

For instance, consider the phenomenon of "storm and stress" in adolescence. G. Stanley Hall, the founder of the study of adolescent development (Hall, 1904), believed that adolescence is a period of intrapersonal stress and interpersonal turmoil. He believed that such storm and stress was universal and inevitable. That is, he argued that all adolescents show such behavior. He maintained this because of his commitment to a theory which tried to reduce all developmental events across the human life span (across *ontogeny*) to certain biological mechanisms, those that characterized the evolution of humans. Such evolution is known as *phylogeny*, or phylogenetic or evolutionary progression.

Hall's theoretical position and the phenomenon of storm and stress will be discussed in several later chapters. The point to see here is that Hall interpreted storm and stress in adolescence in terms of one particular set of ideas. However, while other scientists might recognize that storm and stress occurs, they might interpret it differently. For example, they might relate it to a different theory. Davis (1944), for instance, believed that all human behavior came from learning society's rules. He believed that eventually humans anticipate reward when they emit behaviors which society approves—behaviors consistent with the role society expects of them. Alternatively, they learn to anticipate punishment when they emit socially disapproved behavior, behavior inconsistent with accepted roles. The reason most people obey society's rules, he argues, is that the anticipation of punishment—of something painful and/or unpleasant happening to them—is itself an unpleasant situation. It is an unpleasant feeling-state resulting from learning society's rules. Davis terms this feeling-state *socialized anxiety*, and says that this anxiety is disruptive for people. Accordingly, as humans try to avoid anxiety, they behave in accordance with societal role expectations.

However, Davis notes that the expected role behavior for an adolescent is unclear in our society. Thus, the adolescent will not know precisely what to do or how to behave. One will not always know if what he or she is doing is approved for his or her role, and hence whether there will be punishment. Thus, there is no easy way for the person to reduce socialized anxiety. The individual will not be able then to reduce the disruptive feeling-state, the level of socialized anxiety, and this emotional state will therefore be stressful and "stormy."

INSIGHT INTO ADOLESCENCE

Herman Wouk was born May 27, 1915, in New York City. For a time, he wrote jokes for radio comedians and was a scriptwriter. While on sea duty in 1943, he wrote his first novel about coping with naval traditions and regulations. Here he recalls his feelings as an adolescent.

I do not think I am wrong in remembering the teens as an uncomfortable, on the whole, a wretched, time. To the staggering colt, the world around him must seem a drunkenly reeling nightmare of sights and sounds. I understood very little of what was happening around me. It was like living in a foreign country, vainly pretending to be a native and getting mocked at and fleeced from all sides. And there was this brutal joke that nature had played, springing the feverish puzzle of sex at a time when I was barely learning to read and write and to navigate among the common dangers of existence. Girls were half marvels and half horrors. Adults were unfriendly, nagging nuisances. Education was an old man of the sea, and the social code existed to make a lout of me. I felt I would be a lumpy, pimply fifteen forever. Maybe I had a high old time and was a glamorous, enviable figure. I do not remember it that way.

Source: Wouk, H. "The terrible teens." *Good Housekeeping.* 146:60, 1958.

Thus, Davis also provides an interpretation of storm and stress. But his is one which relies not on a reduction of behavior to biological mechanisms which are universal, but rather on a reduction of behavior to environmental learning mechanisms which are relative to particular rules in a particular society.

It is possible to continue to offer different interpretations of storm and stress in adolescence. For instance, one could offer interpretations from theories which stressed emergent characteristics of adolescence, phenomena unique to the period of life which determine the presence of storm and stress. In fact, such alternative accounts have been given by Anna Freud (1969) and Erik Erikson (1959), and their views about storm and stress will be considered in a later chapter. However, the contrast between the theories of Hall and Davis in regard to the very same phenomenon of adolescent development should suffice here to indicate that alternative theories can be used to interpret the same behavior.

Much of the work in human development has been devoted to trying to advance a particular theory of development. Scholars attempt to show that one theory is better than another. Such endeavors have not proved especially helpful. Alternative views still compete with one another. Adherents of one view usually do not convince followers of another of the error of their ways. And many bright, capable, and creative people continue to work in their own interpretative camps, never attempting to cross the theoretical river to try integrating their ideas collaboratively. This is because, until recently, people attempted to resolve their differences through research, through *empirical* means. But, as just argued, the same behavioral event can always be interpreted in different ways. Thus, trying to resolve theoretical issues at an empirical level has not proved to be, nor may ever be, successful.

A different question recently has been asked about the theoretical differences among human developmentalists (Looft, 1973; Overton & Reese, 1973; Reese & Overton, 1970). Rather than ask which theory is better or worse, people have begun to wonder why scientists differed in the first place about theoretical issues. Why do different scientists subscribe to different theories of human development?

Writers have indicated that theoretical differences exist because scientists are committed to one of the distinct world views described earlier. Thus, if one believes in a mechanistic world view one would be led to construct a theory of human behavior which seeks to reduce that behavior to something else, to another level. As suggested above, one can reduce behavior to biology, as did Hall (1904), or to environmentally based learning principles, as did Davis (1944). That is, a "family of theories" (Reese & Overton, 1970) may be derived from a mechanistic world view. Just as human family members may differ one from the other, it is still the case that there is more within-family similarity in certain characteristics than there is similarity between people from different families. Thus, while members of the mechanistic "family" may differ with regard to just what they reduce human behavior to, the fact that explanation of human behavior involves reduction is one major reason for classification into the same world-view orientation (see Reese & Overton, 1970, for other reasons for classification).

Similarly, scientists committed to an organismic or to a dialectic world view construct different theories of development. The contrasting world views from which all these theories are derived are philosophies. In contrast to scientific hypotheses, philosophical beliefs—like theological or religious ones—cannot be proved right or wrong on the basis of facts. A Hindu does not adhere to a "right" or "true" religion, while a Moslem follows a "wrong" or "false" one, and no amount of empirical data can change this! Similarly, someone with a mechanistic world view does not follow a "wrong" philosophy, while those with a dialectic view follow a "right" one. This is the case because world views are philosophical statements of belief, which, by definition, cannot be evaluated on criteria of truth, correctness, or rightness.

Thus, although world views are not capable of being evaluated in terms of truth criteria, they shape the theories that scientists use to interpret the facts they derive from their studies of the "real" world. Moreover, world views, in shaping theories, shape the very questions scientists ask in their study of the real world. In shaping these questions, another reason may be seen for why empirical evidence is not useful for deciding among theories derived from alternative world views. The questions which follow from different theories are likely to be quite different and, in turn, the data generated to answer these contrasting questions are not likely to provide comparable answers.

For instance, a mechanistic theorist who derives a theory of adolescent development might try to reduce behavior to learning principles, common to people of all ages. Thus, he or she might seek to discover those environment-behavior relations which remain identical from infancy through adolescence and through adulthood. Alternatively, an organismically oriented theorist would attempt to find those phenomena which are unique to and representative of the adolescent period in particular. Anna Freud (1969), for example, is an organismically oriented theorist who emphasizes the *psychological and social* (termed "psychosocial") implications of *puberty*, the event associated with the ability to produce sperms and eggs for reproduction. Obviously then, if one is focusing on such an event, one is considering a phenomenon which only occurs once in life and is thus a unique experience.

A dialectical theorist, on the other hand, would look not just at the adolescent experiencing puberty. Rather, this theorist would try to assess the larger context of puberty. Thus, as will be discussed in Chapter 8, puberty is a unique event in each of our life cycles, and therefore cannot be reduced completely to events involving physical changes at other times in life. However, puberty is not independent of what happens at other times in life.

Puberty is influenced by the cultural and historical changes in society. At the turn of the century the average age that females reached puberty in this country was 13.6 years (determined on the basis of *menarche*—the first menstrual cycle). Today, the average age for puberty is 11.2 years. One of the factors that account for this decrease is that across history our culture has developed the knowledge and technology for improved nutrition and health care. People are better fed and have less probability of certain diseases today than they did at the turn of this century. Moreover, this increased nutrition and medical care occurs not just at adolescence but, as implied above, even before conception with regard to the health status of the potential mother.

Thus, the dialectical theorist would look at the relation of puberty to events at earlier times in the life cycle, as well as to current cultural, environmental, and long-term historical influences. Moreover, the reciprocal nature of these interactions would be considered. The fact that people are becoming sexually mature at increasingly younger ages will have a feedback effect on society, and thus change the history of our culture. As already noted, some of these implications of puberty will be discussed later in this text.

In conclusion, theories derived from alternative world views ask different questions about development. Consequently, they collect data on different topics which may not be very useful in deciding among the different theories. However, it has been argued that attempts to make such decisions are pointless. The idea is *not* to decide which theory is best, or which leads to truth and which does not. Theories from different world views ask different questions because the very nature of reality is conceived differently from the perspective of contrasting world views. Thus, what is a true depiction of reality for one world view may be irrelevant for another.

This means that one can only speak of truth in the context of a particular world view. Truth only has meaning in the construction of reality used *within* a given world view (Kuhn, 1962). Thus, since world views have contrasting perceptions of reality, they will have different truth criteria (Reese & Overton, 1970). This simply means that there is no absolute truth! Truth is always relative to a philosophical context. What is real for one theorist may not even exist for another. The "id" of Sigmund Freud (1949) is seen as a mere fiction by B. F. Skinner (1938).

In sum, where does this trend in social science—the trend that recognizes the relation between philosophy and science—leave scientists? Attempts to compete among alternative theories did not especially advance science. Does this current trend suggest anything fruitful? We think it does.

One major implication of the nature of the philosophy-science relation discussed above is that a criterion other than truth must be used to evaluate interpretations of development. Moreover, since one theory is not seen to be intrinsically better than another, all theories may be said to have an equal opportunity to advance our understanding of human development. Accordingly, it may be suggested that theories should be evaluated on the basis of criteria of *usefulness*.

Thus, *any and all* theories may be found to be of some use. The difficult task is to decide what is and what is not useful from a particular theory. Complicating this evaluation is the fact that traditionally in social science any given theory (1) deals with at most just a few dimensions of behaviors (for example, just common learning principles or just unique implications of puberty), and (2) provides data not readily integrated with data derived from other theories (because different questions are asked). Consequently, theories derived from the mechanistic and the organismic world views are often limited in *scope*. Alternatively, it appears that if a theory can deal with several dimensions of change simultaneously, and thus can provide data which potentially can be integrated with the other data, such a theory would be most useful. Thus, because of its potentially greater scope, a case can be made for the use of a theory derived from a dialectic world view. However, since few scientists have depth of knowledge in more than one discipline, successful use of such an approach probably requires a multidisciplinary effort.

The need for multidisciplinary research

Scholars working within traditional disciplinary boundaries have become increasingly convinced that they are limited in their ability to account for change. For instance, a historical analysis of the traditional ways in which developmental psychologists and family sociologists have studied individual and social change, respectively, indicated a general reluctance to draw on each other's conceptual resources (Hartup, 1978). Changes a family goes through over time were never related to individual development. There were few, if any, attempts to understand how a child's development could influence family change. In turn, of course, the changing context of the child's own development was rarely considered in trying to understand individual development. Little use was made of the idea that in order to understand better the developing person one must view that person in a changing social context.

Because of such disciplinary "isolation," a large share of the changes involved in individual and social development were unexplained. However, by the 1970s such disciplinary isolationism was decreasing (Hartup, 1978). As more interactive theoretical views of development were becoming popular, scholars began considering the interactions of their own discipline's variables with those of other disciplines. Thus, through professional meetings, integrated reviews of the literature, and even some collaborative research (see Lerner & Spanier, 1978a), scholars began to discover that integration of concepts and variables from several disciplines could account better for individual and social change than could attempts to account for such change from a single disciplinary perspective. As such, a pluralism of perspectives was promoted, and a multidisciplinary view of change—of human development—was advanced.

For example, scholars interested in relationships across generational cohorts—of adolescents and their parents—have found it useful to combine ideas about individual psychological development and social change (Bengtson & Troll, 1978). Thus, ideas about how a person functions at particular times (or stages) in his or her life cycle have been combined with sociological notions. These latter ideas relate to the transmission of values from one generation to the next. These ideas consider why one generation has more of a stake than does another in maintaining the existing social value system. Together, these sets of ideas have been found useful in understanding why adolescents tend to see themselves as moving away from their parents in attitudes, beliefs, and behaviors. It can also be learned why, at the same time, parents see their adolescent children as having almost the same attitudes, beliefs, and behaviors as they do.

In summary, many trends in social science have come together to promote a view of development which attempts to link contributions from many interrelated sources of development, as the sources exert their influence over the course of life. In short, a conception which takes an interactive, multidisciplinary, life-span view of change is promoted. *Dynamic interaction* is one such conception. Because this position will be used throughout this book in attempts to describe, and sometimes explain, the life-span, multidisciplinary changes involved in adolescent development, a description of this position follows. It should be emphasized, however, that this view of development is not offered as the only appropriate approach to the study of adolescence. Instead, we offer this approach as one way to organize the many processes involved in a life-span view of adolescence.

DYNAMIC INTERACTIONS OF DEVELOPMENT

The dynamic interactional view of human development stresses that behavior change involves the joint influence of many contributing sources, for example, the biological, the psychological, the sociocultural, and the historical. These levels do not exist in parallel form; one *may not* just add their contributions one to the other to obtain an understanding of development. Instead, each level may be thought of as a circle, part of which is made up of, is embedded within, all other levels. This interpretation is presented schematically in Exhibit 1.2. Here we see four levels of analysis—biological, psychological, sociocultural, and historical. The circle representing each of these is embedded within—is part of—each of the other circles. In other words, the variables and processes which constitute the contribution of each level of analysis are composed of the variables and processes of all other levels. Such embeddedness means that a change in any one level will influence a change in all others. In turn, the change in these other levels will feed back on the initial level to promote further change in it.

From the point of view of this model of development, change is continual. The arrow indicating time in Exhibit 1.2 cuts through all the circles represented, in order to suggest that the interrelation is not a static, one-time-only combination. Rather, it is a constantly changing interaction.

Some examples of relations among sources of development which illustrate the dynamic interactions of behavior change have already been discussed. For instance, the emergence of puberty is not merely a biological event; rather it is a phenomenon

Exhibit 1.2
A model of the dynamic interactional view of development. Four levels of analysis are represented, and changes in one level are both a producer and a product of changes in all other levels.

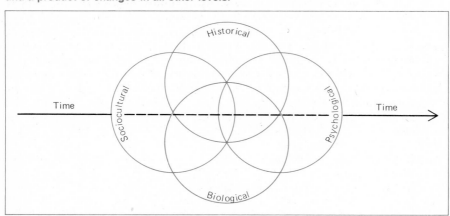

linked to changing sociocultural processes involving nutritional and medical care that begins before conception. Moreover, the resulting change in the emergence of puberty in the life cycle can feed back to affect the culture as it evolves across history. For example, consider the impact on society if 8-year-olds were reproductively mature. Such feedback would also affect psychological development, since the meaning of being pubescent will probably differ for an 8-year-old as compared with a 12-year-old.

Similarly, although the changes associated with puberty invariably lead to bodily changes in the adolescent, the nature, quality, and meaning of these changes may be described usefully with a dynamic interactional framework. Some males reach puberty later than their peers, and for many, they maintain a bodily appearance during much of their early adolescent years which is thin and boney (Jones & Bayley, 1950). Other males reach puberty earlier than their peers, and for many of these youth, a muscular, "athletic" body is characteristic during the early adolescent years. In today's society the thin boys have a body build which is not highly favored, while the athletic boys have a physique which is highly regarded (Lerner & Korn, 1972). Accordingly, the first type of adolescent is likely to get some negative evaluations from his peers and adult supervisors in relation to his body type, while the reverse occurs with the latter type of adolescent (Jones & Bayley, 1950).

The maturation rates of the boys appear to lead then to contrasting social appraisals, and furthermore, these social reactions seem to feed back on the boys to affect psychological attributes such as those of personality development. The thin boys may develop a negative self-concept in relation to the unfavorable evaluations attached to their body type, while positive self-concepts are developed in the athletic boys in relation to the favorable association made to their body build (Mussen & Jones, 1957). In turn, the thin boys might try to change their biological status in order to change their body type and thus break the maturation–body type–social reaction–personality cycle they are involved in. They might change their diet and/or their exercise regimen in order to alter their physique type.

If such an intervention is not attempted, there may be life-span implications of different body types in adolescence. Jones (1949) has shown that the social advantages of early maturation in adolescence and of the athletic build associated with it are maintained by males well into their adult years. Similarly, the negative consequences of early maturation in adolescence are also carried over into the adult years. Further, the model suggests that as society or culture changes with history, so too will all these circular relations involving body build, biology, social evaluations, and personality. Accordingly, in a study by Mussen and Bouterline-Young (1964) it was found that the associations between body build and social evaluations found in the United States are not present in Italian society or in the Italian-American subculture of the United States. As such, they reported that the implications for adolescent personality development of early and late maturation and of different body types were quite different.

To summarize, the major ideas involved in a dynamic interactional view of development are:

1. There are many sources of development.
2. These sources are derived from all levels of phenomena constituting humanity: the biological, psychological, sociocultural, and historical.
3. Each source of development is influenced by and influences each other source.

4. As such, changes in one source will promote changes in all others, and because of this connection feedback will occur.

5. Change, then, is continual, or in other words, all of life is characterized by the potential for change. There are no totally fixed, universal characteristics of development.

CHAPTER SUMMARY

Adolescence is a fascinating period of life about which much can be said. But all that pertains to adolescence is in some way a product of what happened before this period and is in other ways a determinant of what will follow this period. This book recognizes this fact and attempts to put the study of adolescence in a perspective which considers the importance of all phases of the life span. This general approach is known as the *life-span view* of human development.

The life-span view has several important features. First, it is *multidisciplinary.* In other words, it recognizes the contribution of several disciplines. Although much of the study of adolescence is rooted in the fields of psychology and sociology, this book pays attention to information from medicine, biology, history, anthropology, and law.

Second, the life-span view emphasizes change. Individuals change continuously, and adolescence is but one period of change in the life cycle. The life-span view attempts to study changes within an individual over time *(intraindividual change)* as well as differences between individuals over time *(interindividual differences).*

Third, the life-span view implies three activities for researchers, theorists, and practitioners. Human development must be *described.* We must then be able to *explain* what we have described. And finally we must attempt to *optimize* the development which we have explained.

There are, of course, other ways of approaching the study of adolescence. Two which have been prominent in the past are the *adolescent psychological view,* which emphasizes how people of a particular age group perform on a specific task, and the *adolescent developmental view,* which emphasizes the history of the person but usually not in regard to his or her context or the entire life course.

The study of adolescence, or any other part of life, is influenced by the philosophical approaches one brings to such study. Philosophical beliefs about the nature of the universe influence the theories scientists develop, the methods they use, and the way they analyze and interpret their data. These beliefs are sometimes referred to as *world views.*

One world view of human development—the *mechanistic*— suggests that humans can be reduced to atoms and molecules and can be studied at this level. The *organismic* world view proposes that knowledge of humans cannot be gained by reducing events to the atoms and molecules studied by physicists and chemists, but rather must be gained by looking at the whole organism; the constituent parts of the person and the total person must be considered. A third world view is favored in this book: the *dialectic* world view. This view considers not only the interaction of the constituent parts, but also the relationship between the individual and all other aspects of the individual's context.

The dialectic approach forces us to consider the *dynamic interactions* between different aspects of the individual (his or her biological, psychological, historical, and sociocultural influences) and the continual changes that occur within and around the individual.

2
DEFINITIONS OF ADOLESCENCE

CHAPTER

OVERVIEW

There are many ways of defining the period commonly called "adolescence," and the chapter considers the advantages and disadvantages of each type of definition. The implications of the use of each definition for understanding change during adolescence are also discussed.

ISSUES
TO CONSIDER

Why is the adolescent portion of life seen as a transitionary period?

Why must adolescence be seen as involving transitions in several processes?

What are the uses and limitations of an age definition of adolescence?

What are the advantages and disadvantages of focusing on the physical and physiological changes of adolescence as a means of defining adolescence?

What do laws regarding children and adolescents reflect about conceptions of development?

What are the uses and limitations of a psychological definition of adolescence?

What are the unique contributions of sociological approaches to the study of the adolescent period?

How do cultural, anthropological, and historical perspectives enrich understanding of adolescent development?

What does the combination of adolescent developmental transitions imply about the character of adolescents' interactions with others?

How do the interactions adolescents have with others provide a basis of their own development?

n adolescent is not just someone who has attained a given age, reached reproductive maturity, or moved beyond the dependent roles of a child. An adolescent may be all of these things, or none of them, or much more. Adolescence consists of changes among numerous processes involving the biological, psychological, sociological, cultural, and historical dimensions of existence.

In Chapter 1 it was argued that change occurs throughout the life span, and that change occurs on the many interrelated dimensions noted above. This perspective suggested that adolescence usefully may be seen in a life-span, multidisciplinary context. Changes begin at conception and continue until death. Thus, any period of life is a transition from one part of life to another. Accordingly, adolescence is one period involving transitions. As discussed below, adolescence encompasses transitions linking childhood and adulthood.

THE TRANSITIONS OF ADOLESCENCE

Adolescent development involves transitions in all the change processes that make up the person, that is, processes ranging from the biological to the historical. Although by definition these processes always involve change, some changes are concentrated typically within particular ranges during particular portions of life. For instance, some changes occur during a particular range labeled as childhood. When cognitive changes, as studied by Piaget (1970), range from "sensorimotor" through "concrete operational," these changes are labeled as those pertaining to childhood (Chapter 9 will give details of Piagetian levels of cognition). Alternatively, when cognitive changes involve differentiations within an already organized abstract and hypothetical (formal) intellectual structure, the changes are labeled as pertaining to portions of the adult years.

Thus, there are changes in processes which are typically representative of childhood, as it is known at this point in history and in American culture. These are important qualifications to which we will return below. Similarly, there are changes in processes which are typically representative of adulthood. Adolescence is a period of transition, from having changes representative of children to having those changes representative of adults. Thus, adolescence is a *bridge* between the periods of childhood and adulthood.

The childhood period preceding adolescence has attracted the most attention by theorists and researchers of human development, because of the presumed influence that childhood changes have on the rest of life. Adulthood has attracted perhaps the least amount of attention by human development theorists and researchers. This period is certainly the longest one in the typical person's life span. The minimal attention that has been given this period, until recently (Schaie & Gribbin, 1975), stems from some of the theoretical biases spoken of in Chapter 1. These biases state that the course of adult development is determined either in childhood or by late adolescence (A. Freud, 1969; S. Freud, 1949; Piaget, 1972), and thus additional developmental changes are precluded.

Since many contend that such theoretical proscriptions are not absolute—and that therefore developmental change may and does occur throughout life—it can be argued that it is appropriate to view adolescent development as a bridge between developmental periods. Adolescence may be viewed as a period of transition in processes, from childhood change processes to ones of adulthood. However, a more precise specification of the meaning of the adolescent developmental period is necessary.

Many processes are involved in adolescence. These processes change at varying rates. This means that some processes may be making transitions faster or slower than others. A person may have some processes (for example, cognition) that are adultlike, others (for example, emotions) which are still childish, and still others (for example, physical makeup) which are somewhere in between these two. Therefore, to define adolescence one must look across all the processes that are changing, and make a statement about what is considered to be the most frequently occurring characteristics of adolescence.

If one looked at many processes of a person—the physical, motivational, intellectual, emotional, sexual, educational, social, and moral—and found that most of these existed within the range of changes typically representative of a child, one would label the person a child. If most of these processes existed within the range typically representative of an adult, the person would be labeled an adult. If, however, most of them existed at neither the child nor adult state, but, rather, at the state of transition between these two periods, the person would be labeled an adolescent. Accordingly, *adolescent development is that period within the life span when most of the person's processes are in a state of transition from what typically is considered childhood to what typically is considered adulthood.*

Stated differently, when most of one's processes are in the transition period between childhood and adulthood one is an adolescent. Furthermore, it is possible to describe someone as somewhat adolescent, or to say that a person is like an adolescent in some respects. You can be adolescent in terms of your emotions and adult with regard to your level of intellectual development. (You probably have met someone who was judged as quite sophisticated in intellectual endeavors, but who, at the same time, seemed very immature personally or socially.)

From a life-span view, any period of life is defined in terms of what are the typical characteristics of that period. Because of the focus on multiple-change processes, one must look at all processes before categorizing a person's developmental level. If most of the processes exist in the range of transition typical of adolescence, then the person is termed an adolescent.

Thus, from a life-span perspective one focuses on multiple processes of change in order to define an adolescent. Focusing on only one process alone is not sufficient to study adolescent development or to define and understand the adolescent. However, each process of change in adolescence must be understood because each contributes to the person, each interacts with all others.

Often, many of the specific processes of change in adolescence are associated with a particular disciplinary perspective (for example, psychological, sociological, biological). Therefore, in the next portion of the chapter we discuss some of the most important perspectives and consider change processes within each of them. These processes will be treated more intensively in later chapters. For example, an entire chapter will be devoted to cognitive development during adolescence. The present purpose is to indicate the role of each of these processes in an overview of adolescence, and to show the limitations of defining adolescence on the basis of any one of these processes *alone.*

DEFINITIONS OF CHANGE IN ADOLESCENCE

Adolescence traditionally has been defined from the standpoint of a particular attribute of change. But it has been argued that no one attribute alone can define the adolescent period. Accordingly, limitations of each view when considered alone can be noted, and conversely, assets of each, when seen in the context of a multidisciplinary, life-span perspective, may be specified.

Chronological (age) definitions of adolescence

Historically, one way adolescence has been defined is by reference to a chronological age span. For instance, adolescence may be defined as a period that goes from 12 to 18 years or from 13 to 21 years.

The problem with a chronological definition is that it is arbitrary. One person may use the years from 13 to 21 because at 13 years one becomes a "teenager" and because 21 years is the age associated with being an adult to some individuals or in a particular society. But what about states which have said that one is an adult at 18 years of age? Then to be consistent with the rationale for using age limits in the first place, adolescence would now end at 18 years. The point here is that a mere chronological (age) definition of adolescence is an arbitrary one. Any of several age boundaries may be used for any of several reasons, and none of the reasons is likely to be more compelling than the others.

There is also an important conceptual reason for avoiding complete reliancè on a chronological definition. Since the emphasis in the life-span view of human development is on processes of change, a life-span developmentalist rarely looks at age alone. Rather, he or she considers age-*related* changes. The focus is on what happens to you as a consequence of changes in age-related processes. Age is used so often in the literature on human development because it is a convenient, "objective term." But age is not a developmental variable. The passage of time, the movement from one age to another, or having a birthday, does not explain human development. One does not suddenly become "grown up" at 18. If someone magically could switch from 14 to 18 years of age, he or she would not suddenly be as insightful, experienced, and capable as one would have been had he or she undergone the changes that would have occurred during the four-year period. The processes that covary with age are what is important in making us what we are, and not just one's age. Age, then, is just a *marker variable*, a concept merely used to indicate the progression of change.

To elaborate further, it may be recalled that earlier in this chapter it was suggested that one define a period of life in terms of change processes which are typical of the period; however, it was noted that an important qualification of this approach is that what is typical for an age period varies across sociocultural and historical settings. For example, in Chapter 1 it was indicated that the *mean* (statistical average) age of puberty in females is decreasing with history, and it was also seen that the implications of early and late maturation (and of body type) for personality and social development in adolescence varied from culture to culture. Accordingly, if one looked just at age alone, one would be ignoring the important processes that vary and which, in actuality, account for the changes we see in adolescent development.

Several writers have noted that it is not appropriate to focus on age because processes are not perfectly related to age for all times in history, for all societies, or for all people (Baer, 1970; Baltes & Willis, 1977; Wohlwill, 1973). Moreover, processes do not change at necessarily identical rates. Thus, at any one age, processes would be at different points in their respective progressions, and to focus on age alone to the exclusion of process changes would simply ignore this important variation. As a consequence, major differences between adolescents in their individual changes could not be understood adequately.

However, it is sometimes useful to focus on age as a variable in research, but it must be done with a recognition of its limitations. First, at any one point in time, a definition of adolescence which uses some age limits, albeit arbitrary ones, will give one an appreciation for the number of people in that phase of the life span. For instance, by referring to United States census data, one learns that there were more than 21 million persons (with about equal numbers of males and females) between the ages of 15 and 19 in the United States in 1976, and that they made up 9.9 percent of the population (U.S. Bureau of the Census, 1977a). Such knowledge would enable one to know the magnitude of an issue being confronted. For instance, one social problem among adolescents in this age group involves unwanted pregnancies. One nationwide study found that in 1976 more than half of the unmarried females in this age range have had sexual intercourse by age 19 (Zelnik & Kantner, 1977). Research has also found that about 28 percent of the sexually active females (and 12 percent of all females) between 15 and 19 have been pregnant outside of marriage at least once (Zelnik & Kantner, 1978a,b). If one combines all this information about 15- to 19-year-old women, one is able to estimate that about 1.2 million of these young women (and consequently, a nearly equal number of young men) have already been involved in an out-of-wedlock pregnancy.

Second, using age limits to indicate the size of the adolescent population will allow one to consider the effects of historical change on society. As noted above, adolescents between ages 15 and 19 constituted about 9.9 percent of the population in 1976. If one broadened these age limits to include all persons between 10 and 24 years of age in our "adolescent" category, then 28 percent of the United States population would be accounted for (U.S. Bureau of the Census, 1977a). However, as suggested in Chapter 1, although today the United States is a youth-oriented society, such prominence is likely to diminish in the future.

Estimates are that by the year 1990, people in the 10-to 24-years category will constitute only about 23 percent of the population. Although the percentage difference is not very large, this difference translates into approximately three million people. Accordingly, one may ask what changing sociocultural patterns are producing this age distribution change. For example, one may look at changing marriage patterns, use of birth control, and attitudes regarding desired family size. Additionally, one may consider what historical impact will emerge as the age distribution shifts toward the middle-aged and elderly in our society. What impact will the greater number of older people have on the values found in society and in our social institutions and laws? For example, laws regarding retirement age might have to be altered because there may be fewer young people present to enter necessary roles. Thus, one might also consider the feedback to youth that occurs as a consequence of living in a society greatly influenced by the aged. Employing chronological definitions of adolescence can thus be useful as indexes of changing sociocultural and historical processes.

In sum, the first perspective about adolescence has limitations when used alone, but is helpful when put into a broader context. Similar conclusions will be reached about other approaches to defining adolescence.

Adolescence invariably involves anatomical and physiological changes. Changes occur in those physical characteristics that mark the anatomical differences between the sexes, for example in the external genitalia. Such organs and tissues are termed *primary* sexual characteristics. In males, for instance, the penis gets longer and increases in circumference; in females, the coloring of the clitoris changes. Additionally, other characteristics begin to emerge during adolescence. Such characteristics as breast development in females and pigmented facial hair in males emerge. Together, such alterations compose the *secondary* sexual characteristics. These physical alterations are the result of physiological changes involving the production of particular chemicals (hormones) by specific types of glands (the endocrines) of the body.

When the physical and physiological changes that eventually will occur begin to do so, it may be said the adolescent is *prepubescent* (or in prepuberty); during the time when most of those changes are occurring, one may say the adolescent is *pubescent* (or in puberty); and when most of the changes that will occur have done so, the adolescent may be labeled as *postpubescent* (or in postpuberty) (Schonfeld, 1969). Accordingly, many people define adolescence simply on the basis of this range of changes.

For instance, some writers will speak of adolescence as that period of life ranging from the beginning to the end of puberty (see Schonfeld, 1969). To define adolescence in this way requires deciding on an index of when puberty begins and when it ends. Since in both males and females there is a *growth spurt* in adolescence—a period in which there is considerable change over time in body size and height—an often-used criterion for the termination of puberty is the end of the final growth spurt. Typically, the criterion used to index the end of the final growth spurt is when bone growth is complete. Alternatively, the first menstrual cycle in females *(menarche)* and the first ejaculation of seminal fluid in males (usually by *nocturnal emission*, or "wet dream") are used as indexes of the start of puberty (Schonfeld, 1969).

However, there are important limitations of such anatomical or physiological definitions of adolescence. First, there are several problems with using the end of the growth spurt as a criterion for the end of adolescent development. Some people's final growth spurt ends very rapidly, and for others it tails off gradually. In other words, there is a considerable amount of variation among individuals. That is, the time when a person's final growth spurt ends may not correspond at all with that of any of his or her peers. Somebody may be fully grown at 16 years and another person may go on growing through 21 years. In addition, and more importantly, there can be physical changes which affect the nature of one's psychosocial functioning and vice versa. These changes may occur in adolescence, but after the growth spurt is over. They may have to do with those very phenomena (for example, hormonal changes) that are considered important in the adolescent period. Hormone changes may occur, for example, in females with emotionally upsetting personal problems, or from medication being taken on a physician's recommendation. These may affect the nature of their physical changes. It might alter the regularity (the periodicity) of their menstrual cycle, or it may alter the size or tenderness of their breasts, for example. These conditions might be very significant to the young woman, even though they are changes which occur *after* the growth spurt is over. Furthermore, it is readily apparent that physical events such as menstrual irregularity or breast size can have important psychological meaning for some young women.

Similarly, there are some problems involved with choosing criteria to index the beginning of puberty. First, menarche has been thought a reasonable index to use for the presence of puberty in females since it marks the beginning of changes leading to reproductive capability. It is usually noticed, understood, and remembered since it is a dramatic event for the female. But in rare cases, females ovulate before they menstruate, and in most cases, females are actually incapable of reproduction until 12 to 18 months after the menarche. Furthermore, regular ovulation and menstruation may not be established for a few years (Hafez & Evans, 1973).

The use of the first ejaculation as a corresponding index for males also may not be appropriate. The first ejaculation, while in some ways an analogous event for males, is not always understood by the male, or told to someone. It is seldom remembered. Furthermore, even though *spermatogenesis* (sperm production) typically has begun by the first ejaculation, and thus the seminal fluid contains some viable sperms, the concentration of sperms is usually not great enough to impregnate a female. This capability to reproduce typically exists at ages 14 to 15 (Hafez & Evans, 1973). Thus, choice of the first ejaculation, or menarche, or any other biological event (for example, appearance of pubic hair, increased testicular growth, voice changes, or breast size), is just an arbitrary selection.

Complicating the problem of using anatomical and physiological criteria as indexes of adolescence is that such criteria cannot really be considered alone. As noted above, anatomical and physiological changes, especially those pertaining to puberty, are affected significantly by sociocultural and historical changes. Thus, the emergence, nature, and termination of puberty have been altered across history in relation to changing nutrition and medical-related variables. As such, people are reaching puberty earlier and growing more throughout the period (for example, getting taller) than was the case 100 years ago, or even in more recent history.

Accordingly, focusing alone on the anatomical and physiological changes of adolescence is both problematic and limited. However, viewing such changes in their broader sociocultural and historical contexts gives one an appreciation of the dynamic qualities of changes that before now were considered solely biological or maturational. Additionally, the connections among these biological, historical, and sociocultural changes are evident. As noted in Chapter 1, reaching puberty at increasingly earlier ages not only is a product of historical changes in the culture but, in turn, will alter the culture's future history. In short, placing anatomical and physiological changes in their broader context expands their usefulness.

Legal conceptions of adolescence

There is no legal definition of "adolescence." The law in most states recognizes, however, ages of minority (birth until the eighteenth birthday, for instance) and ages of majority (typically 18 years and older). As with a chronological definition of adolescence, such legal definitions of minors (children and "youth") and of adults are arbitrary. Different states or different countries might define children and youth and adults differently. Moreover, within the same state we may find variations in ages at which "adult" behaviors such as voting, drinking, or signing a legal contract may be permitted. But such variation per se has rarely been the focus of concern of those interested in the transitions of adolescence. Although changeable, a law is relatively static, and as such, generally has not been regarded as a dynamic component of a developmental view of adolescence.

It may be argued, however, that the legal status of the person who is a child or an early adolescent is a product of history. Accordingly, a discussion of the legal status of the adolescent may show how even a perspective about adolescence that is not typically seen as relevant to development may have use.

Law typically is not a traditional component of conceptions of adolescence. Yet the laws about children and youth certainly reflect society's conception about the status, obligations, and responsibilities of these people. Moreover, consideration of how such laws changed across the history of a society, or now exist in different cultures, will reveal the evolving and contrasting meanings attached to children and youth across time and geographical area. For example, a review of the philosophical and historical evolution of the notion of "development," and of adolescent development in particular, suggests that for a great span of history no distinctions in physiological or social responsibility were made between children and adults. Accordingly, being just "miniature adults," children were expected to work as long and in some of the same tasks as full-grown adults. If they shirked these or other social and moral responsibilities, they could be punished by the same laws as could adults.

Today, of course, laws protect children with regard to work and legal culpability. In fact, children and youth are not allowed to work at certain jobs in some states, and in all states limits are imposed on how long or hard they may be permitted to work, or below what age work may not be permitted at all. Indeed, in many states youth have to get a "license" (that is, apply for "working papers") in order to be employed in some positions. Similarly, the legal system for youthful offenders is not the same one an adult encounters. Up until the age of majority, youth in many states are not considered totally responsible for criminal acts they may commit. Parents, for example, may be required to pay for damages or legal costs incurred by their children.

Accordingly, the nature of the legal discriminations between children and youth, on the one hand, and adults on the other, reflects the current psychosocial differences society sees or does not see regarding people at different points in their life spans. Furthermore, changes in these perspectives reflect the evolving philosophy about and attitudes toward children, youth, and adults that exist in a culture over time. Such changes may be seen as a product of other biological, cultural, legal, and historical changes that also exist. For instance, the number of persons under age 18 who were arrested more than doubled from 1960 to 1975 (to a total of more than 2 million). The rate of serious crimes almost doubled during this same period (*Uniform Crime Reports*, 1976). One may ask how the changing conceptions of youth, reflected in laws for them, has contributed to this increase. Furthermore, how may this increase influence changes in the present laws? To summarize, focusing on the law allows us to see not only how the adolescent may be a product of his or her social world, but also how he or she may help produce it.

Psychological transitions in adolescence

Adolescent development has been studied predominantly by researchers from within one discipline: psychology. As might be expected, most views of adolescence have been psychological ones and most books about and research studies of adolescents have been psychological in nature. Although such analyses of adolescence have not ignored the other dimensions considered in this book, they certainly have not been emphasized. Furthermore, the dependency of psychological changes on variables associated with these other disciplines generally has not been recognized.

For instance, until relatively recently, with the advent of new methodological techniques for measuring change—for example, sequential research designs (Baltes, 1968; Schaie, 1965)—the importance of history for understanding adolescent changes had not been recognized fully. Although, as will be discussed in Chapter 12, Erikson (1959) indeed had stressed the role of history in shaping the content of personality development in adolescence, the structure (for example, the organization) of this development is believed by him to be universal. Development is believed to be the same in this regard for all adolescents, no matter what historical era or *birth cohort* (year of birth) they are from. However, as suggested earlier, there are no totally fixed, universal characteristics of development. Thus, adolescents of different birth cohorts cannot be expected to develop in a universal fashion.

These expectations about the relationship between adolescent personality change and history have some empirical support. Using a sequential research design—discussed in greater detail in Chapter 7—Nesselroade and Baltes (1974) showed that what occurs in different portions of adolescence is most dependent on historical events similarly affecting people of different birth cohorts. Nesselroade and Baltes studied West Virginia adolescents over the course of two years of their lives, from 1970 to 1972. When first measured, the different groups were 13, 14, 15, and 16 years of age, and when last studied, they were 15, 16, 17, and 18 years of age, respectively. Because of the fact they were in different portions of their adolescent developmental period (early, middle, or late), psychological theories of development such as Erikson's (1959) or Piaget's (1970, 1972) would predict that the subjects would show different psychological structures across these years of measurement. When they reached the last year of measurement they should have been different because of their presumably inevitable different psychological levels of development.

However, although different when first measured, the various groups were more similar by the last time of measurement. They developed to the *same* point in many regards. Despite their age, they all showed some similar patterns of personality change. Thus, as shown in Exhibit 2.1, even though some had been adolescents longer, the groups showed many similar personality outcomes.

Thus, it was not age per se that explained their changes. As such, the idea of universal psychological change in adolescents, changes that occur at specific portions of life and not others, is not supported. Rather, the impact of culture on these differently aged people, as that culture evolved across even this short historical span of from 1970 to 1972, seemed most important. Despite what psychological changes may have been occurring in these differently aged adolescents when they entered the brief historical era between 1970 and 1972, these psychological differences were "overridden" by the historical events occurring for all the groups (for example, the Vietnam war, the beginning of the Watergate political crisis, changes in the nation's economy). Whatever the important events may have been, they were more powerful influences in fostering change in personality than were psychological processes alone.

In fact, the Nesselroade and Baltes (1974) data indicate that it may even be inappropriate to suggest a separation of historical from psychological change. Although one can separate such influences statistically, the point here is that those changes we label psychological are, in the real world, embedded within changing

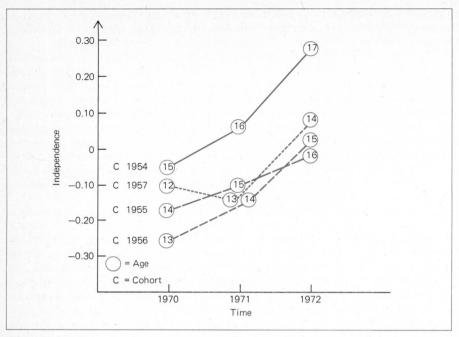

Exhibit 2.1
**Results of a study by Nesselroade and Baltes (1974): Despite being of
different ages from time 1 (1970) through time 2 (1972), most groups of
adolescents showed similar personality developments (here in regard to
independence).** (*Source:* **J. R. Nesselroade and P. B. Baltes, Adolescent
personality development and historical change: 1970–1972.** *Monographs
of the Society for Research in Child Development*, **1974,** *39* **(1, Ser. No.
154), p. 76.)**

historical and cultural settings. Psychological transitions in adolescence are not
universal, but rather appear dependent on the biological, sociocultural, and historical changes with which they interact.

Accordingly, many dimensions of transition of the adolescent (such as cognitive,
personality, motivational, and emotional) have been the focus of psychological
analysis; and for each dimension, alternative theories have been used to account for
the psychological changes. For example, Anna Freud (1969) and Erik Erikson (1968)
have conceptualized adolescent personality in different ways. These analyses focus
on the individual as the "unit" of existence that needs to be explained. Everything of
importance can be explained in terms of the individual. However, on the basis of the
theoretical position outlined in Chapter 1, and on the basis of evidence such as that
provided by Nesselroade and Baltes (1974), it may be argued that such a person-
centered approach to psychology in general, and to adolescent development in
particular, is not advisable. Psychological changes in adolescence arise from a
combination of influences beyond those associated merely with the person.

In summary, the various psychological transitions that occur in adolescence,
involving the person's intellectual, personality, emotional, and moral processes, for
instance, should be studied in a broad, multidisciplinary, interactive context.
Similarly, other disciplinary perspectives on adolescence, although seemingly

broader at the outset, may be enriched also by viewing them within this perspective. For example, sociological and cultural anthropological perspectives can be expanded in this way.

Sociological perspectives

Simply put, a sociological perspective is one which considers human interaction. Sociologists study group functioning at levels ranging from the *dyad* (two persons), to the family, to the community, or to the society. A sociologist might, for instance, focus on those specific social functions of people of a particular social status (or standing) within the group. Considering society as the broad reference group of interest, the sociologist might consider the social functions—the activities or tasks—of people of different status levels, for example, rich or poor, men or women, Black or White. Additionally, the age status of the person (such as child versus adult) might be studied, and a description of the nature of people of different age groups might be undertaken.

Accordingly, because children are often viewed as being directed by, and supported in, their social functions by others, their role as a child is often summarized by the term "dependency." Thus, the status of a child is seen as dependent. In turn, because adults often are considered to be essentially directed by and supported by themselves in their personal and social functions, their role behaviors often are summarized by the term "independence." They would be said to have an independent status. Thus, the sociologically oriented person using these descriptive terms might conceptualize adolescence as a period of transition from the status and role of the child to the status and role of the adult. Adolescence then would be a period when a person makes a transition from having the dependent childhood role and status to having the independent adult role and status.

However, there are several problems with such a sociological definition. If children are dependent and adults are independent, what then is the status and the role of adolescents who are somewhere between? Are they dependent or independent? With this definition, there is no clear role and status for an adolescent.

Perhaps such lack of clarity in the role and status definitions is appropriate, however, in the sense that it reflects the ambiguous way an adolescent may be treated by adults. After all, the adolescent is often treated as a child *and* is often treated as an adult. For example, summer vacation comes and an adolescent male, 17 years old, decides to take off and sit in the backyard and sun himself all summer. His father comes home and the following conversation occurs:

Father: "What are you doing?"

Son: "Well, I'm sunning myself."

Father: "Why aren't you out working?"

Son: "Work! I'm not going to work. I had a tough set of courses this year. I need time to relax."

Father: "You're 17 years old! You're not going to sit there and relax. You're a grown person. You should have a job and bring in some income. I can't be expected to support you the rest of your life."

He is told he is an adult, and so he goes out and gets a job. Later, over the Fourth of July weekend, his friends are going to a resort. He may feel he now wants a little vacation, and so he approaches his father:

INSIGHT INTO ADOLESCENCE

Sylvia Plath was born in Boston in 1932. Her father died when she was a child; she lived with her mother and brother. By the time she was in high school, she wrote stories and poetry which were published in magazines and journals. She graduated from Smith College, and then studied at Cambridge University in England, where she met and married the poet Ted Hughes. They had two children. During most of her adult years she continued to write poetry, and also wrote a novel, *The Bell Jar*, which is about adolescence. In 1963, she ended her own life.

Aurelia Plath, Sylvia's mother, published the letters Sylvia wrote to her. This excerpt appears in the introduction to that book. Sylvia Plath entitled it "Diary Supplement," dated November 13, 1949.

Sometimes I try to put myself in another's place, and I am frightened when I find I am almost succeeding. How awful to be anyone but I. I have a terrible egotism. I love my flesh, my face, my limbs with overwhelming devotion. I know that I am "too tall" and have a fat nose, and yet I pose and prink before the mirror, seeing more and more how lovely I am. . . . I have erected in my mind an image of myself—idealistic and beautiful. Is not that image, free from blemish, the true self—the true perfection? Am I wrong when this image insinuates itself between me and the merciless mirror? (Oh, even now I glance back on what I have just written—how foolish it sounds, how overdramatic.)

Never, never, never will I reach the perfection I long for with all my soul—my paintings, my poems, my stories—all poor, poor reflections . . . for I have been too thoroughly conditioned to the conventional surroundings of this community . . . my vanity desires luxuries which I can never have. . . .

I am continually more aware of the power which chance plays in my life. . . . There will come a time when I must face myself at last. Even now I dread the big choices which loom up in my life—what college? What career? I am afraid. I feel uncertain. What is best for me? What do I want? I do not know. I love freedom. I deplore constrictions and limitations. . . . I am not as wise as I have thought. I can now see, as from a valley, the roads lying open for me, but I cannot see the end—the consequences. . . .

Oh, I love *now*, with all my fears and forebodings, for *now* I still am not completely molded. My life is still just beginning. I am strong. I long for a cause to devote my energies to. . . .

Source: Plath, A. S. (ed). Letters home: Correspondence 1950–1963. New York: Harper & Row, 1975.

Son:	"Say, do you mind if I borrow your car for the weekend? I want to go away with some friends."
Father:	"What do you mean borrow my car? I can't trust you with a car. You're not responsible enough to take the car away for a weekend. What are you going to be doing?"

Thus, one time the adolescent is attributed the role of an independent adult, while at another time he is seen as a dependent child. The adolescent's role is thus uncertain, and because of this vagueness, many writers (for example, Erikson) have said that the major problem confronting the adolescent is finding his or her role in life, his or her "identity."

Additionally, of course, one may even question the view that childhood is a period of total dependency or that adulthood is a period of total independency. Many people have lived in a residential area wherein a little "mistake" is made at a local power plant and an electrical blackout of an entire city (or more) occurs. Or, alternatively, a major service union goes on strike, and people are left without food, or transportation, or safety protection. In such situations one realizes how dependent he or she is on others and how fragile independency is. Although people strive to be independent—to control their own lives— adults may be, in fact, quite dependent on other people and institutions for their everyday existence and long-term survival. Moreover, it is equally true that children are by no means totally dependent.

Although dependency and independency have been used as just an instance of the problems associated with a simple role definition of adolescence, other distinctions (for example, consumer-producer) might have been used to show that similar problems exist. Thus, the meaning of adolescence, in terms of the roles prescribed for the person at this time of life, is unclear, and the clarity of the roles surrounding the adolescent period is also far from unambiguous.

Use of the above illustration provides a basis for noting that the meaning of adolescence must be understood in its social context. An adolescent is not just a person who does certain things. In our society, at this time in history, the precise behaviors and characteristics expected of adolescents are uncertain. Society is not clear about what it wants from the adolescent, what role it wants him or her to play. In fact, it may be said that if there is anything prescribed for adolescents in our current society, it is for them to find some way of defining themselves, so that they will no longer be in the ambiguous role of the adolescent. In other words, it may be that the "role" of the adolescent is to *get out* of the adolescent developmental period!

These observations about the role of the adolescent lead to three assertions. First, if the social meaning attached to the adolescent (for example, in defining the role and status of adolescence) is societally based, then there are not necessarily universal roles for the adolescent. Accordingly, to understand fully the meaning of adolescence, wherever it may occur, one should make comparisons among societies. A cross-cultural perspective should be taken.

Second, even within a given society, the meaning of adolescence changes. Examples of this are the changing legal status of youth and the differing times of physical changes in adolescence. Thus, due to changes in society which accrue over history, the meaning of adolescence changes and, as a consequence, one has to look at the social role of the adolescent as it evolves across history.

Third, of course, one basis for the historical changes in the meaning of adolescence is that the adolescent himself or herself is changing. He or she is a product of the historical influences affecting people in a society, and the adolescent influences changes in the society. Thus, in order to understand the social meaning and role of adolescence, one should understand how the adolescent's own development contributes to changing social functioning.

In summary, with regard to the sociological perspective, sole reliance on the social role of the adolescent is questionable. However, if the social functioning of the adolescent is seen as an outcome of the combined influence of changing biological, psychological, cultural, and historical influences, then its importance becomes clearer. The basis of and implications for the adolescent's social functioning for his or her own and society's continued functioning are more evident.

Cultural anthropology perspectives

A cultural anthropological perspective is one which evaluates how social interaction and societal customs vary from one culture to another. Using this approach to analyze adolescence, one must study the meaning of adolescence in different cultural settings. Anthropological analysis reveals whether or not adolescence is even recognized as a period within the life span in a particular culture, and if not, what age-related distinctions, if any, are used in those cultures. For example, is there a puberty or a fertility rite wherein the person passes immediately from childhood into adulthood (Benedict, 1938; Mead, 1928, 1935)? Additionally, anthropological analysis reveals information about differences among societies that do have some period of adolescence in the way a person is treated during this time. For instance, the relation between the level of technological and industrial development of a culture and its implications for the definition of adolescence might be revealed. Thus, as greater industrialization involves more specialized training, the period of time required for such education would be longer, and consequently, one might expect to see the period of adolescence delayed by extended education.

However, although it has been argued that such anthropological perspectives are necessary for a complete understanding of adolescence, by themselves they are incomplete. To understand why different cultures have different forms of adolescence—or when they may not even have a defined adolescent period—one must see how the prescription for adolescence fits the needs of the culture. How does defining youth in particular ways—for example, in training them for various lengths of time to play various roles—enable the culture to maintain and perpetuate itself? How does adolescence allow the culture to survive? To answer such questions it is important to remember that the needs of a culture change over time, and the characteristics of the people populating the society change also. Accordingly, to understand the diversity of cultural variation in adolescence, the historical influences on the culture, as well as the impact the changing biological and psychological processes of the person contribute to the culture, should be considered.

Historical transitions in adolescent development

The historical perspective of adolescence represents a summary view of all others. All processes—from the biological to the cultural—involve change. Thus, they have a history.

The study of individual development is, of course, the study of a person's life span, or in other words, of the history of his or her changes from conception until death. However, such individual history is linked reciprocally with the history of progressions of all other levels of existence. Accordingly, the study of development includes not only the history of progressions involving the person, but also the history of the person's biological, social, and cultural environment.

Said another way, the study of adolescent development is the study of the history of all the interrelated components of changes constituting human existence as they lead up to, and follow from, the portion of the life span termed adolescence. Such a focus on the dynamics of history suggests why there are numerous, interrelated transitions that may occur in adolescence, and why they may need to be seen in an integrative manner. These recognitions, of course, are the basis of the life-span definition of adolescent development. Moreover, as discussed below, historical changes have other implications for definitions of adolescence.

"Youth" as a new period within the life span

Some human developmentalists have commented that within the current historical context the phenomena of adolescence seem to "begin soon after the tenth birthday and to extend beyond the twentieth birthday" (Muuss, 1975b, p. 1). Muuss (1975b) contends that this prolonged adolescent period occurs most often among people who continue their education past high school. He believes that because the adolescent period has thus lengthened for the majority of today's young people, it is necessary to subdivide the adolescent period into subperiods. For example, he suggests labeling young people in junior high school as "early adolescents," those in senior high school as "middle adolescents," and those in early college as "late adolescents" (Muuss, 1975b).

Keniston (1970) discusses a similar idea. He claims there exists a new transition period in the current sociocultural-historical setting, and he terms this period "youth." This period exists for people who may chronologically have reached the end of adolescence but are still not socially regarded as mature adults. Keniston (1970) contends that there exists in current society groups of young men and women of college and graduate school age who have, as yet, not "settled down." He believes that:

> What characterizes a growing minority of postadolescents today is that they have not settled the questions whose answers once defined adulthood: questions of relationship to the existing society, questions of vocation, questions of social role and life-style.

Youth, then, to Keniston, is a transition period which differs from adolescence in several ways. Keniston (1970) believes that in youth there is a conflict between trying to maintain an autonomous sense of self and being socially involved. This differs from the core adolescent conflict, which involves a struggle for self-definition (Erikson, 1959, 1963; Keniston, 1970). In addition, Keniston claims that adolescents may be characterized as trying to develop toward an "endpoint," that is, an identity or self-definition. Youth, however, already have such a sense of self and continually value development and change. They dislike "being in a rut," or "getting nowhere" with their lives, and value the ability "to keep moving" in life.

Future research will have to document the distinctions Keniston (1970) makes between adolescence and youth. Nevertheless, the point is that historical changes in the social context of young people can both alter the nature of any transitionary period and create or eliminate such periods.

The transitions of adolescence: Summary

Adolescent development has been described as a transitionary period in the life span. The person makes a transition from possessing most processes within the typical range of changes associated with childhood, to having most of the processes typically within the range of changes associated with adulthood. Adolescence, then, is that period when most of the processes of the person are between these two statuses.

This notion of adolescence requires an appraisal of all the processes that are undergoing transition. Additionally, this conception of adolescence requires an understanding of the entire life span. One has to know the modes of childhood and adulthood before one can correctly categorize the person on the basis of whether most of his or her processes are in the period of transition between childhood and adulthood. Moreover, one must recognize that all these change processes are interdependent. As such, one must consider what each process may or may not contribute to an overall, integrated view of this transitionary period. One way that the change processes lead adolescents to both shape and be shaped by their sociocultural environment is considered below.

IMPLICATIONS OF THE TRANSITIONS OF ADOLESCENCE

People typically do not think of themselves in the segmented fashion social scientists do. Rather than apportion their lives into categories such as cognitive, emotional, or biological, it is obvious that adolescents tend to view themselves as whole beings. Although some adolescents may be especially concerned about particular parts of themselves (for example, their body), in typical circumstances the individual does not see his or her body as something not part of the self.

Furthermore, people viewing the adolescent do not make segmentations. Thus, adults such as parents, teachers, or relatives do not speak often of only part of the adolescent as making a transition. Rather, many adults conceive of adolescence as a holistic period of change involving all facets of the person's existence (Anthony, 1969). Accordingly, although the previous discussion in this chapter is certainly consistent with a holistic view of adolescent transitions—in the sense of the need for an integrated understanding of change processes—the meaning of holism from the perspective of adolescents and adults is quite different from the perspective of the person studying adolescence.

Scientists integrate all the changes of adolescence because of a belief that it results in a more scientifically useful depiction of development. Many nonscientists, however, view adolescent changes as a whole for a different reason—a belief in the general, unfavorable nature of this period of life (Anthony, 1969).

An overview of the adolescent's transitional experiences

The most obvious set of changes that the adolescent goes through are the anatomical and physiological ones. New hormones are being produced by the endocrine glands, and these produce alterations in the primary sexual characteristics and the emergence of secondary sexual characteristics. The person thus begins to look different and, as a consequence of the new hormones, feel different. There is also a change in the person's emotional functioning as a consequence of these physical and hormonal changes. New hormones induce sexual changes and produce new drives and new feelings. The new hormonal balance causes the person to feel things that he or she never really felt before. In combination with changing social influences such as peer pressure, the mass media, and interest in members of the other sex, he or she becomes more sexually oriented.

All these physical, psychological, and emotional changes are complicated by the fact that the person is also undergoing cognitive changes. New thought capabilities come to characterize the adolescent. Rather than being tied to the concrete physical reality of what is, the adolescent becomes capable of dealing with hypothetical and abstract aspects of reality. The way the world is organized is no longer seen as the only way it could be. That is, the system of government, the orders of parents, the adolescent's status in the peer group, and the rules imposed on him or her are no longer taken as concrete, immutable things. Rather, as the new thought capabilities that allow the person to think abstractly, hypothetically, and counterfactually come into existence, they allow the person to imagine how things could be. These imaginings could relate to government, self, parents' rules, or what he or she will do in life. In short, anything and everything becomes the focus of an adolescent's hypothetical, counterfactual, and imaginary thinking.

For both psychological and sociological reasons, the major focus of the adolescent's concerns becomes the adolescent himself or herself. The adolescent's inner processes are all going through changes; the physical, physiological, emotional, and cognitive components of the person are undergoing major alterations. Now, with any object being able to be thought of in a new, different, hypothetical way, and with the individual so radically changing, it is appropriate for the person to focus on himself or herself to try to understand what is going on.

The person will ask: What is the nature of this change? What will it do to me? What will I become? Am I the same person that I think I am? As all these uncertainties are being introduced, another set of problems is introduced. That is, at the very time that the adolescent is having all these concerns—at the very time that he or she may be least prepared to deal with further complications and uncertainties, others are imposed. The adolescent in our society typically is asked to make a choice, a decision about what he or she is going to do when grown. Society, perhaps in the form of parents or teachers, asks the adolescent to choose a role. Thus, in today's society, as soon as one gets into junior high or early in high school, one may be asked to choose whether a college preparatory program or a non-college preparatory program is desired. Thus, at about age 13 years or so, one begins to put oneself on a path that will affect what will be done years and years later.

The point is that at precisely the time in life when adolescents are least ready to make a long-term choice, they often are asked to do so. In order to reconcile all the changes being experienced, and to cope with all the demands put on them, American adolescents have to make these choices. To say what they will do, to commit themselves to a role, they have to know what their attributes and capabilities are. They have to know what they can do well and what they want to do. In short, they have to know themselves.

Many adolescents are in a dilemma. They cannot answer the social-role questions without settling other questions about themselves. The answers to one set of questions are interdependent with the answers to the others. A feeling of crisis may emerge, one which requires finding out precisely who one is now. This really is a question of self-definition, of self-identification. Erikson (1959) labels this dilemma the *identity crisis*.

To summarize, the adolescent—because of the impact of all the changes converging on him or her—may be described as in a state of crisis, a state of search for self-definition. Accordingly, the adolescent moves through his or her days attempting to find a place—or role—in society. Such definition will provide a set of rules for beliefs, attitudes, and values (an "ideology") and a prescription for behaviors (a role) that will enable the persons to know what they will "do with themselves" in the world. They will try to find out if they can begin to think like someone who engages in particular behaviors (for example, being a doctor, a lawyer, a nurse, or a telephone operator). They will attempt to discover if they can adopt the ideology of and acquire the behaviors for particular roles.

Of course, adolescents may try out various roles in the course of their search for identity. More will be said about the details of the central self-definition and role-determination processes in later chapters; here issues may be raised about some of the consequences of the processes as they are occurring. What happens to the adolescent at the time of the search? What impact does searching for self-definition have, for instance, on those with whom the adolescent interacts? How does such impact feed back on the adolescent affecting further behavior during this period? Anthony (1969) has provided a basis for addressing these issues. He believes that among adults there is a generalized reaction to, and appraisal of, adolescents. This orientation toward adolescents exists in the form of a social stereotype about the nature of the adolescent developmental period. It is informative to examine the adults's reaction to adolescent development in more detail.

Adult reactions to adolescent development

Anthony (1969) believes that many adults view adolescents with a set of attitudes which are often overgeneralized. The attitudes are applied invariably to any adolescent. No exception is admitted. Such an overgeneralized belief is termed a *stereotype*.

Not all people have stereotypes about adolescents. Even among those who do, it may not always be called into play when dealing with the adolescent. The point Anthony makes is that *if and when* this stereotype is present, it provides a basis of adults' actions toward adolescents and, furthermore, adolescents' reciprocal behavior toward adults.

Anthony says that many people believe adolescence to be a period of upheaval. In fact, as seen in Chapter 1, theorists like Hall (1904) and Davis (1944) stressed this view. More recently, Bandura (1964) also has noted that there is a popular conception of adolescence as being a period of turmoil. Many people who have this stereotyped idea might base their belief, in part, on the observation that the adolescent has not yet established clearly identified "adult" roles. Adolescents are often seen in the midst of deciding what sort of social affiliations they want to have, of deciding what roles they are going to play in society, but as having not yet *committed* themselves to any one set of roles. By not having yet chosen their roles in society, the adolescent is not seen as having made a firm commitment to the maintenance and continuation of society.

Many adults, Anthony believes, see this as confusion in the adolescent, and as a consequence view the adolescent as dangerous. Perhaps he or she has not made a commitment to support society in any particular way. But at the same time, in viewing the adolescent as dangerous, the adult sees the adolescent who is not committing himself or herself to society as endangering his or her own existence. The adult's rationale is that the adolescent does not know that by not committing oneself to society, by not choosing roles that will allow one to contribute to society and hence maintain its existence, one is endangering one's own survival. If one does not contribute to society, society will collapse. Hence, the adolescent will be destroyed by his or her own actions.

This orientation to adolescence culminates in what Anthony labels the first major component of adults' stereotypes about adolescents. The adolescent is seen as *dangerous and as endangered*. The adolescent is both a *victimizer and a victim*. The adolescent is a victimizer of society by not contributing, and a victim of his or her victimizing behavior by not playing a role, by not choosing.

What sort of person would someone be who is both dangerous and endangered? What sort of person would victimize others (society) and at the same time hurt himself or herself? Likely, someone who is maladjusted. Thus, to Anthony, the second component of the stereotype is that adolescence is viewed as a *period of maladjustment,* and *the adolescent* is seen as *maladjusted.*

Why is the adolescent seen as maladjusted? The adolescent is going "back and forth" trying to find a role. Although this may be the nature of role search, the *adolescent* is also seen *as lost*. Anthony contends that because the adolescent is viewed as not having any one direction, especially a positive one, and thus because he or she goes from one role to another (albeit in search of a final role), the adolescent is seen as lost.

But why does the person remain lost? Because he or she is maladjusted. Why is the person maladjusted? Because he or she is dangerous and endangered. Why is he or she both? Because the individual has not committed himself or herself because he or she is lost. And what kind of person remains lost, unable to fit in? A maladjusted person. It can be readily seen how one part of the stereotype reinforces another.

Complicating these perceptions is the fact that there is another dimension of the adolescent stereotype. Along with the above negative characteristics of the stereotype, Anthony argues, the adolescent also is seen as possessing characteristics which are very positive ones in our society. Adolescence is the period in life when one has the greatest likelihood of possessing the physical characteristics and good health which are highly valued in our society. Our society is oriented toward health, physical fitness, and youth. The popularity of sports, the widespread use of techniques which make one slim and fit, and attempts to achieve the "look of youth" are evidence of this orientation (Lerner & Korn, 1972). Thus, while adolescents may be looked at negatively, they may also be seen as *objects of envy*. The best way to summarize this dual orientation to adolescence is to refer to a famous statement by George Bernard Shaw: "Youth is such a wonderful thing; too bad it is wasted on the young."

There is another aspect of this dual, positive-negative orientation to adolescence. There is another reason they may be objects of envy. An adolescent usually has the physical attributes for a successful sex life, with fewer social constraints experienced by many married adults. The body of the adolescent is regarded as sexually desirable. The 18-year-old young man or woman is more likely to be found in the centerfold of current magazines which feature nudity than persons even 10 years more senior. Typically, the 45-year-old or even the 35-year-old man or woman is not presented. Thus, the adolescent is sometimes seen as a *sexual object*. Absence of obligations to spouse or children permits many adolescents the freedom to take advantage of their physical appeal and sexual interests.

In summary, it is the youth, health, and physical fitness of the adolescent that provides part of the basis of attraction. Yet, at the same time, these characteristics may result in an adolescent being considered dangerous, endangered, maladjusted, or lost. An adult holding this stereotype might wonder how adolescents might use their sexuality in light of their maladjusted, victimizing state. The answer would be that sex would be used in the wrong way. Sex outside of marriage and other traditionally nonsanctioned behaviors would come about. Because adolescents are thought by some to be dangerous and maladjusted, some adults fear adolescents might do things that would destroy the fabric of our society.

Stereotypes can be dangerous. Certainly, it is preferable to put all the issues raised above into context. Adolescent crime, sexuality, and rebelliousness do exist, and for some adolescents, these are problematic. But the most responsible approach to these topics would be to include an examination of the range of relevant variables across the spectrum of the adolescent population. How the adult stereotype can affect adolescent behavior may now be assessed.

The outcome of adolescent transitions and adult stereotypes

How may the adult's beliefs about the adolescent's potential behavior affect the adolescent's actual behavior? One major consequence would be to channel the adolescent's behavior so it is consistent with the stereotype. Because of their stereotypes, adults might foster the very behavior in children and adolescents that the stereotype makes them fear will be seen. Parents holding stereotypes about permissive sexual behavior might, for instance, put restrictions on their adolescent child that they believe will decrease the likelihood of undesired sexual behavior. Additionally, they might punish the adolescent severely at the first hint of sexual transgression. Such a step might be seen as necessary to protect both the family and the adolescent. The young adolescent might simply come home a bit late from a group date, but the parents, not believing him or her, might believe that some form of sexual behavior "must have" taken place. The youth conceivably could be punished for two things: for the sexual activity and for lying about it!

The net effects of these parental actions—taken because of their stereotype— might possibly lead to behavior consistent with the stereotype. The adolescent might wonder why the restrictions regarding sex are so severe since even a casual look at the media would indicate that sex is common in society. Accordingly, the newly abstractly thinking adolescent might begin to fantasize about what really is being kept from him or her. Furthermore, being falsely accused and punished for behavior not present might lead the adolescent away from the parents to some extent and toward the peer group. The peer group provides a social milieu which is made up, by definition, of other adolescents, and not parents. Wishing to spend more time with peers and less with parents, the adolescent is thus in a setting less likely to have the same prohibitions on behavior that exist in a parent-dominated setting. Combined with pressures from members of the opposite sex, engaging in sexual behavior becomes more probable. In short, the end result of the parents' stereotype might be to make the undesired behavior more likely.

The stereotype leads to channeling the adolescent's behavior to be consistent with the stereotype. Hence, a *self-fulfilling prophecy* is encouraged. A circular, reciprocal process between the adult's stereotype and the adolescent's behavior is formed. That is, not only does the adult's stereotype foster stereotype-consistent behavior in the adolescent; additionally, when that stereotype-consistent behavior is emitted, even to a small degree, it reinforces (and thus maintains) the adult's stereotype. Hence the stereotype continues to influence the adolescent's behavior, and reciprocally, the adolescent's behavior continues to influence the stereotype. The circular, self-fulfilling prophecy process continues.

In sum, even if there was no initial basis in reality for the adult's stereotype about adolescents—and there need not be one—there soon would be a basis for it, as the self-fulfilling prophecy process began to unfold. To return to a now familiar theme, the adolescent is thus a product and a producer of his or her social world.

However, adolescent behavior is not going to be perfectly consistent with the stereotype of adolescence. There are, of course, many sources of adolescent behavior, and not all adults hold exactly the same stereotypes. This circular model can therefore change in content, or even break down. Thus, although it does not explain every facet of adolescent development, this model is important. It depicts the impact an adolescent may have on others as he or she traverses this transitionary period.

More generally, this model is an instance of a general circular relation among sources of adolescent development. The self-fulfilling prophecy between the changes of adolescents and the social stereotypes of adults is identical in form to circular relations involving other adolescent processes. In later discussions of the cognitive and personality changes involving adolescents, the circular model idea will be applicable.

CHAPTER SUMMARY

Adolescence is that period within the life span when most of the person's processes (such as the biological, psychological, and social) are in transition from what typically is considered childhood to what typically is considered adulthood. There are numerous definitions of adolescence that only focus on one or another of these change processes. Each definition has its limitations, but may contribute to our overall understanding of adolescence.

Age definitions of adolescence are arbitrary. Also, age is not an explanatory variable; it only marks changes that occur in relation to time. However, age definitions allow one to identify the number of adolescents that exist at any one point in history. Thus, one may determine the magnitude of a problem that may affect a part of the adolescent population.

Physical and physiological definitions of adolescence pertain to events associated with puberty. However, there are wide individual differences in the timing of such changes, and therefore criteria for establishing the beginning and end of adolescence this way are often questionable. Nevertheless, looking at changes in the average time of the emergence of events such as menarche gives one an appreciation of the interrelation between biological, sociocultural, and historical change.

Legal definitions of portions of the life span, like childhood or adulthood, are also arbitrary. Although there is no legal definition of adolescence, there are laws which indicate when certain adult behaviors such as voting, drinking, and signing a legal contract may exist. Thus, such laws are an indication of how society sees people at different points in their life spans.

Psychological transitions are the most commonly studied aspects of adolescence. Topics such as personality, intelligence, and moral reasoning have been studied widely. However, the role of sociocultural and historical influences on psychological changes has not been considered adequately. A sociological perspective stresses human interaction and the roles people play at different times of their lives. A cultural anthropological perspective provides information about the comparative meaning of adolescence in different cultural settings. However, whether a society has a culturally defined period of adolescence, and, if so, how that definition may change over time, depends on the survival needs faced by the society.

Historical approaches to the study of adolescence lead to the recognition that as societies change over time, the nature and definition of the adolescent period may vary. Indeed, some scientists have said that due to recent historical changes, the adolescent period may be divided into three periods (early, middle, and late). Others have argued that a new transitionary period between adolescence and adulthood—termed "youth"—has come to characterize the recent historical era.

Because of the numerous changes that occur during adolescence, the person often is pressed into finding a coordinated way to reconcile these changes. Some scientists have depicted this endeavor as the adolescent's search for identity, or self-definition. Others have noted that while the adolescent is searching for self-definition, adults often may maintain stereotypes about adolescence that characterize them in negative ways (for example, as lost or maladjusted). These stereotypes may create a self-fulfilling prophecy, channeling the adolescent's behavior in the very way the stereotype suggests. Although stereotypes cannot explain all facets of adolescent behavior, the idea of a self-fulfilling prophecy is one which has applicability in many areas of adolescent development.

3

THE ADOLESCENT'S SOCIAL CONTEXT

CHAPTER
OVERVIEW

Human life is indisputably social. Perhaps no characteristics set humans apart from lower forms of animal life more than the ability to engage in complex, meaningful relationships and the propensity for social organization. The adolescent is a product of social life as well as a contributor to it. In this chapter some of the most important elements in the adolescent's social world are examined. In particular, some of the *social institutions* which have considerable impact on human development are discussed.

PEER RELATIONSHIPS

The Emergence of Peer Groups
Some Characteristics of the Adolescent Peer Subculture
Institutional Peer Groups
Athletics
When Peer Groups Fail

FAMILY RELATIONSHIPS

The Changing Family
The Influence of the Family
Parents as Models
Other Family Members

THE RELATIVE INFLUENCES OF PARENTS AND PEERS
THE GENERATION GAP

Parent-Adolescent Conflict
Some Family Problems of Adolescence
Studies of Intergenerational Relations

EDUCATION DURING ADOLESCENCE

Functions of the Educational System
Adolescents' Views about the Functions of Education
Family and Peer Influences on Education
Sociocultural and Historical Influences on Education

HIGH SCHOOL DROPOUTS

Magnitude of the Problem
Why Students Leave School
Consequences of Dropping Out

RELIGION IN ADOLESCENCE

Importance of Religion to Adolescents
The Development of Religious Beliefs in Adolescence

RELIGIOUS CULTS

Defection from Traditional Religion
Reasons for Joining
Reasons for Leaving
Other Religious Movements

ADOLESCENTS AS WORKERS
ADOLESCENTS AS CONSUMERS

MILITARY SERVICE
ADOLESCENTS AND THE POLITICAL SYSTEM
Law and Adolescents
Adolescents as Voters
Political Socialization in Adolescence

EFFECTS OF THE MASS MEDIA ON ADOLESCENT DEVELOPMENT
Effects of Manipulated Television Viewing Patterns
Effects of Actual Television Viewing Patterns

What motivates adolescents to form peer groups, and what functions do peer groups perform?

What are some characteristics which are particularly associated with adolescent peer groups?

What types of family change have relevance for the adolescent?

What is the relative influence of parents and peers on adolescent development, and under what circumstances might one group be more influential than another?

In what sense can parent-adolescent conflict be seen as normal, and what are some of the specific issues over which parents and adolescents quarrel?

Is it reasonable for parents to deny their adolescents privileges that they have, such as the right to smoke and drink? What are the arguments speaking to this issue?

Consider the evidence supporting and contradicting the idea that there is a generation gap. What can be concluded about this concept?

How important is the role that the educational system plays in the lives of adolescents?

Why do some adolescents drop out of high school, and in what ways do they differ from those who remain in school?

To what degree is religion important to the contemporary adolescent?

What types of persons join religious cults, why do they join, and why do some leave?

How does the legal system pose a dilemma for adolescents?

What can be concluded about the impact of the mass media on adolescent development?

Does television appear to contribute to violence during adolescence?

 famous poem begins "No man is an island; no man stands alone." This statement recognizes that all humans form *social relationships,* ongoing interactions between two or more people. Social relationships are basic components of individual development. In fact, it might be said that such relationships are absolutely necessary. This is demonstrated by studies which have deprived both nonhuman animals and humans of typical social experiences (Goldfarb, 1945; Harlow & Harlow, 1962; Spitz, 1945; Tobach & Schneirla, 1968). Such research indicates that among these groups abnormal social and nonsocial behaviors develop. There are also isolated reports of children and adolescents who have been deprived of social contact for extended periods of time. Reports of such persons occasionally are found in news stories. The most dramatic cases reported—which are questionable—are so-called "feral" children, separated from their families and supposedly raised by animals

(Krout, 1942; Ogburn, 1959; Singh & Zingg, 1942). Although it is unlikely that such cases of children raised by animals really exist—rather they are probably cases in which the child has been lost or abandoned and discovered shortly thereafter—anecdotal reports are that such children have a retarded rate of development.

This book emphasizes the role of social—as well as biological, psychological, historical, and even philosophical—influences in shaping the developing adolescent. To understand fully the relevance of the social context of the adolescent, one must first specify the nature of social influences and, secondly, consider problems which may arise when social change occurs and individuals and the society experience dysfunctions. The first task, that of discussing the nature and implications of the social context for current adolescent development, is the focus of this chapter. The second task, the identification and and examination of social change and social problems in adolescence, is undertaken in subsequent chapters.

Much of the impact of the social context is influenced by social institutions. A *social institution* is an ongoing aspect of society around which many of life's most important activities are centered. Examples of social institutions are the family, religion, the legal system, the educational system, the mass media, and the political system. All social institutions change from time to time, and much of social change is based on the continuing evolution that can be seen in a society's social institutions. Thus, the social context of adolescents is composed of both other people and social institutions. The influences of both are reviewed in this chapter.

PEER RELATIONSHIPS

Perhaps the most notable social phenomenon of adolescence is the marked influence of peer groups. Peers have the ability to make an adolescent feel on top of the world or at the bottom of the social ladder. Peers hold the key to adolescent popularity or rejection. Peers informally instruct the adolescent on how to talk, how to dress, and how to act. And it is often the intensity of the way one conforms to peer group norms that serves as a basis of parent-adolescent conflict.

The study of peer relations is sometimes referred to as the study of *intragenerational* relationships. The study of adolescent-parent relationships, which crosses generations, is the study of *intergenerational* relationships. A *generation*, like a birth cohort, is a group of people born during one period of history. Usually, if one refers to all people born in just one year, the term "birth cohort" is used. The length of a generation is the span of time between one's birth and the birth of one's children. In the United States, this period averages about twenty-five years. The term "generation," however, sometimes is used in a more general way to refer to spans of time varying from several years to three or four decades. This more general use is applied in this book. Thus, peer relations are sometimes called intragenerational relations, because peers are born within the same generation.

The emergence of peer groups

It is sometimes said that there is strength in numbers. This theme seems to characterize much of peer-group interaction. Peer groups certainly exist in childhood, but they become more central to the individual in adolescence. The adolescent comes to rely heavily on the peer group for support, security, and guidance. Marked peer-group importance probably emerges because there is a great need for such support, security, and guidance during these years of transition, and it is easiest to find such things among others who are undergoing the same transition and with whom much time is spent.

From the standpoint of the adolescent, the peer group has much to offer. It is a sounding board, it gives constant feedback that all is well (or not so well) as adolescence progresses, it answers some of the important questions of adolescence (for example, about sexual relations and drug and alcohol use), and by virtue of its size, it helps legitimize any behaviors or activities in which its members engage.

All peer groups change over time. Moreover, an adolescent may move from one peer group to another, and he or she may belong to more than one peer group. Furthermore all adolescent peer groups in a given culture comprise the adolescent subculture. Thus, when one speaks of peer groups, it is important to recognize the great variability in the existence of peer groups. However, despite such variability, there is much in common among adolescent peer groups.

During adolescence, persons begin new types of interaction with members of the opposite sex. They may move into a new school environment (junior high school or high school), and they engage in a multitude of activities that are new to them (for example, organized sports, dances, after-school clubs). All these new experiences can be mildly threatening if approached alone. The peer group often provides group support to its individual members so that these transitions become less formidable. Thus, it can be argued that influential peer groups emerge during adolescence to help the individual through some new transitions, and to provide support, security, and guidance to the persons involved.

Some characteristics of the adolescent peer subculture

It might seem like an easy task to describe some of the most distinguishing features of the adolescent subculture, but it should be cautioned that the experiences of adolescent development vary considerably from one society to another, and within our own society, from one community or ethnic group or social stratum to another. Nevertheless, there are some aspects of the adolescent subculture in America which never seem to hide.

Automobiles One example is the emphasis on automobiles among adolescent males in particular. Perhaps because a driver's license may be obtained at age 16 in most states, and because automobiles provide mobility and freedom that were not previously available, adolescence and automobiles are closely associated. The parking lots of many high schools throughout the country are full each day, despite the availability of school buses, public transportation, or the nearness of the school to the residences which it serves. Automobiles have taken on symbolic as well as material meaning to many adolescents, and often provide a form of status.

In many communities throughout the country, especially in small towns, adolescents spend weekend evenings "scooping the loop," "dragging main," or "cruising around town." This activity, where the youth of a community drive aimlessly in circles around the town, is annoying, frustrating, and silly to adults—but to the adolescents it may be a primary form of recreation.

Automobiles traditionally have been more important to young men than young women. But both adolescent males and females often derive status from the cars they drive, and many spend much of their spare income on gasoline, repairs, insurance, and special equipment for their cars. The automobile may become a "second home" to the adolescent; it facilitates dating, provides greater opportunities for recreation, and is a ready "escape" when the adolescent wants to get out of the house for a while.

Automobile accident and violation rates are considerably higher for adolescent males than for persons in any other age category; consequently, insurance premiums are higher. Motor vehicle accidents (motorcycle and automobile) are the leading cause of death among adolescents (as drivers *and* passengers).

Groups   Another characteristic of peer interaction is an unusual degree of "mass movement." By this we mean the tendency for adolescents to congregate in groups and to actually move in groups. It is not uncommon to hear a group of several students in the school cafeteria jointly deciding where they will go after school—as if they all *had* to go *somewhere* together. Adolescents can be found congregating in downtown shopping districts, at shopping centers, at athletic events, and on the school grounds. They are often found in large groups, even though there may be no special organized activity which necessitates anyone's presence at the setting. This phenomenon again reinforces the adolescent's feeling of security. To be a part of a group is important, even if the group is engaged in no special activity or has no special purpose.

Cliques   Another characteristic of adolescence is the orientation to be in the "in-group." This orientation is easily understandable, since acceptance is an important human need. Unfortunately, adolescents sometimes satisfy this need by engaging in behavior which not only excludes others, but does so in a hurtful way. All of us can remember persons in our high school who were social outcasts. Very often, persons made fun of these unpopular students, and perhaps had a good laugh at their expense. Adolescents who are cruel in their treatment of others often know that their behavior is wrong, but the need to be a part of the group which is hurting the unpopular individual may be greater than the need to effect social justice in the setting.

In-groups are often referred to as *cliques*. A clique is a closely knit group of persons which tends to systematically exclude others. *Gangs* are another form of an in-group which is selective about who may be considered a member and who may not. Both cliques and gangs are phenomena of adolescence, and reflect the special needs for affiliation that adolescents have. Gangs will be discussed in more detail in Chapter 15.

Institutional peer groups

We tend to think of peer groups as informal affiliations among individuals. However, our society provides for a multitude of more formal associations among adolescents which also serve as important peer groups. Examples are church or synagogue youth groups, boy scouts and girl scouts, YMCA and YWCA clubs, organized athletic teams, community recreation center programs, and other such clubs and organizations.

Most adolescents belong to at least one such group, and these more formal peer associations often serve as important reference groups for the adolescent. As noted earlier, many adolescents may belong simultaneously to both a formal peer group, such as a church youth organization, and a more informal peer group, such as several adolescents of the same sex living in a given neighborhood.

Often, parents especially encourage participation in organized peer groups, perhaps because there may be adult supervision of the activities, and community recognition and status associated with some of the groups. Some parents become concerned, however, when their children become *too* involved with such groups, perhaps worrying that involvement might make excessive time demands on the adolescent, detracting from school performance. Adolescents, however, are usually able to work out an acceptable balance of time commitments among the various activities available to them, and often find institutional peer groups to be rewarding social activities.

Athletics

Special mention of the central role of athletics in adolescent development is warranted. Most adolescent males and a growing number of adolescent females are involved heavily in some form of athletics. Many play on organized teams for the school or in the community, and others simply play in their neighborhoods with friends. Adolescents are physically active, they are perhaps as physically healthy as they will ever be, and they tend to find themselves in environments (such as the school) which place a high value on athletics. Thus, sports activities become central in the lives of many adolescents. Even many of those who are not very accomplished athletically may still participate (for example, as ticket sellers, as team managers, as reporters for the school paper, or as pep club members).

High school athletic teams provide a basis for much of the social life of adolescents. Interscholastic athletic events are important weekend activities in schools, and other social functions such as dances often take place in conjunction with the sporting events.

Some individuals are critical of the central role of athletics in schools. It is argued that it detracts from scholarship or uses up funds that ought to be committed to academics. This is a difficult issue for schools and communities, since an appropriate balance must be found. However, for many students, participation on athletic teams is the primary force which motivates them to remain in school. For other participants, it adds dimensions to their lives which enhance personal and social development. And for nonparticipants, it still provides an opportunity to "be a part of something," by attending such events and sharing in a victory (or loss) through what has come to be known as "school spirit."

The changing roles of women and new federal regulations are encouraging greater athletic opportunities for females in an area that used to be the exclusive domain of the male. Adolescent females are likely to become increasingly attracted to athletics. This trend has already become visible, and public response to female expertise in athletics—especially sports such as gymnastics, basketball, swimming, tennis, golf, and outdoor winter sports—has been extremely positive.

When peer groups fail

Many parents have been known to say that their adolescent got into trouble because he or she got mixed up with some rotten kids—or stated differently, with the wrong peer group. It is not known precisely how an individual becomes affiliated with a particular peer group. Undoubtedly, it is an interactive process, with the peer group becoming open to the individual, and with the individual seeking entrance to the peer group.

Neither is it known what would have happened to adolescents who—as their parents wanted—might have chosen other friends. Whatever the answers, it is clear that peer bonds are strong ones, not easily broken by parents, nor easily terminated on the basis of parental inclination. Many parents have learned after much frustration that adolescents can be influenced some in their choice of peers, but once ties have been formed, parental intervention in the peer relationships usually produces conflict which is unlikely to change the nature of the peer-group ties.

In addition to the peer group's influence, there is another part of the social context that is quiet influential for adolescents. This is the family, and we explore its role next.

FAMILY RELATIONSHIPS

Perhaps no social institution has as great an influence on development as the family. The family is the basic social unit of society, and is the most common location for reproduction, childbearing, and child rearing. Virtually all children in all cultures are socialized by families, although the form of the family unit may vary slightly. Thus, a *family* can be defined as a unit of related individuals in which children are produced and reared.

Children and adolescents may find themselves in more than one family during their socialization. About 1 in 5 children under 18 in the United States do not live with two parents (U.S. Bureau of the Census, 1978a). There are a substantial number of single-parent families, and many children and adolescents live in families with two adults but only one biological parent. These variations in living arrangements and family status come about, of course, as a result of the high rates of marital dissolution found in the United States. Divorce and remarriage are common in the United States today, with about 2 out of every 5 marriages involving recently married persons expected to end in divorce (U.S. Bureau of the Census, 1976). Moreover, about three-fourths of the persons involved in divorce eventually remarry—and those who remarry do so, on the average, about three years after the divorce. Thus, many children and adolescents—perhaps 45 percent—can expect to live in a family setting without both natural parents for a period of time before they reach adulthood.

The changing family

The increase in the divorce rate which occurred in the 1960s and 1970s is but one of the many changes in the family which has had an impact on adolescence. Families of today are in many ways similar to families of earlier generations—but they are also different in many ways. For example, today there is more leisure time available to parents. It is not known to what degree parents use this increased leisure time to enhance family relationships in some way, but it is known that due to shorter work weeks and other changes in life-styles, leisure is a more important aspect of modern family life.

Changes in the birthrates during the 1960s and 1970s suggest that adolescents in the 1980s will have fewer siblings than did adolescents in earlier generations. This may permit closer family ties, since there will be more time available for interaction between each parent and each child—but again, it is not known whether such a result actually will follow from decreased family size in today's families.

The contemporary family is more mobile than the family of earlier generations. Thus, the adolescent of the 1980s is more likely to move from one residence, school, or community to another. Moving undoubtedly has consequences for both peer and family relationships.

Moreover, as the standard of living increases, it is more likely that the problems many families experience in life will shift from those related to economics to those related to interpersonal relationships. Thus, as more families enter the middle class, we might expect that family relationships in general and parent-adolescent conflict in particular may shift in focus.

These are but a few of the recent trends in the American family which may have some impact on adolescence. There are certainly others, some which have not yet adequately been studied, and others which undoubtedly have not yet been identified. It is clear that the institution of the family changes, and that individual families change as well. We may expect to see such change throughout history. But despite such change, there remain some constants. Let us examine some of these.

The influence of the family

Most social scientists would acknowledge the profound impact of the family on the development of the young child. But what about on the adolescent? Does the family play an important role in the socialization and behavior of adolescents? As might be expected, adolescents report that the family has been the most influential social system in their lives (Winch & Gordon, 1974). This influence is particularly great with regard to the acquisition of values. For example, with such traits as thrift and honesty, the family is reported as the prime source of influence by more than 90 percent of respondents in one large study (Winch & Gordon, 1974). Altruism and nurturance are traits often mentioned as being influenced by mothers; and taking pride in one's work, being responsible, and being honest often are mentioned as being influenced by fathers (Winch & Gordon, 1974). All these traits are basic values in society, and even by adolescents' own reports, the family has played a central role in teaching them these values.

Parents as models

Adolescents often find it difficult to resist indulging in behaviors which characterize adulthood. Sexual relations, smoking, drinking, freedom of movement, and independence in decision making are behaviors which the adolescent may desire, but which he or she may learn are prohibited. These and other behaviors thus take on special importance in adolescence. In fact, they may take on undue importance. Adolescents may try to push their sexual partners further than they wish to go in a given relationship, because peer and personal pressures may result in an overemphasis on the importance of such behavior. Adolescents may begin smoking, despite a knowledge that it is harmful and an initial distaste for the habit. They may drink excessively to impress friends, and may come home drunk far more often than they will when they reach adulthood.

These strivings for symbols of adulthood often lead to questions about parents as models. For example, how can a parent who smokes expect his or her adolescent offspring to take seriously the argument that smoking is wrong? Some persons agree that there is an inconsistency in such adult behavior and teaching. Others believe that although there is an inconsistency, adolescents are still "children," and may appropriately engage in such behaviors only when reaching "adulthood." Clearly, discrepancies between parental behavior and teaching may further complicate parent-adolescent interactions if the *adolescent* does not accept the notion that he or she is a "child," but rather believes that he or she is an "adult."

Other family members

Of course, parents are only part of the family system. Adolescents are influenced by siblings and by other relatives such as aunts, uncles, cousins, and grandparents

INSIGHT INTO ADOLESCENCE

Marcel Proust was born in 1871 near Paris. Because he suffered from asthma, he spent his summer holidays as an adolescent at seaside resorts with his family or maternal grandmother. He recreated his life in *Remembrance of Things Past,* an autobiographical novel which he spent most of his adult life writing. In this excerpt, from the second volume of his novel, entitled *Within a Budding Grove,* Proust describes his feelings for his grandmother, who nursed him once when he fell ill during a holiday.

I longed to die. Then my grandmother came in, and to the expansion of my ebbing heart there opened at once an infinity of space. She was wearing a loose cambric gown which she put on at home whenever any of us was ill (because she felt more comfortable in it, she used to say, for she always ascribed to her actions a selfish motive), and which was, for tending us, for watching by our beds, her servant's livery, her nurse's uniform, her religious habit. But whereas the trouble that servants, nurses, religious take, their kindness to us, the merits that we discover in them and the gratitude that we owe them all go to increase the impression that we have of being, in their eyes, some one different, of feeling that we are alone, keeping in our own hands the control over our thoughts, our will to live, I knew, when I was with my grandmother, that, however great the misery that there was in me, it would be received by her with a pity still more vast; that everything that was mine, my cares, my wishes, would be, in my grandmother, supported upon a desire to save and prolong my life stronger than was my own; and my thoughts were continued in her without having to undergo any deflection, since they passed from my mind into hers without change of atmosphere or of personality. . . .

She found a similar pleasure in taking any trouble that saved me one, and in a moment of immobility and rest for my weary limbs something so delicious that when, having seen that she wished to help me with my undressing and to take my boots off, I made as though to stop her and began to undress myself, with an imploring gaze she arrested my hands as they fumbled with the top buttons of my coat and boots.

"Oh, do let me!" she begged. "It is such a joy for your Granny. And be sure you knock on the wall if you want anything in the night. My bed is just on the other side, and the partition is quite thin. Just give a knock now, as soon as you are ready, so that we shall know where we are."

Source: Proust, M. *Within a Budding Grove* (Vol. 2). *Remembrance of Things Past.* Translated by C.S. Moncrieff. New York: Random House, 1970, p. 507.

(Lewis & Feiring, 1978). Every family is different, and so it is difficult to generalize about the roles the various members of the family system play in adolescent development.

Grandparents are often overlooked as a source of influence in adolescent development (Hess & Waring, 1978). Most adults recall fondly their childhood and adolescent interactions with grandparents. The presence of grandparents can be an important source of information about life in earlier times. Grandparents help the adolescent to develop a sense of family history, and their presence may help both form and dispel stereotyped notions about age and aging.

The impact of siblings can be highly variable, depending on such factors as the spacing of the children, one's ordinal position in the family, the number of children, and the sex composition of the children (Hoffman & Manis, 1978; Zajonc & Marcus, 1975). There is a voluminous literature on how development is related to such variables (Sutton-Smith & Rosenberg, 1970). It is important here only to recognize that siblings may play a significant role in one's development. An example or two may highlight the importance of siblings. Sometimes older siblings report that they were disciplined more harshly than their younger brothers or sisters. This may come about because parents become less controlling with subsequent children. Perhaps they learned that more intense discipline is not likely to influence behavioral outcomes. Whatever the reason, parent-adolescent and adolescent-sibling interactions may be different from one child to the next.

Another example of sibling influence occurs when a younger adolescent wants to do something that an older sibling did. It is difficult for parents to deny permission to one child to do something that they permitted another to do—even when they feel they have a good reason for such denial. Of course, an adolescent is sometimes told that he or she may *not* do something because an older sibling was not permitted to do the same thing! Thus, many adolescents feel at an advantage (or disadvantage) because of their siblings. Apart from material rewards which may follow from sibling interaction is the possibility of great friendship and companionship with siblings on the one hand, or great hostility and competitiveness with siblings on the other hand.

In summary, both peers and the family are components of the social context influencing adolescents. Further contributions of these components, as well as an appraisal of their relative impacts, are discussed below.

THE RELATIVE INFLUENCES OF PARENTS AND PEERS

Adolescents exist simultaneously within both family and peer groups, and one may ask how such dual commitments influence the adolescent's behavior and socialization. Do the family and peer relationships that adolescents have contribute in similar ways to development, or is one set of relationships more influential? There are data to suggest that both parents and peers are important. However, depending on the context and meaning of the social relationship, either parents or peers may be shown to be more influential.

Douvan and Adelson (1966) indicate that among 14- to 18-year-old male and female adolescents, there are few, if any, *serious* disagreements with parents. In fact, they report that in choosing their peers, adolescents are oriented toward those who have attitudes and values consistent with those maintained by the parents and adopted by the adolescents themselves. Similarly, Smith (1976), in a study of over 1,000 sixth to twelfth grade urban and suburban Black and White adolescents, found that the family, more so than the peer group, influences the adolescent to seek the advice and consider the opinions of parents. Similar findings have been reported by Kandel and Lesser (1972).

Thus, although there are data indicating that in adolescence the person spends more time with peers than with parents (Bandura, 1964; Douvan & Adelson, 1966), this shift in time commitments does not necessarily indicate a corresponding alteration from parental to peer influence. For instance, Costanzo and Shaw (1966) found that conformity to peer-group norms increased between 7 and 12 years of age for males and for females, but it declined thereafter. Floyd and South (1972) studied sixth, eighth, tenth, and twelfth grade males' and females' orientation to parents and peers. They found less orientation to parents and more orientation to peers in older age groups. Nevertheless, there was a mixed orientation—to both parents and peers—in older age groups. Thus, not only are the influences of parents and peers compatible in the values and behavioral orientations they direct to adolescents (Douvan & Adelson, 1966), but at older ages adolescents show an orientation to be influenced simultaneously by both these generational groups (Floyd & South, 1972).

Indeed, not only does it appear that this dual influence exists, but also it seems that which generational group is more influential at any particular time is dependent on the issue adolescents are confronting. Floyd and South (1972) found that when parents were seen as the better source about a particular issue, adolescents were more parent- than peer-oriented. Larson (1972) also found that the demands of the particular situation determined adolescents' choice, regardless of the direction of parent or peer pressures. Similarly, Brittain (1963, 1969) found that both parents and peers influence adolescents, depending on the issue at hand; adolescent females were more likely to accept the advice of parents concerning the future and the advice of peers concerning school-related issues. Consistent with Brittain's data, Kandel and Lesser (1969) reported that 85 percent of middle-class adolescents and 82 percent of lower-class adolescents were influenced directly by parents in formulating future goals (in this case concerning educational plans).

Other studies also show an orientation to parents and peers, depending on the issue of concern. Chand, Crider, and Willets (1975) found agreement between adolescents and parents on issues related to religion and marriage, but not on issues related to sex and drugs. Similarly, Kelley (1972) found high parent-adolescent similarity on moral issues, but not on issues pertinent to style of dress, hair length, and hours of sleep.

Moreover, several studies indicate that although groups of adolescents and parents have somewhat different attitudes about issues of contemporary social concern (for example, war, drug use, and sexuality), most of these differences reflect contrasts in attitude intensity rather than attitude direction (Lerner, Karson, Meisels, & Knapp, 1975; Lerner & Knapp, 1975; Lerner, Schroeder, Rewitzer, & Weinstock, 1972; Weinstock & Lerner, 1972). That is, rather than one generational group agreeing with an issue while the other group disagrees (a directional difference), most generational group differences involved just different levels of agreement (or disagreement). For example, in regard to a statement such as "Birth control devices and information should be made available to all who desire them," one study found that adolescents showed strong agreement with the item, while their mothers showed moderate agreement with the item (Lerner & Knapp, 1975).

Finally, consistent with the above data indicating influences by both peers and parents, there are data suggesting that adolescents perceive their own attitudes as lying between these two generational groups. In one study, adolescents were asked to rate their own attitudes toward a list of thirty-six statements pertaining to the issues of contemporary social concern noted above; in addition, they rated these same statements in terms of how they thought their peers would respond to them; lastly, they responded in terms of how they thought their parents would answer. The adolescents tended to see their own attitudes as lying *between* those of others of their own generation and those of their parents' generation (with 27 of 36—or 75 percent—of the items). Adolescents tended to place their own positions between the "conservative" end of the continuum, where they tended to put parents, and the "liberal" end, where they tended to place peers. Interestingly, adolescents think their peers are more liberal than they actually are. In essence, this means that adolescents think their friends are, for example, using more drugs and having more sex than is actually the case.

In sum, the above data suggest that adolescents and their parents do not have many major differences in attitudes and values. Apparently, the impact of the intragenerational and intergenerational social contexts often is compatible. Indeed, adolescents tend to perceive that their values lie between those of their parents and peers.

THE GENERATION GAP

Despite the character of the influences of parents and peers that actually exists for the adolescent, there are recurring reports in the media and elsewhere that suggest significant differences between adolescents and their parents. When social scientists discuss such differences between the generations, the term "generation gap" is often used. The presence of such a gap would suggest a basis for conflict between adolescents and their parents.

Parent-adolescent conflict

When one thinks of the relationship between parents and adolescents, conflict—and not the positive interactions—often comes to mind. Adolescents and their parents must cope with a number of dilemmas which seem to have characterized adolescence throughout history (Duvall, 1965). A few of the more persistent conflicts are as follows:

Firm family control versus freedom for the adolescent

Responsibility vested in parents versus responsibility shared with the adolescent

Emphasis on social activities versus academic success

These general areas of conflict must be considered along with the many specific areas of conflict which sometimes crop up in given family situations. Current examples are use of the family automobile, rules concerning having members of the opposite sex over to the house, the acceptable age at which dating may begin, choice of friends and dating partners, curfew times, allowances and use of personal savings, use of drugs and tobacco, problems at school, and use of the telephone. The list may seem endless.

Of course, not all parent-adolescent interactions are hostile or conflict-ridden. Indeed, probably only a small portion of family interaction is negative in the typical family (Bandura, 1964; Douvan & Adelson, 1966). But when conflict arises, it can be a tiresome, unhappy, and sometimes devastating experience for the persons involved. Many parents and adolescents are not able to deal adequately with day-to-day conflict, and others seem to let each quarrel tear their relationship farther and farther apart.

Conflict is normal   In the typical course of events in most families, problems will arise. Some families seem to be better able to cope with such conflict, while others find that it leads to perhaps lasting turmoil in the household. It reasonably can be concluded that it is not conflict itself which marks troubled parent-adolescent relationships, but the family's ability or inability to return to a state of balance following a quarrel. Thus, healthy parent-adolescent relationships may be those in which there is only a moderate amount of conflict (Haan, Smith, & Block, 1968), and in which following conflict, the family is able to return to a state of equilibrium. Unhealthy parent-adolescent relationships may involve more conflict (Haan et al., 1968) and constant bickering and fighting, and can be characterized by an inability to resolve the problem and a continuation of hostility from one quarrel to another.

There are, of course, several possible explanations of why conflict seems so prevalent during the adolescent years. One explanation is proposed by Winch (1971). He argues that in adolescence the young are asked to identify a set of goals; they are then set on the road toward attaining these goals, but they are denied the opportunity to attain these goals until adulthood. Winch likens this dilemma to a dog held on a

INSIGHT INTO ADOLESCENCE

Philip Roth, born in 1933, is a writer of fiction. His stories and novels have brought him recognition in the form of many prizes and awards. *Portnoy's Complaint*, the novel from which the following passage is taken, was published in 1969.

. . . Indeed, during that extended period of rage that goes by the name of my adolescence, what terrified me most about my father was not the violence I expected him momentarily to unleash upon me, but the violence I wished every night at the dinner table to commit upon his ignorant, barbaric carcass. How I wanted to send him howling from the land of the living when he ate from the serving bowl with his own fork, or sucked the soup from his spoon instead of politely waiting for it to cool, or attempted, God forbid, to express an opinion on any subject whatsoever. . . . And what was especially terrifying about the murderous wish was this: if I tried, chances were

I'd succeed! *Chances were he would help me along!* I would have only to leap across the dinner dishes, my fingers aimed at his windpipe, for him instantaneously to sink down beneath the table with his tongue hanging out. Shout he could shout, squabble he could squabble. . . .But defend himself? against *me?* "Alex, keep this back talk up," my mother warns, as I depart from the kitchen roaring like Attila the Hun, run screaming from yet another half-eaten dinner, "continue with this disrespect and you will give that man a heart attack!" "Good!" I cry, slamming in her face the door to my room. "Fine!" I scream, extracting from my closet the nylon jacket I wear only with my collar up (a style she abhors as much as the filthy garment itself). "Wonderful!" I shout, and with streaming eyes run to the corner to vent my fury on the pinball machine.

Source: Roth, P. *Portnoy's Complaint.* New York: Bantam Books/Random House, 1967. 44–45

short leash while a piece of meat is held out of reach but not out of range or sight or smell. "One would hardly expect the dog to be collected and quiescent under such circumstances" (Winch, 1971, p. 428).

Adolescents, it can be argued, are much like members of minority groups. The qualifications of having physical capability, knowledge of the possibilities, and denial of access to them constitute a familiar plight of minority groups. Adolescents, like minority groups, may respond to this dilemma by developing their own language, values, customs, and status system. At the same time they may disparage or completely reject the value system of the adult majority (Winch, 1971). Although this explanation for parent-adolescent conflict may seem to be extreme in its characterizations, it nevertheless suggests why adults see much in adolescence which may not be palatable to them. Thus, adolescent language, dress, and behavior may in part be a result of adolescents' needs to create an "adult" subculture of their own. In this subculture, status is governed by rules the adolescents establish and respect, while the adult (parental) generation become frustrated by the existence of a subculture which does not conform to rules and practices accepted by the society at large.

There are other more specific reasons why one might suppose parent-adolescent conflict may exist. First, parents often are not adequately prepared for the period of their child's adolescence. Many parents prepare for childbirth by taking classes and doing some reading; a small number of parents take classes in the community or in college on child rearing; but it is rare to find parents who have actively prepared for raising adolescents.

Second, most parents take seriously their roles in providing moral direction for their children. Thus, parents often find themselves opposing the very behaviors which often bring status to the adolescent in the youth subculture. In fact, many parents do not permit—or at least actively discourage—behaviors in their offspring in which they themselves engaged as adolescents.

Third, the period of adolescence tends to be longer today than ever before, and this provides a greater period of time during which conflict may arise. There is a great deal of power in money, and parents who are supporting a student through college often find it difficult not to exert control over the youth. This dependence on parents until the early twenties, and the frustrations which may accompany the struggle between emotional emancipation and economic commitments, can be troublesome for members of both generations.

Some family problems of adolescence

There are potentially countless problems that adolescents, their siblings, and their parents may be confronted with during adolescence. In some families, these problems occur rarely and are overcome easily, with little conflict. In other families, however, problems may develop on a daily basis, and may involve bitter quarreling, crying, and even physical punishment or violence. There sometimes appears to be little ability to solve even the most basic of problems. Let us highlight some common family problems of adolescence.

Steve asked me out, and I'm going   Shari just turned 15, and has recently begun high school. She has never been on a date before, and has now been asked out by Steve, a junior, who has his own car. Shari asked her parents for "permission," and they said that Steve is too old for her, that she is too young to be dating, and that they don't want her driving around in this boy's car. After a bitter argument about the problem, Shari announces that she is going anyway.

I'll smoke if I want to   Ted, a 16-year-old, began smoking about eighteen months ago. He started out smoking one cigarette each day on the way home from school with a friend. After about six months of that, he began smoking more often—at parties, at school athletic events, during breaks around the school grounds, and at the shopping center where all the kids "hang out." Ted's parents suspected this because they smelled smoke on his clothes, but Ted denied it every time it came up. Then his parents were told by friends of theirs that they saw Ted smoking at the shopping center. The parents were furious and announced that they forbade Ted to smoke. Ted reported that he planned to continue smoking; but he never smokes at home. Ted and his parents argue daily about the smell of smoke on his clothes.

Get off the phone, or I'll rip it out   Wendy, age 17, talks on the phone about two hours every night. On some nights, she talks even longer. Wendy's parents constantly insist she should restrict her calls to ten minutes. Wendy says that she has as much right to use the phone as anyone, and often talks on the upstairs extension so that her parents don't know she is on the line. Wendy has suggested getting a second phone number, but her parents absolutely refuse.

I'll never do it again   Warren and two of his friends were caught shoplifting by the manager of the supermarket. Warren (age 13) had taken eight candy bars, and the police were called. The manager agreed not to press charges this time, and the police agreed to let the parents handle the situation. Warren had never been in trouble before, and promised not to do it again; but his parents punished him severely for this wrongdoing, including a beating with a belt. They lectured him about shoplifting being the first sign of tendencies toward criminal behavior. Warren was angry at his parents for the beating.

So what if you didn't know about the party? Brenda's parents were out of town for the weekend. Brenda, age 17 and a senior in high school, invited over several of her friends for a Saturday night party—six boys and six girls altogether. During the party, something in the basement caught fire, and after the fire department put the blaze out, $4,000 in damages had been done. Brenda had not told her parents about the party, and there was a bitter argument about Brenda's right to have had such a party. Brenda claimed she would pay for the damage, and insisted that the fire was not the real issue.

We didn't think anyone would get hurt Tony and Bernie, both age 14, often pushed seventh grade boys around in the hallways at the junior high. They felt that the seventh grade boys on the whole were "twerps" and deserved a little pushing around. Between classes one day, Tony bent down on all fours behind a seventh grade boy while Bernie pushed the boy backwards, so that the boy fell over. The boy hit his head on a drinking fountain, and had to be taken to the hospital for seventeen stitches. Tony was punished severely by his parents, but Bernie's parents took a "boys will be boys" attitude. Tony felt the punishment was unfair because he didn't mean to hurt the boy involved. This event was the start of several conflicts between Tony and his parents.

You're a no-good bum Stacy, a 16-year-old sophomore, is a below-average student. She doesn't like school all that well, but she tries. Her father had great aspirations for Stacy, and her academic performance is frustrating for him. He constantly pushes her to achieve and badgers her about homework and grades. Stacy is not sure whether she loves her father or hates him. They constantly quarrel now. Her father's favorite expression is that Stacy is going to be "a no-good bum."

These case studies illustrate just a few of the many problems that adolescents and their parents face. There are no easy answers as to how these problems can be resolved. In all the cases above, it is possible to put oneself in the position of either the parents or the adolescent. The crux of the problem and the most appropriate solution may be different depending on which perspective one takes.

Parents and adolescents, then, may have difficulty in weathering a challenging time in the lives of members of both generations. But the relationship between parents and adolescents need not always be characterized by conflict. Parents can be an important stabilizing influence for adolescents as they mature and face the sometimes rigid demands of the adolescent subculture. And adolescents may provide great sources of pride, satisfaction, and cheer for their parents. Many parents share actively in the accomplishments of their children, and many children wish to please their parents more than anyone else in their day-to-day activities. This is only natural, given the history of intimate interactions which the family shares during the childhood years, and which can be expected to follow during the adulthood years of the developing adolescent.

Moreover, evidence reviewed in preceding sections suggests that for many families the adolescent-parent relationship may not ever be characterized by more than just occasional, and easily removed, conflict. In the following section, additional data supporting this interpretation are presented.

Studies of intergenerational relations

Data reviewed previously suggest that when the *actual* attitudes of adolescents and their parents are compared, few major differences in attitudes can be found, although intensity differences often do exist. However, most studies find even this type of intergenerational disparity to occur in only a minority of attitude comparisons between the generations (Lerner et al., 1975; Lerner & Knapp, 1975; Lerner et al., 1972). These data suggest that the generation gap may not be real after all (Adelson, 1970).

Nevertheless, there are both empirical and theoretical reasons to expect that a generation gap might exist to some degree. There are data showing that adolescents and parents do not perceive the influence of social relationships accurately. Adolescents perceive their parents to be less influential than they actually are, while parents perceive that they are more influential than they actually are (Bengtson & Troll, 1978; Lerner, 1975; Lerner & Knapp, 1975). For example, two studies compared the actual and the perceived attitudes of adolescents and parents (Lerner et al., 1975; Lerner & Knapp, 1975). Actual intergenerational differences in attitudes about issues of contemporary concern occurred with fewer than 30 percent of the comparisons made in either study by Lerner and his colleagues. However, in both investigations, adolescents *overestimated* the magnitude of the differences that existed between themselves and their parents; they saw their parents as having attitudes less congruent with their own than was actually the case. In both studies, parents *underestimated* the extent of differences between themselves and their children; they saw their children as having attitudes very consistent with their own. Thus, although only a small and selective generation gap can be said to actually exist, parents underestimate this division while adolescents overestimate it.

Both psychological and sociological theorists have suggested reasons for the existence of these different perceptions regarding the generation gap. Erikson (1959, 1963) believes adolescence is a period in life which involves the establishment of a sense of personal identity, of self-definition. Other theorists (for example, Elkind, 1967; Piaget, 1950, 1970) believe that adolescence is, as well, a period involving the development of new thought capabilities; these capabilities lead adolescents to believe their ideas are not only new in their own lives, but in general as well. Together, then, adolescents need to establish their own identities, and their own beliefs in the uniqueness of their thoughts. These beliefs may lead them to think they are quite different from those around them—especially their parents. This might result in their overemphasizing and magnifying whatever differences actually exist (Lerner, 1975).

A sociological approach suggests why parents might minimize differences between themselves and their children. Bengtson and Kuypers (1971) suggest that members of the parent generation have a stake in maximizing consistency between themselves and members of their children's generation. The parents have "invested" in society, for example by pursuing their careers and accumulating society's resources. Because they want to protect their investment, they want to rear their children—the new members of society—in ways that will maintain the society in which they have invested. It may be that as a consequence of such a "generational stake" (Bengtson & Kuypers, 1971; Bengtson & Troll, 1978), parents are oriented to believing they have produced children who—because they agree with parental attitudes—will protect their investment. This orientation is consistent with one Erikson (1959, 1963) describes; he believes that adults have a psychosocial need to feel they have generated children who will perpetuate society. This idea, as well as the generational stake idea, suggests that parents may be oriented to minimizing whatever differences exist between themselves and the adolescent children.

In summary, both theory and research combine to suggest that the adolescent's social context is composed of not one generation gap, but several. First, there exists a relatively minor and selective set of differences between adolescents and their parents. However, in addition to this actual gap, there exist two perceived gaps: the overestimated one of the adolescents and the underestimated one of the parents. The potential presence and function of these gaps make the social context of the adolescent a complex, diverse setting; we continue to see this complexity as we examine other dimensions of the social context.

EDUCATION DURING ADOLESCENCE

Enrollment in school is a nearly universal characteristic of adolescence. At the beginning of adolescence, virtually all males and females attend school. About 99 percent of individuals ages 10 to 13 are enrolled in school in the United States, and this figure remains as high as 98 percent for 14- and 15-year-olds (U.S. Bureau of the Census, 1978b). This high rate of school enrollment can be attributed to two factors: the high value Americans place on education and the compulsory laws of school attendance throughout the country.

In most states, however, a student is no longer compelled to attend school upon reaching his or her sixteenth or seventeenth birthday. Thus, only 89 percent of 16- and 17-year-olds are in school. About 85 percent of all males and females now finish high school. About half of all individuals who graduate from high school now go onto college (U.S. Bureau of the Census, 1978b).

Contrary to what many think, females drop out of high school as often as do males. The high dropout rate for females may be due to early marriage and the high incidence of adolescent pregnancy, as well as the many reasons that typically apply to males. These reasons include attraction to employment more so than attraction to school, poor school performance, and peer-group pressures. Despite the notable proportion of individuals who drop out of high school, and the significant portion of the population who choose not to go on to college, education is a major influence in the lives of adolescents. For most of the years that make up the adolescent period, the great majority of youth are enrolled in schools. With such a commitment of time, money, and attention by society to education, one may expect significant functions to be performed by the educational institution.

Functions of the educational system

Schools perform many functions. Ideas about the multiple functions of the educational system have been expressed by several specialists in adolescent development. Ausubel, Montemayor, and Svajian (1977) see education basically as a training institution. They view the school as an agent of cultural transmission designed to perpetuate and improve a given way of life. Schools provide an atmosphere for the transmission and attainment of basic knowledge. McCandless (1970) also considers schools to have a function of skills training and of cultural transmission of knowledge and values. However, he believes schools have at least one other major function, a "maintenance-actualization" role. McCandless believes the educational system creates a setting in which the adolescent can be happy, and yet challenged; schools are a place to develop optimal personal and interpersonal attributes and, as such, maximize the person's ability to contribute to society.

Others have also noted the personal and interpersonal functions of schools. Ausubel et al. (1977) state that schools provide a setting for social interactions and relationship development. Moreover, they facilitate the adolescent's emancipation from parents. School, then affords an opportunity for the adolescent to earn his or her own social status. Status may be earned by demonstrating a mastery of the curriculum, by attaining high class standing, and by interacting with the peer group in nonacademic school activities such as organized athletics or clubs (Ausubel et al., 1977).

Social status may be earned in the future through the training and education attained in school. Johnston and Bachman (1976) point out, for instance, that although far from perfect, there is a positive relation between an individual's advancement in education and the greater likelihood of success, particularly in work. They report educational advancement is positively related to lifetime income, high-status jobs, attractive working conditions, and opportunities for personal development. Johnston and Bachman (1976) also point out that the school also serves a custodial role in society, in that a system of compulsory education such as that found in the United States highly structures the time and activity of students.

Coleman (1965) maintains that the major function of school to today's adolescent is the interpersonal social environment it provides. Thornburg (1969, 1971) found that even during the height of student activism in the late 1960s and early 1970s associated with the Vietnam war, the draft, and civil rights, the dominant concern of college-age youths was their education. In summary, there are individual, interpersonal, and societal functions served by today's educational institutions.

Adolescents' views about the functions of education

Several studies show that adolescents place greater emphasis on the school's role in interpersonal development than on the attainment and cultural transmission of skills and knowledge. In a study of urban and rural high schools having student bodies ranging from 100 to 2,000 students, Coleman (1961) found that academic accomplishment was not a predominant basis of peer popularity. For instance, only 31 percent of the males studied wanted to be remembered by their peers as excellent students, but 45 percent wanted to be remembered as outstanding athletes. Among females, 28 percent wanted to be remembered as excellent students, but 72 percent wanted to be recalled as being popular. Similarly, Snyder (1972) found that among high school juniors the most important criterion selected by both males and females for giving someone peer recognition and status involved personal qualities. Next in importance were material possessions, social activities, and athletics. Academic achievement followed all these qualities in their rankings.

Moreover, Johnston and Bachman (1976), in a study of a national probability sample of 2,227 tenth grade boys and a sample of 2,100 high school teachers, found that both groups had almost identical views regarding what were the actual functions of current high schools. Both groups believed that athletics was the area receiving most emphasis in their schools. Functions related to skill attainment receive less emphasis, and those related to cultural transmission of norms and values still less.

However, other data reported by Johnson and Bachman and other researchers stress these latter functions. Friesen (1968) studied about 15,000 students in 19 Canadian high schools. He found that students saw athletics and popularity as more important for current successful functioning, but they believed academic achievement was more important than either for future successful functioning. Moreover, in addition to seeing a future utility for the skill attainment and cultural transmission roles, data by Johnston and Bachman (1976) suggest that adolescents hope that such functions will become the ones of primary emphasis in the schools of the future. Instead of athletics, the students and teachers in the study agreed that "increasing students' motivation and desire to learn" should be the most important function, and that several issues relating to academic achievement were of utmost priority.

Moreover, among a national sampling of college seniors, there was an even greater stress on skill attainment and cultural transmission functions. Hadden (1969) found that about 75 percent of the students studied saw college as a "symbol of hope in a troubled world" and fewer than 20 percent felt that what they were learning was "silly, wrong, and useless." Individual and interpersonal enhancement functions were emphasized also, however. About two-thirds of the sample agreed that "college has changed my whole view of myself."

Thus, it appears that all the roles of education mentioned are recognized by today's students as important aspects of educational institutions. Moreover, data from a national sample of students show that more than 75 percent believe that schools are doing a good-to-excellent job in providing an appropriate context for students (Harris, 1969).

Family and peer influences on education

The family and peers of adolescents influence both aspirations about and actual outcomes of the adolescent's accomplishments in school. According to information from the U.S. Bureau of the Census (1978b), the college aspirations of high school seniors tend to be correlated with the educational attainment of the head of the household in which they lived. About 70 percent of students who were living in households in which the head had completed at least one year of college themselves had definite college plans. When the head of the household had completed high school, but not any college, only 45 percent of students had definite college plans. Of those living in families having a household head who had not completed high school, only 35 percent had definite college plans.

Sewell and Shah (1968a, 1968b) found that parents' educational attainment is highly related to their adolescent children's educational aspirations, and also to the actual success of adolescents in the school setting. High educational attainment of parents, and particularly fathers, was found to predict similarly high (for example, college) attainment by students.

There are particular types of parent-adolescent interactions that appear to facilitate successful school functioning. Morrow and Wilson (1961) found that high-achieving adolescents, as compared to a group of low achievers, tended to come from families where they were involved in family decisions, where ideas and activities were shared by family members, and where parents were likely to give approval of and praise for the adolescent's performance and show trust in the adolescent's competence. In turn, low-achieving adolescents came from families marked by parental dominance and restrictiveness (Morrow & Wilson, 1961). Moreover, both Morrow and Wilson (1961) and Shaw and White (1965) found that high-achieving adolescents tend to identify with their parents while low-achieving adolescents do not.

Still other data indicate that the type of parental behaviors found by Morrow and Wilson (1961) relate to high adolescent school achievement. Both Swift (1967) and Rehberg and Westby (1967) report that parental encouragement and rewards are associated with better adolescent school performance. Wolf (1964) reports that parent-child interactions that involve encouragement to achieve and development of language skills are highly correlated with intelligence.

Peers also influence adolescents' aspirations and educational performance; in most cases, there is convergence between family and peer influences. Rigsby and McDill (1972), in a study of over 20,000 adolescents, found that there was a positive relation between the proportion of peers perceived to have college plans, the actual proportion with college plans, and adolescents' own likelihood of planning for college.

Similarly, Kandel and Lesser (1969) found that if adolescent peer relationships were characterized by closeness and intimacy, there was a great deal of correspondence between the educational aspirations of the peers and of the adolescent. However, most adolescents (57 percent) had educational plans that agreed with peers and parents. In turn, among those adolescents who disagreed with their parents, there was also a great likelihood (50 percent) that they would disagree with peers as well. Moreover, in those cases when there was a discrepancy between parent and peer orientations, it was most likely that the parental orientation would prevail (Kandel & Lesser, 1969).

Sociocultural and historical influences on education

The political, economic, and environmental changes in society, which are part of the sociocultural context, influence the nature of the educational institution. For instance, changes in political and economic pressures have resulted in a greater number of minority youth being part of the student body of higher educational institutions. For example, only about 26 percent of Blacks who were in their early twenties in the late 1960s had completed a year or more of college. This figure increased to 32 percent for Blacks who were in their early twenties in the late 1970s. Whites, in contrast, attended college in similar proportions over the decade. About 4 in 10 Whites completed a year or more of college during both time periods (U.S. Bureau of the Census, 1977b, 1978b).

The choice of a major also may be influenced by sociocultural changes across history. Economic recessions, difficulty in finding employment, and environmental concerns were examples of social issues in the late 1960s and early 1970s. Changes in the popularity of different college-major fields of study paralleled changes in these social issues. An analysis of the changes of majors found between 1966 and 1974, for example, indicates unpredicted enrollment shifts.

For instance, social science majors increased from about 640,000 to 950,000 between 1966 and 1972, but declined to 770,000 by 1974. The initial increase undoubtedly was related to heightened interest in social services and social change, and perhaps to a desire for more relevance in the lives of college students of that time.

The decline that followed may have occurred partly because of a resulting oversupply of social science majors, given the level of available jobs (U.S. Bureau of the Census, 1978b).

HIGH SCHOOL DROPOUTS

As mentioned earlier, only 85 percent of Americans finish high school. Approximately equal proportions of males and females drop out of school, mostly during the junior and senior years. Since all states have some form of compulsory attendance law requiring school enrollment until age 16 or 17, in the typical case adolescents, parents, and school personnel usually do not have to contend with the problem until midadolescence. But the seeds of a student's unrest which may lead to dropping out may develop at any time. In this section we explore the magnitude of the problem of school dropouts, some of the causes, and some of the consequences.

Magnitude of the problem

Educational attainment of the American population continues to increase. Decade by decade since the turn of the century, an increasing proportion of the population has graduated from high school. The proportion of adolescents graduating from high school reached an all-time high in the 1970s and is now stabilizing. Nevertheless, with about 15 percent of the population not completing high school, a sizable portion of adolescents still must contend with the problems associated with dropping out of school.

More than 800,000 adolescents dropped out of school during the 1975–76 school year. Most dropouts do not return to high school after leaving it, although some finish their high school degree through night school or by taking a high school equivalency examination. In 1975, 3 percent of persons graduated from high school by equivalency examination, and about 1 percent graduated by attending night school or by attending day school part-time (U.S. Bureau of the Census, 1977b, 1978b).

Blacks and persons of Spanish origin have very low rates of high school completion. About two-thirds of Black adolescents finish high school, and about 55 percent of persons of Spanish origin finish high school. The completion rates for male and female members of these minority groups do not differ significantly (U.S. Bureau of the Census, 1978b).

Why students leave school

Many studies of school dropouts are unable to point to a single reason for the problem. Each adolescent who decides not to finish school has his or her own reason, and the causes found in the dropout population as a whole are numerous. One national study, the longitudinal *Youth in Transition* project, conducted at the Institute for Social Research of the University of Michigan, found that family background factors and ability were related to educational attainment (Bachman, 1970). Those most likely to finish high school and enter college were from families with higher socioeconomic standing, were more likely to come from intact homes, and had smaller family sizes. Individuals who dropped out of school had lower intelligence, poorer vocabulary, and poorer reading abilities (Bachman, Green, & Wirtanen, 1971). As might be expected, then, adolescents who find themselves struggling academically through school are most likely to drop out. Indeed, Bachman et al. found that the reasons most often offered by adolescents for why they dropped out pertained to schoolwork and school authority.

There are also other nonacademic reasons for leaving school. Dropouts may find little intellectual stimulation at home. They may encounter a negative evaluation of education by their parents, or pressures from the family to obtain work to help support the family financially. Realistically, however, many adolescents who report that their parents encouraged them to drop out of school may be looking for someone else to blame. Even parents with little education themselves tend to respect the value of education and see educational attainment as a means of improving one's social and financial standing. Probably only a small proportion of parents actually encourage their adolescent children to leave school. Bachman et al. (1971) note that some other reasons that adolescents give for dropping out are a desire for freedom, getting married, a need to earn money, wanting to get a job, and needing to help the family financially.

Other nonacademic reasons may be more influential, however, Dropouts have lower levels of self-esteem and are more often depressed than those who finish high school, while those who did not drop out had higher needs for self-development. These and other personality factors may be involved in leaving school (Bachman et al., 1971).

It is not difficult to understand high school dropouts when one thinks of the adolescent who is doing poorly in school, receives little encouragement at home, perhaps is in trouble from time to time with teachers and administrators, and has to get out of bed every weekday morning for nine months every year to do something that he or she cannot tolerate. Poor school attendance, behavior problems in the classroom and on school grounds, vandalism, and delinquency are consequences which might be expected when one considers the frustration that some adolescents experience in what they consider to be an oppressive environment.

One study suggests that individuals who drop out of school, particularly those from lower-class backgrounds, have failed to achieve middle-class values, which emphasize education (Namenwirth, 1969). Success in school requires acceptance of the traditional middle-class values, and this may be an elusive goal for persons from lower-class families. Indeed, delinquency and other forms of socially deviant behavior are more likely to precede than to follow dropping out (Bachman et al., 1971). Another explanation of failure to finish high school suggests that the school experience simply fails to meet the personal, social, and vocational needs of many youth, particularly those in urban areas and those from lower-class backgrounds (Mussen, Conger, & Kagan, 1974).

It is likely that adolescents who drop out of school very early are different from those who drop out later. There is some evidence that early dropouts have lower than average intelligence, and thus may find it difficult to compete in school, even if they were motivated. Those who drop out later tend to have higher intelligence than those who are early dropouts, although both groups score lower on intelligence tests than do students who finish school (Voss, Wendling, & Elliott, 1966).

One ambitious study of high school dropouts was based on a national sample of 440,000 students attending 1,300 public and private high schools throughout the country (Combs & Cooley, 1968). This study compared dropouts and high school graduates who did not go on to college. Males who dropped out of school were lower on all measures of ability, although the scores were similar for females. Males who finished school had greater interests in science, engineering, math, and related areas, whereas males who dropped out of school tended to have interests in skilled trades, labor, and music. Females showed similar differences. Male and female graduates perceived themselves to be more sociable, vigorous, calm, tidy, cultured, self-confident, and mature than did those who dropped out (Combs & Cooley, 1968).

Thus, it appears that there are significant differences between adolescents who leave high school and those who finish. Certainly in contemporary society, the high school dropout is somewhat stigmatized, since he or she is violating a social norm and rejecting a social status which has come to be highly valued by virtually all segments of society. What, if any, are the consequences of such a decision?

Consequences of dropping out

The consequences of not finishing high school are difficult to assess. One form of evaluation is an economic one. High school dropouts can expect to have lifetime earnings of about $575,000, on the average, based on 1980 dollars. High school graduates are projected to earn substantially more—about $855,000 in their lifetime. Those who obtain college degrees may expect lifetime earnings of about $1,120,000 (U.S. Bureau of the Census, 1977a).

Of course, money is just one measure of the impact of different levels of educational attainment. High school dropouts have higher unemployment rates than do persons with more education. They are more likely to have blue-collar jobs. And they tend to be employed in positions requiring minimal skills (U.S. Bureau of the Census, 1977a).

Thus, one's educational level will usually determine one's employment possibilities. Many jobs require a high school degree, even if specific skills learned in high school are not required for the job. Many employers, then, expect employees to have high school degrees regardless of the job description. Furthermore, some employers require the degree for advancement to higher positions.

There are numerous other circumstances which are related to lower educational attainment. Although these events cannot be directly attributed to an incomplete high school education, they undoubtedly are products of a life-style which often includes dropping out of school. Poverty, early marriage, high fertility, high rates of marital disruption, higher mortality rates, and earlier death are all examples of variables related to educational attainment (Spanier & Glick, 1979; U.S. Bureau of the Census, 1977a). Finally, however, it may be noted that Bachman et al. (1971) report that more often than not those who dropped out regretted this action.

RELIGION IN ADOLESCENCE

Of all the social institutions, none but the family has existed as long as religion. Religion in one form or another is known to exist in all societies and at all periods of history within a given society. Religion, then, is an ever-present aspect of the social structure. So central to our lives is religion that virtually all persons report that they have had a religious affiliation at some point in their lives, and most individuals report a religious affiliation at any given time. And although most surveys find a trend away from formal religion over the past generation, a substantial portion of the population reports that they are active members of a religious denomination.

Most children and adolescents are given some instruction in religion, usually in the faith that the parents have chosen. Christian children are baptised, Jewish children prepare for Bar Mitzvah, and children of most all faiths attend religious school, Sunday school, or other classes which will lead to their confirmation or graduation. But for many, the termination of religious instruction is also the beginning of their movement away from organized religion. It is during adolescence that some individuals begin to question and doubt some of what they have heard, and increasingly feel that as long as the decision is theirs, they will choose not to attend religious services. Adolescence, then, is a period of intense commitment to religion for some. It is a time of rapid movement away from religion for others. And adolescence is a period of conflict about the direction of movement for individuals who are struggling with the formation of their own belief system, which may differ from that of their parents or from that which they were taught earlier.

About 60 percent of all Americans are estimated to be members of religious bodies. There were about 70 million Protestants in 1975, about 49 million Roman Catholics, and about 6 million Jews (U.S. Bureau of the Census, 1977a). Most religious education takes place during childhood and adolescence. Parents who are not active in their religious congregation, or who may not be members at all, often send their children to church or synagogue for religious education.

Thus, in terms of its pervasiveness, religion is a major part of the social context of contemporary adolescents. There is abundant evidence that adolescents identify with this component of their social context, they view it as important, and despite changes over time in the meanings they attach to it, they show religious behaviors very similar to those of their parents.

The identity crisis of adolescence is characterized by a search for self-definition. We have seen that an identity is defined in terms of the ideology associated with it. Both theory and research (Erikson, 1959, 1963; Marcia, 1966, 1967) suggest that adolescents search for a religious ideology as part of their general ideological search. Similar to data indicating that there is no general "storm and stress" during adolescence (Bandura, 1964; Douvan & Adelson, 1966; Offer, 1969), other data indicate there is no crisis in religious behaviors or beliefs in adolescence (Douvan & Gold, 1966; Rice, 1975). Indeed, religious behaviors and beliefs are very important to the adolescent.

Importance of religion to adolescents

Although there are variations by denominational affiliation and sex, data indicate that organized religion as a moral, philosophical, and social institution has been, and continues to be, of central importance to the majority of American youth (Ausubel et al., 1977). This is evidenced by the large proportion of adolescents who rate religion as being important and show a commitment toward religious institutions.

More than thirty years ago, Allport, Gillespie, and Young (1948) found that 68 percent of Harvard students (all males) and 82 percent of Radcliffe students (all females) said yes to the question: "Do you feel that you require some form of religious orientation or belief in order to achieve a fully mature philosophy of life?" More than 20 years later, Yankelovich (1969) also found high ratings for the importance of religion. A large majority of noncollege youth (82 percent) and a large minority of college youth (42 percent) agreed that "Belonging to some organized religion is important in a person's life." Moreover, 91 percent of the parents of the noncollege youths and 81 percent of the parents of the college youths agreed with this statement as well. Similarly, although a larger proportion of adolescents (34 percent) than adults (11 percent) in another study said that belonging to some organized religion was *not* important, the majority of both adults and adolescents disagree with this view (Yankelovich, 1972).

Not only do adolescents rate religious orientation as important, but their behavior shows a commitment to religious institutions as well. During the late 1960s, national polls indicated a trend away from conventional religion among youth (Wuthnow & Glock, 1973). However, in a survey of the religious orientations of college freshmen, it was found that the percentages of youth indicating traditional religious preferences increased from the early 1970s to the mid-1970s. The proportion showing a preference for traditional Judaism increased from 3.8 to 5.1 percent, for traditional Roman Catholicism from 30.1 to 34.3 percent, and for traditional forms of Protestantism from 38.2 to 44.9 percent (*Survey of College Freshman*, 1974).

In addition to increasingly more traditional religious preferences, the proportions of adolescents attending church indicate a high level of religious commitment. Although more so in their early than in their late adolescent years, a large proportion of American adolescents belong to a church—typically the one of their parents (Bell, 1938; Myers, 1951). About half of adolescents regularly attend church. Harris (1971) studied a nationally representative sample of 15- to 21-year-olds. The proportion of high school and college students who attended church regularly was 58 percent and 43 percent, respectively. These and other data (DeBord, 1969; Dutt, 1965; Garrity, 1961; Parker, 1971) indicate that female adolescents attend more regularly than male adolescents. The better educated attend more often than the less educated, and Catholics attend more often than Protestants, who attend more often than Jews (Hassenger, 1967).

Although neither the frequency of religious worship nor the frequency of Sunday school attendance is highly related to moral conduct, for example, likelihood of cheating on a test (Goldsen, Rosenberg, Williams & Suchman, 1960; Hartshorne & May, 1930), "religious" students meet the academic and social expectations of the college environment more so than do nonreligious students (Parker, 1971). Moreover, one study shows that religious commitment is at least somewhat related to psychological development. Mayo, Puryear, and Richey (1969) found that college males who classified themselves as religious were less depressed and less psychotically oriented on a standardized personality inventory than were nonreligious college males. For the females who were studied, ego strength was more characteristic of those with a nonreligious self-classification than of those with a religious self-classification.

The development of religious beliefs in adolescence

Despite the fact that religion is important to most adolescents, and that there seems to be significant parent-adolescent intergenerational continuity in this importance, it does not follow that there are no developmental changes in the role of religion in the lives of adolescents. Adolescents display continuity in their commitment to religious institutions and beliefs across the adolescent period. Kuhlen and Arnold (1944) found that 84 percent of adolescents aged 12 to 18 years believed in God. Remmers and Radler (1957) found that 83 percent of the ninth through twelfth graders they studied believed that God was all-knowing. And Roscoe (1968) reports that 73 percent of the over 4,000 college students he studied believed in a personal God.

While such high levels of commitment to beliefs in God, from early through late adolescence, are an indication of the prominence of religious beliefs throughout adolescence, such findings do not indicate that there are no changes in the quality of these beliefs. In fact, we may expect that although remaining behaviorally committed to religion throughout adolescence, the meaning of and reasons for this behavior might change. As is true for adolescent moral and sexual behavior, qualitatively different reasoning can underlie the same religious behavior at successive portions of adolescence. Thus, the continuity in beliefs about God should be associated with developmental changes in the meanings of these beliefs to the adolescent, *if* religious beliefs follow developmental progressions akin to those associated with reasons for moral and sexual beliefs.

Data from several studies support this reasoning. Research indicates that adolescents' religious beliefs become more abstract, less concerete, more tolerant, and less ritualistic (Kuhlen & Arnold, 1944; Parker, 1971; Wuthnow & Glock, 1973). Similarly, across development, fewer adolescents see virtue in strict observance of specific denominational doctrine. Fewer adolescents view prayer as penance or believe that prayers are answered, and instead see prayer as a vehicle for giving thanks (Brown, 1968; Goldman, 1964; Kuhlen & Arnold, 1944; Pixley & Beckman, 1949; Wuthnow & Glock, 1973).

Kuhlen and Arnold (1944) administered a questionnaire to 547 adolescents, divided into age groups that averaged 12, 15, and 18 years. A greater tolerance in attitudes toward, and less ritualistic thinking about, religious practices and beliefs among older age groups was seen. More 18-year-olds than 15-year-olds and more 15-year-olds than 12-year-olds believed that "Catholics, Jews, and Protestants are equally good," and that "It is not necessary to attend church to be a Christian." Less literal and concrete views about religion and less strict adherence to specific doctrines were evidenced by the fact that fewer 18- than 15-year-olds and fewer 15- than 12-year-olds believed that "Every word in the Bible is true," and that "Young people should belong to the same church as their parents."

This less literal and more personalized belief in what constitutes appropriate religious observance has also been found in studies following the Kuhlen and Arnold (1944) investigation. Young, Dustin, and Holtzman (1966) found that as students proceed through the college experience, they tend to favor organized religions less. Similarly, both Yankelovich (1972) and Wuthnow and Glock (1973) report a trend away from conventional religion among college youth and toward an alternative religion. Some data suggest this trend is minimal. Among freshman in 1970 and seniors in 1971 at the University of California, Berkeley, the number of students who identified themselves with Eastern religions was 3 percent to 8 percent, respectively (Wuthnow & Glock, 1973). Larger proportions of college youth make a less extreme deviation from conventional Western religions, and move toward a more personalized conception of God.

In Roscoe's (1968) study of religious beliefs among some 4,000 college students, only 28 percent of those students who expressed a personal belief in God construed it in terms consistent with the traditional Judeo-Christian biblical concept of God. Moreover, only 25 percent of those studied believed the Bible represented the inspired word of God. Rather, most (about 67 percent) said it was an inspired book, which was historically unreliable but nevertheless served a valid religious purpose.

Furthermore, there is evidence that the type of religious beliefs developed by the end of the adolescent period, whether they are traditional or not, tend to characterize the person well into the adulthood years. Nelson (1956) retested about 900 people in 1950 who had first been assessed about their religious attitudes and beliefs in 1936, when they were college students. After this fourteen-year period, 85 percent showed either little or no shift in religious views or a shift to a more positive regard about religion. Only 14 percent shifted toward showing less positive regard.

Thus, the religious institutions play an important role in the lives of most American adolescents. Although views about religion change over the course of this portion of the life span, adolescents nevertheless attend religious services at least as often as do their parents, and many take a commitment to a belief in God with them into adulthood.

RELIGIOUS CULTS

Although conventional religion plays a central role in the development of many adolescents, for a small but visible proportion of American youth, unconventional religious beliefs develop during adolescence. Youths of post-high school age in particular are sometimes attracted to *religious cults*. Religious cults are small groups of individuals who are together because they share a common set of beliefs, religious in nature. They tend to be unconventional in their life-style, and their forms of worship, methods of recruitment, style of dress, dietary habits, and philosophy of life may be quite variant with the norms of the society. Religious cults often are formed by a single person, who develops a loyal following. The religion may then be based on the beliefs, teachings, and personality of the individual.

For reasons which are not well understood, it is mostly older adolescents and youth who are attracted to religious cults (Doress & Porter, 1978). Younger children and older adults do not often affiliate with such groups. One plausible explanation of this phenomenon is that older adolescents are beginning to achieve emancipation from their parents, but may not yet have become committed to beliefs and philosophies of life which they can identify as their own. Between the time when they are guided by their parents' value system and the time when they must articulate their own, they may be particularly vulnerable to seduction by religions and philosophies which fill this void, but which may be inconsistent with what they were previously taught or will later accept. Erikson (1963) has made a similar argument.

In the 1970s, there were several religious cults which became prominent among American youth: the Unification church of Rev. Sun Myung Moon, the Church of Scientology, the Hare Krishna, the People's Temple, the Children of God, and Eastern religious cults. Sociologists have studied many of these religious cults, and have reached some conclusions about why adolescents join, why they leave, and how the religious cult phenomenon is tied to alienation (Doress & Porter, 1978; Robbins & Anthony, 1978; Roof, 1978).

Defection from traditional religion

One study indicates that defection from traditional religion is not a sign of religious defection alone. Evidence suggests that religious experimentation and defection are associated with psychic stress and with dissatisfaction with the life that traditional society offers. A religious cult, then, may be an attractive alternative to an adolescent who has become alienated with school, with the community in which he or she lives, or with his or her day-to-day activities (Wuthnow & Glock, 1973).

Religious experimenters and defectors differ in some measurable ways from others. They tend to have higher grade point averages and worry less about grades. They are more likely to have been involved in radical politics, to have experimented with drugs, and to believe in sexual experimentation. They display greater problems than the nondefectors in relationships with members of the opposite sex. Finally, it has been suggested that they may have difficulty negotiating some of the typical developmental tasks of later adolescence—identity formation, mate selection, and the establishment of life goals (Wuthnow & Glock, 1973).

Reasons for joining

Doress and Porter (1978) have summarized several reasons why youth join cults, why they stay in them, and why they leave. Cults such as the Unification church emphasize the breakdown of the American family, and promise converts a "perfect family." Other cults so emphasize the family theme that they call themselves "The Love Family" or "Love Israel." Psychologically, some youths may be looking for security in an alternative family.

The religious cult may provide a spiritual search for answers. In other words, the cult may give "perfect" answers to all of life's questions, thus giving structure to the youth's life. Security may be provided by a cult with strict rules, perhaps giving guidance missing from the family unit. The cult provides clear-cut alternatives to the biological family of the adolescent. Doress and Porter (1978) cite the clear differentiations between communal living versus nuclear family living, spirituality versus materialism, austerity versus extravagant spending and new hair styles, new clothing, and elaborate customs and traditions.

Joining a cult may be a way of seeking attention, adventure, or just something new. The robes of the Hare Krishna and the Children of God attract attention; members of the Unification church are taught how to smile. Joining a cult may even be an escape from unemployment or a poor job (Doress & Porter, 1978).

Reasons for leaving

It is not known what proportion of persons joining religious cults eventually leave them, but many do. Many leave because of disillusionment, since the cult was not able to live up to the expectations it promised. Some young people may enter a cult to accomplish certain personal goals, and upon having achieved these goals, will leave. Some leave by force. Parents may arrange to kidnap their children, and sometimes employ professional "deprogrammers" to undo the brainwashing techniques used with indoctrination by some cults.

There have been some interesting legal battles fought over the rights of parents to arrange for deprogramming of their children. The freedom of religion is a prominent belief in the United States, and one court precedent favored the principle of this freedom over the right of parents to have their children deprogrammed. One discussion has argued that the so-called "brainwashing" techniques used by religious cults are really no different than techniques of indoctrination used by more conventional religious groups, and thus should not be used to implicate cults as though they are really any different from other religions (Robbins & Anthony, 1978). Indeed, the brainwashing issue is perhaps the point of greatest conflict between parents whose children have joined a cult and the children themselves.

Other religious movements

There are other religious movements which do not have the flavor of cults. Many fundamental Christian groups, for example, have attracted numerous members in recent years. Groups such as Navigators, Campus Crusade for Christ, Campus Life, and others follow traditional Christian teachings, and tend to make special appeals to adolescents. In addition, they have specific training programs for the members, who are instructed about how to share their beliefs with others.

Unlike the religious cults described above, the fundamental religious groups have teachings which attempt to build on existing social institutions such as the family, rather than attempt to circumvent them. The total commitment individuals make to fundamental Christian movements and the high values placed on sharing one's faith for the purpose of winning converts are a source of conflict in some families and between some adolescents and their peers. But among others, it becomes a mechanism for bringing families or peers closer together.

ADOLESCENTS AS WORKERS

Adolescence is thought of more as a time for schooling than a time for working. However, employment is a common feature of the adolescent years for a sizable segment of the adolescent population. Although most states have laws which restrict the kinds of work younger adolescents can do, some adolescents begin working very early in their lives, doing such jobs as babysitting, mowing lawns, delivering newspapers, selling fruit or lemonade from roadside stands, or shoveling snow. Full-time work and work considered hazardous to youth are usually outlawed for younger adolescents. But by later adolescence, almost all forms of employment are available to youth.

Most adolescents begin working part-time after school or during the summers at odd jobs or at one of the kinds of work mentioned above. Summertime employment is especially attractive to youth in the United States. Often it is considered a means of earning money for luxuries not otherwise affordable by the family, a way of saving toward the purchase of something special, such as an automobile, or part of a plan to save for college. In the mid-1970s, about 4 in 10 persons age 16 to 21 had summer jobs (U.S. Bureau of the Census, 1975).

About three-fourths of persons 16 to 19 years old who are not in school are part of the labor force. More than 9 in 10 males and about 2 in 3 female adolescents not in school are working. Thus, a significant minority of adolescents not in school are unemployed. The rates of unemployment are particularly high for Black adolescents and adolescents of Spanish origin.

In the summer months, about half of all 16- and 17-year-old males can be found working, including those who did not attend school during the year. About 70 percent of all 18- and 19-year-old males can be found working, a figure which also includes those who are no longer in school. These figures are not expected to change very much between 1980 and 1990. Females are not as likely to be employed. About 4 in 10 females 16 and 17 years old and 6 in 10 of those 18 and 19 years old are in the workforce during the summer. As with males, these figures are not projected to change very much between 1980 and 1990. An increase of about 4 percent may be expected for females.

What is perhaps most important about these numbers is not the large proportion of those working, but the significant minority who are not working. Particularly among older adolescents, failure to find a summer job if a student, or failure to find a job at any time if not in school, can be a frustrating experience for the youth. What does one do with his or her free time? How is one to become independent of parents and acquire personal possessions without means of support? Such problems can often lead to normlessness, depression, and delinquent behavior as a solution to the boredom, frustration, and lack of income.

One major focus of adolescence is career preparation. High schools often differentiate between college-bound curriculums and trade curriculums, some schools have counselors specializing in college placement, and most schools make an effort to introduce students to various job opportunities for when they finish their schooling (for example, "career days"). Adolescents are often asked what they want to do when they "grow up." Although most adolescents change their minds from time to time, the importance of the question seems to follow the youth through choices of courses, selection of colleges, and even participation in hobbies. For example, future artists may paint or make pottery. Future musicians may play in the school band or sing in the church choir. Future mechanics may repair automobiles in

---

INSIGHT INTO ADOLESCENCE

Mary Oppen, née Mary Colby, was born at Kalispell, Montana, in 1908. In 1926 she met the poet George Oppen at the Agricultural College at Corvallis, Oregon. Together they traveled widely. They have lived in France, New York City, Mexico City, and San Francisco. In her autobiography, *Meaning a Life*, Mary Oppen frankly discusses their adventures, relationships with other writers and poets, and most of all the choices which shaped her earlier life and her life with her husband. In this excerpt she talks about a time of crisis—a time for choices—in her adolescence.

My parents were away that year because Papa was to have exploratory surgery in order to diagnose some alarming symptoms. Papa and Mama were staying at a friend's house, where Papa was convalescing after the surgery, when he sent for me, and I went on the bus by myself. I sat with him, and he held my hand while he told me, "I may not get well, Mary dear," but I did not really understand what he was saying to me.

With only a year to live, Papa was preoccupied with the store; he planned for it to provide for us all. He was in a race with his death, and in the fall of my fifteenth year he was less and less able to go from the house. Finally he could no longer move about, and the last few days he was in a coma. One night I was called down to find my family gathered around his bed. I was uncomfortable, because I could not find my father in the wasted form gasping for breath. He was alone with his death, and his death left each of us alone too. He was buried from a church he had never entered in life. I had a hard time realizing that he was dead; I could not make the connections between his death, the funeral, and the father I had known.

Before my father died I felt myself a part of a family of six; with his death very suddenly I was alone. We were not a united family after he died, and I struggled with this new way of being. We also stepped down in class; I faced these changes without time to adjust to them. I knew I had to get away from my mother and earn my own living at once. I was willing, even eager, to do this—the only obstacle was my age. I felt a desperate loneliness for my father; I couldn't bear his absence and was pressed to realize his spirit in myself. All my young life, it now seemed, I had been vigilantly avoiding the trap that was Grants Pass, and I now looked for a way into the world. I considered losing myself in wilderness, but no answers came from running away into nothing; I lay beside a spring in the forest with only a bird or squirrel to see me lying there, or I climbed to a hilltop in order to look out at mountains. I pondered a way into the world, into a peopled world.

Source: Oppen, M. Meaning a Life. Santa Barbara, California: Black Sparrow Press, 1977.

their spare time. And future journalists may work for the local radio station or write for the school paper.

Parents play an important role in influencing the career aspirations of their children. There are countless examples of offspring taking over their father's business, of doctors and lawyers who raise their sons to become doctors and lawyers, and of parents who encourage their daughters in particular to plan for marriage and a family, just as they did. But parental influence is more widespread than might be suggested by the phenomenon of following in one's parent's footsteps.

Most parents want their children to achieve a higher social status than they were able to, and educational and occupational attainment is the primary route to greater income and higher social standing. It is not surprising, then, that parents attempt to encourage high aspirations among their children. Furthermore, it is likely that such encouragement plays a significant part in enhancing the standard of living in society. A widespread socialization process which encourages upward career mobility is likely to have the consequence of improving the standard of living from generation to generation, and this, of course, has been a notable characteristic of American society.

ADOLESCENTS AS CONSUMERS

Advertisers constantly remind us of the important role adolescents have as consumers. Newspapers, magazines, radio, and television have much to say to adolescents. The primary message is "spend your money here." As children, most purchasing decisions are made for us by parents, although children do have some influence, particularly with regard to toys and food. But with adolescence comes a new independence in our consumer role. Adolescents often have their own money to spend, and they have lots of items on which to spend their money.

Industries selling appearance-related products take advantage of the adolescent's need for self-esteem, the desire to be attractive, and the need to be accepted. All kinds of beauty treatments, cosmetics, acne medication, shampoos and conditioners, clothing, physique development equipment, athletic equipment, and jewelry are marketed directly to adolescents and the so-called "youth subculture."

Many styles of clothing become popular because certain individuals begin wearing them, and the tendency toward conformity in one's peer group or in school makes the item a "must." Advertisements often are directed toward these needs by portraying such conforming behavior. Magazines directed to young people display new fashions and hair styles and then advertise the products that will permit individuals to have these new fashions and styles. There is a circular relation between what one sees around him or her and what shows up in the mass media. Each reinforces the other until, in a period as brief as several weeks, a new trend can sweep the country.

It is also during adolescence that buying habits are first developed and when many expensive items are purchased for the first time. One's first automobile may be purchased during late adolescence, for instance, and items of lesser expense, such as cosmetics, may influence subsequent buying behavior subtly; we may, for example, be influenced by brand-name recognition during adolescence that can last for years to come.

Adolescents are an unusual group from an economic standpoint. Although adults have higher incomes, most of that income is committed before it is even made. There are monthly mortgage payments or rent; expenses for food, utilities, and medical care; and other fixed expenses, including the costs of raising children.

Adolescents, however, are able to spend most of their earned income. An individual may be saving for college or some other future goal. But this is a choice made only by some. Others simply spend all that they earn, and thus, for some industries, adolescents are the most potent buying force.

MILITARY SERVICE

The relevance of military service in the lives of adolescents varies considerably depending on the historical era. During World War II, virtually all able adolescent males could expect to be drafted by the military, unless they enlisted or were engaged in an important war-related occupation following graduation from school. The United States was in a time of war—one which was supported by virtually all Americans. There were more than 15 million veterans of World War II living in 1950, five years after the war concluded, and by 1976, there were still more than 13 million American men living who had served in World War II (U.S. Bureau of the Census, 1977a). Thus, for many adolescent males of the 1930s and 1940s, service in the military was something that could be planned for before the conclusion of adolescence.

In 1976, there were more than 6 million veterans of the Korean conflict of the early 1950s, some of whom had also served in World War II. The Korean conflict was also supported by most Americans, and therefore adolescents often enlisted or were drafted following completion of their schooling. For those that dropped out of high school, the likelihood of their induction into the Armed Forces was especially great. But in the mid-1960s, the United States became involved in a war in Vietnam which was unpopular, and became less and less popular over time.

Adolescents and young adults, in particular, became heavily involved in protests of the war, many refused to enlist or be drafted, and there were large numbers of "draft dodgers," conscientious objectors, and dissidents in the military service. There were 8 million veterans of the Vietnam war still living in 1976. The majority of them were in late adolescence or early adulthood when they began military service (U.S. Bureau of the Census, 1977a).

Wars tend to be fought by young men. Thus, during unpopular wars, it is logical to expect that adolescents will be among the most vocal of those voicing protests over the war. This was indeed what happened from 1966 to 1971, when there was a yearly average of more than 2 million youths ages 17 to 24 in the military. Thousands of others had refused to serve, and there are still, in 1980, "draft dodgers" from the late 1960s who have refused to return to the United States or who are living in the country but have not come forward to clear their records. Various forms of amnesty have been granted to those who protested, but only some of the thousands who refused to serve have taken advantage of the amnesty plans.

Military service is attractive to many young men and women. The high school dropout, the high school graduate, and the college graduate all may be attracted to military service. The higher the educational level, the greater the likelihood of serving as an officer, particularly if college attendance can be tied to a reserve officer training program (ROTC) or service in a military academy. Both in times of war and in times of peace, many adolescents find that military service is desirable for several reasons. The adolescent may avoid unemployment, he or she may be interested in the opportunities for travel, some may be attracted to the career possibilities and extensive benefits, others may see it as a way of financing an education following military service (through the GI bill), and some may find appeal in the military life-style.

It is likely that adolescents will continue to account for most of the persons enlisting in the military. Since the draft was abolished during the 1970s, the military now is made up entirely of those who volunteer. In 1976, there were about 360,000 persons ages 17 to 19 in the military, about 84 percent of them White, 15 percent Black, and one percent of other races. Women are now found in all branches of the Armed Forces. Women now constitute about 5 percent of the 2 million persons in the military (U.S. Bureau of the Census, 1977a), and their numbers seem likely to increase.

ADOLESCENTS AND THE POLITICAL SYSTEM

Todays's adolescents invariably are influenced by the systems of government they encounter in their local communities and their state and nation. Often they are constrained in their behaviors by these institutions. For example, there may be laws governing use of alcohol. At other times they are encouraged to become involved in their political system. By an amendment to the United States Constitution, for example, 18-year-olds now have the right to vote in national elections. In this section we review the laws pertinent to adolescents and how adolescents behave in regard to their political system.

Law and adolescents

Adolescence has been described as the transitionary period between childhood and adulthood. This definition is particularly appropriate when we consider the legal status of the adolescent. In most states, 18 is defined as the age of majority. In other words, this is the age at which an individual is no longer responsible to parents legally nor are the parents responsible for the children beyond this time. The adolescent legally is *emancipated*.

Many things change for the adolescent upon reaching this age of majority (five states have older ages, either 19 or 21). Although the laws vary from state to state, it is typically at this time when the adolescent would be tried in adult court for commission of a crime. Before this age, he or she would have reported to juvenile court. After this age, adolescents become responsible for their own debts. They can sign legal contracts, buy property, leave home without being defined as runaways, and give consent for surgery or other medical procedures. These and a host of other rights and responsibilities come with legal emancipation.

For many adolescents, reaching the legal age of adulthood comes before they have reached adulthood socially, psychologically, or economically. In other words, the 18-year-old may still be very dependent on parents, but has the legal right to be considered totally apart from parents and family. This poses a conflict in some families, where parents wish to continue to exert influence over their children—influence which may be rejected by the children. The reverse is also true in some cases. Some parents want their children to become self-supporting and independent, but the adolescent may continue to wish to be supported by the parents, both economically and psychologically.

Most parents and adolescents realize that a balance between legal emancipation and psychological emancipation is necessary. College educations can rarely be

Exhibit 3.1

Age of majority, and ages at which state legislation, court action or attorneys general opinions have specifically affirmed the right of individuals to consent for medical care in general, for contraceptive services, for examination and treatment of pregnancy and VD, and for abortion; as of December 31, 1975 (X = any age)*

State	Age of majority	May consent for medical care in general			May consent for:			
		No limitation	If married (M) or emancipated (E)	In emergency	Contraception	Pregnancy-connected care	VD care	Abortion
Ala.	19	14	E[9], M	X	14	X	X	14
Alaska	19, MF	19	E[6,7,8]	X[5,28]	X	X	X	18
Ariz.	18	18	E, M	X[10]	18	18	X	18
Ark.	18	X[2,4]	E, M	X	X[2,4,12]	X[14]	X	18
Calif.	18	18	15E[6], M	X	X[3]	X	12	X
Colo.	18[1]	18	15E[6], M	18	X[2]	18	X	X
Conn.	18	18	E, M	18	18	18	X[18]	18
Del.	18	18	E, M	18	12[11]	12	12	18
Fla.	18	18	E, M	X	X[20]	18	X	X
Ga.	18	18[3]	M[3]	X	XF[3]	X	X	X
Hawaii	18	18	18	18	18	14[27]	14[27]	14[27]
Idaho	18	18	18	18	X[4]	18	14	18
Ill.	18[1]	18	M[7]	X	X[15]	X	12	X[24]
Ind.	18	18	E, M	X	18	18	X	X[24]
Iowa	18, M	18	E, M	X	18[12]	18	X	18
Kans.	18	X[4], 16[5]	18	16	X[4]	X	X	X[4]
Ky.	18	18	E, M[8]	X	X[3]	X	X	X
La.	18, M	X[21,3]	M	X	18[12]	X[3]	X	X
Maine	18	18	E	X	X[23]	18	X	18
Md.	18	18	M[8]	X	X[3]	X	X	X
Mass.	18	18	E[3,6], M[5]	X	18	X	X[19]	X
Mich.	18	X[4]	E, M	X	X[4,12]	X[4]	X	X[4]
Minn.	18	18	E[6], M[8]	X	X[13]	X	X	X[29]
Miss.	21	X[4]	E, M	X	X[16]	X	X	X[4]
Mo.	18[1]	21	E, M[8]	X	21	X[14]	X	18
Mont.	18	X[23,3,14]	E[3,14] M[7,3,14]	X	18	X[14]	X	18[27]
Nebr.	19, M	19	M	19	19	19	X	X[24]
Nev.	18	18	E[3,4,14] M[3,4,14]	X[3,4,14]	18	16	X	18
N.H.	18	X[4]	E, M	X[4]	X[4]	X[4]	14	X[4]
N.J.	18	18	E, M[7]	18	18	X	X	X
N. Mex.	18	18	E, M	X[10]	18[12]	X[17]	X	18
N.Y.	18	18	E, M[8]	X	X	X[4]	X	X[4,25]
N.C.	18	18	E, M	X	18	18	X	18
N. Dak.	18	18	E, M	18	18	18	14	18
Ohio	18	X[4]	18	X[4]	X[12,4]	X[4]	X	18

State	Age of majority	May consent for medical care in general			May consent for:			
		No limitation	If married (M) or emancipated (E)	In emergency	Contraception	Pregnancy-connected care	VD care	Abortion
Okla.	18	X[23,3,14]	E[3,14] M[8,3,14]	X	18[12]	X[3,14]	X	18
Oreg.	18[1], M	15	M	15	15[14]	15[14]	12	18
Pa.	21	18	E[9], M	X	X[26]	X	X	X
R.I.	18	18	E	16, M	18	18	X	18
S.C.	18	16[22]	E, M	X	16	16	X	16
S. Dak.	18	18	E, M	18	18	18	X	18
Tenn.	18	18	18	18	X[3]	18	X	18
Tex.	18	18	16E, M	X	18	X	X	X
Utah	18, M	18	M	X	X	X	X	X[27]
Vt.	18	18	E, M	18	18	18	12	18
Va.	18	18[3]	E	18	X[3,14]	X[14]	X	18
Wash.	18	18	E	18	18	18	14	X
W. Va.	18	18	18	X	18[12]	18	X	18
Wis.	18	18	E, M	18	18	18	X	18
Wyo.	19	19	19	19	19[12]	19	X	19
D.C.	18	18[3]	E, M[3]	X	X[3]	X[3]	X	X
Total At 18	45	35	6	13	21	18	0	24
≤18		12	44	36	27	31	51	26

*The fact that no affirmative legislation, court decision or attorney general's opinion has been found in a particular state does not mean that some or even all categories of minors below the ages shown in the table do not have the right to obtain some or all medical services on their own consent.

Note: Because of reporting lags, the table probably does not include all applicable legislation, cases and attorneys general opinions for 1975. M = Married, F = Female; E= Emancipated.
1. For purposes of signing contracts. 2. Excluding voluntary sterilization if under 18 and unmarried. 3. Excluding voluntary sterilization. 4. If mature enough to understand the nature and consequences of the treatment. 5. If parent not immediately available. 6. Emancipated defined as living apart from parents and managing own financial affairs. 7. And/or pregnant. 8. Or parent. 9. Emancipated defined as a high school graduate, a parent or pregnant. 10. If no parent available, others may consent in loco parentis. 11. If sexually active. 12, Comprehensive family planning law permits (or does not exclude) services to minors without parental consent, 13, Unless parent has previously notified treating agency of objection. 14. Excluding abortion. 15. If referred by clergyman, physician or Planned Parenthood or if "failure to provide such services would create a serious health hazard." 16. If referred by clergyman, physician, family planning clinic, school or institution of higher learning or any state or local government agency. 17. Examination only. 18. In public health agencies, public or private hospitals or clinics. 19. In publicly maintained facilities. 20 If married or pregnant or "may suffer, in the opinion of the physician, probable health hazards if such services are not provided." Surgical services excluded. 21. If minor "is or believes himself to be afflicted with an illness or disease." 22. Except for operation essential to health or life. 23. If physician finds probable health hazard. 24. Parental consent requirement temporarily enjoined by court. 25. In New York City, municipal hospitals perform abortions on minors without parental consent if married, emancipated or at least 17 years old or if seeking parental consent would endanger the physical or mental health of the patient. 26. Minors are being served under a state law which permits doctors to serve minors of any age if delay in treatment "would increase the risk to the minor's life or health." 27. Parent notifications, but not consent, is required, where possible. 28. If parent refuses to grant or withhold consent. 29. County Attorney stated that legislature did not intend to include abortion as pregnancy-related treatment.
Source: Paul, Pilpel, & Wechsler, 1976.

financed without some form of parental support, and for non-college-bound adolescents, starting out on one's own can be difficult without some support from one's family. Although most families are able to conduct this transition in a smooth way, others find that it is a constant struggle to untie the knot that held the adolescent and parents together, whether or not the individuals involved were on good terms when the transition began.

Exhibit 3.1 shows the state-by-state breakdown of ages of majority as of the end of 1975. Also shown are some of the legal conditions applying to the individual's right to consent to medical care, obtain contraceptive services, obtain abortions, be treated for venereal disease, and receive pregnancy-connected care. It can be seen that there is great variability from state to state, and that the intricacies of the law can be complex. The reader is also cautioned that some of the specific ages and rules which apply may have changed since this exhibit was prepared. Furthermore, some of the information may be subject to legal interpretation.

It can be seen from Exhibit 3.1 that some states have also made determinations about what legal rights minors have. Whereas adolescents are often inclined to think about what rights they may gain upon emancipation, there are some rights which they have while still minors. In many states, for example, an adolescent may obtain pregnancy-related care, be treated for venereal disease, or even receive an abortion, regardless of age and without parental consent. Furthermore, most states will allow the adolescent to give consent for medical treatment in an emergency when parental permission may not be readily available.

Upon legal emancipation, parents and adolescents need to investigate the status of health insurance policies, automobile insurance coverage, and any other plans, policies, or services which may no longer include the adolescent. In some cases, the adolescent will need to arrange for his or her own coverage as a result of this new legal status.

Adolescents as voters

Before 1972, only persons 21 and over were permitted to vote in national elections. The right to vote was given to adolescents ages 18 to 21 after a turbulent time in the 1960s, when America's youth became quite politically active and vocal. Thus, beginning with the 1972 presidential elections, persons 18 years old and over have been permitted to vote in national elections. Yet the voter turnout among this newly enfranchised group was low in the 1972 presidential election and even lower in the 1976 presidential election. Thirty-eight percent of young persons 18 to 20 years old reported that they voted in 1976. This compares with the 63 percent of persons 25 and over who voted in the 1976 November presidential election (U.S. Bureau of the Census, 1978a).

Thus, older adolescents who have the right to vote do not seem to exercise this right as often as persons who are older. Several reasons may account for this. In follow-up surveys, some youth simply report that they were not interested in the election. Many reported that they were unable to register. The mobility of youth may affect their voter participation, since they are often away from home at the time of the elections (U.S. Bureau of the Census, 1978a).

Political socialization in adolescence

Earlier in this chapter, we discussed the alleged generation gap between adolescents and their parents in regard to attitudes and values about contemporary social issues.

In that presentation we noted that although adolescents often may believe they have beliefs that contrast with those of their parents, there is, in fact, considerable similarity. Thus, it appears that parents do fairly well in transmitting their own beliefs about social issues to their children. A similar conclusion may be reached in regard to the political socialization of children and adolescents.

Although they often believe otherwise, adolescents tend to hold political attitudes consistent with those of their parents (Niemi, 1973). Indeed, there is evidence indicating that such socialization of political attitudes is evident, and quite resistant to change, by *early* adolescence. Gallatin (1975) notes that high school students' exposure to various types of social studies curricula does not appear to have much impact on political attitudes and behavior. In fact, Jennings and Niemi (1968) and Langton and Jennings (1968) found that high school students who had taken several civics courses did not answer factual questions better than those who had taken only one course. In addition high school students in issues-oriented political courses did not differ greatly from those students in relatively conventional social studies courses in regard to their concerns about social matters and politics. The researchers suggested that by the time people reach high school they may have already been so politically socialized that course work cannot affect their attitudes. This view is supported by research reported by Hess and Torney (1967), who suggest that by the very beginning of adolescence people have acquired their basic orientations to the political system and are unlikely to alter their views thereafter.

However, there do seem to be changes in the *reasons* adolescents offer for their political views. Adelson (1971), Adelson and O'Neil (1966), and Gallatin (1972, 1975) report that in response to questions pertaining to government, law, and political parties, younger subjects were more concrete, authoritarian, and categorical in their thoughts and views, while older adolescents gave more abstract, humanitarian, qualified, and informed responses. Interestingly, Gallatin (1972) found that the older adolescents offered reasons for their answers that incorporated many of the political principles involved in the Bill of Rights of the United States Constitution.

EFFECTS OF THE MASS MEDIA
ON ADOLESCENT DEVELOPMENT

Of all the dimensions of the social context influencing the development of the contemporary adolescent, no dimension is associated so closely with adolescents of the current historical era as are the mass media. Adolescents of other historical eras were exposed to the society outside their own community to some degree. Such instruments for mass communication included the media of newspapers, radio, and film. However, only adolescents living in the most recent decades in this society's history have been exposed to television and have been exposed *extensively* to all forms of mass media simultaneously.

This simultaneous and increasingly greater exposure to contemporary mass media may be illustrated by data on ownership of televisions. About 97 percent of all households have a television set and 61 percent of all households have a color set. Moreover, 45 percent of all households have two or more sets (U.S. Bureau of the Census, 1977a). Similarly, from 1950 to 1975 the number of domestic phones in use in the United States rose from 39 million to 130 million. The average number of daily local conversations rose from 175 million in 1950 to 599 million in 1976. The number of radio stations rose from 2,143 in 1950 to 4,355 in 1975, while the number of television stations increased from 107 to 693 in this same period.

Furthermore, given the vast increase in the use and availability of television, radio, and telephone, it is interesting to note that the number of newspapers published in 1950 (12,115) was not very different from the number published in 1977 (11,089), and the number of periodicals increased from 6,960 to 9,732 (a 40 percent increase). The total circulation of American newspapers has not changed very much, for example, from 1970 (62,108,000) to 1976 (60,976,000). Thus, with the presence of the published media holding fairly steady and other forms of the mass media showing vast increases, Americans are not replacing one sort of mass media with another. Rather, they appear to be increasing the absolute presence of all forms of the media in their lives.

Despite the growing presence and use of the mass media—as a source of information about and communication with large segments of the social network—little research evidence exists about the influence of the mass media on human development. Perhaps because of the increasing prominence of television in modern society, evidenced by the above statistics, the research that does exist pertains mostly to the effects of *television* on adolescents, even though the range of television effects that have been studied is limited. Most of the research deals with the relation of violence in television programs to aggressive behavior in adolescence (Stein & Friedrich, 1975). Thus, we shall focus on the influence of television on adolescent behavior.

Effects of manipulated television viewing patterns

Two major strategies have characterized empirical attempts to assess whether television viewing of violence is related to violent or aggressive behavior in adolescence. One strategy is to manipulate experimentally the viewing patterns of adolescents—by exposing them to regimens or "diets" of violent or nonviolent programming—in order to see the effects on behavior. A second strategy is to assess the actual viewing patterns of youth in order to see if naturally occurring amounts of violent viewing are associated with aggression. McCall (1977) has argued that although experimental studies show whether selected variables *can* influence behavior, they do not necessarily show whether these variables *do* influence behavior in the "real world." Thus, we review studies in this section that show that viewing television violence indeed can influence the adolescent to behave aggressively; in the next section we consider whether such viewing actually does have this influence.

Although experimental studies are useful—in that they indicate the presence of certain effects under controlled conditions—such studies can be limited in several ways (see Chapter 7). One important limitation is that if samples studied are not representative, then effects identified through controlled manipulation cannot necessarily be generalized to broad populations. This is a problem in the experimental studies of manipulated television viewing on adolescent behavior (Stein & Friedrich, 1975). Most studies have used atypical populations of adolescents (for example, delinquents) and/or have only assessed males. As such, these limitations make it even more necessary to be cautious about generalizing results to adolescents as a whole.

Nevertheless, most short-term (for example, one experimental session) studies are consistent in their findings. They show an increase in aggression after exposure to aggressive films. For instance, Leifer and Roberts (1972) showed one of six television programs, varying in amount of violence, to male and female kindergarten, third, sixth, ninth, and twelfth grade students. As the level of viewed violence increased, students indicated on a questionnaire that they were more likely to use physical aggression in conflict situations. However, a second study by Leifer and Roberts (1972), and one by Collins (1973), studying fifth through twelfth grade males and females, found no difference in the incidence of answers about the likelihood of using violence between those students who saw a violent program and those who saw a neutral travelogue. However, three other studies, assessing only adolescent males, found that viewing violent programs led to more violent responses than did viewing neutral programs (Hartmann, 1969; Leifer & Roberts, 1972; Walters & Thomas, 1963).

Thus, although the majority of short-term studies suggest that adolescent aggression can be increased by viewing violent programs, there are some other short-term studies which do not find this relationship. Similarly, studies which have involved longer-term manipulations (several days or weeks of manipulations) are divided on the presence or absence of such a relation. Feshbach and Singer (1971), Wells (1973), and Parke, Berkowitz, Leyens, West, and Sebastian (1977) studied various groups of male adolescents, ranging from 8 to 18 years. All studies involved a repeated exposure, of from several days (Parke et al., 1977) to several weeks (Feshbach & Singer, 1971; Wells, 1973), to either violent programs or neutral ones. The aggression of the males in these studies was rated in several ways, for example, by peer or counselor behavior ratings or by questionnaire responses. For about half the measures of aggression in these studies, it was found that exposure to violent programs led to more aggression than did exposure to nonviolent programs. However, for about the remaining half of the measures, viewing of nonviolent programs led to more aggression than did exposure to violent ones. In fact, in the Wells (1973) study—a thorough investigation involving males from ten schools in different geographical areas and from different socioeconomic levels—there were no significant differences in aggression behaviors between males exposed to the two types of program contents.

Accordingly, the results of the above studies of the effects of manipulated viewing show that adolescents can, at least sometimes, be influenced under somewhat controlled conditions to show aggressive behavior in response to viewing violent programs. A major issue (McCall, 1977) now is whether adolescents in fact do exhibit violent or aggressive behavior in the real world in relation to their actual viewing of violent programs. Studies of effects of actual television viewing patterns provide both indirect and direct evidence that such a "real-world" relation indeed exists.

Effects of actual television viewing patterns

The amount of television actually viewed increases gradually from age 3 years to the beginning of adolescence, after which the total number of hours viewed decreases among high school-aged adolescents (Lyle, 1972). Although the absolute number of violent programs watched also decreases during this period, the proportion of programs watched which are violent, and the preference to watch violent programs, increases throughout adolescence (Lyle & Hoffman, 1972).

Although in childhood males and females watch television about equally, females watch more during adolescence (Lyle, 1972). However, adolescent males still watch more violent programs despite this difference (Stein & Freidrich, 1972, 1975). Although *most* recent research does not find any relation between amount of television watching and either intelligence or school achievement (Stein & Freidrich, 1975), when relationships are found, high amounts of television viewing are associated with low intelligence or poor achievement (Friedrich & Stein, 1973; Stein & Friedrich, 1972). Nevertheless, despite the equivocal nature of the relation between actual television viewing and academic-related functions, there is a far from equivocal connection between actual patterns of viewing violent television and violent and aggressive behaviors.

Adolescents who view a lot of television violence are more likely to approve of it, and to consider it an effective means of conflict resolution, than are adolescents who watch relatively little televised violence (Dominick & Greenberg, 1972). Moreover, adolescents whose favorite programs are violent approve of aggression more than do adolescents with nonviolent program favorites (McIntyre & Teevan, 1972). Since it is known that such aggressive attitudes are positively related to both self-reports and peer ratings of aggressive behavior in adolescence (McLeod, Atkin, & Chaffee, 1972a), this influence of violent viewing may have a great affect on actual adolescent aggressive/violent behavior. This possibility is enhanced by the results of several studies which show that adolescents who view a lot of television violence consider such violence more realistic than do those adolescents who watch only a little televised violence (Lefkowitz, Eron, Walder, & Huesmann, 1972; McLeod et al., 1972a, 1972b). Indeed, about one-third of the adolescents studied by McIntyre and Teevan (1972) believe their favorite television programs were "true to life," regardless of whether these programs were fictional or not. Similar appraisals of the reality of television programs—despite whether they are fictional—also have been found among adults (Gross, 1974).

Thus, television viewing of aggression is related to aggressive attitudes and to the belief that the depiction of aggression on television programs reflects real-life behavior. Moreover, these attitudes and beliefs may be at least indirectly associated with aggressive behavior, since aggressive attitudes and aggressive behaviors have been found related. *Direct* evidence of a relation between viewing violent television and commission of violent behaviors exists also, however.

McLeod et al. (1972a, 1972b) found that the frequency of viewing violence was related positively to self-reported aggression in two samples of male and female sixth to tenth graders. In one sample, peer and teacher ratings of aggression were related similarly to the frequency of violent viewing (although parent ratings were not related). Similarly, McIntyre and Teevan (1972) found that the amount of violence in the favorite television programs of junior high school and high school students was related both to self-reports of aggressive behavior *and* to reports of serious delinquent behavior (such as those requiring police attention). Robinson and Bachman (1972) also found that 19-year-old males' self-reports of aggressive behavior and of serious delinquent acts were associated with preferences for violent television programs.

Furthermore, in a ten-year longitudinal study (Eron, Lefkowitz, Heusmann, & Walder, 1972; Lefkowitz et al., 1972), relating television preference and aggressive behavior (as rated by peers), a positive relation was found between preference for violent television programs and aggressive behavior among third grade males. More interestingly, however, these males' third grade preferences for violent television were also related to aggressive behavior ten years later. However, aggressive behaviors at grade 3 and at the ten-year-later follow-up were not related to preferences for violent *viewing* at the time of the follow-up. Moreover, television viewing preferences were not related to aggression among the females studied.

In summary, most of the evidence indicates that there is a relation between the actual viewing of televised violence and the incidence of aggressive and violent behaviors (Stein & Friedrich, 1975). Although certainly not applying to all adolescents, the recurrence of this relationship in studies assessing effects of actual viewing patterns suggest that altering the incidence of violence on television can change the probability of violent behaviors among today's youth. Thus, as with other aspects of the social context of adolescence we have reviewed in this chapter, television—as a most prevalent mass media influence—has a demonstrated empirical effect on adolescents' functioning. This effect can lead to the greater likelihood of either positive or negative social behaviors. Stein and Friedrich (1975, p. 247) have argued that "the responsibility rests heavily on researchers to inform the public that this ready form of relaxation is, in fact, a powerful teacher. . . . They must also be informed of the great potential inherent in the medium for enhancing the quality of life for individuals and for society as a whole."

CHAPTER SUMMARY

Adolescent development occurs in a social context which includes the family, peer groups, the schools, the church, and the society in which one lives. In society, there are influences such as the political system, the economic system, the legal system, and the mass media. To understand adolescents and their development, it is important to consider each of these influences and the interrelationships between them.

The importance of the peer group is widely known and indisputable. However, there is evidence to suggest that the family is perhaps the most important determinant of adolescent attitudes, values, and political and religious beliefs. We see the impact of the peer group more often in the day-to-day behavior of adolescents. The importance of automobiles and athletics and the presence of cliques and group behavior are results of the powerful force of the peer group. Although conflict between parents and adolescents exists, evidence has been presented to suggest that for most adolescents such conflict actually is minimal. Adolescents actually overestimate the magnitude of the differences that exist between themselves and their parents. Parents underestimate the extent of these differences.

Education is a nearly universal characteristic of adolescence, and about 85 percent of individuals finish high school. However, among those who drop out of school, numerous problems can occur. Males and females have roughly equal dropout rates, although the reasons for leaving school are sometimes different. Females, for example, sometimes leave school because of pregnancy or childbirth. High school dropouts earn less income than those who finish school; obtain less desirable jobs; marry earlier; have higher rates of marital disruption, higher mortality rates, and higher fertility rates; and are more likely to live in poverty.

Most adolescents are given some instruction in religion, usually in the faith that their parents have chosen. The majority of adolescents report that they have a religious affiliation, and about half say that they attend church regularly. Although conventional religions predominate in America, religious cults have achieved growing visibility, in part due to a series of sometimes bizzare incidents in recent years. It is during the late adolescent years that religious cults seem to have the most attraction. The religious cult may provide a spiritual search for answers that the adolescent seeks, or joining the cult may provide attention, adventure, or just something new. Many cults disband, and among those which last, many persons eventually leave.

Americans can now vote at age 18 in national elections, and this right highlights the role of the adolescent in the political system. But adolescents have a sometimes ambiguous role. State laws regarding drinking, signing contracts, and criminal behavior differ, and adolescence actually straddles the legal statuses of "adult" and "minor."

Many adolescents work, usually part-time or during the summers. Working can help provide some of the independence that adolescents seek, as well as some spending money. Such work also may facilitate career preparation. Adolescents also are consumers. They are the targets of much advertising, since in certain markets they are the primary buyers. Adolescents in particular appear to be key purchasers of appearance-related products such as cosmetics.

The mass media, particularly television, have become a powerful force in our society. By adolescence, individuals have watched thousands of hours of television. Researchers have studied how television viewing—particularly viewing violence—influences behavior. Most of the evidence indicates that there is a relation between the actual viewing of televised violence and the incidence of aggressive and violent behaviors.

CHAPTER
OVERVIEW

This chapter highlights the history of ideas about human development. In addition, it traces ideas about adolescent development from their early philosophical roots to contemporary thinking. The chapter emphasizes some of the thinking of early theorists and researchers, as well as some limitations in the first ideas about adolescence.

ISSUES
TO CONSIDER

What has been the key conceptual issue in the study of development over the course of history?

How did Plato and Aristotle contribute to a concept of development?

What is the difference between an ontogenetic and a phylogenetic concept of development?

What was the character of the concept of development during the medieval Christian era?

How did the mind-body problem, as reintroduced in philosophy by Descartes, contribute to advancing ideas about development?

Why did empiricist philosophy represent the first major conception of ontogenetic development, and how did it lead to the scientific study of development?

How does Darwin's theory of evolution, and the concept of adaptation he advanced, contribute to a scientific concept of development?

What was the influence of G. Stanley Hall in advancing a scientific concept of development, and how did this contribution lead to the first theory of adolescent development?

What was the character of scientific concern about development through World War II, and how did the war alter the approach to developmental study?

What is the current role of theory in the study of development?

ave there always been adolescents? Have people always believed that as individuals develop, they pass through a special portion of life akin to what we today term "adolescence"? In fact, have people always believed that there is such a phenomenon as development?

To answer questions such as these it is useful to trace the history of ideas about development in general and about adolescent development in particular. Such historical analysis includes studying the first philosophical statements pertinent to development, statements more than 2,000 years old. The analysis also involves tracing the evolution of scientific studies of development and of adolescence in particular, a period covering little more than 100 years of history. By looking at both the philosophical and scientific roots of ideas of development, several important points can be noted. First, we will see that the life-span view of development discussed in Chapter 1 and the life-span definition of adolescent development given in Chapter 2 are relatively new ideas. Yet they represent outcomes of the more than 2,000 years of philosophical and scientific concern with issues pertinent to human development. Thus, while having what seems like a short history, life-span conceptions actually have a long past (Baltes, 1979).

Second, it may be noted that in both the 2,000 years of philosophy and the 100 years of science to be reviewed, the ideas advanced to explain development revolve around the same few issues. These issues represent the basic concepts in any discussion of development, and differences among philosophers and scientists can be understood by seeing the stances they take in regard to such issues. These issues pertain most directly to one issue: the *nature-nurture controversy*. This controversy relates to the influence of inborn characteristics on human development versus the influence of environment on human development. It is discussed in greater detail in Chapter 5, where it is argued that all the other major conceptual issues of development (the continuity-discontinuity issue and the critical periods hypothesis) derive from the nature-nurture one. The historical analysis in this chapter suggests that although the basic issues involved in any discussion of development have remained the same, the solutions have changed.

Third, then, this chapter discusses how the historical evolution of ideas about development has resulted today in particular views of human, and more specifically, adolescent development (such as the life-span view). As such, the goal of this chapter is to provide historical basis for a life-span conception. However, in order to organize and understand the evolution involved in the philosophical and scientific history of ideas of development, it is necessary first to introduce briefly the nature-nurture issue.

THE HISTORICAL ROLE OF THE NATURE-NURTURE ISSUE

The very first idea about human development involved what is still the most basic issue in development today: the *nature-nurture issue*. Basically, this issue pertains to the source of human behavior and development. Simply, a question is raised about where behavior and development come from. As soon as the first idea was formulated about what human behavior was, and from where it came, a stance was taken in regard to this issue.

In its most extreme form the issue pertains to whether behavior and development derive from *nature* (or in modern terms, *heredity*, *maturation*, or *genes*) or, at the other extreme, whether behavior and development derive from *nurture* (or in more

Exhibit 4.1
Terms associated with nature or nurture conceptions of development

Nature terms	Nurture terms
Innate	Experience
Preformed	Environment
Nativism	Empiricism
Instinct	Acquired
Inborn	Learning
Genetic	Socialization
Heredity	Education
Maturation	
Intrinsic	

modern terms, *environment, experience,* or *learning*). However, whatever terms are used, the issue raises questions about how inborn, intrinsic, native, or in short, *nature* characteristics (for example, genes) may contribute to development, and/or, in turn, how acquired, socialized, environmental, experienced, or in short, *nurture* characteristics (for example, stimulus-response connections) may play a role in development. Exhibit 4.1 lists some terms used in this chapter that pertain to nature and nurture contributions, respectively. This table will be useful to refer to in much of the presentation that follows.

As this chapter proceeds, it will be seen that philosophers and scientists advance ideas about development which pertain to nature, to nurture, or to some combination of the two (and hence they often use terms other than those listed in Exhibit 4.1). It will be argued that all ideas about development relate to this issue and, in turn, that all other issues of development derive from the nature-nurture one. Although a discussion of the relation of the nature-nurture issue to these other core issues of development will be reserved for Chapter 5, the present discussion of the history of philosophical and scientific concern with development can begin with this prominence of the nature-nurture issue in mind. In fact, one can view this historical review as involving the swinging of a pendulum, a pendulum moving from conceptions of human development stressing nature to conceptions stressing nurture. However, it will be argued that a conception stressing either extreme is not appropriate.

PHILOSOPHICAL ROOTS

The beginnings of concern with the phenomena in the world around us can be traced to the first philosophers. Attempts to speculate about the elements in the world constitute philosophical statements, and this first occurred more than 2,000 years ago. It is estimated that in about 600 B.C., a Greek man named Thales of Miletus (640 to 546 B.C.) became the first philosopher through his attempts to speculate about the nature of the universe in order to predict a solar eclipse (Clark, 1957).

This event indicates that when humans first turned their attention to the nature of phenomena in their world, they were concerned with the characteristics of the universe, and not the characteristics of humans themselves. Philosophical concerns about the character of the universe pertain to *cosmology,* and this topic remained the predominant focus of thinkers for several hundred years.

Thus, ideas about the nature of humans, not to mention human development, were not historically the first ideas considered by philosophers. In fact, it was about 200 years later that the first major philosophical statement pertinent to the nature of humans was presented. Plato made this presentation.

Plato (427–347 B.C.)

From Plato's ideas one can derive statements relevant to human development. Yet much of these derivations are indirect. Plato's writings, and those of philosophers for centuries following him, do not reflect a primary concern with human development, although ideas about human changes across life were apparent. The portion of Plato's writing from which one can derive his major ideas relevant to development dealt essentially with the mind-body problem.

This problem—a major concern to philosophers for over 2,000 years—inquires into the relation between the physical, spatial, and temporal body and the nonphysical, nonspatial, and nontemporal mind (or in Plato's term, "soul"). How does something which does not take up matter, space, or time (a soul) relate to something which does (a body)?

Plato reasoned that souls are eternal. He philosophized that there is a "realm of ideas," a spiritual place where souls reside. At birth, however, the body "traps" a particular soul. The soul remains in the body for the life of the person and returns to the realm of ideas when the person dies. Since the soul resides in the realm of ideas, it enters the body with these ideas at birth. That is, the person is born with *innate ideas,* with preexisting, preformed knowledge.

Thus, Plato's idea about the relation between mind and body not only represents the first major statement about what humans are like, but too represents a stance in regard to the nature-nurture issue. Humans are not the way they are because of experience or education. They do not have to learn their knowledge. Rather, their knowledge is built into them; it is innate. Hence, this first major statement about human behavior is a nature one. In sum, Plato said humans are the way they are (that is, having their innate ideas) because they have a soul, and this soul is a nature-based phenomenon.

Additionally, Plato believed that the soul was divided into three layers, and these layers also have implications for a view of human development. The lowest layer of the soul involves humans' desires and appetites. Here passions, emotions, lusts, and physical needs are found (Muuss, 1975a). A parallel can be seen between this layer of the soul and what a man would, more than 2,000 years later, call a structure of the personality. Plato's first layer corresponds to Freud's id (Freud, 1949).

Plato labels the second layer of the soul the spirit. Here courage, endurance, and aggressiveness originate (Muuss, 1975a). Although humans and animals both have the first and second layers, only humans have the third layer. This is the true or real soul. It is, Plato said, reason. It is immortal and, as already noted, only resides temporarily in the body.

What makes this layer idea relevant to a conception of development is that Plato did not believe that the attributes of each layer of the soul were immediately seen from birth. That is, people exercise the attributes of each layer successively, and Plato even noted that although reason is certainly present in all humans, the exercise of reason is not achieved by all people (Muuss, 1975a). Humans have to be trained in order to have their reasoning abilities drawn from them, and such training is what is involved, of course, in the Socratic method of education. This is the method where existing knowledge is drawn from the person on the basis of questions by the teacher.

In sum, Plato's ideas provided the first major statement relevant to human development. This first conception of human development placed the basis of human functioning in a nature conceptual "camp." Moreover, many of Plato's ideas are compatible with ideas about human development expressed by scientists thousands of years later (for example, Freud). Furthermore, although not an explicit theory of development, Plato's idea of layers of the soul did directly suggest that people differ across their life in the attributes they manifest. And, indirectly, Plato's ideas about the soul served as an influence on others to speculate about the makeup of the soul, and how its attributes showed themselves. One whose ideas were so influenced by Plato was his most famous student—Aristotle. Stimulated by his teacher's ideas, Aristotle revised Plato's ideas about the soul and about its relation to the body, and, most important to us, devised ideas explicitly relevant to understanding development.

Aristotle (384–322 B.C.)

Aristotle was also interested in the mind-body problem. His position differed from Plato's, however. Aristotle proposed the *hylomorphic doctrine*, which said that spirit (hylo) and matter (morph) were inseparable although distinct. The soul was present in all living organisms and gave life to matter. Aristotle philosophized that this occurred because there was a nonphysical, nonspatial, nontemporal "force" which "breathed life" into matter. This force was an *entelechy*. In sum, Aristotle proposed the idea of *vitalism*: there is a nonempirical entity present in any living organism which imparts life to that organism and directs its functioning.

Although an entelechy is present in all organisms, not all organisms have the same sort of entelechy. Similar to Plato, Aristotle postulated that layers of the soul existed. But in anticipation of Darwin more than 2,000 years later, Aristotle conceived of these levels in a biological-evolutionary manner (Muuss, 1975a). Aristotle also believed there were three layers of the soul, but identified them as a plantlike layer, an animallike layer, and a humanlike layer. The plant layer was associated with life functions relating to reproduction and nourishment. Although animals and humans had this layer as part of their souls, plants only had this first layer (Muuss, 1975a). Animals had their additional second layer, which was associated with functions such as locomotion, sensation, and perception, but they did not have the third layer of the soul.

This additional layer was found only in humans, who of course had the other two as well. The human layer was associated with thinking and reasoning, and it was the possession of these attributes that Aristotle believed set humans apart from animals and plants. In essence then, Aristotle believed that humans innately possess functions relating to three layers of the soul, and that the layer-related functions pertain to characteristics of life throughout the biological world. Accordingly, Aristotle's postulation is a notion of development, but not one of ontogeny. It is a notion of *phylogeny*.

As noted in Chapter 1, ontogeny refers to the development of a species from its conception to its death. Phylogeny is also concerned with development. But here the concern is with how a particular species came to exist in the first place, or how it came to have the characteristics we see it possessing today. It is a concern with the so-called "evolutionary scale" (Hodos & Campbell, 1969), or the *phylogenetic* (or the *phyletic) scale.* In short, one may talk about either ontogeny or phylogeny and still be concerned with development. When one talks about the latter, however, one speaks of the history of the development of one or more species (from their simpler to their more complex forms).

Accordingly, Aristotle's idea of layers of the soul was related to the idea of phylogenetic development. It considered human attributes in regard to attributes of other (presumably previous) forms of life. Later in this chapter it will be argued that in fact there are important distinctions between Aristotle's position and an appropriate view of phyletic development. Nevertheless, given this important qualification, one may recognize Aristotle's ideas as the first statement directly pertinent to development.

These ideas are not as relevant to ontogenetic development as they are to phyletic development. However, Aristotle *did* offer ideas about ontogeny as well. First, as did Plato, Aristotle believed that the functions associated with each layer of the soul emerged in a sequence from lower to higher. Aristotle was more explicit than Plato about this progression (see Muuss, 1975a), and divided the maturation of the human being into three states of seven years each.

The first seven years were labeled "infancy," and Aristotle saw humans of this age and animals as alike (Muuss, 1975a). Both were ruled by their desires and emotions. Thus, in this first period, Aristotle saw phyletic continuity between humans and animals. The next period of development Aristotle labeled "boyhood," while the last period of development was termed "young manhood" (Muuss, 1975a). After the end of this last stage was reached, development was presumably complete. The person at 21 years was now a mature adult.

One measure of Aristotle's continuing influence through history is that his belief that maturity was reached at age 21 years carried over to modern society. Until recently the age of majority in the United States was 21 years. This arbitrary number was determined by Aristotle's influence. However, Aristotle's influence was even greater than this. Because his philosophy regarding the mind-body problem was adopted by St. Thomas Aquinas, and then subsequently by the Catholic church, Aristotle's views became canonized. They became the only acceptable dogma of the church (Misiak & Sexton, 1966; Misiak & Staudt, 1954).

Until the Protestant Reformation, begun in the sixteenth century by Martin Luther (A.D. 1483–1546), Aristotle's philosophy remained unchallenged. Because the Catholic church was, during these several centuries, a truly *catholic* (that is, universal) institution, and because of the prominence of religion in the lives of people during this period, challenging the dogma of the church was a dangerous act. Challenge could lead to excommunication, and if expelled from the church there was no place else to go. Accordingly, because any one part of Aristotle's philosophy might be seen as related to another, no part was challenged until the Protestant Reformation provided an alternative to Catholicism. Until the sixteenth century then, no view of development other than Aristotle's, regarding either ontogeny or phylogeny, was put forth. At this time, however, another idea relevant to development was advanced.

The medieval Christian era

As exemplified by John Calvin (1509–1564) and the American Puritans (the Pilgrims of the ship *Mayflower*), the medieval Christians had a religious philosophy which stressed the *innate* characteristics of humans. Based on portions of the *Book of*

Genesis, this philosophy stressed the idea of original sin. Humans were said to be born with sin in them. They are born basically evil. A second belief was that humans are basically depraved. The sin in humans will be, they believed, compounded by the inborn tendency to continue to commit sinful acts. In short, the medieval Christian view of human development was, like all others we have met to this point, a nature one.

The nature orientation of this position is best illustrated by the reason given for the presence of innate sin and innate tendencies toward continued badness. The medieval Christian believed in the *homunculus* idea of creation. The reason for innate sin is that a homunculus—a full-grown but miniature adult—is present from birth in the newborn's head. Instantly created with the child, this homunculus contains the sin, and the basic depravity.

Of course, from this view, parents could apply harsh rules and stern punishment to their children. The children—having an adult preformed in them—were only different from other adults in terms of size. Hence, when children were bad it was not because they did not know better—any adult knew how to act—it was because the "devil," the homunculus, made them do it.

While this medieval Christian view does represent a conception of development different from Aristotle's, it still represents a nature view. In fact, from this medieval Christian view, children do not even have to develop at all (except in size), since they have preformed adults within them. Thus, the ideas of Plato, Aristotle, and the medieval Christians do not give us a concept of adolescent development. Furthermore, insofar as the medieval Christian view is concerned, there is no need for a theory of development. However, a philosophical position relevant to a concept of development did develop, and in the span of another 150 years led to a scientific view of development. To reach this philosophical position it is useful to first consider the impact of another view.

Renè Descartes (1596–1650)

Theological changes in the world resulted in the loss of universal acceptance of Aristotelian philosophy and allowed philosophers to return once again to issues that had remained unaddressed for 2,000 years. A Frenchman, René Descartes, led this return. He reconsidered the mind-body problem, and his work marks the beginning of the era of modern philosophy.

In trying to formulate a proof for the existence of God, Descartes found it necessary to raise again the issue of the relation between the physical body and spiritual soul. He saw the two as separate, as dual entities. He proposed that they exist as two separate "lines," but cross at a particular location in the body. He said these separate lines cross at the site of the pineal gland (a small gland near the pituitary gland). Descartes termed this dualistic view of mind and body *interactionism.*

Moreover, in a manner similar to Plato, Descartes said that when the soul interacts with the body at the pineal gland, it gives the body knowledge. Thus, like Plato, Descartes believed in innate ideas. As such, although the first modern philosopher—by virtue of his readdressing issues long unconsidered—he returned to a nativistic (nature) conception of human functioning first put forth by Plato. However, Descartes's ideas stimulated other philosophers to consider also these "old" issues. Other views of the mind-body issue arose. While accepting his dualism, other philosophers rejected his idea of interactionism (Misiak & Sexton, 1966).

One major reason for this rejection was Descartes's attempt to "prove" statements about the mind on the basis of assertions that stressed innate characteristics, characteristics which were said to be "just there," independent of any empirical (observable) proof. There was a group of philosophers who rejected Descartes's nativism. They argued that the only way to explain the existence of a phenomenon—of the mind, for example—was through the formulation of ideas based on empirical events. Together, these philosophers form a school of thought that evolved in Great Britain in the seventeenth century. One may understand the views of this group, and how they led to a concept of development, by focusing on the contributions of one leading thinker in this British School of empiricism.

John Locke (1632–1704)

There were several British philosophers who held similar ideas about the need to use empirical proof (for example, Thomas Hobbes, James Mill, John Stuart Mill, David Hume, David Hartley, Alexander Bain, and John Locke). We focus on Locke's ideas as an example of the British school's position, and also because of the influence his ideas have continued to have on later scientific thinking.

Locke rejected the idea that the mind was composed of innate ideas. Instead, he said that at birth the mind is like a blank slate, or to use his (Latin) terms, a *tabula rasa*. Any knowledge that the mind obtains is derived from experience. And experience makes its impression on the mind—it writes on the blank slate—by entering the body through the senses. Thus, because we experience, or sense, certain observable events—for example, visual, auditory, and tactual stimulation—our mind changes from having no ideas to having knowledge.

Accordingly, here we finally have a philosophical statement which stresses a concept of ontogenetic development. Moreover, it does so through emphasizing, for the first time, nurture. Experiences from the environment provide the basis of development. The newborn is different from the adult because the newborn has no knowledge and the adult does. Thus, there is development—change in knowledge in this case—and the development is based on nurture.

In stressing the role of nurture variables such as sensory stimulation in shaping behavior (or knowledge), Locke is providing a philosophical view quite consistent with a major theory in psychology: the behavioristic, learning approach to development. People like Skinner (1938) and Bijou and Baer (1961) stress that behavior changes can be understood in terms of environmentally based stimulus-response relations. Thus, modern learning theorists are in this regard quite like Locke. In fact, if Locke were alive today, he would have views comparable to those of modern learning theory psychologists. These more modern views will be discussed later in the chapter.

However, Locke's influence extended beyond providing a philosophical and historical basis of learning theory. In fact, his ideas had two more general impacts. First, Locke's stress on the environment caused other philosophers to begin to consider the potential role of the environment in their own ideas. One major figure so influenced was Jean Jacques Rousseau (1712–1778). Rousseau combined both nativistic and environmental ideas in his philosophy—one quite pertinent to a notion of development—and in so doing became the first philosopher to explicitly take the view that a nature-nurture interaction provided the basis of human development. Rousseau said that all children are born innately good (a nature statement). However, in interaction with civilization (their experience, or nurture)

INSIGHT INTO ADOLESCENCE

Jean Jacques Rousseau, born June 28, 1712, in Geneva, Switzerland, was a philosopher and social theorist whose work inspired the leaders of the French Revolution and the romantic writers and philosophers.

He revealed his life in *Confessions,* one of the first modern works of autobiography. In 1728, when Rousseau was 16, he ran away from the master to which he was apprenticed. This excerpt recalls his feelings on that occasion.

However mournful the moment, when terror suggested to me the idea of flight, had appeared—the moment when I carried it into execution appeared equally delightful. While still a child, to leave my country, my parents, my means of support, my resources; to give up an apprenticeship half-served, without a sufficient knowledge of my trade to earn my livelihood; to abandon myself to the horrors of want, without any means of saving myself from it; to expose myself, at the age of innocence and weakness, to all the temptations of vice and despair; to seek, in the distance, suffering, error, snares, servitude, and death, beneath a yoke far more unbending than that which I had been unable to endure—this was what I was going to do, this was the prospect which I ought to have considered. How different was that which my fancy painted! The independence which I believed I had gained was the only feeling which moved me. Free, and my own master, I believed I could do everything, attain to everything; I had only to launch myself forth, to mount and fly through the air. I entered the vast world with a feeling of security; it was to be filled with the fame of my achievements; at every step I was to find festivities, treasures, adventures, friends ready to serve me, mistresses eager to please me; I had only to show myself, to engage the attention of the whole world—and yet not the whole world; to a certain extent I could dispense with it, and did not want so much. Charming society was enough for me, without troubling myself about the rest. In my modesty I limited myself to a narrow, but delightfully select circle, in which my sovereignty was assured. A single castle was the limit of my ambition. As the favourite of the lord and the lady, as the lover of the daughter, as the friend of the son and protector of the neighbours, I was content—I wanted no more.

Source: From *Confessions* by Jean-Jacques Rousseau. An Everymans Library Edition. New York: Dutton.

they become corrupted. Hence, he argued for a "return to nature" in order to avoid the unfavorable effects of civilized experience.

Thus, Locke's emphasis on the environment did influence other philosophers to consider nurture, with the fortunate additional result of leading them to devise other ideas of ontogenetic development. However, Locke's ideas had a second, more indirect, but more important, influence. A concern with empirics, with observation, promotes a concern with science. Science has, as its most basic characteristic, observation. Accordingly, in promoting interest in empirical concerns among intellectuals, Locke was, albeit indirectly, promoting interest in scientific concerns among these people.

During this time, the intellectuals in society were also those who were the leaders of society (that is, they were the ones who had the resources and power to get an education). Moreover, developments in intellectual areas (such as philosophy, literature, and science) were common and popular topics of social conversation. Having knowledge of such developments was a mark of having the status of being an educated and usually rich and powerful person. As such, Locke's influence was to promote a general concern with science among the educated. Accordingly, when new events in science took place, news of them not only would reach other scientists, but also would be likely to get the attention of all educated people. Such information, then, if important enough, not only could influence scientists, but could have implications for all areas of intellectual concern.

There was an event in science which did have such impact. By the middle of the century following Locke's death, an event occurred in science which influenced not only the area of science it pertained to, but all areas of science and of intellectual concern (for example, education, theology, law, and medicine). The event involved the publication of a book by a then relatively unknown British naturalist. The book represented a theory derived on the basis of observations made while the author was on a trip to the Galápagos Islands. The man's name was Charles Darwin. The book was *The Origin of Species by Means of Natural Selection*. Published in 1859, the book represents the transition from philosophical to scientific concern with the idea of development.

SCIENTIFIC ROOTS OF DEVELOPMENT

Locke's empiricism promoted the influence of science, and as such, provided one basis for the impact of Darwin's ideas. Yet historical irony exists. Locke's own ideas stressed a nurture view of ontogenetic development. However, the scientific view of development that Darwin devised stressed a nature view of phylogenetic development. Accordingly, as the transition was made from philosophy to science, we see the nature-nurture pendulum swinging back to nature. However, as in philosophy, the pendulum will not stay there. To see these swings in science a consideration of Darwin's work is useful.

Charles Darwin (1809–1882)

There are several key ideas in Darwin's theory of evolution. The environment in which a type of animal (a species) exists places demands on that animal. If the only food for that animal in that environment exists on the leaves of tall trees, then the animal must be able to reach the leaves in order to survive. The environment

Charles Darwin

"demands" that the animal possess some characteristic that will allow it to reach the high leaves. If the animal has that characteristic, it will fit in with its environment, get food, and survive. If not, it will die.

Imagine, for example, that two species of giraffe existed, one with a long neck (as *is* the case) and the other with a short one. Because the long-neck giraffe would have characteristics that fit in with the demands of the particular environment, it would survive; the short-neck giraffe would not. Of course, if the setting changed—if, for example, only food very low on the ground were available, the short-neck giraffe would have characteristics that best fit the environment—and the outcome would be reversed. The point Darwin stressed is that the characteristics of the natural setting determine which organism characteristics will lead to survival and which ones will not! Thus, it is the natural environment which selects organisms for survival. This is termed *natural selection*.

Hence, Darwin proposes the idea of *survival of the fittest*. Organisms that possess characteristics that fit the survival requirements for a particular environmental setting will survive. In other words, certain characteristics in certain settings have *fundamental biological significance*—they allow the organism to survive. Characteristics that meet the demands of the environment (and hence allow survival) are *adaptive* characteristics.

The giraffe example stresses that various physical characteristics of an organism may be *functional*. In an evolutionary sense, something is functional if it is adaptive, if it aids survival. Thus, the *structure* of an organism (its physical makeup, its constitution, its morphological or bodily characteristics) may be functional. However, while Darwin in 1859 emphasized the function of physical structures of species, he later (Darwin, 1872) pointed out that behavior too had survival value. Showing the emotion of fear when a dangerous bear approaches us and being able to learn to avoid certain stimuli (snakes) and to approach others (food) are examples of behaviors which, if shown, would be adaptive; they would aid our survival.

Thus, behavior also has a function. The function of behavior became the focus of much social scientific concern. This concern was reflected not only in the ideas of those interested in the phylogeny of behavior. Additionally, the idea that the behavior changes characterizing ontogeny could be understood on the basis of adaptation was promoted. Thus, the adaptive role of behavior became a concern providing a basis of *all* of American psychology (White, 1968), and plays a major part in the ideas of theorists as diverse as Hall (1904), Freud (1949), Piaget (1950), Erikson (1959), and Skinner (1938, 1950). However, before the role of ontogenetic changes in adaptation, and hence survival, can be completely discussed, it is useful to return to Darwin's ideas about survival and see how they reflect a concern not with ontogeny but with phylogeny.

Not all species survive. There are several reasons why this might happen. The natural environment might change, putting different demands on species. Species members that have adaptive characteristics will pass them on to their offspring, and therefore the species will continue. Other species, lacking the adaptive characteristics, will no longer be fit to survive, and they will die out. Another reason one species might survive over another is that due to some change in the genetic material (for example, through mutation or cross-breeding) new characteristics might arise and these might favor survival. In either of these illustrations, however, evolution would proceed on the basis of the transmission of adaptive characteristics from parents to offspring. Species would evolve—change with history—as a consequence of the continual interplay between natural selection and survival of the fittest.

The basis of an organism's survival then depends not primarily on what it acquires over the course of its ontogeny that may be adaptive. Rather, its potential for adaptive functioning is transmitted to it by the parents. Accordingly, adaptation is a heredity, or nature, phenomenon. On the basis of evolution—the history of changes in the species, its phylogenetic development—a member of that species either will or will not be born with adaptive characteristics. Thus, Darwin presents a nature theory of phylogenetic development.

In summary, based on his observations, Darwin presents the first major scientific theory of development. As noted, this evolutionary view of species development had profound effects on areas of concern other than science. But it is possible to remain within the scientific realm in order to gauge the impact of Darwin's ideas on those concerned not just with nature, phylogenetic issues, but also with issues pertinent to ontogeny, and finally, to adolescent development as well. Darwin's ideas provided a major influence on the person who both founded the field of developmental psychology and devised the first scientific theory of adolescent development. This man was G. Stanley Hall, and a consideration of his work will bring our discussion—after more than 2,000 years—to a scientific concern with *adolescent* development.

SCIENTIFIC ROOTS OF ADOLESCENT DEVELOPMENT

G. Stanley Hall (1844–1924)

The person who organized the American Psychological Association, and became its first president, was the same person who started the first American journal of psychology (aptly titled *The American Journal of Psychology*) and the first scientific journal devoted to human development (first titled *Pedagogical Seminary*, and then given its present name *The Journal of Genetic Psychology*). This was also the same person who wrote the first text on adolescence (a two-volume work, titled *Adolescence*, 1904). This man was G. Stanley Hall.

G. Stanley Hall

On the basis of these and other accomplishments of similar prominence, Hall was one of the most influential and prominent psychologists at the turn of this century (Misiak & Sexton, 1966). As such, he did much to shape the nature and direction of the relatively new science of psychology. (The birthday of modern psychology is dated as 1879, with the opening of the first psychological laboratory in Leipzig, Germany, by Wilhelm Wundt.)

Hall had his most specific influence in shaping developmental psychology. As implied by the title of the journal he founded—*The Journal of Genetic Psychology*—Hall saw development from a nature point of view. As such, although not many people (including his students) adopted his specific nature-based theory of development, they did follow his general nature orientation. Consequently, Hall's influence was to direct scientific concern to human development, but to do so from a predominantly nature perspective.

In devising his nature viewpoint, Hall was profoundly influenced by Darwin. In fact, Hall fancied himself as the "Darwin of the mind." Hall attempted to translate Darwin's phylogenetic evolutionary principles into conceptions relevant to ontogeny. The ideas by which he believed he could connect phylogeny to ontogeny were derived from those of yet another scientist who was influenced by Darwin, Ernst Haeckel.

The contribution of Haeckel

Ernst Haeckel was a nineteenth-century scientist specializing in the then relatively new area of biology termed *embryology*. When the sperm of the father organism fertilizes the egg (ovum) of the mother, the basis of a new life is formed. The new life will develop in the now pregnant mother for a period of time until birth. The period of time from fertilization until birth is called the *gestation* period, and different species have gestation periods of different lengths (in the human it is about nine months).

There are various phases of development during gestation. The period from fertilization to when the fertilized egg (termed the *zygote*) implants itself in the wall of the uterus of the mother is called the *period of the zygote*. This period lasts for about ten to fourteen days in the human. The next period, from the second week of life through about the eighth to tenth week of life in the human is termed the *period of the embryo*. In this period all organ systems of the organism emerge. This is the period of development before birth that Haeckel studied. There is a third period of gestation, however. In the human, this third period—the *period of the fetus*—ranges from the third through the ninth month of gestation (that is, until birth). In this period there is a continued growth of the organ systems developed in the embryonic period. Additionally, functional (behavior) characteristics of these organ structures begin to appear. The fetus shows body movement (for example, it kicks), and there is even some evidence that from about the eighth month of pregnancy the fetus can *learn*, through classical conditioning (Spelt, 1948).

In studying development in the embryonic period, Haeckel was concerned with the progressive formations of all organ systems present in the organism. Haeckel was concerned with these developments in all species of organism, but particularly in mammals, and this led him to compare embryos of different species. Haeckel looked at the progressive changes that the human embryo went through during about a ten-week-long series of changes, and compared what the embryo looked like at these successive times to the embryos of other species. He saw that the human embryo went through changes that made it look like, first, the fully developed fish embryo; then the frog embryo; then a bit later, the rat embryo; then still later, the monkey embryo; and finally, the ape embryo.

Haeckel reasoned that here was an ontogenetic progression that mirrored the phylogenetic history, the evolution, of the human species. Humans were, he suggested, first fishlike, then amphibianlike, and so on until they were apelike. Thus, when one looks at the changes characterizing an individual member of a species as it progresses across its ontogeny (here, during its embryological period), one will see a *recapitulation* (a repeating, a mirroring) of the evolutionary changes the species went through. In short, Haeckel said that *ontogeny recapitulates phylogeny.*

Haeckel thought that with this idea he had applied Darwinian evolutionary thinking to a study of ontogeny. Hall, in translating Haeckel's ideas about embryological, structural ontogeny into ideas pertinent to *postnatal* (after birth) human behavior ontogeny, thought he was doing the same thing. Yet Haeckel's (and Hall's) translations were incorrect for several reasons. Let us examine why.

Hall's recapitulationist theory

Hall believed that the changes characterizing the human life cycle are a repetition of the sequence of changes the person's ancestors followed during their evolution. Thus, Hall applied to postnatal life the recapitulationist idea Haeckel used for prenatal, embryological development. However, although arguing that during the years from birth to sexual maturity the person was repeating the history of the species, as had been done prenatally, Hall believed that the postnatal recapitulation was more limited (Gallatin, 1975). In fact, according to Gallatin (1975), Hall believed that:

> *Rather than reflecting the entire sweep of evolution, childhood was supposed to proceed in stages, each of which mirrored a primitive stage of the human species. Very early childhood might correspond, Hall speculated, to a monkey-like ancestor of the human race that had reached sexual maturity around the age of six. The years between eight and twelve allegedly represented a reenactment of a more advanced, but still prehistoric form of mankind, possibly a species that had managed to survive by hunting and fishing. (pp. 26–27)*

Furthermore, Hall believed that adolescence represented a specific period in ontogeny after childhood. As such, not only was Hall the first person, within a scientific theory of development, to conceive of adolescence as a distinct portion of the life span (the term had, however, first appeared in the first half of the fifteenth century; Muuss, 1975a), but he did so in a manner consistent with a life-span view of development. That is, Hall saw the capacities and changes of childhood continuing into adolescence, but at a more rapid and heightened pace. Additionally, he saw adolescence as a period of transition between childhood and adulthood. That is, the stages of life previous to adolescence stressed the innate characteristics of humans held "in common with the animals" (Hall, 1904, I, p. 39). However, the stage of life following adolescence was said to raise a human "above them and make him most distinctively human" (Hall, 1904, I, p. 39). In short, adolescence was a period of transition from being essentially beastlike to being essentially humanlike (that is, civilized and mature). This ontogenetic transition mirrored the evolutionary change involved when humans moved, Hall thought, from being essentially like the apes to becoming civilized.

Thus, Hall saw adolescence as a period during which a person changed to become civilized. Human evolution, Hall believed, moved the person through this ontogenetic period, and thus put the person in the position of being able to contribute to humans' highest level of evolutionary attainment: civilization. Hence, Hall (1904, II, p. 71) said that "early adolescence is thus the infancy of man's higher nature, when he receives from the great all-mother his last capital of energy and evolutionary momentum." However, because of the acceleration and heightening capacities in adolescence, and also because of the difficulty in casting off the characteristics of animallike behavior and acquiring at the same time the characteristics of civilization, the adolescent period was a stressful, difficult period. In short, because adolescence was this ontogenetically and evolutionarily crucial "betwixt and between" (Gallatin, 1975) phase of human development, it was necessarily, to Hall, a period of storm and stress.

Criticisms of the recapitulationist idea

It was noted that Hall's theory of ontogenetic development in general, and of adolescence in particular, was not generally accepted. This was because the recapitulationist ideas of both Haeckel and Hall met criticism that severely diminished the usefulness of the ideas.

First, in regard to Haeckel's ideas, it may be noted that his observation that the human embryo was at times the same as that of the fish, or the ape, was faulty. Although to the naked eye the similarity may be striking, due to technological advances with such devices as the electron microscope, one can enlarge the view of these respective embryos considerably. When this is done, one sees that the structures within the cells of each type of embryo are substantially different at *all* times during their respective growth. For instance, from conception through the rest of life, each different embryo has its own specific number of chromosomes (46 in the human). As such, similarities among embryos which seem apparent are not real.

A second criticism of both Haeckel's and Hall's recapitulationist application of Darwinian evolutionary ideas may be mentioned. This second criticism is quite severe. It is that their application is based on a totally incorrect understanding of the meaning of evolution. Darwin's theory of evolution states that humans did not always exist as they presently do. Rather, previous forms of being existed, and through natural selection, some forms were adaptive, at least for a time, and continued to evolve until eventually the human species as it is presently known came to exist. However, this evolutionary process occurs for all animals, and not just humans. Thus, if another animal exists today, it too has had an evolutionary history. It too is as currently adaptive as is the human, albeit to its own environmental setting (or, in evolutionary terms, to its own *ecological milieu*).

Thus, a rat, or a monkey, or an ape, cannot be an ancestor of a human because all are currently existing today. All are equal in evolutionary status. All are equally as evolved and as adaptive. This is not to say that there are not differences among the species. There are, of course, such differences (for example, in level of complexity). However, that is not the point.

The point is that no human had a rat or a monkey as an ancestor; and when one looks at a monkey embryo or at monkey behavior, one is not therefore looking at humans as they existed in a former, lower evolutionary status (Hodos & Campbell, 1969). Although humans and monkeys may have had—millions of years ago—a common ancestor, that creature is long extinct. It no longer exists because it was not fit to survive. Although other forms evolved from it—and some *could* have led to present-day monkeys *while others* could have led to present-day humans—whatever exists today is, by definition, fit to survive and thus adaptive at this point in time (Hodos & Campbell, 1969). Thus, Haeckel and Hall did not appropriately understand the evolutionary process. Humans were never monkeylike in their embryos or in their behavior, since both species have their own evolutionary history and are currently alive and well. Human ontogeny cannot, therefore, repeat a phase of its evolutionary history if that phase simply never occurred.

Finally, even as an analogy, a recapitulationist description of human ontogeny is inappropriate. As initially pointed out by Thorndike (1904), and reemphasized by Gallatin (1975), by 2 or 3 years of age a human child has already exceeded the capacities of monkeys, apes, and prehistoric humanlike organisms (for example, the Neanderthals). Sensorimotor, verbal, and social behavior, for example, are all more advanced in the 3-year-old than in "adults" in any of these other species. Additionally, there is no evidence whatsoever that the events in adolescence are but a mirror of the history of civilization.

In summary, then, Hall's theory that ontogeny recapitulates phylogeny simply was untenable. Thus, although his work is historically quite important in that his is the first scientific theory of human ontogenetic development and of adolescence in particular, it did not lead many to adopt it specifically. However, his ideas were clearly nature ones (human developmental events arise out of the genetic transmission of past evolutionary occurrences). And because of his influence and position in American psychology, his general nature orientation to ontogeny *was* followed even though his specific nature theory was dropped. Thus, Hall influenced his students to use a nature orientation in their work in human development. Since two of his students—Lewis Terman and Arnold Gesell—were among the most important developmentalists in the first third of this century, Hall's influence was to start the scientific study of human development out on a nature theoretical basis.

The contributions of Terman and Gesell

Hall's most prominent students were Terman and Gesell. Their contributions illustrate much of the interest in ontogenetic development through the first three decades of this century. Terman was interested in mental measurement. The first intelligence test was constructed by Binet (Binet & Simon, 1905a,b) in Paris. Terman was one of the first people to translate this test into English (H. H. Goddard in 1910 was the first). Terman, a professor at Stanford University, published the test as the Stanford-Binet (1916), and adopted the intelligence quotient (IQ), suggested by the German psychologist Stern, to express people's performance on the test (IQ = mental age divided by chronological age, multiplied by 100 to remove the fraction).

Terman's interest in measuring intellectual ability was not based just on a concern with *describing* how people differ (that is, individual differences), although in part it was based on this. His interest was also a theoretical one. He believed that intelligence was mostly (if not exclusively) a nature characteristic. Accordingly, not only did he develop an instrument to describe individual differences in intelligence, but also he carried out research to try to determine the genetic component of intelligence. One such study was his monumental *Genetic Studies of Genius*, a *longitudinal* study of intellectually gifted children from 1921 onward (Terman, 1925; Terman & Oden, 1959). A longitudinal study is one in which the same persons are repeatedly measured over time (see Chapter 7 for more details), and Terman's was one of the first such studies begun in this country (Sears, 1975).

Although not proving that intelligence is genetically *determined* (for reasons we shall explore in later chapters), Terman's work, involving nearly fifty years of study and reported in five published volumes over this span (see Terman & Oden, 1959), was quite important for several reasons. First, it encouraged several other longitudinal studies of human development. These studies provided data relevant to life-span changes, and additionally, included much information relevant to adolescent development within a life-span framework. Data from these longitudinal studies will be cited throughout this book. Second, Terman's findings did much to dispel myths about the psychological and social characteristics of intellectually gifted people. Although such people may be stereotyped as weak, sickly, maladjusted, or socially inept, Terman provided data showing them to be healthy, physically fit and athletic, and personally and socially adjusted.

Third, Terman's work did much to make developmental psychology a descriptive, normative discipline. His work with the IQ test and his descriptions of the developments of the gifted involved his making *normative* statements. A *norm* is an average, typical, or modal characteristic for a particular group. If nature is the source of human development, and environment plays no primary role, then all one need do is describe the typical developments of people in order to be dealing with information pertinent to the inevitable (because of its biological, nature basis) pattern of ontogeny. Although there are serious problems with this reasoning (discussed in Chapter 5), Hall's other prominent student, Arnold Gesell, based his work more explicitly on this reasoning than did Terman, and accordingly did even more to make developmental psychology a normative, descriptive field.

Gesell proposed a theory that can be understood by his term *maturational readiness*. This nature-based theory said that maturational changes are independent of learning (Gesell's conception of what nurture amounted to). Sensorimotor behavior and even many cognitive abilities (for example, vocabulary development) were under the *primary* control of maturation. This means that their pattern of development was maturationally determined. Thus, an organism would develop when it was maturationally ready to, and attempts to teach the child before this time could not be helpful.

Hence, in his writing and research (Gesell, 1929, 1931, 1934, 1946, 1954), Gesell stressed the need for the careful and systematic cataloging of growth norms. His work has provided science with much useful knowledge about the expected sequence for, and times of, emergence of numerous physical and mental developments of children and adolescents of particular demographic backgrounds. These descriptions would allow people to know, he believed, the nature-based sequence and timing of development, and as such, the point at which the person was maturationally ready for learning. While this belief will be evaluated in a succeeding chapter, the present point is that Gesell's theory and research did much to make developmental psychology not only a nature-based discipline, but one whose major, if not exclusive, focus was descriptive. Although a nurture-based theory of behavior arose to counteract the predominant nature focus, it will be argued that it did not do much to move the field beyond description. This nurture trend is now discussed.

Behaviorism and learning theory

Just as the pendulum swung between nature and nurture in philosophy, it moved similarly in science. In the second decade of this century and continuing through the 1950s, American psychology, as well as other areas of social science (sociology; Homans, 1961), became strongly influenced by a particular conceptual-theoretical movement: a mechanistic (described in Chapter 1), behavioristic learning theory view of behavior. Philosophically consistent with Locke's empiricist views, this movement stressed that in order for psychology to be an objective science, ideas about behavior had to be derived from empirically verifiable sources. Although this particular view of behavior was not developed by observing children or human development, it was applied to human development. In fact, no learning theory has ever been devised on the basis of information derived *primarily* from children (White, 1970).

John B. Watson, using a learning theory orientation, developed his point of view under the label *behaviorism* (Watson, 1913, 1918). He stressed that stimuli and responses combined under certain lawful, empirical conditions—the laws of classical (and operant) conditioning. By focusing on how stimuli in the environment controlled the behavior of organisms, one could know how behavior was acquired and, by implication, developed. That is, all one had to know in order to understand human development was the way behavior was controlled by the mechanistic laws of conditioning. Watson applied these ideas to children, both in his research (Watson & Raynor, 1920) and in his prescriptions for child care (Watson, 1928).

The nurture view of behaviorism gave psychologists a position which allowed them to be viewed as objective scientists, like their colleagues in the natural sciences (for example, physics and chemistry). As such, behaviorism and variants and extensions of it (Hull, 1929; Skinner, 1938) became the major focus in American psychology. As was the case with Watson's work, ideas and principles were derived from animals such as rats (Beach, 1950; Herrnstein, 1977) and then were applied to humans. As such, ideas about human development arose. Thus, ideas about how humans acquire behavior consistent with the rules of society, that is, how they are *socialized*, were formulated. Such *social learning* theories not only were pertinent to a nurture view of development, but also at times represented some attempt to reinterpret nature conceptions of development in nurture terms (Dollard, Doob, Miller, Mowrer, & Sears, 1939; Miller & Dollard, 1941).

However, this nurture view of development did not integrate nurture and nature concerns. In fact, through the early 1940s there was little integration of ideas by nature-oriented and by nurture-oriented workers. Both "camps" were, in our view, still not moving beyond the descriptive level of endeavor. Although the learning-oriented workers were doing *manipulative* studies—that is, varying stimuli to determine the effect on responses (Chapter 7 gives a fuller discussion of manipulative studies)—their work tended to concentrate only on readily observable aspects of behavior development (such as, aggressive behaviors). This work constituted *in total* no more than a summary, albeit an elaborate and fairly precise one, of how variations in particular stimulus characteristics were related to variations in responses of certain groups of children (basically white middle-class children of highly educated parents).

In sum, then, until the early 1940s the study of human development was in essence a descriptive, normative discipline. There were two theoretical camps that existed, and although both had different reasons for obtaining their descriptions (a nature versus a nurture rationale), these reasons were not really tested within each camp. Proponents within each group continued to work with little concern for integration with the endeavors of the other. A major historical event served to alter all this, and to move developmental science from a primarily descriptive to a primarily theoretical, explanatory-oriented field. The event was World War II.

World War II

The events surrounding World War II irrevocably altered the nature of American social science. First, even before the United States entered the war in December 1941, effects of events in Europe were felt. Nazi persecution led many Jewish intellectuals to flee Europe, and many sought refuge and a new start for their careers in the United States. To the credit of American academicians, great pains were taken to find these refugees positions in American universities and associated institutions, despite the fact that these people brought with them ideas counter to those predominant in the American academic scene (that is, behaviorism and learning theory).

For instance, although Freud himself settled in London (and died there in 1939), many psychoanalytically oriented people, some trained by Freud and/or his daughter Anna, did come to this country. Some of these people, for example Peter Blos and most notably in our present discussion, Erik Erikson, brought with them not only psychoanalytic ideas about development, but, more specifically, ideas pertinent to adolescent development.

In addition, once America entered the war, and numerous soldiers needed to be tested for psychological as well as physical fitness, the federal government gave universities large amounts of money to train clinical psychologists. This program opened the door for many professionals with psychoanalytic orientations to become faculty in universities previously dominated by behaviorists (Misiak & Sexton, 1966), because they were the people with backgrounds appropriate for teaching clinical skills.

Thus, one impact of World War II was to encourage psychoanalytic thinking in many psychology departments. This orientation represented not only the introduction of nature-based thinking into departments where behaviorists previously were in total control of the intellectual domain (Gengerelli, 1976). Additionally, it represented just *one* of many different theoretical accounts of human functioning—accounts which stressed either nature or both nature and nurture as sources of behavior and development—that were now making inroads into American thinking. That is, the academic doors were open to all refugees, not only those with a psychoanalytic bent.

As such, nativistic ideas about perception and learning, introduced by psychologists who believed in the holistic aspects of behavior, were juxtaposed with behaviorist learning ideas. The *gestalt* (meaning "totality") views represented by these Europeans (people like Wertheimer, Koffka, Kohler, Goldstein, and Lewin) were shown to be pertinent also to areas of concern such as brain functioning, group dynamics, and social problems (Sears, 1975). Ideas explicitly relevant to development were also introduced. For example, Heinz Werner (1948) presented to Americans a view of development involving continual nature-nurture interactions.

In summary, the outcome of these changes in ideas about development, fostered by events relating to World War II, was to provide a pluralism of ideas about development. Now there were numerous interpretations of behavior and development, interpretations that were based on substantially different conceptions of the source of human behavior and development. Any given behavior, then, could be explained by a number of different theories, and these various theories were advanced by respected advocates often working in the same academic contexts (Gengerelli, 1976). The simultaneous presentation of diverse interpretations promoted a move away from a mere focus on description and toward a primary concern with theoretical interpretations of development. This focus on explanation was heightened in the post-World War II era, in the late 1950s and 1960s.

The 1950s and 1960s

Because of the *pluralism* of perspectives promoted by events surrounding World War II, developmentalists became less concerned with just collecting data descriptive of development. Rather, they were focusing more on the interpretation, the meaning, of development. As such, they primarily became concerned with the comparative use and evaluation of various theories in putting the facts of development together into an understandable whole. One measure of this change of focus is the rediscovery of the theory of Jean Piaget.

Piaget's theory of the development of cognition was known in America in the 1920s (Piaget, 1923). Yet because of the "clinical" nature of his research methods, his nonstatistical style of data analysis, and the abstract constructs he was concerned with—all of which ran counter to predominant trends in the United States—his theory and research work were generally ignored until the late 1950s. However, due to the European intellectual influences on American thinking occurring from events related to World War II, greater attention was given by Americans to the intellectual resources present in Europe. Thus, the Swiss scientist Piaget was rediscovered, and it can be fairly said that concern with the abstract and conceptual ideas of his theory came to dominate American developmental psychology throughout the 1960s. In fact, his influence continues to this writing as a result both of further substantiation of his ideas and of promoting discussions of alternative theoretical conceptualizations (Brainerd, 1978; Siegel & Brainerd, 1977).

Thus, by the 1960s, the study of development included the use of various theories of development *and* the use of phenomena of development (for example, the cognitive-thought-changes studied by Piaget) that were not only overt, behavioral ones. Bronfenbrenner (1963), in a review of the history of developmental science, similarly notes that from the 1930s to the early 1960s there was a continuing shift from studies involving the mere collection of data toward research concerned with abstract processes and constructs. Accordingly, in describing the status of the field in 1963, Bronfenbrenner said that "first and foremost, the gathering of data for data's sake seems to have lost favor. The major concern in today's developmental research is clearly with inferred processes and constructs" (p. 527).

Similarly, in a more recent review, Looft (1972) found a continuation of the trends noted by Bronfenbrenner. Looft's review, like Bronfenbrenner's, was based on an analysis of major handbooks of developmental psychology published from the 1930s to the time of the review (1972). Each handbook represented a reflection of the current content, emphasis, and concerns of the field. Looft found that in the first handbook (Murchison, 1931) developmental psychology was largely descriptive. Consistent with our analysis and with Bronfenbrenner's conclusion, Looft saw workers devoting their time essentially to the collection of norms. Continually, however, a shift toward more general, integrative concerns was seen by 1946 (after World War II), and the trend continued through 1963 (Bronfenbrenner, 1963) to 1972

(Looft, 1972). Indeed, as a case in point we may note that the editor of a 1970 handbook (Mussen, 1970) pointed out: "The major contemporary empirical and theoretical emphases in the field of developmental psychology, however, seem to be on *explanations* of the psychological changes that occur, the mechanisms and processes accounting for growth and development" (p. vii).

In sum, it may be seen that by the beginning of the 1970s interest was focused on a variety of theories, on explanations, and on processes of development. Such concerns lead to the recognition that there is not just one way (one theory) to follow in attempting to put the facts (the descriptions) of development together. Rather, a pluralistic approach is needed. When followed, it may indicate that more descriptions are necessary. Thus, theoretical concerns guide descriptive endeavors. One gathers facts because one knows they will have a meaning within a particular theory. Moreover, since such theory-based research may proceed from any theoretical base, the data generated must be evaluated in terms of their use in advancing an understanding of change processes. If these conclusions sound like those reached in the presentation of the life-span view of human development in Chapter 1, this is as it should be. The trends emerging and taking hold by the early 1970s combined to promote the life-span view in that decade.

The 1970s through today

The prominence of theory, the evaluation of theories on the basis of criteria of usefulness, findings that developmental changes take many different forms at different points in time, and the recognition that such changes must be understood from a variety of explanatory stances led to the evolution of the life-span view of human development (Baltes & Schaie, 1973b; Datan & Ginsberg, 1975; Datan & Reese, 1977; Goulet & Baltes, 1970; Nesselroade & Reese, 1973). In the conferences and books associated with this orientation, the need for a pluralism of theoretical perspectives was bolstered by the emphasis on how world views of development shape lower-order theoretical and empirical endeavors(Overton & Reese, 1973; Reese & Overton, 1970).

Thus, the life-span approach has fostered a broadened conceptual and methodological awareness among developmentalists (see McCall, 1977), as well as the view that human change may be understood in the context of the changing world within which it is embedded (Baltes & Schaie, 1976; Riegel, 1975). This view has led to the call for understanding human development in its real-world (McCall, 1977; Riegel, 1976a), or ecological (Bronfenbrenner, 1977), context. This context is seen both to provide a basis of human development and, simultaneously, to be shaped by the changing human (Lerner & Spanier, 1978b; Riegel, 1976a, 1976b). The exchanges between the individual and his or her world include processes relevant to biological, psychological, social, and historical changes. For instance, Elder (1974) has shown that children developing during the years of the Great Depression (1929–1930s) in the United States differed from children developing before or after this historical era.

CHAPTER SUMMARY

The history of ideas about adolescent development may be traced to early Greek philosophical statements. These statements, as well as those that followed them, may be organized according to the extent to which they stressed that innate, inborn, or nature, factors were responsible for development, or on the other hand, the degree to which they emphasized that experiential, environmental, or nurture, factors provided bases for development.

Plato (427–347 B.C.) believed that the soul (or mind) entered the body at birth with innate ideas. His nature conception stressed that the soul was divided into three layers: human desires and appetites, the spirit, and the true or real soul. Aristotle (384–322 B.C.) said that the three layers of the soul were a plantlike, an animallike, and a humanlike layer, and that only humans possessed the last layer. However, Aristotle also believed that each layer of the soul emerged in a sequence. In addition, he maintained that humans progress through three 7-year "stages" (infancy, boyhood, and young manhood) until maturity is reached.

Both Plato and Aristotle were nature-oriented since they believed the bases of human abilities lay in preformed characteristics. Similarly, the medieval Christian view of human characteristics—as put forth in the late fourteenth and early fifteenth centuries—also stressed the inborn basis of human characteristics. It was held that humans are born with original sin and have a "little man," a *homunculus,* present in their heads.

The first major nurture-based idea of development was presented by several British philosophers. For instance, John Locke (1632–1704) stressed that a mind at birth was like a blank slate (a *tabula rasa*), and that all knowledge that entered the mind did so as a consequence of the effects experience had on the senses.

A transition from the influence of philosophy to the influence of science set the stage for Darwin's (1809–1882) theory of evolution. Darwin stressed that the development of species (*phylogenetic* development) progressed as a consequence of *natural selection.* Organisms most fit to survive in their ecological setting would pass on these adaptive characteristics to their offspring. Hence, the adaptive characteristics one showed across one's life span (ontogenetic development) came from heredity; as such, Darwin's evolutionary theory was nature-based.

The first theory of adolescent development, formulated by G. Stanley Hall (1844–1924), was based on Darwin's ideas. Hall maintained that the changes in one's life repeated one's evolutionary history (simply, ontogeny recapitulates phylogeny), and that adolescence was an ontogenetic period of "storm and stress" because it corresponded to the portion of evolution when humans made the transition from being animallike to being civilized.

Although there were conceptual and empirical problems with Hall's specific theory, his nature orientation to development influenced many of the early contributors to the science of human development (for example, Terman and Gesell). However, by the end of the second decade of the twentieth century, there arose a nurture-based behavioristic view of human functioning that countered the nativistic theories of Hall's followers.

World War II introduced more theoretical controversy into the study of human development, as Europeans with diverse views about the contributions of nature versus nurture came to the United States. By the 1950s and 1960s, the focus of human development inquiry moved from descriptions of change done from either a nature or a nurture perspective to a focus on contrasting nature, nurture, and nature-nurture interaction explanations of change.

The 1970s were characterized by the growing recognition that the different theories of development should be compared on the basis of their relative usefulness in understanding change, and that it may be necessary to draw from several different theories of change to understand development. This pluralistic orientation has contributed to the evolution of a multidisciplinary life-span approach to the understanding of all developmental periods.

5

CONCEPTUAL ISSUES
OF DEVELOPMENT

CHAPTER
OVERVIEW

There are a number of controversial issues in the study of human development in general and adolescent development in particular. This chapter examines the major conceptual issues in the study of development. These issues are the nature-nurture issue, the continuity-discontinuity issue, the stability-instability issue, and the critical periods hypothesis.

ISSUES
TO CONSIDER

What are the three major ways that questions about the nature-nurture issue have been formulated?

What role does nurture play in influencing the contributions of nature?

What role does nature play in influencing the contributions of nurture?

What are the types of changes pertinent to the continuity-discontinuity issue?

How does the continuity-discontinuity issue pertain to both description and explanation of change?

What is the role of theory in decisions about the continuity and discontinuity of behavior?

What are the types of changes pertinent to the stability-instability issue?

How is the critical periods hypothesis related to the nature-nurture and the continuity-discontinuity issue?

What are the limitations of the critical periods hypothesis?

ike father, like son" and "experience is the best teacher" are both expressions that reflect a view about the basis of behavior. The former represents a nature view and the latter a nurture one. The existence of two such contradictory statements should not be surprising, given the philosophical and scientific debate about the relative contributions of nature and nurture to behavioral development reviewed in the previous chapter. It has been argued that across history views of development have been based on various stances on this issue ranging from extreme nature to extreme nurture views. However, there have also been some conceptions stressing interactions between these two sources.

This chapter focuses on this basic conceptual issue, nature-nurture, because it is our opinion that any conception of development, pertinent to any and all portions of life, must speak to this topic. Any conception of adolescent development will be composed of statements about processes which relate to nature, to nurture, or to some relation between the two. However, the nature-nurture issue is not the only basic issue of development. Two others are identified as important: continuity-discontinuity and the critical periods hypothesis. Yet these other core issues derive from the nature-nurture one. Accordingly, another reason for focus on the nature-nurture issue is that it allows one to understand the interdependence of all issues in development. Additionally, since together these issues have continued to provide the basis of all theory and research in adolescent development, an understanding of them and how they relate to each other is relevant to the material discussed in succeeding chapters.

THE NATURE-NURTURE ISSUE

Our historical review indicated that both philosophers and scientists tended to take extreme, opposite positions in regard to the nature and nurture bases of development. Some stressed nature to the exclusion of nurture (for example, Plato, the medieval Christians, Gesell), while others promoted a nurture view and excluded nature conceptions (for example, Locke, Watson). Although others spoke of both sources of development (for example, Rousseau, Werner), the *predominant* way that the nature-nurture issue was thought of across history was in an *"either-or"* formulation (Anastasi, 1958).

The initial and historically predominant way the issue was formulated may be understood in the form of a question: "Which one (nature *or* nurture) provides the basis of behavior and development?" Anastasi (1958), whose ideas did much to clarify the problems involved in appropriately conceptualizing the nature-nurture issue, was the first to cast the issue in terms of this question. She argued that although one could view most philosophers and scientists as approaching the problem from this "which one" perspective, one had to recognize that their efforts were based on the wrong question.

The "which one" question is based on an *independent, isolated action* assumption of the relation between nature and nurture (Lerner, 1976). To use the terms focused on by Anastasi (see Exhibit 4.1), nature is *heredity* and nurture is *environment*. The "which one" question assumes that nature and nurture are independent, separable sources of influence, and as such, one can exert an influence in isolation from the other. But Anastasi (1958) pointed out that such an assumption is illogical. This is so because there would be no one in an environment without heredity, and there would be no place to see the effects of heredity without environment. Genes do not exist in a vacuum. They exert their influence on behavior in an environment. At the same time, however, if there were no genes (and consequently no heredity), the environment would not have an organism in it to influence. Accordingly, nature and nurture are inextricably tied together. In life they never exist independent of the other. As such, Anastasi (1958) argued that *any* theory of development, in order to be logical and to accurately reflect life situations (that is, to have *ecological validity*), must stress that nature and nurture are always involved in all behavior.

Moreover, she cautioned that it was necessary to understand the contribution of nature and nurture in a particular way. Although some persons recognized that nature and nurture (heredity and environment) were both involved in behavior many asked another wrong question: "How much of each is needed for behavior?" That is, they viewed the issue in terms of an *independent, additive action* assumption (Lerner, 1976). They asked, for any given behavior, how much of it was formed by heredity and how much by environment. In so doing they were still working under the belief that nature and nurture existed independent of each other. Here, however, instead of behavior being either a 100 percent/0 percent or a 0 percent/100 percent issue, some additive contribution of less than these extremes was thought to be involved. For example, people asked whether intelligence was 80 percent heredity and 20 percent environment, or whether personality was 60 percent heredity and 40 percent environment.

This "how much of each" conception may be considered as illogical as the "which one" question, since it is just a less extreme form of the first question. For instance, for the 80 percent of intelligence that might be thought to be nature, one may ask where that 80 percent exerts its influence if not in an environment. And for the 20 percent of intelligence thought to be nurture, how does an organism get that 20 percent acted on if not first having inherited genes?

Thus, the "how much of each" question does not seem to be a useful way to understand the contribution of nature and nurture. Since both must be fully present and involved in all behavior, one needs *100 percent of each* for any and all behavior development. To conceptualize their simultaneous contribution one must ask the question: "How?" One must ask how (100 percent of) nature and (100 percent of) nurture interact to provide the basis of behavior development (Anastasi, 1958). Thus, the relation between nature and nurture may be viewed as involving the *interdependent, interactive action* assumption. From this view heredity and environment do not add together to contribute to behavior, but rather development is seen as a *product* of nature-nurture interaction.

An analogy will help illustrate this. The area of a rectangle is determined by a formula which multiplies the length by the width (area = length × width). To know the area of a given rectangle then, one has to look at the product of a multiplicative relation. It is simply incorrect to ask which one, length or width, determines the area, because a rectangle would not exist unless it had both length and width. Similarly, it is incorrect to ask how much of each is necessary to have an area, because the two dimensions cannot merely be added, but must be multiplied in order to produce a rectangle.

Of course, although length and width must always be completely present in order to have a rectangle, different values of each will lead to different products (or areas). Thus, in determining a particular product (a given area) of a length × width interaction, one must ask *how* a specific value of length in interaction (in multiplication) with a specific value of width produces a rectangle of a given area. More generally then, one must recognize that the same width would lead to different areas

INSIGHT INTO ADOLESCENCE

Francois-Timoleon de Choisy, who lived from 1644 to 1724, was a member of the court of Louis XIV. He loved to wear women's clothes. This eccentricity did not stop him from becoming an abbé, an author, and a member of the prestigious French Academy. In the following passage, he discusses his eccentric habit.

Habits of early childhood are peculiar things, it is impossible to get rid of them: my mother, almost immediately after my birth, had accustomed me to wearing female attire; I continued to make use of them during my youth. I appeared on the stage of a large city for a period of 5 months, playing the roles of young girls; everybody was misled thereby; I have lovers to whom I granted small favors, but I was most reserved with regard to the greater favors; and everybody praised my modesty. I enjoyed this more than anything that life can possibly afford.

Gambling, which has always been a temptation to me, has cured me of these bagatelles for several years, but every time I ruined myself in games of hazard and gave up gambling, I fell back into my former frailty and I became again a woman.

For this purpose I bought a house in the Faubourg Saint-Marceau, right in the middle of the bourgeoisie and the common people, so that I might dress as my fancy dictated among this crowd which would not gossip about anything I was doing. I began by having my ears pierced once more, since the former punctures had closed up again; I put on embroidered corsets and dressing gowns of black gold-brocade, with frills of white silk, equipped with a girdle with stays and a large bow of ribbons in the back to emphasize my figure, a long train, a powdered wig, pendant earrings, beauty spots (*mouches*), and a small bonnet with a top-knot (*fontange*). . . .

I have tried to find out whence I derived so bizarre a pleasure, and arrived at the following: It is God's desire to be loved, adored; man, insofar as his frailty permits, has the same ambition. In other words, since it is beauty which produces love which is ordinarily the lot of women, if men have or imagine they have some attractive traits causing them to be loved, they try to augment such attractions by adopting female attire, which adds to their charm. They then experience the inexpressible pleasure of being loved.

Source: de Choisy, Francois-Timoleon, Memories de L'abbe De Choisy. Translated by E. Hopf in S.K. Paddover (ed.) Confessions and Self Portraits. Paris-Boston, 1895.

in interaction with varying lengths, and in turn, the same length would lead to different areas in interaction with varying widths.

By moving from this analogy back to the question "how?" in regard to the nature-nurture issue, it may be seen that comparable statements may be made. There would be no product—no behavior development—if nature and nurture were not 100 percent present. Thus, the assumptions underlying the "which one" and "how much of each" questions are rejected, and it is recognized that any behavior development is the result of a multiplicative, interactive relation between specific hereditary and environmental influences. Moreover, it should be noted that this means that the same hereditary influence will lead to different behavioral products in interaction with varying environments; furthermore, the same environment will lead to varying behavioral outcomes in interaction with different hereditary influences.

This means that heredity and environment *never* function independently of each other. Nature (for example, genes) never effects behavior directly; it always acts in the context of environment. Environment (for example, stimulation) never directly produces behavior either; it will show variation in its effects depending on the hereditary-related characteristics of the organism on which it acts.

These statements about the reciprocal interdependence of nature and nurture are not just casual matters. It has been argued that major philosophers and scientists have tried to conceptualize behavior and development in terms which are inconsistent with the view reflected by the interactive action conception. Indeed, succeeding chapters will consider theorists who stress that various components of adolescent development (for example, cognition, personality, parent-child relations) can be understood by ideas which stress *either* nature *or* nurture (that is, the "which one" question). Thus, it is important to point out that others do not necessarily agree that the formulation we favor is the best or most useful one.

Accordingly, because of the continuing controversy between nature and nurture interpretations of adolescent development, it will be useful for us to provide a discussion of concepts involved in the resolution of the issues, and our arguments about why we believe that our position in regard to the nature-nurture issue is useful.

Nature interactions with nurture

Discussion of the implications of the question "how?" led to the assertion that there are never any direct hereditary effects on an organism. This view means that heredity never directly gives one structural characteristics such as body build or behavioral functions such as intelligence or personality. Heredity always interacts with an environment, and this means that the same hereditary contribution will lead to different behavioral outcomes under different environmental conditions.

To illustrate, let us represent hereditary contributions by the letter G (for genes), environmental contributions by the letter E, and behavior outcomes by the letter B. As shown in Exhibit 5.1a, it is possible to conceptualize the contribution of heredity to behavior as being direct. Here, a particular combination of genes (G_1) will invariably lead to a particular behavior outcome (B_1). However, it has been argued that this conceptualization is not appropriate. As such, an interactive idea of nature and nurture, illustrated in Exhibit 5.1b, has been advanced. Here the same hereditary contribution (G_1) can be associated with an infinity of behavioral outcomes (B_1 to B_n)

Exhibit 5.1
(a) Heredity (G) does *not* directly lead to behavior (B). *(b)* Rather, the effects of heredity on behavior will be different under different environmental (E) conditions.

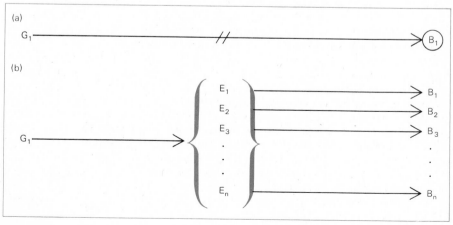

as a consequence of interaction in the infinity of environments (E_1 to E_n) that could exist.

Consider as an example the case of a child born with Down's syndrome. Genetic material (a chemical termed DNA) is carried in genes arranged on stringlike structures present in the nucleus of each cell. These structures are termed chromosomes. The typical cells of the human body have 46 chromosomes, divided into 23 pairs. The only cells in the body which do not have 46 chromosomes are the gametes, the sex cells (sperms in males, ova in females). These cells carry only 23 chromosomes, one of each pair. This arrangement assures that when a sperm fertilizes an ovum to form a zygote, the new human so created will have the number of chromosome pairs appropriate for the species. However, in the child born with Down's syndrome, a genetic anomaly exists. There is an extra chromosome in the twenty-first pair—three chromosomes instead of two.

Thus, children with Down's syndrome have a specific genetic inheritance. The complement of genes transmitted to people at conception, by the union of the sperm and ovum, is termed the *genotype*. This is what constitutes our genetic inheritance. At least insofar as the extra chromosome is concerned, the Down's syndrome child has a specific genotype. Yet even though the genotype remains the same for any such child, the behavioral outcomes associated with this genotype are changeable.

As recently as thirty years ago, Down's syndrome children, who typically are recognized by certain physical (particularly facial) characteristics, were expected to have lifespans of no more than twelve years or so. They also were expected to have quite low IQ scores. They typically were classified into a group of people who, because of low intelligence, required custodial (usually institutional) care. Today, however, Down's syndrome children often live well beyond adolescence. Additionally, they lead more self-reliant lives. Their IQs are now typically higher, often falling in the range allowing for education, training, and sometimes even employment.

How did these vast differences come about? Certainly the genotype did not change. Rather, what changed was the environment of these children. Instead of invariably being put into institutions, different and more advanced special education techniques were provided to the people, often on an outpatient basis. These contrasts in environment led to variation in behavioral outcomes despite the same heredity (that is, *genotypic invariancy*).

That heredity always exerts its effects indirectly through environment in the development of physical as well as behavioral characteristics may also be illustrated. First, consider the disease termed *phenylketonuria* (PKU). This disorder, involving an inability to metabolize fatty substances because of the absence of a particular digestive enzyme, led to a child developing distorted physical features and severe mental retardation. It was discovered that the lack of the necessary enzyme was the result of the absence of a particular gene, and as such, PKU is another instance of a disease associated with a specific genotype.

Today, however, many people—perhaps even some college students reading this book—may have the PKU genotype, and yet have neither the physical nor the behavioral deficits formally associated with the disease. It was discovered that if the missing enzyme is put into the diets of newborns discovered to have the disease, *all* negative effects can be avoided. Again, change in the environment has changed the outcome. In fact, it was found that at about 1 year of age the child no longer needs the added enzyme since either the body no longer needs it to metabolize fat or the enzyme is produced in another way. Here again it may be seen that the same genotype will lead to alternative outcomes, both physical and behavioral, when it interacts in contrasting environmental settings.

Another example may illustrate this further, and more importantly, may provide a basis for specifying the variety of environmental characteristics within which hereditary contributions are embedded. First, imagine that an experiment (improbable for ethical and technological reasons) were done. Say a mother was pregnant with monozygotic (or identical) twins. These are twins who develop from the same fertilized egg, the same zygote, which splits after conception. Hence, the two zygotes have the same genotype. But, importantly, because the zygotes implant on somewhat different parts of the wall of the mother's uterus, there exist somewhat different environments. Further imagine that it was possible immediately after the zygote split into two to take one of them and implant it in another woman who would carry the organism through to birth. Finally, imagine that the first woman, mother A, had lived for the last several years on a diet of chocolate bars, potato chips, and soda pop, had smoked two packs of cigarettes a day, and drank a pint of alcohol each evening. On the other hand, say the second woman, mother B, had lived with a well-balanced diet and neither smoked nor drank. In all other respects the women are alike.

Here is a situation wherein two genotypically identical organisms are developing in quite different uterine environments. Such differences are known to relate to prenatal, birth (perinatal), and postnatal behavior on the part of the offspring, and even have implications for the mother. Thus, despite the genotype identity, the offspring of mother A would be more likely to be born anemic (because of the mother's poor diet), and be more likely to be smaller, less alert, and more hyperactive (because of smoking and alcohol intake) than the offspring of mother B (Hurlock, 1973; Mussen, Conger, & Kagan, 1974).

Although the above study with mother A and mother B is imaginary, the influence of the uterine environment on the offspring is not at all fanciful. The imaginary example was used to illustrate that variations in the environment will cause significant physical and behavioral changes in an offspring, despite the genotype. Even physical characteristics such as eye or skin color may be influenced by environmental variations (albeit extreme ones) no matter what genes are inherited. If mothers are exposed to extreme radiation or dangerous chemicals (as in the case of mothers in Britain in the 1950s who took the drug thalidomide), pigmentation of the eyes or the skin can be radically altered.

In summary then, it is argued that in order to understand the contributions of heredity to development, one needs to recognize that genes influence physical and behavioral characteristics indirectly, by acting in a specific environment. If the same genetic contribution were to be expressed in an environment having other specific characteristics, the same genes would be associated with an alternative behavioral outcome. Accordingly, in order to understand completely nature interactions with nurture, one should know all the ways in which the environment can vary (and as will be argued below, the reverse of this need is also the case).

Certainly, however, there is an infinity of possible environmental variations; and today one cannot even begin to identify all the chemical, nutritional, psychological, and social variables which may vary in the environment, much less identify the ways in which they provide a significant context for development. However, one may at this point note that the environment may be thought of as existing at many levels. One can look at the environment in molecular terms—and talk of chemicals in the body of the mother. Or one can use molar terms—and talk of noise and pollution levels in particular (for example, urban) settings. Consequently, it is useful to specify levels of the environment, because it will (1) allow discussion about where the variables that provide the context for nature interactions may lie; and (2) allow for a consideration of nurture interactions. As such, levels of environmental variation are now considered.

Levels of the environment

An organism does not exist independent of an environment, and it has been argued that as much as the organism is shaped by the environment, the organism shapes the environment. As a consequence of this interdependency, both organism and environment continually change, and it has been suggested that this change involves multiple levels of analysis. These levels—the inner-biological, individual-psychological, physical-environmental, and sociocultural-historical (Riegel, 1975, 1976a)—are elements of both organism and environment. They are used to denote the types of nurture-related variables that may provide the context for nature interactions.

1 The inner-biological level The genotype first is expressed in utero, in the mother's body. Hence, the chemical and physical makeup of the mother can affect the offspring. Chemicals in the mother's bloodstream can enter that of the offspring through the *umbilical cord*, the attachment between mother and offspring. As already noted, poor nutrition, excessive smoking or alcohol intake, and other drug intake can affect the unborn child. Additionally, the contraction of diseases (for example, rubella) can lead to malformations of the heart and limbs and can affect the function of sensory organs (the eyes or ears).

2 The individual-psychological level Independent of her diet, smoking, or drinking habits, or her health status, the psychological functioning of the mother can affect the unborn child. Excessive maternal stress (for example, "nervousness" about the pregnancy) can affect the offspring. Mothers who have excessive stress in about the third month of pregnancy are more likely to have children with certain birth defects (such as cleft palate, hair lip) than are mothers not so stressed (Sutton-Smith, 1973). To illustrate the interrelation between all the levels of the environment, it may be suggested that the way maternal stress exerts an influence on the unborn child is by altering the chemicals (for example, adrenalin) in her blood—at the inner-biological level—at a time in the embryological period when certain organs are being formed.

In addition, previous child-rearing experiences can play a part on the individual-psychological level. Experienced parents (those who already have had a child) are not the same people they were before they had a child. (Firstborns thus have different parents than latter-borns, even though the parents involved may be biologically the same.) Thus, an experienced mother may be less likely to be stressed by a second pregnancy. Not only might this affect the chemicals in her bloodstream, but also, in being less "nervous," she might be less likely to engage in "nervous" behaviors, for example, smoking.

Of course, as more information about prenatal care becomes available in society, and as cultural values change, effects on maternal stress and "nervous" behaviors will change. Thus, again, one level of environment is related to another, the individual-psychological to the sociocultural-historical. Before turning to the latter level, however, let us consider the physical-environmental level.

3 The physical-environmental level Different physical settings have differences in such variables as quality of the air, purity of the water, levels of noise, population density, crowding, and general pollution of the environment. Such variables can affect the inner-biological functioning of the person by producing variations in the likelihood of contracting certain diseases or anomalies (Willems, 1973), and can affect the individual-psychological level as well, by producing various levels of stress, for instance (Gump, 1975). In turn, the quality of the physical setting may be seen as both a product of the values and behaviors of the culture of a society and a producer of changes in the sociocultural setting across time. If values regarding industrialization in the United States had not existed as they did through the early 1960s, and huge levels of industrial waste had not polluted air, land, water, and wildlife, there would have been no basis for the general emergence of countervailing values in the late 1960s and 1970s regarding environmentalism, ecology, and reduction of pollution. The physical-environmental level is not independent of the sociocultural-historical one, and thus this last level may be discussed.

4 The sociocultural-historical level It has been argued that attitudes toward smoking, knowledge about prenatal health care for the mother, and values about pollution may change across time to influence the unborn child. As shown in the example in Chapter 1 in regard to the changing time of puberty, developments related to nature are embedded in history. Thus, with advances in education (remember the case of children with Down's syndrome), medicine, and science (remember the case of children with PKU) and changes in attitudes, values, and behaviors (regarding smoking, drinking, drug use, and pollution of the environment, for example), the outcome of any given hereditary contribution to development will be altered.

In sum, it may be seen that a variety of behavioral outcomes may result from nature interactions with a multilevel environment. Development is thus an outcome of hereditary contributions dynamically interacting with the combined influence of biological through historical changes in an environmental setting. Thus, a genotype is not a blueprint for *a* final behavioral outcome. There is no one-to-one relation between genotype (our genetic inheritance) and phenotype (the observed outcome of development—the outcome of a specific genotype-environment interrelation). Rather, numerous phenotypes can result from the same genotype. The range of potential outcomes that could result from a given genotype's potentially infinite interactions with environments is termed the *norm of reaction* (Hirsch, 1970).

Just as the effects of heredity on behavior can best be understood in relation to environment, the effects of the environment on behavior can best be understood in relation to the nature of the organism. Up to this point in the chapter we have stressed nature interactions with nurture; nurture interactions with nature also may be considered.

Nurture interactions with nature

Just as the effects of nature on behavior are influenced by nurture, environmental contributions to behavior are moderated by the nature of the organism. From this view, the same environmental event (for example, contraction of a disease, exposure to a particular stimulus) or group of events (for example, those associated with middle-class as opposed to upper-class membership) will lead to different behavioral outcomes depending on the nature of the organism. Using the same symbols as in

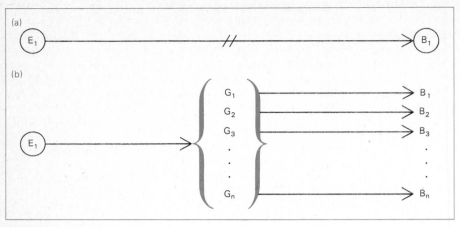

Exhibit 5.2
(a) Environment (E) does *not* directly lead to behavior (B). *(b)* Rather, the effects of environment on behavior (B) will be different in interaction with organisms having different natures (G).

Exhibit 5.1, one may see this view illustrated in Exhibit 5.2. As shown in Exhibit 5.2a, it is possible to conceptualize the contribution of environment to behavior as being direct. Thus, a particular environmental event, or set of events, (E_1) is seen as directly leading to a particular behavioral outcome (B_1). However, as with the former argument regarding nature contributions, this view does not hold up. We have argued for a dynamic interactive view of nature and nurture, and the environmental contribution component of this view is illustrated in Figure 5.2b. Here the same environmental contribution (E_1) can be associated with an array of behavioral outcomes $(B_1$ to $B_n)$ as a consequence of interaction with organisms having different natures $(G_1$ to $G_n)$. A basis of *plasticity* (the potential for change) in development is thus promoted, and this may be illustrated in several ways.

First, consider a very general set of experiential events associated with being a child of upper-middle-class parents. Imagine if such parents had two children, *dizygotic twins*, also called *fraternal twins*. Such siblings are born of the same pregnancy but are from two separate ova which are fertilized at the same time. Thus, although born together, these siblings have different genotypes (unlike monozygotic twins). If one of these twins was born with the genetic anomaly discussed earlier, Down's syndrome, while the other was born with a normal complement of genes, then a situation would result wherein children born of the same parents, at the same point in time, would potentially be exposed to the same environmental events.

However, despite whatever experiences the Down's syndrome child encountered, the effects of those experiences could not be expected to result in behaviors falling within a range identical to that of the sibling. Despite advances in special education, noted earlier, one still cannot expect the Down's syndrome child to have an IQ score within the normal range (that is, between 85 and 115), and one would not expect the child to attain a high-status vocation. However, such expectations could appropriately be maintained in regard to the sibling born with the normal genotype. Thus, the hereditary nature of the organism imposes limits on the possible contributions of environment.

Other illustrations of this interaction may be drawn from the information presented above about the prenatal maternal environment. It was noted that if the mother contracted rubella during pregnancy, adverse physical and functional outcomes for the infant might follow. However, this same experience (contraction of the disease) may or may not lead to these outcomes depending on the maturational level of the organism. If the experience occurs during the embryological period, these negative effects are likely to occur; if it happens in the late fetal period, they are not likely to happen. Similarly, excessive maternal stress will or will not be more likely to lead to certain physical deformities (like cleft palate) depending on the maturational level of the organism. Thus, here again, the nature of the organism moderates the influence of experience on development.

It may be concluded, then, that even if one is talking of very narrow sorts of environmental experiences (as in encountering a specific stimulus in a specific transitory situation) or very broad types of experiences (as are associated with membership in one culture versus another), the effects of these environmental influences would not be the same if they interacted with hereditarily (genotypically) different organisms. Nor would the effects be the same even if it were possible to assure that these different organisms had identical experiences. As long as the nature of the organism is different, the contributions of experience will vary.

It is important to note then that all humans are genotypically unique! A conservative estimate is that there are over *70 trillion* potential genotypes (Hirsch, 1970, p. 73). This means that there are no two living people who share the same genotype, with the possible exception of identical twins. However, even for these people, the differences in experience they encounter—differences which begin as soon as their respective zygotes implant at different points on the placental wall of the mother—contribute to their diversity too.

This argument is highlighted by noting that a genotype immediately becomes a phenotype at the moment of conception. The genotype is expressed in one and only one environment. Hence, although a norm of reaction exists for the genotype, once it is expressed in one particular context, all the other alternative phenotypes it *could* have resulted in are excluded. Thus, even identical twins become, at least a bit, phenotypically different from each other at the moment of implantation.

To summarize, because of genotypic uniqueness, all individuals will interact with their environments (be they the same or different) in unique, specific ways. Thus, the environment always contributes to behavior, but the precise direction and outcome of this influence can only be completely understood in the context of an appreciation of the genetic individuality of the person. This view agrees with that of Hirsch (1970), who argued that "extreme environmentalists were wrong to hope that one law or set of laws described universal features of modifiability. Extreme hereditarians were wrong to ignore the norm of reaction" (p. 270).

THE CONTINUITY-DISCONTINUITY ISSUE

Given that behavior and development have some basis in the combination of nature and nurture, one may ask whether that basis remains the same across the life span or, alternatively, if as people develop, their behavior has a different basis. Given that there are "laws" or "rules" which account for behavior during development, do the same laws apply across the life span, or at different times in life do different rules apply? Here, then, the continuity-discontinuity issue is raised.

In a general way one may say that if things stay the same, *continuity* exists, and if things change, *discontinuity* exists. However, greater precision and clarification of the continuity-discontinuity issue are necessary. It may be recalled from Chapter 1 that in a life-span approach to human development, goals are to describe, explain, and optimize development. The continuity-discontinuity issue pertains to all these goals. Indeed, the continuity-discontinuity issue is that basic concern of development which pertains to the "intraindividual change" focus of these goals.

Description of intraindividual change

In seeking to systematically represent the changes a person goes through across time—that is, in trying to describe intraindividual change—one may ask if the behavior being described takes the same form across time. Simply, does the behavior look the same? When engaging in peer-group relations, when playing, do a child, an adolescent, and an adult do the same things: If behavior seen at one point in the life span can be *described* in the same way as behavior at another point, then *descriptive continuity* exists. If behavior seen at one point in the life span cannot be *described* in the same way as can behavior at another point, then *descriptive discontinuity* exists.

The former situation would exist if what a person did with his or her peers in order to "have fun" were the same in adolescence and adulthood, while the latter situation would exist if what was done to "have fun" were different for the person at these two times. Further illustration of descriptive continuity and discontinuity is seen in Exhibit 5.3. Part *a* of the figure illustrates no change in intraindividual status (continuity), while Part *b* shows change in intraindividual status (discontinuity).

Explanation of intraindividual change

Changes in the description of behavior across a person's life can occur for many reasons. In fact, even the *same* change—whether it is continuous *or* discontinuous—can be explained with many reasons. This possibility was illustrated earlier when it

Exhibit 5.3
(*a*) If behavior can be represented in the same way at two times in the individual's life span, then descriptive continuity exists between these two points. (*b*) If behavior cannot be represented in the same way at two times in the individual's life span, then descriptive discontinuity exists between these two points.

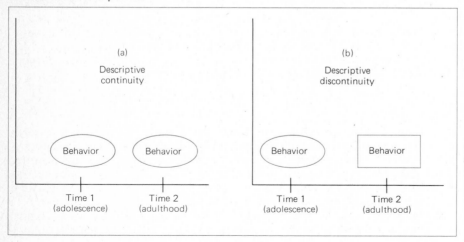

was noted that storm and stress in adolescence could be explained by very different theories. Chapter 6, in fact, in explaining different theories of adolescent development, shows how different reasons for the existence of the same developments may be given.

If the same *explanations* are used to account for behavior across a person's life, then this means that behavior is interpreted as involving unchanging laws or rules. In this case there is *explanatory continuity*. If, however, different *explanations* are used to account for behavior across a person's life, then there is *explanatory discontinuity*. In other words, if the variables used to account for behavior change processes *do not* vary from time 1 to time 2 in a person's life, explanatory continuity exists; if the variables used to account for behavior change processes *do* vary from time 1 to time 2 in a person's life, explanatory discontinuity exists.

Descriptive and explanatory combinations

It is possible to have any combination of descriptive continuity-discontinuity and explanatory continuity-discontinuity. For instance, suppose one were interested in accounting for a person's recreational behavior at different times in his or her life, and tried to explain this behavior through use of motivational ideas. There might or might not be changes in the main recreation behaviors from childhood (for example, bicycle riding) to adolescence. There might be descriptive continuity or discontinuity. In *either* case, however, one might suggest a continuous or a discontinuous explanation. For instance, it might be argued that recreational behavior is determined by curiosity motivation. Bike riding in childhood and adolescence, or bike riding in the former period and dancing in the latter, may just be determined by how curious the person is about seeing where the bike ride can take him or her (in the former case) or about seeing what the new dance steps are (in the latter case). Thus, one would be accounting for behavior based on an explanatory, continuous interpretation.

Alternatively, it might be argued that recreational behavior in adolescence is determined not by curiosity motivation, but rather by sexual motivation. That is, although curiosity led to bike riding or disco dancing in her childhood, the female now rides bikes or goes dancing to meet males. Here, then, one would be accounting for behavior based on an explanatory, discontinuous interpretation.

Further illustration of explanatory continuity and explanatory discontinuity is seen in Exhibit 5.4. Part *a* is an illustration of no intraindividual change in the explanations of behavior over time (continuity). In Part *b* intraindividual change in the explanations of behavior over time (discontinuity) is shown. However, in both portions of the figure the behavior being described is continuous. As indicated above, however, descriptive continuity or discontinuity and explanatory continuity or discontinuity can occur. Intraindividual change may take a form fitting into any of the quadrants shown in Exhibit 5.5.

With change form 1, descriptions of behavior would remain the same (for example, the person plays in the same way); similarly the reasons used to explain why the behavior did not change would remain the same also (for example, the same motive is present). Change form 2 would involve the same descriptions of behavior (for example, bike riding as the major form of recreation) across time, but the explanation of the identical behaviors would change from time 1 (for example, the person rides to master a motor skill) to time 2 (for example, the person rides to meet members of the opposite sex). Change form 3 would involve the behavior changing from time 1 (for example, bike riding) to time 2 (for example, dancing), but the

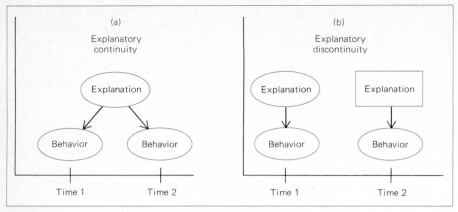

Exhibit 5.4
(*a*) If behavior can be accounted for in the same way at two times in the person's life span, then explanatory continuity exists between these two points. (*b*) If behavior cannot be accounted for in the same way at two times in the individual's life span, then explanatory discontinuity exists between these two points.

explanation of behavior remains the same (for example, motivation to master motor skills). Finally, change form 4 involves the behavior being understood on the basis of different reasons (for example, time 1 behavior involves a motor skill motive and time 2 involves a heterosexual interest motive).

The role of theory

It may be seen that a change may take any one of several forms, and that even the same descriptive change can be interpreted (explained) in different ways. The primary reason why people interpret a given change in contrasting ways is that theoretical differences exist among them. As discussed in Chapter 1, events of adolescence may be interpreted as continuations of processes present in earlier

Exhibit 5.5
Intra-individual change may take a form reflecting any combination of descriptive and explanatory continuity or discontinuity.

	Explanatory continuity	Explanatory discontinuity
Descriptive continuity	1	2
Descriptive discontinuity	3	4

ontogenetic periods or as results of processes specially present in adolescence. Thus, Davis (1944) explained storm and stress behavior in adolescence (behavior which, by the way, was regarded as descriptively discontinuous) by proposing social learning principles that were present in earlier ontogenetic periods. He used explanatory continuity. Hall (1904), moreover, coupled descriptive discontinuity with explanatory discontinuity, saying the adolescent period recapitulated a special portion of phylogeny.

The point in recasting the ideas of Davis and Hall in terms of the continuity-discontinuity issue is to indicate that whether a given behavior is seen as continuous or discontinuous is not primarily an empirical issue. It is a theoretical issue (Langer, 1970; Werner, 1957). Furthermore, since theoretical differences affect the ways in which one collects and analyzes data, even descriptions of behavior as continuous or discontinuous are primarily matters of theoretical interpretations and not empirical "reality."

For instance, suppose one researcher believed in a theory that learning in adolescence involved general laws leading to smooth, continuous, incremental learning steps; and suppose another followed a theory that suggested adolescent learning was discontinuous, that it involved jumps or spurts in knowledge and that different people spurted ahead at different times. Both researchers might do the same experiment to test their respective views, but the way they handled their data—and what their data proved—would reflect their theoretical biases and not empirical reality.

Suppose that to study learning in adolescents, ten high school students were selected on the basis of those factors which might influence their ability to learn (for example, their IQs, ages, educational level, etc.). Each student would be presented a list of ten "nonsense syllables," two consonants and a vowel for which no previous knowledge existed. Syllables like "guz," "wog," or "zek" might be used. After seeing the list, students would be asked to recall the items, and the number of words correctly recalled would be the score the researcher would record for each student on each of three trials.

The researcher who believed in general laws and continuity might decide to pool the responses across students because of the belief that learning was generally the same for all people. Thus, in graphing the results, the research might use the group average for number of items correct on trial 1 (see Exhibit 5.6a). Suppose that on trial 1, subject 1 recalled all items correctly, but all other subjects recalled no items. The *total* number of items recalled for this trial would be 10, and the average number for the ten subjects would be 1. Thus, the point on the graph of Exhibit 5.6b would be entered. If we further suppose that on trial 2, subject 1 continued to recall all ten items correctly, and that now subject 2 did the same, while all others continued to score zero, then the situation in Exhibit 5.7 would occur. The total number of correct items would be 20, the average would be 2, and the second point on the graph (see 5.7b) would be entered. Similarly, if on the third trial, subject 3 now got all correct, as subjects 1 and 2 continued to, but all others still scored zero, one would have a situation like that in Exhibit 5.8.

If such patterns continued and the researcher connected the points in the figure, he or she would see evidence that learning was smooth and continuous. Because of the belief in general laws of learning (that all people learn in the same manner), the researcher might not be prone to look at the individual differences in the learning of the subjects, and the data graphed would be group scores. Thus, in this example (which is intentionally extreme in order to make a point of the theoretical basis of

(a)

Subject	Number correct on trial		
	1	2	3
1	10		
2	0		
3	0		
4	0		
5	0		
6	0		
7	0		
8	0		
9	0		
10	0		
Average number correct on trial	1		

(b)

Exhibit 5.6
Results of a study of learning in adolescence: the data collected and graphed for the group for trial 1.

Exhibit 5.7
Results of a study of learning in adolescence: the data collected and graphed for the group for trial 2.

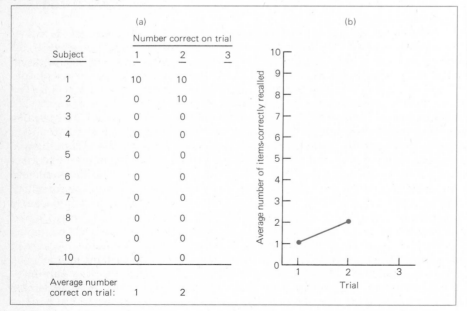

(a)

Subject	Number correct on trial		
	1	2	3
1	10	10	
2	0	10	
3	0	0	
4	0	0	
5	0	0	
6	0	0	
7	0	0	
8	0	0	
9	0	0	
10	0	0	
Average number correct on trial:	1	2	

(b)

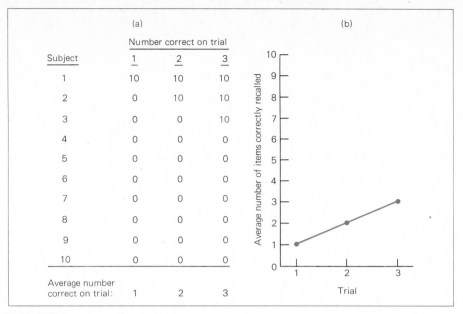

	(a)				(b)
	Number correct on trial				
Subject	1	2	3		
1	10	10	10		
2	0	10	10		
3	0	0	10		
4	0	0	0		
5	0	0	0		
6	0	0	0		
7	0	0	0		
8	0	0	0		
9	0	0	0		
10	0	0	0		
Average number correct on trial:	1	2	3		

Exhibit 5.8
Results of a study of learning in adolescence: the data collected and graphed for the group for trial 3.

decisions about continuity-discontinuity), the group data would support a continuity view of learning. Yet if analyzed differently, the very same data could support a discontinuity interpretation.

If the researcher who believed in discontinuity would graph the data shown in Exhibits 5.6 to 5.8, he or she would emphasize the individuality of learning processes, that people show discontinuous spurts in learning after varying lengths of time in which no learning was evidenced. Thus, from the same data as above, a graph like that of Exhibit 5.9 could be drawn, and as such, the individual data would now support the discontinuity view of learning.

It has already been stated that this example is extreme. Experienced, competent researchers would invariably be sensitive to such major trends in their data. However, this is precisely the point. Most often trends in data are *considerably* more subtle than those in Exhibits 5.6 to 5.9. As such, the impact of theoretical orientation on collecting and handling the data is not as readily obvious to researchers. This situation not only requires a vigilance about the way researchers—because of their biases—may affect the nature of the "reality" they "discover," but also highlights the need to be aware of how depictions of one's data relate *primarily* to theoretical issues and not to empirical ones.

In summary, in both explaining and describing intraindividual change as continuous or discontinuous, theoretical perspective is a major determinant of what particular change format (see Exhibit 5.5) is advanced as representative of development. Furthermore, it is important to note that even among those who agree that development is to be explained by discontinuous terms, there are important

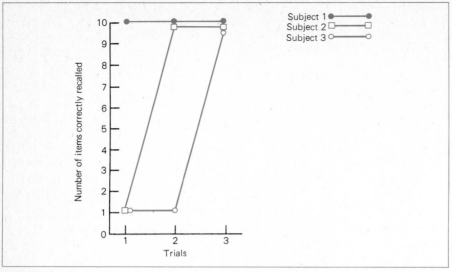

Exhibit 5.9
Results of a study of learning in adolescence: the data collected are the same as those of Figures 5.6, 5.7, and 5.8, but here they are graphed to show individual (as opposed to group) performances across trials.

differences in the discontinuities they specify as being involved in change. But here too the basis of these differences involves theoretical contrasts.

Quantitative versus qualitative changes

Explanatory discontinuity can be put forth for either of two reasons. One can assert that it is necessary to interpret development as involving discontinuity because a *quantitative* change has occurred. Quantitative changes involve differences in how much or how many of something exists. For example, quantitative changes in adolescence occur in such things as height and weight—since there is an adolescent growth spurt—and these changes are often interpreted as resulting from quantitative increases in the production of particular hormones.

In turn, one can assert that it is necessary to interpret development as involving discontinuity because *qualitative* change has occurred. Qualitative changes involve differences in *what* exists, what sort of phenomenon is present. The emergence in adolescence of a drive-state never before present in life, that is, a reproductively mature sexual drive (Freud, 1969), and the emergence in adolescence of new and abstract thought capabilities not present in younger people (Piaget, 1950, 1970) are instances of changes interpreted as arising from qualitative alterations in the person. It is believed that the person is *not* just more of the same; rather, the person is seen as having a *new* quality or characteristic.

It is possible to offer an explanatory, discontinuous interpretation of development involving *either* quantitative *or* qualitative change. When particular types of explanatory, discontinuous qualitative changes are said to be involved in development, the third major conceptual issue of development is raised. This third issue to be examined shortly is termed the critical periods hypothesis, and involves the view that development is characterized by qualitatively distinct changes. On the basis of adherence to a particular theory of development, qualitative changes are believed to characterize ontogeny, and because of this, discontinuous explanations of change are needed.

It is important to recognize that any particular description or explanation of intraindividual change is the result of a particular theoretical view of development. This implies that commitment to a theory which focuses on only certain variables or processes will restrict one's view of the variety of changes that may characterize development.

THE STABILITY-INSTABILITY ISSUE

The changes one person makes do not necessarily match the changes others make. One adolescent's major recreational activity may change from playing chess to playing pinball, while another's may change from bicycle riding to reading. Another example of such interindividual differences in change is that although two adolescents may go through the same change sequence (for example, from chess to pinball), one may make the change faster than another.

The life-span approach to human development is concerned partially with the description, explanation, and optimization of interindividual differences. Whenever one is concerned with differences between people on how they change across time, the stability-instability issue is raised.

Because the stability-instability issue focuses on a person's change relative to that of other changing people, it basically is an issue that pertains to a group level as opposed to an individual one. To illustrate, people are measured on a particular characteristic (for example, height at puberty), and from these measurements a distribution of scores is obtained. In other words, not all people would be the same height at puberty. Rather, some would be shorter, some taller, and some of average height. People with different scores (in this case, heights) would have different positions (or locations) in the group. Thus, there are differences between people in their scores (their heights), and this set of differences is termed a *distribution*.

The issue of stability-instability arises when the group is tested at a second time (for example, height measured at the end of the final growth spurt in adolescence). Although heights may have changed for most, if not all, people, each person's relative position in the group could have stayed the same. If persons A, B, and C each grew 4 inches, and so too did all the other people in their group, then despite the *absolute* increase in height, their relative positions in the group would have stayed the same. Despite intraindividual change, there were no interindividual differences in such change. This illustration is an example of stability.

Stability occurs if a person's rate of change relative to the others in the group stays the same over time. However, if a person's rate of change relative to the others in the group changes over time, there is *instability*. Thus, if person C has grown 8 inches in height while everyone else grew only 4, then person C would have changed more than those in the group, and instability (for this person) would have occurred.

These relations are diagramed in Exhibit 5.10 for distributions of height score. Notice that in the illustrations of both stability and instability for height, the score of the target person *increased* between time 1 and time 2. This illustration allows an important point implied above to be made explicit. Whether stability or instability occurs says nothing whatsoever about whether or not any absolute change took place.

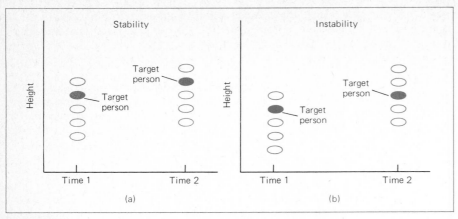

Exhibit 5.10
Examples of (a) stability and (b) instability in development. (Adapted from Lerner, 1976, p. 128.)

A person can change, and this change may still be labeled stability. This could occur if others in the group also changed but the target person's rate of change was the same as the others in the group. On the other hand, a person could remain the same between time 1 and time 2 and yet his or her position relative to the group could be termed unstable. This could occur if others in the group changed while the target person did not. Hence, the terms stability and instability describe *relative*, not absolute, changes. Again, the terms relate to whether or not differences present at time 1 among people in a group persisted at time 2 (and hence stability occurred) or were altered, with the group distributed differently at the second time (and hence instability occurred). However, as suggested above, stability or instability may occur in several ways. Stability between two times in a person's development can occur when (1) the person remains the same and so does the group, or (2) the person changes and so does the group to corresponding extents. On the other hand, instability between two times in a person's development can occur when (1) the person remains the same but the group changes, or (2) the person changes and so do members of the group, but to extents not corresponding with the person's degree of change.

In sum, stability-instability is an issue which applies to groups. A person is not stable or unstable within himself or herself. Rather, depending on the distribution of scores in a group over time, the individual's location may be stable or unstable. Yet in either case, one still does not know if the person has or has not changed and/or why this change has or has not occurred. To know this, one has to examine the continuity-discontinuity issue in both its descriptive and its explanatory aspects. As implied above, any combination of continuity-discontinuity and stability-instability may characterize development.

Relations of stability-instability to continuity-discontinuity

The continuity-discontinuity issue describes and explains intraindividual change. At the same time, the stability-instability issue *describes* differences between people within groups that arise as a consequence of such within-person change. Thus, two types of alterations involving people are occurring simultaneously. All people are changing over time, *and* because not all people change in the same way or at the same rate, people's locations relative to others alter too. Accordingly, to understand *all* dimensions of a person's alteration over time, both aspects of change should be considered simultaneously. Only through such a joint, simultaneous focus can life-span development best be understood.

Such joint focus is complex because a person's developmental processes may be either continuous or discontinuous (on explanatory and/or descriptive levels), and the progression of these processes may result in a person's change relative to his or her group being stable or unstable. Thus, development may be characterized by any one of four types of change-difference patterns (Baltes & Nesselroade, 1973; Emmerich, 1968; Lerner, 1976). There may be *(a)* continuity and stability, *(b)* continuity and instability, *(c)* discontinuity and stability, and *(d)* discontinuity and instability.

Changes characteristic of development

A person may show stability of location when in one group (for example, distributions formed by measuring height at age 17 years and at age 21 years), but may show instability when considered in the context of another group (for example, distributions formed by measuring knowledge of calculus at age 17 years and at age 21 years). Not only does this underscore the point that stability-instability is a group consideration, and not the property of a person, but also it suggests that when different measures of characteristics are taken, different statements about stability-instability may appropriately be made.

Within the same portion of the life span, people may show stability in regard to measures of some processes and instability in others. Any of these differences may, of course, involve either continuity or discontinuity. Thus, one cannot speak of adolescence as a period that includes just *one* particular type of change.

Any statements about the nature of change depend on the particular change process being focused on. More importantly, however, since the same change phenomenon (for example, storm and stress in adolescence) may be understood and measured in different ways, depending on the theoretical orientation of the researcher, statements about the nature of change relate primarily to theoretical issues.

Accordingly, to describe fully the types of changes that may characterize any portion of the life span, one should pay attention to all the levels at which change can exist, and how concepts drawn from theories pertaining to processes at all these levels together may provide a more complete picture of life-span development. In turn, these ideas have implications for theories about development which suggest that *only* certain changes can exist. This is illustrated in discussing the critical periods hypothesis.

THE CRITICAL PERIODS HYPOTHESIS

The critical periods hypothesis rests on two ideas; the first is a descriptive statement, and the second is an explanatory one. First, there are qualitatively discontinuous periods in life. Second, the meaning these periods have for later life is fixed and universal. Although it is possible to agree that there well may be qualitatively discontinuous portions of life, it will be argued that the major problems with the critical periods hypothesis come from the second idea, *fixity* (the opposite of plasticity).

Although there are several ways of formulating a critical periods hypothesis (Caldwell, 1962; Lerner, 1976; Sluckin, 1965), the thrust of it remains identical. The hypothesis suggests that the potential for development is *not* the same across the life span. Rather, there are certain times during which certain developments must occur if those developments are ever to occur optimally or adaptively; or there are times in life *beyond* which certain developments will not occur optimally or adaptively if they have not already occurred (Erikson, 1959, 1964; Lorenz, 1965). Thus, it is critical for these particular developments to occur within their necessary periods. Simply, the critical periods hypothesis states that if you do not develop what you should develop when you should develop it, then you will never develop it!

Because the life span is divided into these special periods, theorists using this hypothesis are obviously taking a discontinuity position. Moreover, since these theorists try to account for different outcomes of experiences on the basis of when these experiences occurred—that is, within or outside of critical time limits—they are using the critical periods hypothesis in an explanatory manner. They are offering an explanatory, discontinuous account of why experiences will not lead to the same developmental outcome at different times in a person's life. Thus, they are saying that not all times of life are the same. Rather, different periods in life are special and unique. The critical periods impose particular limits on development. Thus, these periods represent *qualitatively distinct* portions of the life cycle.

However, because theorists using a critical periods hypothesis are advancing a notion based on qualitative explanatory discontinuity, and are thus saying that the same experience will lead to different outcomes depending on the time of life the experience occurs, a specific stance is taken in regard to the nature-nurture issue. The critical periods hypothesis indicates that it is not experience (or nurture) that determines what outcomes will arise from developmental progressions. Rather, the critical periods hypothesis indicates that phenomena independent of experience determine the influences and outcomes that experience can result in (that is, adaptive or maladaptive)—a nature view.

Thus, critical periods theorists typically take a stance stressing nature over nurture. For example, Erikson (1959, 1964) divides the life span into eight critical periods. He says that certain phenomena must develop within each respective period in order for healthy development to proceed. However, a person does not have an infinite length of time to develop what is supposed to be developed within each critical period. Rather, the person's development is governed by a "maturational ground plan," or in Erikson's (1959) terms, the "epigenetic principle." This maturational plan is innate in each person. Such genetically based limits may differ from person to person because of hereditary differences, but in all people this plan sets the time limits of each period. If the person does not develop as he or she is supposed to develop within the fixed time, then in accordance with the maturational ground plan, development will move on. Experiences that could have led to healthy development if they had acted before development became refocused will not now be able to have such an adaptive influence.

For instance, Erikson (1959) says that in the critical period of life termed adolescence, one has to develop a sense of identity. If one does not achieve this sense of self-definition during one's innately fixed time limit—a time limit which, Erikson (1959) implies, cannot be known in advance (because different people do have different, but not measurable, inheritances)—then identity will *never* be adequately achieved. Additionally, the rest of development will be unfavorably altered (Erikson,

1959). Thus, to Erikson, it *is* quite critical to develop appropriately within a critical period.

There will be much more to say about Erikson's ideas throughout this book. His general ideas about critical periods, and his particular concerns with adolescence as a critical period, will be considered later. In fact, it shall be argued that more often than not adolescence has been seen as a critical period in the human life cycle.

A critique of the critical periods hypothesis

As exemplified by Erikson (1959), the basis of a period being seen as critical lies in the idea that *nature acts independently of nurture* in imposing limits on development at certain times of life. Although this idea leads critical periods theorists to infer that development is qualitatively discontinuous, it is not this inference which is a problem. Development may, for instance, proceed through qualitatively different levels as a consequence of the interaction among nature and nurture variables. In our opinion, a conceptual problem with the critical periods hypothesis exists because it stresses fixity in development as a consequence of the independent, isolated action of nature. It has been argued that nature and nurture are dynamically interactive and that conceptions of development which contend that one source influences behavior independently of the other are not consistent with data showing the plasticity of behavior development across the entire life cycle. Indeed, it is not surprising to learn that when critical periods ideas are put to empirical test, they are found to be untenable interpretations of animal behavior (Moltz & Stettner, 1961; Sluckin, 1965), human behavior (Schneirla & Rosenblatt, 1961, 1963), and for present interests, adolescent behavior.

However, despite the limitations of the critical periods hypothesis, theorists like Erikson (1959) have provided ideas of some use. Erikson has discussed how developments at earlier periods of life influence developments at later periods. Although events in earlier periods may not critically affect development in later life—in the sense of inevitable sources of particular behavior—earlier events can influence development in one direction as opposed to another. For example, negative experience with a dentist in early life may make it less likely that dentistry will be chosen as a profession in later life. Or exposure to traditional socialization pressures in childhood that relate to the sex-appropriateness of behavior (for example, females become nurses, males become physicians) may make it likely that males and females will enter "sex-appropriate" vocations after adolescence. Yet although events in earlier periods may make one *sensitive* to particular events in later periods, such sensitivity does not necessarily imply that intervention during these later periods cannot alter development. Positive later experiences with a dentist or changes in the socialization pressures in society (due to revised social values, new laws, or other historical alterations) can lead to modification of development.

Plasticity and optimization of development

The above criticism of the critical periods hypothesis leads to some ideas about the optimization of development across the life span. If behavior is changeable, events in any period of life may be targets of intervention. Moreover, because the nature of change within and among developmental periods can be conceptualized as continuous or discontinuous, depending on which of many theories is used to explain change, one may intervene at any time in life to affect development.

One may try to encourage females to choose socially nontraditional vocations (for example, surgeons, engineers, or diplomats) in adulthood by intervening during adolescence through changing rewards they encounter. Such intervention, based on a nurture, continuity view, is but one of many, however. If a discontinuity view is taken, then strategies for modification would be tried at the time that choice of career is made. Moreover, because different theories lead not only to different views of the continuity or discontinuity of sources of development, but also to different methods (for example, data analysis strategies) used to study development, many different techniques or mechanisms for effecting developmental optimization may be used. One may intervene at the individual-psychological level by applying particular rewards to the female who chooses a nontraditional role. Or one may intervene at the sociocultural level by enacting laws making employers seek women to engage in nontraditional careers. Either strategy, it should be noted, might change the distribution of males and females in particular vocational groups. Thus, intervention strategies also relate to the stability-instability issue.

CHAPTER SUMMARY

The nature-nurture issue is the basic conceptual issue involved in understanding adolescent development. Other key issues, such as the continuity-discontinuity issue and the critical periods hypothesis, derive from the nature-nurture issue. Formulations about the relation of nature and nurture variables to development vary. Those formulations that see nature (for example, heredity) and nurture (for example, environment) as independent and additive were judged inadequate on conceptual and empirical grounds. No one in the environment is without heredity, and one cannot see the effects of heredity without the environment. Environmental variations have been shown to influence the effects that a given genetic inheritance has on behavior, and in turn, the same environment does not have identical effects on all organisms.

Environmental variables may be derived from several levels of analysis—the inner-biological, the individual-psychological, the outer-physical–environmental, and the sociocultural-historical. Particular combinations of variables from these levels create for each *genotype* a potentially unique context within which it develops. Given this fact, the *phenotype* that develops is also unique.

One may ask if behavior may be described in the same or different ways across the life span (the issue of *descriptive continuity-discontinuity*). One also may ask if the reasons for behavioral development stay the same or change across the life span (the issue of *explanatory continuity-discontinuity*). Any combination of continuous-discontinuous descriptions and explanations may be offered in research and theory.

The *stability-instability* issue involves the differences between people as they change over time. Stability occurs when a person's changes lead him or her to maintain a similar position, relative to others, over time. Instability occurs when a person changes his or her position, relative to others, over time.

Some theorists believe that because of particular maturational or genetic processes that are independent of experience, there are particular times in life when certain changes must occur in order for development to proceed optimally. Such an idea is termed the *critical periods* hypothesis. It is a nature-based explanation that claims there are qualitatively discontinuous periods in the life span. Although many scientists describe adolescence as a critical period within the life span, such an idea ignores data which show the plasticity and complexity of development. Nevertheless, such a conception is useful in pointing up the possibility that the adolescent period, as it exists in its current sociocultural and historical context, may present unique issues and problems.

6

THEORIES OF ADOLESCENCE

CHAPTER
OVERVIEW

Theories about adolescent development are varied, and sometimes contradictory, concerning some fundamental assumptions about human development. This chapter discusses several noted theorists and their ideas. How each theory relates to the nature-nurture issue and the idea of storm and stress in adolescence is considered.

Does the popular belief that adolescence is universally a period of storm and stress correspond to the data about adolescents' behavior and social relations?

What are the characteristics and limitations of nature theories of adolescence, such as those of Hall and Lorenz?

What are some major differences among nurture theories of development?

How do social learning theories, like those of Davis and McCandless, explain development in adolescence?

What are the major distinctions among weak, moderate, and strong interaction theories of adolescent development?

How does the nature of development within and across the stages of psychosexual development, specified in Sigmund Freud's theory, represent a weak interaction theory?

What are the key characteristics of the psychoanalytic theory provided by Anna Freud, and how do the changes she discusses form her theory of adolescent development?

Why is Piaget's theory of cognitive development an example of a moderate interaction theory?

I n the preceding chapters it has been emphasized that adolescent development is a changeable phenomenon. Yet there are many other views of adolescence which suggest a less malleable view of the person. This latter conception is consistent with some current ideas of adolescence in our society.

To illustrate, Bandura (1964) notes that the average person on the street associates adolescence with storm and stress, tension, rebellion, dependency conflicts, peer-group conformity, black leather jackets, and the like. The professional and popular literature on adolescence also advances the belief that adolescence is, indeed, a unique and stormy developmental period.

This consistency between the lay person's and the conventional scientific view of adolescence is illustrated also by Gallatin (1975):

> There can be little doubt that the prevailing image of adolescence is a romantic one. The teenager of the commercial film and weekly T.V. series emerges as a fascinating bundle of contradictions—self-centered yet sensitive, sexually driven yet reticent, hostile yet vulnerable. In all likelihood, much of the responsibility for this popular conception can be assigned to those who have formulated theories of adolescent development. While they may disagree about the actual causes of storm and stress, many theorists appear to assume that it is a virtual certainty during adolescence, and this assumption seems somehow to have permeated American society at large. (p. 28)

Despite the prevalence of this assumption, there are those who do not see adolescence as a stormy period. This chapter reviews some interesting data showing that most adolescents do not regard their own development in this way (Bandura, 1964; Douvan & Adelson, 1966; Offer, 1969). Furthermore, we shall consider the research and ideas of scientists who, like the present authors, do not see the period as inevitably filled with conflict and turmoil (for example, Bandura, 1964; Douvan & Adelson, 1966; Gallatin, 1975; Kohlberg, 1969; Offer, 1969).

Thus, the particular phenomena of adolescence are issues of debate, rather than mere facts. Moreover, as Gallatin (1975) indicated, even among those who agree on what behaviors characterize adolescence, there are differences in the explanations given to account for the behavior. These differences derive from theoretical differences among scientists, and as will be argued, one can organize these theoretical differences in terms of where various theorists stand in regard to the nature-nurture issue.

In fact, whether one sees behaviors in adolescence as invariant or variant depends also on the stand taken in regard to the nature-nurture issue. In Chapter 5 it was argued that such "factual" disputes are not primarily empirical matters, but instead are matters of theoretical interpretation. The contribution of nature and/or nurture, the continuity or discontinuity of adolescent behavior, and the critical nature of the period are all issues resting on theoretical, and not primarily empirical, differences.

A number of theories can be used to explain adolescent development. Those theories which historically arose first (for example, those of Hall, 1904, and Freud, 1904, 1905) promoted the view that there are universal features of development, and that such features involved adolescence storm and stress. Because of (1) the theories being historically first, (2) the influence of Hall on other early contributors to the field, (3) attention by the public media, and (4) especially, the fact that few other theorists in the United States developed ideas pertinent to adolescence, these nature-based issues were the ones that influenced popular conceptions, and account for the consistency between scientific and public ideas about adolescents. Nevertheless, as theorists with other (that is, nurture or nature-nurture interactional) viewpoints began to turn their attention to adolescence, and as *research* about adolescence became more prevalent (Bandura, 1964; Douvan & Adelson, 1966; Offer, 1969), views and information arose to counter the nature position.

As has been emphasized throughout this book, to understand the phenomena of adolescence, we need to focus on the meanings, the interpretations, of the behavior of people. It is useful to understand what theories have been and could be offered to account for adolescent development. As already noted, one can organize these theories in terms of their stance on the nature-nurture issue.

In order to show the relations between theoretical interpretation and data, it is appropriate to focus on one area of adolescent behavior. This focus will illustrate how the same "fact" may be interpreted differently in contrasting theoretical contexts. In some theoretical contexts, a fact may not even be accepted at all. The area of adolescent development most useful to focus on in these illustrations is the alleged storm and stress of adolescence. Major theoretical and popular conceptions of the period claim that there is storm and stress. In addition, it has been suggested that there are theoretical as well as data-based reasons to dispute the universality of adolescent storm and stress.

In the next section some data on storm and stress in adolescence are reviewed, and then in succeeding sections, various nature, nurture, and interactional theories of adolescent development are presented and appraised for their ability to account successfully for this information.

ADOLESCENT STORM AND
STRESS: FACT OR FICTION?

G. Stanley Hall proposed the first scientific theory of adolescent development. In Chapter 4 the characteristics of this position as well as its limitations were presented. Hall depicted adolescence as a recapitulational transition period between an uncivilized, beastlike state to a civilized, humanlike one. Such a transition, he argued, gave an emotional and behavioral texture to the period that inevitably involved storm and stress (Hall, 1904; Gallatin, 1975). Despite the limitations of the recapitulationist theory and the faulty appraisal of adolescence it therefore involved, Hall's general nature position did have an influence on thinking about development. Accordingly, for the historical reasons noted earlier, Hall's influence was to create a general impression of adolescence as being universally stormy and stressful. Yet like the nature-based recapitulationist theory from which it was derived, this conception is inconsistent with a wealth of data derived from diverse sources.

As early as the 1920s and 1930s data were available from cross-cultural studies of adolescence that spoke against the universality of storm and stress. Indeed, these cultural anthropological studies (for example, Mead, 1928, 1930) demonstrated that in some societies adolescence is one of the most pleasurable periods of personal and social development. Additionally, these studies showed that in some other societies there is no period of life corresponding to what Western civilization labels as adolescence. As a consequence of a puberty or a fertility rite, there is a rapid, abrupt transition from child to adult status (Mead, 1930). As such, there is no time for any prolonged turmoil.

However, it is possible that nature theorists such as Hall would argue that using events from non-Western societies to evaluate the character of adolescence in Western societies is not appropriate because of the possibly different genetic backgrounds of the two groups. As discussed in Chapter 5, there is as much genotypic diversity within any one group as between any two groups (see also Hirsch, 1970; Lewontin, 1976), and thus such a view would not be supported; nevertheless, one may look at studies done within Western civilization and still find evidence inconsistent with the idea of universal storm and stress.

Bandura (1964; Bandura & Walters, 1959) interviewed middle-class families having adolescent boys. The findings of this research run counter to the idea that adolescence is a typically stressful period. For instance, although it is stereotypically believed that parents of adolescents become more controlling and prohibitive of their children, Bandura (1964) reports that by the time of adolescence the males had so adopted parental values and standards that parental restrictions actually were reduced. Similarly, Bandura notes that although the storm and stress idea of adolescence suggests a struggle by youth to free themselves of dependence on parents, independence training had begun during childhood for the males in his sample. As such, independence was largely accomplished by adolescence. Finally, although adolescence is a time when people begin to move from having primary ties with parents to having primary ties with peers, Bandura did not find that choosing friends was a major source of friction between parents and adolescents. He found that adolescents tended to form friendships with those who shared similar values, and as such, the peers tended to support those standards of the parents that the boys already adopted.

Bandura points out, however, that these data do not mean that adolescence is a stressless, problemless period of life. He is careful to note that no period of life is free of crisis or adjustment problems, and any period of life may present particular adjustment problems for some people and not for others. Thus, one has to be careful about overgeneralizing problems associated with one sample to all samples of adolescents. Indeed, Bandura (1964) notes that in that portion of his study that assessed a sample of antisocial boys whose excessive aggression did lead to their adolescence being associated with storm and stress, one could not appropriately view their problems as resulting just from adolescence. Bandura found that their problem behaviors were present through their childhood as well. However, when the boys were physically smaller, the parents were able to control their aggressive behavior better than they could during adolescence.

From Bandura's data (1964; Bandura & Walters, 1959) it may be concluded that (1) even when storm and stress is seen in adolescence, it is not necessarily the result of events in adolescence, but instead may be associated with life-span developments; and (2) storm and stress is not necessarily characteristic of the adolescent period—many possible types of adolescent development can occur. The existence of such plasticity is supported by data from other studies.

Offer (1969), also studying adolescent boys, found three major routes through the adolescent period. He notes that there is a *continuous-growth* type of development. This involves smooth and nonabrupt changes in behavior. Subjects here were not in any major conflict with their parents, and did not feel parental rearing practices were inappropriate, or that parental values were not ones that they themselves did not share. Most adolescents fell into this category, and such a pattern is like the one we have seen Bandura (1964) describe. A second type of pattern is *surgent growth*. Here development involves an abrupt spurt, much like some transitions in cultures having puberty or fertility rites. Such rapid progression does not necessarily involve the turmoil associated with storm and stress. Finally, however, Offer (1969) did identify a *tumultuous-growth* type of adolescent development. Here crisis, stress, and problems characterize the period. For such adolescents, "storm and stress" aptly characterizes the nature of their change.

Thus, only for some people is the adolescent period one of storm and stress. Indeed, based on the Bandura (1964) and Offer (1969) data it may be assumed that such a tumultuous period is involved with only a minority of adolescents. Moreover, although this conclusion is derived from these two studies of male adolescents, it is bolstered by the data of Douvan and Adelson (1966), who studied both male and female adolescents. As in the previously noted studies, most males and females shared the basic values of their parents and were satisfied with their family life and the style of treatment by their parents. Indeed, girls exemplified this pattern even more so than boys. Douvan and Adelson found few signs of rebellion or conflict, and most girls regarded parental rules as fair and appropriate. Only 25 percent of the females had *any* reservation at all about parental rules, for example, and only 5 percent considered these rules unjust or severe. Moreover, about 50 percent of the girls studied took part in setting their own rules, although whether they participated did not relate to their degree of satisfaction with their parents.

In summary, available data indicate that adolescence is not universally a stressful period. To the contrary, more often than not it seems adolescent experiences do not involve major upheavals, maladaptive developments, or angry, conflicting interpersonal relations with parents. Yet some adolescents do experience some of these negative events, and others experience all of them. Accordingly, there is a range of potential experiences that can characterize adolescent development within even the same cultural setting. The following section assesses the degree to which theories of adolescent development are useful in understanding and integrating the data of storm and stress in adolescence. As nature, nurture, and interactional theories of adolescent development are reviewed, we shall not attempt to mention each possible formulation that could be placed in each category. Instead we focus on those ideas that are most representative of each category *and* that have had the most importance for the study of adolescence.

NATURE THEORIES OF ADOLESCENT DEVELOPMENT

Hall's theory revisited

In turning first to nature theories of adolescent development, it may be noted that although such an approach was historically the first to be put forth (in the recapitulationist ideas of Hall), such an approach does not find wide support today. Hall's theory, although the ideal model of a nature-based theory of adolescence, quickly lost favor in social science. Hall viewed the human life span as mirroring evolutionary transitions of the human species. The events of ontogeny were determined, he believed, by phylogenetic history. In their nature humans had the basis of their developmental course.

In Chapter 3 it was noted that there were two major reasons for discarding this recapitulationist nature theory. First, it was based on an inappropriate understanding of the character of evolution (Hodos & Campbell, 1969); and second, human ontogeny is more complex at early age levels (for example, 3 years of age) than is even high primate behavior at adult levels (Gallatin, 1975; Thorndike, 1904). Thus, because of such major problems, Hall's specific nature theory was not tenable.

The instinctual theory of Konrad Lorenz

Because of limitations mentioned, a completely nature-based theory of adolescence has not become popular or influential. However, another nature-based conception has been influential, although not specifically in regard to adolescence. The position of Konrad Lorenz has influenced people to believe that human behavior, even at the adolescent and adult levels, is governed by *instincts*. Lorenz believes that instincts are preformed, innate potentials for behavior and are in no way influenced by environment, experience, learning, or any variable tied to nurture (Lorenz, 1965).

Lorenz is known today for his study of instincts in *precocial* birds (birds that can walk upon hatching), such as ducks or geese. He coined the termed *imprinting* to describe early social and emotional attachments formed by such birds to the first moving object they see (usually, but not necessarily, their mother). He explains such an attachment on the basis of the presence of an instinct for attachment. However, he says that proof for the innate basis of imprinting is that attachments seem to be invariably formed; but he also says that the reason the attachments are formed is because of the presence of an instinct. Why does imprinting exist? He reasons that it exists because there is an instinct for it. How does one know that the instinct is present? Because one sees imprinting.

Thus, Lorenz uses tautological, circular reasoning. In addition to this logical problem, there exists ample evidence, some of which was reviewed earlier regarding the modifiability of critical periods (Moltz & Stettner, 1961; Schneirla & Rosenblatt, 1961, 1963), that imprinting is quite capable of being influenced by experiential variation. It was contended that *any* concept that stresses the sole influence of nature, to the exclusion of an interacting nurture, is flawed. It is a concept based on inappropriate logic and inadequate attention to the empirical literature.

Accordingly, one could dismiss Lorenz's ideas of instincts for these reasons, and not bother to discuss them here, if it were not for the fact that Lorenz applies his ideas to humans. In fact, Lorenz's *initial* interest in instincts was not to explain the basis of behaviors in species of birds. Rather, it was to explain the behavior of different types of humans: Jews versus the so-called "Aryan race." Writing in Nazi Germany in 1940, Lorenz (as translated by Eisenberg, 1972) wrote:

> The only resistance which mankind of healthy stock can offer . . . against being penetrated by symptoms of degeneracy is based on the existence of certain innate schemata. . . . Our species-specific sensitivity to the beauty and ugliness of members of our species is intimately connected with the symptoms of degeneration, caused by domestication, which threaten our race. . . . Usually, a man of high value is disgusted with special intensity by slight symptoms of degeneracy in men of the other race. . . . The immensely high reproduction rate in the moral imbecile has long been established. . . . This phenomenon leads everywhere . . . to the fact that socially inferior human material is enabled . . . to penetrate and finally to annihilate the healthy nation. The selection for toughness, heroism, social utility . . . must be accomplished by some human institution if mankind, in default of selective factors, is not to be ruined by domestication-induced degeneracy. **The racial idea as the basis of our state has already accomplished much in this respect.** The most effective race-preserving measure is . . . the greatest support of the natural defenses. . . . We must—and should—rely on the healthy feelings of our Best and charge them with the selection which will determine the prosperity or the decay of our people. . . . (p. 124) (Emphasis added.)

Although switching his focus from Jews to geese after the Nazis lost the Second World War, Lorenz maintained an interest in human instincts. Perhaps because of his war-related views or experiences, he wrote a book, a quarter of a century after his 1940 statement, which argued that aggression was instinctual in humans. In fact, this book, titled *On Aggression* (Lorenz, 1966), not only sees social conflict as an innate component of all humans, but makes specific statements about adolescents' instinctual "militant enthusiasm" (Lorenz, 1966). Although in this writing Lorenz suggests that civilization must find methods for ritualizing and containing aggressive instincts (for instance by having people of different races get acquainted), he basically is suggesting we need to make the best of an inevitably negative situation (Schneirla, 1966). He sees humans, and perhaps particularly youth, as universally and unalterably destructively aggressive.

Although Lorenz calls for social reform, for example to get youth involved in "genuine causes that are worth serving in the modern world" (Lorenz, 1966), and although we would not dispute such a broad social value, we do contend that his call is based on a totally false premise. As there is no evidence for solely nature-based

Konrad Lorenz

critical periods or instincts in nonhuman animals, there is no evidence for it among humans. Lorenz's speculations about innate aggressive tendencies in adolescents are as faulty logically and empirically as his ideas about instinctual imprinting in geese or instinctual moral degeneracy in Jews. Rather than scientifically studying *how* nature and nurture interact to provide an endless variety of behavior developments, and attempting to discover which combination of variables may lead to aggression in adolescence, Lorenz simply asserts that aggression is innately present. In sum, theories of adolescence based solely on the influence of nature are not especially useful for science. Furthermore, when they take the form that Lorenz's argument took, they may have dire social consequences. We agree with a review of Lorenz's *On Aggression* book written by T. C. Schneirla, a person who led the way in showing the shortcomings of positions such as that of Lorenz. Schneirla (1966) wrote:

> It is as heavy a responsibility to inform man about aggressive tendencies assumed to be present on an inborn basis as it is to inform him about "original sin," which Lorenz admits in effect. A corollary risk is advising societies to base their programs of social training on attempts to inhibit hypothetical innate aggressions, instead of continuing positive measures for constructive behavior. (p. 16)

NURTURE THEORIES OF ADOLESCENT DEVELOPMENT

Nurture theories of development stress the influence of experience and environment on behavior change. Most generally, such theories suggest that behavior is a response to stimulation. The link between stimulus and response is conceptualized in terms of learning or conditioning. However, it is important to understand that such a conception of nurture theories is a broad one. Not all nurture theorists would call themselves learning theorists, nor would they have a commitment to precisely the same view of what learning is. In other words, they might differ about what is involved in the acquisition of behavior as a consequence of experience.

Hence, there is great diversity among nurture theorists. Some, for instance, tie their accounts of behavior to the "laws" of classical and operant conditioning, and thus tie their views of behavior change to functional relations between external stimuli that can be manipulated and responses that can be verified objectively (Bijou, 1976; Bijou & Baer, 1961). Such an approach is often called a functional analysis of behavior (Bijou, 1976, 1977) because behavior (actually responses, R) is seen to be a function (f) of stimulation (S), or simply R = f(S).

Because of the commitment to completely empirical stimulus-response (S-R) relations, nurture theorists who take a functional analysis approach to behavior do not necessarily consider themselves "learning theorists" (Bijou, 1977). Learning theorists are instead those who include in their systems phenomena which are not directly (extrinsically) empirically observable. For instance, such theorists might talk about internal "mental" or "cognitive" responses and stimuli (for example, Hull, 1952; Kendler & Kendler, 1962). Thus, by including phenomena in their theories which, although derived from previous experience, are not present for empirical observation, such learning theorists differ from those nurture theorists who take a functional analysis view.

Moreover, further differences can be found among those committed to a nurture view. Some theorists believe behavior change involves *reinforcement* (any stimulus which produces or maintains behavior, or in other words, makes a behavior more probable; Skinner, 1950). Some believe that nurture controls behavior, independent of any reinforcing stimulus (for example, Bandura & Walters, 1959, 1963). In other words, one can differentiate on the basis of the role given to reinforcement, or to other nurture phenomena—for instance the experience of observing others—in the control of behavior.

Bandura and Walters (1963), for example, assert that by observing others behave, a person can acquire new responses, or show a response that had previously been dropped. By observing a model behave, they argue, a person can show such changes, although there is not direct reinforcement to the person. Seeing the consequences of response for the person who serves as the *model* of behavior (that is, the person who displays the behavior a subject observes), and the social status of the model, can affect the observer's behavior independently of any direct reinforcement (Bandura & Walters, 1963). Thus, free of specific reinforcement for a particular response, some nurture theorists say, an observer may imitate a model's behavior if the status of the model is high (Bandura & Huston, 1961) and the consequences of response for the model are positive. Such theorists are often termed *observational learning* theorists. Alternatively, however, those who consider themselves reinforcement theorists say that an observer who is influenced by a model does indeed receive direct reinforcement, although it is a more general response than that involved in a specific, single act by a model (Gewirtz & Stingle, 1968).

Differences between the functional analysis position and the learning theory position, on the one hand, and reinforcement theory versus observational learning theory, on the other, are just two of the many areas of difference that might be mentioned. Thus, although other theoretical differences could be mentioned, the point is that there is no consensus about what is the nurture view of behavior.

Complicating this situation is the fact that there has never been a nurture theory devised *solely* to deal with phenomena of either human development in general or adolescent development in particular (White, 1970). Moreover, whatever theoretical statements are made about the nurture basis of adolescent development are taken from data primarily collected from organisms other than humans. Thus, not only is there no consensus on a nurture theory of behavior change, but there is no consensus on a theory of adolescent development.

Social learning theories of adolescent development

In the 1940s and 1950s, some theorists (for example, Dollard & Miller, 1950) used nurture-based learning principles to explain how the social environment controls human behavior. Although the principles that were eventually developed in such *social learning* interpretations of human behavior were primarily derived from data collected on laboratory rats, they represent influential views of how nurture is involved in human functioning, and provide us with nurture conceptions of development.

As with the nurture view in general, there is no one social learning theory of human functioning, or of adolescent behavior in particular. In Chapter 1, for instance, one such position—the theory of socialized anxiety (Davis, 1944)—was presented. It was argued that what people learn in their social environment is to anticipate reward for approved behavior and punishment for disapproved behavior. Anticipation of punishment represents an unpleasant feeling-state for the person— termed socialized (learned) anxiety—and people behave in ways which will diminish or avoid this anxiety. In adolescence, however, Davis argues that the behaviors society will now reward and/or punish are less certain for the person, and thus there is no definite way to decrease socialized anxiety. Accordingly, storm and stress may be involved in this period.

The theory of McCandless

Although Davis's (1944) theory is a nurture one, and one that does speak directly to adolescence, other social learning theories also relate to this period of life. McCandless (1970), a person whose ideas we shall meet throughout this book, has proposed a "drive theory" of adolescent behavior. He views a drive as an energizer of behavior, and specifies that several drives exist in the person (for example, a hunger drive, a drive to avoid pain, and emerging in adolescence for the first time in life, a sex drive). The nurture part of McCandless's theory involves the direction that behavior takes as a consequence of being energized by a particular drive.

One learns in society, through the principles of classical and operant conditioning, that certain behaviors appropriately will *reduce* drive-states. Certain behaviors will reduce hunger, or pain, or sexual arousal. McCandless asserts that those behaviors that reduce drives are most likely to be learned (repeated again in comparable social situations). Drive-reducing behaviors are those that are rewarded (as a consequence of having the drive diminished), while behaviors which do not diminish a drive-state are therefore punished behaviors. Such behaviors are less likely to be repeated.

As a consequence of repeating behavior, people form habits. Thus, when a particular drive-state is aroused, it is probable an individual will behave by emitting the habit. Thus, like Davis, McCandless says people learn to show certain behaviors (habits) because they reduce an internal state. However, unlike Davis, these states involve more than just socialized anxiety, which is a learned association to behavior.

Boyd R. McCandless

To McCandless, the states individuals act to reduce are drive-states, and these states (such as hunger or sex drive) need not be learned. They may be biologically based. Nevertheless, what people do in response to the arousal of *any* drive is a socially learned phenomenon.

Moreover, like Davis, McCandless sees a specific relevance of his ideas to adolescent development. Again, however, this relevance differs from the one that Davis specifies. For instance, as already implied, adolescence is special for McCandless because of the emergence of a new drive: sex. New social learning, new habits, must be formed to reduce this drive in a way that will be rewarded. However, McCandless specifies that society does not reward males and females for the same drive-reducing habits. Consequently, males and females are channeled into developing those habits which are socially prescribed as sex-appropriate. Thus, because of the sex drive, adolescence becomes a time of defining oneself in terms of new, sex-specific habits—habits which are socially defined as leading to reward for people of one or the other sex. Until new habits are formed, and thus new self-definitions are attained, McCandless (1970) would argue that adolescence could very likely be a period of undiminished drives and hence of stress and emotional turmoil.

Later chapters will present a more detailed discussion of how the social learning theory of McCandless leads to a nurture conception of personality and self-concept development, and of sex differences in these developments. Moreover, how these ideas parallel those derived from the more nature-oriented theory of Erikson (1959, 1963) will be discussed. This relation to personality development and to other theories of adolescent functioning is a major reason that McCandless's (1970) drive theory of adolescence has become so prominent. However, at this point it may be noted that as with the nurture view in general, and with social learning theories more specifically, there may be several different social learning conceptions of adolescent functioning.

Nurture theories as part of the mechanistic family

Although there is no *one* nurture theory, but rather a number of nurture theories, it may nevertheless be asserted that all such theories can be integrated into one theoretical family (Reese & Overton, 1970). This synthesis can be made because of an idea in common among these theories that behavior can be explained in terms of stimulus-response connections. In other words, whether we are contrasting the functional analysis approach with the learning theory one, or the reinforcement view of how behavior is produced or maintained with the observational learning conception, or Davis's conception of social learning with the view expressed by McCandless, we see one essential theme running through each conception: Behavior is an environmentally conditioned stimulus-response phenomenon. Because behavior can always be reduced to a stimulus-response connection, the theories we have considered can be placed, despite their diversity, within the same conceptual "camp."

Nurture theories: strengths and weaknesses

Although there is much in these nurture theories to advance the science of human development, there are also some limitations. First, in terms of the assets, we may note that by linking behavior change to observable events, nurture theories at least in part allow for scientific analyses of development. Unlike the nature conceptions of Lorenz (1965), nurture theories of development do suggest variables that can be observed independently of the behaviors these variables are thought to explain. Thus, some of the problems of circular logic and hence of explanation, as exemplified by Lorenz, are avoided. Changes in rewards associated with the behaviors of males and females when entering adolescence can be manipulated independently of the behaviors themselves in order to see whether such alteration can affect behavior change.

Moreover, nurture theories are useful because in stressing the environmental basis of behavior change, they promote a notion of plasticity. As the environmental stimuli change in a variety of ways, behavior, conceived of as a response to such stimulus modification, should also change. Although the recognition of plasticity in the nurture conception of behavior is to be applauded, the *basis* of this plasticity is limited in our opinion by a total reliance on a nurture point of view.

Environmental variation is only one source of organism plasticity. It was argued earlier that as a consequence of genotypic uniqueness, and of nature-nurture interactions more particularly, a basis of plasticity of behavior was provided. The same environmental stimulus cannot have the same effect on all organisms because their interactional history is unique. Nurture theories do not pay sufficient attention to such interaction. Instead they stress the general, invariant effects of stimulation on behavior, and in so doing, do not consider adequately the individual differences in outcomes that even identical nurture histories would involve. Consequently, nurture theories are incomplete since they do not take into account the dynamic interactions of nature and nurture.

Complicating this problem are issues relating to the unit of analysis: stimulus-response connections. Not only are these connections identical across life, but behavior, no matter how complex, is reduced to these connections. This means that all behavior must be understood in terms of these connections. While some components of change do of course involve stimulus-response connections, it may be suggested that adolescence involves a complex of biological, psychological, sociocultural, and historical changes. Such a complex of changes cannot easily or adequately be understood by reduction to a simple stimulus-response unit *or* by reference to a theoretical orientation that only considers one source of behavior change.

Not all theories emphasizing nature-nurture interaction in adolescent development place equal stress on both sources of development. Lerner and Spanier (1978) have noted that there are at least three types of interaction theories of development: "weak," "moderate," and "strong" types.

A *weak interaction theory* places primary stress on one source, usually nature. This source determines the sequence and character of development. In such conceptions, development proceeds in accordance with a "maturational ground plan" (Erikson, 1959), or with some other nature-based scheme. Nurture can speed up, slow down, or even stop ("fixate") development (Emmerich, 1968), but it can in no way alter the ordering or characteristics of change.

A *moderate interaction theory* places equal stress on nature and nurture, but sees the two sources as independent of each other. Although they interact to provide a basis for any and all behavior development, one does not change the quality of the other over the course of their interaction (Sameroff, 1975). Piaget's influential cognitive development theory is presented in this chapter, and in greater detail in

---

INSIGHT INTO ADOLESCENCE

Charles Maurice de Talleyrand, born in 1754 in France, had a most unhappy childhood, which he described in his book *Memories*. Nevertheless, at 19 he became an abbé, at 34 a bishop, at 35 a revolutionist, at 42 a minister, and at 52 a duke. He served and wrecked a number of governments, and made a fortune in office by accepting enormous bribes. On one occasion he said, "The only good principle is to have none."

At the age of 16 he was sent to the College of Saint-Sulpice. This experience, described in *Memories*, is quoted here.

I spent three years at Saint-Sulpice, and hardly spoke at all during the whole time; people thought I was supercilious and often reproached me with being so. This seemed to me so to point out how little they knew me, that I deigned no reply;they then said that my arrogance was beyond all endurance. Good Heavens! I was neither arrogant nor proud: I was merely a harmless young man, extremely miserable and inwardly irritated. *People say*, I often thought to myself, *that I am fit for nothing*. . . . Fit for nothing. . . . After giving way to despondency for a few moments, a strong and comforting feeling cheered

me, and I discovered *that I was fit for something, even for good and noble deeds*. What forebodings, a thousand times dispelled, did not then cross my mind, always placing me under a spell which I was unable to explain!

The library of Saint-Sulpice had been enriched by gifts from Cardinal de Fleury; its works were numerous and carefully selected. I spent my days there reading the productions of great historians, the private lives of statesmen and moralists, and a few poets. I was particularly fond of books of travel. A new land, the dangers of a storm, the picture of a wreck, the description of a country bearing traces of great changes, sometimes of upheavals, all this had deep interest for me. Sometimes, when I considered these voyages to distant lands, these dreadful scenes described so vividly in the writings of modern explorers, it seemed to me that my lot was not so hopeless as I had thought. A good library affords true comfort to all the dispositions of the soul.

My . . . really useful education dates from this time; it was self-taught in lonely silence.

Source: Talleyrand, C. M. Memoirs of the *Prince de Talleyrand*. Translated by Beaufort in S.K. Padover (ed.) *Confessions and Self Portraits*. Paris-Boston, 1895.

Chapter 9, as the ideal model of a moderate interactional theory, and one which has much relevence for adolescent development (Elkind, 1967).

Finally, a *strong interaction theory* is one which not only sees both nature and nurture as inextricably involved in all behavior development, but sees the two as reciprocally related. Part of that which we call nature is nurture and vice versa (Overton, 1973). This strong view of nature-nurture interaction is consistent with the idea of dynamic interactionism.

The role of weak interaction theories

Perhaps no other type of theory has been more influential in the study of adolescent development than has the weak interaction type. Here the contributions of Sigmund Freud, Anna Freud, and Erik Erikson stand out.

The classic examples of such weak interaction theories are found in the psychoanalytic literature. Sigmund Freud's theory of psychosexual development and the extension of his work to adolescent development by his daughter, Anna Freud, are examples of such theories. Additionally, Erik Erikson's theory of psychosocial development (1959, 1963, 1964, 1968) is also a prime example of this type of theory. Considerable attention will be devoted in succeeding chapters to Erikson's theory because of the importance it has for adolescence. Because Erikson's ideas build on those of Sigmund and Anna Freud, this chapter is intended to provide a basis for future discussion of Erikson by focusing on the ideas of the two Freuds.

SIGMUND FREUD'S THEORY OF PSYCHOSEXUAL STAGE DEVELOPMENT

Sigmund Freud was born in Freiberg, Moravia, in 1856 and died in London, England, in 1939. He lived most of his life, however, in Vienna, where in 1881 he obtained his medical degree. In fact, the only time he ever set foot on United States soil was to visit G. Stanley Hall at the twentieth anniversary of Clark University (in 1909), of which Hall was the founder and president.

Although trained as a physician, and earning most of his fame in the field of psychiatry, Freud was also a well-versed research scientist. As such, he was well acquainted with and influenced by work in many areas of scientific inquiry. In the field of physics, ideas relating to the concept of energy were being investigated. One idea—the law of the conservation of energy—had a profound influence on Freud. This principle states that physical energy can be neither created nor destroyed, but only transformed. For example, steam energy from beneath the earth's surface is used to generate mechanical energy in turbines of power plants, which in turn transforms the spent mechanical energy into electrical energy, which is used to create heat energy, boiling the water on a pot on a stove to create steam energy again.

The concept of libido

Freud saw a parallel between the transformation of energy in the physical world and events that occur in mental life. Freud hypothesized that humans are really complicated energy systems (Hall, 1954), and that they are energized just as are other physical systems. Life, he hypothesized, is governed by a human mental (or psychic) energy, termed *libido*. Libido cannot be created or destroyed. Humans are born with a certain amount of libido, and instead of it being transformed into another type of energy, a transformation occurs involving changes in location within the body over the course of development.

Rather than being distributed evenly in all body parts, at different points in life libido is localized in specific body zones. Such concentration of energy leads to an excessive amount of tension if there is not some way for the tension to be released. Freud specified that tension could be released if stimulation were applied to the bodily area where libido was centered. An unpleasant feeling-state (tension) would be relieved, and in turn, a pleasurable feeling (tension reduction) would occur. The tension reduction resulting from appropriate stimulation is *gratification*. In short, stimulation to the appropriate bodily zone would provide libidinal gratification.

But what determines what body zone has the libido? Freud said that there was a universal, biological sequence of libido progression. In accordance with a person's nature, libido would be centered in particular body zones for certain predetermined lengths of time (critical periods). Thus, where the libido was concentrated would determine what sort of stimulation to the person would be appropriate (that is, gratifying), and what sort of stimulation would not be appropriate.

Although it may be apparent that the experiences the person encounters determine whether appropriate stimulation is given, such experiences do not alter the order of bodily concentration of libido—or in Freud's terms, the stage of psychosexual development. Thus, experience can help or hinder the development of certain feeling-states, but it is nature which determines where and when libido moves.

To see this interrelation between nature and nurture the sequence of changes that Freud specified will be considered. He saw libido moving through five "sites" of bodily localization. Thus, there are five stages of psychosexual development.

The oral stage

Freud said the first erogenous zone in development is the mouth region. The libido remains here for approximately the first year of life. In this stage the infant obtains gratification through stimulation of the mouth in one of two ways. The infant can bring things into its mouth and suck on them (for example, the mother's breast), or later, when teeth develop, can bite on things. However, it is possible for such gratification not to occur. An infant might be deprived of needed stimulation because of frequent or prolonged mother absence. When the infant's attempts to obtain appropriate stimulation are blocked or frustrated, problems in the infant's psychosexual development may occur. If frustration is extensive enough, *fixation* may result. Some of the infant's libido will remain *fixed* (will stay) at the oral zone, and when the infant moves to the next stage—in accordance with "nature's" timetable— all the libido that could have moved on to the next body zone will not now do so. Some libido always will be tied into the person's oral zone for the rest of life. Such an oral fixation will mean that for the rest of life the person will attempt to obtain the gratification missed earlier. Thus, the emotional problems the person has as an adult will be based on these early fixations.

For instance, a fixation in the sucking portion of the oral stage might result in an adult who is always attempting to acquire or hoard things (Hall, 1954). This might show itself through attempts to acquire wealth or power or, more obviously, through eating excessive amounts of food. Other examples might be an older child who relentlessly sucks his or her thumb or an adult who chain-smokes. Alternatively, a fixation in the oral biting (or oral aggressive) period of this stage might result in an adult who continually is aggressive verbally. Someone who constantly makes "biting remarks" about others—an extremely sarcastic or cynical person—might be fixated in the oral biting portion of this stage.

The anal stage

From about the end of the first year of life through the third year, the libido is centered in the anal region of the body. Here the child obtains gratification through exercise of the anal muscles opening and closing the sphincter, allowing fecal waste products to be let out or retained. In this stage Freud also spoke of two subperiods: an anal explusive period, where one obtains gratification from loosening the anal muscles and allowing the feces to be discarded, and the anal retentive period, where gratification is obtained through retention of the feces.

Fixations may result from frustrating experiences in this stage also. Since this stage usually corresponds in our culture to the time in which people are toilet trained, anal explusive fixations may result from too severe toilet training. This may result in an adult who "lets everything hang out"—a messy, disorderly, or wasteful person (Hall, 1954). Alternatively, an anal retentive fixation might result in an adult who is excessively neat and orderly. Such an adult might also be seen to be "uptight," keeping everything in, including his or her emotions.

The phallic stage

Here one must distinguish between the development of boys and girls. For both sexes, the phallic stage, which to Freud spans the period from about the third to the fifth years, involves the libido moving to the genital area. However, it is necessary to discuss the sexes separately because of the structural differences in their genitalia.

The male phallic stage The libido moves to the boy's genital area, and gratification is obtained through manipulation and stimulation of the genitals. Although masturbation certainly would provide a source of such gratification, Freud believed that the boy's mother is most likely to provide this stimulation. Because mother is providing this stimulation, the boy comes to desire his mother sexually (incestuously). But he recognizes that his father stands in the way of his incestuous desires, and this arouses negative feelings for the father.

Freud labels this emotional reaction the *Oedipus complex*. Oedipus was a character in Greek mythology who (unknowingly) killed his father and then married his mother. Freud saw a parallel between this myth and events in the lives of all humans. He believed that the psychosexual stages applied universally to all humans, and that phenomena occurring within each stage—such as the Oedipus complex— were nature-based and hence unavoidable. Thus, he argued that all males experience an Oedipal complex. All experience incestuous love for their mother and feelings of antagonism toward their father.

But when the boy realizes that the father is his rival for his mother's love, the boy comes to fear that the father will punish him for his incestuous desires in the form of castration. As a result, the boy experiences *castration anxiety*. Because of the power of this anxiety, the boy gives up his desires for his mother; in turn, he identifies with his father.

Identification with father is a most important development. As a result of identification, the boy comes to model himself after the father. The boy forms a structure of his personality which Freud terms the *superego*. The superego has two components. The first, the *ego-ideal*, is the representation of the perfect, or ideal, man (the "father figure"). In modeling himself after father, the boy thus becomes a "man" in his society. The second part of the superego is the *conscience*, the internalization of society's standards, ethics, and morals. Thus, this internalization brings about moral development (Bronfenbrenner, 1960).

At many points in the series of events of this stage, experiences can unfavorably alter the outcome. If for some reason the boy does not successfully resolve his Oedipal complex, he may not give up his love for his mother. As an adult he may be inordinately tied to her, or he may identify with her instead of with his father. If this occurs, he might incorporate part of the mother's superego, possibly in regard to choice of sexual partner in adulthood. Part of the mother's ego-ideal involves the type of person she wants or has as a mate. Being a mother, she has chosen a male in this regard. The boy, in adopting his mother's ego-ideal, might also choose a male sexual partner when an adult. Thus, one possible outcome of an unresolved Oedipal complex would be male homosexuality.

The female phallic stage Freud himself was never satisfied with his own formulation of the female phallic stage (Bronfenbrenner, 1960). As the libido moves to the genital area, gratification is obtained through manipulation and stimulation of the genitals. Although presumably it is the mother who provides the major source of this stimulation for the girl, the girl (for reasons not perfectly clear even to Freud himself) falls in love with her father. Then, analogous to what occurs with boys, she desires to possess incestuously her father, but realizes that her mother stands in her way. At this point, however, the similarity with male development is markedly altered.

The female is afraid that the mother will punish her for the incestuous desires she maintains toward the father. Although it is possible that the girl first fears that this punishment will take the form of castration, her awareness of her own genital structure causes her to realize that, in a sense, she already has been punished. That is, the girl perceives that she does not have a penis, but only an inferior (to Freud) organ, a clitoris.

Sigmund Freud

Hence, the girl is unable to resolve her Oedipal complex in the same way as the male. This is one reason the conflict is sometimes labeled differently for girls, as the *Electra complex*. The male experiences castration anxiety and this impels him to resolve his Oedipal complex. Since the girl does not have a penis, she cannot very well experience this emotion. The girl experiences only a roughly similar emotion, *penis envy*. The girl envies the male for his possession of a genital structure of which she has been deprived.

Penis envy still impels the girl to resolve the Oedipal conflict. She relinquishes her incestuous love for her father, and identifies with mother. She then forms the superego component of her personality, which, again, is composed of the ego-ideal (here the ideal female, or "mother figure") and the conscience. However, Freud believed that only castration anxiety could lead to complete superego development, and thus, because females experience penis envy and not castration anxiety, they do not attain full superego development. This lack, Freud believed, takes the form of incomplete conscience development. In short, to Freud (1950), females are never as morally developed as males. We will consider this provocative idea in Chapter 10.

Finally, as with males, difficulties in the female's phallic stage could have profound effects on adult psychosexual functioning. Thus, in a manner analogous to males, female homosexuality could result from extreme difficulties occurring in the female's phallic stage.

The latency stage

After the end of the phallic stage—at about 5 years of age—the libido submerges, in a manner analogous to an icéberg. The libido is not localized in any body zone from the end of the phallic stage until puberty occurs—typically at about 12 years of age. Freud said that the libido is latent. Because it does not localize itself in any bodily zone until puberty, no erogenous zones emerge or exist.

The genital stage

At puberty the libido again emerges. Again it emerges in the genital area, but now it takes a mature, or adult, form. If the person has not been too severely restricted in his or her psychosexual development in the first five years of life, adult sexuality may now occur. Sexuality can not be directed to heterosexual union and reproduction. Although remnants—or traces—of the effects of the earlier stages may significantly affect the person at this time in life, it is only when the genital stage emerges that the person's libido can be gratified through directing it into reproductive functions.

A critique of Freud's ideas

For Freud, the form of adolescent and adult development was determined in early life. To him, the first five years of life, involving the first three psychosexual stages, were critical stages for functioning in later life. As such, Freud's concerns with adolescence and adulthood were only secondary ones. The behaviors in these periods were shaped in earlier life, and if one wanted to understand an adolescent or an adult, one had to deal with the fixations, conflicts, and frustrations that had occurred in the first five years.

Several objections to these conclusions from Freud's ideas can be raised. Freud was a critical periods theorist. As such, he saw nature as having a primary role in development independent of the contribution of nurture. Why such a conception is inadequate on both logical and empirical grounds was discussed in Chapter 5. Indeed, one may object to Freud's ideas precisely because of the sources of information he used to form his ideas.

Freud had a very biased source of "data." He worked in Victorian Europe, a period in history noted for its repressive views about sexuality. As a practicing psychiatrist, his main source of data was the memories of *adult* neurotic patients, people who came for treatment of emotional and behavioral problems interfering with their everyday functioning. Freud used his psychoanalytic therapy methods to discover the source of his patients' emotional problems. Through work with such patients he attempted to construct a theory of *early* development. But these patients were adults from one particular historical period—*not* children. Thus, Freud constructed a theory about early development in children without actually observing them.

Freud's adult patients reconstructed their early, long-gone past through *retrospection*. With Freud's help they tried to remember what happened to them when they were 1, 2, or 3 years of age. This is how Freud obtained the information to build his theory. But it is quite possible that adults may forget, distort, or misremember early memories. Therefore, because his data were unchecked for failures of early memories, Freud likely obtained biased information. Furthermore, Freud's patients cannot necessarily be viewed as representative of other nonneurotic Victorian adults or, for that matter, of all other humans living during other times in history.

Thus, one may question whether Freud, if he were working today, would devise the same theory of psychosexual development. For example, would Freud today find females viewing their genital structure as inferior and thus experiencing penis envy? Would he still maintain that females are not as morally developed as males, and would he find no evidence of psychosexual functioning during the years of latency?

Finally, even if one were to ignore all the above criticisms, one might question whether Freud's ideas represented all the possible developmental phenomena that could occur in each stage of life. Is latency necessarily a period of relative quiet, a time when few significant events occur for the child? Is adolescence just a time when events in preceding life make themselves evident? Or are there characteristics of adolescence that are special to that period? Interestingly, although accepting most of Freud's ideas as correct, it was other psychoanalytically oriented thinkers who led the way in showing that Freud was incomplete in his depiction of developmental phenomena within and across stages. Erikson (1959, 1963), for instance, showed that by attending to the demands placed on the individual by society as the person developed, important phenomena could be identified in latency, in adolescence, and across the rest of the life span as well. Similarly, Anna Freud (1969) said that if one focused on events that occurred only at puberty, one would see special characteristics of the adolescent period.

Erikson and Anna Freud did not so much contradict Freud as did they transcend him. Both reached this point not by adding anything new to Freud's basic ideas, but rather by focusing on the implications of one aspect of Freud's theory to which he himself did not greatly attend. We now consider Freud's ideas about the structure of personality; the different focus taken by Anna Freud is discussed in order to illustrate the implications of this focus for an interactional theory of adolescence. Again, this presentation is intended as preparation for the ideas provided by Erikson as a consequence of his corresponding focus.

Freud believed that the human personality is made up of several different mental structures. One of these structures, the superego, arises out of the resolution of the Oedipal conflict. Another of these, termed the *id*, was defined as an innate structure of the personality. The id "contains" all the person's libido. The id is thus involved in all the person's attempts to obtain pleasure, or gratification, through appropriate stimulation. In fact, because the id is the center for the libido, and since the libido creates tensions that require appropriate stimulation, resulting in pleasure, Freud said that the id functions in accordance with the *pleasure principle*. Thus, in emphasizing the implications of the gratification of libidinal energy, Freud emphasized implications of the biologically based id on human functioning. In addition to the superego and the id, Freud specified a third structure of the personality, the *ego*.

The function of the id is solely to obtain pleasure. Thus, the id compels a person in the oral stage to seek appropriate stimulation—for example, the mother's nipple. When the stimulation is not available, the id functions in a particular way which Freud termed the *primary process*. Simply, the primary process is a fantasy, or imaginary, process. When the mother's nipple is not present, the child imagines that it is there. But such fantasies are not sufficient to allow the child to obtain appropriate stimulation. One cannot just fantasize. One must interact with reality. Accordingly, another structure of the personality is formed, a structure whose sole function is to adapt to reality, to allow the person actually to obtain needed stimulation and hence survive. This other structure of the personality is the ego.

Because the ego develops only to deal with reality, to allow the person to adjust to the demands of the real world and hence to survive, Freud said the ego functions in accordance with the *reality principle*. The ego has processes that enable it to adjust to and deal with reality. This *secondary process* involves such things as cognition and perception. Through the functioning of these processes, the ego is capable of perceiving and knowing the real world, and thus adapting to it.

Although Freud spoke about the implications of all three of the structures of the mind—the id, the ego, and the superego, the sum of which comprises a person's personality structures—he emphasized the implications of the id on human functioning. Thus, in describing human psychosexual development, Freud was viewing human beings as essentially biological and psychological in nature. On the other hand, Freud did not spend a good deal of time discussing the implications of the ego. This focus is what Erikson (1963) and Anna Freud provide.

ANNA FREUD: ADOLESCENCE AS A DEVELOPMENTAL DISTURBANCE

In agreement with her father, Anna Freud (1969) notes that all structures of the personality are present when the ego and the superego form to join with the innately present id. Moreover, like her father, she believes that all three of these structures are present by the end of the third psychosexual stage, the phallic stage, or in other words, by about the end of the fifth year of life.

Both Freuds contend that when all structures are present, they present different directives to the person. The id only "wants" pleasure (gratification). It is not concerned with either survival or morality. The superego, at the other extreme, contains the conscience and cares nothing for pleasure. Only morality (and a stern

Victorian view of it at that!) is important. Thus, while the id might pressure the person for sexual gratification, the superego would condemn the person for such a desire. The ego, however, has to balance these two counterdirected types of pressures.

The ego's only role is survival. It must defend itself from dangers to that survival, whether those dangers are from within or without. The conflict between the id and the superego represents a danger to survival. If the person would spend all his or her time in conflict about action, there would be no energy left to deal with the demands placed on the person from outside the self (for example, from society). Accordingly, the ego develops *defense mechanisms,* that is, ways to avoid dealing with at least one set of the conflicting demands imposed from within. Such avoidance would rid the person of the internal conflict, and "free up" energy for external adaptive demands.

The defense mechanisms developed by the ego (mechanisms like *repression, rationalization, substitution, projection*) involve taking the pressures imposed by the id and placing them in a particular area of the mind, the *unconscious.* This area contains material most difficult to bring into awareness (into the conscious). The reason that the id pressures are defended against, and not those of the superego, is that the latter's pressures represent the demands and rules of society. If one got rid of these demands—internalized as one's conscience—this would mean that one would get rid of one's morality. We term people who apparently have no internalized morality, who do not obey rules of society, *sociopaths.* Typically, society has severe sanctions against sociopaths, often defining their behavior as illegal, and sometimes imprisoning them. Accordingly, it would not be adaptive for the ego to put the superego in the unconscious, and so it is the id material which is placed in this area of the mind.

To both Freuds, the typical person establishes a balance among the id, ego, and superego by 5 years of age. By the time latency has been reached, ego defenses appropriate for dealing with all pressures, or drives, from the id have been established. The person is thus in equilibrium. However, although people may differ in regard to the character of this balance, depending on events in the first three stages of life, all people will, Anna Freud (1969) claims, have their balance destroyed in adolescence.

Anna Freud

Unlike her father, Anna Freud sees adolescence as a period in life presenting demands for the person which are not *just* those relating to earlier life. These demands involve new pressures being put on the ego, and require new adaptational solutions for the person. The new demands on the ego are universal, she contends, because the pressures that create them are universal too. To understand this, let us consider the special alterations that Anna Freud (1969) associates with adolescence.

Alterations in the drives

With puberty comes an adult genital drive. Thus, the balance among the id, ego, and superego is upset as this new feeling-state comes to dominate the person's being. Because this alteration is an inevitable, universal one, Anna Freud argues that an inescapable imbalance in development occurs. As such, adolescence is necessarily a period of *developmental disturbance*. Although for theoretical reasons that differ from Hall, Lorenz, Davis, or McCandless, Anna Freud also says that adolescence is a period of storm and stress.

In sum, because of the universal emergence of the genital drive at puberty, the adolescent is necessarily involved "in dangers which did not exist before and with which he is not accustomed to deal. Since, at this stage, he lives and functions still as a member of his family unit, he runs the risk of allowing the new genital urges to connect with his old love objects, that is, with his parents, brothers, or sisters" (Freud, 1969, p. 7). Since such incestuous relations are not condoned in any known culture (Winch, 1971), some defense against it must be established. The genital alteration thus requires a personality alteration.

Alterations in the ego organization

Anna Freud claims that the new drive throws the person into upheaval. It causes unpredictable behavior, as the person tries out all the formerly useful defenses to deal with the new drive. This, she contends, puts strain on the person since what is involved is using a set of mechanisms, balanced for one state, on another, quantitatively greater and qualitatively different state. As such, not only does the adolescent try more of the same defenses, but also he or she eventually forms new types of mechanisms. For example, in relation to the new cognitive abilities which emerge in adolescence, the adolescent comes for the first time to use highly abstract, intellectual reasons to justify his or her behavior. This new ego defense mechanism is thus termed *intellectualization*. However, such alterations are still not sufficient to resolve the adolescent disturbance.

Alterations in object relations

Despite the new ego defenses, the danger of inappropriately acting out the genital drive is so great that "nothing helps here except a complete discarding of the people who were the important love objects of the child, that is, the parents" (Freud, 1969, p. 8). Indeed, the new defenses are useful in helping the adolescent to alter the relations he or she has had with these "love objects." Defenses like intellectualization often involve quite involved rationales for why the parents are "stupid," are "ineffective," or possess "useless . . . beliefs and conventions" (Freud, 1969, p. 8). Of course, in moving away from parents as the major object of social relations, the adolescent does not necessarily become nonsocial. To the contrary, in fact, there is a last alteration that follows from the break in ties with parents.

Alterations in ideals and social relations

When the adolescent has broken the ties with the parents, he or she has also rejected the attitudes, values, and beliefs formerly shared with them. Anna Freud argues that the adolescent is thus left without social ties or ideals. Substitutes are found for both of these in the peer group, she suggests. Moreover, these new social relations are "justified" not only on the basis of shared ideology (for example, in accordance with the intellectualization defense, adolescents might say that the peers understand them while parents do not). More importantly, attachment to the peer group provides a mechanism wherein the new genital drive—which started all alterations initially—may be dealt with in a setting less dangerous to the adaptation of the adolescent than is the family setting.

A critique of Anna Freud's ideas

Anna Freud, her father, and others who use nature bases for their ideas share the limitations of such a conception. Moreover, because she sees the alterations of adolescence as being biologically imperative and hence universal, she clearly describes adolescence in terms which acknowledge little plasticity within people, and few differences between people. She is led to the depiction of adolescence as necessarily stormy and stressful.

It has been argued, however, that such statements simply are not consistent with a vast amount of existing data. Contrary to what she indicates, the data of Bandura (1964), Douvan and Adelson (1966), and Offer (1969) clearly indicate that most adolescents (1) do not have stormy, stressful periods; (2) do not break ties with parents; (3) continue to share the ideals of their parents; and (4) choose friends who, like they do, have ideals consistent with those of their parents.

By taking a weak interactionist stance in regard to the nature-nurture issue, both Sigmund and Anna Freud are led to describe human (and consequently adolescent) development in a manner inconsistent with the known character of the adolescent transition.

MODERATE INTERACTIONS AND PIAGET'S THEORY OF DEVELOPMENT

As already noted, theories which stress moderate interaction see both nature and nurture variables as equally involved in development, but view each source as independent of the other. Although both sources are always necessary, each remains unaltered by the other over the course of their interaction. In a sense, this idea of interaction is akin to the "how much of each" question regarding nature-nurture interaction that was rejected in Chapter 5. Both this question and the moderate interaction view see nature and nurture (heredity and environment, or organism and experience) as independently manipulated, independently existing sources.

Such theories are useful in that they lead to studies wherein factors associated with organism and environment can be assessed for the separate, main effects on development, as well as for their combined ("interactive") contribution. One can study the effects of age (or stage) of development and of training experiences (for example, various types of learning programs) on test scores of educational achievement. Thus, one might learn how the organism's stage and particular experiences contribute to achievement alone and in combination with each other. Questions could be answered about whether stage, experience, or some particular combination of the two most facilitates achievement.

Yet in reviewing the logic and data concerning nature-nurture interaction, the problems with viewing variables such as nature and nurture, or organism and environment, as independent were suggested. Organisms cannot be separated from experience, and thus although studies designed to be consistent with a moderate interaction view might give information about questions such as those above, this information will be limited.

Piaget's view of nature-nurture interaction

Jean Piaget is the leading theorist in the area of cognitive development. Much of Chapter 9 will be devoted to a fuller discussion of his ideas. Here we shall look at issues relating to his moderate interaction views. According to Piaget (1950, 1970), cognitive development progresses through four stages. In each stage of development the *structure* of thought is qualitatively different. For instance, it has been already stated that adolescence is a period in which new hypothetical and abstract ("formal") thought capabilities emerge. Like Sigmund Freud, Piaget believes the stages he defines are universal. One proceeds through these stages in an invariant sequence. However, seemingly unlike Freud, Piaget claims that the stages come about as a consequence of a mutual influence of nature and nurture on each other. Specifically, cognitive development is said to arise from the action of the organism on the environment *and* from the action of the environment on the organism.

Thus, Piaget's (1950, 1970) theory is one which does seem to accept a fuller role for experience in providing an interactive basis of stage progression, and thus may be seen as a more moderate stance in regard to interaction. However, because, under close analysis, there is not as full a consideration of environmental or experiential changes as there is of organism changes, Piaget's theory is, as Brainerd (1978) has asserted, perhaps quite close to the maturational (or in present terms, weak interactionist) position of Freud.

Although Piaget continually emphasizes that developmental structural change arises from an interaction between organism and environment processes, it is only the organism that is seen as going through changes. Although the organism's *conception* of the environment changes, constant flux of the physical and social world is never simultaneously considered by Piaget. Additionally, the impact of these physical and social environmental changes on the structure of the stages is totally disregarded. Environmentally based interindividual differences can only affect the rate of change and the final stage of development reached. Changes in the environment do not affect the sequence and characteristics of the stages themselves. Thus, as Riegel (1976b) asserts, for Piaget, the organism changes but the environment does not.

By disregarding the impact of continual social and physical changes in the environment, Piaget ignores what he claims is the source of developmental progression: organism-environment interactions. If only the organism's changes are considered and the environment's are not, then no variation in structural change may be attributed to variation in the environment, and nothing can be related to environmental change. The only source of variation can be the organism, and only organism changes can predict organism changes. A problem of circular logic is raised because of Piaget's failure to consider environmental changes as actively contributing to development.

STRONG INTERACTION THEORIES

If it is maintained that the environment—in both its physical and its social aspects—is continually changing, and if such continual alterations are as influential in developmental progression as those changes having their primary focus in the organism, then it seems that a nature-based analysis of development is inappropriate. Moreover, if environmental processes are given a coequal status, then since there is an infinite variety of environmental variations that can occur, particular progressions associated with any one set of ideas need not be the only developmental change processes and sequences that may occur. Piaget's four stages and the five psychosexual stages of Freud, and the respective sequences of each, represent only instances of a much larger class of stages and sequences which could occur. In other words, if one takes a complete or strong view of interaction between nature and nurture variables, then the potential for plasticity in developmental sequencing and outcomes is emphasized. Consequently, there is a lack of focus on (or even hope for) universals in developmental progression.

Moreover, it follows that if one stresses that behavior changes arise from the combined influence of all levels of organization (inner-biological, individual-psychological, outer-physical, sociocultural-historical), then to explain adolescent development fully, data must be collected from all interacting levels. It is the interdependence among the levels, and not any one level itself, that provides the basis of development (Sampson, 1977).

Research studies designed from this point of view may often be complex. Research methods useful to study change at all levels of analysis are required. In the next chapter the many dimensions of developmental research that may be used in such a pluralistic, multidisciplinary effort will be considered.

CHAPTER SUMMARY

Major debates in science revolve around differences in the interpretation of facts. Alternative theories provide contrasting explanations for why particular behaviors characterize adolescents. A case in point is the phenomenon of storm and stress in adolescence. Although most recent studies indicate that stormy, stressful episodes are not characteristic of most adolescents' lives, nature-, nurture-, and interactionist-based theories of adolescent development all attempt to account for the absence or presence of such behavior. The characteristics of this range of theories are reviewed in this chapter.

Hall's recapitulationist theory is offered as a prime example of a nature-based conception of adolescent development, as is Lorenz's instinct theory of human behavior. Here adolescents are depicted as oriented to aggression because of the "innate militarism" of youth.

Some of the nurture theories stress the functional relations that exist between stimuli and responses—and do not use terms that pertain to mental or cognitive links between these elements. Other theorists stress such terms. In addition, some nurture theorists stress the role of reinforcement in linking stimuli and responses, while others stress that observations of modeled behavior in the absence of reinforcement can lead to the acquisition of responses.

McCandless proposes a social learning theory of adolescent development that involves learning in society—through principles of classical and operant conditioning—that certain behaviors will reduce drive-states. In adolescence one learns those drive-reducing behaviors that are associated with the socially specified roles for an adolescent male or female.

In addition to various nature or nurture theories, there are several types of interactionist theories. Such theories may be categorized on the basis of the strength of the interaction thought to exist between nature and nurture. The leading interactionist theories of adolescent development see nurture as only an inhibitor or facilitator of primarily nature-based developments. Erikson, Sigmund Freud, and Anna Freud all have theories that fall in this *weak-interaction* category.

Sigmund Freud's theory of psychosexual development sees psychic energy, or *libido,* as moving to various areas of the body in an invariant, universal sequence. Where libido is centered determines the type of gratification needed; the role of environment is to provide experiences that may or may not offer gratification. Sigmund Freud divided *psychosexual* development into five stages *(oral, anal, phallic, latency,* and *genital)* and proposed that all interactions important for adolescent development occurred within the first three stages. Thus the genital period—which begins with puberty—is seen to involve only developments whose nature was determined in earlier life.

Anna Freud, however, revises her father's ideas. She sees adolescence as a universal developmental disturbance precisely because of the emergence of the genital drive at puberty. This alteration in drive level requires the ego to change its defense mechanisms in order to deal adaptively with the new impulses associated with an adult genital capacity. In turn, this alteration in ego organization leads to changes in object relations and in ideals and social relations.

Other interactionist theories see nature and nurture interacting, but being unchanged by each other over the course of their relation; these are termed *moderate interaction* theories. The theory of Piaget is suggested as an instance of a moderate interaction theory. Still others see nature and nurture as dynamically interactive in that each is both a product and a producer of the other; these are termed *strong interaction* theories. This is the point of view the present authors favor.

7

RESEARCH METHODS
IN THE STUDY OF
ADOLESCENT DEVELOPMENT

CHAPTER OVERVIEW

To understand adolescence fully, it is necessary to know something about the way in which researchers go about investigating human development and social relations. This chapter discusses various observational techniques, data collection procedures, and research designs used to study adolescence. In addition, some common problems often encountered in research are presented.

DIMENSIONS OF RESEARCH METHODS IN ADOLESCENT DEVELOPMENT

The Normative-Explanatory Dimension
The Naturalistic-Manipulative Dimension
The Atheoretical-Theoretical Dimension
The Ahistorical-Historical Dimension

DESIGNS OF DEVELOPMENTAL RESEARCH

The Longitudinal Design
The Cross-Sectional Design
The Time-Lag Design
Sequential Strategies of Design
A Sequential Study of Adolescent Personality Development

SOME GENERAL METHODOLOGICAL PROBLEMS OF ADOLESCENT DEVELOPMENTAL RESEARCH

Contamination
Researcher Effects on Subject Responses
Reconstruction through Retrospection
Faulty Logic
Inadequate Definition of Concepts
Sampling
Overgeneralization

ISSUES TO CONSIDER

What is the role of research in science?

What are the differences among studies located along the normative-explanatory dimension of adolescent developmental research?

What are the differences among studies located along the naturalistic-manipulative dimension?

What are the assets and limitations of research studies using questionnaires and interviews?

How do studies that are atheoretical differ from those that are theoretical?

Why is the ahistorical-historical dimension central in developmental research?

What are the three major designs for developmental research that have been used traditionally, and what are the assets and limitations of each?

What is the nature of sequential research designs, and how do they avoid confounding the contributions of the three components of developmental change?

What are the general methodological problems of adolescent developmental research?

What are the characteristics of the various types of sampling procedures that exist?

What are the major problems of overgeneralization that exist in the developmental research literature?

hy must the study of adolescent development involve research? What is wrong if people just sit back in their armchairs and tell others what adolescents are like, and never actually study if what they say corresponds to actual behavior? Why would a scientist be more likely to believe a statement about development based on the observation of adolescents than a view which is in no way backed up by observations?

The answers to all these questions rest on the commitment to the *scientific method*, an approach used by researchers to study the phenomena of the world. The basic characteristic of scientific study is *empiricism*, a view that knowledge is achieved through the systematic collection and analysis of data. This characteristic is the major difference between philosophy and science. Those who are not scientists may find knowledge in ways independent of empirical research (for example, through spiritual beliefs). However, for a scientist to know something about the development of adolescents, people must be observed, questioned, interviewed, or in some way examined. One cannot rely *just* on what one believes or wants to believe about behavior. Rather, one's beliefs must be tested by determining whether such beliefs are supported when actual behavior is studied.

Up to this point in the text, concepts and theories about adolescent development rather than "facts" about adolescents have been emphasized. However, once understood, any theory must be related to facts in order for it to have use. A scientific *theory* is a statement of the way in which variables are related to each other and from which hypotheses can be drawn. Stated differently, a theory is simply an idea which leads to the generation of additional facts (Hempel, 1966; Lerner, 1976; Winch & Spanier, 1974). Theory must be tied to the examination of data in order for it to have a use in science. The set of specific procedures by which a science makes observations and collects and examines data may be termed its *research methods*.

There are several problems typically encountered in research on adolescence and in research on human development generally. Preceding discussions have suggested that many factors contribute to development and that, as a consequence, development may take many forms and directions. To observe such plasticity, it is unlikely that any one means of observing adolescent development would be appropriate for all contexts, times, or people. Indeed, there are many research methods that may be used to study development. And although each method has its special advantages, each also has limitations.

In order to understand the range of methods that may be used in the life-span, multidisciplinary study of adolescent development, and to become sensitive to the problems in existing data and the dangers such problems present for future data, this discussion will be organized in two parts. First, the variety of research methods that can be used to study adolescent development will be discussed. Second, general problems in research, and especially those in human developmental research, will be considered. Ways to avoid such problems are suggested. A general theme throughout this presentation will be that the method one uses depends on the issues of theoretical interest. In other words, it will be argued that the questions about development one asks determine what methods one ought to use; the questions one asks should not be determined by the particular method one likes to use. Theory should determine method and not the other way around.

DIMENSIONS OF RESEARCH METHODS
IN ADOLESCENT DEVELOPMENT

In this portion of the chapter various developmental research methods are discussed. It is useful to present these methods as varying along four dimensions. A dimension is an imaginary line continuously running between two end points. For instance, psychologists often talk of personality dimensions like active-passive, or dominant-submissive. A person can have a characteristic at either extreme or anywhere in between the two ends on any dimension. Any given person can fall (be located) at one point on one dimension (for example, the middle) and at some other point on another (for example, the extreme). Another person could have other locations along these dimensions, depending on his or her individual characteristics.

Any developmental study has characteristics which allow it to be located along some point of four dimensions of research. Location at one point on one dimension does not necessarily imply a location on the other dimensions. The fact that any one study could fall along different points of each dimension means that an almost limitless array of strategies of research is available to the developmental researcher. To see this variety let us turn to the first dimension of developmental research methods.

The normative-explanatory dimension

McCandless (1967, 1970) was the first to present the four independent dimensions of developmental research in one unified statement. Although he consistently presented these four dimensions in a particular order, there is no necessary sequence. All are equally important to consider. The normative-explanatory dimension is presented first for historical reasons. As discussed in Chapter 4, human development was until the 1950s a largely *descriptive* discipline aimed at finding norms of behavior. Increasingly since that time, however, there has been a shift to a focus on theoretical issues, and hence a concern with research aimed at *explaining* behavior change. Because this dimension pertains to a major historical shift in science, it is considered first.

Normative studies are those which describe the typical (mean, median, or modal) behavior of people of particular age levels and specific populations. Such work *describes* some typical characteristics associated with certain groups of people. For example, normative research might be aimed at describing the average height or weight for White middle-class, 13-year-old males and females from the Midwestern United States. Indeed, norms such as these have been obtained. Barnett and Einhorn (1972) report that the average height for 13-year-old males is 61.3 inches and for 13-year-old females is 62.2 inches. Similarly, the average weight for these two groups is 98.6 pounds and 105.5 pounds, respectively. In both height and weight, the average early adolescent female has higher scores than the average early adolescent male.

By providing typical descriptions of characteristics, norms are useful in indicating what may be expected to occur in groups of people at particular points in their development. Thus, if we look at the height and weight norms for 18-year-old males and females, we see that the average male height is 70.2 inches and the average weight is 144.8 pounds. The corresponding measures for 18-year-old females are 64.4 inches and 126.2 pounds. Thus, for 18-year-olds there is a reversal of what was seen at age 13. By looking at the growth norms for these two age levels, we can expect that the average late adolescent male will be taller and heavier than the average late adolescent female.

The above height and weight norms were published in 1972. Corresponding norms, collected earlier and later in history, would likely reveal that what was average for a particular group of adolescents at a particular age has changed across history. Accordingly, not only does normative research give the researcher an appreciation of the developmental characteristics of people over the course of their life, but also as norms are repeatedly collected over history, they allow the researcher to see the interrelation of individual development with sociocultural change.

But why do norms change over either individual or historical time? Why do height and weight typically change from early to late adolescence? Why have adolescents tended to be taller across history? Why do some researchers believe that such trends are ending? Although these questions will be answered in Chapter 8, the present point is that descriptions of behaviors are not explanations. Normative research does not explain why behavior changes in the typical manner that it does.

Such explanation is the goal of studies that lie toward the explanatory end of this first dimension. *Explanatory studies* attempt to account for the "why" of social and behavioral development. Such studies, however, clearly depend on the identification of norms. After all, if researchers do not have any ideas about how to describe the typical occurrence of the behavior under study, they will have difficulty explaining it. Thus norms are necessary for explanatory research. However, in and of themselves they are not sufficient; they just present a catalog of descriptions, a collection of unaccounted-for facts.

Then where do explanations come from? As emphasized in preceding chapters, explanations come from theory. Researchers attempt to integrate the norms of development within a particular theoretical formulation. They devise an empirical test of their theory, carry out this test, and in this way determine if their explanation is valid. Thus, theory is useful in that it provides a basis for doing the type of research that will allow for an accounting of the facts of the discipline.

For example, there are normative differences in the IQ scores of Black and White children and adolescents (Loehlin, Lindzey, & Spuhler, 1975). White samples have higher average scores than the Black samples. Various theories have been advanced to explain this difference (Burt, 1966; Hirsch, 1970; Jensen, 1969, 1973; Lerner, 1976; Palmer, 1968), and one such interpretation rests on social class and cultural differences between the groups. To simplify for purposes of illustration, the gist of this explanation is that variables that exist in different sociocultural settings account for the difference in IQ. For instance, differences in health, nutrition, and education explain why the average Black youth—who is more likely than the average White to be in a sociocultural setting having lower levels of these variables—scores lower on IQ tests. The average Black youth is not as well-educated, well-fed, or healthy as the average White youth. If it were found that normative IQ differences disappeared for particular samples of Blacks and Whites who were equated on such variables, then the explanation above of the basis of the norms would find support. Indeed, evidence supporting this explanation has been presented (Kagan, 1969; Palmer, 1968).

In sum, the first dimension of research sorts studies on the basis of relative emphasis on either description or explanation. When the latter type of study is done, the researcher attempts to relate one set of observations (the normative ones, the descriptions) to another set of observations in particular ways. That is, the researcher will argue that if the descriptions are to be explained by a particular theory, then certain relations between the described behaviors and other, independently observed behaviors should be seen. If social class differences explain IQ differences, then particular changes in social class-related variables (for example, increased quality of education) should be related to certain changes (that is, increases) in IQ scores.

In essence, in explanatory studies the researcher makes a prediction, or forms a *hypothesis*, about how the variables are related to each other. Many different types of data collection techniques are available to the researcher testing such hypotheses. The range of techniques is associated with the second dimension of research.

The naturalistic-manipulative dimension

Although it has been noted that all scientific inquiry rests on the collection and analysis of data, we have suggested there are many different, useful ways in which scientists may obtain these data. Our choice of a data collection technique is determined partly by our interest in avoiding *reactivity*—an unwanted influence on a subject's responses. Reactivity exists when a subject's behavior or responses are influenced by the fact that he or she is participating in a research study. One useful way of avoiding reactivity while studying development is to go into the real world to observe behavior. Observation of behavior as it occurs in its natural setting is termed *naturalistic* observation. In such observation, the researcher avoids manipulation of the ongoing behavior. Rather, after deciding what to observe, the researcher attempts to find such behavior as it naturally exists.

There are two general types of naturalistic observation. *Participant observation* is a technique mostly used by sociologists and anthropologists to discover the nature of social relationships in real-life settings. In this type of research, the researcher becomes a part of the setting for weeks, months, or even a year or two, and systematically observes what he or she sees and hears. The participant observer may also do some informal interviewing and may supplement his or her observations with other data available in the setting. The researcher usually writes up very comprehensive notes each day about what was said and about what happened in the setting. These notes are analyzed carefully later. Many important social science studies have used this technique, since it allows the researcher to observe social phenomena first-hand. This technique, however, has not been used widely to study adolescents.

The second type of naturalistic observation is more structured. Psychologists in particular often wish to examine the relationship between a very small number of variables in a given study. Thus, it might be necessary to isolate the specific behaviors of interest and systematically observe only those behaviors of interest in a more structured naturalistic study. Although it is clear that such an observational technique gives the researcher an excellent chance of discovering how behavior really develops, such research also has some limitations. The behavior of interest may occur at infrequent or irregular intervals, and the researcher may not be able to attend to everything that is possible to observe—even with the help of such apparatus as cameras. Such observations are sometimes difficult to use as a basis for explanations.

For example, suppose a researcher is interested in how adolescents form heterosexual dating relationships and wants to know if people of similar levels of physical attractiveness tend to form relationships with each other (Berscheid & Walster, 1974; Huston & Levinger, 1978). If the researcher chooses to study such development with the use of structured naturalistic observations, he or she might go out and find an appropriate sample of adolescents and then watch them, for example, at a high school dance. Of course, a good deal of behavior might be occurring at a very rapid pace. To try to cope with such an enormous input of information, the researcher might look at the adolescents for only thirty seconds at a time in five-minute intervals. Moreover, a wide-angle-lensed camera might be used to record these observations. However, despite these techniques, the researcher avoids manipulating the behavior of the subjects. Thus, if too few adolescents are forming new relationships, for example, dancing repeatedly with one another or leaving the dance together, the researcher does not intervene to increase the frequency of the behavior of interest.

Indeed, because no planned intervention in behavior occurs in naturalistic observation, the researcher cannot cancel out or control for the influences of other variables which might relate to the formation of relationships. For example, things other than the physical attractiveness of a potential partner might influence relationship formation in adolescence. Such things as prior acquaintance, mutual friends, or even dancing ability could determine if one person repeatedly dances with or leaves with another. Since the researcher cannot control the role of such other potentially influential variables, it is sometimes difficult to use structured naturalistic observations to support explanations. For example, it would be difficult to assert that people of similar physical attractiveness levels formed relationships in adolescence, because even if sufficient observations of relationship formations occurred, and even if comparable physical attractiveness levels did seem to link people together, the researcher would not be able to tell if attractiveness (or another possible but uncontrolled-for influence) was the key determinant.

Thus, the lack of control over behavior—in terms of its frequency and its influence by other variables—is one reason why naturalistic observation cannot be the only observational technique in developmental research. Another reason is that there are some behaviors that are not readily available for naturalistic observation. For instance, to use a somewhat unusual topic for developmental inquiry but nonetheless a legitimate one, suppose the researcher is interested in observing masturbation behaviors among adolescents. The occurrences of such behaviors among this age group, within situations ethically available to the researcher, would be expected to be extremely low.

Controlled and experimental observations   Some changes in behavior which are of interest require more controlled observational techniques. The adolescent might be put into a situation which maximizes the likelihood that the researcher will see the relevant behavior. Variables that could potentially influence the relevant behavior, but which are not of current interest, would be controlled in the research, or excluded altogether.

For example, suppose that a researcher is interested in seeing if adolescents form heterosexual relationships in school on the basis of similar levels of physical attractiveness. Here a group of male and female adolescents unacquainted with each other might be placed in a classroom in order to form two-person study groups to examine a topic about which they have little background. The researcher could have observers rate the physical attractiveness of the people and see who paired up with whom. In this study, then, the researcher has exerted greater control over his or her observations. Although no attempt has been made to manipulate (that is, change) the adolescents' behaviors *directly*, the situation within which the adolescents interact has been controlled, and even some characteristics of adolescents within the situation have been arranged.

Researchers who opt for techniques that allow more control over their observations are conducting research toward the *manipulative* end of the dimension. When the research situation is controlled by the researcher, but the behavior of the person is not directly manipulated, we label this *controlled observation*. In *experimental observation*, maximum control over observations and direct manipulation of behaviors are involved.

In the controlled experiment, one excercises as much control over the *situation* as possible. One manipulates conditions such that only the variables whose effects on behavior one wants to ascertain would vary, and this variation itself is also controlled. Everything else that could possibly affect the behavior of interest would be either held constant in all conditions or balanced across the research conditions. In other words, one would control any variable in the situation that could influence the behavior of interest.

For example, suppose one wants to know the extent to which each of three types of instructional techniques affects learning in 14-year-old adolescents. Since variables such as the sex, age, social class, IQ, race, religion, and type of school could all be related to any effects the instructional techniques might have on learning, one would want to control these variables. Thus, subjects might all be 14-year-old, White, middle-class, Protestant males of average IQ, attending a public junior high school in the South. The only variables that would be different would be the type of instruction the adolescents were exposed to. Thus, the precise effects of instructional techniques on learning could be determined.

However, this information would be known only under the conditions of the study. The effects of such instructional techniques on males or females of different racial and social class backgrounds, attending schools in different sections of the country, for example, would be unknown. Moreover, the known effects of instructional technique even on the subjects assessed would be limited. In the real world, the variables which the researcher was able to control in the study vary naturally. The reason such variables are controlled in the first place is that they are expected to affect learning. Thus, how the results of a controlled, manipulated experiment reflect what actually happens in the real world could not fully be determined from this one study. One would have to see if the results could be generalized. The researcher might have to return to a real classroom situation to see how the instructional techniques of interest affect learning in adolescents at the age of interest when such adolescents are actually learning in real-life settings.

It may be concluded that observational techniques always involve a trade-off. One trades precise control over behavior for real-life validity when one uses the naturalistic observational method; on the other hand, one loses such validity when one gains control through manipulation in controlled or experimental observations. However, both types of observational techniques are needed. The researcher who begins with manipulated, controlled observations may recognize the necessity of seeing if and how the results may actually occur in the natural world. The naturalistic observer, on the other hand, may find it necessary to move into the laboratory and make controlled observations in order to verify the impressions of behavior gained in the field setting and to attempt to understand the independent effects of particular variables on specific behaviors.

Questionnaires and interviews   Observational techniques are most useful when social interaction or behavior is of interest, and when such behavior is ethically open to scientific scrutiny. However, different techniques may be needed if (1) there is no overt social interaction or behavior to observe; (2) the behavior is not one which is readily or ethically seen through observation; or (3) the presence of a researcher when the behavior of interest is occurring would influence that behavior in a way that would not have otherwise occurred had the researcher not been present.

An example of the first problem would be if the researcher was interested primarily in feelings, attitudes, values, or recollections of earlier events. In regard to the second problem, researchers may not study behaviors which harm or embarrass their subjects. Thus, trying to observe directly certain behaviors—for example, sexual acts—might be prohibited. In addition, some behaviors (for example, those associated with adolescent car accidents) are not often readily available to naturalistic observation, and for obvious ethical reasons cannot be "controlled" by the researcher. Furthermore, other events occur only once in life (such as loss of virginity) and at times and in situations making them unavailable for direct observation. Indeed, if a researcher went beyond the bounds of ethics, and tried to be present at such an event, it is assured that the adolescents' interaction would differ from what it would have been had the researcher been absent.

The presence of the researcher is the third problem with making direct observations. Often, there are issues and behaviors of interest to the researcher of adolescent development that cannot be directly observed by him or her because doing so would distort the behavior. Sexual interactions among adolescents are obvious examples of the sort of behavior that would be distorted if a researcher were present. However, drug use and alcohol consumption, voting behavior, and parent-child interaction are other examples of social interaction and behavior that could be influenced by the presence of an outside observer.

Although one possible solution to the introduction of an outside observer would be, as described earlier, to become a participant observer—that is, actually become a real part of the social setting—such a technique is difficult in adolescence development research. Unless the researcher can pass for an adolescent, he or she may not readily be accepted in research where the presence of an adult would be awkward or disruptive.

Thus, because of the difficulties involved in direct observation, other methods sometimes are used. These take the form of questionnaires and interviews. These techniques involve written or verbal responses to questions. A questionnaire is usually self-administered, but may be completed in a group setting with the questions read out loud. Interviews may be conducted in face-to-face settings, by telephone, or by other means. Both questionnaires and interviews can have fixed-choice questions, in which the possible answers are specified, or open-ended ones, in which any answer is possible and the precise response given by the respondent is recorded. Questionnaires and interviews are the techniques of *survey research*.

There are numerous issues in adolescent development that only can be studied through the use of survey research methods. However, responses to questionnaires and interviews are not expected to reflect perfectly behavior as it would occur if directly observed. Without a direct assessment of the correspondence between actual behavior and reported behavior, one cannot be certain of how well reports of behavior agree with actual behavior. Adolescents might forget, distort, or not really know the answers to various items in these instruments. Although it is *possible* to take steps to assess how much distortion takes place in their answers, such steps are difficult. For example, one could compare adolescents' answers to questions about their behavior with their actual behavior. However, often the unavailability of such direct observation of behavior is, as noted, the reason that indirect assessment devices were used in the first place.

Survey research, however, is most valuable when one is interested in adolescent reports or recollections, values, attitudes, or other unobservable information. Furthermore, it allows the researcher to study large numbers of people in a shorter time than observation often permits and to collect data on a large number of variables in a short time span. Questionnaires are often answered very honestly and accurately since anonymity can be assured. Interviews allow the respondent and researcher to get better acquainted, and the technique allows the researcher to probe issues or change directions in the midst of the data collection.

As with all other research techniques, questionnaires and interviews have assets and limitations. Again there is a trade-off. One is able to investigate behaviors not readily available for observation, but has to use techniques whose correspondence with the actual behaviors of interest is often uncertain. Yet because of their assets such methods tend to be the most frequently used among social scientists (Cattell, 1973). Finally, one additional value that these techniques have is their ability to combine with other (for example, observational) techniques. For instance, one could see if an adolescent's attitudes or values, as measured by a questionnaire, changed as a consequence of various experimental manipulations.

Nonobtrusive measures   Much research can be done without observing, testing, or talking to people directly. There are data all around us, waiting to be collected, and we often don't even know it. Whenever we use data which already exist in our environment, we are using *nonobtrusive* measures.

There are numerous examples of such research studies (Webb, Campbell, Schwartz, and Sechrest, 1966). Reading habits on campus could be studied by examining wear on library books; sexual attitudes could be examined by reading the grafitti on bathroom walls; divorce could be researched by analyzing records available at the county courthouse. We could study radio listening preferences by having auto mechanics find out how car radios are set. And popular versus unpopular magazines in libraries or waiting rooms could be determined by looking at which ones collected the most dust.

A good researcher is creative and takes advantage of whatever evidence is available to study the research problem best. With the various forms of data collection techniques open to a researcher, a variety of potential strategies are available for observing adolescents. Although every method has specific strengths and weaknesses, any method may be used depending on the nature of the research question being investigated. But what determines the question of any research effort? There is some rationale for every research effort, and this question is addressed by the third dimension of developmental research.

The atheoretical-theoretical dimension

This dimension of developmental research identifies studies on the basis of their relative emphasis on theory as the basis of the research. There may be various reasons that lead a researcher to conduct a particular study. Some research may be done simply on the basis of interest in some particular phenomenon. The researchers may be curious about the way something develops. They may have a hunch about some aspect of development. Or they simply may want to see what happens when a variable is manipulated or assessed. In addition, research may be used as a way of solving a practical problem (McCandless, 1970). In these cases research is not being conducted from a theoretical perspective. The research is not based on hypothetical statements drawn from a theory (hypotheses), and the research ideas, when tested, will not necessarily support, clarify, or refute a theory. Rather, atheoretical research is, by definition, carried out on a theory-independent basis. Although such research may be found to have some relevance to theory after it is completed, this is usually not intended. In fact, the data from such an atheoretical study may end up being just a piece of scientific data that has no meaning or relevance to any given theoretical formulation.

Because of such potential limitations for the study of adolescence, theoretically relevant research is stressed in this book. As indicated in our historical review of the changing emphases in the study of human development, studies based on theoretical conceptions of development may be seen as most useful in advancing the science. The data resulting from such research are expected to have some direct relevance for understanding development. The purpose of theory is to integrate existing knowledge and to obtain new knowledge. New knowledge results from the tests of hypotheses derived from such theories. Thus, theory-related research always has the promise of providing information which expands our understanding of development.

How does one study the effects of several influences on human development across the life span? The issue is how one can design research to measure intraindividual change, or individual development, as that development is influenced by many variables. Although the preceding discussion offered different techniques of observations, there was no statement about how these techniques could be used in a study to assess the nature of developmental change. This concern is addressed in the discussion of the fourth dimension of developmental research. It is this dimension alone which determines whether a research effort is or is not a developmental one.

The ahistorical-historical dimension

This dimension sorts studies on the basis of their relative concern with change. As discussed earlier in the text, some studies are concerned with behavior at one particular time in an adolescent's development. Such studies were labeled adolescent-psychological ones. In such studies there may be no interest whatsoever in how the behavior at this point in development came to take the form that it does or what form this behavior may take later. Such studies may be termed *ahistorical*, because behavior is studied at only one point in time (McCandless, 1970). For instance, a particular study might be concerned with the effects of a certain type of social reinforcement on aggression in 14-year-olds. If the study is ahistorical in its orientation, it will not be concerned about how the child's earlier development contributed to this relation or about the future status of this relation.

However, as research becomes more concerned with the origins and the future course of behavior, it moves closer to the historical end of the continuum. Thus, historical research is concerned not only with the status of a relationship between two or more variables at a particular point in development, but also with the basis of that relation, as well as the future status of that relation. Historical research wants to know what variables in the 14-year-old youth's developmental history provided a basis for the relation between reinforcement and aggression, and what implication the relation at age 14 has for later adolescent and adult relations between social reinforcement and aggression. In summary then, historical research is concerned with the change in behavior over time.

Without historical investigation, basic issues of development could not be studied empirically. The developmentalist would be unable to determine either the continuity-discontinuity or the stability-instability of behavior. Thus, although an ahistorical study allows us to know the relations among the variables of sex, social class, race, and IQ at a given age, for example, it in no way allows us to know anything about the previous or the eventual interrelations among these variables. A historical research study is thus the most appropriate for developmental inquiry. However, there are several ways to design historical research, and not all such research designs are, in fact, appropriate for developmental research.

Indeed, although there are three types of historical designs typically noted by developmentalists, none of these conventional methods is fully adequate for developmental research. These three conventional research designs—termed the longitudinal, cross-sectional, and time-lag designs—each have important limitations when applied to developmental research. Because of the need to understand the reason why conventional research designs are inadequate for studying change, the next section focuses on the nature of design in developmental research.

DESIGNS OF DEVELOPMENTAL RESEARCH

Many people who attempt to understand an individual's development do so by specifying age-related developmental progressions. An example is attributing storm and stress to the adolescent stage of life. Although age-related progressions or "stage" progressions may be one source of a person's change, they are not the only processes which provide a basis for change. For example, if a major event occurred in society at a particular time—for instance the Watergate political crisis, the assassination of President Kennedy, or the 1929 crash of the Stock Market—behaviors of people might be affected despite the stage or age of development they were in. If one were measuring attitudes toward the government during the time of the Watergate political crisis, the events in society at this time of measurement may have influenced children, adolescents, and adults. As such, it is possible that time of measurement, as well as age-related phenomena, can influence development.

In addition, not only may age and time affect change, but so too may history. Again imagine that attitudes toward government were being measured and that the subjects of the study were people born during the Great Depression in the United States (1929 through the late 1930s). During this historical era many of the institutions that provided economic security to American citizens (banks, for example) failed, and existing governmental policies were not able to deal with this situation. Accordingly, it may be expected that people born in the 1920s who experienced the effects of the Depression during childhood might have developed differently than people born well before or well after this historical era. Indeed, research has found this to be true (Elder, 1974).

As mentioned in an earlier chapter, a *cohort* is a group of persons experiencing some event in common. People born in a given year are members of a particular *birth cohort*. By virtue of being in a particular birth cohort, one may have specific experiences that might not be part of the experiences of people born in other historical eras. Such birth cohort-related influences can affect the character of behavior people show across their lives. People who were children during the Great

Depression may continue to be more wary about the stability of the economy and of the ability of the government to safeguard citizens than may people who were children during eras of affluence and prosperity (the late 1950s in the United States, for example). Because of membership in a certain birth cohort, people may continue to differ from those of other cohorts, no matter at what age they are measured or what exists in the sociocultural setting at a particular time of measurement.

It may be seen, then, that there are at least three components of developmental change. *Birth cohort-related events*, as well as *time of measurement* and *age-related phenomena*, can contribute to developmental changes. Recognizing that reference is always made to phenomena that change in relation to these components, we label these components *age*, *time*, and *cohort* for convenience. Thus, when intraindividual change is seen from one point in the life span to another, one must be able to determine how processes associated with each of these three components may influence change.

Until relatively recently (Baltes, 1968; Schaie, 1965), the three most popular designs of developmental research did not allow for an adequate determination of the contributions of these three components. The three designs—the longitudinal, cross-sectional, and time-lag methods—typically involve a *confounding* of two of the three components of change. When a variable is confounded, its influence on behavior cannot be separated from that of another variable that could be influencing behavior at the same time.

For instance, if one wanted to know if males or females could score higher on a test of reading comprehension, one would not want all the males to be college-educated and all the females only grade school-educated. It is known that education level can influence reading comprehension as well as can sex-related variables. If one did not equate the two sex groups on education level (if one did not "control" for the contributions of education), then one would not know if differences between the groups were influenced by their sex or by their educational disparities (or some combination of the two). Thus, sex could be confounded with education. In other words, one could not separate the effects of the two variables. When the separate influence of two variables cannot be determined, these variables may be confounded, and any study that involves such a confounding has a potential methodological flaw.

Unfortunately, the three commonly used designs for developmental research confound two of the three components of developmental change and, as a consequence, their utility is severely limited. In Exhibit 7.1 the particular confounding factors in each of these designs are presented. Reference to this exhibit will be useful as the discussion turns to an explanation of the characteristics of each of these designs, and an explanation of why they confound what they do.

Exhibit 7.1
Some characteristics of longitudinal, cross-sectional, and time-lag designs of developmental research

Design	Study involves:	Confounded components of developmental change
Longitudinal	One birth cohort	Age with time
Cross-sectional	One time of measurement	Age with birth cohort
Time lag	One age	Time with birth cohort

The *longitudinal design* (also known as a *panel design*) involves observing the same group of people at more than one point in time. The main asset of this approach is that since the same people are studied over time, the similarities or changes in behavior across their development can be directly seen. However, this method, particularly since it involves repeated observations of the same people over an extended period of time, leads to some limitations.

It obviously takes a relatively long time to do some longitudinal studies. If researchers wanted, for instance, to do a longitudinal study of personality development from birth through late adolescence, they would have to devote about 20 years of their own lives to such a research endeavor. Such a commitment would be expensive, as well as time-consuming, and thus it may be easily seen why relatively few long-term longitudinal studies have been done.

Other limitations of longitudinal studies pertain to the nature of the people studied and to problems with the measurements that may be used. Not everyone would be willing to be a subject in a study that required their continual observation over the course of many months or years of their lives. Hence, samples tend to be small in such studies. Those people who are willing to take part may not be representative of most people. Thus, longitudinal studies often involve unrepresentative, or "biased," samples of people. Results of such studies may not be applied easily, or "generalized," to a broader population. In addition, longitudinal samples typically become increasingly biased as the study continues. Some people drop out from participation, and one should not assume that those people that do remain are identical to the former group. After all, the group that stays may be different just by virtue of the fact that they continue to participate.

Another problem with longitudinal studies is that after some time people may become used to the tests of their behavior. They may learn "how to respond," or they may respond differently than they would have if they had never been exposed to the test. Hence, the meaning of a particular test to the subjects may be altered over time through the repeated use of the instrument with the same sample. Such an occurrence would make it difficult to say that the same variable was actually being measured at different times in the subjects' lives.

Often the purpose of using this method is to determine the developmental time course for a particular type of behavior or psychological function. One also wants information which may be applied to understanding development about future generations of people. Yet with a longitudinal study, one is only studying people who are born in one historical era and who are measured at certain points in time. One does not know if findings about this one cohort can be generalized to people in other cohorts.

A confounding of age and time exists when one cohort is studied. Since a longitudinal study involves assessing one particular cohort of people (for example, a group of males and females born in 1965), such people can be age 15 at only one time of measurement (1980 in this case). Thus, their behavior at age 15 may be due to age-related phenomena or to pheonomena present at the time of measurement (or to both). Similarly, members of one birth cohort can only be age 20 at one time of measurement. Thus, as noted in Exhibit 7.1, age and time are confounded in a longitudinal study. One does not know if results of a longitudinal study can be applied to other 15- or 20-year-olds who are measured at other times.

Hence, the findings about development that one gains from a longitudinal study reflect age-related changes, or alternatively, they may reflect only characteristics of people born and studied at particular points in time. One does not know in a longitudinal study whether the findings are due to universal rules or "laws" of development (that is, rules which describe a person's development no matter when it occurs), or to particular historical events that may have influenced the research subjects, or to the particular times the subjects are measured, or to some combination of all these influences.

To summarize, although longitudinal studies are useful for describing development as it occurs in a group of people, such studies have expense, sampling, and measurement problems, and may present results not applicable to similarly aged people who grew up in different historical eras, or who were measured at different points in time. Because of such problems, alternatives to the longitudinal method are often used.

The cross-sectional design

The most widely used developmental research design is the *cross-sectional design*. Here different groups of people are studied at one point in time, and hence all observations can be completed relatively quickly. The design is less expensive than longitudinal research and requires less time. Because of these characteristics, some have argued that the method allows for a very efficiently derived description of development. However, there are important limitations of cross-sectional research.

If one wanted to study the development of aggression in individuals who range in age from 2 to 20 years, one could use the cross-sectional method. Instead of observing one group of people every year, for example, for 18 years, groups of individuals at each age between 2 and 20 could be observed at one point in time.

However, it is difficult to fully and adequately control for all variables that may affect behavior differences. One may not be certain if differences between the various age groups are reflections of real age changes, or merely reflections of the groups not being really identical to begin with.

Sometimes the researcher attempts to match the individuals on a number of important variables other than age to ensure some degree of comparability. However, such comparability is difficult to achieve. Moreover, although it is possible to get less biased, more representative samples for cross-sectional research than for longitudinal studies (people will cooperate more readily since they are only committed to be observed or interviewed once), such better sampling may still not lead to a useful description of the components of developmental change. This failure occurs because of a flaw in the rationale for the use of a cross-sectional method instead of a longitudinal one.

The expectation in some cross-sectional studies is that they yield results comparable to those obtained from studying the same group of people over time, and do so more efficiently, so long as the only differences among cross-sectional groups are their ages. However, despite how adequately subjects are matched, it is rarely the case that the results of cross-sectional and longitudinal studies are consistent (Schaie & Strother, 1968).

For example, when studying intellectual development with a cross-sectional design, most researchers report that highest performance occurs in the early twenties or thirties and considerable decreases in performance levels occur after this period (for example, Horn & Cattell, 1966). With longitudinal studies of these same variables, however, often no decrease in performance is seen at all. In fact, some studies (for example, Bayley & Oden, 1955) have found some increase in performance levels into the fifties. As has been pointed out, it may be suggested that the nature of the subjects typically used in the longitudinal design is considerably different from that of subjects used in the cross-sectional study.

Longitudinal studies, as has been noted, may be composed of a select sample to begin with, and as the study proceeds, some people will drop out of the research. Such attrition may not be random. Rather, it may be due to the fact that subjects of lower intellectual ability leave the study. Hence, in the example of research on intellectual development, this bias could account for lack of decreases in level of performance. In addition, as Schaie and Strother (1968) point out, these longitudinal studies have not assessed intellectual development in the sixties and seventies, the age periods during which the greatest performance decreases have been seen in the cross-sectional studies (for example, Jones, 1959). Thus, comparisons of the age-associated changes found with the two methods are not appropriate.

On the other hand, cross-sectional samples have not escaped criticism. Schaie (1959) has argued that such samples do not give the researcher a good indication of age-associated changes because of the fact that it is difficult to control for extraneous variables in the samples used to represent people of widely different age ranges.

Although these arguments appropriately may be used to reconcile the differences (or perhaps to explain them away), Schaie (1965) suggests that these arguments miss an essential point: they do not show a recognition of an essential methodological problem involved in the consideration of longitudinal and cross-sectional designs. Just as longitudinal studies are confounded (between age and time), cross-sectional studies also are confounded. As seen in Exhibit 7.1, the confounding is between age and cohort. Because the two types of studies involve different confounding, it is unlikely that they will reveal the same results.

The confounding of age and cohort which exists in cross-sectional studies occurs because at any one time of measurement (for example, 1980) people who are of different ages can only be so because they were born in different years. To be 20 in 1980, one has to have been born in 1960, while to be 25 at this time of measurement one has to be a member of the 1955 birth cohort. Consequently, because cross-sectional studies focus only on one time of measurement there is no way of telling whether differences between age groups are due to age-related changes or to differences associated with being born in historically different eras.

To summarize, like the longitudinal method, the cross-sectional method has important limitations. Because of these shortcomings it is difficult to decide whether one or the other of these methods gives a more useful depiction of developmental changes. Both methods may potentially introduce serious, but different, distortions into measures of developmental changes. This is perhaps the major reason why information from the two techniques often is not consistent (Schaie & Strother, 1968). Similarly, data derived from the third conventional design of developmental research, the time-lag design, are not necessarily consistent with those of the former two. This is because yet another type of confounding is involved.

The time-lag design

Although not as frequently used in research as the cross-sectional or longitudinal designs, the *time-lag design* allows a researcher to see differences in behavior associated with particular ages at various times in history. That is, in contrast to focusing on one cohort or one time of measurement, the time-lag design considers only one age level, and looks at characteristics associated with being a particular age at different times in history.

For example, earlier in this chapter, when differences were discussed between the 1970s and earlier decades in the normative height and weight of 13-year-olds, a time-lag design was actually being indicated. When the focus of research is to determine the characteristics associated with being a particular age (for example, 15 years old) at different times of measurement (for example, 1950, 1960, 1970, and 1980), a time-lag design is implied.

Of course, such a design involves cross-sections of people, and has all the problems of control, matching, and sampling associated with such designs. But there are also additional problems. As indicated in Exhibit 7.1, because only one age is studied at different times, the different groups are members of different birth cohorts. Thus, in a time-lag design, time and birth cohort are confounded, and one does not know, for example, if the behaviors of 15-year-olds studied at two points in time are associated with events acting on all people—no matter what their age—at a particular test time, or are due to historical events associated with membership in a specific cohort.

In sum, none of the three types of conventional designs of developmental research allow for the unconfounded assessment of the contributions of the three components of developmental change. Although each design has some advantages, the problems of each places limitations on the ability of developmental researchers to describe adequately how individual, sociocultural, or historical influences can influence change. This might lead some to conclude that a bleak picture exists for the study of human development, since the three conventional designs of developmental research have some methodological problems.

However, due to the influence of K. Warner Schaie (1965), Paul B. Baltes, and John R. Nesselroade (Baltes, 1968; Nesselroade & Baltes, 1974), a more positive view exists. Schaie (1965) demonstrated how the conventional methods were part of a more *general developmental model* for developmental research design. Presentation of this model allowed him to offer a new type of approach to designing developmental research. These are the sequential methods of developmental research.

Sequential strategies of design

The problems of confounding involved in the cross-sectional, longitudinal, and time-lag designs may be resolved, Schaie (1965) argues, through use of *sequential methods*. By combining features of longitudinal and cross-sectional designs, the researcher may assess the relative contributions of age, cohort, and time in one study, to know what differences (or portion of the differences) between groups are due to age differences, to cohort (historical) differences, or to time of testing differences. In addition, a sequential design allows these sources of differences to be determined in a relatively short period of time.

Research based on sequential designs is complex, due in part to the usual involvement of *multivariate* (many variable) statistical analyses and the numerous measurements that have to be taken of different groups. But a simplified example of such a design may be offered. It will suggest how use of such a design allows the developmental researcher to avoid the potential confounding involved with traditional cross-sectional and longitudinal approaches.

Basically, a sequential design involves the remeasurement of a cross-sectional sample of people after a given fixed interval of time has passed. A researcher selects a

K. Warner Schale

cross-sectional sample composed of various cohorts, and measures each cohort longitudinally (with the provision that each set of measurements occurs at about the same point in time for each cohort). In addition, if, for example, three times of testing are included (as the longitudinal component of the design), then control cohort groups, assessed, for instance, only at the third testing time, may be used to control for (to assess) any retesting effects. Hence, this design calls for obtaining repeated measures from each of the different cohort groups included in a given cross-sectional sample, and for obtaining data from retest control groups to assess effects of retesting. The researcher is thus in a position to make statements about the relative influences of age, cohort, and times of measurement on any observed developmental functions in the results.

To see how this works, it is useful to consider a sample design of such a sequential study. Such a design is presented in Exhibit 7.2 and recast in the form of a matrix in Exhibit 7.3. Different cohort levels are composed of different groups of

Exhibit 7.2
The design of a sequential study

Birth cohort	Time of measurement 1	Age at time 1	Time of measurement 2	Age at time 2	Time of measurement 3	Age at time 3	Time of measurement of retest control group	Age of control group
1957	1970	13	1971	14	1972	15	1972	15
1956	1970	14	1971	15	1972	16	1972	16
1955	1970	15	1971	16	1972	17	1972	17
1954	1970	16	1971	17	1972	18	1972	18

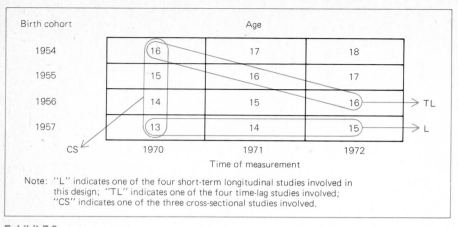

Birth cohort   Age

1954   16   17   18

1955   15   16   17

1956   14   15   16 ——→ TL

1957   13   14   15 ——→ L

CS   1970   1971   1972

Time of measurement

Note: "L" indicates one of the four short-term longitudinal studies involved in
       this design; "TL" indicates one of the four time-lag studies involved;
       "CS" indicates one of the three cross-sectional studies involved.

Exhibit 7.3
**The design of a sequential study put into the form of a matrix (the same
design as that shown in exhibit 7.2 is presented).**

people born at different historical periods (1954, 1955, 1956, or 1957). Thus, at the time of the first testing (1970 for this design), the study has the attributes of a cross-sectional study. Indeed, there are three such cross-sectional studies in this particular design, one for each time of measurement (see Exhibit 7.3). However, the sequential feature is introduced when these same subjects are again measured in 1971 and 1972. Thus, for each cohort there is now a longitudinal study. As seen in Exhibit 7.3, each cohort in a sequential design of this sort is involved in its own short-term longitudinal study (there are four of these in the design shown in Exhibit 7.3). Additionally, it should be noted that the diagonals of the design matrix of Exhibit 7.3 represent time-lag studies; people of the same age are studied at different times. Thus, a sequential study involves all combinations of observations of other designs in one integrated matrix of observations.

With such a matrix, the researcher can answer a number of questions involving the potentially interrelated influences of cohort, age, and time. Referring to Exhibits 7.2 and 7.3, if, for example, the cohort composed of people born in 1955 underwent changes between times of measurement 1 and 2, and were found to be different at age 16 from the people in the 1954 cohort group when they were 16, then there must be some historical difference between these two cohort levels. In other words, if differences are due simply to age-related changes, then people of the same age should perform the same no matter what cohort they are from or when they are measured. A younger cohort group should perform similarly to that of an older cohort group as members of each group age, *if* there are no historical differences between cohorts and if time of testing does not matter. Again from Exhibits 7.2 and 7.3, the 1957 cohort should show a level of performance on its second measurement comparable to that of the first measurement for the 1956 cohort, *if* there are no historical differences between the generations.

In turn, if time of testing were a source of change, then people should respond the same despite their age or cohort. If events in 1972 were the strongest influence on behavior, then one should see that people of all cohorts represented in Exhibits 7.2 and 7.3 respond the same way.

Finally, of course, if birth cohort were of most importance, then people of a particular cohort should respond in a given way no matter what age they are and no matter at what time they are measured. As illustrated by the example of children born in the Great Depression (Elder, 1974), membership in a particular cohort would override influences due to age or time of measurement.

Additionally, it should be noted that by including groups of subjects to be tested for the first time at the end of the study (see Exhibit 7.2), sequential researchers provide a way to judge the effects of repeated use of the measuring instruments, noted earlier. If subjects in the core sample did not respond differently as a consequence of their having been repeatedly measured (for example, by the same tests of personality or IQ), then their behavior at the end of the study should be comparable to a group of subjects matched in every way with them except for the fact that no repeated testing was given. If there are differences, however, between the core sample and these "retest" controls, then there are statistical techniques available to researchers to measure the effects of retesting (Nesselroade & Baltes, 1974).

Despite the complexity of data analysis, and the more complex research design and reasoning process associated with it, the sequential approach has advantages not associated with other techniques. It allows for the unconfounding of the components of developmental change in one descriptive effort. As such, it allows the contributions of variables associated with multiple levels of influence to be evaluated adequately.

In fact, although sequential research studies are relatively few in number, one such study discussed in earlier chapters may be recalled here in order to illustrate the use of sequential designs for assessments of adolescent development. Indeed, the design illustrated in Exhibits 7.2 and 7.3 was used because it corresponds to the one used by Nesselroade and Baltes (1974) in their sequential study of adolescent personality development.

A sequential study of adolescent personality development

Noting that most conceptions of adolescent personality development suggest that age-related progressions are influential in this period of life, Nesselroade and Baltes (1974) argue that historical (cohort) and specific sociocultural (time) influences may be involved also. As such, they applied sequential methodology to see how these three components contributed to changes in personality in the period from 1970 to 1972.

About 1,800 West Virginia male and female adolescents were measured in 1970, 1971, and 1972. These adolescents were from birth cohorts 1954 to 1957, and thus, as in Exhibits 7.2 and 7.3, ranged in age at the time of first measurement, from 13 to 16. Personality questionnaires and measures of intelligence were administered to these subjects.

Contrary to what is stressed by those theorists who focus on personological components of adolescent development (for example, Anna Freud, 1969), Nesselroade and Baltes found that change at this time of life was quite responsive to sociocultural-historical influences. In fact, age by itself was not found to be a very influential contributor to change. Rather, for these groups of adolescents, developmental change was influenced more by cultural changes over the two-year historical period than by age-related sequences.

For instance, adolescents as a whole, *despite their age or birth cohort*, decreased in "superego strength," "social-emotional anxiety," and achievement during the

1970–1972 period. Moreover, most adolescents, regardless of age or cohort, increased in independence during this period.

Accordingly, the Nesselroade and Baltes (1974) data show that it was the time at which all these differently aged adolescents were measured that was most influential in their changes. Perhaps due to the events in the society of that time which were associated with the Vietnam war, all adolescents performed similarly in regard to these personality characteristics. Despite where they were upon "entering" the 1970–1972 historical era, members of different cohorts changed in similar directions due to events surrounding them at the times they were tested.

Without sequential methodology, the importance of the specific sociocultural setting at that time could not have been suggested. This suggestion is supported by data obtained from other sequential studies which have shown the influence of birth cohort on intellectual developments in children (Baltes, Baltes, & Reinert, 1970) and adults (Schaie, Labouvie, & Buech, 1973). These data suggest that to understand developmental change, one should consider the interactions among individual and sociocultural-historical processes.

SOME GENERAL METHODOLOGICAL PROBLEMS OF ADOLESCENT DEVELOPMENTAL RESEARCH

As already noted, methodological problems involve issues of how data are obtained and interpreted. Developmental researchers recognize that any study can be biased or faulty if certain issues of method are not confronted. Although certain data collection procedures may be appropriate, others may yield data with serious problems of interpretation. If one collects data in wrong or in biased ways, little confidence may be placed in such data, and thus the data will be of little use. However, if the potential problems are recognized, and steps are taken to successfully deal with them, the researcher will have confidence in both the accuracy of the data and the interpretations drawn from them. Some of the important methodological problems of developmental research are discussed below.

Contamination

McCandless (1970) has detailed several prominent methodological problems of developmental research. The first is *contamination*. When data are contaminated, they are influenced by variables other than those which are being studied. That is, the results of the study may be due not only to the actual relations among the variables investigated. Contamination may occur in several ways.

In some studies, subjects are tested successively, one after the other. If one subject reveals the intent of the study to a succeeding subject, or in some way tells this later subject what to expect, this revelation might influence the second subject's responses. If this second subject's behavior is influenced by this information, then his or her responses would not be due only to the variables being studied.

Researchers also may contaminate their own data. Suppose a researcher believes that there is a relationship between the type of body an adolescent has and that person's personality or temperament. To test this belief, the researcher might develop a method to rate body type and temperament. However, it is possible that if the researcher himself or herself does both of these ratings for all the subjects, any relation discovered between body type and temperament might be contaminated by the researcher's hypothesis about this relationship. To illustrate this possibility, the work of William Sheldon (1940, 1942) may be noted. Sheldon developed a theory relating a person's physique type to the person's temperament. He specified that there are three essential components of body build, and that it is possible to characterize the body in terms of the relative contribution of these three components. Thus, some people are predominantly fat—their bodies are composed essentially of adipose (fat) tissue. Other people's bodies are composed mainly of muscle and bone tissue—they have an athletic-looking body. Finally, other people's bodies are composed essentially of neither fat nor muscle tissue but of nervous-system tissue; such a body build would appear thin and linear.

Sheldon also specified that certain types of temperament go along with each of these three body types. He then devised ways to measure the body builds and temperaments of his subjects (4,000 Harvard University male undergraduates). However, Sheldon himself performed both of these sets of measurements. He rated body build, and then, even though he knew the hypothesized relation between body build and temperament, he rated temperament. Thus, there is the strong possibility that the high relation Sheldon found between these two sets of ratings was contaminated. Of course, Sheldon did not set out intentionally to contaminate his ratings. Such errors may often occur among well-trained, but perhaps unvigilant, researchers. Hence, researchers must take precautions to ensure that their subjects' responses are not affected by anything extraneous to the research situation. Furthermore, the relations found among their data should not be influenced by their own hypotheses. In science, a question should not determine the answer.

Researcher effects on subject responses

Another related type of methodological problem involving the researcher occurs when the investigator unintentionally affects the responses of his or her subjects. These researcher effects have been investigated by Rosenthal (1966), who suggests that such errors may play an important part in much research.

Suppose one wants to conduct a study of the racial attitudes of White adolescents toward Black people and chooses to use the interview method. Each adolescent and the researcher sit alone in a small cubicle to conduct the interview. If the interviewer were Black, he or she might get verbal responses from the respondents which are different from what might be obtained if he or she were White. White adolescents may be more candid about expressing any hostile or negative racial attitudes when interviewed by a White person than when interviewed by a Black person. Thus, in this example the race of the researcher might affect the answers of the respondents.

Although it is difficult to determine such researcher effects, the investigator should always be aware of the potential for such bias and should design the method of the study with safeguards. For instance, in the racial attitude study, the researcher might want to use two interviewers, one Black and one White, in order to control and test for any possible biasing effects introduced by the race of the interviewer.

Reconstruction through retrospection

There are many ways to obtain information about the events that characterize people's development. In Chapter 6, the method used by Freud was discussed. By asking his adult neurotic patients to recall the events of their early childhood, Freud reconstructed their developmental histories. However, it was noted that such a method has a strong potential for introducing serious problems into one's data. Such events may be recalled incorrectly, partially forgotten, distorted, or even lied about. However, there is usually no way to check on these distortions. The actual events and interactions are not being observed empirically with the retrospective method but are merely being reconstructed through use of a subjective verbal account.

Thus, when one reconstructs the past developmental history of a person through retrospection—by having the respondents look back upon their life and recall previous events—one is using a subjective, and perhaps distorted, account of the developmental history. Hence, the reconstruction through retrospection method is a limited way of obtaining information about the events that characterize people's development. Because the data collected through this method may be inaccurate, and because it is difficult to determine the level of inaccuracy, theories and inferences drawn on the basis of such information may have limitations.

However, there is another way of obtaining information about the events that characterize people's development, the *anterospective construction* method. In this method, behavior is measured at or about the very time that it occurs. Hence, any descriptions of the course of development are based on actual, empirical observations of behavior as it develops. This anterospective method thus offers empirical data which objectively may be verified for accuracy.

Faulty logic

Another important problem is presented in developmental research when the investigator uses faulty reasoning techniques in interpreting data. In fact, such faulty reasoning may actually influence the design of the study itself and the method used to collect data.

Although faulty logic is by no means unique to developmental research, such problems do play an all too prominent role in such investigations. The potential problem may be illustrated by offering the following syllogism:

1. Boats float on water.
2. X is floating on water.
3. Therefore, X is a boat.

Obviously this is an example of faulty logic. On the basis of the initial premise, one cannot exclude the possibility that things other than boats float on water; thus, it is not logical to conclude that just because X floats on water, X is a boat. However, if one asserts that boats *and only* boats float on water, then it *would* follow from this premise that X is a boat.

Although it is clear that the first syllogism is not logical, it is possible to just alter the words of the syllogism (the content) and leave the logic (or lack of logic) intact. Thus, a second syllogism might be:

1. Infants deprived of their mother's breast milk in the first year of their life overeat at age 15.
2. John, a 15-year-old, overeats.
3. Therefore, John was deprived of his mother's breast milk during the first year of his life.

Clearly, this conclusion also does not follow from the premise. There may be sources of overeating among 15-year-olds other than breast milk deprivation. Yet when this logically faulty syllogism is cast in terms of developmental events between mother and child, it all too often acquires an air of believability.

Perhaps one reason for such faulty logic in developmental research is that development deals with sequential events. There may be a belief in *post hoc, ergo propter hoc,* "after the fact, therefore because of the fact." Clearly, no one would assert that if one rises at 4:00 A.M. every day, and then with astonishing predictability the sun rises just a few hours later, one's personal rising is the source of the sun's rising. Yet when such faulty reasoning is couched in terms of sequential events that occur over the course of development, such lack of logic may all too often slip by unnoticed.

A researcher may wish to determine the source of development of a particular behavior. Thus, the researcher might collect data about events that occurred during the first few years of a child's life and then relate this information to data collected at a later time in life. If a relation between these early and later measures is found—perhaps expressed in terms of a correlation coefficient—the researcher might infer that the early behavior provided a source of the later behavior. Yet it has been argued that simply through the use of the method of data collection, sufficient information was not obtained to make this inference necessarily correct.

Inadequate definition of concepts

This problem pertains to how researchers define and measure the concepts they are investigating. A *concept* is a term used to represent some aspect of the physical or social world. Concepts, of course, may be more or less abstract. Thus, a concept used to represent such things as cars, wagons, and trains—that is, the concept of vehicle—might be considered relatively concrete. The empirical referents of the concept (whatever are being referred to) generally are understood. Other relatively concrete concepts might be animal, body, or height. Yet not all concepts are similarly concrete. Some concepts do not have commonly understood empirical referents. Thus, when psychologists use concepts such as aggression, learning, or personality, it is absolutely necessary that they precisely specify what they mean. Then anyone interested in the researcher's work will know exactly what is meant by the use of a term. If such operational definitions are not used, however, considerable problems of communication may result. Two different researchers may be studying the same phenomenon, but if they define and measure it differently, their results may not be comparable. If they do not communicate these different meanings clearly, this lack of comparability may never be recognized.

For example, suppose a researcher is interested in studying the "generation gap." What exactly does the term mean? On a simple level one may suppose that it refers to a set of differences that allegedly exist between adolescents and their parents. But this definition is not sufficient because it does not specify what the differences are. Adolescents and their parents may differ from each other in many ways. Are the differences referred to by this term differences in the physical appearances of the generational groups—for example, in their respective styles of dress and hair lengths? Or does one mean divisions between the generations in their support for radical political causes? Or does one mean differences between the generations in attitudes about such issues as drug use, sexual behavior, and racism?

If researchers anchor their concepts in precise, empirical terms, considerable confusion may be avoided. For example, some studies (for example, Lerner, Karson, Meisels, & Knapp, 1975; Lerner & Knapp, 1975) have defined the generation gap in terms of attitude differences between adolescents and their parents occurring on a list of thirty-six statements dealing with contemporary issues such as sex, war, and drugs. In these studies, reviewed in Chapter 3, differences were found between the adolescents and their parents. But if someone else used a different definition of the generation gap, the comparability of findings between this other study and those noted above would not be direct. So long as researchers take pains to define clearly what they mean by their use of a concept, and design their study with such clear definitions in mind, any confusion about the use of the same term to represent different things may be eliminated.

Sampling

Another methodological problem deals with obtaining subjects for developmental research and making inferences about development based on results from a particular sample. If one wants to do a study of the racial attitudes of White and Black 15-year-olds, one obviously needs groups of White and Black 15-year-olds to study. The procedures used to obtain such samples will affect the conclusions one appropriately can make from the data.

Ideally one would like to measure the attitudes of all such adolescents. However, this is clearly an economic and practical impossibility. Therefore, researchers must often draw a sample from the large population—that is, a group of persons from the population that may feasibly be studied. Through the study of this sample, the researcher hopes to obtain results that could be generalized to the entire population.

Thus, the researcher must be sure that the sample used is representative of the entire population. If the sample is not representative, if it is *biased,* then the researcher may not appropriately infer that results obtained with the sample are characteristic of the entire population. For example, if the researcher conducting a study of racial attitudes among 15-year-old Blacks and Whites chooses as his or her sample White and Black adolescents from a small Southern city, then it would be inappropriate to infer that such adolescents are representative of all White or Black adolescents living elsewhere.

Standard procedures are available for obtaining unbiased samples. With *probability sampling,* all persons in the population have a known, nonzero chance of falling in the sample. In *nonprobability sampling,* not everyone in the population of interest may have a chance of being sampled.

There are three types of probability sampling. In *simple random sampling,* everyone in the population has an equal chance of being selected. Drawing names from a hat and using a computer to generate random selections are examples of simple random sampling.

Stratified sampling involves proportionately dividing the population according to the categories of a variable of interest, and then randomly sampling from within those categories. For example, if race is an important variable in the study, and only 10 percent of the population is Black, then one would only obtain one Black respondent for every nine White respondents using simple random sampling techniques. By using stratified sampling, one could choose equal numbers of Blacks and Whites for comparison, even though their numbers in the population were different.

The third type of probability sampling is *cluster* (or *area*) *sampling.* This technique involves dividing a state, for example, into areas. First, areas are sampled (for example, counties), then areas within these areas are sampled again (towns, for example). Then after a specified number of towns have been sampled, individuals or households within the towns may be sampled further. Thus, a statewide study could be conducted by sending observers or interviewers to only a few communities.

There are also three types of nonprobability sampling. *Availability samples* are used often in research in adolescent development, and unfortunately do not allow for any generalization. Availability sampling involves using whoever is available for the research—whoever is around and volunteers.

Judgmental (or *purposive*) *sampling* is similar, except that the researcher chooses subjects who fit a specific definition for the study. If, for example, the researcher wanted to study contraceptive use among adolescent females, he or she might look specifically for sexually active females between the ages of 14 and 18. But there would be no guarantee that the girls who are found would be representative of others.

Quota sampling, the third type of nonprobability sampling, involves the selection of individuals on the basis of whether they can be used to fill a predetermined quota which is set up to represent the population in question. For example, the researcher might want to do a national study without the great expense associated with probability samples. He or she might try to construct a sample which appears to be representative of the nation as a whole by establishing quotas of certain numbers of Blacks and Whites; Jews, Protestants, and Roman Catholics; males and females; the college-educated and those with high school educations or less; and married and unmarried adults. Any person can be selected for the sample so long as he or she fulfills the quota. The sampling ends when all the quotas have been met, and those selected are then studied. This method is often used by national polling organizations and can be quite accurate, even though it is a nonprobability method.

Although such procedures are well known to researchers, it is still often the case that studies are done with knowingly biased, unrepresentative samples. Why? To answer this question it should be noted that there are often ethical, economic, and practical problems that interfere with the researcher's desire to obtain a truly representative, unbiased sample. For example, it should be obvious that not all 15-year-old Black and White adolescents are available to the researcher. The researcher is located in a particular part of the country, and thus only youth living in that area are usually accessible for study. Even then, not all persons may be available. Schools may not allow a researcher to study the adolescents there. And even if a school does cooperate, the researcher is ethically bound to obtain the informed consent of those responsible for the person. Usually, then, the parents, and in most cases the adolescent as well, will have to give consent for participation, and lack of consent may lower response rates and the representativeness of the sampling.

The results of any developmental study are limited to the extent that biased sampling procedures interfere with obtaining a representative sample. Accordingly, the results of any such study may be generalized to broader populations only with extreme caution. Thus, because of methodological problems of sampling, the researcher always encounters a related problem, that of generalization.

Overgeneralization

It may be concluded that if limitations imposed on developmental research by sampling are not recognized, the researcher may try to interpret the study's results as being more representative than they actually are. As noted by McCandless (1970), there are other types of overgeneralization. The results of a particular study might indicate that there exist small, but reliable, differences between two groups. Yet the researcher may speak of these differences as if they reflected wide disparities between the groups. If such statements occur, one may also term this overgeneralization. For instance, suppose that a particular researcher is interested in the attitudes that adolescent males and females maintain about their own bodies. To study such body concepts, the researcher might ask a large group of adolescent males and females to rate several body characteristics (for example, arms, legs, face, body build, height, general appearance) in terms of how important each is in determining the person's satisfaction with his or her body's appearance (Lerner, Karabenick, & Stuart, 1973). Now suppose that female adolescents have a mean importance rating for the face of 4.20 (on a 5-point scale, with 5.0 being extremely important), and the corresponding rating for the male adolescents is 3.95. Because of the fact that many adolescent responses went into the calculation of these means and thus only small differences are needed for statistically significant differences to occur, the researcher might find that such a small difference between males and females is noteworthy. However, such *statistical* significance may not correspond to *psychological* significance. Can one say that on the basis of only a 0.25 point difference (out of a possible 4.0 point difference) that this one aspect of adolescent females' body concept is considerably different than the adolescent males' body concept? Probably not, and in fact, if such an assertion were made, it might be seen as an instance of overgeneralization.

Other types of overgeneralization also exist. Suppose that in the above study, the researcher also is interested in learning what parts of the male body are most important to females in deciding that a male is attractive, and what parts of the female body are most important to males in deciding that a female is attractive. The researcher can again ask the adolescent males and females to rate each of the body parts, but this time in terms of its importance for establishing the attractiveness of the opposite sex. Suppose that it is found the females rate general appearance as the most important characteristic of the male's body in determining male attractiveness, while males rate face as the most important part of the female's body in determining a female's attractiveness. Would the researcher be justified in concluding that when adolescent males go about choosing a female for a dating partner they make their judgments on the basis of the female's face, and that when females choose a male dating partner they make their judgments on the basis of the male's general appearance? May these ratings be generalized to choice of partners in dating situations? Since the findings of the study pertain to ratings obtained about females and males in general, not about choices of dating partners, such generalization would appear unwarranted.

As McCandless had indicated, "applying findings gathered in one situation to circumstances different in essential characteristics" is an instance of unsound generalization (1970, p. 55). Whenever one applies specific results to situations that may be different in important ways, one is guilty of overgeneralization.

To avoid unsound generalization, researchers must avoid (1) generalizing their results to situations different from those to which their data apply; (2) attributing more meaning, clarity, or significance to their results than is actually indicated; and (3) applying their findings to groups of people not actually represented in their sample (McCandless, 1970).

For example, due to both an intense interest in studying child development and the difficulty of readily obtaining samples of children to study, many university and other research institutions set up laboratory schools in earlier decades of this century. Many of the "facts" of development (at that time mostly "normative facts") were obtained through the study of children at these schools. Yet these children were often the children of the employees in that university or research organization. Hence, they were primarily White middle-class children of highly educated parents. Certainly, while the "facts" of development of such children are important, these "facts" may not be generalizable to all other children.

CHAPTER SUMMARY

Researchers in adolescent development have a wide variety of research strategies available to them. Yet no one choice is ideal for all problems or issues. Moreover, in any research effort there exist numerous methodological problems of data collection and interpretation that can affect negatively even those studies which have been designed carefully.

With such problems, it may be easy to see why there is not a large body of unequivocal data to support any theoretical idea in adolescent development. Indeed, as the various change processes of adolescent development are discussed in the rest of this book, it often will be noted that much research is flawed by the problems identified in this chapter. In addition, research about some topics often is unrelated to the theoretical statements that have been made about that topic (Gallatin, 1975).

Research on adolescent development can be classified on each of four distinct dimensions. The *normative-explanatory dimension* distinguishes between studies which describe the typical characteristics of adolescents and studies which attempt to account for the "why" of behavior. The *naturalistic-manipulative dimension* pertains to the degree to which a researcher studies behavior in its naturalistic (real-life) setting versus in a contrived laboratory setting. In the former case, the researcher usually interferes little with ongoing behavior, while in the latter setting, the researcher may need to manipulate certain variables so that change in the outcome variables may be studied. The *atheoretical-theoretical dimension* helps to identify studies on the basis of their relative emphasis on theory. The *ahistorical-historical dimension* sorts studies on the basis of their relative concern with change.

Much developmental research involves persons in a given *cohort.* A cohort is a group of individuals experiencing some event in common—and a *birth cohort* is the most common type of group studied in developmental studies. When individuals or groups are studied over time, the research has a *longitudinal* design. When individuals or groups are studied at only one point in time, the research has a *cross-sectional* design. The *time-lag* design provides for the examination of persons of a given age at different times in history.

Sequential methods combine the features of both longitudinal and cross-sectional designs. A sequential study has the greatest promise of discovering the answers to some of the fundamental questions asked about development. This is true because this design helps the researcher untangle the potentially interrelated influences of cohort, age, and time.

Besides issues of data collection and design, there are other potentially troublesome problems in research. *Contamination* occurs when data are influenced by variables extraneous to those which are central to the study. *Researcher effects* exist when a subject's responses or behavior is influenced by the researcher. Errors can crop into research when persons are asked to reconstruct past events and to report them from memory. *Faulty logic* is a problem when the investigator uses faulty reasoning techniques in interpreting data. Concepts may be defined inadequately. Finally, improper or inadequate *sampling* techniques may severely limit the ability of the researcher to generalize the findings beyond the small number of individuals studied.

8

PHYSICAL AND PHYSIOLOGICAL
CHANGES DURING ADOLESCENCE

CHAPTER
OVERVIEW

When one thinks about the characteristics which distinguish adolescence from other aspects of life, physical and physiological changes may readily come to mind. This chapter describes these changes and the implications they have for other aspects of adolescent development. The role of one's appearance in social relations is also discussed.

BODILY CHANGES IN ADOLESCENCE

Neuroendocrine Mechanisms of Adolescent Bodily Change
Prepubescence
Pubescence
Postpubescence
The Role of Sociocultural Variation
The Role of Historical Variation

INDIVIDUAL, SOCIOCULTURAL, AND HISTORICAL
IMPLICATIONS OF ADOLESCENT BODILY CHANGES

Implications of Early versus Late Maturation in Males
Implications of Early versus Late Maturation in Females

RELATIONS BETWEEN BODY TYPE AND PERSONALITY AND SOCIAL DEVELOPMENT

Sociocultural Influences on Body-Behavior Relations
Body-Build-Behavior Stereotypes

ISSUES
TO CONSIDER

What are the major phases of adolescent bodily change?

How do neuroendocrine mechanisms provide a basis of bodily change?

What are the major changes involved in the prepubescent, pubescent, and post-pubescent phases of male adolescent bodily change?

What are the major changes involved in the prepubescent, pubescent, and post-pubescent phases of female adolescent bodily change?

What is the nature of the relation between adolescent bodily change and sociocultural and historical variations?

What are the implications and limitations of existing longitudinal and cross-sectional research on the importance of early versus late maturation?

Why is it hypothesized that the physical appearance resulting from adolescent bodily changes is an important source of subsequent behavior?

What evidence supports the view that the interactions between body appearance and social stereotypes are involved in body-behavior relations?

Many social scientists specializing in adolescent development have observed that, to a great extent, "adolescents *are* their bodies, and their bodies are they" (for example, McCandless, 1970). This phrase denotes the special importance the adolescent attaches to the body, and the physical, physiological, and psychosocial changes associated with it. Bodily changes are the most noticeable and rapid changes that characterize adolescence. Indeed, they are the most noticeable and rapid set of physiological changes that occur across the life span. Moreover, as mentioned earlier, some major theorists of adolescent development—for example, Anna Freud (1969)—stress that the physical and physiological alterations associated with adolescence are the primary changes initiating further development.

Thus, there is ample justification for viewing the bodily changes of adolescence as especially important. An additional reason is that these physical and physiological changes are a major source of the adjustment problems confronting the adolescent. In Chapter 2 the general nature of changes in adolescence was noted. It was suggested that all dimensions of adolescent functioning, ranging from the biological to the sociocultural and historical, undergo transition. From this view, the person must reestablish a self-definition in order to adapt to the combined impact of all these alterations. Because these changes are dramatic, the adolescent is confronted with discovering who he or she is. However, establishing an identity is made more difficult if how one physically looks and internally feels is changing simultaneously. The changes in height, weight, sexual characteristics, and hormonal distributions complicate the adolescent's attempt to find an identity.

Many people have treated adolescent development as if it were equivalent to a study of physical and physiological changes (Schonfeld, 1969). In fact, the word "adolescence" itself comes from the Latin verb *adolescere*, which means to grow into maturity (Rogers, 1977). Although the life-span, multidisciplinary view of adolescent development involves much more than these physical and physiological changes, these alterations are, as has been noted, nevertheless quite important.

Accordingly, to detail the characteristics of the physical and physiological changes of adolescence, we shall focus first on the concept of puberty. Especially among those who equate adolescence with physical and physiological changes, the importance of puberty is great. Puberty describes particular types of physical and physiological changes in the person, and it is associated with several other changes as well (Schonfeld, 1969). However, equating puberty with adolescence, or even with the sum of the physical and physiological changes of adolescence, may be inappropriate. There are numerous aspects of physical and physiological changes in adolescence, and those associated with puberty are only one set of these.

BODILY CHANGES IN ADOLESCENCE

As a matter of convenience, the physical and physiological changes of adolescence may be labeled as "bodily" changes. These changes do not begin or end all at once. However, there is a general order to these changes that applies to most, but certainly not to all, people (Katchadourian, 1977). Although divisions in this sequence are quite arbitrary because of the fluidity of bodily change (Schonfeld, 1969), it is convenient to speak of phases of bodily change in adolescence in order to draw important distinctions among various degrees and types of change.

Bodily changes involve alterations in such things as height, weight, fat and muscle distribution, glandular secretions, and sexual characteristics. When changes in one or more of these characteristics have begun, but the majority of changes that

INSIGHT INTO ADOLESCENCE

Anne Frank died March 1945 in a Nazi concentration camp at the age of 15. When Hitler came to power in 1933, the Frank family moved from Germany to Amsterdam. In July 1942 they went into hiding with a few friends. For more than two years they hid from the Nazis; during this time Anne kept a diary. The entries appear in the form of letters to an imaginary girl named Kitty. Anne Frank meant to write a book after the war based on this diary and other sketches, called *The House Behind*.

Wednesday, 5 January, 1944

Dear Kitty,

I have two things to confess to you today, which will take a long time. But I must tell someone and you are the best one to tell, as I know that, come what may, you always keep a secret. . . .

Yesterday I read an article about blushing by Sis Heyster. This article might have been addressed to me personally. Although I don't blush very easily, the other things in it certainly all fit me. She writes roughly something like this—that a girl in the years of puberty becomes quiet within and begins to think about the wonders that are happening to her body.

I experience that, too, and that is why I get the feeling lately of being embarrassed about Margot, Mummy, and Daddy. Funnily enough, Margot, who is much more shy that I am, isn't at all embarrassed.

I think what is happening to me is so wonderful, and not only what can be seen on my body, but all that is taking place inside. I never discuss myself or any of these things with anybody; that is why I have to talk to myself about them.

Each time I have a period—and that has only been three times—I have the feeling that in spite of all the pain, unpleasantness, and nastiness, I have a sweet secret, and that is why, although it is nothing but a nuisance to me in a way, I always long for the time that I shall feel that secret within me again.

Sis Heyster also writes that girls of this age don't feel quite certain of themselves, and discover that they themselves are individuals with ideas, thoughts, and habits. After I came here, when I was just fourteen, I began to think about myself sooner that most girls, and to know that I am a "person." Sometimes, when I lie in bed at night, I have a terrible desire to feel my breasts and to listen to the quiet rhythmic beat of my heart.

I already had these kinds of feelings subconsciously before I came here, because I remember that once when I slept with a girl friend I had a strong desire to kiss her, and that I did do so. I could not help being terribly inquisitive over her body, for she had always kept it hidden from me. I asked her whether, as proof of our friendship, we could feel one another's breasts, but she refused. I go into ecstasies every time I see the naked figure of a woman, such as Venus, for example. It strikes me as so wonderful and exquisite that I have difficulty in stopping the tears rolling down my cheeks.

If only I had a girl friend!

Yours, Anne

Source: Excerpt from *Anne Frank: The Diary of a Young Girl*. Copyright © 1952 by Otto H. Frank. Reprinted by permission of Doubleday & Company, Inc.

---

will take place have not, the person may be labeled as being in the *prepubescent* (or prepuberty) phase. When most of those bodily changes that will eventually take place have been initiated, the person is in the *pubescent* (or puberty) phase. Finally, when most of those bodily changes have already occurred, the person is in the postpubescent (or postpuberty) phase. This phase ends when all changes are completed.

The bodily changes of adolescence involve a period of alteration of physical and physiological characteristics during which the person reaches an adult level of reproductive maturity. But puberty is not synonymous with all maturational changes. In fact, some authors (for example, Schonfeld, 1969) see puberty as only one point within the pubescent phase. Puberty is the point at which the person is capable of reproducing (Schonfeld, 1969).

As noted in Chapter 2, this point is *not* synonymous with menarche (the first menstrual cycle) in females or with the first ejaculation in males. The initial menstrual cycles of females, for instance, typically are not accompanied by ovulation. Thus, the early adolescent female usually is not able to conceive. Ovulation and the ability to conceive, which we have labeled puberty and others sometimes term *nubility,* occur one to three years after menarche (Hafez & Evans, 1973; Montagu, 1946). Even with puberty, however, regular ovulation typically is not established until several years after menarche (Hafez & Evans, 1973). Nevertheless, exceptions are increasingly evident. In one recent year (1975), for example, 30,000 females age 14 and under became pregnant in the United States (Alan Guttmacher Institute, 1976).

Similarly, for males there is a period of time between the first ejaculation, which usually occurs between 11 and 16 years of age (Kinsey, Pomeroy, & Martin, 1948), and the capability of fertilizing. At the time of first ejaculation the male is usually sterile, and it is not for one to three years after this time that there are enough motile sperm in the ejaculate so that the male could be fertile (Schonfeld, 1969).

Thus, neither menarche, the first seminal emission, nor puberty itself is commensurate with all the bodily changes associated with the prepubescent, pubescent, and postpubescent phases of adolescence. In the following sections some of the major changes associated with each of these phases will be detailed. These changes will relate to both the *primary* and the *secondary* sexual characteristics of the person. Primary sexual characteristics are present at birth and involve the internal and external genitalia (for example, the penis in males and the vagina in females). Secondary sexual characteristics are those which emerge to represent the two sexes during the prepubescent through postpubescent phases (for example, breast development in females and pigmented facial hair in males). Moreover, these changes all involve nervous system and endocrine system mechanisms. After these general *neurohormonal* processes involved in all phases of adolescent bodily change are briefly described, some of their outcomes will be considered.

Neuroendocrine mechanisms of adolescent bodily change

There are two types of glandular systems. *Exocrine* glands have an opening (a duct) to the world outside the body. Examples of such glands are the salivary and the sweat glands. *Endocrine* glands, however, have no such external duct. Rather, they secrete a substance, *hormones,* directly into the bloodstream. The role of the endocrine glands is most important in understanding the changes associated with adolescent bodily changes.

The hormonal influences on adolescent bodily change begin to occur as a result of stimulation from the central nervous system. On the basis of stimulation from some still unknown higher, cerebral cortex brain center, a structure of the brain termed the *hypothalamus* is stimulated. The hypothalamus in turn stimulates a major endocrine gland, the *pituitary.* More specifically, the front part of the pituitary (the *anterior*) is stimulated. As a consequence, the anterior pituitary gland secretes certain hormones.

First, a *growth-stimulating hormone* (sometimes labeled as GSH or termed *somatotropin*) is secreted. This hormone acts on all body *(soma)* tissues to stimulate their rate of growth and nourishment *(trophe)*. A second type of hormone that is secreted is termed a *trophic* hormone. Such a hormone stimulates specific tissues. In fact, the role of such hormones is to stimulate other endocrine glands to produce their own specific hormones. Although there are several trophic hormones released by the pituitary in order to initiate adolescence (Katchadourian, 1977; Schonfeld, 1969), two specific trophic hormones, *gonadotropic* hormones, act on those glands in males and females that are associated with each sex, respectively. These glands are the testes in males and the ovaries in females, and they are termed *gonads*. *Follicle-stimulating hormone (FSH)* encourages ovulation in the female and spermatogenesis in the male. In addition, it encourages releases of estrogen in the female. *Luteinizing hormone (LH)* also encourages ovulation in the female and testicular development in the male. Furthermore, LH encourages the secretion of *progesterone* in the female and *testosterone* in the male. Thus, gonadotrophic hormones produced by the anterior pituitary act specifically on the gonads of males and females, causing the production of particular hormones. These latter hormones provide a basis for the sexual maturation of males and females.

The hormones secreted by the gonads most generally are termed *androgens* (for males) and *estrogens* (for females). Their relative concentration in the body influences the changes we associate with prepubescence through postpubescence. The changes we typically find with males result from greater concentrations of androgens than estrogens, while more estrogens than androgens are necessary to produce the changes we typically find with females. However, it should be noted that males and females have both types of hormones, and that both play a role in fostering changes across the phases of adolescent sexual maturation. For instance, for both males and females, androgens initially stimulate growth and muscle development, but both androgens and estrogens are eventually needed to terminate growth (Schonfeld, 1969).

In sum, through the functioning of these hormones, the alterations associated with bodily change in adolescence occur; as such, sexual maturation proceeds. Thus, interplays between gonadotrophins and androgens and estrogens lead to the emergence of mature, reproductively fertile sex cells in males and females: the sperm of the male and the ovum of the female. However, this maturation is just one aspect of the physical and physiological changes involved in the phases of adolescent bodily change we have identified. To learn of the others, the characteristics of change associated with each respective phase are now discussed.

Prepubescence

Because of the general orderliness of the sequence of bodily changes in adolescence, Schonfeld (1969) suggests that the beginning and end of prepubescence can be marked by the first evidence of sexual maturation and the appearance of pubic hair, respectively. In males, there is a progressive enlargement of the testicles, an enlargement and reddening of the scrotal sac, and an increase in the length and circumference of the penis (Schonfeld, 1969, p. 29). These changes all involve primary sexual characteristics. Insofar as secondary sexual characteristics are concerned, no true pubic hair is present, although the male may have downy hair.

In females, the changes marking prepubescence typically begin an average of two years earlier than with males. At the level of the cells and tissues of the body, the first sign of female development in this phase is the enlargement of the ovary and the ripening of the cells (termed *primary graffian follicles*) that will eventually evolve into mature reproductive cells *(ova)*. However, in contrast with males, these changes in primary sexual characteristics typically are not visible for clinical or scientific inspection, and as such, changes in secondary sex characteristics are the indexes often used to mark prepubescent changes. In this phase there is a rounding of the hips and the first visible sign of breast development. The rounding of the hips occurs as a result of increased deposit of fat, while the first visible signs of breast development are marked by an elevation of the areola surrounding the nipple (Schonfeld, 1969). This raising produces a small conelike protuberance, known as the breast "bud." As with the male, there is no true pubic hair, although down may be present.

Pubescence

Schonfeld (1969) uses as an index of the onset of the pubescent phase the appearance of pubic hair and, in turn, defines the end of this major phase to be when pubic hair development is complete. Whether or not one agrees with the appropriateness of these indexes, there is wide agreement that such pubic hair changes are important

Exhibit 8.1
Stage of pubic hair development in adolescent girls: (1) early pubescent (not shown) in which there is no true pubic hair; (2) late prepubescent–early pubescence in which sparse growth of downy hair is mainly at sides of labia; (3) pigmentation, coarsening, and curling with an increase in the amount of hair; (4) adult hair, but limited in area; (5) adult hair with horizontal upper border. (*Source:* Redrawn from J. M. Tanner, *Growth at adolescence*, 2d ed., Oxford: Blackwell, 1962.)

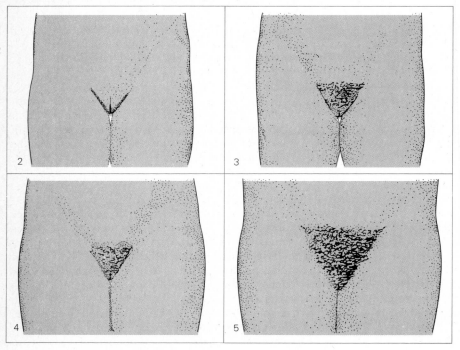

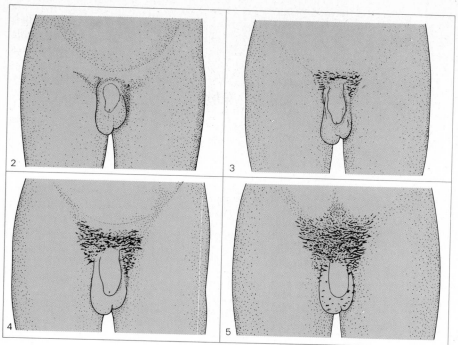

Exhibit 8.2
Stages of pubic hair development in adolescent boys: (1) early prepubescent (not shown) in which there is no true pubic hair; (2) late prepubescent—early pubescent in which sparse growth of downy hair is mainly at base of penis; (3) pigmentation, coarsening, and curling, with an increase in amount of hair; (4) adult hair, but limited in area; (5) adult hair with horizontal upper border and spreading to thighs. (*Source:* Redrawn from J. M. Tanner, *Growth at adolescence*, 2d ed., Oxford: Blackwell, 1962.)

markers of the range of changes characteristic of this phase of major bodily changes (Katchadourian, 1977). Exhibit 8.1 shows the progressive changes involved in pubic hair development for adolescent females, and Exhibit 8.2 shows these changes for adolescent males.

In addition to pubic hair development, pubescence is marked by a growth spurt. The peak time of growth in height and weight occurs during this phase. Thus, as seen in Exhibit 8.3, there is a marked increase in the amount of height gained in the age range typically associated with pubescence for both males and females in the United States today. A corresponding increase in weight in males and females is presented in Exhibit 8.4. In both Exhibits 8.3 and 8.4 it should be noted that the components of the adolescent growth spurt occur about two years earlier in females than in males. Exhibit 8.5 also shows the relative changes in growth from infancy through the adolescent growth spurt and on to maturity. This figure is based on the North American and Western European populations. The growth rates for males and females are shown at regular intervals from infancy to maturity, and the relative appearance of each sex as a consequence of this growth is illustrated.

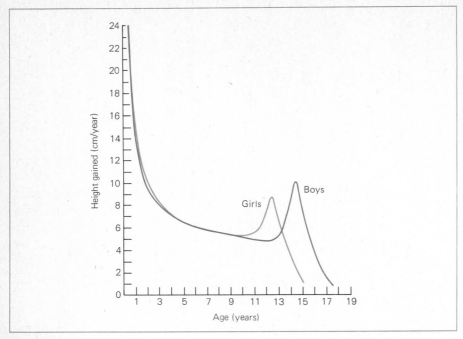

Exhibit 8.3
Typical individual curves showing velocity of growth in *height* for boys and girls. (*Source:* Redrawn from J. M. Tanner, R. H. Whitehouse, and M. Takaishi, *Archives of Diseases in Childhood,* 1966, *41,* 466.

Exhibit 8.4
Typical individual curves showing velocity of *weight* gain in boys and girls. (*Source:* Redrawn from J. M. Tanner, R. H. Whitehouse, and M. Takaishi, *Archives of Diseases in Childhood*, 1966, *41,* 466.)

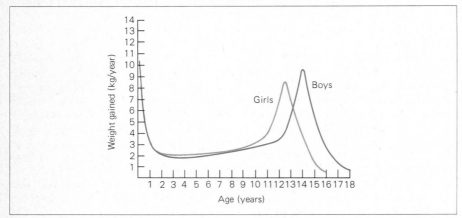

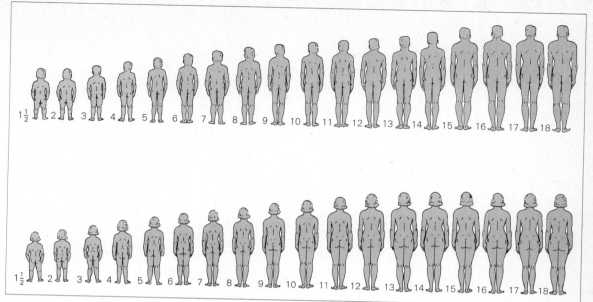

Exhibit 8.5
Rates of growth in development of boys and girls, shown at regular intervals from infancy to maturity. Note the change in the form of the body as well as the increase in height. (*Source:* Redrawn from *Growing up* by J. M. Tanner. Copyright 1973 by Scientific American, Inc. All rights reserved.)

Other changes characterize people during pubescence. Menarche occurs in females, usually about 18 months after the maximum height increment of the growth spurt (Schonfeld, 1969). In addition to this functional change, there are structural alterations in the primary sexual characteristics of females. For instance, the vulva and clitoris enlarge. Moreover, in regard to the secondary sexual characteristics of females, there is increased breast development. Thus, there is a change from having breast buds to having the areola and nipple elevated to form the "primary" breast (Schonfeld, 1969). This range of changes is described and illustrated in Exhibit 8.6.

The primary and secondary sexual characteristics of males also change during pubescence. With regard to secondary characteristics, there is a deepening of the voice, due to growth of the larynx. Both pigmented axillary and facial hair appear, usually about two years after the emergence of pubic hair (Schonfeld, 1969). With regard to primary sexual characteristics, the testes continue to enlarge, and the scrotum grows and becomes pigmented. Similarly, the penis becomes longer and increases in circumference (Schonfeld, 1969). These changes are described and illustrated in Exhibit 8.7.

In summary, the pubescent phase of adolescent development involves a series of structural and functional changes in both the primary and secondary sexual characteristics of both sexes. Although not all such changes have been described, what most authorities see as the major ones have been depicted (Katchadourian, 1977; Schonfeld, 1969; Tanner, 1973).

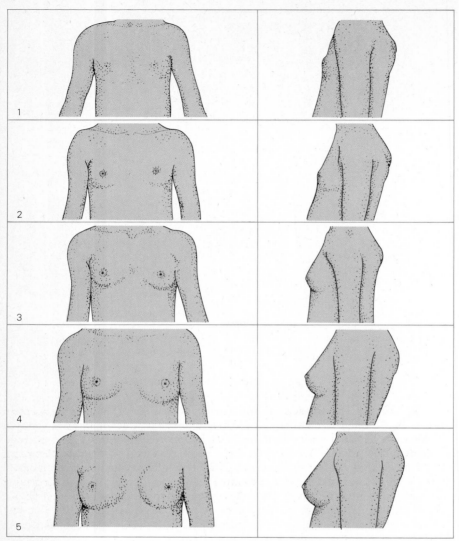

Exhibit 8.6
Stages of breast development in adolescent girls: (1) prepubescence flat appearance, like that of a child; (2) small, raised breast bud; (3) general enlargement and raising of breast and areola; (4) areola and papilla (nipple) form contour separate from that of breast; (5) adult breast— areola is in the same contour as breast. (*Source:* Redrawn from J. M. Tanner, *Growth at adolescence*, 2d ed., Oxford: Blackwell, 1962.)

Postpubescence

According to Schonfeld (1969, p. 28), the postpubescent phase of adolescence may be marked as starting when pubic hair growth is complete, when there is a deceleration of growth in height, and when there is completion of changes in the primary and

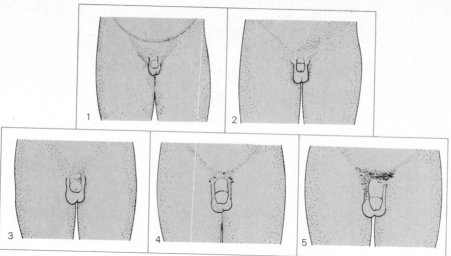

Exhibit 8.7
Stages of male genital development: (1) prepubescence, in which the size of the testes and penis is similar to that in early childhood; (2) testes become larger and scrotal skin reddens and coarsens; (3) continuation of stage 2, with lengthening of penis; (4) penis enlarges in general size, and scrotal skin becomes pigmented; (5) adult genitalia. (*Source:* Redrawn from J. M. Tanner, *Growth at adolescence*, 2d ed., Oxford: Blackwell, 1962.)

secondary sexual characteristics and the person is fertile. Despite the extent of the completed changes, there continue to be changes in the primary and secondary sexual characteristics. In males, the beard usually starts to grow in this phase, and for females, there is further growth of axillary hair and breast development.

Thus, the physical and physiological changes characterizing adolescence involve much more than just puberty. Rather, they include alterations spanning perhaps an entire decade of the life span and involve at least three phases of bodily change. Exhibit 8.8 summarizes the normative sequence of bodily changes for males in current United States society, and Exhibit 8.9 presents corresponding information for females. While the information in these two exhibits represents norms that can be generalized across most segments of current United States society, there are important qualifications to these data. There is in some cases considerable variation in the rate and quality of changes involved in all phases of adolescent bodily change, and this variation is associated with both sociocultural and historical differences. These sources of variation are considered in the next two sections.

The role of sociocultural variation

There are abundant data indicating that the body changes associated with adolescence vary in relation to their sociocultural environment. To illustrate, data for one aspect of bodily change—menarche—will be considered.

As shown in Exhibit 8.10, there is a vast difference in the age of menarche in different cultures, and further, in different social strata within a culture. Thus, the median age at menarche for Cuban Blacks or Whites is 12.4 years—the lowest age

Exhibit 8.8
Normative sequence of bodily changes in males

Phase	Appearance of sexual characteristics	Average ages	Age range*
Childhood through prepubescence	*Testes* and *penis* have not grown since infancy; no *pubic hair*; growth in *height* constant. No spurt.	——	——
Prepubescence	*Testes* begin to increase in size; *scrotum* grows, and skin reddens and becomes coarser; *penis* grows in length and circumference; no true *pubic hair*; may have down.	12–13 years	10–15 years
Pubescence	*Pubic hair* is pigmented, coarse, and straight at base of penis, becoming progressively more curled and profuse, forming at first an inverse triangle and subsequently extending up to umbilicus; *axillary hair* starts after pubic hair; *penis* and testes continue growing; *scrotum* becomes larger, pigmented, and sculptured; marked spurt of growth in *height* with maximum increment about time pubic hair first develops, decelerating by the time fully established; spontaneous or induced *emissions* follow but *spermatozoa* inadequate in number and motility (adolescent sterility); *voice* beginning to change as larynx enlarges.	13–16 years	11–18 years
Postpubescence	*Facial* and *body* hair appear and spread; *pubic* and *axillary hair* become denser; *voice* deepens; *testes* and *penis* continue to grow; *emission* has adequate number of motile *spermatozoa* for fertility; growth in *height* gradually decelerates, 98 percent of mature stature by 17¾ years ± 10 months, indention of frontal *hair* line.	16–18 years	14–20 years
Postpubescence to adult	Mature, full development of *primary* and *secondary sex* characteristics; *muscles* and *hirsutism* may continue increasing.	Onset 18–20 years	Onset 16–21 years

*This age range includes 80 percent of cases.
Source: Adapted from Schonfeld (1969, p. 30).

listed—while the median age for the Black Bundi tribes-people of New Guinea is 18.8 years—the highest age shown. Not only do the data of Exhibit 8.11 underscore that age per se is an inappropriate focus in an attempt to understand development, but also these data indicate that sociocultural differences are not related to race. As observed by Katchadourian (1977), for example, Blacks were observed to have both early (in Cuba) *and* late (in New Guinea) maturation.

In addition, a study by Halbrecht, Sklorowski, and Tsafriv (1971) shows that significant differences exist within a given cultural group. In Israel, the age of menarche was found to be different for females born in Europe or the United States, or whose father had been born in these different settings.

The variables accounting for these differences might relate to nutritional or health care differences associated with various sociocultural settings. There is evidence for this view. Differences in age of menarche within the same country are often seen between urban and poor rural areas. Tanner (1970) reports that in Rumania

Exhibit 8.9
Normative sequence of bodily changes in females

Phase	Appearance of sexual characteristics	Average age	Age range*
Childhood through prepubescence	No *pubic hair*; *breasts* are flat; *growth* in height is constant, no spurt.		
Prepubescence	Rounding of *hips*; *breasts* and nipples are elevated to form *bud* stage; no true pubic hair; may have down.	10–11 years	9–14 years
Pubescence	*Pubic hair* is pigmented, coarse, and straight primarily along labia, but becomes progressively curled, and spreads over mons and becomes profuse with an inverse triangular pattern; *axillary hair* starts after pubic hair; marked growth spurt with maximum *height* increment 18 months before menarche; *menarche: labia* become enlarged, *vaginal secretion* becomes acid; *breast* development begins with areola and nipple elevated to form "primary" breast.	11–14 years	10–16 years
Postpubescence	*Axillary hair* in moderate quantity; *pubic hair* fully developed; *breasts* fill out, forming adult-type configuration; *menstruation* well established; *growth* in height is decelerated, ceasing at 16¼ ± 13 months.	14–16 years	13–18 years
Postpubescence to adulthood	Further growth of *axillary hair*; *breasts* fully developed.	Onset 16–18 years	Onset 15–19 years

*This age range includes 80 percent of cases.
Source: Adapted from Schonfeld (1969, p. 33).

the average age of menarche is 13.5 years in towns and 14.6 years in villages. Corresponding differences between town-reared and rural-reared children have been found in the Soviet Union (13.0 and 14.3 years, respectively) and in India (12.8 and 14.2 years, respectively). In all these contrasts, nutritional resources are less abundant in the rural setting. That such scarcity generally may delay menarche is possible in light of the fact that females who have many siblings (and thus a higher probability of scarce resources) also have delayed menarche.

The availability of resources in different socioeconomic strata within a society is also associated with variation in age of menarche. In Hong Kong the age at menarche is 12.5 years for children of the rich, 12.8 years for those of average income levels, and 13.3 years for children of poor families (Tanner, 1970). However, different studies of the relation between age of menarche and social class define social class differently. Thus, there is often a situation where the poor in one country may be starving while the poor in another society may have relatively adequate nutrition (Katchadourian, 1977). Nevertheless, a relation between socioeconomic status and menarche typically is found. Thus, in European countries, the range of socioeconomic status from rich to poor is associated with a range of about 2 to 4 months in age of menarche (Katchadourian, 1977).

Exhibit 8.10
Median age at menarche in several populations.

Population or location*	Median age, years	Population or location	Median age, years*
Cuba		Tel Aviv, Israel‡	13.0
Negro	12.4	London, U.K.	13.1
White	12.4	Assam, India (city	
Mulatto	12.6	dwellers)	13.2
Cuba†		Burma (city dwellers)	13.2
Negro	12.9	Uganda (wealthy Kampala)	13.4
White	13.0	Oslo, Norway	13.5
Mulatto	13.0	France	13.5
Hong Kong (wealthy		Nigeria (wealthy Ibo)	14.1
Chinese)	12.5	U.S.S.R. (rural Buriats)	15.0
Florence, Italy	12.5	South Africa (Transkei	
Wroclaw, Poland	12.6	Banfu)	15.0
Budapest, Hungary	12.8	Rwanda§	
California, U.S.	12.8	Tutsi	16.5
Colombo, Ceylon	12.8	Huru	17.1
Moscow, U.S.S.R.	13.0	New Guinea (Bundi)	18.8

*Data from Tanner (1966) unless otherwise indicated.
†Pospisilova-Zuzakova, Stukovsky, and Valsik (1965).
‡Ber and Brociner (1964).
§Hiernaux (1965).
Source: Jean Hiernaux, Ethnic Differences in Growth and Development, *Eugenics Quarterly*, 1968, *15*, 12–21. Copyright 1968 American Eugenics Society.

The role of historical variation

Adolescent bodily changes are also related to history. This relation, often termed the *secular trend* (Katchadourian, 1977; Muuss, 1975b), can be illustrated by considerable data, some of which were discussed in earlier chapters. In addition, it may be noted that since 1900, children of preschool age have been taller on an average of 1.0 centimeter and heavier on an average of 0.5 kilogram per decade (Katchadourian, 1977). Furthermore, the changes in height and weight occurring during the adolescent growth spurt have involved increased gains of 2.5 centimeters and of 2.5 kilograms, respectively (Falkner, 1972; Katchadourian, 1977). It has been noted that these changes occur in the context of increasingly earlier ages for the start of adolescent bodily changes (Muuss, 1975b; Schonfeld, 1969). Thus, these alterations happen among present birth cohorts during a pubescent period which both begins and ends earlier in life than was the case with past birth cohorts. Because adolescent bodily change stops earlier and earlier as history progresses, the absolute increases in final adult height and weight across history are not great (Bakwin & McLaughlin, 1964; Maresh, 1972). However, there is as yet no final decision about whether this historical trend for increasingly earlier adolescent bodily changes is continuing (Katchadourian, 1977; Schonfeld, 1969; Tanner, 1962).

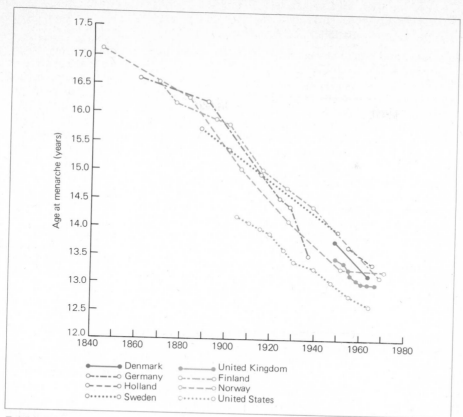

Exhibit 8.11
Declining age of menarche. Redrawn from *Growing Up* by J. M. Tanner.
Copyright 1973 by Scientific American, Inc. All rights reserved.

Plasticity continues to characterize bodily changes in adolescents in some sociocultural settings, at least through the early 1970s, as illustrated by the data in Exhibit 8.11. Here, the declining age of menarche across history in different countries is illustrated. In Norway, for example, it may be noted that females of the 1840 birth cohort reached menarche at about 17 years, while Norwegian females in more current cohorts reach this point about four years earlier in life. As noted previously, the rate of decreased age of menarche in this country has been about four months per decade (Muuss, 1975b). Similarly, it may be noted in the exhibt that in the United States, women of a birth cohort around 1890 had menarche at about age 14 years. Today, however, females in the United States reach this point between one and two years earlier.

In sum, the bodily changes of adolescence can be influenced by variables associated with sociocultural and historical variation. In turn, these bodily changes may reciprocally have an impact on these other factors which influence them, and it may be that the *nature and rate* of adolescent bodily change may have important implications for the individual, the society, and history. This idea is evaluated in the following sections of this chapter.

The quality and rate of any aspect of individual development influence the person. The type of thinking ability one possesses (for example, whether it is concrete or abstract) and how quickly one changes from one type of thought to another (for example, whether one attains the ability to think abstractly sooner than peers do) may be expected to influence a person's functioning. Similarly, the type of body characteristics one develops as a consequence of the prepubescent through postpubescent changes (for example, whether the body is fat or muscular) and how fast one proceeds through these phases of adolescent bodily change (for example, whether one has slower or faster breast development than one's peers) will influence one's personal and social functioning. Thus, the inference that the nature and rate of bodily changes should influence psychological and social levels of analysis is just one instance of a more general view that the types and rates of all developmental changes are important in human functioning.

This general view has a long tradition of study within adolescence, insofar as it has been raised in the context of bodily changes. Generally, the issue has been studied when the implications of *early versus late maturation* have been examined. Adolescent bodily changes involve, in a functional sense, an alteration toward reproductive capability; this is an adaptive capability which obviously allows the species to survive. When an organism is capable of reproductive function, it is termed *mature*. Thus, the physical and physiological changes associated with the prepubescent through postpubescent phases are labeled *maturational*, in that they are involved with reproductive capability.

We stress this definition of the term because it implies that maturational changes are not just nature-based phenomena. In Chapter 5 it was suggested that many people mistakenly have considered that any change or *growth* (a term *usually* associated with changes in structure, as opposed to function) which could be labeled as maturational was a nature phenomenon. Not only do the arguments and data presented in Chapter 5 suggest the limitations of such a view, but the data reviewed in preceding sections of this chapter—regarding the sociocultural and historical influences on bodily changes—also speak against the view.

Simply, it is our position that although prepubescent through postpubescent bodily changes may be labeled as maturational in order to indicate their association with the attainment of reproductive capability, the use of the term maturation in no way implies a solely nature-based phenomenon. Indeed, it has been argued that all changes, whether they be associated with adolescent maturation or with maturation at any time in life, are products of interactions among nature and nurture processes.

Thus, the study of *early maturers* focuses on people whose nature-nurture interactional history has led them to go through the phases of adolescent bodily change faster than usual. They show instability in that their bodily changes relative to their same-age peers are more rapid. In turn, the study of *late maturers* assesses people who as a result of their interactional history have gone through the phases of adolescent bodily change slower than usual. Late maturers also show instability; but here it is because their bodily changes relative to their same-age peers are slower. Although of the same age, the early maturer is accelerated in bodily growth (he or she is in a more advanced change phase), while the late maturer is delayed (he or she is in a less advanced phase).

Such differences in rate of development lead to quite distinct differences in bodily appearance. As seen in Exhibit 8.12, all the females are of the same age, but 1

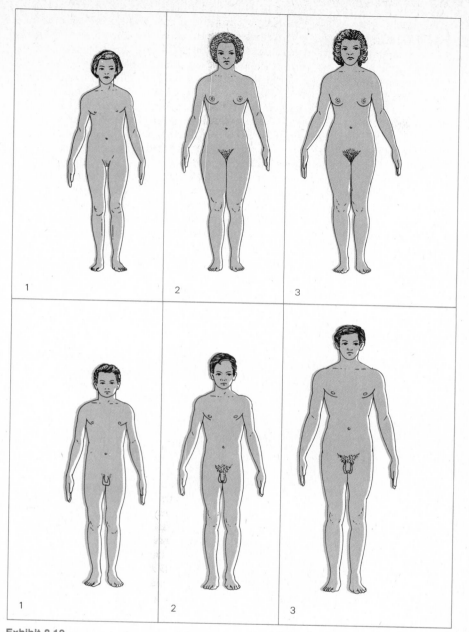

Exhibit 8.12
Variations in pubescent development. All three females are 12¾ years old, and all three males are 14¾ years old, but in different phases of change. (*Source:* Redrawn from *Growing up* by J. M. Tanner. Copyright 1973 by Scientific American, Inc. All rights reserved.)

has the characteristics of prepubescence, 2 of pubescence, and 3 of postpubescence. Similar differences are seen with the three identically aged males shown in the exhibit. Although the adolescents depicted in Exhibit 8.12 are shown at one point in their development, the contrasts in bodily appearance between early and late maturers become increasingly more pronounced over time. These developmental differences are shown for males in Exhibit 8.13 and for females in Exhibit 8.14.

It should be noted that at any given age in adolescence, it is possible to describe in different ways the *types* of bodies early and late maturers possess as a consequence of their contrasting rates. For example, the early maturing male at age 16.5 has a body build which is muscular and which appears strong and athletic-looking (see the first 16.5-year-old male in Exhibit 8.13). However, the most extreme late-maturing male at this time has a body type which is not muscular (see the second 16.5-year-old male in Exhibit 8.13). Indeed, such extreme late maturers often have a thin body type and a frail appearance (Jones & Bayley, 1950), often seen as "not having filled out." In addition, others who are late maturers, but not to the extreme extent of the first group, have a plump body (Tanner, 1962), and are regarded in these cases as "not having lost their baby fat." With females, early maturation typically results in a bodily appearance that combines both muscularity with some fatness, while late maturing is associated with thinness, as in males (see the two 14.5-year-olds, respectively, of Exhibit 8.14). These contrasts in the physical appearance of the body, in the type of build that results from bodily changes, will be important when we discuss the idea that both the types and rates of bodily change in adolescence affect individual and social functioning.

To evaluate this idea it should first be noted that there has not been a great amount of research on the psychosocial implications of early versus late maturation. What data do exist come mostly from longitudinal studies conducted at the

Exhibit 8.13
Contrasts between an early- and a late-maturing boy, age 11½ to 16⅗ years. (*Source:* Drawing based on photograph in F. H. Shuttleworth, The adolescent period: A pictorial atlas. *Monographs of the Society for Research in Child Development*, 1951, 14, Serial No. 50, 1949, p. 24.)

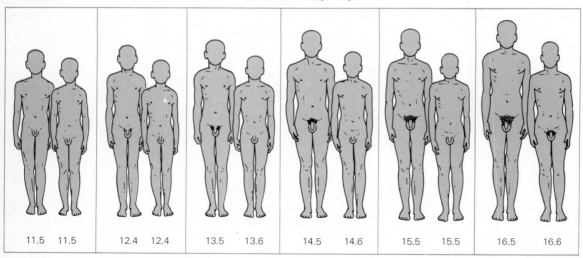

| 11.5 11.5 | 12.4 12.4 | 13.5 13.6 | 14.5 14.6 | 15.5 15.5 | 16.5 16.6 |

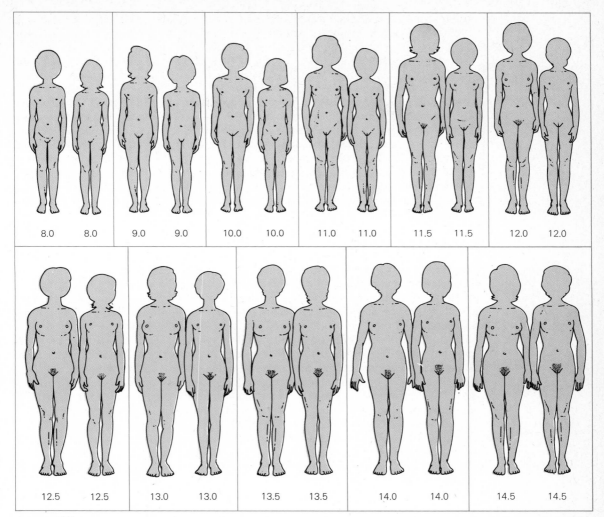

Exhibit 8.14
Contrasts between an early- and a late-maturing girl, ages 8 to 14½ years
(*Source:* Drawings based on photographs in F. H. Shuttleworth, The adolescent period: A pictorial atlas. *Monographs of the Society for Research in Child Development*, 1951, 14, Serial No. 50, 1949, pp. 13–14.)

University of California at Berkeley. These studies, labeled the California Growth Studies, have the limitations of all studies with longitudinal designs. They involve a confounding of age and time effects, they may have biased samples, and there may be effects associated with repeated testing.

Moreover, the data about early and late maturers from the California Growth Study involve extremely small samples of subjects in most cases. Further, these samples consist mostly of middle-class persons. Thus, the data from these studies can, at best, serve as a tentative basis for generalizations. Because there are important differences in the findings associated with early and late maturation in males and females, the data for each sex will be considered separately.

Implications of early versus late maturation in males

In one of the first studies of early and late maturation derived from the California Growth Study, Jones and Bayley (1950) classified a group of ninety males on the basis of their rate of maturation. To judge this rate, x-rays were taken of bones in various parts of the body. This index reliably indicates the phase of adolescent bodily change and corresponds to other measures of such change, including phase of pubic hair growth or testicular enlargement (McCandless, 1970). It is interesting to note that the use of this x-ray index of maturation level has varied across history. Researchers in current cohorts recognize the possible dangers of x-ray use more so than those who worked in the 1930s, when the subjects of the California Growth Study were children and adolescents (McCandless, 1970). Because of its danger and expense, less exact measures of rate of maturation are used today. For example, indexes relating to pubic hair growth and even just general physical appearance are used.

Nevertheless, on the basis of their x-ray indexes, Jones and Bayley (1950) were able to find two groups within the original sample of ninety males who most consistently were accelerated (those whose maturation rate was in the top 20 percent of the distribution) and who most consistently were delayed (and thus in the lowest 20 percent of the distribution) in their respective maturational changes. There were sixteen males in each of these two groups. It was this group of early and late maturers that was studied extensively regarding the psychosocial implications of their maturational rates. Unfortunately (because of its limitations), the data from these thirty-two males provide much of what we know of these implications.

Jones and Bayley obtained ratings of the members of each group from two sources. First, a group of adults judged the males in terms of their social and personal characteristics. Second, some of the peers of these early- and late-maturing males made the same type of judgments. The early maturers—those whom it may be remembered had the athletic-looking type of build—were judged more positively by the adults than were the late maturers—those who had primarily a thin body type. The early maturers were seen as more physically attractive, more masculine, better groomed, and less needful of status striving than the late maturers. On the other hand, the delayed males were regarded as more tense, more seeking of attention, more affected, and more childish than their early-maturing age-mates (McCandless, 1970). In addition, the late maturers were seen by the adults as less mature in heterosexual relations than their accelerated peers.

However, the adults did not judge the two groups to be different in regard to popularity, leadership, cheerfulness, and assurance. The peers of the males in these two groups did not quite agree with the adults here. In fact, they were quite a bit more negative about the late maturers than were the adults.

Their peers judged the late maturers to be more restless, more bossy, more attention-seeking, less assured, less likely to have a sense of humor about themselves, less physically attractive, and less likely to have older friends than the early maturers. In addition, the peers saw the late maturers as less popular and as less likely to be leaders than the early maturers. This means that members of the former group were *in fact* less popular and less often leaders than were members of the latter group, because such attributes are based on peer group appraisals (McCandless, 1970). Independent data support this view. Latham (1951) found that junior high school boys who were more physically mature, and were therefore taller, heavier, and more muscular than their peers, were more likely to be chosen sport team captains. In addition, these more mature boys were the dominant people in the leading social groups in school.

In summary, members of their adult and peer society gave adolescent boys different social and personal evaluations in accordance with whether such boys reached puberty before or after their group norm. If social interactions and appraisals contribute to individual functioning, then it may be expected that these contrasting social evaluations would affect the two groups' psychological development.

The results of a second study, done by Mussen and Jones (1957), confirm this expectation. These researchers studied the same males assessed by Jones and Bayley. Mussen and Jones, however, administered the Thematic Apperception Test (TAT) to the males. This test is a *projective* personality test. In such a test, a relatively ambiguous stimulus is presented to a person (in the case of the TAT, pictures are presented). It is *assumed* that in describing the stimulus the person will reveal his or her underlying personality "dynamics." In other words, his or her current conflicts, fears, desires, feelings, and thoughts about self and others will be revealed, or "projected," into the descriptions.

Although many of the interpretations of the subjects' projections did not show distinctions between the two groups, there was one major and statistically significant set of differences between early and late maturers. More often than was the case with the early maturers, the late maturers gave responses suggestive of feelings of inadequacy, weakness, rejection, rebelliousness toward their families (often seen as a desire to get free of parental restraint), and feelings of disapproval by parents and authorities. Yet at the same time, the late maturers were more likely than the early maturers to give responses that suggested dependency. Since late maturers are rejected by the peers, it is to the parents that the late-maturing male must turn if anyone will meet his dependency needs. Thus, the late maturer is dependent on the very social objects—the parents—toward whom he holds negative attitudes. There is thus both a need to approach and a desire to avoid the parents. In short, this means the late-maturing male exists in a state of conflict. In sum, very much more so than is the case with early-maturing males, late-maturing males have negative self-concepts. Indeed, although not statistically significant, the late maturers' tendency to feel they had a less attractive body, and their feelings of being less relaxed and assured and more restless, are consistent with this interpretation.

Early maturers tended to be characterized as having positive self-concepts. They lacked rebellious feelings toward their parents, and gave responses indicative of self-confidence, independence, and the ability to play an adult role in interpersonal relationships. Although these males evidenced more aggressive themes in their responses than did the late-maturing males, such a feeling is quite consistent with the traditional masculine stereotype in our society of a dominant, aggressive, instrumentally effective person (Kagan & Moss, 1962; Lerner & Korn, 1972).

In summary, the adult and peer social appraisals of the two maturational groups were related to the way the groups functioned on the individual-psychological level. Information independent of the California Growth Study data set indicates that early and late maturers have personal characteristics consistent with those reported by Mussen and Jones (1957). On the basis of an essentially qualitative analysis of their data, Kinsey et al. (1948) report that early and late maturers formed two quite distinct groups. Rate of maturation was indexed by the age at first ejaculation, as reported by the respondent through recall. Although this event is a questionable index of maturational rate, and the recall may be faulty, the Kinsey et al. data are consistent with other information. The early maturers in the Kinsey et al. sample were seen to be perhaps the most alert, energetic, spontaneous, active, extroverted, and aggressive males studied. The late maturers, however, were appraised as slow, quiet, mild, unforceful, reserved, timid, introverted, and socially inept.

It should be noted that these differences were discerned among males who were several years postpubescence. Most were in late adolescence or early adulthood. This fact suggests that the individual and social advantages of the early maturer, and the problems of the late maturer, may have implications for later development across the life span. There is ample evidence supporting this inference.

Weatherly (1964) reported data, independent of those from the California Growth Study, comparing early- , average- , and late-maturing college males on several measures of personality. The late maturers were found to have more responses that indicated feelings of guilt, inferiority, and depression, and more responses showing needs for being encouraged and obtaining sympathy and understanding, than males in other groups. On the other hand, members of the late-maturing group were less oriented toward leading, dominating, or controlling than were males in the two other maturational groups. However, Weatherly found that despite their need for support for others, late maturers were more rebellious and unconventional than were average or early maturers. Thus, the conflict between dependency and independency, seen among the late maturers in the Mussen and Jones (1957) study, is identifiable in this independent, and older, sample of late maturers.

Still other evidence, from the California Growth Study data set, indicates that, at least for the early adult years, the differences between early- and late-maturing males remain stable. Ames (1957) interviewed early- and late-maturing males when they were in their early thirties. The major trend in the results of the study was that rate of maturation in adolescence was a better predictor of social and vocational behaviors in the males' thirties than were any *social* measures of such behaviors taken during childhood or adolescence. Basically, the direction of Ames's findings was that the earlier the age of maturation (the more mature the male in adolescence), the higher the social and personal success in adulthood. The earlier the maturation was in adolescence, the higher was adult occupational status, informal and formal social activity, and business social life. In addition, of the forty males Ames studied, fifteen had supervisory or leadership business roles. Twelve of these fifteen were early maturers. Similarly, eight of the subjects held some office in a club or a civic group. All eight were early maturers.

In sum, although there were no known intellectual or social class differences between the early- and late-maturational groups (McCandless, 1970), the early maturers led personally and socially more positive lives than the late maturers. Indeed, there was only one hint of disadvantage for the early-maturing males during this period of their life. Ames (1957) found a very slight tendency for this group to report they were less happy in their marriage than was the case with the late maturers.

Jones (1957) also studied these males when they were in their thirties, but through administration of several psychological tests. However, she did not find such a marital quality difference as did Ames. Jones also reported that differences in physical attractiveness between the two groups were no longer present. The groups did not differ in attractiveness, grooming, marital status, family size, or education level. However, the early maturers showed, as Ames also reported, earlier patterns of job success. In addition, on a personal level, these males scored higher on a test designed to measure their attitude toward and ability for making a good impression on others.

Interviews revealed that the late maturers seemed to be less settled at age 33, and on the basis of tests, they showed themselves to be less self-controlled, dominant, and responsible, and more rebellious, touchy, impulsive, self-centered, and dependent on others than were the early maturers. However, Jones (1957) did find the late maturers to be more insightful and assertive than the early maturers.

Thus, there is marked stability in the psychological and social implications of rate of maturation from adolescence into the fourth decade of the life span, but there is evidence that by the end of this decade and the beginning of the next, these contrasts become unstable. In a follow-up study of the California Growth Study males (Jones, 1965), done when they were in their forties, the advantages for the early maturers seemed to diminish. Possibly due to the fact that the bodily assets of the early maturers also tended to diminish relative to the late maturers at this time of life (middle age), the social and personal superiority of the early maturers, which seemed based on bodily appraisals, also decreased to a point where the psychosocial functioning of early- versus late-maturing males was almost identical. However, although the psychological implications of early versus late maturation may disappear in the middle adulthood years, the above data still indicate clear and *relatively* long-term effects of maturational status on the psychosocial development of adolescent males. Before we attempt to interpret this relation between maturational rate and individual and social functioning, however, the nature of this relation for females is considered.

Implications of early versus late maturation in females

The data for females are not as complete as those for males. Early- and late-maturing females have not been followed over a similar duration of their lives as is the case with males. Moreover, what data do exist are somewhat more complicated.

Jones (1949) studied groups of early- and late-maturing females. Jones did not find the psychological and social advantages of early maturation with females that were found with males. In fact, the reverse seemed to be the case. In females, late maturation seemed to be associated with positive social appraisals and personality, and early maturation had correspondingly negative consequences. However, as was seen in Exhibit 8.14, early-maturing girls tend to have a body type which is more chubby, and hence *less* attractive in American society (Staffieri, 1972), than have late-maturing girls, whose thinner, less plump body is more attractive (Staffieri, 1972). Thus, since it was the late-maturing boys who had a more unattractive male physique (Lerner & Korn, 1972), and it was early-maturing girls who had a more unattractive female physique, relative to their respectively sexed but alternatively paced maturing peers, it may be that it is the socioculturally judged attractiveness of the body one derives from one's maturational retardedness or advancement, rather than this retardedness or advancement itself, which is most important in providing a source of the relationship between personality, social status, and the body. How one's body is appraised by one's society, and not the rate or age of maturation that gives one this appearance, may be the basis of body-behavior relations.

The usefulness of this appearance–societal attitude interaction interpretation is considered in the following section. But it should be pointed out that although early-maturing females differ from late-maturing females in social and personality

INSIGHT INTO ADOLESCENCE

Sara Davidson, a journalist and author of *Loose Change: Three Women of the Sixties,* begins her book by asking, "What happened to us in the sixties?" One of the three women of the book is herself; the other two are women friends with whom she went to college at Berkeley in the early sixties. Ten years later she followed up the lives of her two friends, and through extensive interviews with them, she chronicles *their and her* changes from the sixties to the present.

But perfection and control were useless when applied to one area: the beanstalk-like growth of my body. In Los Angeles in the fifties, few people believed they looked as they should. My younger sister, Terry, became convinced she needed a nose job when her best friend underwent the operation. My mother to this day believes her right hand is too large and her neck too long, and when she saw me grow six inches in the eighth grade, shooting up from 5'2" to 5'8", she took me to a doctor who gave me painful hormone shots that were supposed to close my growth centers.

From the moment the doctor first stung my behind with a giant dose of hormones until perhaps six years later, there was not a day that I did not feel disadvantaged because of the misfortune of my height. Looking back, I can see that at sixteen I had a willowy, beautifully proportioned body, but at the time I was only aware of what I considered its unnatural elongation. When the shots failed to work and I grew to be 5'10", I calculated that 90 per cent of the men in the world were inaccessible to me because they were shorter. I daydreamed of going to Sweden to have an operation on my legs that would diminish me by three inches. When friends offered to fix me up, my first question was always "Is he tall?" followed by "Is he cute?" (Later I would ask, "Is he bright?" and still later, "Is he sensitive?")

I devised ways of gauging whether a boy was as tall as I when we were seated in cars cruising Hollywood: I would scan the length of his forearm hanging out the car window and then scan my own. Sometimes I miscalculated. He would walk to my car, open the door, and as I stood up his head would swivel backward like the short clown watching the tall clown unfold from a midget car. "God, you're tall."

Source: Excerpt from *Loose Change* by Sarah Davidson. Copyright 1970, 1977 by Sarah Davidson. Reprinted by permission of Doubleday & Company, Inc.

development, such differences seem to disappear by 17 years of age. Jones and Mussen (1958) studied the TAT responses of early- and late-maturing females when they were 17 years old, and no major differences in projective personality responses were seen as a function of their different maturational backgrounds.

Together, the Jones (1949) and Jones and Mussen (1958) studies suggest that whatever differences may exist initially between early- and late-maturing females, these contrasts tend to diminish much sooner in life than is the case with early- and late-maturing males. Other studies of implications of early and late maturation in females present data generally consistent with those reported by Jones (1949) about the relative advantages of a rapid maturation rate for adolescent psychosocial functioning. The data also indicate that these differences in early adolescence tend to disappear by late adolescence or early adulthood.

Stolz and Stolz (1944), in a longitudinal study, found that early-maturing females tended to be embarrassed more than their peers. Reasons for their greater embarrassment centered around their being bigger and taller than others—including their male peers, who matured from six months to two years later. Further, the females were embarrassed about their menstrual cycle. Thus, like those of Jones

(1949), the Stolz and Stolz data indicate disadvantages for early-maturing females. Again, one reason for the disadvantage of the early maturers may be that as a consequence of their maturational rate, they possess a physique type (an overly large, somewhat heavier one relative to peers) that is negatively evaluated by others in their social world (Lerner & Gellert, 1969; Lerner & Schroeder, 1971; Staffieri, 1972). However, as noted, these maturation-related differences among females tend to disappear.

Faust (1960) studied sixth to ninth grade females cross-sectionally. The females' maturational status was indexed by age of menarche, and the peers of the subjects were asked to make attributions of positive characteristics about them. In the sixth grade, the early-maturing females received fewer positive peer attributions. Thus, they received more peer rejection than did the premenarche sixth grade females. However, in the seventh grade cohort, and markedly so in the older two grade cohorts, there was a tendency for positive peer attributions to be associated with postmenarche females. The difference suggests that, as reported by Jones (1949) and Stolz and Stolz (1944), females who mature at an average or even late rate (for example, the seventh and the eighth and ninth graders, respectively) are more likely to have a psychosocial advantage in their early adolescence than are those females who mature early (for example, the sixth graders).

Again, that these contrasts disappear by middle to late adolescence is supported by information independent of those derived from the California Growth Study data reported by Jones and Mussen (1958). Nisbet, Illsley, Sutherland, and Douse (1964), although finding (contrary to the above) that females who matured earlier than others were in fact superior at age 13 years on some intellectual ability measures, noted these differences had largely disappeared by 16 years of age. Similarly, Shipman (1964) found that age at menarche was unrelated to a measure of timidity or of emotional maturity among adult females.

In sum, the effects of early versus late maturation seem to be more transitory in females than in males. Yet for either sex it may be that the type of body one develops as a consequence of rate of maturation has the major implication for social and personal functioning. If one develops a type of body that is viewed as attractive by members of one's society, as is the case with early maturation in males and late maturation in females, then this development may promote correspondingly favorable personality and social developments. Alternatively, development of a physique type considered unattractive by members of one's society, as in the case of late-maturing males and early-maturing females, may be associated with negative personality and social development. Let us consider the evidence for such relations.

RELATIONS BETWEEN BODY TYPE AND PERSONALITY AND SOCIAL DEVELOPMENT

Early and late maturational status is generally associated with specific physique or body types. It has been seen that with male early maturers, a body type which is muscular, which has strong bones, and which is "athletic-looking" tends to develop. A person who has such a body type may be termed a *mesomorph*. On the other hand, very late maturing males tend to have a body type which generally is thin, has little muscle mass, has thin but noticeable bones, has little fat, and appears "frail-looking" (see Tanner, 1962). A person who has such a body type may be termed an *ectomorph*. Still another type of body is generally associated both with somewhat late-maturing males (Tanner, 1972) and with early-maturing females. A person with a chubby or

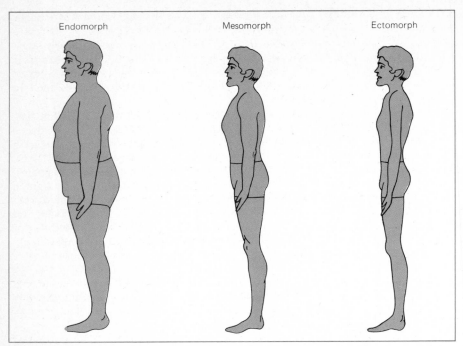

Exhibit 8.15
A late adolescent male endomorph, mesomorph, and ectomorph.

plump build, whose body tends to be fat and rounded in appearance, may be termed an *endomorph*. Exhibit 8.15 shows drawings of late adolescent males representing an extreme endomorph, mesomorph, and ectomorph body type.

The terms endomorph, mesomorph, and ectomorph were derived from the work of William Sheldon (1940, 1942), a psychologist (who was also a physician) who theorized that the relation between such body types and personality and social behaviors of a person is largely genetically predetermined. Sheldon noted that in the *gastrula* (an early) stage of embryonic development, the embryo is divided into three layers of cells: the endoderm, the mesoderm, and the ectoderm. From the endoderm arises one's fat (adipose) tissue and one's digestive (visceral) organs. From the mesoderm the muscles and bones of the body develop. And from the ectoderm the nervous system and the sensory organs of the body arise. Although every human's body is thus necessarily contributed to by all three layers, Sheldon (1940, 1942) believed that the layers might not contribute equally to the formation of a given person's body. Rather, distinct *somatotypes* (*soma* means body, and thus the term means body types) will develop.

If a person's body is composed of a major contribution from the endoderm, and minor ones from the mesoderm and the ectoderm, then fat and viscera will predominate. Here, the somatotype will be *endomorphic* (*morph* is also a term meaning body, and thus the term means body made up of endoderm). Because of the predominance of adipose and visceral tissue, the body type will appear chubby, round, and plump.

If a person's body is composed of a major contribution from the mesoderm, and minor ones from the other two layers, then muscles and strong bones will dominate the body. Sheldon believed a *mesomorphic* somatotype would then occur.

In turn, if a person's body is composed of a major contribution from the ectoderm, and minor ones from the other two layers, there will be neither fat nor muscles and bones to give the body girth or mass. The *ectomorphic* somatotype that thus results is thin and frail-looking.

Sheldon believed that the only source of one's somatotype was the contribution of the three embryonic layers, and he held that this contribution is a solely nature-based phenomenon. Thus, he ignored the fact that there exist many sources of body shape and growth, and some of these, like the ones relating to socioeconomic status, social class, and history that we have reviewed earlier in this chapter, are clearly not solely nature-based contributors. Moreover, not only is Sheldon's assertion about the genetic basis of body type incorrect, but so too is his belief about the relation between body type and personality (to him, *temperament*) formation.

Sheldon (1940, 1942) believed that along with every somatotype there was a *temperament* type. In other words, he believed a set of activity patterns was tied to what he considered innately formed body types. Thus, the endomorph was said to love to relax and to eat, and was slow of movement. The mesomorph was athletic and liked exercise. The ectomorph was said to be unable to cushion himself or herself from stimulation because of the absence of fat or muscle, was withdrawing and introverted, and rather than being social, was dominated by thought (cerebral) functions.

Chapter 7 indicated that to test his ideas about the necessary relation between body build and personality, Sheldon (1940, 1942) rated the physiques and temperaments of 4,000 Harvard male undergraduates. His method was criticized on the basis of researcher bias. He knew what he wanted to prove, he did all measurements himself, and indeed he found what he thought he would. The high relation between body build and personality he found (about two-thirds of the variation in personality was associated with variation in body builds, in predicted directions) may have been more in his eyes than in the subjects' behavior.

Nevertheless, studies done after Sheldon's that have linked body build and behavior by having independent groups of people rate body build and temperament, without telling (at least some) of the raters the hypothesis under investigation, have also found relations between body build and behavior (for example, Walker, 1962). However, the relations have not been of the magnitude Sheldon reported. For example, about 4 to 25 percent of the variation in personality and social behavior has been found to be associated with predicted variation in body build. There is no argument about whether one's body has implications for one's personality and social functioning. It certainly does. Indeed, it has been the point of this chapter to discuss this relation, insofar as it relates to the rate and type of bodily change at puberty. Thus, the present quarrel with Sheldon is not with whether or not a body build–personality relation exists, but rather with whether this relation is determined solely by nature.

In Chapter 7 it was argued, in reviewing the Nesselroade and Baltes (1974) study and associated information, that personality and social behavior may derive from sources relating to birth cohort and time of measurement. Moreover, throughout previous chapters the problems associated with viewing the adolescent's development as arising solely from nature (or nurture, for that matter) have been suggested. A view of adolescent development which sees development as arising from the combined influence of all levels of analysis has been suggested. Accordingly, while one may accept, as do other researchers (see McCandless, 1970, for example), using the terms endomorph, mesomorph, and ectomorph as *descriptive* labels representing body types which appear essentially fat, average (or muscular), and thin, respectively (Lerner & Korn, 1972), it is our view that the relations between body type and personality which Sheldon thought to be determined genetically can be better accounted for by reference to interactionist ideas.

Earlier in this chapter evidence was presented that the bodily changes of adolescence are dependent on sociocultural and historical variations; however, the data on the implications of these bodily changes for personal and social functioning have not been shown to be similarly dependent. One reason for this is that the overwhelming majority of studies of these implications have been done in the United States. More problematically, many of these studies have involved assessment of only one cohort (from the California Growth Study). Thus, with age and time confounded, assessment of the contributions of variables from multiple levels of analysis is difficult. Furthermore, although some cross-cultural data do exist (for example, Iwawaki & Lerner, 1974, 1976; Lerner & Iwawaki, 1975; Lerner, Iwawaki, & Chihara, 1976; Lerner & Pool, 1972), much of it shows no sociocultural differences in the meaning of body type. Fortunately, one study does exist which will allow for an evaluation of whether an interaction theory can account for the relations between body and behavior.

Sociocultural influences on body-behavior relations

In the discussion above it was noted that Mussen and Jones (1957) studied the implications of early maturation for personality development among White, essentially middle class males from California. The parents of these boys were (presumably) also all born in the United States. Mussen and Bouterline-Young (1964) studied two additional groups of early-maturing boys. First, they studied early-maturing Italian adolescents, boys who had grown up in Italy and who had Italian parents. Second, they studied early-maturing Italian-American adolescents. These were boys who had grown up in the United States but who were the sons of parents who had grown up in Italy. All male subjects—both those in the Mussen and Jones study and those from the Mussen and Bouterline-Young study—were White and had Western European backgrounds. A limited inference may thus be drawn: despite the different cultural backgrounds of the three groups (American, Italian, and Italian-American), the groups had a similar or common genetic background or "gene pool."

If Sheldon's theory were correct—if it *is* merely genes which provide the basis of body-behavior relations—then the same relations between early maturation, and thus mesomorphy, and personality should be seen in the three cultural groups. If, however, it is *sociocultural* background—for example, values attached or not attached in a particular society to a given body type—which provides the major basis of body-type behavior and personality relations, then despite any genetic similarity that may exist among the three cultural groups, body-behavior relations should be different in people from the different cultural settings.

The findings of Mussen and Bouterline-Young (1964) supported the idea that body-behavior relations are based on an interaction between body type and sociocultural appraisal. It will be recalled that the TAT responses of early-maturing American males revealed positive attitudes toward parents *and* positive self-concepts (Mussen & Jones, 1957). However, although among the Italian early maturers there were also positive attitudes toward parents, these youths did not have very positive self-concepts. In this cultural group, mesomorphy was thus *not* related to positive self-regard. However, in the final cultural group, the Italian-American sample, early maturation was associated with positive feelings about the self. But on the other hand, this group tended to have negative feelings toward their parents.

It may be suggested, then, that the relation between a given body type and the personality and social developments that are associated with it appears to find its basis in the cultural "meanings" attached to that body type. Specifically, if it can be shown that in a given culture particular appraisals are associated with a given body type, then one may argue that such social expectations and evaluations—such social stereotypes—may provide a basis of relations between that body type and personality development. The nature of the relations between social stereotypes about body build and the behavior developed by someone with a particular body type would involve the functioning of a self-fulfilling prophecy phenomenon. As discussed earlier in this book, stereotypes can provide a basis of behavior through channeling, or delimiting, alternative behavioral possibilities. For example, late-maturing thin boys—believed only capable of excelling at nonathletic hobbies—may be urged to engage in such sedentary activities. A chubby late maturer—believed incapable of group leadership—may never be chosen to lead precisely because of this belief. Never having the opportunity to demonstrate or develop leadership skills, the person would not be able to show them. Thus, the stereotype eventually fosters in people the very behavior it predicts, and this process is summarized by the term "self-fulfilling prophecy."

Body-build–behavior stereotypes

Several studies have demonstrated that, indeed, general social stereotypes exist about behavior associated with endomorphy, mesomorphy, and ectomorphy, respectively (for example, Lerner, 1969a; Lerner & Korn, 1972). As shown in Exhibit 8.16, which summarizes the behavior and personality expectations generally associated with each body type, the attitudes typically held toward the mesomorph are overwhelmingly positive and favorable; the appraisals of people having endomorphic body types are overwhelmingly negative; and the attitudes shown toward those with ectomorphic physiques are predominantly negative as well. That these body-build stereotypes, represented by the data in Exhibit 8.16, are general attitudes held in our society toward these three body types is seen in the results of studies which show that the same findings are obtained from samples of people who are different in age (Lerner, 1969a; Lerner & Korn, 1972), sex (Lerner, 1969b; Lerner & Gellert, 1969), race (Lerner, Knapp, & Pool, 1974), and geographical area of residence within the United States (Lerner & Schroeder, 1971). In fact, the favorableness of the mesomorph stereotype and the negative attitudes associated with endomorphy and ectomorphy can be generalized to the body build stereotypes found among both Mexican (Lerner & Pool, 1972) and Japanese (Lerner & Iwawaki, 1975) adolescents. Moreover, these stereotypes are markedly similar to the attributions and evaluations already seen to be associated with early and late maturers.

If these social stereotypes do exert an influence on personality development—presumably through the functioning of a self-fulfilling prophecy—then one should see evidence of personality development conforming to the stereotypes among people of specific body types. One set of evidence that can be offered is, of course, the data on the personality and social development of early and late maturers, especially

Exhibit 8.16
Typical stereotypes associated with the mesomorph, endomorph, and ectomorph

Mesomorph	Endomorph	Ectomorph
Healthy	Sad	Sick
Brave	Worst ballplayer	Afraid
Best ballplayer	Ugly	Weak
Has most muscles	Least wanted as a friend	Small
Good-looking	Not to be picked leader	Light
Be picked leader	Large	Has least muscles
Most want as a friend	Sloppy	Eats the least
Has many friends	Is left out of games	Thin
Happy	Has few friends	Doesn't fight
Others like him	Heavy	Quiet
Neat	Fat	
Clean	Eats the most	
Likes others	Slow	
Fast	Forgets	
Fights	Kind	
Remembers	Stupid	
Teases	Dirty	
Smart		
Nice		
Honest		
Helps others		

Source: Adapted from Lerner & Korn, 1972.

males, already reviewed in this chapter. The evaluations of early-maturing males and the stereotypes about mesomorphs are virtually identical. Thus, given this evidence that early-maturing males have the positive personal and social attributes expected of them, support is found for a self-fulfilling prophecy–circular-function notion between person and society. Of course, the data pertaining to the endomorph and ectomorph stereotypes and to the evaluations of late maturers and their concomitant personality and social development can also be used to support a circular-function notion.

However, evidence independent of that associated with the early- and late-maturing literature exists, and these data deal directly with the impact of body-build stereotypes. Lerner and Korn (1972) reported evidence for negative self-concepts, in correspondence with negative endomorphy stereotypes, among chubby adolescent males. Alternatively, evidence for positive self-concepts, in correspondence with the positive mesomorphy stereotypes, was found among average-build adolescent males. Moreover, it has been found in data derived from the responses of early adolescents both in the United States (Lerner, Karabenick, & Meisels, 1975) and in Japan (Iwawaki, Lerner, & Chihara, 1977) that social behavior consistent with these stereotypes occurs. Subjects from both cultural settings tend to use more interpersonal space toward the negatively evaluated, unattractively regarded endomorph than they do toward the positively evaluated, attractively regarded mesomorph.

Tentative evidence for development consistent with such social behavior comes from a study by Lerner and Lerner (1977). Not only do attractive early adolescents have more favorable and fewer negative interactions with their peers than is the case with unattractive early adolescents, but physical attractiveness differences help account for the psychological functioning of the early adolescents as well. Physically attractive children achieve better grades in school than do their physically unattractive age-mates (Lerner & Lerner, 1977). This relation was found for both males and females.

Finally, cross-cultural evidence exists for this individual-psychological implication of body characteristics. Douglas and Ross (1964), in a longitudinal study of 5,000 children born in Britain in the first week of March 1946, found that early-maturing males and females (who were mesomorphic) showed a slight, but significant, tendency to have higher intellectual and reading abilities, as measured by scores on standardized tests.

In summary, the appearance of the adolescent's body does have an important affect on psychological functioning. The changes that the body undergoes in puberty, the rate of change at which these alterations occur, and apparently, most prominently, the appearance of the body as a consequence of these changes have significant social and psychological implications. Different bodily appearances are associated with contrasting social appraisals by the adults and peers in the adolescent's world. More importantly, however, these different social reactions to their bodies affect the ways in which adolescents feel and think about themselves.

CHAPTER SUMMARY

The bodily changes of adolescence may be divided into three successive periods. Changes in all these periods are promoted by the release of chemical substances, termed *hormones*, from ductless glands of the body, termed *endocrine glands*.

The first period of bodily change in adolescence is termed *prepubescence*. This period begins with the first evidence of sexual maturation and ends with the appearance of pubic hair. Signs of this stage in males are the progressive enlargement of the testicles and an increase in the length and circumference of the penis. In females signs are a rounding of the hips and the first visible indications of breast development.

In *pubescence* there is the growth of pubic hair and growth spurts in height and weight that occur for both sexes. However, as is the case for most bodily changes across all three periods, these changes occur about two years earlier in females than in males. For females the first menstruation (*menarche*) occurs, and breast development continues. For males there is continued growth of the penis and testes and a change in the coloration of the scrotum. *Postpubescence* begins when pubic hair growth is complete and ends when all changes in primary and secondary sexual characteristics are complete.

There also exist sociocultural and historical differences, presumably due to variables relating to health and nutritional statuses of children and adolescents. The age of menarche, for example, varies today in relation to the cultural context within and differences between countries. Moreover, there has been a historical trend downward in the average age of menarche. A decrease of several months per decade from about 1840 to the present has been found.

Variation in the rate of bodily change in adolescence is related to psychological and social developments. Studies of early-maturing and late-maturing adolescent males indicate that, in comparison to the latter group, the former group is better adjusted and has more favorable interactions with peers and adults. These advantages of early maturation, and the possession of a body type that has strong muscles and bones (a *mesomorph*), and disadvantages of late maturation, and either a plump *(endomorph)* or thin *(ectomorph)* body type, tend to continue through the middle adult years for males.

For females, however, somewhat different relations exist. Early maturation is associated with more psychosocial disadvantages than is late maturation. These relations for female adolescent rates of physical maturation, bodily appearance, and personality and social functioning have not been determined in later adult life.

It has been found that for males, mesomorphy is the most positively regarded body type, and that endomorphy and ecotomorphy are the least favorably evaluated. For females, however, mesomorphy is not seen as the most favorable body type. Instead a build closer to ectomorphy is seen as more desirable.

Although theories exist which link body build and personality on the basis of genetics (for example, the constitutional theory of Sheldon), there are findings that the psychosocial implications of an adolescent's body type vary in relation to sociocultural attitudes about the attractiveness of that body type. In America, where mesomorphy is given positive social evaluations and endomorphy negative evaluations, adolescent male mesomorphs develop positive self and body concepts while endomorphs do not. However, in other countries, such advantages for early-maturing mesomorphs and disadvantages for those with the body types associated with late maturation may not exist.

Moreover, in American society there is considerable evidence that the general physical attractiveness level of male and female children and adolescents not only provides a basis of others' reactions to them but, in addition, is related to their personality, social, and intellectual development. Thus, evidence appears to exist for a self-fulfilling prophecy between stereotypes about body build, attractiveness, and adolescent psychosocial development.

COGNITIVE DEVELOPMENT IN ADOLESCENCE

Cognitive development refers to changes in mental abilities, such as intelligence and knowledge. This chapter discusses two major ways in which adolescent cognition has been studied. These approaches, the psychometric and Piagetian approaches, are described and evaluated.

What are the major characteristics of and distinctions between the quantitative and the qualitative approaches to studying adolescent cognition?

What is the role of cohort effects in contributing to cognitive stability? How stable are cognitive abilities across the life span?

How does the age-differentiation hypothesis help explain the structure of cognitive abilities in adolescence?

On what cognitive abilities do male and female adolescents differ, and how consistent are these differences across adolescence?

What role may social interactions play in moderating intelligence test scores?

How does the equilibration model provide a continual basis of development across all the stages of cognitive development?

What are the major assets and limitations of thought within each stage of cognitive development that Piaget specifies?

What are the major characteristics of formal operational thought, and how is it measured?

What is the nature of the intraindividual and interindividual differences associated with the development of formal operations?

What are the components of adolescent egocentrism, and what processes are presumed to be associated with its decrease?

ll college students are familiar with the concept of intelligence. In early childhood, and certainly by the time one enters grade school, a person becomes aware that he or she is being evaluated on the basis of how much he or she knows, or how bright or smart he or she is. Presence in college means in part that a person has had a history of favorable evaluations regarding his or her intelligence, knowledge, or mental aptitude, or that he or she values the further development of this dimension of functioning. Thus, on the basis of other people's reactions, and because of our own appraisal as well, we deem intelligence or knowledge as a prominent aspect of our lives.

However, it also may be noted that ideas about our lifelong association with intellectual appraisal and knowledge development differ from person to person. The tests one may take in the early school years to measure intellectual aptitude do not coincide with those taken for similar reasons as adolescents or adults; moreover, those who are interested in intelligence or knowledge at one particular time of life often do not administer the same test to evaluate different individuals. Thus, it may seem that what people mean when they say they are evaluating intelligence, or brightness, or knowledge, may be quite different.

There are many definitions of intelligence, and of what it means to undergo development of one's intelligence or one's knowledge. Yet despite the many theories, definitions, and tests, two broad approaches to the study of intellectual/knowledge development can be identified. Within these two major approaches, many of the major issues, findings, and problems in the study of the adolescent's intellectual functioning and knowledge development may be presented. The two major approaches in this area of study are the quantitative one, typically associated with the administration of intelligence tests and the derivation of IQ scores, and the qualitative one, typically associated with the developmental theory of cognition of the Swiss scientist Jean Piaget (Elkind, 1968). To deal with these two approaches one must first arrive at a definition of intellectual/knowledge development that will be useful across both of these formats of study.

A DEFINITION OF COGNITION

Within both the quantitative and the qualitative approaches to the study of intellectual/knowledge development, there is a basic concern with the same fundamental issue: What is the character of the person's knowledge? However, the two approaches differ in regard to the formulation of this concern. In the *quantitative approach* there is an emphasis on *how much* the person knows relative to his or her age group, and as will be indicated, this emphasis leads to the derivation of a score (an intelligence quotient, or IQ) from a mental test used to represent the quantity of knowledge. Yet despite this emphasis on measuring whether a person knows more, as much, or less than others of his or her age group, advocates of this approach do not deny that the type of thinking or knowledge that a person shows may differ at various points in development (Elkind, 1968). Indeed, in constructing the mental tests from which IQ scores are derived, different tests often are used at different developmental levels (Bloom, 1964).

The recognition of different modes, types, or qualities of thought is the emphasis of the second approach, however. Here, rather than stressing whether a person knows more or less information than his or her peers, the emphasis is on the way the person knows whatever he or she does know. Thus, rather than emphasize the number of correct answers to test items, people using the *qualitative* approach to intelligence will consider the type of thinking a person uses to deal with information. Despite whether the answer to a question is correct, there will be a manner of thinking about the issue—for instance, in an abstract or hypothetical way or in a concrete manner—which will be used by a person. It is this mode of thought—this quality—and not the correctness of the answer, that will be the focus in the second approach.

Thus, both approaches are concerned with knowledge, with changes within people, and with differences between people in their knowledge. Those following a quantitative approach will be concerned with how much knowledge a person has across his or her life and with differences between people in how much they know. Those looking at intelligence qualitatively, however, will be concerned with changes in the type of thinking shown by a person across his or her life, and the differences among people (for example, of different ages) in the quality of their thought. Hence, although the kinds of changes and differences emphasized within the two approaches differ (Elkind, 1968), both approaches are concerned with characteristics of knowledge, with what and/or how a person "knows."

Accordingly, scientists specializing in this area of study all are concerned most basically with knowing and with the psychological and behavioral processes involved in the development and use of knowledge (Elkind, 1968). Those working within the quantitative approach traditionally have used the term "intelligence" to reflect their area of study. Those working within the qualitative framework traditionally have used the term "cognition" most often, although they have considered the study of cognitive development and intellectual development as interchangeable endeavors (Neimark, 1975; Piaget, 1950, 1970). Thus, one may find a common concern with knowledge and its development. Furthermore, there is a conceptual and empirical (DeVries, 1974; Kuhn, 1976) compatibility between each approach. As a result, the term cognition may be used to represent the concern with intelligence and knowledge found within each of the two approaches identified.

To reiterate, the study of cognitive development is defined here as the assessment of the change processes involved with the acquisition and use of knowledge (Elkind, 1968). From this view, the terms "intelligence" and "knowledge" are just synonyms of "cognition." People show intraindividual changes in the quantitative and qualitative aspects of their cognition, and there are differences between people in these changes as well. Although these changes and differences exist across the life span (Baltes & Schaie, 1974, 1976; Lerner & Ryff, 1978), many of these changes are especially prominent in adolescence. Accordingly, in considering cognition we focus on some of these intraindividual changes and the differences between people that characterize each of the dimensions of adolescent functioning.

QUANTITATIVE DIMENSIONS OF ADOLESCENT COGNITIVE DEVELOPMENT

That the quantitative approach to cognition emphasizes the *measurement* of mental functioning has already been noted. For this reason it is also labeled the *psychometric* approach. Evaluation of cognitive status and development is based on scores derived from intelligence tests.

The first intelligence test was devised in France in 1905 by Alfred Binet. His purpose was to devise a technique to screen children from the French public schools who were not mentally competent to profit from education. Intelligence tests were brought to the United States by Lewis Terman of Stanford University. Terman revised the scale of Binet by standardizing it on American samples. This new version was published as the Stanford-Binet in 1916. Since its introduction it has been restandardized and revised several times. The Stanford-Binet is an individual test of intelligence. It is administered by a single administrator to a single person. But it has not remained the only intelligence test available. There are other individual intelligence tests, such as Wechsler's Intelligence Scale for Children (WISC) and Wechsler's Adult Intelligence Scale (WAIS). Furthermore, there are numerous group-administered intelligence tests.

One reason that there are a number of instruments to measure cognition quantitatively is that there are a number of definitions about what constitutes intelligence, even among those who study it within the quantitative tradition (Anastasi, 1970). Accordingly, there is no one way in which intelligence tests are constructed, and there is no consensus about what sorts of items should be included in these tests. Moreover, there is little agreement about whether it is useful to try to express intelligence with one score (Burt, 1954, 1955; Garrett, 1946) or with scores from several measures of different intellectual abilities (Thurstone & Thurstone, 1962). Furthermore, if multiple measures of abilities are sought, as is often the case (Horn, 1970; Horn & Knapp, 1973), there is no consensus about what abilities to measure and at what point in the life span to measure them (Fitzgerald, Nesselroade, & Baltes, 1973; Horn, 1970; Reinert, 1970).

Because of these controversies involving rather complex conceptual and methodological arguments (Baltes & Schaie, 1976; Horn & Donaldson, 1976, 1977; Schaie & Baltes, 1977), there is no one statement that can be made about the nature of the quantitative assessment of cognition that will be applicable in all contexts. As a consequence, what follows is a general depiction of some of the issues involved in the evaluation of quantitative intelligence, and the reader is cautioned to refer to, for instance, the references made above for a fuller discussion.

Derivation of an IQ score

Depending on the particular definition of intelligence being used, a person constructing a test of intelligence will devise items which presumably will provide measures of the particular cognitive abilities being evaluated. The validity of these measures typically will be determined with large groups of people. As a consequence, standards of performance will be developed.

The groups of people used in this test construction process will have particular demographic characteristics. For example, they may be White middle-class Protestant males and females between 3 and 25 years of age living in urban areas in the Midwestern United States. The performance of these groups will become the standard, against which other performances will be measured. That is, the average and range of responses seen with this group will become the norms of performance on the test.

With such normative information we can know how a person having the characteristics of particular segments of the standardization population should perform. For instance, one can know what the typical 5-year-old from this population should score. Furthermore, one can appraise the performance of any given person relative to the performance of those in the standardization group. For example, one can see how the target person's actual score on the test items compares with the expected average score for his or her age group (Matarazzo, 1972). From such a comparison one can derive an IQ score.

There are several ways in which this score can be computed (Matarazzo, 1972). More recent methods use somewhat complicated statistical procedures, compared to the simpler methods associated with the technique originally employed. Although these more recent calculation procedures are necessary in constructing and interpreting test scores, the simpler, original formula for calculation will be used to illustrate the basic idea behind the derivation of the IQ score.

The purpose of the IQ score is to reflect in a single value how much knowledge, ability, or cognitive aptitude a person has relative to others in his or her group. The "group" corresponds to the standardization population, and typically in the study of human development, the person is compared to others of the same age. In short, one expresses with the IQ score a person's cognitive status relative to his or her age group.

Using the formula for the intelligence quotient (IQ) first developed by Stern (1912), one can express this relative standing as:

$$IQ = \frac{MA}{CA} \times 100$$

where MA = mental age, or in other words, one's actual score on the test, and CA = chronological age, or in other words, the mean score that would be normatively expected for one's age. By dividing MA by CA, the formula allows for this relative evaluation, and by multiplying by 100 one avoids dealing with fractions and instead treats only whole numbers. Moreover, use of this formula assures that the average IQ score for any age group will be 100.

Thus, if one's score is greater than the score expected for one's age, one's IQ score would be better than the average person of one's own age (an example is a 10-year-old that knows what the average 12-year-old knows). One would always have in such a case an IQ above 100 (for example, 120 in the above example). On the other hand, if one knew less than what was average for one's age, one would always have an IQ less than 100 (an example is a 12-year-old that knows what the average 10-year-old knows, and who would have an 83 in this instance). If one's score at any age is the same as the average score for people of that age (if you are 10 years old and know as much as the average 10-year-old), then one's IQ would be 100. Said another way, at any age level, the average IQ equals 100.

This fact means that IQ scores are always relative appraisals. An IQ score expresses one's location in an age-based distribution of other IQ scores. As such, IQ is not an indication of any absolute level of knowledge. Indeed, it takes much more knowledge to attain an average score as a 12-year-old than it does as a 5-year-old, and thus, for example, a 12-year-old with an IQ of 100 knows much more than does a 5-year-old with an IQ of 120. Yet one says the 5-year-old is "brighter" than the 12-year-old because, *relative* to their respective age groups, the 5-year-old scores higher.

Recognize that we have illustrated just one way of deriving an IQ score. Even if one agreed on one method of IQ score derivation, there would be differences in the tests these scores could be derived from. One major dimension of these test differences is that people use different tests at different ages to derive IQ scores. But one may still ask if any general developmental trends can be found in an individual's IQ scores. Data pertinent to this question are evaluated below.

DEVELOPMENTAL COMPONENTS OF IQ SCORES

It is not necessary to focus on IQ scores from a developmental perspective. Indeed much of the major work on the measurement of cognitive abilities has not traditionally been developmental (see Horn, 1967, 1968, 1970, 1978, for a discussion). Furthermore, the research that has been developmental has, with but a few exceptions (for example, Baltes, Baltes, & Reinert, 1970; Schaie, Labouvie, & Buech, 1973), confounded age, cohort, and time. This has made interpretation of data difficult (Baltes & Schaie, 1974, 1976). Thus, if one asks questions about the development of intelligence, one is confronted with problematic data sets.

Nevertheless, a variety of issues may be raised from a developmental perspective. Some of the major issues deal with the constancy and stability of IQ scores over time, the differentiation of cognitive abilities across the life cycle, the nature of the variables that moderate cognitive changes across life, and the relation between psychometric intelligence and the qualitative view of cognition. Although this list of issues is not exhaustive, it does highlight key topics that have been identified by developmentalists (Elkind, 1968; Neimark, 1975), especially in their appraisal of cognitive development in adolescence. Indeed, focus on these issues will highlight the role of the adolescent period in cognitive development across the life span.

Constancy and stability of IQ scores across life

By virtue of the ability to read and understand this book, it may be assumed that the reader has an above-average level of intelligence. Did a correspondingly high level of intelligence exist prior to the late adolescent/early adulthood years? Said another way, would a measure of one's cognitive ability taken in the very early school years have served as a good basis for predicting one's current intellectual level?

In turn, does the level of intelligence a person displays in late adolescence or early adulthood tell anything about ability in later life? Will people, in their aged years, continue to display the above-average intellectual level they may now show? Or will they change, perhaps in the direction of decline? In short, what does a measure of intelligence taken at one level allow one to predict about intelligence at another age level?

At least for age levels from infancy through late adolescence, data derived from both cross-sectional and longitudinal research suggest a similar course of changes in IQ scores. The data in Exhibit 9.1 are adapted from a longitudinal investigation (Bayley, 1949). Illustrated here is a period of greatly increasing relations among scores from the early years of life through late childhood (about 9 to 10 years of age) with intelligence measured at 18 years; after this period, there is a slower increase in the relations among scores to about age 16 or 17 years. From this portion of middle adolescence through the early adult years, the curve tends to flatten out, indicating no differences in the relations among scores between measured years. The data suggests a person's IQ score becomes increasingly stable from birth through middle adolescence, and at about age 18 a maximum score is reached and maintained for some time.

Bayley (1949) studied a group of people from birth to age 18 years. Although she had to employ different tests of intelligence at succeeding age levels in order to measure subjects appropriately, the number she used (five) was relatively few for research of this kind (Bloom, 1964). Bayley related IQ scores at one age to those of other ages through use of a statistic, termed the *correlation*. A correlation may vary

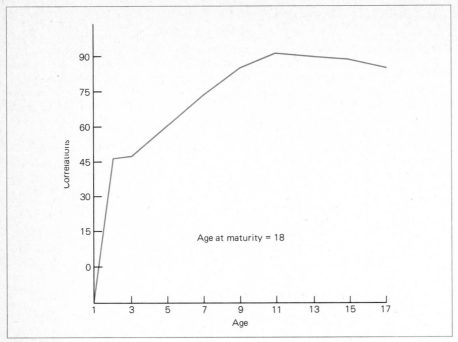

Exhibit 9.1
Correlations between intelligence measured at each age and intelligence
at age 18. (*Source:* Longitudinal data collected by Bayley, 1949.)

from −1.0 to +1.0, with values closer to +1.0 indicating a strong positive relation between two sets of scores. A positive correlation means that as scores in one set of measures increase, so do scores in the other set. A negative correlation means that as scores in one set increase, scores in the other decrease. Thus, a correlation "coefficient" of +.75 between height and weight, for instance, would mean that greater height was associated with greater weight.

Bayley (1949) found that intelligence at age 1 year was not related to intelligence at age 18 years. The correlation between IQ scores from these two age levels was 0.0 (there was no relationship whatsoever). However, the correlation between IQ scores at 2 years and at 18 years was +.41. The correlation between scores at 4 years and 18 years was +.71. Between 11 years and 18 years it was +.92. Thus, there is a rapid movement toward stability of IQ scores across the early years of life. This movement toward stability slows during adolescence. By age 18 years, IQ scores have become stable for a time.

One reason for the low relation between early childhood measures of intelligence and adolescent intelligence is that what is measured at age 1 is not akin to what is measured at age 18. At the earlier period, measures involve sensorimotor behavior, while at the later period they involve such abilities as verbal reasoning and mathematical concepts. There is little reason to expect scores on these two types of tests to relate to each other across age, since even when such tests are administered at the same point in life (for example, adulthood), they are not correlated (Bloom, 1964;

Cronbach, 1960). However, as tests at age levels beyond 1 year come increasingly to include measures of abilities similar to those measured at age 18 years, there is corresponding increase in the correlation. Thus, between ages 1 and 18 years there seems to be an increasingly greater "overlap" (Anderson, 1939; Bloom, 1964) in IQ scores.

What is the course of intelligence after middle adolescence? Does performance on intelligence tests improve or deteriorate after this time? Some cross-sectional data indicate decreases in IQ scores from middle adolescence into adulthood, although data from longitudinal research indicate stability or increases in scores. The confounds involved in cross-sectional and longitudinal studies may provide a basis of these different trends. In Chapter 7 the benefits of sequential methodology were discussed. If such methodology could be used, differences relating to birth cohort membership might be taken into account.

In 1956 Schaie (see Baltes & Schaie, 1974) began to study 500 people ranging in age from 21 to 70. He administered two tests of cognitive ability, the Thurstone and Thurstone Primary Mental Abilities test and Schaie's Test of Behavioral Rigidity. Seven years later 301 of the people were retested with the same instruments. Using elaborate statistical techniques (termed "factor analysis"), Schaie and his colleagues found that four different types of cognitive abilities were being measured by these tests:

1. *Crystallized intelligence*, which measures knowledge attained through education and socialization (for example, verbal comprehension, number skills). This is the type of intelligence measured by most traditional IQ tests (Baltes & Schaie, 1974).

2. *Cognitive flexibility*, which measures the ability to shift from one way of thinking to another.

3. *Visual-motor flexibility*, which measures a similar shifting ability, but in tasks requiring a coordination between vision and muscle movements.

4. *Visualization*, which measures the ability to organize and process visual information.

When Schaie and his colleagues analyzed their data cross-sectionally, they saw the adolescent-to-adulthood decline typically seen in such studies. However, when they looked at the longitudinal data within each of the birth cohort groups in their sequential design, they found a decline on only *one* of the four measures (visual-motor flexibility). In fact, for the most important abilities—those involved in crystallized intelligence (Baltes & Schaie, 1974) and visualization—a systematic *increase* in scores for all age groups was seen. Even those people over 70 years of age improved from the first testing to the second. Thus, as seen in Exhibit 9.2, older people scored lower than younger ones on the four measures of intelligence in both 1956 and 1963. However, for both crystallized intelligence and visualization, scores increase between these two times of testing, even for the older groups.

Similarly, data from a study by Schaie, Labouvie, and Buech (1973) show that when members of the same cohort are tested at succeeding times, there are many scores which increase. Yet if these within-cohort curves are not analyzed, and just cross-sectional curves are considered, then the typical adolescent-to-adult decline is seen. The graphs in Exhibt 9.3 illustrate these findings.

Clearly then, the course of intellectual change from adolescence onward is not

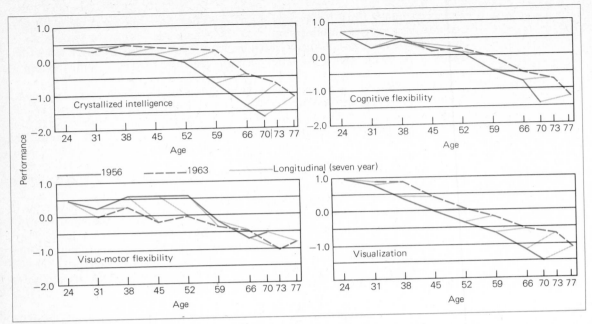

Exhibit 9.2
Age, time, and cohort components of change for four types of cognitive abilities: the solid lines slope downward, indicating that in both 1956 and 1963, older people scored lower than younger ones on various dimensions of intelligence. However, the dashed lines, which show how a given age group's performance changed from the first test to the second, reveal that in older groups crystallized intelligence and visualization go up, not down. (*Source:* Adapted from Baltes & Schaie, 1974.)

just an age-related phenomenon. The above data indicate that differences in scores and patterns of change in scores from one time of measurement to another are associated mainly with membership in different cohort groups. In other words, how well a person performed at any one time, and whether that performance was stable or not, was associated more with generational (cohort) differences and not with chronological age. It appears also that as the absolute level of ability scores is concerned, the measured intelligence of the general population is increasing across history. Perhaps because of better educational techniques, more geared to those cognitive attributes being measured in current tests, members of younger cohorts are more likely to achieve higher absolute scores than are members of older cohorts.

As such, not only do today's adolescent and young adult have a higher level of cognitive ability—as measured by tests such as those used by Schaie, Baltes, Labouvie, and their colleagues—than do members of older cohorts, but as is the case with members of *all* cohorts, they are likely to maintain much of this level of functioning across their life span. On the basis of findings from sequential studies, one may expect that many of the levels and types of ability present in adolescence will be maintained, or be enhanced, in the adult and aged years.

However, this conclusion raises another issue. It has been argued that early measures of intelligence do not measure what is assessed as intelligence in

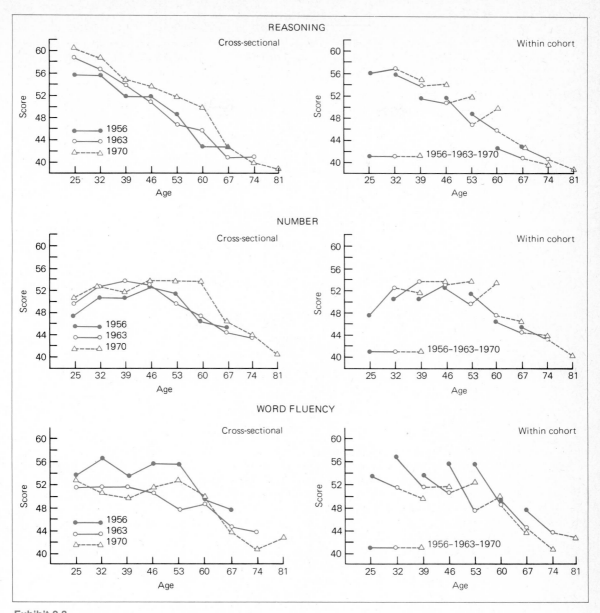

Exhibit 9.3
Cross-sectional (left) and within-cohort sequential (right) curves for scores on ability tests for reasoning, number, and word fluency, respectively. (*Source:* Adapted from Schaie, Labouvie, & Buech, 1973.)

adolescence. Are those types of abilities seen present in adolescence and thereafter first present in this period of life? In other words, is there continuity or discontinuity in the type of cognitive abilities present from childhood to adolescence? This question raises the issue of the age-differentiation hypothesis.

The differentiation of cognitive abilities

The number of different abilities that make up psychometric intelligence has been a continuing source of controversy. Estimates have ranged from one (Spearman, 1927) to over one-hundred (Guilford, 1967). From a developmental perspective, the number of abilities that characterize the person at different points in the life span also has been controversial, especially insofar as adolescence is concerned. Burt (1954, 1955) and Garrett (1946) formulated the age-differentiation hypothesis of intelligence to address this controversy.

As originally put, this idea suggests that a global ability structure emerges in childhood. That is, there is a general sort of intelligence, with all measures of cognitive ability highly related. Furthermore, it is argued that although all measures of cognitive ability remain correlated across the life span, there are groupings of abilities that form (as we saw in Schaie's sequential research). In other words, there is a *differentiation* from one to several groups of abilities, and it is held that this change characterizes the adolescent period.

According to Fitzgerald, Nesselroade, and Baltes (1973), there are data which suggest a revision of this general idea. A sequence of *integration* (early childhood), *differentiation* (childhood through adolescence into adulthood), and *dedifferentiation* or *reintegration* (late adulthood) is suggested. This ordering involves increasingly higher interrelations in childhood among whatever mental abilities are present, and as such, the presence of one global or general ability dimension is hypothesized. After this, by late childhood and into adolescence, there is differentiation into several ability dimensions. In late adulthood, there is a return to the less differentiated structure.

Fitzgerald et al. (1973) note that the existence of this life-span process is uncertain, since there have been studies both finding it and not finding it. In fact, reviews of this research (Anastasi, 1970; Reinert, 1970) show that studies divide about equally between supporting and rejecting the age-differentiation hypothesis. However, these reviews have indicated that several methodological problems exist in this research (for example, use of small, homogeneous samples, use of tests that are not sensitive to changes in the number of abilities present, and failure to include control groups). As such, to decide whether the differentiation hypothesis is a useful one, at least insofar as adolescent development is concerned, Fitzgerald et al. conducted a study which avoided such methodological problems.

From a stratified probability sample of about 2,100 junior high and high school students in West Virginia, a group of 1,891 volunteers was studied. Students were divided into three grade level groups: grades 7–8 (sample size, N, was 783), grades 9–10 (N= 630), and grades 11–12 (N=478). Within each group, subjects were divided about equally by sex.

The age-differentiation hypothesis suggests that there is a gradual change through adolescence in the structure of intelligence from the global nature of childhood to the differentiation of adulthood. Consequently, Fitzgerald et al. used the Thurstone and Thurstone (1962) conception of the primary mental abilities of adulthood to define the structure of adult intelligence. This conception of adult intelligence sees cognitive abilities as grouped into four categories (verbal, number, reasoning, and space factors). Using this structure of abilities as a target, Fitzgerald et al. assessed whether there was an increasingly greater correspondence across the grade groups with the target, adult structure, as would be expected on the basis of the age-differentiation hypothesis.

The results of this matching failed to find evidence for differentiation. At all grade levels, the same number of factors (four) were found. Thus, from early through middle adolescence, the same level of differentiation was present. In addition, the four factors present in each group were found to be clearly the same as those that Thurstone had indicated composed adult intellectual structure. Data within and across groups indicated that the factors constituting adult ability were already present among adolescents within the seventh grade. In short, from early adolescence to adulthood, people have a stable ability structure, and thus, if there is differentiation of cognitive abilities, it emerges prior to adolescence.

Variables that moderate intellectual change

What are the variables that influence or moderate the stability or instability of psychometric changes across the child-adolescent-adult span? Researchers have moved beyond mere description of the course of intellectual changes across life and have attempted to discover those personal, social, and environmental variables which may moderate these changes.

Achievement   From late childhood and through adolescence, a relationship exists between scores on intelligence tests, grades earned in school, and scores on standardized *achievement tests* (Lavin, 1965). Such tests are designed to measure what has been learned already (Brody & Brody, 1976). Thus, one may distinguish between *aptitude tests*—such as intelligence tests, which are designed to measure one's *capacity* to learn—and achievement tests, which measure previous intellectual accomplishment.

The correlation between IQ scores and grades, for instance, is usually reported to be about +.5 (Brody & Brody, 1976). However, this relation tends to be higher in high school than in college. In college there is presumed to be a more intellectually homogeneous background among students; thus with less variation in IQ scores there is less chance of finding a high correlation between IQ and grades (Brody & Brody, 1976). Consequently, the differences in grades that do exist among college students are probably due to many personal and social factors. Moreover, even when the correlation between aptitude (IQ) scores and achievement test scores has been found to be highest—about +.7 in the late childhood and early adolescent portions of life (Crans, Kenny, & Campbell, 1972)—it is still true that more than half of the difference in people's achievement scores is associated with factors other than IQ score.

Nevertheless, there are some longitudinal data which suggest that among people who have very high IQ scores there is a tendency to show especially high "achievement." Terman (1925; Terman & Oden, 1959) longitudinally studied several hundred males and females from their late childhood–early adolescence through their adult years. At the time of their recruitment into the study the average IQ score for this large group was 151, and very few had scores less than 140. The accomplishments of this group turned out to be impressive. Numerous men and women published novels, poetry, short stores, and plays, as well as scientific and scholarly papers and books. Many achieved national recognition, for example, by

INSIGHT INTO ADOLESCENCE

Benjamin Franklin was a printer, publisher, author, inventor, scientist, and diplomat—one of the best known and admired men in this country and in Europe during the last half of the eighteenth century. He helped write the Declaration of Independence and the U.S. Constitution. The following selection is from his autobiography.

While I was intent on improving my language, I met with an English grammar (I think it was Greenwood's) having at the end of it two little sketches on the arts of rhetoric and logic, the latter finishing with a dispute in the Socratic method; and soon after I procured Xenophon's *Memorable Things of Socrates,* wherein there are many examples of the same method. I was charmed with it, adopted it, dropped by abrupt contradiction and positive argumentation, and put on the humble inquirer; and being then, from reading Shaftesbury and Collins, made a doubter, as I already was in many points of our religious doctrines, I found this method the safest for myself and very embarrassing to those against whom I used it; therefore I took delight in it,

practiced it continually, and grew very artful and expert in drawing people, even of superior knowledge, into concessions, the consequences of which they did not foresee, entangling them in difficulties out of which they could not extricate themselves, and so obtaining victories that neither myself nor my cause always deserved. I continued this method some few years, but gradually left it, retaining only the habit of expressing myself in terms of modest diffidence; never using, when I advanced any thing that might possibly be disputed, the words certainly, undoubtedly, or any others that gave the air of positiveness to an opinion; but rather said, I conceive or apprehend a thing to be so and so; it appears to me, or I should not think it so or so; or it is so, if I am not mistaken. This habit, I believe, has been of great advantage to me when I have had occasion to inculcate my opinions, and persuade men into measures that I have been from time to time engaged in promoting.

Source: Benjamin Franklin, *Autobiography,* ed. Leonard W. Labaree et al. (New Haven, 1964), 64–65.

---

being listed in *Who's Who in America* and/or by becoming governmental, business, military, or educational leaders.

However, it should be emphasized that not *all* people in this high IQ group showed such achievement. For instance, most of the women in the sample chose to be housewives and not to pursue a career outside the home. Thus, again it is seen that IQ and achievement do not stand in any one-to-one relation.

Sex differences Another popular variable that has been considered is sex. Researchers have been concerned with whether males and females tend to show similar patterns of development of intellectual abilities. Sex, like age, may be regarded as only a marker variable for processes of behavior change. However, a rationale for looking at sex differences in cognitive development has been that the discovery of such differences would provide a reason for looking at how biological, sociocultural, psychological, or social processes may vary in relation to sex. Thus, a search for the bases of cognitive changes might be made more efficient.

However, the sexes do not differ consistently in tests of total or composite abilities (Maccoby & Jacklin, 1974). In fact, in a major review of the research literature on sex differences, Maccoby and Jacklin (1974) can draw only a few tentative generalizations about the presence and direction of sex differences. Although Block (1976) has shown that even these generalizations are quite problematic, she does agree with Maccoby and Jacklin that boys and men *tend* to score higher than girls and women in tests of spatial and quantitative ability, and in turn, girls and women score higher than boys and men on measures of verbal ability.

Yet even these generalizations are only first approximations of trends in the literature and need to be qualified. For instance, the generalization that females are better on verbal tasks must be qualified by noting that this advantage does not become marked until about grade 10 or 11. Although the difference is seen through the rest of adolescence and into young adulthood, it is not found in every study. For example, although Hakstian and Cattell (1975) found that a group of 142 grade 11 and 12 girls were better in spelling and word fluency than a group of 138 boys in these grades, the study by Fitzerald, Nesselroade, and Baltes (1973) reported no marked sex differences in verbal abilities among seventh grade to twelfth grade adolescents. Yet on the other hand, Droege (1967), in a longitudinal study from the ninth to the twelfth grade, found the verbal superiority of females increasing throughout this period.

Similarly, the generalization that males show better quantitative ability must be qualified, since Maccoby and Jacklin (1974) find no evidence of such a sex difference in the preschool years. Moreover, there appears to be no sex difference in mastery of numerical operations and concepts in the early school years. In fact, the majority of studies using representative samples show no sex differences up to adolescence. However, when differences are found after this age level, they tend to favor males. Although Maccoby and Jacklin reach similar conclusions about the age-related emergence of sex differences insofar as visual-spatial abilities are concerned, we must again emphasize that the data are uncertain.

Not only did the Fitzgerald et al. (1973) study report no sex differences in regard to adolescent number and space factors, but Waber (1977), studying 40 male and 40 female 10- through 16-year-olds, found no significant sex differences on either spatial or verbal ability measures. In turn, in the Hakstian and Cattell (1975) study noted above, females, who did surpass males on verbal measures, also did better than males on visual-motor dexterity and perceptual speed scores.

Together, these studies of sex differences suggest that a search for processes that *consistently* may vary with sex may not be fruitful. In addition to methodological differences and problems in the various studies of sex differences (Block, 1976; Maccoby & Jacklin, 1974), it may be that these studies have contrasting findings because the contexts within which females and males develop are different. However, these context differences are often not studied. Some of what is known about these effects is summarized next.

Social interaction effects   When one does consider those studies which evaluate behavior change processes in various settings, many variables that seem to affect intellectual change are uncovered. Although there are various dimensions along which researchers have evaluated the influence of these variables on psychometric intelligence (Bijou, 1976), one dimension that has attracted considerable attention is the role of social interactions and IQ scores. Basically, the issue addressed here is whether people who develop in different settings have different IQ scores. Several research directions indicate the anwer is yes.

Wolf (1964) noted that although the correlation between socioeconomic status and IQ is generally reported to be +.4, there is no indication of what produces this relationship. Wolf hypothesized that parent-child interaction may be involved; children at different socioeconomic levels may interact with their parents in different ways. Wolf measured thirteen variables pertaining to parent-child interaction in a group of sixty mothers and their sixty fifth grade children. The variables related to categories such as pressures for achievement and pressures for general learning. The combined (multiple) correlation among these thirteen parent-child interaction variables and IQ score was +.76, indicating that children differing in their social interaction context also differ in their psychometric intelligence.

These results suggest that if a person interacts in a setting where pressures for certain behaviors are maintained about him or her, then he or she may perform in accordance with these pressures. These pressures may be behavioral urging or prompting, as in Wolf's (1964) study. In addition, there may be expectations about performance which are based on attitudes about the person (recall our discussion in Chapters 2 and 8 about the role of stereotypes in creating a self-fulfilling prophecy). In other words, people's attitudes about a target person's behaviors may create a social climate which channels the target's behavior in a way consistent with the attitudes (Rosenthal, 1966).

Moreover, a target person's own expectations about the social interactions involved in intellectual performance can contribute to the self-fulfilling prophecy. Kagan (1969) notes that Black children's poor performance on standard IQ tests may be due to social factors, as well as to the bias in test construction against Blacks (the tests were standardized on White middle-class populations). Kagan says that Blacks may not interact comfortably in a test where they are appraised by White examiners. They may anticipate stress and in fact feel uneasy in such a situation, and this may interfere with performance. Kagan (1969) cites unpublished data which show that when Blacks are made to feel comfortable in a test situation, their performance improves.

Thus, one may speculate that if Blacks could anticipate a favorable interaction with their White evaluator (or if the evaluator were Black), their test performance would improve, at least insofar as attitudes about the interaction influenced behavior. Results of a study by Piersel, Brody, and Kratochwill (1977) support this idea. These investigators gave the WISC to sixty-three disadvantaged minority children (64 percent Black, 25 percent Mexican-American, and 11 percent of mixed ethnicity). Children were divided into three groups. One group was administered the test by a White tester. A second group was given feedback for correct and incorrect responses. A third group was allowed to view another minority child being given the test by a White tester. Presumably, the vicarious experience involved in this third condition should have reduced any fears the minority children had about the situation, and lead to better test performance. Indeed, not only did the children in this third group have higher test scores than those in the other two groups, but also as the amount of apprehension about evaluation decreased, IQ scores increased.

Thus, the attitudes of both teachers and students involved in an interactive situation can influence IQ scores. Although race is an obvious cue for bringing out attitudes about social interaction, there may often be cues that are more subtle. There may be aspects of either person involved in the parent-child or teacher-student interaction that lead to interactions which may affect IQ scores. These aspects need not be physical cues like race or sex. In fact, a study by Gordon and Thomas (1967) indicates that as far as teachers are concerned, an important cue may be an aspect of the students' personality.

Gordon and Thomas (1967) noted that different children tend to show characteristic styles of behavior in the classroom. They were able to describe four such styles of reactivity, or "temperament" types, among a group of kindergarten children. Students were rated as:

1. *Plungers*, who jump right into any new activity
2. *Go-alongers*, who participate after the activity is begun
3. *Sideliners*, who participate only partially
4. *Nonparticipators*, who do not take part at all

Experienced teachers, who had taught the children, were asked to rate each child's temperament and to estimate his or her intelligence. Gordon and Thomas then took an actual measure of intelligence. However, the teachers did not know a child's score when making the intelligence estimates.

The results showed that although there was only a very low correlation between temperament and IQ (a correlation of about +.2), the teachers estimated a very high relation to exist (about +.6). Moreover, the teachers saw the plungers as brightest, the go-alongers as next brightest, the sideliners as next brightest, and the nonparticipators as least intelligent. Yet there was *no* such IQ difference among these groups.

Thus, teacher expectations based on a variable like temperament can lead to a self-fulfilling prophecy. A circular process is suggested by data from a cross-sectional study by Lerner and Miller (1971). These researchers repeated the procedure of Gordon and Thomas except that the subjects were all seventh grade students in a small suburban Midwestern junior high school. At this age level there was a high correlation between temperament and intelligence (about +.6). This latter study is consistent with the idea that variables that may relate to different processes of social interaction may influence a person's IQ score.

In summary, psychometric intelligence scores appear to be influenced by interactions in a particular social context and by broader sociocultural and historical influences associated with birth cohort membership and time of measurement. Although such plasticity has led some developmentalists to focus on the situational or cohort influences on IQ (Baltes, Cornelius, & Nesselroade, 1978), it has led others to reject psychometric intelligence as a useful topic of inquiry (McClelland, 1973).

Still others taking a less extreme view have been intrigued by an alternative conception of intellecutal functioning—the qualitative approach developed by Jean Piaget. Although this approach will be discussed shortly, the point of Elkind (1968), that the quantitative and the qualitative approaches to cognition are compatible, may be repeated here. Indeed, in order to understand the qualitative approach, we first consider an issue which serves as a bridge between the two approaches—the correspondence, if any, between psychometric and Piagetian assessments of cognition.

Relations between quantitative and qualitative cognition

DeVries (1974) studied 143 bright and average children, aged 5, 6, and 7 years, through the administration of several psychometric measures of intelligence (for example, the Stanford-Binet) and several measures designed to assess the type of cognition evaluated by Piaget. Although scores on the two types of tests overlapped to some degree, DeVries was able to conclude that to a very great extent, Piagetian-based tasks measure a different type of intelligence than do psychometric tests.

Kuhn (1976) provides data showing that even the minimal correspondence identified by DeVries (1974) tends to diminish by adolescence. As we shall see, Piaget describes four general stages of cognitive development. Kuhn found that among fifty-two middle-class 6- to 8-year-olds, a high correlation existed between mental age and development into the third stage in Piaget's theory—concrete operations—a stage associated with middle to late childhood. However, among fifty-six middle-class 10- to 12-year-olds, there was no correlation between mental age and progression to the last stage of cognitive development in Piaget's theory—the formal operational stage—the one associated with adolescence (Elkind, 1968; Neimark, 1975). In short, there was no relation between psychometric intelligence and that type of intelligence studied by Piaget and his followers among adolescents.

Piaget has provided the only comprehensive theoretical description about adolescent cognition (Elkind, 1968; Neimark, 1975). Because most current research on the thinking of adolescents in some way recognizes the work of Piaget, and of his major collaborator, Inhelder (Inhelder & Piaget, 1958), it is important to study this approach in its own right.

THE QUALITATIVE ASSESSMENT OF ADOLESCENT COGNITIVE DEVELOPMENT

The theory of Jean Piaget has become almost synonymous with the qualitative approach to the study of cognition (Elkind, 1968), especially in the adolescent developmental period. In fact, in a relatively recent review of the literature on intellectual development during adolescence, Neimark (1975) devoted her whole attention to Piaget's theory (Inhelder & Piaget, 1958) and to research derived from it. Accordingly, in the presentation to follow, the contributions of Piaget, his followers, and his critics will be emphasized.

Piaget's theory is a most complex one. As noted, he divides the course of cognitive development into stages, and sees the last stage of development as one associated with adolescence. However, to understand the quality of thought possessed by the adolescent, one must understand the character of thought existing in each of the three preceding stages. Furthermore, to understand his theory, one must recognize that Piaget has concepts which cut across the stages. He has concepts which are thus stage-independent, and in fact are used to explain the basis of a person's development from one stage to another. Finally, however, in order to deal with all this complexity, one has to recognize that Piaget comes to the study of human cognitive development from a unique intellectual perspective. He was not trained as a social scientist and hence does not use a vocabulary typical of many psychologists or sociologists. Perhaps it would be helpful first to know something of Piaget's personal background.

Piaget: A biographical overview

Jean Piaget was born in Switzerland in 1896. Piaget was intellectually precocious. He published his first scientific paper at the age of 10. During his own adolescence he had published so many high-quality research papers on mollusks (sea creatures such as oysters and clams) that he was offered the position of curator of the mollusk collection in the Geneva museum (Flavell, 1963). To culminate these early achievements, Piaget received a doctorate in the natural sciences at the age of 22.

After receiving his doctorate in 1918, Piaget, maintaining a broad intellectual interest, became involved with work in psychology and maintained an active interest in *epistemology*, the philosophy of knowledge. Perhaps because it seemed that the

Jean Piaget

best way to understand knowledge was to study how it develops, Piaget began studying the development of cognition in his own children. From these initial studies, his first books resulted, and in them he began to devise a developmental theory of cognition. He viewed cognition as a developmental phenomenon rather than all development as a cognitive phenomenon.

Since Piaget came to his interest in cognitive development from his training in natural science and his interest in epistemology, his theory is colored by these intellectual roots. As a consequence, Piaget's theory uses many philosophically based terms and has a strong biological basis. These emphases will become apparent as his theory is considered.

PIAGET'S THEORY OF COGNITIVE DEVELOPMENT

Piaget proposes that cognitive development progresses through phases. He casts this proposal in the form of a stage theory of development. In Chapter 6 Sigmund Freud's stage theory of psychosexual development was discussed. Piaget's theory is like Freud's, in that they both use a stage theory formulation. Within developmental psychology, a stage theory is one which holds that all people who develop pass through a series of qualitatively different (discontinuous) levels of organization in an invariant sequence. Thus, stages are seen as universal levels of progressions. Within a stage theory, stages may not be skipped or reordered. The only interindividual differences possible are in the rate one passes through stages and the final level of development reached. Some people's development may not proceed, for instance, because of fixation; but *if* they did develop, they would have progressed in the specified sequence.

All stage theorists propose some mechanism by which a person changes from one level to another. Freud claimed, for example, that the movement of libido into specific bodily zones was the basis of a stage emerging. Piaget has his own ideas about general principles of development which apply at all stages and which, at the same time, account for progression from one level of functioning to the next.

INSIGHT INTO ADOLESCENCE

Jean Piaget was born in Switzerland in 1896. Intellectually precocious, he published articles on mollusks (sea creatures such as oysters and clams) during his teenage years. However, he became world famous for integrating ideas from philosophy and biology in order to formulate a biological theory of the development of knowledge. The selection below describes an experience with his godfather that motivated him to devote his energies to devising such a theory.

My godfather, Samuel Cornut, a Romanish man of letters, invited me about that same period to spend a vacation with him at Lake Annecy . . .

But my godfather had a purpose. He found me too specialized and wanted to teach me philosophy. Between the gatherings of mollusks he would teach me the "creative evolution" of Bergson. (It was only afterward that he sent me

that work as a souvenir.) It was the first time that I heard philosophy discussed by anyone not a theologian; the shock was terrific, I must admit.

First of all, it was an emotional shock. I recall one evening of profound revelation. The identification of God with life itself was an idea that stirred me almost to ecstasy because it now enabled me to see in biology the explanation of all things and of the mind itself.

In the second place, it was an intellectual shock. The problem of knowing (properly called the epistemological problem) suddenly appeared to me in an entirely new perspective and as an absorbing topic of study. It made me decide to consecrate my life to the biological explanation of knowledge.

Source: From *Jean Piaget, the Man and His Ideas* by Richard Evans, translated by Eleanor Duckworth. Copyright © 1973 by Richard I. Evans. Reprinted by permission of E. P. Dutton.

Stage-independent conceptions of cognitive development

Piaget proposes principles of cognitive development that apply to all stages of development. These are general laws describing phenomena that continually function to provide a source of cognition throughout ontogeny. To understand them we must focus on the biological basis of Piaget's theory.

To Piaget (1950, 1970; Inhelder & Piaget, 1958, Piaget & Inhelder, 1969), cognition is an instance of a biological system, just like digestion, respiration, and circulation. As such, cognition is governed by laws that apply to any biological system, and has functions and characteristics identical to any biological system.

Like all biological systems, cognition has two components that are invariant: *organization* and *adaptation*. Cognition is always organized, and it is always an adaptive system. Its functioning allows the person to adapt to his or her environment, and thus to survive. Although he recognizes the fundamental importance of both of these characteristics of cognitive functioning, Piaget devotes the major portion of his work to adaptation. By understanding the adaptation involved in relations between person and environment, one may understand the bases of cognitive development.

The process of adaptation is divided into two *always* functioning complementary processes: *assimilation* and *accommodation*.

Assimilation When a cell assimilates food, it takes the food in through its membrane, breaking it down to fit the needs of the cell. In other words, in assimilation an object taken in does not retain its original form or structure. It is altered to fit the existing structure. Hence, as Piaget has said: "From a biological point of view, assimilation is the integration of external elements into evolving or completed structures of an organism" (1970, pp. 706–707).

Cognitive assimilation involves changing an object, external to the subject (the person), to fit the already existing internal knowledge structure of the subject. For example, an infant may have knowledge of its mother's breast, gained through its *actions* on this external stimulus object. The infant has sucked on its mother's nipple, and has come to "know" the mother's breast through the actions it performs in relation to it. The subject develops an internal cognitive structure from its actions on an external stimulus. Thus, to Piaget the basis of knowledge lies in action.

Assimilation occurs when, for instance, the infant discovers its thumb and begins to suck on it. Knowledge of this external stimulus may be gained by the infant acting on the thumb as it did the nipple. The infant would integrate the thumb into the already existing cognitive structure pertaining to the mother's breast, by altering actions on the thumb, or rather fitting actions on the thumb, so as to incorporate the actions into an already existing cognitive structure. The infant would be changing the object to fit, or match, the structure of the subject, and thus the infant would be assimilating.

Accommodation The process that is the complement of assimilation is termed *accommodation*. Accommodation involves altering the subject to fit the object. Cognitive accommodation involves altering already existing cognitive structures in the subject to match new, external stimulus objects.

The infant could accommodate to its thumb, rather than assimilate it, by acting on the thumb not as it did to its mother's nipple but rather by altering its actions. Such a change in action would modify the already existing cognitive structure. This structure is altered to include the different actions on this new object, and thus there is a gain in knowledge. By the subject's altered actions on the different object, a corresponding alteration in the subject's cognitive structure occurs. Rather than matching the object to the subject, the subject—through differential actions—matches the object. Hence, accommodation occurs.

Equilibration Assimilation and accommodation are seen as complementary processes because Piaget postulates that there exists a fundamental factor in development, termed *equilibration*. Piaget proposes that a person's adaptation to the environment involves a balance—an equilibrium—between the activity of the person on the environment (assimilation) and the activity of the environment on the person (accommodation). In other words, when a person acts on the environment, he or she incorporates the external stimulus world into an already existing structure, and this is assimilation. At the same time, when the environment acts on the person, the person is altered in order to adjust to the external stimulus world, and this is accommodation.

Piaget hypothesizes an intrinsic orientation in people to equilibrate their actions on the environment with the environment's actions on them. Piaget proposes that neither of these two tendencies must always override the other if the person is to be adaptive. Thus, equilibration is, to Piaget, the balance of interaction between subject and object (Piaget, 1952). He has stated:

> *Cognitive adaptation, like its biological counterpart, consists of an equilibrium between assimilation and accommodation. As has been shown, there is no*

assimilation without accommodation. But we must strongly emphasize the fact that accommodation does not exist without simultaneous assimilation either. (Piaget, 1970, p. 708)

Piaget proposes that equilibration is the moving force behind cognitive development. Whenever the person alters the environment, incorporating it into an already existing internal structure, there must also be an alteration of the person's structure to match the objects in the external environment. There must be a balance in action—the basis of all knowledge—between person and environment.

Functional (reproductive) assimilation However, if cognitive development moves toward equilibration, then why, when such a balance is reached, does cognitive development not just stop there? It is not enough to argue that there are many things in the infant's world that need further assimilations and accommodations. If the infant is in equilibrium, there would seem to be no reason to bother with other stimulation.

To address this problem Piaget specifies that there exist several other aspects of assimilation. Discussion of one of these—*functional* (or *reproductive*) *assimilation*—will illustrate how cognitive development continues to progress. The concept of reproductive assimilation refers to the fact that any cognitive structure brought about through assimilation continues to assimilate. Any biological system's equilibrium is necessarily temporary; the system must continue to function if adaptation is to be maintained. Ingested food may place the digestive system in equilibrium, but such balance is temporary since the food must necessarily be assimilated if digestion is to continue to fulfill its adaptive function (to provide energy). Similarly, when a simple cognitive structure is developed on the basis of assimilation—such as that involved in our example of the infant's sucking on the mother's nipple—it continues to assimilate. It functions to reproduce itself. Such structures "apply themselves again and again to assimilate aspects of the environment" (Flavell, 1963, p. 55). Thus, the concept of functional assimilation indicates that a basic property of the assimilation function is to continue to assimilate.

Hence, any equilibrium the infant establishes will be only temporary. The child would then assimilate other components of the environment, and this, in turn, would require accommodation. While an equilibration is reached again, it too is short-lived, because a *disequilibrium* will inevitably result when the child continues to assimilate. Because of the disequilibrium resulting from continued functional assimilation, higher levels of cognitive development are reached when the child next equilibrates.

In summary, the occurrence of disequilibrium (through the process of reproductive assimilation) provides the source of cognitive development throughout all stages of life. This equilibration model provides a set of stage-independent concepts about cognitive development that account for a person's continued cognitive development. A consideration of Piaget's stage-dependent concepts follows.

STAGES OF COGNITIVE DEVELOPMENT

As noted, Piaget (1950, 1970) describes four stages of cognitive development. People may differ in their rate of development through a stage, but some rough age boundaries for each stage can be indicated.

The sensorimotor stage

Piaget labels the first stage *sensorimotor*, and suggests that it lasts from birth through about 2 years. Changes in this stage involve the development of what Piaget terms *schemes*. A scheme is an organized sensorimotor action sequence. As such, the schemes existing throughout this first stage conveniently may be thought of as reflexive in nature. Similar to a reflex, a scheme is a *rigid* cognitive structure. The direction of the sequence involved in the scheme is always the same. Analogous to a reflex such as an eye blink, wherein a puff of air always precedes and leads to an eye blink, a scheme is also unidirectional; the motor component of the schematic sequence cannot be reversed.

For much of the early portions of the sensorimotor stage, the infant's cognitive development could be described as "out of sight, out of mind." The infant interacts with objects in the external world, but acts as if their existence depended on his or her sensing them (Piaget, 1950). When objects are not in the infant's immediate sensory world, the infant acts as if they do not exist. The infant is thus *egocentric*. There is no differentiation between the existence of an object and sensory stimulation provided by that object (Elkind, 1967). There is no knowledge that objects exist permanently independently of the subject. Thus, there is no scheme of object permanency.

All stages of cognitive development contain functioning that may be described as egocentric. Overcoming *sensorimotor egocentrism* involves the most important cognitive attainment of the child during this stage. All remaining portions of this stage contain schematic structures that involve the infant's developing knowledge that there is object permanency in the world.

There are numerous instances of the infant's lack of a scheme of object permanency. For example, the child acts as if a person or object appears and disappears by virtue of going into and passing out of sight. Only as a consequence of repeated sensorimotor actions will a child develop an internalized representation of an object, and come to know that it exists even though he or she is not perceiving it. When this occurs the child has "conquered the object" (Elkind, 1967). The child's egocentrism has diminished enough to now know the difference between an object and the sensory impression it makes. This knowledge implies *representational ability*, an ability to represent internally an absent object and thus to act as if one knows it continues to exist. This major cognitive achievement enables the infant to progress to the next stage.

The preoperational stage

The age range associated with this second stage is usually 2 through 6 or 7 years of age. The major cognitive achievements in this stage involve the elaboration of the representational ability that enabled the child to move beyond the sensorimotor stage. In the preoperational stage, true systems of representation, or symbolic functioning, emerge. In fact, Elkind (1967) has termed this stage the period of the "conquest of the symbol."

The most obvious example of the development of representational systems is language. Words are used to symbolize objects, events, and feelings. Other indications of the representational ability in this stage involve the emergence of *symbolic play* (as when the child uses two crossed sticks to represent a jet plane) and the emergence of *delayed imitation* (as when a child sees daddy smoking a pipe and pacing across the room and repeats the act hours later).

Cognitive development in the preoperational stage also has limitations. The child in this stage is also egocentric, but here the egocentrism takes a form different from that seen in the previous stage. As always, egocentrism involves a failure to differentiate adequately between self and other; but in this stage egocentrism involves a failure to separate the symbol of the object from the actual object in the real world. The child has the ability to symbolize objects with words, but fails to differentiate between the words and the things to which the words refer. For example, the child believes that a word which is used to refer to an object is an integral part of that object, and that an object cannot have more than one word to symbolize it (Elkind, 1967). In other words, the child does not know that an object and the word symbolizing the object are two independent things.

One consequence of this type of egocentrism is that the child acts as if words carry more meaning than they actually do (Elkind, 1967). The inability to separate words from objects is part of a general inability to hold two aspects of a situation separately in mind at the same time. This inability is also reflected in the preoperational child's failure to show conservation.

Conservation is the ability to know that one aspect of a stimulus array has remained unchanged, although other aspects of the stimulus array have changed. To illustrate, imagine a 5-year-old is presented with a mommy doll and a daddy doll. Six marbles are then taken and placed in a row beside the mommy doll and then six more marbles are placed beside the daddy doll in positions directly corresponding to the mommy doll's marbles. The materials would look like those in Exhibit 9.4a. If the 5-year-old is shown this arrangement and asked, "Which doll has more marbles to play with—the mommy doll or the daddy doll, or do they both have the same?" the child would probably say that both dolls have the same. However, if the mommy doll's marbles are spread out in the same position, so that an arrangement as in Exhibit 9.4b is achieved, and the same question is asked, the preoperational 5-year-old child will answer that the mommy doll has more!

This is an example of the inability to conserve number. The child does not know that one aspect of the stimulus array—the number of marbles—has remained unchanged, although another aspect of the array—the positioning of the marbles—has changed. It seems the child cannot appreciate these two dimensions of the stimulus array at the same time. The child fails to show knowledge that the actions with the mommy doll's marbles can be *reversed* and be put back to the original stimulus array. When the next stage of cognitive development—the concrete operational stage—is discussed, it will be learned that the preoperational child

Exhibit 9.4
Examples of a test of number conservation.

cannot understand this *reversibility* of action yet. Thought is still dominated by schemes, and such structures are rigid and unidirectional. Thus, even though one spreads out the marbles right in front of the child, the child still maintains that the altered array has more marbles. One might even return the array to its original form and again ask the same questions. The child would now probably say once again that they both have the same number, and even if one repeats these steps several times, the child's answers might correspondingly alternate between "same" and "more."

In sum, the preoperational child's lack of conservation ability manifests itself in respect to several quantitative aspects of stimuli, such as mass, area, and volume. Although the preoperational child's thought has progressed well beyond that of the sensorimotor child—due mostly to extensive representational abilities—the preoperational child's cognition still has these limitations—due mostly to an inability to understand such things as the negation or reversibility of actions, as performed on the stimuli in the conservation tests. When one can mentally represent such reversible actions, one shows the ability that is the hallmark of the next stage.

The concrete operational stage

Up to the point when a child enters the concrete operational stage (which spans from about 6 or 7 years of age through 11 or 12 years), the child's cognitive structure is composed predominantly of schemes. Being a unidirectional structure, there is no ability to mentally reverse various physical actions.

The emergence of *operational structures* gives the child this ability. An operation is an internalized action that is reversible. As opposed to schemes, operations allow the person to know that actions can be counteracted by reversing them. Moreover, operations *are* internalized actions. People in this stage do not have to see the marbles rearranged to know that one can return them to the distribution. They can just think of the action. Their thought about concrete, physical actions does not require that they actually see these actions. They can reverse the action in their heads and come to the same conclusion about the actions if they actually, concretely viewed the reshaping actions.

Operational cognitive ability extends the child's capacity to deal with the world. Because thought is now reversible, the concrete operational stage is the period in which the child begins to show the conservation abilities lacking in the preoperational stage. Moreover, because operations are internalized actions, the child's cognitive abilities are also extended in that now one need not actually see actions performed in order to know about them. Simply, operations extend the scope of action by internalizing it.

Despite the accomplishments involved in the concrete operational stage, there are limitations. The label for this stage is concrete operational, and this denotes that thought is bound by concrete, physical reality. Although the child can deal with objects internally, actions and objects must have a real existence. Things or events that are *counterfactual* —that are not actually represented in the real world—cannot be understood by the concrete operational child.

An illustration of this point offered by Elkind (1967) is helpful. If someone asks you to imagine that coal is white, and then asks you to indicate what color coal would be when burning at its hottest, you would most probably have an answer to this counterfactual question. You might think that since coal is actually black and when burning at its hottest is white, then if it were white, it would be black when burning at its hottest. The point here is *not* the particular solution, but the fact that you can deal with the counterfactual question. The concrete operational child, on the other hand, cannot do this. For example, the response might typically be, "But coal is black!" (Elkind, 1967). In essence, a major limitation of concrete operational thought is that it is limited to thinking about concrete things.

Other limitations of concrete thought exist. The concrete operational child is also egocentric (Elkind, 1967). For such children, egocentrism takes the form of an inability to differentiate between actions and objects *directly experienced* and the actions and objects one *thinks about*. Although the child can think independently of experience, and can deal with an action whether it is experienced or just thought about, the child does not distinguish between knowledge gained through experience and knowledge gained from thought alone. If given some information about a physical situation (say a scientific problem) and asked to give a solution to the problem, the child will not have to see the actual physical objects in order to reach a solution. The child will think about it and form an answer. But the child will not recognize the answer as just one possible solution to the problem. Rather, the child will think the answer is one and the same with the physical situation. The child will not see any difference between what he or she thinks and what is! Even if the child's ideas about experience are challenged and/or evidence is presented contradicting those ideas, the child will not alter the answer, but will just reinterpret the opposing evidence to fit his or her ideas (Elkind, 1967). Rather than accommodate to the new data, the child will assimilate it to his or her already existing structure, but will not recognize the hypothetical nature of this process. When the child attains the ability to think counterfactually, to see that reality and thoughts about reality are different, and can generate and recognize hypotheses about reality, the fourth stage in Piaget's theory is reached. This stage is the one associated specifically with adolescence (Elkind, 1967, 1968; Neimark, 1975).

The formal operational stage

The last stage of cognitive development in Piaget's theory is termed the *formal operational stage*. It begins at about 11 or 12 years of age, and continues for the rest of life, according to Piaget (1972). It is because of the lower age limit typically associated with this stage, in both theory and research (see Neimark, 1975), that the study of the qualitative aspect of adolescent cognition is associated with the evaluation of formal operational development.

In this stage, thought becomes hypothetical in emphasis. Now discriminating between thoughts about reality and actual reality, the child comes to recognize that his or her thoughts about reality have an element of arbitrariness about them, that they may not actually be real representations about the true nature of experience. Thus, the child's thoughts about reality take on a hypothetical "if, then" characteristic: "*if* something *were* the case, *then* something else would follow." In forming such hypotheses about the world, the child's thought can be seen to correspond to formal, scientific, logical thinking. This emergence accounts for the label applied to this stage—the formal operational stage.

Another perspective on the quality of this stage is provided by Neimark (1975). She explains the distinctive quality of adolescent thought by noting:

> *Although the properties and relations at issue during the concrete operational stage are abstract in the sense of being derived from objects and events, they are still dependent upon specifics of the objects and events from which they derive;*

that is, they are empirically based abstractions rather than pure abstractions. In this sense the elements of concrete operational thought are "concrete" rather than "abstract" or "formal." On the other hand, propositions, the elements of formal operational thought, are abstract in the sense that the truth value of a statement can be freed from a dependence upon the evidence of experience and, instead, determined logically from the truth values of other propositions to which it bears a formal, logical relationship. This type of reasoning, deriving from the form of propositions rather than their content, is new in the development of the child: deductive rather than inductive thought. (Neimark, 1975, pp. 547–548)

In other words, because the concrete operational child can only form abstractions relevant to phenomena or problems that exist, thoughts about a given topic cannot be integrated with *potentially* relevant but nonempirical (that is, hypothetical) aspects of the problem. In this sense, mental operations are not coordinated, and the child cannot reach solutions by means of general theories or the postulation of all possible solutions to a problem (Wadsworth, 1971). In turn, the formal operational person shows these qualities of thought.

Thus, to be able to deal with all potentially relevant aspects of a problem, the person has to be able to *transform* (that is, alter, or rearrange) the problem so as to contend with all its possible forms. The cognitive structure that characterizes formal operations allows such complete transformations. This structure is termed the *INRC group* by Piaget (Inhelder & Piaget, 1958). That is, all transformations of a problem may be obtained through the application of the components of this group: identity, negation, reciprocal, and correlative transformations. Simply, one can think of all aspects of a problem by, for instance, recognizing the problem in terms of its singular attributes (an identity transformation), canceling the existence of the problem (a negation operation), taking its opposite (a reciprocal transformation), or relating it to other problems (a correlative transformation).

Since only the coordinated use of all these transformations allows all potentially applicable aspects of a problem to be dealt with, it is not until the INRC group is established that the person possesses a cognitive structure appropriate for dealing with pure abstractions, with the set of all propositions pertinent to a problem that is the "object" of thought in the formal operational stage. To indicate the attributes of thought characteristic of people in the formal operational stage, some examples of tasks typically used to measure such cognitive functioning are discussed.

The measurement of formal operational thought

In discussing preoperational thinking, some of the various conservation tasks used to index the child's level of functioning were noted. Different types of problems are presented to children and adolescents in order to assess whether they show the types of mental functions that represent formal operational thought. Inhelder and Piaget (1958; Piaget & Inhelder, 1969) describe several such formal operational tasks.

One of these tasks tests *combinatorial thought.* To explain the meaning of this term, Piaget and Inhelder (1969) describe a task wherein a subject is presented with five jars, each containing colorless liquids. Combining the liquids from three particular jars will produce a color, while any use of the liquids from either of the other jars will not produce a color. The subject is shown that a colored liquid can be produced, but is not shown which combination will do this.

Concrete operational children typically try to solve this problem by combining liquids two at a time, but after combining all pairs, or possibly trying to mix all five liquids together, their search for the workable combination usually stops. However, the formal operational child will explore all possible solutions, and typically tests all possible combinations of two and three liquids until a color is produced.

Tasks involving certain types of *verbal problems* cannot usually be solved without formal operational ability (Piaget & Inhelder, 1969; Wadsworth, 1971). One such verbal problem is represented by the question, "If Jane is taller than Doris, and is shorter than Francine, who is the shortest of the three?" (Wadsworth, 1971). Although concrete operational children may be able to solve an analogous problem, for example, one dealing with sticks of various lengths, when the elements of the problem (the sticks) are physically present, abstract verbal problems are usually not solved until formal operations have emerged.

Although formal operational thought can be illustrated by particular solutions to problems presented by many other tasks (Inhelder & Piaget, 1958), we may mention one other task, the *pendulum problem*, to illustrate the quality of thought at this period of functioning. A pendulum can be made to swing faster by shortening the string holding it. Conversely, it can be made to swing slower by lengthening the string. Concrete operational children typically adjust the *weight* of a pendulum when asked to alter its speed (Wadsworth, 1971). Alternatively, they may adjust string length and weight simultaneously, and attribute any change in speed to the weight alteration (Wadsworth, 1971). However, in the formal operational period, subjects separate weight and string length, deal with them separately, and show knowledge that it is string length which is the variable relevant to the speed of swinging (Inhelder & Piaget, 1958).

In summary, with formal operations the child's thought is completely free from any dependence on concrete reality. Now the child can and does think not only in the "if then" or "as if" manner, but counterfactually and completely abstractly as well. In her review of research on adolescent intellectual development, Neimark (1975) notes that there exists strong research evidence for the validity of formal operational thought as an empirical phenomenon distinct from concrete operational thought. There have been repeated demonstrations of age-related improvements in formal thought during adolescence (for example, Martorano, 1977). Indeed, presentations by Moshman (1977) and Flavell and Wohlwill (1969) support Piaget's ideas about the structure of adolescent thought, as well as of the way this stage is formed. Similarly, Roberge (1976) found that the formal operational structures necessary to solve complex problems and deal with conditional reasoning arguments emerge in early adolescence, and a report by Strauss, Danziger, and Ramati (1977) shows that formal thoughts, which dominated college students' thinking, cannot easily be changed back to concrete operational. Thus, formal operations emerge as a distinct stage in adolescence and continue to characterize thought thereafter. However, several qualifications of these conclusions are necessary.

Issues in the assessment of formal operations

As will be noted below, the emergence of formal operations in adolescence does not say anything about whether another stage of cognition follows. Moreover, there is evidence that the emergence of a formal operational thought structure is not a characteristic of all people. As reviewed by Neimark (1975), studies done with older adolescents and adults in Western cultures show that not all individuals attain the level of formal operations. For instance, Jackson (1965) found that only seven of sixteen persons 13 to 15 years old reached a conventional stage of formal thought, and less than 75 percent of the 15-year-olds that Dale (1970) studied reached such a stage. In fact, on the basis of results from two studies (Elkind, 1962; Towler & Wheatley, 1971), Neimark (1975) notes there is evidence that only about 60 percent of samples of college students show appropriate performance on tasks requiring the conservation of volume. Similarly, Martorano (1977) found that in a sample of sixth to twelfth grade females, there was a grade-associated improvement on average scores for ten different tests of formal operations. However, not even the oldest group of subjects showed formal operations across all ten tasks.

Moreover, although not all people may attain the formal operations level, once attained in adolescence it may not be continuous throughout the rest of life. Papalia (1972) found that less than 60 percent of her 65- to 82-year-old sample conserved volume, and Tomlinson-Keasey (1972) found evidence of formal operations in just about 50 percent of her middle-aged female sample. These latter two studies could be interpreted as showing that formal operations are not present in the postadolescent life periods of people of some (older) cohorts. This may be due either to their never reaching this stage or, after having attaining it, to their losing their ability. However, without ontogenetic-historical data on subjects' life-span performance, this issue presently cannot be decided.

Not only are generalizations about the course of formal operations across the life span within a culture tentative, but so too are such statements when made from a cross-cultural perspective. As summarized by Neimark (1975), people in many cultural settings do not attain formal operational abilities at the average, early adolescent time that it occurs within Western cultural settings. For example, Douglas and Wong (1977) reported that American adolescents (13- and 15-year-olds) were more advanced in formal operations than Hong Kong Chinese youth of corresponding ages. In fact, in some non-Western groups there is a failure ever to attain such thinking ability. Piaget (1969b, 1972) himself notes such failures. Reasons for these differences have been suggested to lie in the contrasts in experience found between rural and urban settings (Peluffo, 1962; Youniss & Dean, 1974), and the kind of schooling experiences encountered (Goodnow, 1962, Goodnow & Bethon, 1966; Peluffo, 1962, 1967).

Although these explanations might lead one to expect socioeconomic or educational differences to be associated with formal operational attainment, the data do not support such a view. Neimark (1975) finds that socioeconomic status has no known effect on the development of formal thought, and in addition, she notes that only *very* profound differences in education seem to be associated with the development of formal thought. Moreover, variables such as sex and psychometric intelligence, which might be thought to mark differences in experience associated with formal thought development, do not seem useful. Some studies find sex differences (for example, Dale, 1970; Elkind, 1962), and some do not (for example, Jackson, 1965; Lovell, 1961). Moreover, IQ score differences do not, as we have already seen, relate to differences in formal operational development (Kuhn, 1976). Indeed, it seems that after some minimal level of psychometric intelligence is reached, variables other than those associated with IQ scores contribute to formal operational development (Neimark, 1975).

It has just been suggested that the variables readily thought of as possible facilitators of such progression do not seem consistently functional. Thus, it might be appropriate to try *directly* to train formal operational thought. But few studies have attempted this. Although Tomlinson-Keasey (1972) facilitated formal thought through training on one task, subjects did not generalize formal thinking ability to other tasks. Schwebel's (1972) attempt at training also met with limited success, and Lathey (1970) had no success at all in attempting to produce volume conservation in 11-year-olds. Kuhn and Angelev (1976) did succeed in their intervention attempt, however. Fourth and fifth graders were given a fifteen-week program where they confronted problems requiring formal operational thought. The frequency of exposure to the problems (once every two weeks, once a week, or twice a week) was related directly to amount of advancement on three formal operational problems.

In sum, formal operations does not represent a level of thought reached universally by all people in all cultures. Even though uncertainty remains about the variables which provide a transition to this level of thinking, there is strong evidence that formal operations does represent a distinct level of thought beyond concrete operations. Moreover, for most adolescents living in contemporary Western culture—and for all those people now reading these words—formal operations represents an *attained* stage of thought. Although we have seen the assets of this type of thought, it must be noted that, as is the case with preceding levels of thought, formal operational thinking also has limitations. These are now considered.

Adolescent egocentrism

Because anything and everything can become the object of the adolescent's newly developed abstract and hypothetical cognitive ability, the person not only may recognize his or her own thoughts as only one possible interpretation of reality, but also may come to view reality as only one possible instance of a potentially unlimited number of possible realities. The concrete predomination of what *is* real is replaced by the abstract and hypothetical predomination of what *can be* real. All things in experience are thought about hypothetically, and even the adolescent's own thoughts can become objects of his or her hypothesizing.

In other words, one can now think about one's own thinking. Since the young person spends a good deal of time using these new thought capabilities, the person's own thought processes thereby become a major object of cognitive concern. This preoccupation, or *centration*, leads, however, to a limitation of the newly developed formal operational thought. It leads to egocentrism within the formal operational stage. Elkind (1967) has labeled the egocentrism of this stage *adolescent egocentrism*, and sees it as having two parts.

First, we have seen how the adolescent's own thoughts come to dominate his or her thinking. Because of this preoccupation, the adolescent fails to distinguish, or discriminate, between his or her own thinking and what others are thinking about. Being preoccupied with self, and not making the above discrimination, the adolescent comes to believe that others are as preoccupied with his or her appearance and behavior as he or she is (Elkind, 1967). Thus, the adolescent constructs an *imaginary audience.*

An illustration of the functioning of the imaginary audience and of some emotional consequences of this cognitive development may be seen if one thinks back to his or her days of early adolescence. Assuredly, some new fad, perhaps in regard to a particular style of clothing, sprung up among peers. Some adolescents perhaps were stuck with wearing the old, outdated style, and were literally afraid to be seen in public. They were sure that as soon as they walked about without the appropriate clothes, everyone would notice the absence.

A second component of adolescent egocentrism also exists. The adolescent's thoughts and feelings are experienced as new and unique. Although to the adolescent they are in fact new and unique, the young person comes to believe that they are *historically* new and unique. That is, the adolescent constructs a *personal fable*, the belief that he or she is a one-of-a-kind individual—a person having singular feelings and thoughts.

Here, too, it is easy to think of an illustration of the personal fable. Think back to your early adolescent years and your first "love affair." No one had ever *loved* as deeply, as totally—no one had ever felt the intense compassion, the devotion, the longing, the overwhelming fulfillment that you felt for your one true love! Then remember a few days or weeks later, when it was over! The pain, the depression, the agony—no one had ever *suffered* as deeply, no one had ever been so wrongfully abused, so thoroughly tortured, so spitefully crushed by unrequited love! You sat in your room, unmoving, and your mother would say, "What's wrong with you? Come and eat." The inevitable answer: "You don't understand. What do you know about love!"

Although the formal operational stage is the last stage of cognitive development in Piaget's theory, the egocentrism of this stage diminishes over the course of the person's subsequent cognitive functioning. According to Piaget (Inhelder & Piaget, 1958), the adolescent decenters through interaction with peers, elders, and—most importantly—with the assumption of adult roles and responsibilities: "The focal point of the decentering process is the entrance into the occupational world or the beginning of serious professional training. The adolescent becomes an adult when he undertakes a real job" (Inhelder & Piaget, 1958, p. 346).

Quite interestingly, it may be noted that Piaget sees the end point of adolescence as the adoption of a role in society. Earlier discussions also have stressed the centrality of role attainment as the major psychosocial task of adolescence; it will be seen that this emphasis dominates the views of adolescent development of Erik Erikson (Chapter 12). In short, from many theoretical perspectives—including those stressing cognition and personality—the linkage of the adolescent with his or her society through the processes of role search and attainment is a core component of development.

In sum, with the attainment of formal operations, Piaget (1950, 1970, 1972) claims the person has reached the last stage of cognitive development. To him and his followers, no new cognitive structures emerge over the course of life (Flavell, 1970; Piaget, 1972), although the person may change through a differentiation or specialization of abilities within the common, formal structure (Neimark, 1975; Piaget, 1972). As a way of summary, Exhibit 9.5 presents the four stages in Piaget's theory and shows the cognitive achievements and limitations involved in each stage. However, to close this chapter it is important to note that Piaget's is not the only view about the character of qualitative change in adolescence and later life.

IS THERE A FIFTH STAGE OF COGNITIVE DEVELOPMENT?

Although unquestionably seen as one of the greatest contributions to the study of human development, Piaget's work has not escaped criticism. These critiques have involved many dimensions of inquiry. For example, criticism has centered on measurement and other methodological problems in Piaget's work, and the issue of whether the idea of a "stage" is useful, at least insofar as Piaget employs it (Brainerd,

Exhibit 9.5
Piaget's stages of cognitive development

Stage	Approximate age range	Major cognitive achievements	Major cognitive limitations
Sensorimotor	Birth to 2	Scheme of object permanency	Egocentrism: lack of ability to differentiate between self and external stimulus world
Preoperational	2 to 6 or 7	Systems of representation: symbolic functioning for example, language, symbolic play, delayed limitation	Lack of conservation ability. Egocentrism: lack of ability to differentiate between symbol and object
Concrete operational	6 or 7 to 12	Ability to show experience-independent thought (reversible, internalized actions) Conservation ability	Egocentrism: lack of ability to differentiate between thoughts about reality and actual experience of reality
Formal operational	12 on	Ability to think hypothetically, counterfactually, and propositionally	Egocentrism: imaginary audience, personal fable

Source: Adapted from Lerner, *Concepts and theories of human development.* © 1976, Addison-Wesley Publishing Co., Reading, Massachusetts.

1978). Insofar as adolescent development itself is concerned, the major issue of criticism has involved whether formal operations is indeed the last stage of cognitive development. Is there a fifth, and qualitatively distinct, level of thought that may follow formal operations?

Theorists like Riegel (1973, 1976b) and Arlin (1975) have pointed out that formal operational thought involves finding solutions to problems—it involves being able to generate and evaluate all possible combinations of hypotheses about an issue. However, they do not believe that such thinking allows one to recognize new problems and issues. Arlin (1975) proposed a fifth stage of development, involving a new level of thought, may follow formal operations for some people, and presented data showing that such a "problem-finding" stage existed. Arlin's (1975) ideas have been criticized (Fakouri, 1976), and as is the case with formal operations, some data speak against the presence of such a fifth stage in some late adolescents (Cropper, Meck, & Ash, 1977). But there is some reason to believe that future research moving beyond the concerns emphasized by Piaget may indicate a fifth-stage.

In Chapter 6 Piaget's theory was classified as a moderate interactional view. This means that although Piaget emphasizes that an *interaction* between organism and environment provides the basis of stage progression, he does not place as much stress on the changes in the environment as he does on those changes occurring within the organism. However, Riegel (1976b) suggests that if such a dynamically changing environment were indeed considered, then the sequence and end point of cognitive development that Piaget specifies would have to be altered. Riegel (1973, 1976b) proposes then that a fifth stage of cognitive development—termed *dialectical operations*—may follow the formal operational period. By attending to the person's dynamic interactions within a changing environment—a concern largely omitted by Piaget—Riegel (1973, 1976b) suggests that new information may be provided about the qualitative nature of cognitive development in and after adolescence. It is for future research, however, to determine the appropriateness of this fifth-stage idea.

CHAPTER SUMMARY

Cognition refers to knowing, and *cognitive development* involves changes in the processes involved in the acquisition and use of knowledge. Two approaches exist to the study of adolescent cognitive development. In the *quantitative* approach there is an emphasis on how much the person knows relative to his or her age group, and in the *qualitative* approach there is consideration of the type of thinking a person uses to deal with information.

Those studying cognition, or intelligence, from a quantitative perspective typically measure a person's knowledge on a standardized test, and then usually compare the person's performance with others in the person's age group. Often, the level of performance is expressed as a relative score, termed an intelligence quotient, or IQ score.

Several changes characterize the development of cognition. Correlations between measures of intelligence taken very early in life and those taken at age 18 are not very high. However, this correlation increases with age. Research shows that whether one sees increases, decreases, or stabilities in such correlations across the life span greatly depends on variables related to the social and historical context of individual development.

Intelligence is a *differentiated* phenomenon. Prior to the adolescent years, a global set of intellectual abilities exists. However, through childhood, adolescence, and early adulthood, a differentiation of mental capacities occurs. The variables that appear to moderate such changes are difficult to assess. However, several studies show that the types of interactions children and adolescents engage in, for example between parents and children or students and teachers, are related to differences in IQ scores.

The study of cognition from a qualitative point of view is most associated with the theory and research of Jean Piaget. Piaget proposes that cognition develops through four stages: the *sensorimotor, preoperational, concrete operational,* and *formal operational.* One's progression through these stages involves the person's attempt to maintain a balance, an *equilibration,* between *assimilation* (changing external stimulation to fit already existing knowledge) and *accommodation* (changing already existing knowledge to fit external stimulation).

The sensorimotor stage involves developing the knowledge that external stimulation (objects) continues to exist even when not sensed by the person. When the person mentally can represent absent objects and can use symbols to represent objects, the major characteristics of the preoperational stage are evident. However, although thought about objects in the world is internalized mentally, it is not reversible.

Knowledge about the reversibility of actions occurs in the concrete operational stage. Operations—internalized actions which are reversible—now exist. But thought is limited in that the person can only think about objects which have a concrete, real existence. The person does not have the ability to deal adequately with counterfactual, hypothetical phenomena, and does not recognize the subjective and arbitrary nature of thought.

Such recognition characterizes the formal operational stage, the stage most representative of adolescents in modern Western society. Here the person can think of all possible combinations of elements of a problem to find a solution—the real and the imaginary. However, because the person centers so much on this newly emerged thinking ability, some scientists believe the adolescent is characterized by a particular type of egocentrism. An adolescent may believe others are as preoccupied with the object of his or her own thoughts—himself or herself—as he or she is (this is termed *imaginary audience*). Because of the attention, the adolescent comes to believe he or she is a special, unique person (this is termed *personal fable*).

Research pertaining to Piaget's theory and adolescence has taken several directions. Data indicate that not all people within and across cultures attain formal operations, or attain it completely. Other data suggest that in later life formal operational abilities may be lost. However, since there are data showing that formal operational ability may be achieved through intervention, such loss may suggest the presence of nonoptimal contexts. Finally, both research and theory suggest that cognitive changes proceed beyond adolescence and that this may involve the emergence of a fifth stage of cognitive functioning.

10

MORAL DEVELOPMENT IN ADOLESCENCE

CHAPTER
OVERVIEW

How the adolescent comes to obey society's laws, follow its customs, and act and think in a manner judged as moral is an issue of both practical and scientific significance. Major theories of moral development are reviewed in this chapter. In addition, both theory and research relating to how adolescents develop high levels of moral reasoning are evaluated.

ISSUES
TO CONSIDER

What are the strengths and weaknesses of the nature and nurture conceptions of moral development, as reflected in the theories of Freud and McCandless, respectively?

Why do interactionist cognitive developmental theories of moral development, such as that of Piaget or Kohlberg, focus on moral reasonings instead of moral responses?

What are the strengths and weaknesses of Kohlberg's method of assessing moral reasoning?

What are the levels and stages of moral development in Kohlberg's theory, and what are the major characteristics of moral reasoning stage development?

What evidence exists that moral reasoning develops in the sequence that Kohlberg suggests?

What evidence supports the features of universality and irreversibility that Kohlberg describes?

How do other individual-psychological processes appear to moderate adolescent moral reasoning?

How does the social environment influence adolescent moral behavior and reasoning?

here are many reasons why the morality of adolescents is a major concern. Adolescents sometimes are said to be maladjusted, lost, and dangerous to the institutions of society. Similarly, as noted earlier, many people view adolescence as a period of storm and stress, and hence of rebellion and upheaval. There are several theories which agree with popular conceptions about the general turmoil and/or dangerousness of adolescents (Freud, 1969; Hall, 1904; Lorenz, 1966). Nevertheless, evidence for such general maladjustment and turmoil does not exist in the scientific literature (Bandura, 1969; Douvan & Adelson, 1966; Offer, 1969). Thus, there are both practical and scientific reasons to question whether and how the adolescent will come to obey laws, conform to established social institutions, and think in a manner that adults might judge as "correct," "good," "ethical," or "moral."

There are also additional scientific reasons for focusing on adolescent moral behavior and thought. Most developmental theorists see morality as a basic dimension of the person's adaptation to his or her world. Although different theorists define moral behavior and development in markedly distinct ways, all ideas about moral functioning suggest an adjustment of the person to the social world, an adjustment which serves the dual purpose of fitting the person to his or her society, and at the same time, contributing to the maintenance and perpetuation of that society.

Thus, moral development appears to be a basic component of human adaptation and societal survival. This view is reflected in the position taken by Hogan and Emler:

> The capacity of human groups to survive and to extend their domination over the environment is a direct reflection of their ability to solve the problems of social organization and cultural transmission.
>
> Most scholars who have thought seriously about these problems have concluded that they are rooted largely, if not mainly, in the moral socialization of the group. The great social philosophers of recent times—Émile Durkheim, Karl Marx, Max Weber, L. T. Hobhouse, and Sigmund Freud—have all taken the view that human societies are at their core embodiments of moral orders. If we wish to understand that uniquely human invention, culture, we must analyze the relation of the individual to this moral issue. (1978, p. 200)

However, despite this general agreement, the substantive differences involved in this bidirectional relation require that one understand the different meanings attached to the term "moral development" in order to describe the characteristics of adolescent morality.

DEFINITIONS OF MORAL DEVELOPMENT

Despite the practical and scientific importance given to adolescent moral functioning, there is no consensus about what constitutes such functioning. What is morality? How does one know if the adolescent is or is not moral? When and how does morality develop, and what are the changes that people go through as they show this development? Theories derived from the nature, nurture, and interactionist conceptions discussed in previous chapters provide different answers to these questions. Indeed, there are three major types of theories of moral development that are present in the current study of human development: theories which stress the role of *nature*, of *nurture*, or of *interaction*. Theorists whose ideas have already been discussed may be used to illustrate each of these types.

Freud's nature-oriented theory

Sigmund Freud's (1949) psychoanalytic theory of psychosexual stage development (Chapter 6) takes a weak interactionist stance regarding nature and nurture, and as such sees each stage emerging in an intrinsically determined, universalistic manner. Accordingly, all people experience an Oedipal conflict in their third psychosexual stage (the phallic stage). The successful resolution of this conflict will result in the formation of the structure of the personality Freud labeled as the superego. This structure, it may be recalled, has two components, the ego ideal and the conscience. The latter represents the internalization, into one's mental life, of society's rules, laws, codes, ethics, and mores. In short, by about 5 years of age (with the end of the phallic stage), superego development typically will be complete. When this occurs, the person's conscience will be formed as much as it ever can be, and this in turn means that by about 5 years of age the person will have completed his or her moral development.

Of course, there are reasons for incomplete moral development. Freud (1949) specified that females did not experience the same type of conflict in the phallic stage that males underwent. Males' developments were thought to be based on castration anxiety, while females, not having an identical genital structure, had developments based on penis envy. Freud held that *only* castration anxiety could eventually lead to full superego development (and hence conscience formation). Because of their biologically fixed anatomical difference, females could not ever have complete conscience formation. Females would not ever be as morally developed as would males (Bronfenbrenner, 1960). In addition, moral development could be hampered by particular experiences occurring within the third psychosexual stage (for example, if absence of an appropriate same-sex model led to an inability to resolve the Oedipal conflict). However, because such an experience is moderated in its possible influence on the basis of whether or not it occurs within the third stage, even this experience is shaped by the nature of the person.

Hence, Freud's view of moral development is a nature-based one, and one which emphasizes the completion of moral development in early childhood. Thus, as is generally the case with his theory, Freud saw no special relevance for adolescence in regard to moral development. Whether or not one would have the internalized mental structures enabling one to behave in accordance with society's rules was dependent on developments which emerged and which are completed prior to adolescence.

This theory allows one to recognize two attributes of Freud's psychoanalytic view of moral development. First, Freud would identify a person as morally developed or not on the basis of whether that person showed *behavior* consistent with society's rules. Because of the internalization involved with conscience formation, Freud only would be able to know when a person had completed this formation on the basis of behavioral consistency with these external social rules. Accordingly, to Freud (1949), moral development involves increasing behavior consistency with society's rules, and as soon as a person shows such behavioral congruence (at about 5 years of age), he or she is completely morally developed. This conception indicates then that as long as two people—say a 5-year-old and a

20-year-old—show an identical response in a moral situation, they are identically morally developed.

This observation raises the second point about Freud's views on morality. Freud does not deal with the *content* of behavior. He does not concern himself with whether a particular response in a situation should be judged as moral in some universalistic sense. Rather, as long as the response conforms with the particular rules of the society, then that response shows internalization, conscience formation, and thus moral development. Hence, because different societies can and do prescribe different sorts of rules for behaviors, Freud says there is no universal moral behavior. Rather, what is seen as moral behavior is defined *relative* to a particular society.

In summary, Freud's nature-based view focuses on response consistency with society's rules as an index of moral development and takes a *moral relativism* stance about the ethical appropriateness of any given behavior. Interestingly, a theoretical position often seen as diametrically opposed to Freud's takes an identical stance regarding moral responses and moral relativism. Nurture-based social learning theories converge with psychoanalytic conceptions of moral development.

Nurture-oriented social learning theories

Social learning theorists see behavior as a response to stimulation (Davis, 1944; McCandless, 1970). Such responses may arise either from external environmental sources, such as lights, sounds, or other people, or from internal bodily sources, such as drives (McCandless, 1970). Nevertheless, in either case, responses become linked to stimulation on the basis of whether reward or punishment is associated with a particular stimulus-response connection (Bijou & Baer, 1961). Those responses leading to reward stay in the person's behavioral repertoire, while those associated with punishment do not. The social environment determines which responses will or will not be rewarded, and as such, behavior development involves learning to emit those responses leading to reward and not to emit those responses leading to punishment.

Although social learning theorists differ in regard to the details of how such learning takes place (Bandura & Walters, 1963; Davis, 1944; McCandless, 1970; Sears, 1957), there is general consensus that development involves increasingly conforming behavior to social rules. Thus, the comparability of this position with that of Freud's is evident. Moreover, it is clear that behavior development and moral development are virtually indistinct. There is nothing qualitatively different between behavior labeled as moral and behavior labeled as social, personal, or anything else for that matter. All behavior follows the principles of social learning, and as such, all behavior involves the conformity of the person's responses to the rules of society.

Thus, like all classes of behavior, moral development involves increasing response consistency to the rules of society; and since there is an *arbitrary* relation between a response and a reward—that is, any particular society may reward any given behavior—there are no responses which necessarily (universally) have to be rewarded. Hence, any response may be defined as moral in a given society, and this means that a morally relativistic stance is taken by social learning theorists. By focusing on how nurture processes come to control the person's behavior, social learning theorists derive a conception of moral development that, like the nature-based psychoanalytic one, stresses increasing response consistency with society's rules as the index of moral change. This view also takes a moral relativism stance regarding the content of moral behavior.

Although basing their views on quite distinct ideas about the *basis* of response conformity to societal rules, both psychoanalytic and social learning theorists would judge that if a young child and an adolescent emitted the same response in a moral situation, they would therefore be equally morally developed. Moreover, theorists from both persuasions might say that if in a particular society killing of certain other people were condoned and, in fact, rewarded (for example, the murder of Jews in Nazi Germany or the institutionalized killing of some female infants in some primitive societies), this would be morally acceptable behavior, insofar as that society was concerned. That is, because of moral relativism, any society may establish any behavior as moral.

Interactionist cognitive developmental theories

Another view of moral development has become increasingly prominent in American social science since the late 1950s. This conception not only rejects the focus on responses as an index of moral development, but also stresses that a *universalistic* view of moral development must be taken.

This view rejects moral relativism, and might lead to the claim that those societies which condone killing of other humans are in fact immoral societies. This third theory type was based on the work of Jean Piaget. The position has, however, become more prominently advanced by theorists who, working from a cognitive developmental position like Piaget's, have expanded his initial conceptions.

Piaget (1965) became a major contributor to the topic of moral development by offering a theory that, consistent with his general theory of cognitive development, saw a child's morality as progressing through phases. However, he saw the child as having "two moralities," that is, as progressing through a two-phase sequence. However, the target of concern in this sequence is not behavior that might require moral action, but rather it is *reasoning* about moral responses in such situations. Thus, in his major statement of his views regarding moral development, Piaget (1965, p. 7) cautions readers that they will find "no direct analysis of child morality as it is practiced in home and school life or in children's societies. It is the moral judgment that we propose to investigate, not moral behavior. . . ."

Kohlberg (1958, 1963a, 1963b), Turiel (1969), and other followers of the cognitive developmental view believe that there must be a focus on reasoning and not on responses since the same moral response may be associated with two quite distinct reasons for behavior. Unless one understands the *reasons why* people believe an act is moral or not, one will not be able to see the complexity of moral development that actually exists (Turiel, 1969).

On the basis of his research, Piaget (1965) formulated two phases of moral reasoning development in children. In the first phase, labeled *heteronomous morality*, the child is *objective* in his or her moral judgments. An act is judged right or wrong solely in terms of the consequences of the act. If one breaks a vase, one would be judged by a child in this phase as morally culpable, whether or not the breaking was an accident. This type of judgment is based, Piaget believes, on the *moral realism* of the child. Rules are seen as unchangeable, externally (that is, societally) imposed requirements for behavior; these rules are imposed by adults on the child, and require unyielding acceptance. Such a "relationship of constraint" is seen as necessary because punishment for disobedience to rules is seen as an automatic consequence of the behavior. In short, acts are judged objectively as good or bad, and if a bad act is emitted, there will be *imminent justice,* that is, immediate punishment that occurs automatically.

However, in the second phase, labeled *autonomous morality,* children become *subjective* in their moral judgments. This means they take the *intentions* of the person into account when judging the moral rightness or wrongness of an act. If one breaks a vase out of spite or anger, one would be judged morally wrong. But if one breaks the vase because of clumsiness, then no moral culpability would be seen. This second type of judgment Piaget believes is based on the child's *moral rationality.* Rules are seen as outcomes of agreements between people who are in a relation *not* of social contraint, but rather of cooperation and autonomy. That is, each person is an equal in such a relation, and as such, rules are made in relation to the *mutual* interest of those involved. Thus, acts are judged good or bad in terms of the principles of this "contract." Whatever punishment is associated with violation of contract rules is determined by humans, and is not a consequence of some reflexive, automatic punisher.

Accordingly, although a 5-year-old and an 18-year-old might behave in similar ways in a moral situation, for example, neither might cheat on an exam or steal from a friend, the similar responses would not mean that the reasons underlying the responses were similar. The younger child might not cheat or steal simply because of a belief that he or she would be physically punished for it.

However, the 18-year-old might see such reasoning as "immature." Here the reason for not stealing might involve an *implicit* agreement among friends to respect each other's rights and property. The fact that there may be physical punishment associated with stealing would be *irrelevant* to a reason based on a conception of such mutual trust. Thus, to Piaget, because of the presence of such different types of moral reasonings, the 5- and the 18-year-old would not have similar levels of moral development, despite their similar responses.

In summary, Piaget (1965) believes that all people pass through these two phases of moral reasoning. In other words, he suggests a sequence that first involves an objective and concrete morality based on constraints imposed by the powerful (for example, adults) on the nonpowerful (for example, children). Second, a subjective morality follows, based on an abstract understanding of the implicit contracts involved in cooperation and autonomy relationships.

Piaget's denial of the importance of focusing *just* on the moral response, and his stress on orderings to morality, represented an approach to the study of moral development that was quite distinct from the morally relativistic, response-centered approaches of psychoanalysis and social learning theory. As such, it stimulated considerable interest among developmental researchers, especially because it offered a provocative framework for assessing changes in morality beyond the level of early childhood. However, the interest it stimulated soon led to Piaget's theory being replaced as the focus of developmental research inquiry. Following Piaget's general cognitive developmental theoretical approach, Lawrence Kohlberg (1958, 1963a, 1963b) obtained evidence that Piaget's two-phase model was not sufficient to take into account all the types of changes in moral reasoning through which people progressed. Kohlberg devised a theory involving six stages of moral reasoning development in order to encompass all the qualitative changes he discerned. Interest in moral development in the 1960s and 1970s was centered on assessing the usefulness of Kohlberg's universalistic theory. Accordingly, to determine what is currently known about adolescent moral development, one must deal with the research and theory generated in relation to Kohlberg's stage theory.

KOHLBERG'S THEORY OF MORAL REASONING DEVELOPMENT

Kohlberg's theory of moral development, like Piaget's, is based on the idea that by focusing only on the response in a moral situation, one may ignore important distinctions in the moral reasoning of people at different points in their life span, reasoning differences that in fact may give different meaning to the exact same response at various developmental levels. Because the response alone does not necessarily give a clue about underlying reasoning, "an individual's response must be examined in light of how he perceives the moral situation, what the meaning of the situation is to the person responding, and the relation of his choice to that meaning: the cognitive and emotional processes in making moral judgments" (Turiel, 1969, p. 95).

Because of these issues, Kohlberg rejected response-oriented approaches to understanding moral development and chose to investigate the reasons underlying moral responses (Kohlberg, 1958, 1963a). He devised a way to find the underlying reasons through his construction of a moral development interview. Information from this interview provided the data for the theory he formulated. As such, to understand the empirical origin of Kohlberg's ideas, one must consider his method of studying moral reasoning.

Kohlberg's method of assessing moral reasoning

To study moral reasoning, Kohlberg devised a series of stories, each presenting imaginary moral dilemmas. We will present one such story and then evaluate the features it offers in providing a technique for assessing moral reasoning.

> One day air raid sirens began to sound. Everyone realized that a hydrogen bomb was going to be dropped on the city by the enemy, and that the only way to survive was to be in a bomb shelter. Not everyone had bomb shelters, but those who did ran quickly to them. Since Mr. and Mrs. Jones had built a shelter, they immediately went to it where they had enough air space inside to last them for exactly five days. They knew that after five days the fallout would have diminished to the point where they could safely leave the shelter. If they left before that, they would die. There was enough air for the Joneses only. Their next door neighbors had not built a shelter and were trying to get in. The Joneses knew that they would not have enough air if they let the neighbors in, and that they would all die if they came inside. So they refused to let them in.
>
> So now the neighbors were tying to break the door down in order to get in. Mr. Jones took his rifle and told them to go away or else he would shoot. They would not go away. So he either had to shoot them or let them come into the shelter.

What are the features of this story that make it a moral dilemma? First, as is true of all of Kohlberg's moral dilemma stories (Turiel, 1969), the story presents a conflict to the listener. In this particular story the conflict involves the need for a choice

Lawrence Kohlberg

between two culturally unacceptable alternatives: killing others so that you might survive or allowing others and yourself and family to die. The story presents a dilemma because it puts the listener in a conflict situation such that any response is clearly not the only conceivable one that is acceptable. As such, the particular response is irrelevant. What is of concern is the reasoning used to resolve the conflict. Thus, Kohlberg asks the listener not just to tell him what Mr. Jones should do, but why Mr. Jones should do whatever the listener decides.

Thus, Kohlberg would first ask, "What should Mr. Jones do?" Next he would ask, "Does he have the right to shoot his neighbors if he feels that they would all die if he let them in since there would not be enough air to last them very long? Why?" Then, "Does he have the right to keep his neighbors out of his shelter even though he knows they will die if he keeps them out? Why?" And finally Kohlberg would ask, "Does he have the right to let them in if he knows they will all die? Why?"

On the basis of an elaborate and complicated system for scoring the reasons people give to questions about this and the other dilemmas in his interview (Kohlberg, 1958, 1963a; Kurtines & Grief, 1974), Kohlberg is able to classify people into different reasoning categories. This classification led him to formulate the idea that there existed a sequence in the type of reasons people offered about their responses to moral dilemmas. The types of moral reasonings people used passed through a series of qualitatively different stages. However, contrary to the two cognitive developmental phases Piaget (1965) proposed, Kohlberg (1958, 1963a) argued that there are six stages in the development of moral reasoning and asserted that these stages were divided into three levels, with each level being associated with two stages. However, both the levels and the stages involved within and across them were seen to form a universal and invariant sequence of progression. These levels and stages of moral reasoning development are discussed in the next section.

STAGES OF MORAL REASONING

There are no age limits typically associated with Kohlberg's stages or levels. However, since the very first stage does seem to rest on some minimal representational ability, we may presume it does not emerge prior to the preoperational period in Piaget's ideas, that is, somewhere between 2 to 6 or 7 years of age. Moreover, many of the subsequent stages of moral reasoning seem to be dependent on formal operational thinking (Kohlberg, 1973). As such, they may be expected to be involved more typically with adolescence, at least insofar as Western culture is concerned (Simpson, 1974).

Level 1   Preconventional moral reasoning

Within the first level, the first two stages of moral reasoning emerge. Although these two stages involve qualitatively different thought processes about moral conflicts, they do have a general similarity. For both stages a person's moral reasoning involves reference to *external* and *physical* events and objects, as opposed to such things as society's standards, as the source for decisions about moral rightness or wrongness.

Stage 1   Obedience and punishment orientation   The reference to external, physical things is well illustrated in this first stage of moral development. Kohlberg sees this stage as being dominated by moral reasoning that involves reference merely to obedience or punishment by powerful figures. Thus, an act is judged wrong or right if it is or is not associated with punishment. Reasoning here is similar to what we have seen involved in Piaget's first phase of moral reasoning. In stage 1, a person reasons that one must be obedient to powerful authority *because* that authority *is* powerful; it can punish you. Acts, then, are judged as not moral only because they are associated with these external, physical sanctions.

Stage 2   Naïvely egoistic orientation   Reference to external, physical events is also made in this stage. However, an act is judged right if it is involved with an external event that satisfies the needs of the person, or sometimes, the needs of someone very close to the person (for example, a father or a wife). Thus, even though stealing is wrong—because it is associated with punishment—reasoning at this level might lead to the assertion that stealing is right *if* the act of stealing is instrumental in satisfying a need of the person. For example, if the person was very hungry, then stealing food would be seen as a moral act in this instance.

Thus, although this second stage also involves major reference to external, physical events as the source of rightness or wrongness, the perspective of self-needs (or sometimes the needs of significant others) is also brought into consideration (albeit egocentrically). Thus, the development in this second stage gradually brings about a transition of perspective, a perspective involving people. This transition then leads to the next level of moral reasoning.

Level 2   Conventional moral reasoning

In this second level of moral reasoning, the person's thinking involves reference to acting as others expect. Acts are judged right if they conform to roles that others (that is, society) think a person should play. Thus, an act is seen as moral if it is in accord with the established order of society.

Stage 3   Good-person orientation   Here the person is oriented toward being seen as a good boy or a good girl by others. The person sees society as providing certain general, or stereotyped, roles for people. If you act in accord with these role

INSIGHT INTO ADOLESCENCE

Will D. Campbell wrote an autobiography entitled *Brother to a Dragonfly*. This work describes growing up in a small town in the South. At the age of 16 Will Campbell became a preacher. Besides being a writer, he is still a minister and a farmer.

But my debut as a real preacher man had nothing to do with my relationship to the pastor. It started as a joke. In April the eleven members of our graduating class had gone the hundred yards from the schoolhouse to the churchhouse to practice for our forthcoming baccalaureate exercises which, as always, would be held in the East Fork Baptist Church. Mr. Ray Turner was in charge of the rehearsal. His wife, the meanest woman I had ever encountered, and the best English teacher, was assisting.

Someone had played the Washington and Lee March on the piano as we filed down the aisle, and we had remained standing to sing "Follow the Gleam." Something had gone wrong and it must be repeated. Somehow I had made my way to the dais and sat on the double chair reserved for the preacher. It was a holy position and I felt presumptuous and insecure sitting there. I had borrowed from Holland Anderson, one of our classmates, his big, black hat, looking like those worn by Italian priests and it, two sizes too large, covered my head and ears. When the class finished the singing of "Follow the Gleam," they were supposed to sit down. At the precise moment they sat, like a jack-in-the-box, I stood up, placing my hands firmly on the pulpit and looking down at them in judgmental fashion. I had intended to be cute, but not funny. At least not as funny as it apparently was. As they roared with laughter my ears burned with embarrassment. And yet I was more than pleased that I had made them laugh. I glanced quickly in the direction of the principal and his wife. I feared I had committed an act of sacrilege. But they were bursting with uncontrollable guffaws. I was a hit! There was no stopping me then. I went into contortions and gyrations, flailing away at the pulpit, making the veins stand out on my neck. It was a pantomime which would have been a credit to Billy Sunday at his best.

Source: From Brother to a Dragonfly *by Will D. Campbell. Copyright © 1977 by the author. Used by permission of The Seabury Press, Inc.*

prescriptions, you will win the approval of other people, and hence you will be labeled a good person. Thus, acts that help others, that lead to the approval of others, or that simply *should*—given certain role expectations by society—lead to the approval of others, will be judged as moral.

Stage 4 Authority and social-order-maintenance orientation A more formal view of society's rules and institutions emerges in this stage. Rather than just acting in accord with the rules and institutions of society to earn approval, the person comes to see these rules and institutions of society as ends in themselves. That is, acts that are in accord with the maintenance of the rules of society and that allow the institutions of social order (for example, the government) to continue functioning are seen as moral. The social order and institutions of society must be maintained for their own sake; they are ends in themselves. A moral person is one who "does his or her duty" and maintains established authority, social order, and institutions of society. A person simply is not moral if his or her acts are counter to these goals.

Thus, reasoning at this level involves a consideration of a person's role in reference to society. But at stage 4, in contrast with stage 3, moral thinking also involves viewing the social order as an end in itself. The self has to maintain these institutions in order to do one's duty and be moral. However, this thinking may lead the person to consider the reverse side of the issue. The person may begin to think about what society must do in order for it to be judged as moral. If and when such considerations begin to emerge, the person will gradually make a transition into the next level of moral reasoning.

Level 3   Post conventional moral reasoning

This is the last level in the development of moral reasoning. Moral judgments are made in reference to the view that there are arbitrary, subjective elements in social rules. The rules and institutions of society are not absolute, but relative. Other rules, equally as reasonable, may have been established. Thus, the rules and institutions of society are no longer viewed as ends in themselves, but as subjective. Such postconventional reasoning, which, as seen below, is related to formal operational thinking and thus to adolescence as well, also develops through two stages.

Stage 5   Contractual legalistic orientation   In this stage, the person recognizes that a reciprocity, an implicit contract, exists between self and society. One must conform to society's rules and institutions (do one's duty) because society in turn will do its duty and provide one with certain protections. Thus, the institutions of society are seen not as ends in themselves but as part of a contract. From this view a person would not steal because this would violate the implicit social contract, which includes mutual respect for the rights of other members of the society.

Thus, the person sees that any specific set of rules in society is somewhat arbitrary. But one's duty is to fulfill one's part of the contract (for example, not to steal from others), just as it is necessary for society to fulfill its part of the contract (for example, it will provide institutions and laws protecting one's property from being stolen). Hence, the person sees an element of subjectivism in the rules of society, and this recognition may lead into the last stage of moral reasoning development.

Stage 6   Conscience, or principle, orientation   The presence of this stage is controversial even to Kohlberg and his coworkers (Kohlberg, 1978). Here there is more formal recognition that societal rules are arbitrary. Thus, one sees not only that a given, implicit contract between a person and society is a somewhat arbitrary, subjective phenomenon, but also that one's interpretation of the meaning and boundaries of this contract is also subjective. One person may give one interpretation to these rules, while another person may give a different interpretation. From this perspective, the ultimate appeal in making moral judgments must be to one's own conscience.

The person comes to believe that there may be rules that transcend those of specific, given social contracts. Since a person's own subjective view of this contract must be seen as legitimate, a person's own views must be the ultimate source of moral judgments. One's conscience, one's set of personal *principles*, must be appealed to as the ultimate source of moral decisions. To summarize, stage 6 reasoning involves an appeal to transcendent, *universal* principles of morality, rules that find their source in the person's own conscience.

Characteristics of moral reasoning stage development

Kohlberg and his associates (for example, Turiel, 1969) have done more than just describe the ordering and nature of the above six stages. They also have attempted to describe the nature of intraindividual *change* from one stage to another. Turiel (1969), for example, notes that development through the stages of moral reasoning is a gradual process. Transition from one stage to another is not abrupt; rather, movement is characterized by gradual shifts in the most frequent type of reasoning given by a person over the course of development. Thus, at any given point in life a person will be functioning at more than one stage at the same time. As such, one must have a large sample of a person's moral reasonings in order to accurately determine that person's stage of moral reasoning. Only such a large sample will allow one to discover the most frequently occurring type of reasoning the person uses to make moral decisions.

However, the point is that people have the ability to reason at many of the stages Kohlberg specifies. Labeling the person as existing at one or another stage is, in reality, a matter of classifying the person on the basis of his or her most often used type of reasoning. In short, people do not exist at one stage of reasoning, but rather, "stage mixture" exists.

Turiel (1969) has indicated that stage mixture is a *necessary* component of the development of moral reasoning. From a cognitive developmental perspective, changes in moral reasoning level should come about as a result of disequilibrium, which of course would necessitate the reestablishment of an equilibration. That is, using the equilibration model of cognitive development advanced by Piaget (1950, 1970), described earlier, Kohlberg (1973) and Turiel (1969, 1974) see moral development as proceeding on the basis of the person attempting to maintain a balance between assimilation and accommodation. Because of functional assimilation, the person will attempt to incorporate moral reasonings into his or her already existing cognitive structure. However, if these reasonings are at a higher stage, then they should eventually *conflict* with the existing cognitive organization of the person (Langer, 1969; Turiel, 1974). As such, disequilibration should occur, and this would require accommodation, hence rebalancing, and as a result, movement to a higher reasoning level. In support of this model change, Turiel (1969) has demonstrated that when children are exposed to reasoning at a level one stage higher than their own, the child perceives a contradiction between his or her own level of moral reasoning and the next higher one, and the conflict produced by this recognition produces disequilibrium.

But how is the person able to perceive a discrepancy between his or her own reason and the one that is from one stage higher and thus not modally the child's? Turiel suggests that the answer lies in stage mixture. Since the person is functioning at more than one stage at the same time, there are reasoning structures available from this higher stage that enable the person to perceive this discrepancy. Stage mixture, then, is not only an ever-present, but a necessary, component of moral reasoning development. As Turiel has said, "Stage mixture serves to facilitate the perception of contradictions, making the individual more susceptible to disequilibrium and consequently more likely to progress developmentally" (1969, p. 130).

However, people may experience differing degrees of cognitive conflict—and therefore disequilibrium—in their lives. Accordingly, they may pass through the stages of moral reasoning at different rates if, in fact, they pass through them at all. Thus, different people are likely to reach different levels of moral thinking at any one time in their life. In fact, Turiel (1969) has said that his research indicates that most Americans are at stage 4 in their moral reasoning development. That is, for the majority of today's Americans, moral correctness is evaluated in reference to the maintenance of established social order and the institutions of that order. Yet there are some groups of people living in today's world that are, research indicates, likely to reason at more advanced levels. Interestingly, these are groups of today's adolescents and youth who are embedded in particular family and social settings (Haan, 1978; Haan, Smith, & Block, 1968).

This last observation leads beyond just description of the attributes of Kohlberg's theory. We are led to consider whether his formulations are useful for indicating what processes lead or do not lead to advances in moral reasoning. Why do some adolescents advance, while other people living today do not typically show such thinking?

To deal with these issues it is necessary to review the formulations and data generated in relation to Kohlberg's work. This review will speak to the methodological and empirical issues involved in his approach and, in so doing, will lead us to a formulation of moral development somewhat different from that of Kohlberg's moral universalism theory.

A CRITIQUE OF KOHLBERG'S THEORY

Evaluations of Kohlberg's work can be classified into two areas. First, there are those who have considered Kohlberg's method of evaluating moral reasoning development. Second, there are those who have tried to determine if moral reasoning follows the stagelike sequence Kohlberg formulated. Consideration of the first area of evaluation will make us cautious about generalizing information about moral reasoning derived from use of Kohlberg's interview. Consideration of the second area will support the idea that there are indeed qualitative changes across life in moral reasoning (although not necessarily completely consistent with the order Kohlberg suggests), and that these changes are related to behavior change processes ranging from the psychological to the sociocultural and historical.

Methodological appraisals of Kohlberg's theory

A major methodological critique of Kohlberg's approach to studying moral development was presented by Kurtines and Greif (1974). They identified several major problems with how scores from Kohlberg's interview are derived. The scores represent the basic data for evaluating a person's level of moral reasoning. Kurtines and Greif contend that because there are many areas of methodological concern associated with his interview, it is most difficult to unequivocally evaluate the usefulness of Kohlberg's theory. Because several of the major objections Kurtines and Greif raise about Kohlberg's method are unanswered (see Kuhn, 1976, and Colby, 1978, for some exceptions), it is important to remain appropriately cautious.

First, Kurtines and Greif (1974) note problems with the administration and scoring of Kohlberg's interview. Together, these problems relate to the reliability of the interview. A measure is *reliable* when consistent scores are repeatedly obtained from administration of the measure. Because of issues relating to lack of standardization, subjectivity, and ambiguity, there may be problems with getting consistent appraisals of moral reasoning from Kohlberg's interview.

In regard to administration of the interview, Kurtines and Greif note that the questioning process is quite time-consuming and is not standardized, and that precise instructions for administration are difficult to obtain. The instructions are presented in an unwieldy manual, and it is often necessary to learn how to use the manual from Kohlberg or one of his associates. This makes independent use of the interview quite difficult. Moreover, the questions used to evaluate people's reasonings are different for different people, and this makes comparing data across subjects problematic, since different subjects are being measured in different ways. Furthermore, since the content (and number) of dilemmas presented in the interview is different in different studies, it is again difficult to generalize the results of one investigation to another, because, in effect, different measuring devices, of unknown comparability, are used (Kurtines & Greif, 1974).

Complicating the administration problems are scoring problems. The classification of answers to interview questions is based on a subjective evaluation by the researcher (Kurtines & Greif, 1974). Thus, the introduction of scorer bias into the results is great. Furthermore, because of the subjectivity in scoring there is considerable variability in scoring. Moreover, because the rules for scoring are often ambiguous (Kurtines & Greif, 1974), there is again a reason for independent researchers not to use the interview.

A study by Rubin and Trotter (1977) illustrates some of the problems with the reliability of measuring moral reasoning through Kohlberg's approach. Elementary school children in grades 3 and 5 were administered three of the interview dilemmas. Two weeks later the children were retested. This time one-half of the children were given these interview stories, while the other half received a multiple-choice-type test based on the interview (that is, rather than ask open-ended questions, the children were asked to choose an answer to a dilemma from among some alternatives). Across the two-week period there was low to moderate consistency in reasoning scores for the children, but those in the second group had significantly higher scores. Moreover, since there were several answers given to each dilemma, Rubin and Trotter (1977) wanted to see if consistency in moral reasoning was shown by a person within a given dilemma. Looking at all the answers within each dilemma for the first time of testing, the researchers found no consistency in the moral reasoning scores obtained by a subject answering different questions about the same dilemma.

In addition to administration and scoring problems, Kurtines and Greif identify problems with the *content* of the dilemmas. These problems relate to the *validity* of the interview measure. A measure is valid if it assesses what it is supposed to assess. Does the interview provide, as Kohlberg claims (1958, 1963a, 1971), a measure of *universal sequences* of moral reasoning (sequences that apply equally to all people of all cultures at all times of measurement)? Kurtines and Greif (1974) note that the main characters in the dilemmas are male. If a person recognizes the different role expectations for males and females in traditional Western culture, then the gender of the main character in the dilemma may influence that person's moral reasonings. In light of this, it is not surprising that some research using Kohlberg's scale shows females to be less morally mature than males (Kohlberg & Kramer, 1969), although it must be noted that most studies using Kohlberg's measures show males and females to be quite similar in their reasonings (Maccoby & Jacklin, 1974, pp. 114–117). Yet Kurtines and Greif's criticism of sex bias in the content of the dilemmas is consistent with other objections to the content of the interview.

Eisenberg-Berg (1976) notes that all dilemmas pertain only to constraint situations, that is, to a person's being pressured by two moral values affecting himself or herself. However, prosocial issues, such as risking one's own life to save someone else's, are never evaluated. Thus, there is a value bias in Kohlberg's interview.

A broader, and more profound, bias is noted by Simpson (1974). She sees

Kohlberg's dilemmas *and* his past scoring system to be culturally biased. Simpson (1974) notes that while dilemmas were revised in content for cross-cultural research, this procedure was not sufficient because the scoring system was kept the same. This was done because of the belief in the universality of principles and issues in moral reasoning. However, she argues that Kohlberg sees morality from an American viewpoint, and as such, only those answers which are consistent with American moral values can be scored as moral. Thus, if the context of a dilemma raises an issue not relevant to a given culture, or if the culture has different moral values, then lower moral reasoning would be scored.

To illustrate this cultural bias in the content and scoring of the interview, Simpson (1974) notes that one typical dilemma contrasts *property rights* with the *value of human life*. A man's wife is dying from a disease for which a pharmacist has developed a drug to cure the disease. However, the drug is quite expensive and because the man cannot afford its price, he breaks into the pharmacy to steal the pharmacist's property (the drug) in order to secure it so that his wife may be saved.

Simpson sees cultural bias in the content and the scoring of this dilemma. First, not all cultures have notions of property rights that would make the above situation a dilemma. She notes that: "The Americans who believe that one has a right to anything one can pay for and that taxes on income and private property and restrictive use laws are wrong or bad have very little content in common with members of a culture where little or no property is seen as private and rights over it are group rights and held in common" (Simpson, 1974, p. 96). In turn, Simpson notes that the scoring attached to this interview story is also biased in that Kohlberg (1971, p. 174) believes that "anyone who understands the values of life and property will recognize that life is morally more valuable than property." Simpson contends that this view not only falsely reflects actual moral practice *even in the United States,* but too reflects a lack of appreciation of the nature of other cultures.

First, she notes that in America it is *human* life, and not all life, that is seen as sacred. However, even the value of human life may be secondary to other values. Those who kill or rape others are often put to death, and insofar as property is concerned, those "who steal secrets from the government to give to other governments" (Simpson, 1974, p. 97) are liable to the death penalty. In turn, second, in cultures such as that of the Eskimo, it is appropriate to kill the aged or the newly born because they might consume resources needed for the survival of the major part of the group.

In sum, because of the various biases in the content and scoring of his dilemmas, there is reason to be wary about whether Kohlberg has offered a technique to validly assess universal sequences in moral reasoning development. In addition, the lack of standardization in administration and scoring procedures involved with the interview, and the subjective component involved in scoring, leads to questions about the reliability of the interview. Despite these limitations, Kohlberg's approach continues to be an important one in studying moral development, especially since he and his coworkers are currently addressing many of the above criticisms of his work. They are revising the system of interview scoring and even the number and definitions of the stages themselves (Colby, 1978; Kohlberg, 1978). Furthermore, there is *some* empirical support for the specifics of Kohlberg's theory, and for the more general idea that there are indeed qualitative changes in moral reasoning across life. Keeping the methodological limitations of this work in mind, we now turn to research relevant to Kohlberg's theory.

Empirical appraisals of Kohlberg's theory

Two major, interrelated issues have been involved in the empirical assessment of Kohlberg's theory (1958, 1963a,b, 1971, 1973). First, does moral reasoning progress through a sequence similar to that suggested by Kohlberg? Second, if such a sequence does exist, is it universal and irreversible in sequence, as is a requirement of all stage theories of development like Kohlberg's (Lerner, 1976)? Finally, a third issue has arisen as a consequence of interest in the first two. What are the variables that may affect the sequence of stages of moral reasoning?

Sequences in moral judgments   Most research relevant to Kohlberg's ideas has dealt with whether reasoning proceeds in a sequence consistent with his theory. Although many studies have not used his exact measures, there is strong evidence that there is an age-associated development toward postconventional reasoning. Older people are more likely than younger people to offer principle-based moral judgments that take into account the intentions, rather than the mere actions, of a person.

Weiner and Peter (1973) studied 300 people, age 4 to 18 years. In making moral judgments, subjects were asked to take the outcome of the act and the intentions and abilities of the actor into account. At higher age levels the main determinant of moral evaluation was the subjective intentions of the actor, rather than the objective outcome of his or her act. Similarly, Hewitt (1975) read Dutch male children and early adolescents, aged 8 to 12 years, stories about a harm doer. The harm doer's intentions were either good or bad, and the results of the harm were either minor or serious. The older males differentiated the harmer's behavior as being naughty or not on the basis of intentions and provocations for the harmful act. The younger males did not make these distinctions. This developmental trend of giving abstract reasons for judging moral acts as one gets older is supported with data reported by Keasey (1974). Preadolescent and late adolescent (that is, college) females rated responses to Kohlberg's dilemmas. Their ratings were given in the context of being presented with (a) an *opinion* about how the dilemma should be resolved, and (b) a moral *reason*, at various stages, that supported the opinion. There was a greater relative influence of opinion agreement, rather than stage of moral reasoning, in shaping the ratings of the preadolescents as opposed to the college students.

Similarly, evidence for development toward a more abstract conceptualization of morality is provided in a report by Edwards (1974). Seven hundred 7- to 15-year-olds were asked to define terms like "right" and "wrong." Older groups had higher moral development scores. Although there were no socioeconomic status differences, females did better on these evaluations than did males. This finding is consistent with the higher verbal ability noted for females of the age range studied (Maccoby & Jacklin, 1974), and suggests that depending on how moral thinking is measured, there may be either no sex differences or differences favoring females (which is counter to Freud's view, of course).

Further evidence exists for a sequential movement to stages involving more abstract, principle-based, and intention-oriented forms of judgment. Davison, Robbins, and Swanson (1978) studied 160 people ranging in school level from junior high school through graduate school. To measure moral reasoning they used a scale developed by Rest, Cooper, Coder, Masanz, and Anderson (1974). As will be discussed in more detail below, this scale represents an attempt to objectively measure Kohlberg's stages. Using this device, Davison et al. found that subjects' patterns of stage scores were generally consistent with the ordering of stages in Kohlberg's theory, and that as one instance in support of this, reasoning at adjacent stages (for example, stages 3 and 4) was more similar than reasoning at nonadjacent stages (for example, stages 3 and 5).

Recall Turiel's (1969, 1974) claim that movement from one stage to another is dependent on information that causes conflict, and hence a disequilibration. This, he contends, requires a reevaluation of the existing way of thinking, and the construction, therefore, of a new, higher stage of thought in order to reestablish balance (Turiel, 1974). If this idea is correct, we should see people at a given stage of reasoning respond differently to reasons below or above their own. The former should be seen as inferior (or "immature"), while the latter, causing conflict, should influence the subjects intellectually or be seen as better. Turiel and Rothman (1972) reported stage 4 subjects to be influenced in their responses by reasoning above but not below their own level. Although this finding supports Turiel's (1969, 1974) ideas about cognitive conflict, the fact that the Turiel and Rothman (1972) subjects who predominantly reasoned at stages 2 and 3 were unaffected by moral justifications does not lend such support.

However, some additional support for the idea of cognitive conflict is provided by the data reported by Lazorowitz, Stephen, and Friedman (1976). Subjects were a large group of college students. These late adolescents tended to be positively influenced (to show altruism to a partner in a laboratory experiment) by reasoning above their own. Moreover, those subjects at the highest levels of moral reasoning did react negatively to reasoning below their own. However, inconsistent with the idea of cognitive conflict was the finding that those subjects at the lowest levels of moral reasoning (stages 1 and 2) were not differentially affected by reasoning similar to their own (that is, a stage 2 reason given to a stage 1 person) and, in fact, reacted somewhat negatively to reasons above their own (that is, stage 3).

Thus, there is some evidence to indicate that although people generally seem to progress toward intentional, principled reasonings, they do not necessarily conform to a stagelike progression. Data reported by Surber (1977) support this view. Surber studied kindergarten through adult subjects. At all these age levels—not just at the older ones—the intentions of the actor and the consequences of the act influenced judgments. As Kohlberg might predict, as age increased, there was a decrease in the importance of consequences in making moral judgment. Yet the fact that intentions were used continuously from early childhood through adulthood indicates that moral reasoning is less stagelike than suggested by Kohlberg's universalistic theory. Further evidence of the lack of universalism of Kohlberg's ideas is derived from cross-cultural studies. We now turn to them.

The universality of Kohlberg's stages Most cross-cultural studies of moral development have been cross-sectional in design. Although they provide data somewhat consistent with the ideas of stage progression outlined by Kohlberg for the first four stages, they do not tend to show invariant progression into the highest level of moral reasoning, that is, the principled one. This in itself is not necessarily contrary to a stage theory. Such a theory does not say that people will necessarily reach the highest levels, but only that if they do they will go through the specified sequence. Yet since cross-sectional studies confound age and cohort effects, by testing at only one measurement time, they cannot be regarded as providing unequivocal support for Kohlberg's theory. Indeed, in the one cross-cultural study that used a sequential design (White, Bushnell, & Regnemer, 1978), time of testing effects were seen to contribute most to moral reasoning scores.

To be specific, all cross-cultural research before 1978 had been cross-sectional in design. For instance, studies done in British Honduras (Gorsuch & Barnes, 1973), Canada (Kohlberg & Kramer, 1969), Kenya (Edwards, 1974), Great Britain (Kohlberg & Kramer, 1969), the Bahamas (White, 1975), and Taiwan (Kohlberg & Kramer, 1969) had consistently indicated age differences in moral reasoning through Kohlbergian stages 1 to 4. However, stage 5 and 6 reasoning appeared so infrequently in these studies that their age-related development in populations other than those derived from the United States remains uncertain.

This cultural difference may be due to the absence of particular, but largely unknown, variables which may moderate reasoning development in cultures other than the United States. Some support for this idea is found in the data of Edwards (1975), who reported that people in highly industrialized settings move through lower stages more rapidly, and achieve higher stages more often, than people in less industrialized and less urban settings (see also Salili, Maehr, & Gillmore, 1976). In turn, the cultural difference may be due to the cultural bias in Kohlberg's theory and scoring system, identified by Simpson (1974). Other cultures may not include as morally relevant the types of situations or values used by Kohlberg to score the higher stages of moral reasoning.

Although current data cannot decide between these two alternatives, the study by White et al. (1978) suggests that any changes in moral reasoning scores are more attributable to events occurring in the cultural milieu when people are tested than to age-related or stage-related phenomena. White et al. studied 426 Bahamian males and females, aged 8 to 17 years. All subjects were interviewed repeatedly over a three-year period using Kohlberg's interview. That is, their design was sequential in that they repeated testing their initial cross-sectional sample over the course of the three-year period. There was an upward stage movement within and between birth cohort groups. In other words, the cross-sectional data at each year showed age group differences; older age groups showed higher scores. Moreover, *within* each cohort there was an upward movement in reasoning scores from inital to final testing.

However, not only did none of the subjects in the sample show reasoning above stage 3, but the age differences in reasoning scores were associated much more with time of testing than age or cohort. The time of testing effect was 3½ times greater than the age effect. This was the major effect found in the study; for example, there were no sex differences found. Thus, the results of the within-cohort longitudinal comparisons, which involved a confounding of age and time effects, suggest that variables in the environment of the subjects at the time they were tested, rather than those variables that may covary with age, account for the age differences found in the study.

It is clear that with such time-related effects playing the major role in contributing to changes in moral development, the universality of Kohlberg's stages is in doubt. The few studies that directly assess the irreversibility of the stages cast similar doubt about the adequacy of his stage theory.

The irreversibility of Kohlberg's stages Kuhn (1976) used a short-term longitudinal design to assess the continuity in moral reasoning of 5- to 8-year-olds as measured by Kohlberg's interview. Across each of two six-month intervals subjects were as likely to show progressive change (an increase in scores) as regressive change (a decrease in scores). However, over the longer, one-year period encompassed by the study, subjects tended to show progressive change, most of which involved *slight* advancement toward the next stage in Kohlberg's sequence. Although these data bear only on the sequence irreversibility of the first three stages of Kohlberg's theory—since these were the stages subjects reasoned at—they do provide partial support for his theory.

The considerable short-term (that is, six months) fluctuation could have been due to several sources. Other studies (Bandura & McDonald, 1963) have shown that children can be *induced* to move forward or backward in their moral reasoning. Since subjects have reasoning structures at several stages available to them, such inducement would be expected to be obtained on the basis of stage mixture (Turiel, 1969). However, the subjects in Kuhn's (1976) study were not prompted to show either continuity or discontinuity in their reasoning. Thus, the observed fluctuation could be due either to measurement unreliability associated with Kohlberg's interview or to genuine fluctuation in judgment (Kuhn, 1976), fluctuation perhaps naturally moderated by variables that happened to be acting at the particular times at which Kuhn's subjects were tested. Indeed, such a testing effect in a longitudinal study is likely, given the data of White et al. (1978).

However, despite what variables may be operating to produce fluctuation or continuity in reasoning, there are data suggesting that when the irreversible sequencing of Kohlberg's stages are evaluated at age levels beyond childhood, their universal ordering does not hold. Holstein (1976) studied the individual developmental sequences of fifty-two middle-class adolescents, and of forty-eight of their fathers and forty-nine of their mothers. These family groups were followed longitudinally for a three-year period. Over this sequence there was a stepwise progression in moral reasoning development, *but not from stage to stage*. Rather, people progressed from level to level. However, even this held only for levels 1 and 2 of Kohlberg's theory; that is, people only progressed sequentially from preconventional to conventional morality. Moreover, insofar as irreversibility is concerned, regression in reasoning was found in the higher (postconventional) stages. Furthermore, since the subjects in Holstein's study were of different ages and from different cohorts, and since all these groups nevertheless showed the progression limitations and reversibility characteristics, we may infer that time of testing effects again are most associated with whatever age differences were obtained.

In conclusion, there do not seem to be characteristics of universality and irreversibility associated with Kohlberg's stages. Rather, variables acting in the particular historical context of people at particular times seem to be most related to whether one sees qualitative changes in moral reasoning, and what direction those changes take. In other words, although evidence exists for a general progression from objective morality to subjective, intentional, and principled reasoning, it appears that the nature and direction of this sequence are changeable phenomena. They are dependent on other than stage-related variables. In the next section, we consider evidence pertaining to those nonstage-related variables which may moderate the shift in moral thinking from objective to principled reasoning.

Variables moderating stage progression   As noted earlier, Rest et al. (1974) attempted to construct a scale that could be scored objectively to measure Kohlbergian moral development. To do this, statements were written to exemplify each of Kohlberg's stages, and subjects were asked to pick the statement defining the most important issue in a moral dilemma. The importance attributed to principled (stages 5 or 6) moral statements (a measure termed the "P score") showed age-related differences. In a group of junior high school through graduate school students, the *P* score correlated about +.6 with age, with comprehension of social and moral concepts, and with the scores from Kohlberg's interview. While the first correlation is consistent with an age-progression or stage-progression theory and the last correlation shows some validity for Kohlberg's interview measure, the correlation between *P* score and moral and social comprehension suggests that perhaps intelligence plays a major moderating role in moral reasoning.

However, although the *P* score did correlate with IQ, it was a much lower correlation. Alternatively, there was an indication that subjects chose important moral issues on the basis of attitudes and values rather than just intelligence. The *P* score correlated about +.6 with various political attitude measures. Rest et al. repeated most of these findings in a second, independent sample of students and adults, and across time, there was high consistency within the same people in their *P* scores.

Similarly, an independent study by Eisenberg-Berg (1976) considered the relation of moral reasoning to prosocial dilemma moral reasoning, and to various political and humanitarian attitudes. Subjects were seventy six White adolescents ranging in grade level from 7 to 12. Not only did she find a significant relation between constraint reasoning and prosocial moral reasoning, and a grade-associated increase toward more principled judgments, but she also found that attitudes may moderate these moral reasoning differences. Political liberalism significantly related to both constraint and prosocial moral reasoning, while humanitarian political attitudes related to prosocial, but not constraint, reasoning.

Rest (1975) reports longitudinal data bearing on the relation of attitudes to moral reasoning and on the role of other moderating influences. After two years, eighty-eight adolescents (aged 16 to 20 years) were retested with the scale Rest et al. (1974) devised. In addition, they were retested with the measure of their comprehension of social and moral concepts, and with a measure of their "law and order" political attitudes. Both younger and older adolescents showed increases in their *P* scores, and the younger group showed shifts from preconventional to conventional thinking. Moreover, there were also increases in the measures of comprehension and attitudes that coincided with the reasoning differences. While again suggesting the possible role of attitudes, Rest's (1975) data indicated that variables other than psychological ones (such as attitudes) may exist in the environment of adolescents to foster the development of moral reasoning. Among those adolescents in his sample who were high school graduates, those who went away to college changed twice as much in principled reasoning as did the noncollege subjects. Rest (1975) found that at the time of their first testing in 1972:

> The college-bound subjects were not significantly different from the noncollege-bound subjects on any of the three measures. By 1974, however, the college group was different from the noncollege group on the P score, and on the Law and Order test score. (The college group also showed greater average gains on the Comprehension test, but was not significantly different from the noncollege group in 1974.) In fact, on the P score each group gained significantly over two years, but the college group gained over twice as much as the noncollege group. (p. 745)

Thus, although both college and noncollege adolescents did not differ at the first testing, and even though they maintained nonsignificantly different levels of comprehension regarding social and moral concepts, and despite the fact they both advanced toward more principled reasoning levels, there was something in the college environment which facilitated the development of adolescents.

Although other studies have shown also that the moral reasoning of adolescents varies in relation to their situational context (McGeorge, 1974), there have been no *direct* tests of just what variables might lead the adolescent who is in one setting to advance and an adolescent who is in another setting not to. There are some indirect clues, however.

Perspective taking, formal operations, and principled reasoning

Yussen (1976) studied thirty subjects at each of grades 9, 10, 12, and college. He asked the subjects to answer a moral reasoning questionnaire for the social roles of "self," "average policeman," and "average philosopher." As expected by Kohlberg's theory, there was an age-associated increase in principled responses, and this held for answers in regard to all three roles. In addition, however, there was also an age-associated increase in differentiation among the contrasting social roles. Older subjects were more able than younger ones to take the moral perspective of people playing different social roles. Similarly, Costanzo, Coie, Grumet, and Farnill (1973) found that an age-associated increase from 5 to 11 years in use of information about intentions in making moral judgments coincided with an increase in social perspective-taking ability in this age range. Moreover, Eisenberg-Berg and Mussen (1978) found that a measure of *empathy* (the ability to take the perspective of another and feel what that person feels) was related to measures of both constraint and prosocial moral reasoning among seventy two adolescents in grades 9 to 12.

Together these studies suggest that the ability to take the perspective of someone in another social role or social situation may be related importantly to the presence of principled moral reasoning. Such a relation is consistent with the quality of postconventional morality, in that a mutual pact, a reciprocal relation, among equal partners in a social relation is involved as a basis of such an orientation. It might seem that if one could not take another's perspective, and see the world from the role orientation of the other, the reciprocal social relation that provides the basis of principled moral thinking could not emerge.

Three ideas are therefore suggested. First, inability to take another's perspective should be associated with a failure to show advanced moral reasoning, while in turn, perspective-taking ability should be related to principled reasoning. The above-noted studies by Yussen (1976), Costanzo et al. (1973), and Eisenberg-Berg and Mussen (1978) support this idea. Also supporting this idea are data reported by Moir (1974), who found that scores of 11-year-old females on Kohlberg's interview were correlated with scores on nonmoral-role-taking tasks.

Similarly, data by Arbuthnot (1975) bear on this first idea. College students showed both immediate and delayed increases in moral judgment scores when required to role-play a moral dilemma against an opponent who used reasoning above the subject's reasoning stage. These data suggest that role playing at a higher moral level than one's own may encourage reasoning change. It is possible that such role playing produces cognitive conflict and induces disequilibrium. But disequilibrium from what level?

Here the second idea is raised. Moir (1974), in the above-noted study, suggested that role playing coincides with principled judgment, because being able to take another's perspective requires being able to overcome a form of *egocentrism* involving seeing oneself as central (imaginary audience) and quite special (personal fable). In other words, principled morality rests on overcoming the egocentrism of the formal operational stage of cognitive development because such egocentrism involves an inability to take others' perspectives and hence to show the cognitive ability apparently necessary for more advanced moral thinking.

Thus, Arbuthnot's (1975) data may be interpreted as showing that required role playing led to moral reasoning increases because it simulated a typical, naturally occurring process wherein conflict produced by having to take others' roles makes the person decenter from his or her adolescent egocentrism. In support of this idea, it may be noted that Arbuthnot found that those college students who were reasoning at levels below the highest ones were the ones who showed the most change toward principled reasoning through role playing.

Together the above data and reasoning suggest that processes of cognitive change typically associated with adolescence in Western culture may be those most involved with advances to higher levels of moral reasoning. In other words, principled morality rests on the attainment of cognitive processes typically associated with adolescence, that is, formal operations. Indeed, not only did Kohlberg (1973) himself advance such a hypothesis, but data reported by Tomlinson-Keasey and Keasey (1974) support it. Among subjects who had just begun to acquire formal operations (30 sixth grade females) and subjects who were assumed to be well practiced in formal thought (24 college females), there were high positive relations between being at advanced levels in both areas of functioning. Similarly, Langford and George (1975) found that among sixty-five females, aged 12 to 15 years, there were positive relationships between scores at Kohlberg's higher stages and scores on a task of formal operational ability. Comparable relationships have been reported among male and female college students (Faust & Arbuthnot, 1978).

If principled morality seems to be so related to that form of cognition most associated with adolescence, then it may be that those sociocultural and historical influences that promote one type of functioning also promote the other. This observation leads us back to the third idea involved in interrelating perspective taking and principled morality. This idea suggests a reason why the college students in Rest's (1975) study showed more advancement in principled morality than their noncollege peers. Earlier, we noted Turiel's (1969) report that certain groups of people living in today's world were more likely than were other groups to show advanced moral thinking. These groups are late adolescents and young adults who are involved in a college environment. It may be that the demands of college involve more intense perspective-taking requirements for adaptation than is the case in other settings. Being exposed to people from varied backgrounds, and being required at least in part to interact with these others (for example, in dormitories or in class projects), as well as being exposed to and tested about thoughts (for example, of philosophers, about other cultures) typically quite different from one's own, requires personal adaptation. The functional assimilation of this information would require accommodation and thus a movement away from knowledge of the world through one's own, possibly egocentric, point of view.

Although it is *certainly* the case that people outside of the college setting can obtain the information necessary for decentering, and hence perspective taking and principled morality (Rest's noncollege subjects *did* show an increase in P scores), it appears that the college setting facilitates this process.

Of course, given the fact that there is a relation between IQ, formal operations, and principled morality (Rest et al., 1974), and that there are marked individual differences in the attainment of formal operations, not all adolescents who go to college will show similar changes in moral reasoning. Thus, one must take into account characteristics of the person as well as characteristics of the situation in order to understand the course of moral development. This conclusion is complicated by the fact that it is not just the cognitive egocentrism processes of the person which interact with the situation to foster moral development. Other psychological variables, even beyond those of attitudes which we have already noted, interact with sociocultural variables to facilitate moral functioning.

VARIABLES RELATING TO MORAL DEVELOPMENT

Cognitive conflicts which reduce adolescent egocentrism by promoting perspective taking are not the only variables related to moral development. In indicating that moral development does, however, involve an orientation of the person toward others in his or her world, such variables do suggest the social relation character of morality. In earlier chapters it was noted that the central phenomena of adolescence involved the person's attempt to find a role in society, and indeed it might be expected that such role search requires the ability to try to see the world from the perspective of alternative roles. Thus, perspective taking would seem to be as much involved in the search for adolescent identity as it is in overcoming egocentrism, and hence moving to higher levels of formal thinking and of principled morality.

Personality–moral reasoning relations

This interaction among individual-psychological processes relating to identity, formal operations, and morality has found theoretical and empirical support. In regard to theory, it will be recalled that in Chapter 9 we noted that Piaget believes that the transition from earlier to later formal operational thought involves attainment of a role (Inhelder & Piaget, 1958). Piaget believes that an adolescent becomes an adult cognitively when he or she has attained a firm role to play in society. In Erikson's (1959, 1963) terms, the adolescent has found an identity; Erikson (1959) believes that transition to a stage beyond adolescence also involves such identity achievement. Kohlberg (1973) too has said that identity achievement is a prerequisite for principled morality.

Stage theories of personality and social development other than Erikson's (1959, 1963) illuminate the relation between moral and other psychological developments (for example, emotional and ego developments). Indeed, Loevinger's (1966; Loevinger & Wessler, 1970) stage theory of ego development includes milestones of development that appear to correspond to the stages Kohlberg sees as involved in moral reasoning. Loevinger (1966; Loevinger & Wessler, 1970), following the psychoanalytic conception of seeing the ego as a personality structure involved in controlling impulses from the id, describes seven stages of ego development and the type of control the ego, at each of these stages, can exert on impulses. As seen in Exhibit 10.1, the stages of ego development appear to involve many of the functions Kohlberg relates to moral stages. This seems to be especially the case in the last five stages. The last column of Exhibit 10.1 represents the possible relation between the ego stages in Loevinger's (1966; Loevinger & Wessler, 1970) theory and the moral reasoning stages in Kohlberg's theory. In sum, the ideas of Loevinger, as well as those of Piaget and Erikson, suggest interrelation among ego, cognitive, and moral processes.

There is some empirical support for these hypothesized interrelations among

Exhibit 10.1

Some possible relations between Loevinger's stages of ego development and Kohlberg's stages of moral reasoning development

Loevinger's stages	Impulse control involved in the stage	Possible relation to the stages in Kohlberg's theory	
Presocial	——	Level 1	Preconventional reasoning
Impulse-ridden	Impulse-ridden, fear of retaliation		Stage 1 Obedience & punishment
			Stage 2 Naïve egoistic orientation
Self-protective	Expedient, fear of being caught		
Conformity	Conformity to external rule	Level 2	Conventional reasoning
Conscientious	Internalized rules, guilt		Stage 3 Good-person orientation
			Stage 4 Authority and social maintenance orientation
Autonomous	Coping with conflict, toleration of differences	Level 3	Postconventional reasoning
			Stage 5 Contractual legalistic orientation
Integrated	Reconciling inner conflicts, renunciation of the unattainable		Stage 6 Conscience or principle orientation

individual-psychological processes. Tomlinson-Keasey and Keasey (1974) found that older adolescents (female college students) who should be more practiced in formal operational thought showed more advanced moral judgments than younger adolescents (sixth grade females) who had just begun to acquire formal operations. The findings were interpreted as suggesting that although formal thought may be a prerequisite of higher levels of moral reasoning, there may be a time lag between the acquisition of formal thought and its use in moral reasoning.

Evidence also exists about relations between ego functioning and moral reasoning level. Podd (1972) studied a group of about 100 White middle-class male college students. Subjects who had achieved an ego identity were generally characterized by the higher levels of moral judgment, while those with a relative lack of ego identity were generally characterized by either the least advanced level of moral reasoning or a transitionary level between intermediate and high levels of reasoning. Moreover, those who were in a crisis over their identity were inconsistent in their reasoning levels.

While Podd's data are consistent with the ideas of Piaget, Kohlberg, and Erikson, there are some studies in the literature which provide either no support (Cauble, 1976) or only indirect support for the interrelation between identity and morality (Bachrach, Huesmann, & Peterson, 1977). In the latter study, for instance, if it can be assumed that feeling one's destiny is controlled by oneself is an emotion consistent with feeling a sense of self-knowledge (identity), then the relation between these feeling data (labeled "internality" by the authors) and intentionality-based moral reasoning is consistent with an identity-morality relation. Among 130 7- to 11-year-olds, Bachrach et al. (1977) found that intentionality of judgments and internality of control develop in a related manner, and that heightened internality significantly enhances the ability to attain intentionality in moral reasonings.

There is theoretical justification and some empirical support for an interrelation among those individual processes that pertain to the person's role search and attainment; yet none of the above information involves measures of the *behavior* implications of these psychological orientations. Data pertinent to these implications do exist, however. Harris, Mussen, and Rutherford (1976) administered both Kohlberg's interview and an intelligence test to 33 fifth grade boys. In addition, the peers of these boys rated their moral conduct, and the boys' honesty was evaluated in a structured test. Higher levels of moral reasoning were associated with better cognitive ability. Moreover, on a behavioral level, higher reasoners showed greater resistance to temptation and were rated by their peers as behaving in a prosocial manner (for example, as being concerned with the welfare of others).

Not only are moral reasoning differences associated with behavioral differences in late childhood, but such associations exist among late adolescents and young adults as well. Haan, Smith, and Block (1968) studied about 500 University of California and San Francisco State College students and Peace Corps volunteers in-training, about equally divided into male and female groups. Because of the study's prominent empirical and theoretical implications, we shall consider its details quite carefully. All subjects in the study had responded to Kohlberg's interview. The students participated in various campus activities and groups. They showed a wide range of *behavioral* and social involvement. Some students had been arrested as a consequence of their participation in a protest advocating free speech.

INSIGHT INTO ADOLESCENCE

Jean-Paul Sartre is a leading intellectual in the world today, an accomplished philosopher, novelist, playwright, essayist, and psychologist. He was born in Paris in 1905. In 1964 Sartre was offered the Nobel Prize for Literature. He refused the Nobel Prize, saying, "A writer who takes political, social or literary positions must act only with the means that are his. Those means are the written word. A writer must not accept official awards because he would be adding the influence of the institution that crowned his work to the power of his pen. That is not fair to reader. . . ."

In this excerpt from *Words*, Sartre writes about himself at the age of 12.

One morning, in 1917, at La Rochelle, I was waiting for some companions who were supposed to accompany me to the *lycée;* they were late. Soon I could think of nothing more to distract myself, and I decided to think about the Almighty. He at once tumbled down into the blue sky and vanished without explanation: He does not exist, I said to myself, in polite astonishment, and I thought the matter was settled. In one sense it was, because I have never since had the least temptation to revive Him. But the Other, the Invisible, the Holy Ghost, he who guaranteed my mandate and dominated my life through great, anonymous, and sacred forces, he remained. I had all the more trouble freeing myself from his because he had lodged himself in the back of my head among the made-up notions I used to understand, place, and justify myself. For a long time, writing was asking Death or Religion in disguise to tear my life away from chance. I was of the Church. As a militant, I wanted to save myself through works; as a mystic, I tried to unveil the stillness of existence through a counteracting murmur of words, and, above all, I confused things with their names: that is belief. I was dim of sight.

Source: Sartre, J.-P. The *Words*. Translated by Bernard Frechtman. New York: George Braziller, Inc., 1964, pp. 250–251.

Others were members of such groups as Young Democrats, Young Republicans, California Conservatives for Political Action, a student-body-sponsored Community Involvement Program, or a tutorial group. On the basis of answers to Kohlberg's interview the subjects were divided into one of five "pure" moral-type groups, basically one for each of the stages from 2 to 6.

Haan et al. (1968) obtained several biographical, behavioral, and cognitive-personality test measures on the subjects. Together, the data provide a profile of the behavioral as well as the personality characteristics of members of each moral reasoning group. In addition, the data provide clues about the bases of differences among these groups.

Characteristics of principled reasoners   The members of the *principled reasoning* groups were more likely to have interrupted their college careers, to live in apartments or houses on their own, to be politically more radical, and to have been in strong support of the protest movement. Indeed, the political-social activity of these people was the highest of all groups studied. They affiliated with more organizations—and thus played more roles as members of different groups—and were more involved with them. They were active participants in a lot of groups, and were not just passive joiners.

In addition to these behavioral characteristics, male members of this principled group described their own personality as being "idealistic," and conceived of the ideal good man in society as being perceptive, empathic, and altruistic. These ideas emphasize their commitment to taking the roles of others (Haan et al., 1968). The principled women saw themselves as guilty, doubting, restless, impulsive, and altruistic. Their idea of the ideal woman is one who is rebellious and free.

Characteristics of conventional reasoners   The members of the *conventionally reasoning* moral groups were the least likely to interrupt their college careers, lived mainly in institutional, adult-approved arrangements, were politically more conservative, and were the groups least in support of (although still approving) the protest movement. Members of these groups affiliated with few political-social organizations and were relatively inactive.

The self-descriptions that coincided with these behaviors for the males in these groups reflect traditional social values: conventional, ambitious, sociable, practical, orderly, and not curious, individualistic, or rebellious. The women saw themselves as ambitious and foresightful, and not as guilty, restless, or rebellious. Both sexes shared an idea of the good person in society as one who had efficient control of the self and had social skillfulness.

Characteristics of preconventional reasoners   Finally, with those people who reasoned predominantly at a *preconventional, naïve egoistic* moral level, Haan et al. found a high likelihood of college career interruption. Although the men in this group were more likely than the women to live on their own, both men and women strongly supported the protest movement. The men in this group belonged to only a moderate number of organizations, but they participated intensely. On the other hand, the women in this group joined the most organizations but had been the most inactive.

The personal descriptions of these behavioral orientations showed that both men and women see themselves as rebellious. The men's self-descriptions reflect a lack of involvement with others, and their ideal person is someone who is aloof, stubborn, uncompromising, playful, and free. Similarly, women also reject interpersonal obligations, see themselves as stubborn and aloof, and idealize such characteristics as practical and stubborn.

Conclusions To summarize the Haan et al. (1968) findings, it seems that differences in moral reasoning level indeed relate to contrasts in attitudes, personality, and behavior. Principled thinkers are actively involved in the role orientations of others, and see themselves as altruistic and idealistic. Their principled view of the person's relation to his or her social world permeates their own self-conceptions and provides a basis for their active involvement in their world. Alternatively, preconventional thinkers, although showing *some* behavioral similarities to principled thinkers (for example, living alone, engaging in protests), do so for entirely different reasons (ones consistent with their naïve egoistic orientation). They are unconcerned with the welfare of others, show little concern for interpersonal obligation, and engage in protest behaviors to abet their individual rights or goals. In contrast, the conventional thinkers are not actively involved in many organizations, tend to live in situations and behave in accordance with traditional and adult-approved values, and show additional ideas and values that are consistent also with their conventional reasoning and behavior.

In sum, as a final instance of the moral reasoning and behavior differences among these groups, we may consider the data in Exhibit 10.2. This exhibit presents the percentage of men and women in the Haan et al. sample from each moral reasoning group who were arrested in a protest demonstration regarding the free speech movement. As expected, the conventional thinkers (stages 3 and 4) were by far the group having the lowest proportion of arrests. Similarly, the postconventional group (stages 5 and 6) had the highest percentage. However, while the preconventional thinkers (stage 2) also had a high proportion of arrests, their involvement was for reasons qualitatively different than those used in the principled groups. Consistent with their egoistic, nonsocially concerned orientation, the stage 2 thinkers were mostly concerned with their individual rights in a power conflict. The principled thinkers apparently used their perspective-taking abilities behaviorally, and based their involvement on concerns with basic issues of civil liberties and rights, and on

Exhibit 10.2

Percentage of subjects from each of five of Kohlberg's moral reasoning stages who were arrested in a free speech movement protest

		Stage*			
	2 Naïvely egoistic	3 Good person	4 Authority and social order maintenance	5 Contractual legalistic	6 Conscience or principled
Men,	60	18	6	41	75
Women,	33	9	12	57	86

*There were no stage 1 thinkers reported in the sample.
Source: Adapted from Haan, et al. (1968). Copyright 1968 by the American Psychological Association. Reprinted by permission.

the relation of students as citizens within a university community. Thus, these data show that there are behavioral consequences of moral thought. But as stressed by Piaget (1965), Kohlberg (1958, 1963a), and Turiel (1969), it is necessary to focus on the *thought*, because the same *behavior* (for example, protest) can be based on qualitatively and developmentally different individual-psychological levels of functioning.

These conclusions indicate that adolescents and youth who may be described as differing in their levels of moral reasoning may be also described as differing in their personal (for example, identity, attitudes, values) and behavioral attributes. However, these descriptions do not suggest an explanation for these differences. Some of the elements for a potential explanation lie in some of our previous discussion as well as in other data from the Haan et al. (1968) study, presented below.

SOCIAL INTERACTIVE BASES OF MORAL DEVELOPMENT

In reviewing the Rest (1975) data about college youth's greater increase in principled reasoning than their non-college-age peers, it was suggested that if one brings certain characteristics to a social situation having facilitative characteristics, then moral development would be fostered. Interacting in an environment that fosters social perspective taking may foster moral development among those adolescents who have certain levels of formal operational egocentrism, IQ, and identity. The time of testing effects found (White et al., 1978) or implicated (Holstein, 1976; Kuhn, 1976) in moral development research may in fact represent the outcome of a time-specific interaction between individuals having such predispositions and the forces in the setting that promote such change.

However, a question remains as to what brings an adolescent into a facilitative setting, such as college, with a predisposition amenable to influence. Why do some adolescents show principled morality as a consequence of their college experience, while others remain at levels not as high? Indeed, why do people enter into their college years with different levels of morality? One suggestion we may make is that adolescents show such differences because of differences in their history of social interactions. It may be that if adolescents experience different interactional histories, they will develop at different rates after entering potentially facilitative settings.

Although the sequential research needed to test this idea has not been done, there are data that suggest, at the very least, that adolescents and youth who do have different levels of moral reasoning also have different types of social interactional experiences. Most of these data relate to adolescent-parent interactions.

Adolescent-parent interactions

Haan et al. (1968) found that the preconventional, conventional, and postconventional subjects they studied all reported different types of family interaction patterns. Subjects were evaluated on how different their own political views were from each of their parents (for example, in regard to commitment to various issues), how different their views were from those of their parents on various social issues pertinent to the two generational groups, and how much conflict they had with their parents. These measures were combined to form one index of conflict and disagreement.

As seen in Exhibit 10.3, there is a curvilinear relation between conflict and moral

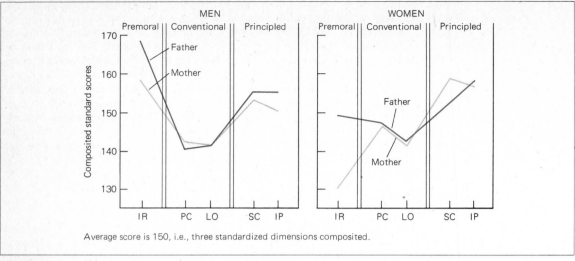

Exhibit 10.3
Degree of conflict and disagreement with parents for males and females
from preconventional, conventional, and postconventional groups.
(*Source:* Haan, Smith, and Block, 1968.)

reasoning for the men. Intense family conflict, especially with the father, is associated with preconventional thinking. Alternatively, and as expected on the basis of their moral orientation, there is least conflict found with the conventional thinkers. A moderate level of conflict exists for those with principled reasoning. For the women, there is a trend toward increased conflict with mother being associated with higher moral reasoning. Although this trend is not as evident with the father, it seems that for both males and females, conflict with the parent of the same sex is most related to moral reasoning.

Thus, among students measured at one point in time, there is a relation between differing reports of conflict in family interactions and contrasts in moral reasoning. From such data we do not know if differing levels of conflict produced moral development, or the reverse. Hoffman (1975), however, in a study of fifth and seventh grade White middle-class children and their parents, concluded that differences in the moral orientation of children (for example, in their consideration for others, feelings of fear or guilt upon transgression) are at least in part due to different discipline and affection patterns of parents.

Data reported by Santrock (1975) provide direct support for this idea. Subjects were 120 six- to 10-year-old, predominantly lower-class boys from either an intact home environment or a family where the father was absent (due to separation, divorce, or death). Based on reports by the subjects, the sons of divorced women experienced more power-assertiveness discipline (as opposed, for instance, to love withdrawal discipline) than did the sons of widows. Such interaction differences influence moral behavior. According to teachers' ratings, the sons of divorced women have more social deviation, but more advanced moral judgment, than do the sons of widows. Moreover, in relation to interaction differences associated with being in a father-absent or a father-present home, there were also differences in moral functioning. Teachers rated the former group of boys as less advanced in moral development than the latter group.

Thus, social interactions involving parents and children do seem to provide a basis for differences in moral development. Yet such family social interactions are not the only ones that an adolescent experiences. Not only do adolescents show development toward more social interactions with peers, but even insofar as their interactions with parents are influential, they do not seem to imitate the moral reasoning orientations of their parents. Haan, Langer, and Kohlberg (1976) found that in a large sample of children ranging in age from 10 to 30 years, and their parents, there was little relation between moral stages among family members. Although husbands' and wives' moral stages were correlated at a low level, there was no relation among siblings' moral levels. Parents' and daughters' stages were also unrelated, and parents' and sons' stages were related only among younger sons. Thus, although family interactions do contribute to moral functioning, they do not seem to shape it totally.

Adolescent-peer interactions

Social interactions outside the family may be more likely to advance moral development, because by avoiding the inevitable power differences between parents and children, they more readily may promote the reciprocal and mutual interactions involved in decentered, morally principled thinking. It may be that adolescents' greater interaction with their peers, who by definition are equal to them, provides them with the precise context necessary to facilitate moral development.

Data reported by Haan (1978) support this position. Six adolescent friendship groups (sexually mixed, but either all Black or all White) participated in a series of moral "games" to see if moral behavior was accounted for better by Kohlberg's formal, abstract reasoning ideas or by an interpersonal formulation stressing that "moral solutions are achieved through dialogues that strive for balanced agreements among participants" (Haan, 1978, p. 286). The games presented to subjects, aged 13 to 17 years, included having to role-play life in two cultures, competing or cooperating as teams in a game having only one winner, constructing a society, and role playing being the last survivors on earth and deciding what to do.

Haan scored the subjects on the Kohlberg and "interpersonal" measures of morality across games. Although these scores fluctuated between games, the interpersonal scores were more stable than the Kohlberg scores, particularly in games involving stress (for example, the competition one). Moreover, in all situations requiring action, all subjects used interpersonal morality—which required a balance of positions among all those who were interacting—more than the measures of moral reasoning associated with Kohlberg's theory. Thus, insofar as moral behavior was concerned, moral reasoning involved establishment of social interaction agreements among the adolescents, and was not primarily based on principled thoughts independent of the group consensus.

Yet the use of such interaction-based, social reciprocity morality facilitated development of both the interpersonal and Kohlberg-related measures of morality. After the games the levels of scores for both these explanations of morality increased for all six adolescent groups, as compared to a control group that did not play any moral games. This suggests that any explanation of moral development should take into account the interaction between abstract reasoning and the demands of the particular social situation.

CHAPTER SUMMARY

The various definitions and theories of moral development can be divided on the basis of their stress on nature or nurture variables. Both S. Freud's nature-oriented psychoanalytic views and nurture-oriented social learning views stress that moral development involves increasing response conformity to socially specified behavior. Freud, however, believes this conformity is associated with superego development, while social learning theorists stress that rewards, punishments, or observations of a model are the basis of response acquisition.

Some cognitive developmentalists believe that individuals may have similar moral behavior in a given situation yet have different reasons for their behavior. Thus, Piaget and Kohlberg, among others, have studied the development of moral reasoning. Piaget proposed that moral development proceeds through a two-phase sequence involving judging right or wrong on the basis of the objective consequences of an act and then judging right or wrong on the basis of the actor's subjective intentions for committing the behavior.

Kohlberg has elaborated Piaget's views, and has proposed a six-stage theory of moral reasoning development that today serves as the impetus for most research and discussion about moral development. Kohlberg presents a moral dilemma—a situation where there is no right or wrong answer—and asks subjects to give their reasons for their particular responses to the situation. He reports a progression in moral reasoning which involves *preconventional morality,* involving the stage of punishment and obedience reasoning and the stage of naïve egoistic reasoning; *conventional morality,* involving the good-person orientation to morality and the stage of social order and institutional maintenance morality; and *postconventional morality,* involving the stage of contractual legalistic moral reasoning and the stage of conscience and principle orientation.

Kohlberg's work has been criticized for the validity, reliability, and cultural bias of both his measure of moral reasoning and the stages he has suggested. Nevertheless, there is some empirical support for his ideas. Data indicate that there is a general, sequential progression to more abstract, principle-based, and intentionality-oriented forms of judgment. However, the universality Kohlberg claims for his stages seems in doubt. Most people do not progress beyond the conventional level of moral reasoning, and cross-cultural research indicates that reasoning beyond stage 3 occurs infrequently.

In addition to research aimed at checking the validity of Kohlberg's theory, research has been directed at determining variables which may moderate moral reasoning development. Politically liberal and humanitarian attitudes have been found to be related to higher levels of moral reasoning, and going to college seems to expose people to experiences which facilitate more abstract and principled levels of moral reasoning. Moreover, formal operational thinking ability, empathic abilities, and the attainment of ego identity appear related to the development of principled moral reasoning. Finally, several studies indicate that principled, as opposed to both conventional and preconventional, moral reasoners engage in different social, heterosexual, and family interactions.

11

ADOLESCENT SEXUALITY

CHAPTER OVERVIEW

Sex is an important topic for the study of adolescence because it is a central part of human development. During adolescence, it can be a source of great satisfaction, great frustration, or great problems. This chapter discusses sexual socialization, sexuality in America today, the consequences of sexual involvement, and sex education.

ISSUES TO CONSIDER

What are the components of the sexual socialization process, and how do they differ?

What is the difference between homosexuality, transsexuality, and transvestism?

Why might the definitions of sexuality that we apply to infants and young children differ from the definitions of sexuality that we might apply to adolescents and adults?

What arguments favor the position that there has been a sexual evolution rather than a sexual revolution?

How much sexual activity actually exists among adolescents, what forms does this sexual behavior take, and to what degree do active incidence and cumulative incidence differ?

Under what circumstances does sexual intercourse begin?

Why is contraception an important topic in the study of adolescent sexuality, and to what degree do adolescents practice contraception in their sexual behavior?

What are the sexual standards that an adolescent might possibly have, and how does guilt play a role in moving from one sexual standard to another?

What are the consequences of adolescent sexuality, and what problems do they pose for the individual and for society?

How significant is the problem of venereal disease for adolescents? Can the problem be said to be improving or worsening?

What is the best advice to parents and schools about when sex education should begin?

What should be taught in sex education programs, and what arguments are there in favor of such programs?

S ex is one of the greatest concerns of adolescents and of the adults who worry about them. It is not difficult to imagine why this is so. Although sexual development begins in childhood, it is not until adolescence that sexuality becomes an important focus in the lives of most individuals.

The adolescent's hormonal balance changes throughout this period of life. The genitals develop to their nearly adult form. And both males and females begin to experience new feelings, including new bodily functions such as menstruation for females and ejaculation of seminal fluid for males. Perhaps more important than these physical changes, however, are the social and psychological changes which accompany adolescence. Sexual *behavior* and sexual *interaction* take on meaning as the adolescent begins to think about social events in school, parties outside of school, love, and dating.

Society has taken a special interest in the topic of adolescent sexuality in recent years, undoubtedly because of the vast changes that have taken place in the extent of sexual behavior among young persons. In addition, there is growing concern about the potential consequences of sexual involvement during adolescence. Not only is sexuality sometimes a source of anxiety for the individuals who must negotiate adolescence, but it is also the source of some of our society's most troublesome social problems. Pregnancy outside of marriage is an increasingly prominent feature of the adolescent years for a sizable segment of American youth. The consequences of pregnancy—abortion, illegitimacy, and early marriage—are all significant social issues. Moreover, many topics pertaining to sexual development, such as homosexuality, are of considerable interest and controversy. Finally, some of our most fervent religious and moral debates revolve around issues such as the acceptability of adolescent sexual behavior.

SEXUAL SOCIALIZATION

We begin our discussion with an examination of the many elements of the sexual socialization process. *Sexual socialization* is the process of becoming sexual, taking on a gender identity, learning sex roles, understanding sexual behavior, and generally acquiring the knowledge, skills, and dispositions that allow a person to function sexually in a given culture (Spanier, 1977). Sexual socialization, then, is the entire developmental process that forms the basis of our sexuality, our masculinity or femininity, and our maleness or femaleness. As this definition implies, sexuality is more than just what a male and a female do together in bed or in a park. Each dimension of our sexual socialization contributes something to the dynamics of our sexual functioning. There are five important components of sexual socialization (Spanier, 1977):

Development of sex-object preference This component involves the way in which an individual learns to direct his or her sexual interest toward persons of the same or opposite sex. Both biological-hereditary and social-psychological factors contribute to the determination of sex-object preference. Research is not clear about how males and females come to a decision about which sex will become the focus of sexual interest, but it seems likely that socialization influences during childhood and adolescence interact powerfully with whatever biological-hereditary contributions may exist to direct our sexual orientation.

Most persons are *heterosexual*, meaning that they are attracted sexually to persons of the other sex. A small, but significant, portion of the population is *homosexual*, meaning that such persons are sexually attracted to persons of the same sex. As Kinsey and his colleagues pointed out many years ago (Kinsey et al., 1948), there is undoubtedly a continuum ranging from exclusively heterosexual to exclusively homosexual, with individuals at various positions along the continuum. Furthermore, although most persons remain on one end of the continuum or the other throughout their lives, some persons have feelings placing them at different ends of the continuum at different times in their lives.

Homosexuality is a topic of concern to some adolescents, either because of fears that one may be homosexual or because the individual actually has had a homosexual experience. Eleven percent of adolescent boys and six percent of the girls report that they had at least one homosexual experience during adolescence (Sorensen, 1973). However, even though they have not had actual homosexual experiences, many others—25 percent in all—report that they have had homosexual advances made to them by other adolescents or adults (Sorensen, 1973).

It is not known how many persons who had homosexual experiences in adolescence continued such sexual activity or retained such an orientation into adulthood. One estimate is that only 4 percent of men and an even smaller percent of women remain exclusively homosexual throughout their lives, even though a substantially larger proportion have at least some homosexual experience (Kinsey et al., 1948, 1953).

Development of gender identity How does a child come to identify himself or herself as a male or female? The social definition given to a child at birth customarily follows the anatomical sex of the child, but one really acquires gender identity through a lengthy process during the first several years of life (Money & Ehrhardt, 1972). The physician's first words, "It's a boy" or "It's a girl," and the announcement of sex which shows up in birth notices are but the first important cues to the child and persons in his or her environment that the child is similar in one way to about half the population and different in one way from the other half. Children learn early in life that they are boys or girls, and they are taught in both direct and subtle ways to behave according to norms appropriate for their sex (Kohlberg, 1966; Mischel, 1966).

In rare cases, there are discrepancies between the person's anatomical designation and the internal feelings and self-definition that a person develops. A *transsexual* is a person who believes he or she is trapped inside the wrong kind of body. A male-to-female transsexual is someone who has a male's anatomy, but who believes he (she) is a female. A female-to-male transsexual has a female's anatomy, but believes she (he) is a male.

Studies done with *hermaphrodites* and *pseudohermaphrodites*, persons born with ambiguous, damaged, or both male and female genitals, provide some evidence about the development of gender identity. This research suggests that regardless of what the chromosomes say a person is (chromosomal sex), what reproductive organs the child has (gonadal sex), or what the hormonal balance is (hormonal sex), the decision of the parents in infancy about whether the child will be brought up as a boy or girl will generally determine the individual's gender identity throughout life (Money & Ehrhardt, 1972). This research also concludes that gender identity becomes fixed during, and is essentially unchangeable after, a period beginning at about 18 months of age and ending by age 4 or 5 years.

When a transsexual adult wishes to have his or her external genitals conform to his or her gender identity, or when a hermaphrodite requires an alteration of the genital structures, surgery is often used to make such alterations. Clinics which specialize in such surgery are called *gender identity clinics,* and are generally affiliated with medical schools. Psychological and legal counseling is generally provided to the person undergoing the "sex-change" operation, and hormonal treatments also may be involved.

Transvestism is sometimes confused with transsexualism and homosexuality. Transvestites are persons (more often males than females) who enjoy dressing as members of the opposite sex. They may receive sexual pleasure from such cross-dressing, and they may or may not be homosexual besides. Technically, however, homosexuality, transsexualism, and transvestism are three distinct variations of the customary sexual socialization process, although some social scientists have identified background characteristics and experiences which these individuals have in common (Stoller, 1968).

Development of sex roles This component involves the process by which individuals learn to define roles as "masculine," "feminine," or unrelated to sex-linked distinctions, and furthermore, how persons conceptually affiliate with and behaviorally perform these roles. We shall discuss sex roles more fully in Chapter 13.

Acquiring sexual skills, knowledge, and values It is not enough to understand that we are males and have sexual preferences for females, or vice versa. Part of sexual socialization guides our learning about sex. There is, of course, formal sex education—that which we might learn in settings such as public schools. But there is also informal sex education—that which we learn from parents, friends, and siblings, or from books, magazines, and the mass media, and even dating and sexual partners. This component, then, involves what we learn about sex and all the ways in which we acquire such information. We learn not only what sex is all about, but also *how* to be sexual—how to engage in the behaviors that are considered sexual. Furthermore, we must learn *values* which guide our sexual behavior. Of course, the extent of knowledge acquired before, during, and after adolescence varies widely, and the guidance provided adolescents by differing value systems will also vary much from one person to the next.

Development of dispositions to act in sexual contexts This component refers to a process which leads the individual to specific sexual behavior. How do values, knowledge, and skills, under the influence of certain sexual stimuli (such as pleasurable sensations, peer or partner pressure to act sexually, sexual drives), lead to specific sexual behavior? This component is the link between "what is in one's head" and "what one does." Given adolescents with similar amounts of knowledge, similar sexual "skills," and exposure to similar values, we know that there may be different behaviors which follow. Many factors in the social situation, in the dating relationship, and in the adolescent's past may influence how knowledge is translated into behavior. We shall attempt to examine the dynamics of this component in more detail later in this chapter.

Sexual socialization before adolescence

Freud (1923) suggested that all persons are born with an innate sexuality which must be channelled during the life course. He believed that people are innately bisexual and that their homosexuality or heterosexuality is determined by progression through the various developmental stages (Freud, 1949). Freud's ideas, however, met with much disfavor, since he suggested that infantile sexuality existed, an idea which was abhorrent to many. Although Freud's ideas about sexual development were rather controversial, they did make us aware of the possibility of a sexual component of early socialization. Comprehensive data adequate to examine some of the issues raised by the possibility of childhood sexuality only became available, however, in the 1940s, when the work of Alfred Kinsey and his colleagues was first published.

Alfred Kinsey, the first director of the Institute for Sex Research at Indiana University, was a zoologist by training. In the 1930s, he and his colleagues began the most massive investigation of sexual behavior ever accomplished. Despite a small staff and limited resources, he interviewed thousands of American men and women about their sexual experiences. His work was published after many years of interviewing and tabulating. Two volumes summarized the findings: *Sexual Behavior in the Human Male* (Kinsey et al., 1948) and *Sexual Behavior in the Human Female* (Kinsey et al., 1953). Not only was the study a bold undertaking, but some of the findings shocked those who read the reports. Because of the unrepresentative nature of his sample, we must be cautious about generalizing from his findings. However, his data serve as a useful starting point for our discussion.

Among the findings of Kinsey's research was that there was a considerable amount of sex play during the childhood years for both males and females, much of it with persons of the same sex. Thus, Kinsey was able to confirm in one way what

Alfred Kinsey

Freud first suggested—that sexuality was an aspect of childhood development which merits attention. Let us address some of the issues raised by both Freud and Kinsey.

More recent data confirm what Kinsey found—that children engage in acts adults would define as sexual, such as masturbation and sex play, which might include kissing, petting, and even sexual intercourse. We know that boys can obtain erections from infancy onward (but they cannot ejaculate seminal fluid until puberty), and both boys and girls can experience pleasurable feelings which *could* be defined as sexual.

Sexuality in childhood does exist, then, if we consider the specific *behaviors* which occur. Thus, Freud's more general ideas about infantile sexuality can be supported *if* we are willing to think about sex as any activity involving physically pleasurable feelings. At first glance, such a definition of sexuality might seem appropriate. But closer examination of what we mean by sexuality highlights the profound difference between childhood sexuality as discussed above and adolescent and adult sexuality. The key to understanding the distinction lies in the social and psychological definitions given to seemingly identical sexual acts. Strictly speaking, very little direct empirical support for Freud's (1923) theorizing and thinking about infantile sexuality exists today. Childhood sexuality cannot really be equated with adolescent sexuality because the child has not yet attached the same *meanings* to the act in which he or she engages. For example, two 5-year-old girls who are "playing doctor" and touching each other's gentials are engaging in behaviors that would be defined very differently if they were performed by two 18-year-old females. Even though they might sense that their behavior would not be approved, the 5-year-olds play secretly without a full understanding of why the behavior is disapproved.

A 6-year-old boy and a 5-year-old girl who are wrestling in the backyard probably attach different meanings to their activity than would a 17-year-old male and a 16-year-old female doing the same thing. The key difference is in the social definition attached to these activities. In other words, any given behavior is thought of as sexual only when we attach sexual meaning to it. Furthermore, an activity is best defined as sexual or not, depending on the definition the participants themselves attach to it. Even identical acts among adults (for example, a gynecologist conducting a pelvic exam and a husband touching his wife's genitals during sexual foreplay) are defined quite differently, depending on the context and social and personal definitions of the situation.

The childhood years, then, mostly involve activities which are not sexual by adult definitions. Nevertheless, children do begin to learn that their body can produce pleasurable feelings for them. Children may masturbate, even though they do not consider it a "sexual" activity. They may play doctor, hold hands, kiss, or even fondle members of the same or opposite sex. But they would not typically think of these activities as homosexual or heterosexual until they have enough knowledge about and exposure to sexuality to understand the implications of their behaviors and the social and personal meanings for them.

As adolescence approaches, however, all this changes. Informal sex education from friends, parents, the school, and the mass media quickly teaches the adolescent that sexuality is an important part of one's life. Learning about sex accelerates. By the early adolescent years, the individual may be experiencing much confusion about what he or she is hearing. Pressures from parents and peers may come into conflict. And the adolescent may experience great anxiety while struggling to reconcile his or her social and familial pressures with newly discovered sexual feelings, previously learned values, and an awareness of the increasing amount of sexuality among young people in our society.

One other factor begins to complicate the sexual socialization process. *Guilt* is a powerful emotion for some young people. The discrepancy between one's values, one's behaviors, and parental expectations is often highly related to the guilt one will encounter. Our society confuses many adolescents. The mass media present an inherent contradiction with regard to sex. Television, books, magazines, and movies may portray sex either as something desirable, to be sought at every opportunity, or as a sinful, mysterious, lustful, or clandestine activity. The adolescent must reconcile these contradictions as he or she begins to put sex in perspective and give it a place among the many other aspects of adolescent development.

Sexual behaviors of adolescence

Sexual expression may take many different forms. When we think of adolescent sexuality, we often think first about heterosexual intercourse. However, many forms of sexual activity short of intercourse are important during adolescence.

For males, the beginning of adolescent sexuality is often a *nocturnal emission* (or "wet dream"), a discharge of semen during sleep. The experience is accompanied by an orgasm and is often associated with sexually colored dreams. Although females

---

INSIGHT INTO ADOLESCENCE

Margot Fonteyn (neé Margaret Hookham) is a famous ballerina with the Royal Ballet (of England). With her mother's encouragement, she studied ballet, starting in her early years. As an adolescent, she danced the lead role in many ballets. The passage that follows describes her feelings during that time.

Young people usually pass through a period of extreme ideals, and I decided that only the live theatre, classical music and serious authors were worth attention. Since I disdained the movies, thus missing a lot of the best films ever made, I was not well informed on the mechanics of kissing. In fact, I had given the matter no thought at all until one day an escort suddenly kissed me on the mouth. It was a quite disagreeable shock, not related in any way to my unspecific dreams of love and happiness. In a quick reaction of fright at this unexpected happening, I slapped the boy's face. I never thought for a moment how odd it was that, in the ballet, I would not hesitate to embrace passionately whichever dancer represented my loved one. Real life seemed often so much more unreal than the stage; or maybe I should say that my identity was clear to me only when I assumed some make-believe character. For myself, I was influenced this way and that, thinking in turn that I should be sparkling, or tragic, or intellectual—depending on the person last described with approval in some overheard conversation. Needless to say, I was none of those things.

It was so easy for me to step out into the limelight through the plywood door of Giselle's cottage and suffer her shyness, ecstasy, deception and madness as if it was my own life catching me by surprise at each new turn. It was a fresh, living experience for me at every performance as the drama unfolded. But when I left the stage door and sought my orientation among real people, I was in a wilderness of unpredictables in an unchoreographed world.

Source: Fonteyn, M. *Margot Fonteyn: An Autobiography.* Alfred A. Knopf, Inc., 1977.

may also have sexual dreams, and are capable of experiencing orgasm during sleep, they do not have a similar discharge.

Masturbation is another normal, adolescent sexual activity (Kinsey et al., 1948, 1953; McCary, 1978). As noted earlier, masturbation for some begins in childhood, but it is a widespread phenomenon during adolescence. It is nearly universal among males, and a majority of adolescent females report masturbating at some time. Whereas it tends to become a regular activity for males once they begin, it ranges from a rather sporadic event for some females to a regular occurrence for others.

Contrary to common assumption, there is no evidence that masturbation is a harmful activity. Some adolescents develop an acute sense of guilt about masturbation, feeling ashamed or embarrassed. Parental threats to their children to avoid such sexual release will generally intensify feelings of guilt and are unlikely to prevent the practice. Adolescents have sexual tension which can be relieved through masturbation, and it is unlikely that an adolescent would easily abandon the activity. Furthermore, some women are able to achieve orgasm only by masturbation, and others report more intense orgasms from masturbation than from coitus (Ellis, 1958; Hite, 1976; Masters & Johnson, 1966).

Research shows that heterosexual activity progresses through a sequence of steps for the typical adolescent (Spanier, 1976). Kissing, light petting, heavy petting, and coitus are encountered in sequence for most persons. There is great variation as to when a person has his or her first romantic kiss, how quickly one progresses from slight involvement to complete sexual involvement, and when in the life cycle the sequence is completed. Indeed, some individuals have already had sexual intercourse by the time they reach puberty; others have never kissed someone (or had a date) by the conclusion of the adolescent years; and still others may go through the entire sequence of sexual involvement on their first date (Spanier, 1977; Zelnick & Kantner, 1977).

Petting is rarely discussed, but it is an important topic. For married persons or adolescents who are having sexual intercourse regularly, petting may only be a form of foreplay—a prelude to sexual intercourse. But for many adolescents, petting is the sexual focus of a relationship. We have many terms in our vocabulary to describe the phenomenon—making out, feeling up, going to third base, Russian hands and Roman fingers, etc. Many adolescents readily engage in petting since they find it a pleasurable and stimulating activity. In many cases, it is an indication of the affection and interest a male and female have for each other.

However, petting may lead to a level of arousal which makes it difficult not to advance further. Consequently, many adolescents, particularly males (Kanin, 1970), find it difficult to be satisfied with petting as an end in itself. Indeed, it is not uncommon for the sexual tension generated in petting to lead to orgasm for males and females, without intercourse. Unrelieved sexual tension may sometimes result in pain in the region of the testes in the male, a condition known as *orchialgia* or *testalgia*. It is pain probably due to congestion in the prostrate gland (Cawood, 1971). Such pain is uncomfortable, but disappears in a short time after the stimulation. Under similar circumstances of stimulation without sexual release, some females also have discomfort due to congestion and tension in the pelvic region. This condition is known as *vasocongestion*. As with males, it can be relieved through orgasm or it will dissipate soon after the stimulation ceases.

Traditionally, males have been put in the position of aggressors in social and sexual relationships. Females have had the role of holding the males off. Much evidence suggests that this traditional stereotype is still applicable. Men are more active in every form of sexual behavior and still tend to assume that females are the ones who must set the limits in a given sexual relationship. Although the generalization still holds, it is clear that the times are changing. Females seem to be narrowing the gap in all forms of sexual behavior, and there seems to be more willingness on the part of females to play a more nearly equal role in sexual involvement. The extent of this change is difficult to monitor, however, since all such changes have been overshadowed in recent years by the great increase in adolescent coitus. We now consider the extent of adolescent coital involvement in America today.

SEXUAL REVOLUTION OR EVOLUTION?

Whether or not we conclude that there has been a sexual revolution depends on our definition of revolution. If we are thinking about changes that have occurred since Puritan days, our conclusions may be different than if we think about changes since the 1960s. More importantly, our conclusions will be influenced by whether we look at how many people have *ever* had sexual intercourse or how many people have sexual intercourse *regularly*, perhaps with many partners.

The term *"sexual evolution"* may be more appropriate than "sexual revolution" in describing what has happened and is happening in American culture. Since parts of culture are interrelated, sexual changes will occur as other aspects of social life change. When this change is so dramatic that it creates an imbalance between or threatens the normal evolution of other basic societal institutions, then perhaps a revolution has occurred. But when change is consistent with, follows from, or is compatible with other societal changes, then we can say evolutionary change has occurred. It is undoubtedly this latter form of social change which has occurred with regard to human sexual behavior during the last couple of decades in North America (Spanier, 1979).

But there is no conclusive evidence that the evolution has occurred in all social strata of life at the same rate or to the same degree. People adhere to, accept, or resist a multiplicity of ideas, standards, and ways of life. Ours is a diverse society. This is no more apparent in any aspect of American life than sexual behavior. Perhaps one of the most important results, if not the most important result, of sexual evolution is the growing, but not yet universal, acceptance of this fact of diversity. Difference increasingly is tolerated, even encouraged.

Kinsey's reports signaled the beginning of the most recent phase of sexual evolution. As a result of his research, Americans became more aware of the extent of some sexual practices and increasingly became willing to talk about them. However, as persons came to talk more and more about sex, many also came to the conclusion that there was actually more and more of it occurring.

Many factors tended to reinforce the belief that the incidence of adolescent sexuality had increased. There was an assumption that changes in attitudes toward sex must necessarily reflect changes in behavior. Sometimes changes in attitude follow changes in behavior, and sometimes the reverse is true. For example, attitudes toward homosexuality have changed without any demonstrated change in the incidence of homosexuality. Thus, acceptance of a given type of behavior may neither reflect nor produce changes in that behavior.

Freedom of discussion has increased public awareness of various types of sexual activity. The mass media did their share to contribute to the belief that adolescent sexuality was increasing. Sex is a marketable commodity, a salable product. Thus, as television and the cinema became more popular and widely available, sex became a more public topic. The widespread availability of magazines with nude pictures and the visibility of X-rated movies are reflections of the increased openness about sex.

There were some studies before Kinsey's, and there have been many since. These studies give us some insight into sexuality and social change. The evidence available suggests that adolescent sexuality has been characteristic of a significant portion of the population from the time of the first studies on the subject. It is obvious through literature that it has always existed in America, although it has never been possible to determine precisely how widespread it has been at any given time.

It appears now that the sexual "revolution" that so many persons thought they were witnessing in the 1950s and early 1960s was really a revolution in attitudes, values, and openness about sexuality in the society. There is no evidence to suggest that there was any major shift in actual sexual behavior during those years. The best evidence suggests that there was no significant increase in adolescent sexual behavior during the fifty-year period beginning around World War I. Almost every study since the mid-1960s, however, indicates a rather significant and consistent increase since then in the number of sexually experienced adolescents and young adults. The increase applies to both males and females, but it has been more dramatic among females. Virtually all married men in contemporary America have had premarital intercourse, but the experience of females has traditionally been more limited. The "catching-up" phenomenon that can be observed among females is to be expected in a time of greater sexual freedom, women's liberation, and increasing equality between the sexes.

In the past fifteen years then, it appears that the total number of persons who become sexually experienced during adolescence has increased in the United States. The precise extent of such change will be documented in the next section. This trend can be expected to continue, we believe, since increased equality between males and females will be likely to result in still more similarities in the nature and extent of male and female sexual behavior. There is some agreement that most of the increase can be attributed to individuals having sexual relations with persons to whom they are emotionally committed or with whom they are in love. A smaller portion of the increase involves individuals having sexual contacts promiscuously or with casual dates (Cannon & Long, 1971; Sorensen, 1973). We must await future research, however, to know whether there will be a shift toward more adolescent sexual activity being accounted for by persons having casual sex.

There is other, indirect evidence for the recent upward trend in adolescent sexual behavior. There has been a marked rise in venereal disease, especially among young people. The number of illegitimate births has increased among adolescents. Adolescent females are obtaining more abortions. A growing number of women are requesting contraceptives. And the incidence of nonmarital cohabitation ("living together") has increased dramatically (Clayton & Voss, 1977; Jaffe & Dryfoos, 1976; Sullivan, Tietze, & Dryfoos, 1977; Zelnik & Kantner, 1977, 1978).

SEXUALITY TODAY

There can be little doubt that the nature and extent of adolescent sexual activity has changed in recent years. Although the definition of what constitutes a sexual revolution varies from person to person, most researchers who study adolescent sexuality would now agree on at least one fact—that a greater number of adolescents have sexual intercourse before reaching adulthood than at any previous time in this country's history.

Incidence of sexual activity

A recent national survey of never-married females aged 15 to 19 found that 55 percent of the 19-year-olds interviewed had already had sexual intercourse. Among all females aged 15 to 19, 35 percent were sexually experienced by the time of the interview (Zelnik & Kantner, 1977). In a five-year period between an earlier survey which used a comparable national sample and the more recent study, there was an increase of 30 percent in coital experience for all females between ages 15 and 19. By age 15, 18 percent of American females have already had sexual intercourse, suggesting that many of the concerns we have about pregnancy outside of marriage are justified for younger as well as older adolescents.

Exhibits 11.1 and 11.2 display the steady increase in sexual involvement through the adolescent years. Figures for 1976 and 1971 are shown to indicate the magnitude of change which has resulted in just five years. These figures are the best we have to date, since they are from national probability samples of almost 4,000 young females in 1971 and 2,000 young females in 1976. Actually, the estimates are conservative, since they do not include adolescents who were married by the time of the interview, females who are likely to have had an even higher incidence of coital experience.

This study interviewed females only, and there are no comparable data for males. However, virtually every earlier study of adolescent sexuality conducted over

Exhibit 11.1
Percent of never-married women aged 15 to 19 who have ever had intercourse, by age, 1976 and 1971. (*Source:* Adapted from Zelnik & Kantner, 1977.)

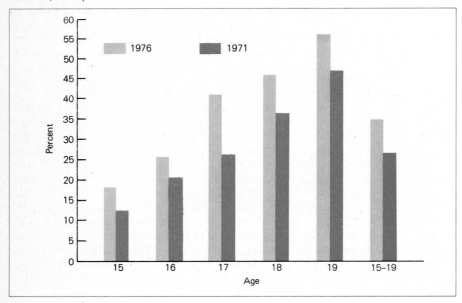

Exhibit 11.2
Percent of never-married women aged 15 to 19 who have ever had intercourse, by age and race, 1976 and 1971

Age	1976			1971		
	All	White	Black	All	White	Black
15–19	34.9	30.8	62.7	26.8	21.4	51.2
15	18.0	13.8	38.4	13.8	10.9	30.5
16	25.4	22.6	52.6	21.2	16.9	46.2
17	40.9	36.1	68.4	26.6	21.8	58.8
18	45.2	43.6	74.1	36.8	32.3	62.7
19	55.2	48.7	83.6	46.8	39.4	76.2

Source: Adapted from Zelnik and Kantner, 1977.

the past fifty years has shown the corresponding figures to be higher for males (Bowman & Spanier, 1978). Thus, it can be reasonably assumed that this generalization still holds true for today's adolescents.

We need to be clear about what these data say and what they do not say. These figures reflect *cumulative incidence*. This refers to the total number of persons who have engaged in sexual intercourse at least once by the time of the interview. Cumulative incidence figures, shown in Exhibit 11.2, do not tell us how often, with how many partners, or under what circumstances such sexual involvement took place. Cumulative incidence figures are sometimes misleading to the unwary reader, because they may erroneously be interpreted as *active incidence* figures, which indicate the number of persons who are sexually active at a given time. Of course, active incidence is always lower than cumulative incidence. Let us now consider some of the other aspects of adolescent sexuality today.

About half of the females who were sexually experienced indicated that they had not had intercourse during the month prior to the interview, and fewer than 3 in 10 had had intercourse as many as three times in the month (Zelnik & Kantner, 1977). Thus, we see that a good deal of adolescent sexual activity is rather sporadic. In fact, 15 percent of all sexually experienced adolescent females report that they had sexual intercourse *only once*. Thus, only a portion of the 35 percent of all adolescents aged 15 to 19 who are sexually experienced are having coitus on a regular basis.

The findings that more than a third of all middle and older adolescents and more than half of the oldest adolescents are sexually experienced has caused great concern for many parents, teachers, school administrators, community agencies, and government policymakers. One fear is that many adolescents are indiscriminately having sexual relations with very little thought about its consequences and about the personal meaning it has for them. Actually, the data suggest that this is not what is happening. About half of all sexually experienced adolescents have had sexual intercourse with only one partner. Less than one-third have had two or three partners. Only 10 percent of all sexually experienced adolescents have had six or more partners. Thus, if we consider sexually experienced and sexually inexperienced adolescents together, less than 4 percent have engaged in coitus with six or more partners.

However, we also observe, in Exhibits 11.3 and 11.4, that the number of partners with whom adolescents had sexual intercourse increased during the five years between the two surveys of American females. Furthermore, as we mentioned before, other research has shown that the figures are higher for males in all forms of sexual activity (Carns, 1973; Kinsey et al., 1948, 1953; Spanier, 1973). Thus, it can be concluded that the number of partners for males of corresponding ages will likely be higher on the average. Finally, we also should note that as we examine the individual age groups across adolescence, the number of partners increases. Thus, among 19-year-old sexually experienced females, 14 percent have had six or more partners.

There are some notable racial differences in sexual activity (see Exhibit 11.2). By age 15, 38 percent of Black females have had sexual intercourse. By age 19, the figure is 84 percent. For a substantial number of Black females, sexual activity actually begins *before* the female is even capable of conception. By the conclusion of adolescence, sexual experience is quite prevalent among Blacks, although our same caution about the differences between cumulative and active incidence is applicable in this discussion.

However, lest we think that these higher cumulative incidence figures suggest that Blacks are any more promiscuous than Whites, we point to the figures on number of partners. Although Blacks are more likely to have had more than one sexual partner than are Whites, they are less likely than Whites to have had six or more sexual partners. Only 6 percent of sexually experienced Black adolescent females have had six or more partners, compared to more than 11 percent for Whites.

Exhibit 11.3
Percent of sexually experienced never-married women aged 15 to 19, by number of partners ever, 1976 and 1971. (*Source:* Zelnik & Kantner, 1977.)

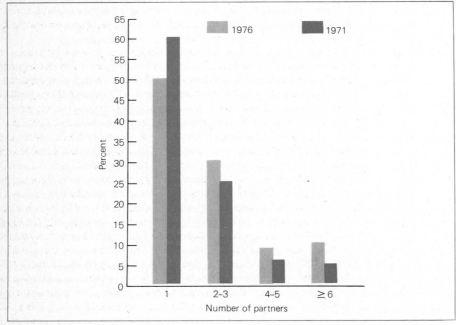

Exhibit 11.4
Percent distribution of sexually experienced
never-married women aged 15 to 19,
according to number of partners ever,
by age, 1976 and 1971

Number of partners	Age		
	15–19	15–17	18–19
1976			
1	50.1	54.0	45.3
2–3	31.4	31.5	31.3
4–5	8.7	8.4	9.1
≥6	9.8	6.1	14.3
Total	100.0	100.0	100.0
1971			
1	61.5	66.5	56.1
2–3	25.1	22.7	27.7
4–5	7.8	5.9	9.9
≥6	5.6	4.9	6.3
Total	100.0	100.0	100.0

Source: Adapted from Zelnik and Kantner, 1977.

The initiation of sex

When and under what circumstance does sexual activity begin? We have already indicated that nocturnal emissions and masturbation typically are the earliest sexual experiences for males. At some time during the adolescent years, males and females usually begin their progression of heterosexual involvement in conjunction with dating relationships. In the typical case, sexual intercourse first occurs with a steady dating partner. For most adolescents, intercourse usually follows a period in which kissing and petting were the primary forms of sexual expression. Of course, there is considerable variation, with some adolescents having their first sexual experiences very early in a dating relationship or outside of one altogether.

Exhibit 11.5 shows that among sexually active adolescent females, the median age at which coitus first took place was 16.2. This finding is very important when we consider sex education and the availability of contraception. As we shall discuss later, sex education and contraceptive information and availability are too late to be of utmost benefit if provided only in the last years of high school. It is clear from these recent data that many adolescents need detailed information about reproduction and contraception during junior high school, at the very latest.

Research shows that for Whites there is no relationship between first coitus and the age at menarche, but there is a correlation for Blacks (Zelnik & Kantner, 1977). In other words, for Blacks, the earlier the age at menarche, the earlier sex tends to begin. There are also some interesting seasonal variations. Nearly two-fifths of American females report that they first experienced sexual intercourse during the summer months (Zelnik & Kantner, 1977).

Exhibit 11.5
Median age at first intercourse of sexually experienced never-married women aged 15 to 19, by age, 1976

Age at survey	Median age at first intercourse
15–19	16.2
15	14.7
16	15.5
17	16.4
18	16.8
19	17.1

Source: Adapted from Zelnik and Kantner, 1977.

Exhibit 11.6
Percent distribution of sexually experienced never-married women aged 15 to 19, according to place of occurrence of first intercourse, 1976

Place of occurrence	Percent
Respondent's home	16.3
Partner's home	41.6
Relative or friend's home	21.4
Motel or hotel	5.2
Automobile	9.5
Other	6.0
Total	100.0

Source: Adapted from Zelnik and Kantner, 1977.

Parents of adolescents have always been curious about where sexual activity among adolescents takes place. Some parents encourage their children to bring dates home, presumably because the couple is less likely to become sexually involved if they are in a more supervised setting. Other parents, though, encourage their children to go out, thinking that places of greater social activity will discourage sexual activity. The data in Exhibit 11.6 tells us that the male's residence is the most common location for the first coital experience. It is likely, however, that in a large proportion of the cases, no one other than the young couple is at home at the time. A relative's or friend's home is a distant second, and the female's home is the third most common place. Fifty-eight percent of initial coital experiences, then, occur in the homes of the male or female, and almost eighty percent take place in someone's home. Only 5 percent occur in motels or hotels, less than 10 percent in automobiles, and the remaining 6 percent in other places, such as in the "great outdoors" (Zelnik & Kantner, 1977).

Data from an earlier national survey of college students provide us with additional information about the nature of the relationships between males and females at the time they begin sexual activity (Carns, 1973). Males tend to have their first sexual experience at earlier ages than do females. Their first partner is more likely to be a pickup or casual date than is a female's first partner. A female's first partner is more likely to be someone to whom she is seriously committed or with whom she is in love. The first intercourse is less likely to be planned among males, and less likely to be discussed if planned ahead of time. Males are more likely to report that they enjoyed their first sexual experience than are females. They are less likely to do it again with their first partner, they talk about it sooner, tell more people, and are more likely to receive an approving reaction from the persons they tell. Males tell their parents more than females do. They have a greater frequency, they have more partners before they are married, and they report less guilt about having had sexual intercourse than females.

These differences persist throughout the remainder of sexual activity in the adolescent years. It is not until marriage that males and females become more nearly

INSIGHT INTO ADOLESCENCE

Jerome David Salinger was born in New York City in 1919. He began writing at the age of 15, and published his first story in *Story* magazine in 1940. He began writing *The Catcher in the Rye,* from which the following passage is taken, in 1941. It was published as a novel ten years later. At present J.D. Salinger leads a secluded life.

I just kept laying there on Ely's bed, thinking about Jane and all. It just drove me stark staring mad when I thought about her and Stradlater parked somewhere. . . . Every time I thought about it, I felt like jumping out the window. The thing is, you didn't know Stradlater. I knew him. Most guys at Pencey just *talked* about having sexual intercourse with girls all the time—like Ackley, for instance—but old Stradlater really did it. . . .

The trouble was, I knew that guy Stradlater's technique. That made it even worse. We once double-dated, in Ed Banky's car, and Stradlater was in the back, with his date, and I was in the front with mine. What a technique that guy had. What he'd do was, he'd start snowing his date in this very quiet, *sincere* voice—like as if he wasn't only a very handsome guy but a nice, *sincere* guy, too. I damn near puked, listening to him. His date kept saying, "No—*please.* Please, don't. *Please.*" But old Stradlater kept snowing her in this Abraham Lincoln, sincere voice, and finally there'd be this terrific silence in the back of the car. It was really embarrassing. I don't think he gave that girl the time that night—but damn near. *Damn* near.

Source: J. D. Salinger, *The Catcher in Rye.* New York: Bantam Book/Little, Brown, 1945, pp. 48–49.

---

equal in frequency of sexual intercourse. Then, of course, marital coitus would by definition provide equal experience for men and women. However, data on extramarital sexuality (Hunt, 1974; Kinsey et al., 1948, 1953) show that male-female differences in total sexual outlet still persist throughout the remainder of the life span, since extramarital coitus is more common for males, and masturbation, which continues to some extent for many persons during marriage, is also more common for males.

These data on male-female differences from first sexual intercourse through adolescence and into adulthood further persuade us to consider modern sexual change as evolutionary rather than revolutionary. Adolescent heterosexual activity is still dominated by males. Sex is much more important in the adolescent male subculture than the adolescent female subculture. Males talk about sex more openly with each other, joke about it more, and experience greater peer pressure to perform sexually. Females traditionally have not discussed sex very much with their friends, and have been quite secretive about their own activities. Although adolescent males and females are converging on these dimensions, the narrowing of the gap can probably be attributed more to changes in the female subculture than in the male.

But until males and females have a more nearly equal role in the initiation of sexual relationships or in the task of postponing sexual relations, a sexual revolution cannot be said to have occurred. We believe that a true sexual revolution would be characterized by greater equality among males and females in the *nature* of sexual interaction. Similarity in the numbers of sexually experienced persons will not signal a sexual revolution until the content and dynamics of the social *relationships* in which the sexual acts occur are more equal. In short, social and sexual relationships must change *qualitatively*, not just quantitatively.

Contraceptive use

It should be evident from the figures presented above that researchers no longer need to concern themselves with the question of whether adolescents do or do not engage in sexual intercourse. The answer is yes. Many do. The research topic which is now probably more important than any other in the study of adolescent sexuality is contraceptive use. Why do some adolescents use contraception while others do not? What leads an adolescent to be contraceptively prepared and protected? What can be done to help adolescents who have decided to have sexual relations avoid the unfortunate consequences of veneral disease, unwanted pregnancy, and perhaps abortion (Thompson & Spanier, 1978)?

In 1976, one-fourth of sexually experienced adolescent females had *never* used contraception. An additional 45 percent had used contraception only sometimes, and only 30 percent reported that they had always used it. These figures represent a significant improvement in contraceptive use since 1971, as Exhibits 11.7 and 11.8 show, but they still point to the serious problem of nonuse among adolescents. Almost 2 in 3 adolescents reported that they had not used any form of contraception during their last sexual experience. Even by age 19, only a little more than two-thirds of the respondents report that they were contraceptively protected at the last intercourse.

Exhibit 11.7
Percent of sexually experienced never-married women aged 15 to 19 who used contraception at last intercourse, by age, 1976 and 1971. (*Source:*** Zelnik & Kantner, 1977.)**

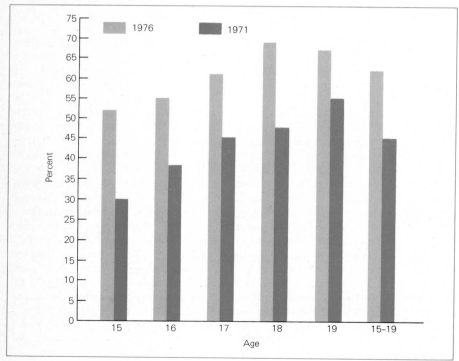

Exhibit 11.8

Percent of sexually experienced never-married women aged 15 to 19, according to contraceptive use status, by age, 1976 and 1971

Age	Use status			
	Never	Sometimes	Always	Last time
1976				
15–19	25.6	44.5	30.0	63.5
15	38.0	32.5	29.5	53.8
16	30.9	38.7	30.5	56.3
17	29.4	41.4	29.3	61.8
18	20.8	49.1	30.1	70.3
19	15.1	54.4	30.5	68.8
1971				
15–19	17.0	64.6	18.4	45.4
15	32.9	47.4	19.7	29.9
16	20.6	58.9	20.5	38.8
17	12.2	70.8	17.0	45.2
18	13.0	70.1	16.9	48.8
19	14.6	66.4	19.0	55.3

Source: Adapted from Zelnik and Kantner, 1977.

Among adolescent female contraceptive users, oral contraceptives (birth control pills) are the most commonly used method. Pills were reported as the method used at last intercourse by almost one-third of the females. Condoms and withdrawal were next in popularity, with IUD use, douche, and other methods used by a small percentage. The figures presented in Exhibits 11.9 and 11.10 suggest that less than half of adolescent women are using effective methods of contraception (pills, condoms, IUDs). Withdrawal, douche, and some of the methods included in the other category (rhythm, creams, foams, jellies) have relatively high failure rates, and thus many of the adolescents using these methods are actually at risk of pregnancy (Hatcher et al., 1976). And almost 37 percent of the adolescents used no contraception at all at last intercourse.

Zelnik and Kantner (1977) report that the older a female is at the time of first intercourse, the more likely it is that she will begin to use contraception at the same time she begins to have sex. However, there is no evidence that the gap between age at first intercourse and age at first contraceptive use has declined for females as a whole in recent years. A study of the relative influences on males and females to use contraception demonstrated that partner influence was most important, parental influence least important, with peer influence in between (Thompson & Spanier, 1978).

Much has been said about oral contraceptives contributing to the increased incidence of adolescent sexuality. The fact that only a minority of sexually experienced adolescent females use oral contraceptives should suggest to us that pill use is not a major or even contributing factor in the *initiation* of sexual activity for most American adolescents. It may be true, however, that once sexual activity has begun, the availability of the pill makes sexual involvement easier and less

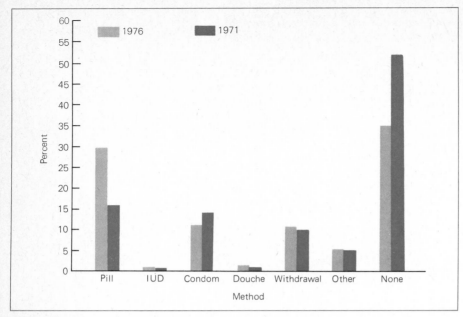

Exhibit 11.9
Percent of sexually experienced never-married women aged 15 to 19,
according to method used at last intercourse, 1976 and 1971. (*Source:*
Zelnik & Kantner, 1977.)

worrisome. About half of the unmarried teenage women who have used or
contraceptives got their first prescription from a clinic rather than a private
physician. According to Zelnik and Kantner, this contrasts with the practice of older,
married women, who rely much more on the private physician for contraception.

Exhibit 11.10
**Percent distribution of sexually experienced
never-married women aged 15 to 19, according
to method used at last intercourse by age,
1976**

	Age		
Method	15–19	15–17	18–19
Pill	31.2	21.6	42.9
IUD	2.2	1.3	3.4
Condom	12.6	15.2	9.3
Douche	2.3	2.4	2.3
Withdrawal	10.6	14.9	5.4
Other	4.5	3.0	6.3
None	36.6	41.6	30.4
Total	100.0	100.0	100.0

Source: Adapted from Zelnick and Kantner, 1977.

Reasons for inadequate protection

Many young women feel that it is awkward, presumptuous, or unromantic to be contraceptively protected. Young men and women report a variety of reasons why they did not adequately prepare. For some, sexual intercourse is something which is supposed to happen "naturally" in a romantic context. Some females are reluctant, when asked to have coitus, to be in a position to reply, "Why yes, I was hoping you would ask, and therefore, I was fitted for a diaphragm yesterday," or "Sure—and I'm OK as far as the pill is concerned. I began taking it last month since I expected that our relationship would come to this." Many men and women feel that the romance is taken out of the situation if they have anticipated it or prepared for it. A woman does not want to appear as though she were expecting to have coitus, even though she perhaps was.

Since it is the female who gets pregnant, she must be especially concerned about possible pregnancy. However, the male also has a role. Men need to take an active role in contraceptive preparation. It is not unreasonable for a female to suggest that intercourse be delayed an hour or so, or even a full day, until the couple acquires contraception. Many females feel that they are not necessarily "bad girls" if they are overcome with passion and have sexual intercourse, but that they would be "bad" if they were contraceptively prepared for it.

Studies have brought to light a variety of reasons why people have premarital intercourse without adequate contraceptive protection (Lehfeldt, 1971; Sandberg & Jacobs, 1972; Shah, Zelnik, & Kantner, 1975). Among them are ignorance of which contraceptive methods are effective and where to get them; rejection of a method prescribed by a physician because the patient thinks it unsafe; objection to contraception on religious or moral grounds; denial that contraception works; irresponsibility; immaturity; willingness to take risks; availability of abortion; rebellion against society or parents; hostility toward the other sex; equation of love with self-sacrifice; a belief that intercourse is sinful and pregnancy is the punishment; a feeling that pregnancy is a gift of love; the belief that sex is for procreation only; unwillingness to deny oneself or to delay intercourse; a desire of the female to become pregnant; the feeling that "it can't or won't happen to me;" the belief that intercourse is a demonstration of love; the belief that the girl was too young to become pregnant; and the belief that intercourse was too infrequent or occurred at the wrong time of the month.

In future years, it will be increasingly important for parents and persons working with adolescents to pay attention to education about contraception and motivation for contraceptive use. The widespread lack of contraceptive use among adolescents comes at a time in history when the most effective methods of protection ever known to exist are readily available, when state laws restricting the distribution of contraception to minors have finally been eliminated (Paul et al., 1976), when there are family planning clinics and other health services within driving or commuting distance for virtually all American adolescents, and when adolescent knowledge about contraception is at an all-time high.

Factors influencing sexual involvement

In recent years there has been a controversy about whether sex education in the public schools encourages adolescent sexual behavior. This policy-related question is part of a larger one which social scientists have also been interested in recently:

What is the process that eventually leads to premarital intercourse? Do parents play a part? Do the mass media have an influence? Do magazines, X-rated movies, or pornography play a part? What about pressures from friends or dating partners? There are now some research data to help answer these questions (Spanier, 1973, 1976a, 1976b).

Data on sexual socialization obtained during interviews with a national sample of about 1,200 college students were grouped into three categories:

1. Formal sex education—sex education taught within school classrooms, for example in health, biology, physical education, or family relations classes.

2. Informal sex education—sex information obtained from family members, peer groups, or other sources. Examples of informal sex education are a girl who has seen an older man expose himself, two children who are "playing doctor," an adolescent who discovers that touching his or her genitals is pleasurable, a mother telling her daughter about contraception, and a high school student who reads a *Playboy* magazine.

3. Dating experiences—frequency of dates, degree of closeness to persons dated, total amount of dating experience, and pressures and influences associated with dating.

The findings of the study showed that of all three types of influence, dating experiences were the most influential in explaining the nature and extent of adolescent sexual behavior. Persons who had a greater dating frequency, were more emotionally involved with the partners they dated, and those who had the most extensive dating history had the most active sex lives. Informal sex education experiences were not as strongly related to a person's sexual behavior, and formal sex education was least related of all.

These findings suggested that it is the *context* of the person's involvement at the present time which is most influential. What the person was taught when growing up does not seem to be as important as what is happening in that person's life at the moment. For example, parents who were very strict and conservative about sexual matters and taught their children accordingly did not have as great an influence as the pressures from a current dating partner. Religiosity at present was more important than religiosity while growing up.

Attendance in sex education classes did not seem to influence sexual behavior one way or another, regardless of when the course was taken, what kind of class it was, who taught it, and whether coitus or birth control was specifically mentioned. (This finding should allay the fears of some persons critical of sex education.) Exposure to erotic materials was related to greater sexual activity, but it is probable that exposure to erotic materials and sexual behavior are correlated, but not causally related. In other words, they both seem to be an increasingly likely occurrence, but one cannot be attributed as the cause of the other. This research suggests that the pressures and influences an individual faces in a given relationship can be powerful enough to outweigh all other teaching to the contrary.

SEXUAL VALUES

Most young people are brought up with the value that sexual intercourse is something to be reserved for marriage. Even if sex never was discussed in the home, most college students can recall that when they were younger, they believed sex was to be practiced only with one's husband or wife. The fact that the majority of these individuals have sexual intercourse before the termination of their adolescence suggests that values must be changeable. Sexual values in particular seem to change during adolescence in the direction of greater openness to the possibility of sexual relations before marriage. As discussed above, the stimulus that provides a basis for such change is often the intimacy associated with a serious dating relationship.

As might be expected, guilt is a common by-product of the change in values that most adolescents experience. It can be worrisome, if not traumatic, to have sexual intercourse after being taught that it is wrong, after learning from clergymen that it is sinful, or after hearing sad stories about unwed mothers. Thus, the sexually active adolescent typically goes through a process of guilt resolution. The task is to rethink and redefine one's values to be consistent with new behaviors. Most individuals make this transition without too much difficulty. Others, however, have a lot of trouble reconciling old values, new behaviors, and new values. Parents and other significant persons in the adolescent's life might disapprove of some of his or her new behaviors, and the adolescent must struggle with this thought. It is always difficult to engage in behaviors which would disappoint others.

This conflict undoubtedly accounts for why most adolescents do not discuss their sexual activities with their parents. In fact, many parents would like to discuss personal topics with their children, although they often would rather avoid such discussions if the topic is sex. Many parents of adolescents hesitate to talk about sex with their children for fear that they will find out that it has already begun.

Of course, not all adolescents have sexual intercourse. Some persons reach adulthood before they first have coitus, and some individuals still do wait until marriage. However, most of the same issues of guilt resolution and parental communication are still applicable to other forms of sexual involvement, such as kissing and petting, which are even more prevalent. Sex is a topic of slight discussion in the home, and yet it is one domain of social functioning for which adolescents feel the need for some guidance. They rarely turn to their parents; instead, they will be more likely to turn to peers or partners for advice. Sometimes not finding guidance there either, many adolescents begin sexual relations without any serious thought about what it means to them. In this section, we discuss briefly the standards of sexual behavior that are found among today's adolescents.

Sexual standards

Every person has a sexual standard. This standard may change during a person's life. Individuals often begin with a more restrictive standard—one which instructs us that sex is to be reserved for marriage. Yet one may then develop a new standard, perhaps after falling in love or coming to college, which permits him or her to have sexual intercourse before marriage in certain circumstances. Reiss (1960) differentiates between two types of sex: *body-centered* sex has its emphasis on the physical nature of sex, and *person-centered* sex has its emphasis on the emotional relationship between the individuals who are engaged in the sex act. Furthermore, *individuals* may be classified according to one of the four sexual standards:

1. *Abstinence.* Premarital intercourse is wrong for both men and women, regardless of circumstances.

2. *Permissiveness with affection.* Premarital intercourse is right for both men and women, as long as there is emotional attachment, love, or strong affection.

3. *Permissiveness without affection.* Premarital intercourse is right for both men and women whenever there is physical attraction, regardless of whether affection is present.

4. *Double standard.* Premarital intercourse is considered right for men but wrong for women.

Sociologists have debated whether the double standard or the abstinence standard was dominant throughout modern Western history. Even though it has always been stated, since the emergence of Christianity, that abstinence was the norm, it is certainly true that it was never fully practiced. It is probably correct to say that, until recently, abstinence has been the culturally approved standard, whereas the double standard existed in reality for a significant portion, perhaps a majority, of the population. Today, most young persons adhere to a permissiveness-with-affection standard, although it is likely that the commitment necessary for "affection" has been relaxed somewhat in recent years. The double standard is on its way out, although remnants of it must surely still be around, since male-female differences continue to be evident. The abstinence standard is reported by many young persons, although it appears that this standard is replaced by one of the permissiveness standards sometime before marriage for a majority of American youth. A minority of persons adhere to the abstinence standard, particularly those of strong religious conviction and those under strict parental influence.

The permissiveness-without-affection standard has never been dominant. It probably involves only a small portion of the population, but is undoubtedly increasing. There have been many times in history when young people were accused of advocating "free love" and sexual promiscuity. In the 1950s, some such persons were called "beatniks" in the mass media. In the 1960s they were called "hippies." In the 1970s, some were known as "freaks." Whatever term was applied, it is incorrect to conclude that young people have ever held one universal standard. And the permissiveness-without-affection standard never ran rampant. There are a variety of sexual standards among American youth, and our society is becoming increasingly willing to allow each individual to choose his or her own standard.

One study of the moral judgments of college students found that there were six categories of sexual philosophy which could be identified on a campus (D'Augelli, 1972). These categories are not really sexual standards, as are those mentioned above, but rather are descriptions of the sexual experiences or potential for sexual experience found in a given setting (D'Augelli, 1972; D'Augelli & Cross, 1975):

1. *Inexperienced virgins.* These individuals usually have little dating experience until college. Their dating relationships have not been serious or involved. They have not thought much about sex, about the relationship they desire, or about themselves. They may be moralistic about sex, although not necessarily. They have a close relationship with their parents and do not want to hurt them. Their sexual experience has usually been kissing, necking, or light petting.

2. *Adamant virgins.* These individuals are set in their idea that intercourse should be saved for marriage: "Virginity is a gift for the spouse" is a predominant theme. However, they may say that premarital intercourse is permissible for others—it is up to the individual. They say that they do not feel guilty about light or heavy petting but say they would feel guilty about going further. They often attribute control to the partner and presently pet with someone special. They do not

usually confine themselves to one partner. There is a sense that the marriage license is important in assuring that the partner is the "right" one. Their family or religion is often mentioned as directly influencing their sexual views.

3. *Potential nonvirgins.* These individuals often say that given the right situation, they would have intercourse. They say that they have not yet been in the right situation and/or have not yet met the right person. They feel that premarital intercourse is morally acceptable, but they have a high fear of pregnancy. They seem to want more security than they have in their present relationships, at least at the point of development in the relationship, and the ideas of commitment of some sort and love are important to them. They seem frustrated by their cautiousness or inconsistency.

4. *Engaged (or committed) nonvirgins.* These individuals have had intercourse usually with one person only, although not necessarily. This person is usually considered someone very much loved and may be the financé(e). Often, marriage or some future commitment is mentioned, but the important thing in justifying the sexual behavior is the love and commitment to the relationship between the partners. The relationship is described as very close and very important, and the development of that relationship is of high value to them. They usually have discussed sex with their partner. Morality is considered an individual's personal concern.

5. *Liberated nonvirgins.* These individuals engage in sex in a freer way than others. They have a freer, looser life-style and are not interested in the security of the relationship as much as in the relationship itself. Sex within the context of the meaning of the relationship is important, and what is stressed is the agreed-upon meaning for the two partners. The physical act itself is valued for its pleasure. Reciprocal pleasure-giving as well as other reciprocities is important.

6. *Confused nonvirgins.* These individuals engage in sex without real understanding of their motivation, the place of sex in their lives, or its effects on them. There is usually some ambivalence about having had intercourse under these circumstances, especially if there have been many partners. The relationships between them and their partners gradually terminate. They seem generally confused about themselves and may be characterized as having a diffuse identity. Sex is seen as a pleasure and a need; it also seems to be the means to an end, an attempt to establish relationships.

CONSEQUENCES OF ADOLESCENT SEXUALITY

Let us acknowledge first of all that many adolescents find great satisfaction in their sexual relationships. Those who are having coitus willingly, without guilt, perhaps as a part of a steady, love-oriented relationship, may feel that sex ia a natural expression of the feelings they have for their partner. Furthermore, if these individuals are contraceptively protected, they may have very little worry about their involvement. Thus, not all the consequences of adolescent sexuality can be considered negative, unless a particular religious or moral criterion is used. However, there are many unfortunate consequences of adolescent sexuality that have become such important social issues that they tend to overshadow whatever positive consequences come to mind. Pregnancy outside of marriage and its possible outcomes—abortion, illegitimacy, forced marriage—constitute a prominent social problem in America today. Venereal disease is another possible consequence which we shall discuss.

Life entails risk. But apart from the circumstance of rape, the risk of pregnancy outside of marriage is entirely avoidable. Yet when abstinence is rejected as a sexual standard, an element of risk is always a consideration in sexual intercourse. The failure to use adequate contraception or any contraception at all drastically increases the risk of pregnancy, and our earlier discussion documents the magnitude of the potential problem. Thus, it should not be surprising to learn that pregnancy and childbirth among adolescents have come to be described in the last decade as a problem of epidemic proportions.

Extent of the problem

There is no way at present to get a complete and accurate picture of premarital pregnancies. But there are useful statistics giving some indication of frequency. If we assume a reasonable degree of validity in available statistics and we (1) combine figures for births recorded as illegitimate, (2) add children born within marriage but conceived before the wedding, (3) assume the addition of an unknown number of premarital pregnancies terminated by abortion before or after the wedding, and (4) realize there are an unknown number of such pregnancies ending with miscarriage or a stillborn child, we could conservatively estimate that there are at least 1 million *premarital* pregnancies each year in the United States. Certainly the major proportion of these pregnancies are likely to be among adolescent females. Zelnik and Kantner (1978b) estimate that almost 800,000 premarital pregnancies occur among females in the 15-to-19 age group each year. Contraceptive use is carefully considered in their analysis. They estimate that almost 700,000 additional adolescents would become pregnant each year if they did not use contraception. Furthermore, an additional 300,000 pregnancies could be prevented each year if contraception were used consistently by the sexually active females or their partners in this age group. They estimate that 9.3 percent of adolescent females aged 15 to 19 who have not yet married have been pregnant at least once.

Some adolescent females do not feel that the risk of pregnancy is very great for them. Exhibit 11.11 dramatically shows how mistaken this belief is. Fifty-eight percent of sexually active adolescents who have never used contraception had already been pregnant at least once by the date of the survey. Forty-two percent of the sometimes users had been pregnant. And even 11 percent of those always using contraception had been pregnant. The lowest pregnancy rates—about 6 percent— were for females who had always used an effective medical method, such as birth control pills. Another analysis of adolescent pregnancy considered females below the age of 15. Jaffe and Dryfoos (1976) estimated that 30,000 young girls under age 15 become pregnant each year in the United States.

Most recent studies of pregnancy among adolescents indicate a trend suggesting that females are becoming more regular and effective contraceptive users. Thus, there can be some optimism for the future with regard to adolescent pregnancies. With better accepted and more widespread sex education in the public schools, greater availability and use of effective contraception, and increasing social concern about the problem of adolescent sexuality and pregnancy, we can expect a gradual decrease in out-of-wedlock pregnancies among adolescent females. Nevertheless, the magnitude of the problem at present is still very great.

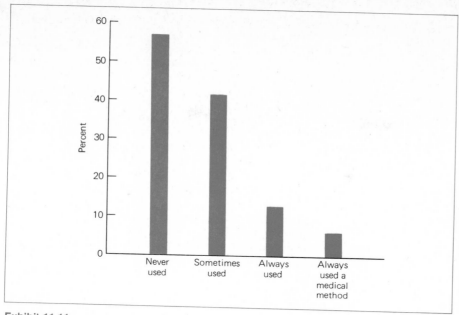

Exhibit 11.11
Percent of sexually active young women who ever had a premarital pregnancy, by contraceptive-use status. (Source: Zelnik & Kantner, 1977.)

Outcome of premarital pregnancy

Females facing a premarital pregnancy have four options.

1. They may marry.
2. They may have an abortion.
3. They may give birth to the child and keep it.
4. They may give birth to the child and give it up for adoption.

Actually, there is a fifth possibility that does not involve a decision on the part of the female—*miscarriage* (the technical name is *spontaneous abortion*). The third and fourth options lead to what is known as an *illegitimate* birth, a term referring to any birth outside of marriage.

What do American adolescents do when faced with a pregnancy? Of the females who had ever been pregnant by the time they were interviewed in 1976 (Zelnik & Kantner, 1978a), 28 percent married before the outcome of the pregnancy. An additional 9 percent married after the outcome of the pregnancy, and the remaining 63 percent never married by the time of the interview. Eleven percent of the females who had ever been pregnant were pregnant at the time of the interview, and they are included in the above figures.

In this national study of females aged 15 to 19, the researchers found that among White females, about half of all first pregnancies terminated in abortion. About 3 in

10 of the pregnancies culminated in live births, about 1 in 6 pregnancies ended in miscarriage, and 1.6 percent of the females had stillbirths.

There are some significant racial differences in how the outcome of a pregnancy is managed. Whites are about four times as likely as Blacks to marry after discovering that they are pregnant. Data on abortion among Blacks are not as reliable as that available for Whites, but Zelnik and Kantner (1978b) estimate that Blacks are much more likely to carry a premarital pregnancy to term, while Whites are much more likely to have an abortion. About 5 out of every 6 Black adolescent females who report ever being pregnant state that they continued the pregnancy and had the child. Considering this tendency to continue a pregnancy and their lesser likelihood of marriage following a pregnancy, it is easy to understand why young Black females have an illegitimacy rate which is substantially higher than the rate of Whites. Let us now examine the various options following premarital pregnancy, beginning with an illegitimate birth.

Illegitimacy There are three categories of births of interest to us when we examine the overall phenomenon of adolescent fertility. Since some individuals marry while in the adolescent years, births to these individuals are considered legitimate and do not show up in discussions of adolescent illegitimacy. Other births are conceived outside of marriage but occur following a hasty, or, in some cases, an already planned, marriage. But other births are conceived and delivered out-of-wedlock (Baldwin, 1976). In 1974, 85 percent of births to females under 15 were out-of-wedlock. Forty-eight percent of births to females aged 15 to 17 were born out-of-wedlock. And 27 percent of births to females aged 18 to 19 were delivered before the female married (National Center for Health Statistics, 1976). In the most recent ten-year period studied, the proportion of teenage births which were out-of-wedlock more than doubled (Baldwin, 1976). Stated differently, marriage is becoming a less popular solution to a premarital pregnancy.

In 1975, there were 11,000 females in the United States under age 15 who gave birth outside of marriage. In addition, 222,500 unmarried females aged 15 to 19 gave birth that year. These births account for more than half of all births outside of marriage to American women. These figures increased by more than 15 percent in a five-year period and more than tripled in a twenty-year period (U.S. Bureau of the Census, 1977a). The illegitimacy rate has decreased in recent years for women in all age and racial groups except for White females under 20 (National Center for Health Statistics, 1977a). Remember that these figures are for *births* and not pregnancies.

In 1976, the overall fertility rate for all women in the United States reached an all-time low. Corresponding to this change, the fertility rate for all adolescent females also decreased. However, looking just at those who are unmarried still shows that in this year of record low fertility, unmarried adolescent White females maintained the same level of illegitimacy, while Black adolescent females experienced a decrease of 4 percent in their illegitimacy rate (National Center for Health Statistics, 1978). Blacks historically have had higher illegitimacy rates, and this still is so today. However, for several years now, the Black-White differential in illegitimacy has been decreasing, and it seems likely that the rates will continue to converge in coming years.

As we mentioned above, young women giving birth to a baby can either keep the child or give it up for adoption. Approximately 18 percent of babies born to unmarried White adolescents are given up for adoption, and an additional 6 percent live with other relatives or friends of the mother (Zelnik & Kantner, 1978a). Thus, more than three-fourths of illegitimate White babies are not given up for adoption. This may account for the relative scarcity of White babies available for adoption in a period when many married couples are becoming increasingly willing to adopt children (Baldwin, 1976). Only 6 percent of the infants born to unmarried adolescent Black females live with anyone other than their mothers. Thus, Black females are even less likely to give their children up for adoption.

The consequences of adolescent childbearing are great. We shall document in Chapter 15 the extent of the social and economic problems presented by adolescent childbearing. Among the problems are higher infant mortality, greater health risks for both mother and baby, and a number of social and economic consequences for the mother and child throughout a significant part of the life span.

Marriage As mentioned earlier, only a minority of adolescent women now marry as a result of an unexpected pregnancy. If the female was engaged when the pregnancy started and her fiancé is the father of the child, the situation is as favorable as it could be under the circumstances. If she marries a man whom she would not otherwise marry, the marriage gets an unfavorable start. If she marries a man she knows is not the father of the child and does not tell him she is pregnant, in some states the man has grounds for annulment or divorce, should that fact become known after the wedding. At best, such a procedure is a serious form of misrepresentation. A woman may, and in some cases does, marry a man who accepts the child even knowing that he is not the father.

If a couple have intercourse when they are not ready to marry, will they be more ready if a pregnancy leads them to marry earlier? There is evidence to suggest that marriages entered in order to camouflage a premarital pregnancy may be more than ordinarily unstable. The divorce rate is more than twice as high for those marriages in which childbirth occurs before the wedding. The difference in divorce rates is not as great, however, when conception, but not childbirth, occurred before marriage (Grabill, 1976).

Abortion More than 1 million legal abortions are now performed in the United States each year (Sullivan, Tietze, & Dryfoos, 1977). In 1976, there were 1.1 million abortions among all American women. Approximately one-third of these abortions were given to females aged 19 and under. An additional third of abortions are performed on young women age 20 to 24. Adolescent females are accounting for an increasingly larger share of abortions in the United States each year (Center for Disease Control, 1977).

Abortion is recognized by professionals as a safe procedure with very low complication rates. Only about 1 percent of abortions performed legally in the United States result in any complications. However, the risk of complication increases with the length of the period of gestation, and adolescent females for a variety of reasons often delay obtaining their abortion until beyond the thirteenth week of pregnancy, before which abortion is relatively simple and safe. The delay may be related to inadequate information about the diagnosis of pregnancy, ignorance of the early symptoms and signs of pregnancy, an unwillingness to admit that it might have happened, or fear of telling someone. As a result, adolescent females seeking abortions may experience higher complication rates than women in the other reproductive years (Baldwin, 1976).

The fact that nearly 400,000 adolescent females (including at least 15,000 under the age of 15) have an abortion each year in the United States suggests that it ought to be a topic of discussion and concern among parents and those who work with adolescents. Less is known about the social and psychological consequences of abortion than of the medical and health consequences. Although research suggests that abortion is not usually a traumatic experience for females, anecdotal reports illustrate that some young females are troubled by the experience for some time after the abortion.

Consequences for males

Since females get pregnant and males do not, we tend to think mostly about the consequences of pregnancy for the female. However, the male and his feelings should not be neglected. Sexual relationships during the adolescent years have potential rewards and potential pitfalls for the male as well. Whether or not a pregnancy results, the consequences can be troublesome. Let us review those which are possible.

An unwanted pregnancy The greatest risk that a man faces is a possible pregnancy for the female. He may disclaim any involvement with her, but in the typical case, men acknowledge their involvement and are affected by the pregnancy. The female carries the greater burden because, after all, she is pregnant and will usually be considered legally responsible for the child. The man, however, may be faced with the expenses of an abortion, a forced marriage, or a wedding which is moved up quickly. Above all, perhaps, he must at a more personal or emotional level deal with the problem he has had a role in creating. But the consequences for the male may be even more severe.

Accusation of rape by force Most cases of rape are violent acts committed by troubled men. However, cases are not unknown in which a woman voluntarily has sexual intercourse, and afterward, because she feels guilty, or because the fact is discovered, or for some other reason, she claims rape (see MacDonald, 1973). Usually there are no witnesses to intercourse. Hence, it is the man's word against the woman's. She may not succeed in making her accusation hold up in court. But even after the fire is put out, so to speak, the odor of smoke remains in the air, and there may be people who still wonder whether the man was guilty and justice miscarried.

Accusation of statutory rape Typically, state law specifies an "age of consent." This is the minimum age which an unmarried girl must have reached in order legally to give consent to sexual intercourse. If she is below the age of consent, she cannot legally consent to having intercourse even though she voluntarily says the words agreeing to it. A comparable situation is found in an individual's inability to sign a valid legal contract before age 18 or 21 even though his or her name is on the contract form.

Let us assume that in a given state the age of consent is 16. A physically well-developed 15-year-old girl claims to be 17. A 21-year-old man takes her at her word. She voluntarily has sexual intercourse. Her parents discover this fact and make known her correct age. The man with whom the girl had intercourse is liable to prosecution for statutory rape, which constitutes a felony.

Accusation of paternity If a woman becomes pregnant, any man who has had intercourse with her within a given time span is a possible candidate for an accusation of paternity.

Contrary to common assumption, paternity cannot be unequivocably ascertained by means of blood tests. It is true that blood types are hereditary. Blood tests made upon a man or men, mother, and child can ascertain whether a given man could or could not be the father. That is not equivalent, however, to determining that a given man *is* the father. For example, suppose Ms. X has a child. She admits having had intercourse with three men, namely, A, B, and C. Blood tests are made on all five persons. The tests indicate that Ms. X could not have had that child, with its particular blood type, with A or B. She could have had that child with C. That still does not prove beyond all doubt that C is the father. Miss X may not have mentioned D, with whom she also had intercourse and whose blood type is the same as C's.

Blood tests can establish *nonpaternity* as a certainty in some cases, but paternity only as a possibility. The scientific definition of "fact" and the legal definition of "fact" are not the same. The former implies certainty, while the latter implies only "beyond a reasonable doubt." The former is based on proof, the latter on evidence. Therefore, "proof" of paternity may reach a level of probability that is acceptable in a court (Krause, 1971).

Pressure to marry in case of acknowledged paternity   Pressure to marry in such cases may be "external" or "internal." It may come from parents, fear of gossip, or concern for reputation. Or it may come from a sense of responsibility.

If the couple are engaged, there may be no pressure in the usual sense of the term because they plan to marry anyway. Their problem is relatively simpler, involving only an actual or asserted change of wedding date. In some cases, however, marrying earlier than they had expected is a serious upset to a couple's families and to their educational and occupational plans.

If, on the other hand, the couple had not planned to marry, would not be good choices as marriage partners for one another, do not know each other well enough, or are not in love, marriage to camouflage a pregnancy or to give a child a legal father and a name may be damaging to all three persons.

Venereal disease

When an infection is transmitted primarily by sexual intercourse, it is called a *venereal disease*. Such diseases are named after Venus, the goddess of love, because their primary mode of transmission is through sexual activity (Katchadourian, 1977). There are several common infections of the genital tract which are transmitted through sexual intercourse. Trichomoniasis, herpes simplex virus type 2, vaginal thrush, the "crabs," and prostatitis are common infections of the genital tract that are often transmitted by sexual intercourse with an infected person. These infections induce discharges and/or irritations which are a nuisance and sometimes difficult to treat (Goldstein, 1976). Space does not permit going into detail regarding the organisms that cause these diseases or their symptoms, cures, and effects. Our point of focus will be the risk of contracting one of the two most serious types of venereal diseases, *syphilis* and *gonorrhea*.

Syphilis and gonorrhea are both very contagious. Of reported cases of syphilis, 95 percent are contracted through intercourse, and the other 5 percent are contracted through kissing when there is a cut or scratch in the mucous membrane of the lips or mouth, by oral-genital contact, by prenatal transmission, or by transfusion. Gonorrhea is almost always contracted through sexual intercourse. Reports of contagion by means of bathtubs, swimming pools, and toilet seats are without foundation in fact. It is difficult to get accurate statistics on the incidence of syphilis and gonorrhea

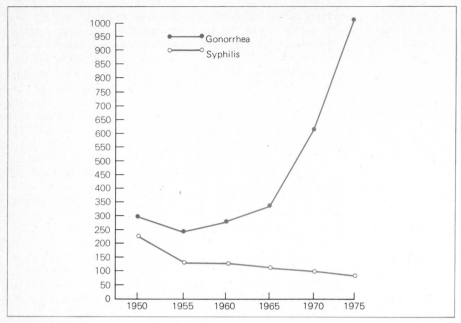

Exhibit 11.12
Cases of gonorrhea and syphilis reported in the United States, 1950–1975. (*Source:* U.S. Bureau of the Census, *Statistical Abstract*, 1977, p. 114.)

because only a proportion of cases are reported. This fact must be kept in mind in interpreting figures indicating changes in incidence. It is possible that part, although by no means all, of any apparent increase in incidence is due to better reporting. Thus, the data reported in Exhibit 11.12 suggest both a possible marked increase in gonorrhea and in addition perhaps a greater willingness to bring these diseases to the attention of health authorities. The reported incidence of syphilis, however, has declined.

There is evidence that the incidence of venereal disease, particularly gonorrhea, is increasing dramatically among adolescents. In 1975, there were 1,000,000 *reported* cases of gonorrhea for the population as a whole, an increase of more than 100,000 over the previous year. There were 80,000 new cases of syphilis reported (U.S. Bureau of the Census, 1977a). There are no accurate data available on other forms of venereal disease. A major portion of the increase in venereal disease is accounted for by adolescents. There has been a particularly striking increase among males and females in the 10-to-14 age category, although the prevalence for individuals of this age group is small compared to the 15-to-19 and 20-to-24 age groups. The majority of the cases of venereal disease reported in the United States occur among persons younger than 25 years (Johns, Sutton, & Webster, 1975). One in ten in this age group contracts venereal disease in a given year.

There is now what may be interpreted as an epidemic. The World Health Organization ranks gonorrhea as the most prevalent communicable disease after the common cold. The situation concerning venereal disease is serious any way it is considered, but there are several facts that further complicate it relative to premarital intercourse. Reported cases of gonorrhea and syphilis are about twice as numerous among males as among females. As many as 80 percent of females and a small proportion of males who have gonorrhea are asymptomatic; that is, they have the disease and can transmit it to others, but they themselves show no symptoms of it (American Social Health Association, 1975). Of course, the presence of the disease can be detected by laboratory tests. Asymptomatic individuals are generally not aware of the fact that they have gonorrhea. Syphilis may become asymptomatic only after the primary and secondary states of the disease have passed, and this may be several years after the original infection (American Social Health Association, 1975).

There is a not uncommon tendency to treat gonorrhea as being no more serious than, say, a cold. But complications of the disease in women account for 175,000 hospital admissions totaling 1,200,000 hospital-patient days per year. On any given day, an average of 3,200 patients are hospitalized and an estimated 5,750 girls are absent from school as a result of gonorrhea infections (American Social Health Association, 1975).

At one time it was thought that penicillin would prove to be the ultimate cure for syphilis and gonorrhea. It is still effective in most cases. But some gonorrhea organisms are becoming partially resistant to it. Other antibiotics are being used with some success, but the final answer has not yet been found (Neumann & Baecker, 1972; Rudolph, 1972; Schroeter & Lucas, 1972).

The only contraceptive that is even partially effective in preventing venereal disease contagion is the condom. Fiumara (1972) mentions conditions (some of which would be likely to make intercourse less than satisfactory) to be met before the condom is effective against gonorrhea. There must be no preliminary sex play involving the genitals before putting the condom on; the condom must be intact before and after use; it must be put on and taken off correctly. Even if all these conditions are met, the condom is more protection against gonorrhea than against syphilis because it does not cover all the areas of the couple's bodies that may come into contact (Hart, 1975). With the increasingly widespread use of contraceptive methods (especially the pill) designed for women, a reasonable guess would be that more men will leave the responsibility for contraception to the woman, and consequently fewer men will use the condom. Some investigators believe that this is now happening and that it is one of the reasons for the rising incidence of venereal infection.

SEX EDUCATION

Sex education is a topic of special importance in the study of adolescent development. *Sex education* is the process of teaching an individual to understand and accept himself or herself as a person with sexual feelings and reproductive capabilities. Sex education includes learning to interact with individuals in a healthy, constructive, and meaningful manner. It also involves learning to fit sexuality into a pattern of behavior which allows the person to function as a responsible member of society. Many believe that an important objective of adolescent development is to achieve a balance between socialization and conformity on the one hand and individual freedom, growth, and realization of one's potential on the other. Nowhere is the need for such a balance more apparent than in connection with sex education.

In light of the high and increasing prevalence of sexual relations before marriage, society's stigma against pregnancy outside of marriage, and the data indicating lack of contraceptive use among many sexually active adolescents, sex education has become strongly advocated by some, although others find sex education controversial and approach it cautiously.

Why sex education?

The most powerful argument of sex education is that children and adolescents engage in sexual activity (including masturbation, childhood sex play, and heterosexual kissing, petting, and intercourse), and will continue to do so throughout their lives. Advocates of sex education believe that an informed adolescent is better off than an uninformed adolescent. All humans need to learn about sex sometime, and most experts now agree that sex education should begin early.

The most controversial aspects surrounding sex education are not really whether it should be given, but where. Most would agree that the home is a proper place for sex education, but many parents don't have the knowledge and skills to impart such knowledge to their children in a complete way. Some parents are ill-informed themselves, and some are too bashful to bring up the topic in front of their children. As a result, many adolescents have never had a discussion about human sexuality with their parents.

Some believe sex education belongs in church. But not everyone attends church, and many religious denominations or individual congregations do not have a plan for sex education or specific programs that can be used. Since the social institutions of family and church in most instances do not provide adequate sex education, many look to the school for such instruction. It is here that the controversy emerges. Although schools throughout the country now offer sex education in some form, many school districts are reluctant to initiate such programs, and parents in some communities feel strongly that it should be avoided.

One fear is that by discussing sex, adolescents will get ideas that they did not have previously. Research indicates that influences from dating partners and peers are the most profound influences on adolescent sexuality, while sex education is not at all influential (Spanier, 1976a). Perhaps fears that an adolescent who hears about sex in the classroom will therefore experiment with sex should be laid to rest. Fears about sex education must be considered against the possible benefits.

It has been argued by sex educators that adolescents who are well-informed at least are able to make a choice. If they do decide to have sexual intercourse, for example, their sex education may instruct them about contraceptive preparation. They may have a more clear idea about what is involved in a sexual relationship, and may have been provided the opportunity to think about what it means to them. Consequently, they may feel better about the decision they have made and may be better able to put sex in a realistic perspective.

Many would argue that even if some adolescents participated in sexual relations more freely as a result of sex education, this would be tolerable by society if it also meant that many other adolescents could avoid an unwanted pregnancy, an early forced marriage, or the possibility of an abortion. Of course, our purpose in this discussion is not to debate the moral issues involved in sexual behavior, sex education, or the consequences of either. Rather, it is important to point out what some of the issues are in communities and school systems.

When should sex education begin?

Social scientists and sex educators almost universally recommend that sex education begin in the home very early in the child's development. Sex education should then be a collaborative effort between the family and the school, with the school taking on progressively more responsibility for the academic aspects of sex education. Some might wonder how or why a young child would receive sex education. Most sex educators believe that persons should obtain knowledge about sex and reproduction at the ages at which they can understand reasonably well the various aspects of the topic. A 3- or 4-year-old child may simply wonder where babies come from, or why his or her mother's tummy is swollen. Such a child only needs to be told that there is a baby growing inside the mother, and have explained in very general terms how this event came about.

There is a story of the 3-year-old who asked his mother where he came from. The concerned mother, who had been preparing for this moment for over a year, gave the overwhelmed child a 20-minute talk on sperms and eggs, fertilization, labor and delivery. The child responded, "Oh, I thought I came from Chicago. Johnny says he is from New York." The story illustrates that this child needed perhaps only the briefest of answers. At age 10, however, the child would, of course, require a more detailed and complex answer, and at age 14 or 15, a different answer still.

What should be taught?

Sex education, then, may begin early in the home, and continue in the school, with lessons on family relationships, basic biology, and later, human physiology and anatomy. Females need to learn about menstruation before they begin menstruating. Men would best learn about nocturnal emissions before they begin to contend with them. And males and females both ought to have some understanding of the entire reproductive process before they are likely to experience it firsthand. It is also argued that a female should know of the potential consequences of pregnancy out of marriage, and how to avoid such an event. Males have a role in reproduction, even though we are most readily aware of the consequences for females. Thus, the trend has been toward mixed male and female classes for health and sex education.

The degree to which the school should be involved in teaching the values that accompany sexual behavior receives less agreement from experts. Some argue that sexuality cannot be taught outside of a context of values, but others argue that the school should stick to the facts, and let the parents and religious institutions teach the values.

It is likely that sex education will become nearly universal in coming years. Many states now require some form of sex education. Some schools teach sex education as a part of a health education program. And some school systems have comprehensive sex education programs beginning with kindergarten and continuing through the end of high school.

Formal versus informal sex education

Most sex education traditionally has taken place outside of the home, religious institution, and school classroom. Adolescents for centuries have learned about sex mostly from peers. In modern times, information from peers is commonly supplemented by the mass media and by independent reading. Of course, information obtained in these ways often leads to misconceptions about human sexuality, since peers often are unreliable sources of information on the topic, and impressions from the mass media may be very biased.

Independent reading can be a profitable source of information for the adolescent—if the material is accurate. But much of what can be bought is not prepared for the purpose of informing adolescents about reproduction and normative sexual behavior. To the contrary, much written material is prepared for adults, and may feature nonnormative forms of sexual relationships and behaviors.

The movement toward sex education in the schools, then, may have the advantage for future adolescents of informing them, before they are faced with decisions about their own sexual behavior, about accurate information which they may profitably use in making such decisions. Adolescents of the future may be able to avoid some of the conflict and confusion that their older siblings and parents experienced when they were younger. They may be spared the process of having to unlearn incorrect facts, and reformulate ideas based on misconceptions. However, there will likely always be a mystique surrounding sex which will for some time in the future make sexual behavior and relationships a topic of special interest to adolescents.

LOVE AND INTIMACY

A discussion of all of the "facts" about adolescent sexuality can lose sight of one very important fact that relates to most of the others. Typically adolescent sexuality is associated with an intimate relationship between two persons who care about each other very much. There are exceptions, of course, and we have pointed out how variable adolescent sexuality is. But sex most often occurs in the context of a union which at the time is thought by the adolescents to be fairly stable. Love and intimacy, therefore, are topics which are very important to any consideration of sexual behavior.

Love has different meanings to different people. One's definition of love will vary depending on the background and experiences of the person involved, the nature of the love object, the period in the individual's life, the intensity of the individual's attraction to the love object, and the importance the individual places on being in love. Most adolescents have had some experience with romantic love. The intensity, duration, and frequency can all be quite variable, but the emotion seems to be recognizable to most adolescents. Love can often be a justification for sex. Adolescent males, probably more than females, have been known to profess love to their partner or to exaggerate it in order to encourage the partner to become more sexually involved than he or she otherwise might. For many males and females, love is the crucial component in the reasoning process that leads to the reduction of guilt and the redefinition of values discussed earlier in the chapter. Finally, love is the key that allows some individuals to alter the meaning of sex, for example, from a body-oriented activity to another-person-oriented status.

Love is a powerful emotion. When sex is seen by the adolescent as an expression of this emotion, the likelihood of sexual intercourse is great. Some adolescents are taught, and continue to believe, that marriage is the appropriate time when coitus, as an ultimate expression of love, is appropriate. Other adolescents do not readily differentiate between recreational sex and procreational sex, and consequently believe that sex must wait until marriage since that is the appropriate time to begin procreating.

INSIGHT INTO ADOLESCENCE

James Joyce was an Irish writer born in 1882; he died in 1941. His novel, *A Portrait of the Artist as a Young Man*, describes a boy's life from early childhood to young manhood. It is also the story of the growth of an artist who is trying to see his life. In writing this novel, Joyce obviously vividly remembered his own experiences, feeling them at the same time.

A girl stood before him in midstream, alone and still, gazing out to sea. She seemed like one whom magic had changed into the likeness of a strange and beautiful seabird. Her long slender bare legs were delicate as a crane's and pure save where an emerald trail of seaweed had fashioned itself as a sign upon the flesh. Her thighs, fuller and softhued as ivory, were bared almost to the hips where the white fringes of her drawers were like featherings of soft white down. Her slateblue skirts were kilted boldly about her waist and dovetailed behind her. Her bosom was as a bird's soft and slight, slight and soft as the breast of some darkplumaged dove. But her long fair hair was girlish: and girlish, and touched with the wonder of mortal beauty, her face.

She was alone and still, gazing out to sea; and when she felt his presence and the worship of his eyes her eyes turned to him in quiet sufferance of his gaze, without shame or wantonness. Long, long she suffered his gaze and then quietly withdrew her eyes from his and bent them towards the stream, gently stirring the water with her foot hither and thither. The first faint noise of gently moving water broke the silence, low and faint and whispering, faint as the bells of sleep; hither and thither, hither and thither: and a faint flame trembled on her cheek.

—Heavenly God! cried Stephen's soul, in an outburst of profane joy.

He turned away from her suddenly and set off across the strand. His cheeks were aflame; his body was aglow; his limbs were trembling. On and on and on and on he strode, far out over the sands, singing wildly to the sea, crying to greet the advent of the life that had cried to him.

Her image had passed into his soul for ever and no word had broken the holy silence of his ecstasy. Her eyes had called him and his soul had leaped at the call. To live, to err, to fall, to triumph, to recreate life out of life! A wild angel had appeared to him, the angel of mortal youth and beauty, an envoy from the fair courts of life, to throw open before him in an instant of ecstasy the gates of all the ways of error and glory. On and on and on and on!

Source: Joyce, J. *A Portrait of the artist as a young man*, Viking Press, 1976.

The intimate nature of sexual intercourse and that which precedes it often produce anxiety for sexually inexperienced adolescents and young adults. Socialization for modesty has to be overcome, fears about sexual performance need to be managed, and a concern about awkwardness is common. Many males and females do not find their first sexual experiences enjoyable because of these factors. Indeed, the anxiety of early sexual experiences may be associated with brief impotence among males and poor vaginal lubrication among females. Tension and fears surrounding the experience heighten these complicating responses. Although these symptoms of "sexual dysfunction" tend to be short-lived and of little lasting consequence, they do not help make the adolescent's transition to his or her new experience very smooth. Indeed, some adolescent males and females find that their relationship falters or terminates following sexual intercourse. In some cases, the episode so disrupts the relationship that it does not recover. How and why this happens in some cases has not been studied.

On the other hand, for many adolescents, the transition from virginity to nonvirginity is practically unnoticeable, since coitus may be physically a very small increment in the progression of the individual's sexual behavior. In other words, persons who are very involved physically with their partner but have not yet had intercourse may find that intercourse is a slight increment in the intensity of their involvement. In these cases, the event may occur without much thought, anxiety, or concern at the time.

The intense feelings which accompany intimate love relationships have implications for other aspects of the adolescent's life. Romantic love may exist coincidentally with love for parents, siblings, and others. How the adolescent deals with these types of love depends both on the adolescent's personal characteristics and on the larger social system of which the individual, the family, and friends are a fundamental part.

CHAPTER SUMMARY

It is with adolescence that sexual development, sexual behavior, and sexual interaction take on special importance to the individual. Society too has a great interest in the sexuality of adolescents, since some of our greatest social problems—abortion, illegitimacy, and early marriage—are all related to adolescent sexuality.

Sexual socialization is the process all persons go through which results in our ability to function sexually in a given culture. This process has five components: development of *sex-object preference*, which determines our orientation toward *homosexuality* or *heterosexuality*; development of *gender identity*, which identifies us as male or female; development of sex roles, which leads us to define roles as masculine, feminine, or some other way; acquiring sexual skills, knowledge, and values, which involves sex education, the attainment of actual sexual skills, and acquisition of a value system; and development of dispositions to act in sexual contexts, which establishes the link between one's attitudes and values and actual behavior.

Adolescence is different from childhood in that behaviors which appear to be sexual to adults now may take on sexual meaning for the adolescents themselves. In childhood, both heterosexual and homosexual play is common, but it is not until adolescence that adult sexual *meaning* is attached to these behaviors. It was Kinsey and his associates that first provided comprehensive data on these various behaviors, and now ample research confirms the nature and extent of childhood and adolescent sexual behavior.

Masturbation for both males and females and nocturnal emissions for males only are two forms of sexual behavior found normally in adolescence. Holding hands, kissing, and *petting* are forms of sexual interaction that become increasingly prevalent in adolescence. Sexual intercourse is now experienced by the majority of adolescents in the United States, although for many the event does not occur until late adolescence, and for others the frequency of such involvement and the duration of the relationships involved may be very short. Although there is now more sexual behavior during adolescence than at any previous time in history, it is still debatable whether there has been a sexual revolution. It can be argued that the term *sexual evolution* is a more appropriate notion, since the changes that have occurred in American society have really been gradual and in many ways consistent with other social change.

Sexual intercourse begins in early adolescence for a small number of persons, but by late adolescence, about half of White females and five-sixths of Black females (and even higher proportions of males) have become sexually active. Sexual intercourse usually first takes place in someone's home, most often the home of the male. Contrary to what some might believe, most adolescents who are sexually active have had only a small number of partners, with half having had only one partner. Unfortunately, most adolescents are not contraceptively protected when they begin sexual activity, and a large proportion are inadequately protected throughout adolescence. As a result, there are a great number of pregnancies among adolescent females.

Adolescents have differing sexual standards. Those having an *abstinence* standard believe that sex before marriage is wrong for both males and females, regardless of the feelings involved. The *permissiveness-with-affection* standard says that sex before marriage is acceptable for both males and females as long as there is emotional attachment or love. The *permissiveness-without-affection* standard proposes that premarital intercourse is right whenever there is physical attraction, regardless of the degree of affection. The *double standard* exists when sex is considered right for men but wrong for women. Other sexual standards also exist.

There are hundreds of thousands of premarital pregnancies each year in the United States. Adolescent females who become pregnant have four options: they may marry, have an abortion, give birth to the child and keep it, or give birth to the child and give it up for adoption. Abortion is the most common alternative, and the large majority of abortions performed in the United States are on unmarried females, mostly adolescents. There are many consequences of an unwanted pregnancy for *both* males and females.

Sex education is perhaps the most promising way of reversing the trend of increasing unwanted pregnancies among adolescents. Education can also be helpful in alerting adolescents to the possibility of venereal disease, and to some of the biological facts and social-psychological issues relevant to adolescent sexual development. Sex education may also provide an opportunity for adolescent males and females to discuss the relationships between dating, love, and sex. Such discussion is important since love and intimacy are topics which are not separated easily from the topic of sex.

12

PERSONALITY DEVELOPMENT IN ADOLESCENCE

CHAPTER
OVERVIEW

There are many ways in which scientists define personality. This chapter presents a definition derived from a life-span view. The ideas of Erik Erikson are then used to describe personality. The issue of identity, central to Erikson's theory, is discussed and related to theory and research on personality development in adolescence.

ISSUES
TO CONSIDER

Why is the definition of personality a primary issue in the study of personality development?

How may adolescent personality development be conceptualized from a life-span view?

In what ways does the theory of Erik Erikson provide a description of adolescent personality development that is consistent with a life-span definition?

How does society impose changing adaptational demands on the developing person?

What are the major characteristics of Erikson's stage theory of psychosocial development? How do stages prior to adolescence contribute to development in this period? How are succeeding stages influenced by events in adolescence?

Why is the issue of ego identity the core one in the adolescent period?

Does research evidence support Erikson's ideas about the sequence of ego development?

What are the types of ego identity statuses adolescents may attain, and what is the developmental course for each of these?

How is the development of adolescent identity affected by other psychological processes?

How do social interactive processes affect the development of adolescent identity?

«P ersonality" is a term in the vocabulary of most people. It is also a concept used by many social scientists. However, the way most people use the word differs from the manner in which it most typically is used by scientists. In its common, everyday use personality is often seen as something which helps one "win friends and influence people," something which can be turned on or off at will (as in "turn on your personality when you go for a job interview"). Often, personality also is seen as something a person develops to make up for deficits in other areas (for example, we hear people say that a person is not good-looking but that he or she has a good personality). Yet despite this range of everyday "definitions" of personality, no conception within this range corresponds to the use of the term in science.

Most social scientists use the term personality to refer to some *relatively* enduring characteristics of an individual. Yet in trying to describe and explain the basis and nature of these characteristics of individuality, there is as much variety of opinion among social scientists as there is among non-scientists. Indeed, Wiggins (1968) wrote more than a decade ago that the primary scientific issue in the study of personality was one of defining the term. This problem still exists today.

The issue is not one of asking whether people have particular patterns of thoughts, feelings, and behaviors. Rather, it is one of asking where the particular set of characteristics that typifies a person comes from, and precisely what are these characteristics. We may recognize the former concern as the nature-nurture issue. Some theorists, like Lorenz (1965) or Hall (1904), see the characteristics that make up the person as lying in instincts, while other theorists, like Davis (1944), Mischel (1970), or Bijou (1976), see external stimuli as shaping the person. Thus, while the former group of theorists emphasizes bases of personality lying within the person, the latter emphasizes bases of personality lying within the situation. Still another group of theorists stresses that a person's behavior derives from an interaction between person and situation (Bowers, 1973), and a range of opinion exists also about the type of interaction between person and context that is involved in individuality.

Not only do scientists disagree about the bases of personality, but they do not have similar ideas about what the component thoughts, feelings, or behaviors of the individual are, or in fact, whether all these things are necessary to study in the assessment of personality. One way of understanding this controversy is to focus on an often-cited observation by Kluckhohn and Murray (1948, p. 35), that in certain respects every person is (*a*) like all other people; (*b*) like some other people; and (*c*) like no other person (Gallatin, 1975). Most existing ideas of personality have tended to focus on only one of these three aspects of the individual and have downgraded or ignored the other two.

For instance, the stage theory of Sigmund Freud (1949) emphasizes that all people pass through the specified psychosexual stages in an invariant sequence. Hence, in stressing such universality, Freud is indicating that any person is like all others. The constitutional typology of William Sheldon (1940, 1942) emphasizes that people exist in personality (or temperament) groups, depending on their possession of a physique that is predominantly either endomorphic, mesomorphic, or ectomorphic. Thus, in stressing that such types of people exist, Sheldon is indicating that a given person is like some, but not all, others.

Finally, the mechanistic, social learning theories we have described (Bijou, 1976; Bijou & Baer, 1961; Davis, 1944; McCandless, 1970) are conceptions which have the potential of showing that any person is unique. Although the basis of behavior—the nurture laws of S-R learning—remains the same for all people, any given person may encounter any particular S-R, reward-punishment history. As such, any person could have a unique repertoire of behavior. Indeed, Mischel (1973), a leading representative of this social learning position, has argued that in the real world, such differences in learning history invariably occur. As a consequence, a given person is like no other (Mischel, 1973).

In summary, because of differences in ideas about the basis of personality and about the characteristics that make up personality, there is no single definition of personality that can be agreed on. Yet a *useful* conception of personality can be advanced. In our view, such a conception would not focus on *just* universal, or group, or individual characteristics. This would be incomplete. For example, although the views of Freud, Sheldon, and Mischel are useful in depicting the universal, group, and individual characteristics of a person, respectively, their use is limited by the fact that they do not consider how these three types of characteristics interrelate. Every person has (1) universal characteristics, for example, those relating to continual orientations to adaptation and survival; (2) group characteristics, for example, those relating to society and culture membership; *and* (3) individual characteristics, for example, those pertaining to the unique genotype-environment interaction of the person. Accordingly, it appears that a most useful definition of personality would be one which considers the range of individual (or *idiographic*) *and* general (or *nomothetic*) characteristics a person may possess, and how these characteristics are related to the person's social world. This chapter attempts to offer such a definition.

A life-span view of development emphasizes that change is constant across life, and that any one part of life is a consequence of preceding portions and an antecedent of following portions. Second, the context within which the person develops is constantly changing also. This indicates the need for a multidisciplinary orientation, and suggests that a *personological* analysis of personality is limited. Such a view seeks to understand individual changes by looking at individual phenomena only.

Consistent with discussions in earlier chapters, personality can be assumed to have the following attributes:

1. Personality is seen as a life-span process.

2. As such, any particular portion of the life span is understood in terms of how it is textured and shaped by the developments in life preceding it, and in turn, how it similarly contributes to the portions of the life span following it.

3. This life-span progression is understood best by examining processes lying at all levels of analysis. This leads to a view encompassing both general (for example, adaptational) and specific (for example, familial) aspects of the person throughout the life span, including adolescence.

Although as transitionary as is any portion of the life span, the adolescent period, involving so many changes (in cognition, physiology, physique, morality, and sexuality, to name just a few), may produce special adaptational demands on the person. The body looks and feels different, the person thinks differently, may judge right and wrong differently, engages in different types of social relationships, and acquires a new genital capacity. The combination of all these transitions has a dramatic effect. Prior to adolescence the person's characteristics changed in less rapid ways (for example, the quantitative changes involved in height and weight), and were thought of by the person in relatively concrete, nonabstract terms. Thus, while going through such changes relatively gradually, the person's definition of self could be based on relatively continuous, concrete cues.

However, in adolescence, the attributes defining the person are in a state of change, and their eventual developmental end point is far from certain. Yet the adolescent must integrate all these changing cues by reestablishing a definition of self. This will provide a basis for contending with all the various pressures of biological, psychological, social, and cultural changes.

Thus, defining or identifying oneself becomes a central task in adolescence. Who one is, one's identity, gives the individual an integrated specification of what he or she will *do*: with one's body, with one's sexuality, with one's mind, with one's relationships, and with one's morality. In short, having a self-definition, or an identity, gives one a *role* to play.

THE ROLE OF ERIKSON'S THEORY

The theory of Erik Erikson (1959, 1963, 1968) places primary stress on the attainment of a role as a basis for the adolescent's successful achievement of an identity. Erikson sees adolescence as a stage of development having universal features. He *explains* the universality of these features by relying on a maturationally based, critical-periods-hypothesis conception of stage progression.

Erikson's account of personality development includes many of the attributes of a life-span conception. Erikson *describes* personality development as a life-span process, sees adolescence as a major transition between childhood and adulthood, and uses multidisciplinary ideas to understand the adolescent (identity is based on attaining a role, which is a socioculturally based set of behavior prescriptions).

Erikson divides the life span into eight stages of development. Like Freud, on whose theory he bases his own ideas, Erikson sees these stages as proceeding in a fixed, universal sequence. Moreover, within each stage a person is supposed to develop a particular component of his or her personality—specifically, a part of the ego—*if* he or she is to develop adaptively. However, a person does not have an infinite amount of time in which to accomplish this development. In accordance with one's innately fixed maturational timetable, Erikson (1959) believes that stage progression will continue independently of whether one has developed as expected. Since the focus of development shifts when a new stage emerges, it is *critical* that one

Erik H. Erickson

develop appropriately in each stage. Since there is no environmental interaction that can alter the maturational timetable of progression, if one does not develop as expected in a critical period, then (1) that part will never be developed as adequately as it might have been, and (2) the rest of development is altered unfavorably (Erikson, 1959).

Thus, while Erikson (1959, 1963, 1968) offers insightful and useful *descriptions* of phenomena associated with adolescence, his *explanations*, being based on weak interactional, universalistic, critical periods notions, suffer the shortcomings of such ideas. Yet it is possible to use Erikson's ideas at least as an *initial* framework for describing the phenomena associated with adolescent personality development. Indeed, much of the recent research literature on adolescent personality has taken these descriptions as a starting point (for example, Adams, Shea & Fitch, in press; Donovan, 1975; LaVoie & Adams, in press; Marcia, 1964, 1966, 1976; Munro & Adams, 1977; Schenkel, 1975; Toder & Marcia, 1973; Waterman & Goldman, 1976; Waterman, Kohutis, & Pulone, 1977; Waterman & Waterman, 1971) and is integrated by reference to this descriptive framework.

Some roots of Erikson's ideas

Erik H. Erikson was born in Frankfurt, Germany, in 1902, and moved to the United States in the early 1930s. As a young man, Erikson served as a tutor to the children of some of the associates of Sigmund Freud. While working in this capacity, Erikson came under the influence of both Sigmund Freud and his daughter Anna. Accordingly, Erikson received training in psychoanalysis, and after moving to the United States and settling in the Boston area, he soon established his expertise in the area of childhood psychoanalytic practice.

Through his practice, as well as through the results of some empirical investigations (Erikson, 1963), Erikson began to evolve a theory of affective (or emotional) development which complemented the theory of Sigmund Freud. Erikson's theory altered the essential focus of past psychoanalytic theorizing, from a focus on the id to one on the ego.

When one changes focus from the id to the ego, one immediately recognizes the necessity of dealing with the society around the person. The function of the ego is survival, adjustment to the demands of reality. That reality is shaped, formed, and provided by the society that the person is a part of. An appropriate adjustment to reality in one society, allowing the person to survive, might be inefficient or even totally inappropriate in another society. Hence, when one says that the child is adapting to reality, one is saying, in effect, that the child is adapting to the demands of his or her own particular society. To understand this societal shaping of adaptational demands, it may be noted that society itself is an adaptive phenomenon.

THE ADAPTIVE NATURE OF SOCIETY

A society would not exist if humans could survive in complete social isolation. Social interaction, including sexual behavior, provides a combination of behaviors which allow humanity to be perpetuated and social relations to be maintained.

Thus, males and females may have formed social relations as a consequence of obtaining social and sexual rewards, and these relations led to reproduction, and hence perpetuation of the species. In addition, because of the rewarding aspects of social as well as sexual interaction, and the dependence of human infants on adults, the relations tended to endure over time, and this perhaps provided the basis of the first family units. A division of labor according to sex probably came about since men, as the physically stronger members of the family unit, needed to do the hunting, fishing, gathering, and physically demanding agricultural tasks characteristic of primitive societies. Similarly, females were more tied to their home as a result of pregnancy, childbirth, and breast feeding.

Because it was rewarding to at least some members of the social unit for other members to survive, particularly the adult man and woman, different behaviors had to be prescribed. In this way roles were probably invented, and we can speculate that the first such social roles were sex roles. In any event, to survive as a unit—which it must be reemphasized was individually rewarding—social roles were established, and with their emergence a society was created. A society may be defined as any continuing system of social rules governing the behavior of people interacting within the system.

As the settings within which humans lived changed and became more complex, more differentiated and complex adaptational demands were placed on people in order for them to maintain and perpetuate themselves. One social unit could not, for example, produce all the resources necessary for survival. As such, different units took on different roles, some people becoming hunters, others cooks, others shepherds, and still others builders of homes or protectors of them. Thus, role structure became more complex, more specialized, and more interdependent as society evolved.

Furthermore, in order to assure that the roles maintaining society would be performed by people having the skills and commitments necessary for social survival, people engaged in behavior to perpetuate the social order. Children born into society were instructed in the rules and tasks of that society in order to ensure their eventual contribution to society's maintenance. The process by which members of one generation shape the behaviors and personalities of members of another generation is termed *socialization*; and one function of socialization is to assure that there will be members of society capable of meeting the adaptational (survival) demands of people in that society. Thus, children are taught what is necessary to do in order to coexist with others and to survive. Although all societies teach its new members what to do, the precise attributes of what one has to do in order to survive will differ from one society to another.

For instance, although it is held by Freud and Erikson that all infants pass through the same oral stage and need to deal with reality in order to obtain the appropriate oral stimulation, the way they obtain it may be different in different societies. In one society, for example, there may be prolonged breast feeding by the mother. The infant need only seek the mother's breasts, which may never be very far away, in order to obtain the needed oral stimulation. In another society, however, infants may be weaned relatively early. A few days after birth the mother might return to work and leave the infant in the care of a grandparent or older sibling (DuBois, 1944). Although the infant might also still need oral stimulation, adjustments to reality different from those involved with the former infant will have to be made. Thus, the specifics of a child's society must be understood when one considers the implications for adaptation. In some societies we must learn to hunt, fish, and make arrowheads in order to survive. In other contexts, such skills are not as useful as learning to read, write, and do arithmetic.

In sum, society, the roles it evolves, and the process of socialization within society are all components of adaptive individual and social functioning. To Erikson, the part of the person that can attain the competency to perform these individual-social linkages is the ego, that part of the personality believed in psychoanalytic theory to be governed by the reality principle. Despite whether or not one chooses to talk of an ego as being involved in these linkages, the person must attain those skills necessary for survival in his or her society.

Yet it is clear that the demands placed on the person (or the ego) are not constant across life. Although society may expect certain behaviors of its adult members—behaviors which both maintain and perpetuate society—similar expectations are not maintained for infants, children, and in some societies, adolescents. In other words, the adaptive demands of an infant are not the same as those of a child or adolescent.

Changes in adaptive demands across life

Erikson believed that the implications of the ego for human psychological functioning were not given sufficient attention by Freud. When such attention was given it seemed clear that humans are not only biological and psychological creatures, but *social* creatures as well. To Erikson, a child's psychological development can be fully understood only when considered within the context of the society in which the child is growing up. Thus, one can see why Erikson's most famous book is entitled *Childhood and Society* (1963).

By changing the focus of Freud's psychoanalytic theory from the id to the ego, and thus stressing the interrelation of the ego and the forces in society affecting it, Erikson is concerned with a person's *psychosocial* development throughout life. However, as psychosocial development proceeds, new adjustment demands are placed on the ego.

Society alters its specification for adaptive behavior at different times in a person's life. As noted above, in infancy, society (specifically the family) expects "incorporation" from an infant. All that an infant must do in order to be deemed *socially* adaptive is to be stimulated and consume food from caregivers. We would not expect a person of this age to do much more than this. Certainly, we would not expect the infant to get a summer job, or follow career goals. Yet we may expect such behavior from an 18-year-old. Indeed, if *all* one did on one's summer vacation from college is take in the stimulation (from the sun) and incorporate the food (from the kitchen), this would not be considered very appropriate behavior by one's parents.

Thus, a behavior deemed adaptive at one time in life is not necessarily going to be seen as functional for the rest of life. Rather, new behaviors must emerge. Although we still have to be incorporative at age 18, we have to be more. Identity-related behaviors may have to come to predominate at this time of life. Unless one shows these behaviors, and shows them to sufficient degrees, one may not be judged as adaptive. One may not meet the demands of his or her society. In summary, the person must always meet the societally shaped demands of his or her world, but these demands are altered continually across the person's life span.

A similar conception has been advanced by Havighurst (1951, 1953, 1956). He believes that as people progress across their life span there are certain tasks they must master at different portions of life. He terms such change-related requirements *developmental tasks*, and notes that the specific tasks that occur at each particular portion of life arise out of particular combinations of pressures from inner-biological (for example, physical maturation), psychological (for example, aspirations in life), and sociocultural (for example, cultural expectations) influences (Havighurst, 1956). These pressures require an adjustment on the part of a person. Since at different times in the life span the combination of pressures from each of the levels is different, at each successive portion of life a distinct set of adjustment demands is placed on the developing person. Consequently, a developmental task:

> . . . arises at or about a certain period in the life of an individual, successful achievement of which leads to his happiness and to success with later tasks, while failure leads to unhappiness in the individual, disapproval by society, and difficulty with later tasks. (Havighurst, 1953)

The particular combination of pressures from the inner-biological, psychological, and sociocultural levels of analysis that exists during adolescence will vary as a consequence of historical changes (Thornberg, 1970). Tasks that may have been developmentally necessary for adolescents at one period of history (for example, selection of an occupation) may be delayed or accelerated in other eras. Nevertheless, many of the developmental tasks that Havighurst (1953) saw as appropriate for adolescents in mid-twentieth-century America have been seen in preceding chapters still to be relevant to today's adolescents. These tasks include achievement of appropriate peer-group relations, achievement of socially appropriate roles, preparation for a vocational role, development of intellectual skills, and development of an ethical or moral orientation (Havighurst, 1953).

Returning to Erikson's terminology, we may note that although the ego has to develop the capabilities of dealing with its society, the capabilities society expects are altered across life. Erikson believes that there are eight different capabilities that have to be developed. In other words, society places eight successive demands on the ego, and thus there are eight stages of psychosocial development. Within each stage, the ego must develop that capability necessary for adaptive functioning in order for development of further ego capability.

Indeed, it has been seen that Erikson asserts that at each stage it is critical for an adequate capability to be attained. Erikson theorized that until the demand within each stage is—or is not—met, the ego is in a state of *psychosocial crisis*. If the developing ego attains the appropriate abilities, the emotional crisis will be resolved successfully and healthy ego development can proceed. In turn, of course, if the appropriate attributes of the ego are not developed, negative emotional consequences will result.

To assess these ideas, as well as the utility of Erikson's stages for understanding adolescent personality development, we turn now to an overview of the psychosocial stages. After this presentation we shall focus on research relevant to the adolescent period in particular.

ERIKSON'S THEORY OF PSYCHOSOCIAL DEVELOPMENT

As a follower of Freudian psychoanalysis, Erikson sees the stages of psychosocial development as complementary to Freud's psychosexual ones. Accordingly, the id-based psychosexual stages exist along with the ego-based psychosocial ones. But although these psychosocial stages have some similarity to the psychosexual ones, they go beyond them in that they compose stages in the ego's continual functioning.

Stage 1 The oral-sensory stage

Freud's first stage of psychosexual development is termed the oral stage. In that stage the infant is concerned with obtaining appropriate stimulation in the oral zone. Erikson believes, however, that when one changes one's focus to the ego, one sees that the newborn infant is concerned not merely with oral stimulation. Rather, all the newborn infant's senses are being bombarded with stimulation—its eyes, ears, nose, and all other sense-receptor sites. Thus, in order to begin to deal effectively with the social world, the infant must be able to incorporate all this sensory information effectively. Hence, Erikson terms this psychosocial state the *oral-sensory stage*. The ego must develop the capability of dealing with the wealth of sensory stimulation constantly impinging on it.

However, the necessity of dealing with all this stimulation creates an emotional crisis for the infant. If the infant experiences the sensory world as relatively pleasant or benign, one sort of emotion will result. Alternatively, if the child's sensory stimulation experiences are negative or harsh, then another type of feeling will result. The infant who has relatively pleasant sensory experiences will come to *feel* that the world is a relatively benign, supportive place, that it will not hurt or shock him or her. To Erikson, the infant will develop *a sense of basic trust*. If, however, the infant experiences pain and discomfort, he or she will feel that the world is not supportive, but that there is pain and danger in the world. The infant will develop *a sense of mistrust*.

The infant thus faces an emotional crisis, precipitated by the nature and quality of the sensory world he or she attempts to incorporate. The emotional crisis is between *trust versus mistrust*. (We may delete the phrase "a sense of" for the sake of brevity of presentation, with the understanding that this phrase is always to be applied to all the various stage-specific feelings.) Erikson thinks of these two feelings as being bipolar, alternative end points along a single dimension. Erikson would represent the trust versus mistrust continuum as:

trust   mistrust

The ends of this continuum represent the alternative emotional outcomes of this stage of psychosocial development, but Erikson stresses that people do not, and should not, develop *either* complete trust *or* complete mistrust.

If a person develops complete trust, Erikson points out, this will be as unadaptive as developing complete mistrust—the person will not recognize the real dangers that exist in the world (for example, the person will never look when crossing the street because he or she will trust that no driver would ever hurt him or her, or the person might never strive to provide for himself or herself because of a feeling that the world will surely provide). However, a person whose feeling falls on the far end of the mistrust side of the continuum will never attempt to interact with the world because of feelings that assuredly the world will be hurtful. Erikson notes that such a person feels that there is no chance of anything but pain resulting from social interactions in the world. Thus, we see that it is necessary to develop a feeling that lies somewhere between the two end points of the continuum. If one develops more trust than mistrust, then Erikson believes that healthy ego development will proceed. If, however, one develops greater mistrust than trust, then unhealthy, nonoptimal ego development will proceed.

Having a feeling located closer to the trust end of the continuum means that the ego has developed the appropriate capabilities, allowing it to deal effectively with the sensory input from the world. Having a feeling located closer to the other side of the continuum, however, means that the appropriate ego capabilities have not developed. This location will affect the ego's functioning as the child enters the next stage of psychosocial development.

Stage 2 The anal-musculature stage

Freud's second stage of psychosexual development is termed the anal stage. Here we may remember that the infant obtains gratification through the exercise of his anal musculature. To Erikson, however, psychosocial development involves the other muscles of the body as well. Psychosocial development thus involves developing control over all of one's muscles. Analogous to use of the anal muscles, however, the infant must learn when to exercise and when not to exercise all his or her bodily muscles (Erikson, 1963).

Accordingly, if the child feels in control of his or her own body, the child will develop *a sense of autonomy*. On the other hand, if the child finds himself or herself unable to exert this independent control, if he or she finds that others have to do for him or her what one is expected to do for oneself, then one will develop *a sense of shame and doubt*. One will feel shame because one is not showing the ability to control one's own movements (for example, bowel movements, movements involved in feeding oneself), and this may evoke disapproval from significant other persons (for example, parents). Moreover, because one is experiencing this inability to control the self, one will feel doubt about one's capabilities for so doing. Shame is felt because others do things for the person that both the individual and others feel should be done for oneself.

Stage 3 The genital-locomotor stage

If the child has developed appropriately within the anal-musculature stage and has gained the ability to control his or her own movements, the child will now have a chance to use these abilities. This third psychosocial stage corresponds to Freud's psychosexual phallic stage. Although Erikson does not dismiss the psychosexual implications of the Oedipal conflict, he specifies that such a development also has important psychosocial implications. If the child is to resolve successfully the Oedipal conflict, he or she must begin to move independently away from the parental figures. The child must begin to use the previously developed self-control over the muscles, take his or her own steps into the world, and thereby break the Oedipal ties. What Erikson says is that society expects the child not to remain "tied to the mother's apron strings," but rather to locomote (walk off) by oneself and thereby eliminate such attachments. The child must be able to move freely in interaction with the environment.

Accordingly, if the child is able to step into the world without the parent being there to guide or prod, the child will develop *a sense of initiative*. He or she will feel that the self can decide when to use locomotor abilities to interact with the world. On the other hand, if the child does not move off on his or her own, if he or she remains tied to the parent for directives about locomotor functioning, the child will not feel a sense of initiative. Rather, the child will feel *a sense of guilt*. To Erikson, this is because the child's Oedipal attachments remain relatively intact. To the extent that they continue to exist while society expects evidence of their being eliminated, the child will feel guilt.

Stage 4   Latency

Freud did not pay a good deal of attention to the psychosexual latency stage because of his belief that the libido is submerged. Consequently, the stage had little if any psychosexual importance to Freud. However, Erikson attaches a great deal of psychosocial importance to the latency years. Erikson believes that in all societies children begin at this stage to learn the tasks necessary for being adult members of society. In our society this psychosocial orientation in part takes the form of the child's being sent off to school. In other societies this same psychosocial orientation may take the form of teaching the child to farm, cook, hunt, or fish.

Accordingly, if the child learns these skills well, if he or she learns what to do and how to do it, he or she will develop *a sense of industry*. The child will feel that he or she knows what to do to be a capably functioning adult member of society. On the other side of the continuum lies the feeling associated with failures in these psychosocial developments. If the child feels that he or she has not learned to perform capably the necessary tasks of the society (while the child feels others around him or her have acquired this), he or she will feel *a sense of inferiority*.

Stage 5   Puberty and adolescence

This stage of development corresponds to the genital stage of psychosexual development in Freud's theory. Erikson also is concerned with the implications of the emergence of a genital sex drive occurring at puberty. But as with the previous stages of psychosocial development, Erikson here looks at the broader, psychosocial implications of all the physical, physiological, and psychological changes that emerge at puberty.

Erikson sees all the changes occurring at puberty as presenting the adolescent with serious psychosocial problems. The person has lived for about twelve years and has developed a sense of who he or she is and of what he or she is and is not capable of doing. If the person has developed successfully, he or she will have developed more trust than mistrust, more autonomy than shame and doubt, more initiative than guilt, and more industry than inferiority. In any event, all the feelings developed have gone into giving him or her a feeling about who one is and what one can do. Now, however, this knowledge is challenged. The adolescent now finds himself or herself in a body that looks and feels different, and further finds that he or she is thinking about this and all things in a new way. Thus, all the associations the adolescent has had about the self in earlier stages may not now be relevant to this new person one finds oneself to be. Because of the need to have a coherent sense of self in order to be adaptive, the adolescent asks a crucial psychosocial question: Who am I?

Moreover, at precisely the time when the adolescent feels unsure about this, society begins to ask related questions about the adolescent. For instance, in our society the adolescent must now begin to take the first definite steps toward career objectives. For example, one has to make a decision about whether or not one will enter into college preparatory courses. Society asks adolescents what role they will play in society. Society wants to know how these soon-to-be-adult persons will contribute to society's maintenance. Society wants to know what *socially prescribed set of behaviors*, functional for the adaptive maintenance of society, will be adopted. Such a set of behaviors is a *role*, and thus the key aspect of this adolescent dilemma is one of finding a role. Yet how can one know what one can do and wants to do to contribute to society, and meet its demands, if one does not know who one is?

In summary, this question—Who am I?—is basically a question of self-definition, necessitated by the emergence of all the new feelings and capabilities arising during adolescence (for example, the sex drive and formal thought), as well as by the new demands placed on the adolescent by society. The adaptive challenge to find a role one can be committed to, and thus to achieve an identity, is the most important psychosocial task of adolescence. The emotional upheaval provoked by this crisis is termed by Erikson the *identity crisis*. To resolve this crisis and *achieve a sense of identity*, Erikson (1959) sees it as necessary to combine psychological processes and societal goals and directives:

> At one time, it will appear to refer to a conscious sense of individual identity; at another to an unconscious striving for a continuity of personal character; at a third, as a criterion for the silent doings of ego synthesis; and finally, as a maintenance of an inner solidarity with a group's ideals and identity. (Erikson, 1959, p. 57)

To achieve identity then, the adolescent must find an orientation to life that both fulfills the attributes of the self *and at the same time* is consistent with what society expects of a person. As such, this orientation must be both individually and socially adaptive. That is, such a role cannot be something which is self-destructive (for example, sustained fasting) or socially disapproved (for example, criminal behavior). Indeed, Erikson terms the adoption of a role such as the latter *negative identity formation*, and notes that although such roles exist in most societies, they are by definition ones which have severe sanctions associated with them. Thus, in trying to find an orientation to life that meets one's individual and societal demands, the adolescent is searching for a set of behavioral prescriptions—a role—that fulfills the biological, psychological, and social demands of life. Said another way, a role represents a synthesis of biological, psychological, and social adaptive demands. This is why Erikson (1959, 1963) sees ego identity as having these three components.

However, to find such an identity, the adolescent must discover what he or she believes in, what his or her attitudes and ideals are. These factors, which can be said to define one's *ideology*, provide an important component of one's role. When we know who we are, we know what we do, and when we know what we do, we know our role in society.

Along with any role (for example, wife, father, student, teacher) goes a set of orientations toward the world which serves to define that role. These attitudes, beliefs, and values give us some idea of what a person engaged in a particular role in society thinks of and does. Thus, there is an ideology that serves to define a societal role. We know fairly well what the ideology of a Catholic priest is and how it is similar to and different from the ideology associated with a military general, or a professional artist, or a professional politician. The point is that along with any role goes a role-defining ideology. To solve one's identity crisis, one must be committed to a role, which in turn means showing commitment toward an ideology. Erikson (1963) terms such an emotional orientation *fidelity*.

If the adolescent finds his or her role in society, if he or she can show commitment to an ideology, he or she will have achieved a sense of identity. Alternatively, if the adolescent does not find a role to play in society, he or she will remain in the identity crisis. He or she typically might complain: "I don't know where I'm at" or "I can't get my head together." In an attempt to resolve this crisis, the adolescent might try one role one day and another the next, perhaps successfully, but only temporarily, investing the self in many different things. Accordingly, Erikson maintains that if the adolescent does not resolve the identity crisis, he or she will feel *a sense of role confusion* or *identity diffusion*. These two terms denote the adolescent's feelings associated with being unable to show commitment to a role, and hence to achieve a crisis-resolving identity.

In summary, it may be seen that the identity crisis of adolescence is provoked by individual and societal changes and can only be resolved through commitment to a role balancing the individual and social demands raised by these changes. The terms "crisis" and "commitment" become the hallmarks of the fifth stage of psychosocial development. Yet the adaptive struggle in this stage not only is preceded by events in earlier ones but also is influenced in its outcome by them. As Constantinople (1969) points out:

> In order to achieve a positive resolution of the identity crisis, the adolescent must sift through all of the attitudes toward himself and the world which have occurred over the years with the resolution of earlier crises, and he must fashion for himself a sense of who he is that will remain constant across situations and that can be shared by others when they interact with him. (p. 358)

Furthermore, the identity the adolescent attains as a consequence of the psychosocial crises preceding and during adolescence will influence the rest of the life span. To Erikson, self-esteem is a feeling about the self which tends to remain constant across life, and thus gives the person a coherent psychological basis of dealing with the demands of social reality. In one essay (1959) in which he discussed identity in terms of self-esteem Erikson says:

> Self-esteem, confirmed at the end of each major crisis, grows to be a conviction that one is learning effective steps toward a tangible future, that one is developing a defined personality within a social reality which one understands. (p. 89)

Constantinople (1969) elaborates that in adolescence:

> This self-esteem is the end product of successful resolutions of each crisis; the fewer or the less satisfactory the successful resolutions, the less self-esteem on which to build at this stage of development, and the greater the likelihood of a prolonged sense of identity diffusion, of not being sure of who one is and where one is going. (p. 358)

Where one is going is on to the early portion of one's adulthood. There yet another psychosocial crisis will be faced. As implied, successful resolution of it, as well as of the remaining crises of the adult years, will rest on the attainment of an adequate identity.

Stage 6 Young adulthood

In this and psychosocial stages 7 and 8, Erikson departs from the psychosexual model. He provides a description of the psychosocial stage changes involved with the rest of the human life span. In young adulthood, the person is oriented toward entering into an interpersonal union. The society now requires that most persons enter into an institution that will allow the society to continue to exist. Accordingly, the formation of a new family unit must be established, usually through marriage. The young adult must form a relationship with another person which will allow such an institution to prosper.

Considered in terms independent of Erikson's theory, society demands more from an adult than just behaviors that allow the society to be maintained. If adults do not behave to perpetuate the society, it will not survive. Thus, as soon as one adopts a role—which we may now define as a maintenance role—role requirements become more differentiated, and hence more complex. The young adult is required to take on a perpetuation role. The young adult must create an interpersonal relationship wherein—in the typical case—reproduction can occur, and hence a new member of society can be created.

However, it is not true that society traditionally approves of any sort of union leading to reproduction. The adaptive function of reproduction is survival of the species. From a human social perspective, reproduction must occur within a context that maximizes the likelihood of socially approved socialization. In order for society to survive, the new members must be committed to its maintenance and perpetuation. As such, society must assure that new members are taught values that promote these goals. As a consequence, an institution is created in all societies which is the most efficient one for socializing new members. This core socialization unit is what we call the *family*, and it is given the function of bringing new members into the society within a context that ensures the stable continuation of the society.

For this reason, we have termed the family the basic unit of society, and its role as the core socialization unit explains why the young adult is prompted to form an interpersonal relation, leading to reproduction, and other functions, within the institution of the family.

If children are born outside of marriage, then not only are they born of parents who have behaved in defiance of basic and adaptive societal rules, but also, because of this situation, they are not in a context that seems the most likely to assure societally approved socialization. Accordingly, the young person is prompted by society to form not only an interpersonal relationship, but one that will, through marriage, create a new family, and a new, stable context for socializing new members. However, in order to fulfill this perpetuation role, the young person must be able to maintain a stable interpersonal relationship. If such stability is lacking, then there is no assurance that children will be socialized appropriately, and the function of perpetuating society will not be served.

Accordingly, to return now to Erikson's terminology, there is a psychosocial pressure for a person during this period of life to form a close, stable interpersonal relationship. This demand, however, causes a new crisis.

Erikson argues that to enter into and successfully maintain such a relationship, one must be able to give of oneself totally. Such openness is not limited only to sexual relations. Rather, Erikson means that by giving of oneself totally, all the facets of one person (for example, feelings, ideas, goals, attitudes, and values) must be unconditionally available to the other person; moreover, the person must be unconditionally receptive to these same things from the partner. Accordingly, to the extent that one can attain such interchange, one will feel *a sense of intimacy*. Again, not limited just to sexual intimacy, this exchange includes the mutual interchange of both partners' most intimate feelings, ideas, and goals.

If, however, one has not achieved an identity in stage 5 and thus does not have the ability to give completely, then of course one will not be able to achieve this sense of intimacy. One cannot give of oneself if one does not have a self to give. Thus, rather than being able to have a complete mutual interchange, one will be restricted in what one is capable of giving. Accordingly, there would be limits to being intimate with another person. If one cannot (for whatever reason) share and be shared, then one will feel *a sense of isolation*.

Stage 7   Adulthood

If a successful, intimate union has been developed, the person can now attempt to meet the next set of psychosocial requirements, presented by adulthood. In this stage, society requires the person to play the role of a productive, contributing member. Farmers must grow crops, artists must paint pictures, and professors must generate ideas.

Accordingly, if the person successfully plays the role society expects of him or her, if he or she is contributing and producing what is expected, then the person will have *a sense of generativity*. One will feel he or she is performing a role appropriately. On the other hand, if the person finds that he or she is not fulfilling the requirements of the role, and is not producing as one should, then *a sense of stagnation* results. The person will find that his or her output is below expectations.

Of course, generativity goals can be attained from creating those products associated with one's maintenance role *and/or* one's perpetuation role. One can be generative by producing *and rearing* children in order that society may be perpetuated, and one can be generative by creating those products (for example, goods or services) associated with one's maintenance role. Indeed, some people can fulfill their generative goals by playing a perpetuation role with children other than their own, for example, in the case of the socialization performed by a schoolteacher.

However, despite the different ways in which people can fulfill generativity goals, traditionally all possibilities have not been equally available to all people. American society historically has drawn important distinctions between men and women as to what behaviors they may appropriately engage in. Thus, how men and women achieve feelings of generativity differs. While men's generative feelings could be achieved through engaging in professional or business activities as well as through engaging in parenting, women's generative feelings could traditionally be attained only through the generation (or production) and rearing of children. Women who chose not to have children or opted for entering the "men's world" (of business or professionalism) were negatively evaluated by society, and viewed as inappropriately fulfilling the roles of women. While this situation is changing, of course, there are components of Erikson's (1964) ideas that suggest this may be dangerous for the survival of society.

Erikson believes adaptive role choices made in adolescence are based on an integration of biological, psychological, and social orientations. The roles that *adaptive* women and men adopt in adolescence successfully achieve such integration. Women have traditionally adopted roles which are based on child caring and rearing, and thus combine maintenance and perpetuation functions, while men conventionally separated these functions. Consequently, since society has survived with these differences, traditional role adoptions are biosocially adaptive and should be maintained (Erikson, 1964, 1968). Thus, the role searches and attainments of adolescents should necessarily show sex differences because they are based on the alternative biological demands that pertain to males and females (Erikson, 1964, 1968). Chapter 13 discusses the nature of sex differences, and the presentation is organized around this provocative idea of Erikson's.

Thus, Erikson describes differences in the content of role adoption, and not in role function. Indeed, in succeeding sections of the present chapter we shall note that studies of identity status and development do not find consistent sex differences. That is, despite whatever roles are adopted in adolescence and followed in young adulthood and adulthood, males and females appear equally capable of achieving identities. As such, members of both groups may progress into the last stage of psychosocial development without a sex-related disadvantage.

Stage 8   Maturity

Maturity, to Erikson (1959), is "the acceptance of one's one and only life cycle . . . as something that had to be and that, by necessity, permitted of no substitutions" (p. 98). However, Erikson believes that this feeling *only* can be attained by someone who has successfully resolved the generativity versus stagnation crisis of stage 7.

In this last stage of psychosocial development, the person recognizes that he or she is reaching the end of the life span. If one has successfully progressed through the previous stages of development—if one has experienced more trust than mistrust, more autonomy than shame and doubt, if one has had an identity, has had an intimate relationship, and has been a productive, generative person—then one will face the final years of life with enthusiasm. The person will be childlike, says Erikson, in his or her enthusiasm for life. Thus, Erikson argues that he or she will feel *a sense of ego integrity*. He or she will feel that a full and complete life has been led.

Alternatively, if the person has not experienced these events—if, for example, he or she has felt mistrustful, guilty, or inferior, or has felt a sense of identity diffusion, isolation, or stagnation—then he or she will not be enthusiastic about these last years of life. Rather, the person perhaps will feel cheated or bitter. He or she might be "childish" in behavior, as if trying to go back to earlier years and attain the feelings that were never experienced. In this case, Erikson says, the person would feel *a sense of despair*. He or she would feel that time was running out and that one had not gained everything out of life that was felt was needed.

Conclusions

Erikson offers descriptions of development which suggest that the events and outcomes of adolescence are central. The processes of behavior change that exist prior to adolescence converge to create a crisis of self-definition. That is, the adolescent must establish an identity to maintain—or recreate—an integrated sense of self in the face of these alterations. This must be done at a time when social demands are also changing. This process involves the adoption of a set of behaviors and an ideology which will carry the potential for allowing the person to meet the psychosocial demands of the rest of the life span.

We have argued that Erikson's descriptions not only allow adolescent personality to be studied from a life-span framework, but also allow this study to be focused on what Erikson and others believe to be the basic aspect of personality in this portion of life: identity. Not only does our brief summary in the preceding paragraph support this view that identity is central in the study of adolescent personality, but the history of the scientific study of adolescence reflects a corresponding emphasis. Although the first edition of a major work presenting the main theories of adolescence (Muuss, 1966) barely made mention of Erikson's ideas, a more recent edition (Muuss, 1975c) devotes more discussion to the ideas of Erikson than to any of those of several other theorists mentioned.

Thus, Erikson's ideas about adolescent development have become quite influential, and as such, there has been considerable research on the study of identity and its development, correlates, and bases. This research has, however, extended far beyond the issues and ideas raised by Erikson himself. As noted about other major theorists like Piaget and Kohlberg, a major use of their ideas lies in the works he or she stimulates in others. As such, the next sections consider the nature of empirical findings about adolescent identity development.

IDENTITY DEVELOPMENT IN ADOLESCENCE: RESEARCH DIRECTIONS

Research about adolescent identity processes has fallen into three inter-related categories. First, research has been conducted to determine whether ego identity occurs in a stagelike progression such as Erikson specifies. Do issues of industry versus inferiority invariably precede those of identity versus role confusion, and, in turn, do these issues always become of concern prior to problems of intimacy versus isolation? If such universality of sequencing were to be found, then Erikson's (1959) ideas about the critical importance of successful development in a prior stage for subsequent stage functioning would be supported. If such universality were not found, then a search would be appropriate for those variables which provide a basis of the various sequences of ego development that could occur.

A second direction that research about adolescent identity processes has taken has been to focus on what changes, if any, occur in a person's identity status over time. Erikson describes the identity crisis (as he does the basic crisis of each stage) as a bipolar continuum ranging from identity to role confusion. Thus, a person may occupy any position along this continuum, or in other words, have any one of a number of statuses along this dimension. Researchers (for example, Marcia, 1964, 1966) have tried to describe the array of different statuses a person may have along this dimension and how, across life, these statuses may change.

Because Erikson's sequences have not been found to be universal, and because one's identity status within the adolescent stage of life also has been found to change, a third area of research pertinent to ego identity has arisen. People have been concerned with what variables are related to changes in ego development and identity status. Although such work has been largely descriptive, we shall see that it provides ideas about the explanation of these changes.

Sequences in ego development

Does the emergence of an identity crisis in adolescence occur in a stagelike manner? Is the adolescent crisis, as Erikson described it, inevitably preceded by the specified childhood crisis and followed by the adult ones? Although much research supports the idea of adolescence as a time of crisis in self-definition, the universal stagelike characteristics of this crisis are in doubt.

Several studies, independent of Erikson's framework, do show adolescence to be a period of change in self-definition. Montemayor and Eisen (1977) found that self-concept development from childhood to adolescence followed a sequence from concrete to abstract. This change was assessed by analyzing responses to the question "Who am I?" a question we have seen to be of central importance in the identity crisis. Significant increases from grades 4 through 12 were seen in self-definitions relating to occupational role, individuality of one's existence, and ideology. All these are concerns of the adolescent role search as Erikson (1959, 1963) describes it. Decreases in self-definitions pertaining to territoriality, citizenship, possessions, resources, and physical self were also seen across this grade range.

Additional support for the view that adolescence is a time of personal reorganization, and one involving ego development, is found in studies by Haan (1974) and by Martin and Redmore (1978). In the former study, involving a longitudinal study of ninety-nine adolescents, it was found that being able to cope with adaptive demands in adulthood was apparently preceded by progressive reorganization of personality characteristics during adolescence. In the latter study, of thirty-two Black children studied longitudinally from the sixth to the twelfth grade, thirty showed an increase in level of ego development, and these increases showed intraindividual stability (the correlation in ego scores between the two grades was +.5).

Thus, people's egos do develop, their personalities reorganize, and their self-definitions come to include occupational and ideological concerns. But such alterations do not necessarily correspond to stagelike progressions. Research aimed directly at assessing such a conception has not provided complete support for Erikson's ideas. In the largest study involving an assessment of the presence of stagelike qualities in adolescent development, Constantinople (1969) tested more than 900 male and female college students from the University of Rochester. Her study was complex, involving both cross-sectional and longitudinal comparisons. In 1965 she tested members of the freshman through senior classes, and then in 1966 and again in 1967 she retested portions of these original groups.

To study Erikson's stages of ego development, she devised a test containing sixty items. She wrote five items for each of the first six stages in Erikson's theory to reflect the successful, or positive, end of the bipolar continuum, and five items to reflect the negative end. Although there was some evidence that people's answers were somewhat influenced by how socially desirable a particular response to an item seemed, Constantinople (1969) nevertheless concluded that high scores on the positive continuum ends (for example, industry, identity) and low scores on the negative continuum ends (for example, inferiority, diffusion) indicated successful resolution of a stage's crisis. Because our concern is adolescence, we focus on Constantinople's (1969) findings regarding the crisis of industry versus inferiority, identity versus identity diffusion, and intimacy versus isolation.

Insofar as the scores for these crises are concerned, it appeared that, in general, scores on the positive continuum ends increased while those for the negative ends decreased across groups. There was increasingly more successful stage resolution among males and females having higher college standing. Moreover, since between-cohort differences (people studied at different times but in the same college class) did not appear great, it seems that the age-group differences may reflect age changes.

Another characteristic of the cross-sectional data was a trend that indicated that stage resolution was less evident for the intimacy versus isolation crisis, a finding consistent with Erikson's idea that identity issues must be solved first before intimacy ones can be dealt with. These college students may have just resolved their identities and made career plans by the senior year, and just begun to focus on intimacy. But although seniors scored higher than freshman on the positive industry and identity crisis ends, and lower on the negative inferiority end, there were no college class differences for intimacy, or for diffusion, or isolation—negative crisis ends that should have been lowered if successful development in accordance with Erikson's stage theory had occurred. This failure to show the expected developmental trend was particularly evident for females (Constantinople, 1969).

Constantinople (1969) undertook longitudinal follow-ups of the subjects in order to provide further information about the differences in successful resolution of stages found in the cross-sectional data. These three-year repeated measurement studies gave unqualified support to the suggestion of developmental changes in the cross-sectional data insofar as alterations in identity and identity diffusion were concerned. There were consistent increases in the successful resolution of identity from the freshman to the senior year across subjects *and* from one year to the next within subject groups. Even here, however, there are problems for Erikson's theory. Only males showed consistent decreases in the scores for identity diffusion. Changes in scores for the other crises did not always decrease or increase in accordance with Erikson's theory, and furthermore, the changes that did occur were often accounted for by time and cohort effects. Exhibit 12.1 shows the increase in identity scores for males and females from their freshman through senior years, as well as the degrees of decrease in the diffusion scores for these subjects during this period.

Constantinople's (1969) data provide, at best, only partial support for the stagelike character of ego development. Similarly, Ciaccio (1971), studying ego development in 5-, 8-, and 11-year-old boys through use of a projective test, found only partial support for Erikson's theory. In support of Erikson, the youngest group showed the most *interest* with stage 2 crisis issues (autonomy versus shame and doubt), while the older two groups showed the most *interest* for the crises of stages 3 and 4. But support for Erikson's idea that the ego develops as it meets the different crises of succeeding stages was not found, since despite their varying interests, all groups showed most *conflict* for the stage 2 crisis.

Similarly, LaVoie (1976) studied sophomore, junior, and senior male and female high school students with Constantinople's (1969) measure of stage crisis resolution. LaVoie classified these adolescents on the basis of their degree of successful stage 5 crisis resolution (identity achievement) and found that although those who were high on identity scored higher on the positive crisis ends for stages 1 and 4, there were no differences between high- and low-identity achievers for the positive scores for stages 2, 3, and 6. Moreover, although LaVoie and Adams (in press) found that positive resolution of industry, identity, and intimacy crises, as measured by Constantinople's (1969) test, is related to adult attachment (that is, liking and love) scores, negative crisis scores were not so related.

In summary, it appears that ego development does not proceed in the stagelike manner that Erikson suggests. Thus, the ego identity crisis does not necessarily arise after the crisis typically associated with earlier portions of life or precede those typically associated with later portions. Instead, a more plastic ordering of crises seems to exist between individuals (Douvan & Adelson, 1966; Gallatin, 1975). There seems to be a progressive increment in resolution of issues dealing with identity. For

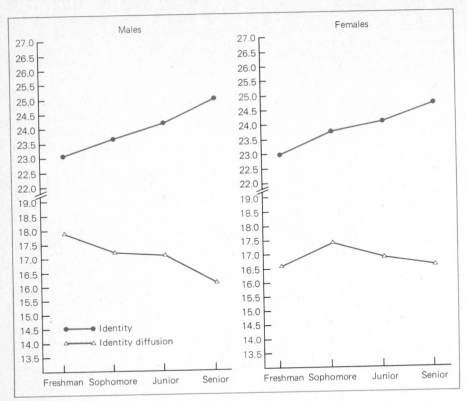

Exhibit 12.1
Changes in identity and indentity diffusion scores for male (left graph)
and female (right graph) college subjects. (*Source:* **Adapted from**
Constantinople, 1969, pp. 364–366. Copyright 1969 by the American
Psychological Association. Reprinted by permission.)

instance, the major consistency between cross-sectional and longitudinal data that Constantinople (1969) reported was the general movement across life toward a change in location along the identity–identity diffusion continuum. Most students changed in the direction of increased identity and decreased diffusion scores.

Hence, developmental progressions do seem to be involved in the resolution of the identity crisis of adolescence. Adolescents' changing status along the crisis continuum has thus become the second major focus of research on adolescent identity development.

The differentiation of identity status

What are the major types of ego changes adolescents go through in meeting the challenge of the identity crisis? Are there adolescents who occupy locations along the identity-identity diffusion continuum other than at or near these two extremes? If so, what is their location or status? These were the major issues that James Marcia (1964, 1966) confronted as he began a series of provocative studies of identity development

James Marcia

in adolescence. Rather than viewing identity as a global phenomenon, Marcia (1964, 1966) hypothesized that more differentiation existed. Erikson (1959) suggested this possibility, and in this idea Marcia found the basis of his own ideas about identity status.

Erikson noted that the adolescent period involves a *crisis* in self-definition, and in order to resolve this crisis one must *commit* oneself to a role. As discussed earlier, such commitment means adoption of an ideology (attitudes, values, beliefs) that coincides with the behavioral prescriptions for one's adopted role or occupation. Accordingly, to determine the adolescent's identity status, one should appraise his or her degrees of crisis and commitment. Using a semistructured, open-ended interview, Marcia (1966) evaluated adolescents' levels of crisis and commitment insofar as issues of occupational choice, religion, and political ideology were concerned.

Using eighty-six male college students as subjects, Marcia (1966) found evidence for four identity statuses. As Erikson (1959, 1963, 1968) said, two of these statuses were those adolescents who had *achieved identity* and those who were in a state of *identity diffusion*. The former group had had a crisis period but now showed commitment to an occupation and to an ideology. The latter group may or may not have had a crisis; however, their defining characteristic was their lack of commitment. Moreover, they were not concerned about this lack of commitment.

The first of the two other statuses Marcia identified he labeled as *moratorium*. Students here were in a crisis, and had, at best, vague commitments to an occupation or to an ideology. However, moratorium status adolescents were actively trying to make commitments. They were in a state of search.

The last identity status Marcia identified was termed *foreclosure*. Adolescents in this status had never experienced a crisis. Yet they were highly committed. Their interviews showed they had adopted the identities their parents had wanted them to take, and that they had done so with little or no question and with no crisis.

Marcia (1966) found some evidence that there were differences among these four groups that were consistent with Erikson's theory. As such, his research attests to the validity of each status. Identity achievers were found to have the highest scores on an independent test of ego identity, and did not follow authoritarian values (for example, the belief that one should conform, a stress on obedience to authority) as much as members of some other statuses (for example, foreclosure adolescents). In addition, the achievers maintained their feelings of self-esteem (that is, positive self-regard) more than did members of other groups in the face of experimental manipulations having negative information about them. Foreclosure adolescents endorsed authoritarian values more than did other groups, and had a self-esteem more vulnerable to negative information than had the identity achievers.

Evidence regarding the validity of the other two statuses was not as compelling. In a concept attainment task involving experimentally induced stress, the moratorium subjects showed more variability than others, but were otherwise not distinguishable from the identity achievers. Furthermore, the identity diffusion subjects performed lower than did the identity achievement subjects on the stress task, but in no other way did their behavior conform to theoretical expectations (Marcia, 1966).

However, other studies have provided more evidence that these four identity statuses exist. Schacter (1968) found that even among emotionally disturbed adolescent males, resolution of the identity crisis was positively related to attainment of occupational commitment. Marcia (1967) found that identity-achieving and moratorium adolescent males were less vulnerable to attempts to manipulate their self-esteem than were foreclosed or diffusion males, and Marcia and Friedman (1970) found that identity-achieving adolescent females choose more difficult college majors than do identity diffusion females. In addition, foreclosure females, although like identity achievers in many respects, were higher in authoritarianism. However, they also had higher self-esteem and lower anxiety than did the achievers, a finding not seemingly consistent with others.

Similarly, partial support for the four identity statuses comes from a study by Toder and Marcia (1973). In an experiment, attempts were made to have sixty-four college females conform to group demands. Identity achievers conformed less than those having unstable statuses (the moratorium and diffusion subjects). However, the foreclosure subjects also conformed less than those in the other two groups. Although this lack of conformity to group pressure would be expected on the basis of the foreclosure subjects' stable identity status, it would not be expected by virtue of their authoritarian, and hence conforming and obedient, values.

These data are far from unequivocal in showing distinctions among the four different statuses. Other data, however, provide more compelling support. Several studies have shown that when adolescents are studied longitudinally, they progress through the four identity statuses in ways consistent with theoretical expectations. For instance, Waterman and Waterman (1971) longitudinally studied ninety-two male college adolescents through the course of their freshman year. Using Marcia's (1966) interview, changes in occupational and ideological status were assessed. In regard to occupational commitment, there was a significant increase in the number of moratorium subjects, that is, those people actively searching, and a significant decrease in the number of identity diffusion subjects, that is, those people not caring to search for commitment. Hence, there was a group movement toward trying to make commitments, and thus play an adaptive, functional role in society.

However, insofar as ideology was concerned, there was a significant increase in the number of identity diffusion subjects. Indeed, about 44 percent of the subjects changed identity status for occupation over the course of the freshman year, and about 51 percent did so in regard to ideology; but people who had an identity achiever status at the beginning of the freshman period were just as likely to change as those who initially had other statuses.

These one-year longitudinal data do not provide compelling support for general progression toward more adaptive identity statuses in adolescence. However, the freshman year of college may involve demands on the person that produce instability in identity. Progressively more stability in identity achievement might be found if adolescents were followed beyond the freshman year. Longer-term longitudinal assessments support this expectation.

Waterman, Geary, and Waterman (1974) studied fifty-three male college seniors, all of whom had been subjects in the Waterman and Waterman (1971) study of identity development in the freshman college year. Over this longer time period there were significant increases in the frequency of subjects falling in the achievement status, for *both* occupation and ideology ratings. Moreover, although about 50 percent of these subjects stayed in the same status from the freshman to the senior year, the achiever status was the most stable across this period. In turn, the moratorium status was the least stable. Similarly, Marcia (1976), in a reinterview of thirty males who were given identity status interviews six to seven years earlier, found the moratorium status to show a 100 percent rate of change. Moreover, Waterman and Goldman (1976), reinterviewing eighteen seniors first studied as freshman in 1970 and forty-one seniors first studied as freshman in 1971, found with both cohorts that there were significant increases in the frequency of identity achievement and decreases in moratorium and diffusion statuses. In summary, there was a very high probability for resolution of the identity crisis. About 75 percent of those youth studied over the entire period of their college experience reached a status of identity achievement.

We conclude, therefore, that there is some evidence for differentiation among ego identity statuses within adolescence. Most people move adaptively from other statuses toward identity achievement, and hence crisis resolution, by virtue of occupational and ideological role commitment. However, it is clear that this pattern is variable. Not all people go through this sequence. For instance, some begin and end adolescence as foreclosure youth. People differ in their rates of development, and some never seem to attain an identity of either achievement or foreclosure. For example, Waterman, et al. (1974) found that a substantial proportion of subjects completed their college years in the identity diffusion status. In their study, 13 percent of seniors were diffuse on both occupational and ideology ratings, and an additional 33 percent were diffuse in one or the other of these areas.

In summary, not only is there considerable plasticity of when in the sequence of other psychosocial crises the identity crisis occurs, but there also is plasticity in developments within this adolescent crisis. Because of this variability, the third area of research pertaining to adolescent identity has arisen. Researchers have become concerned with what variables may interrelate with those pertaining to identity processes. Through describing how identity may be affected by those other variables to which it is related, this research provides an explanation of the basis of adolescent identity, and as such, its changing character.

Identity: Psychological dimensions

Processes of cognitive and moral development are intertwined with those of identity. Podd (1972) found that principled moral reasoning, formal operational thought, and identity achievement were positively related. Those whose identity status was diffuse tended to show preconventional moral thought (Podd, 1972). Furthermore, independent data show the interrelation between advances in identity development and other theoretically relevant psychological functions.

Advances in formal operations involve progressions in dealing with abstract thought. If such development is indeed related to identity formation, then one should expect to see those who engage in abstract processes tending to have the identity achievement status. If one considers that writing poetry is an activity at least in part based on abstract thought, then support for this relation is found in a report by Waterman, Kohutis, and Pulone (1977). In two studies of college students, these investigators found that those people who wrote poetry were more likely to be in the achievement status than those who did not write poetry. Moreover, poetry writers were less frequently found in the foreclosure and diffusion statuses than people who did not write poetry. Yet writing per se was not related to identity status, since there were no identity differences among students who did or who did not keep a personal journal or diary.

Similarly, Waterman and Goldman (1976) found that among the two cohorts they studied longitudinally from the freshman to the senior college year, an interest in literary and art forms was predictive of becoming an identity achiever by the end of college for those who were not in this status as freshman. Moreover, that identity status is related to intellectual achievement as well as to abstract cognitive functions is a finding reported by Jones and Strowig (1968). A group of 150 female and 167 male rural Wisconsin high school seniors were asked the "Who am I?" question, and answers were scored for identity development. Higher scores were positively related to achievement.

Thus, advanced cognitive performance is associated with an advanced identity status. This relation suggests that a generally greater level of adaptive functioning is associated with identity attainment. Data reported by LaVoie (1976) support this idea. High school male and female students who were measured as having high identity had lower scores on measures of defensiveness, general maladjustment, and neurosis than did students measured as low in identity. Moreover, the self-concepts of the high-identity scorers were more positive than those of the low-identity scorers. Similarly, Matteson (1977) found that among ninety-nine Danish youth, aged 17 to 18 years, more advanced identity status was related to the ability to control the expression of impulses among males, and to rejection of compliance to authority among both sex groups. It may be that in rejecting authority, high-identity youth see themselves as more capable of controlling their own lives.

Two studies support these interpretations. Waterman, Beubel, and Waterman (1970) found that identity achievers (and also moratorium subjects) saw their own behavior more controlled by phenomena internal to and thus dependent on them than by events external to and thus independent of their control (for example, luck or "fate"). In turn, the reverse ideas about the center of control for one's behavior were held by subjects in the foreclosure and diffusion statuses. Similarly, Schenkel (1975) found that identity achievers were least dependent on extraneous cues from the environment in performing a perceptual task, while the reverse was the case with identity diffusion adolescents.

Thus, the development of identity is associated with cognitive, adjustment, perceptual, and other psychological processes. However, the character of these psychological interactions may be moderated by their relations with interindividual social processes.

Identity: Social dimensions

Since achieving an identity denotes finding a role that meets society's demands, identity processes are basically interpersonal ones. They link the person to society in a way that facilitates both individual and social maintenance and survival. One might expect, then, that people who have achieved identity should engage in interpersonal relationships useful in advancing this individual and social functioning, that is, intimate relations. Orlofsky, Marcia, and Lesser (1973) found evidence of just such a relation. In a study of fifty-three college males, it was found that those subjects who were in the identity achievement status were among those who had the greatest capacity for intimate interpersonal relationships. The interpersonal relationships of foreclosed and diffusion students were stereotyped, superficial, and hence not very intimate. The searching moratorium students showed the most variability between these two extremes. Similarly, Kacerguis and Adams (in press) studied forty-four male and forty-four female college students, and found that those people of either sex who were in the identity achievement category were more likely to be engaged in intimate relationships than were males or females in the foreclosure, moratorium, and diffusion categories. People in these latter three groups were much more variable in their level of intimacy.

Because identity links the adolescent to his or her social world, a basis of the different interpersonal styles of adolescents who differ in identity status may lie in their social interaction history; perhaps this involves the family, since it is the major social institution delivering those societal demands to which the person must adapt. Recalling Erikson's (1959) conception of identity as being in part composed of self-esteem, O'Donnell's (1976) finding, that in eighth and eleventh grade adolescents the degree of positive feelings toward parents was generally more closely related to self-esteem than degree of these feelings to friends, may be taken as support for the importance of family interaction in identity development. Other studies show that different family structures, for example, presence of a working or a nonworking mother (Nelson, 1971) or father absence (Santrock, 1970), are associated with contrasts in levels of adjustment in adolescence or in ego development prior to adolescence, respectively. However, neither these reports nor that of O'Donnell suggests what sort of parental or familial functions may foster ego identity development.

Several studies suggest that parental personal and interpersonal characteristics may be transmitted to their offspring, in the context of the family setting the parents help create, to foster identity development. LaVoie (1976) reports that male high school students high in identity reported less regulation and control by their mothers and fathers, and more frequent praise by their fathers, than did males low in identity. Similarly, LaVoie found that high-identity high school females reported less maternal restrictiveness and greater freedom to discuss problems with their mothers and fathers than did low-identity females. Thus, high-identity adolescents appear to be characterized by a family setting that involves less parental restrictiveness and better child-parent communication than do low-identity adolescents. Waterman and Waterman (1971) and Matteson (1974) provide further data to support this conclusion.

In their longitudinal study of college freshman, Waterman and Waterman (1971) found that those students who showed stable identity achievement status for the entire year—and it will be recalled that many did not—scored significantly higher on a measure of family independence than did those students who changed out of the

INSIGHT INTO ADOLESCENCE

Sören Aabye Kierkegaard was born in Denmark in 1813. When Kierkegaard was 24, his father died. This event provoked a crisis. He questioned his youth and adolescence—all of his life up to that moment. As Kierkegaard was a religious man, and believed somewhat in predestination, he was haunted by some terrible "sin" he felt his father had committed. Kierkegaard became an eminent religious philosopher who inspired many twentieth-century thinkers, particularly the Existentialists.

My father died Wednesday the 8th at 2 A.M. I had so deeply wished him to live a few years longer, and I regard his death as the last sacrifice he made to his love for me, for he died not from me, but for me, in order that perhaps something might still come of me. Of all he left me, his memory, his transfigured image, transfigured not through the poetic inventions of my imagination (of that it had no need), but transfigured through many personal touches that I only now learn about, this memory is the most precious thing to me and I will endeavor to keep it concealed from the world, for I do feel that at this moment there is only *one* person (E. Boesen) with whom I can truly speak of him. He was "a deeply faithful friend."

August 11, 1838.

1848.

Everything my father has told me comes true, yes. "There are sins from which a human being can be saved only by extraordinary divine succor." From a human viewpoint I owe my father everything. He has made me as unhappy as possible in every way, made my youth a torment without peer, caused me, inwardly, not to be far from feeling scandalized by Christianity, or, rather, I *was* scandalized, but out of reverence for it I decided never to breathe a word about it to anyone, and out of love for my father to represent Christianity as being as true as possible in contrast to the senseless nonsense which in Christendom passes for Christianity; and yet my father was the most affectionate father and I always had and always will have a deep yearning for him whom, morning and evening, I have never once failed to remember.

Source: Kierkegaard, S. *The Diary of Sören Kierkegaard* New York: Philosophical Library, 1960.

achievement status. In addition, those students who initially were foreclosured and then left this status by the end of the freshman year were also significantly higher scorers on a measure of family independence than those students who did not change out of this status.

In the study by Matteson (1974), involving ninth grade students, a measure of adolescent self-esteem and of communication with parents was taken. In addition, the parents of the adolescents completed questionnaires about parent-adolescent communication and their own marital communication. Matteson reported that adolescents with low self-esteem viewed communication with their parents as less facilitative than did adolescents with high self-esteem. Moreover, parents of low self-esteem adolescents perceived their communication with their spouses as less facilitative, and rated their marriages as less satisfying, than did parents of adolescents with high self-esteem.

Thus, family setting variables that relate to communication quality among *all* family members and to patterns of parental control appear to relate to identity development. A family setting having open communication and low restrictions on the individual seems to be most facilitative in providing a context for successful resolution of role search. Of course, settings having such characteristics need not be just conventional American family ones. Although there have been few studies, other types of family structures, on the one hand, or other types of social settings, on the other, can promote such development.

Long, Henderson, and Platt (1973) studied fifty-one Israeli male and female adolescents, aged 11 to 13 years, reared in a *kibbutzim*, and compared them to two groups of same-aged youth reared in more traditional family settings. In the kibbutzim family system, children are reared collectively by adults who are not necessarily their parents. In fact, in this system children may often spend at most a few hours a day with either biological parent. Yet in the kibbutzim system, the individual's contribution to the group is emphasized, as is equality of all group members despite their age or role. The adolescents reared in this setting showed more social interest and higher self-esteem than those adolescents reared in the other setting.

Moreover, the college environment may be seen as a nonfamily social setting where open communication of ideas and minimal restrictiveness of search for roles are involved. Sanford (1962) has speculated that because of these properties the college experience promotes movement toward identity achievement. The longitudinal data of Waterman and Waterman (1971), Waterman et al. (1974), and Waterman and Goldman (1976) support this view. Most college students experience an identity crisis during their college years, and of these, 75 percent reach the achievement status.

Although future research is needed to evaluate the appropriateness of these interpretations, it does appear that if an adolescent is placed in a social setting involving openness of social communication and minimal restrictiveness on role search, an adaptive coordination between self and society will be attained. An identity will be achieved.

CHAPTER SUMMARY

Erik Erikson's stage theory of psychosocial development offers descriptions of personality development that are consistent with a life-span perspective. Although Erikson's explanations of psychosocial development are limited on both conceptual and empirical grounds, his descriptions have served as the major basis for research about adolescent personality.

Erikson sees the person as having to develop the capacities (the ego functions) to meet the demands of society. However, as the person develops, society expects different behaviors to be shown. Thus, Erikson describes eight stages of psychosocial development; with each stage there is an "ego crisis" pertaining to whether the person will meet the demands of society and successfully develop the appropriate capability. Erikson's eight stages are the *oral-sensory*, the *anal-musculature*, the *genital-locomotor*, *latency*, *puberty and adolescence*, *young adulthood*, *adulthood*, and *maturity*.

In adolescence the person needs to adopt a role and thus adopt a set of behaviors that will contribute to the maintenance and perpetuation of society. Yet because of all the changes that characterize adolescence, the person is unsure of who he or she is; and unless the person feels he or she has such self-knowledge, any role adoption cannot be made with assurance. Thus, the crisis of adolescence is between *identity* at one extreme and role confusion (or identity diffusion) at the other.

Research on identity development in adolescence primarily has been derived from these ideas of Erikson. One direction that research has taken is to determine if the identity crisis emerges in adolescence in the stagelike manner that Erikson suggests. Although most research indicates that adolescence is indeed a time for personal definition and reorganization, the sequence that Erikson offers does not seem to hold. Some adolescents, for instance, attain intimacy—the characteristic supposedly associated with the succeeding stage of successful ego development—simultaneously with or prior to the development of identity.

Another direction that research has taken is to indicate the types of identity statuses a person may possess during adolescence. Marcia has indicated that in addition to the *identity achievement* and the *identity diffusion* statuses, some adolescents fell into a *moratorium* category (they were experiencing an identity crisis but were actively striving to make a commitment to a role), while others were in a status Marcia labeled as *foreclosure* (adolescents here had never experienced a crisis and yet they were committed). Data indicate that over the course of the college years people change their identity status more toward achievement and away from moratorium. Indeed by the end of college most people are identity achievers. Moreover, over time the achievement category tends to be the most stable ego status.

A third direction that research has taken is to explore the variables that may affect the development of particular ego statuses in adolescence. Data indicate that formal operational ability, principled moral reasoning, positive self-concept, and an internal center of control are related to the attainment of identity achievement. Furthermore, particular types of social interactions (for example, warm, facilitative ones with parents) and relationships (for example, intimate, friendly ones with peers) in particular contexts (such as college) appear to be positively related to the development of identity achievement.

13

SEX DIFFERENCES IN ADOLESCENT PERSONALITY AND SOCIAL DEVELOPMENT

CHAPTER
OVERVIEW

Some differences between males and females—reproductive functioning for example—are obvious and universal. The presence and basis of differences in personality and social development are, however, controversial. This chapter examines theory and research on such sex differences, and identifies some important areas in which contemporary male and female adolescents are thought to differ.

ISSUES
TO CONSIDER

In what ways do the ideas of Erikson provide a nature view of sex differences in personality and social development?

In Erikson's view, what are the implications of the inner-space orientation of females and the outer-space orientation of males?

What are the major dimensions of sex differences predicted by Erikson's theory, and how do these predictions compare with those derived from McCandless's nurture, social learning theory of such differences?

How do the sex-role stereotypes that exist currently in Western societies correspond to social and personality differences predicted by Erikson and McCandless?

How may sex-role stereotypes influence socialization, and how do cultural and historical changes in socialization influence the evolution of sex roles?

To what degree are the data from current research studies that pertain to adolescent body attitudes consistent with the theoretical ideas of Erikson and McCandless?

Do male and female adolescents differ in their self-esteems and self-concepts in ways consistent with the theories of Erikson and McCandless?

What are the characteristics of vocational role behaviors and orientations among male and female adolescents? Do the characteristics correspond to those predicted by Erikson and McCandless?

There are obvious differences between the sexes. Structural differences in primary and secondary sexual characteristics and functional differences in reproduction are universal contrasts between males and females. Only women can *menstruate, gestate* (carry children), and *lactate* (breast-feed). Only men can *impregnate* (Money & Ehrhardt, 1972). However, to social scientists interested in the total development of individuals, it is important to try to discern both the obvious and the subtle characteristics that give the person his or her distinctiveness.

This chapter examines some major dimensions of differences between males and females. Some theorists have suggested that personality and social functioning are innately tied to the physical and physiological characteristics of males and females (for example, Erikson, 1964, 1968; Freud, 1923). Such a *nature* view says that there are inevitable differences between the sexes, since there are universal biological contrasts between them. Just as it is biologically adaptive (for species survival) to engage in male or female reproductive functions, it is also "biologically imperative" (Freud, 1923, 1949) to engage in those personal behaviors which are linked innately to one's biological status as a male or female. It is in this sense that sex differences in personality and social relations are seen as universal. To proponents of this position, such as Erikson (1964, 1968), *anatomy is destiny!*

Another idea about the possible basis of such sex differences is found in social learning interpretations of behavior development (for example, McCandless, 1970). Because any behavior is, from this point of view, a phenomenon shaped through social rewards and punishments, there are no necessarily universal sex differences. Nevertheless, because males and females are seen to be rewarded and punished for different sets of behaviors, proponents of this view still predict that males and females will show different personal and social behaviors.

Indeed, one goal of this chapter is to show that both nature theorists such as Erikson, and nurture theorists, such as McCandless, make similar predictions about the status of sex differences in behaviors (albeit for different reasons), especially during adolescence. Both theorists claim that adolescents are prompted to choose a role linking them to their societies. We shall indicate that there are three sets of predictions regarding sex differences in adolescent personality that may be derived from Erikson's (1959, 1964, 1968) nature-based theory. These predicted sex differences in the adolescent pertain to (1) body concept, (2) self-concept and self-esteem, and (3) vocational role orientation. We shall also see that the same predictions may be derived from the nurture view of McCandless (1970).

The topic of sex differences in personality and social development is a controversial and complex one. Moreover, it is an area with hundreds of recent research studies and theoretical papers which are relevant (Block, 1973, 1976; Maccoby, 1966; Maccoby & Jacklin, 1974). Clearly, not all sex differences can be reviewed precisely in one chapter. Our discussion focuses on major theorists' ideas about sex differences, and on research studies which help clarify these ideas. We shall attempt to extend these ideas by interpreting data within a general framework which describes an individual's behavior development, and differences between persons, as products of biology, psychology, society, culture, and history (Block, 1973; Sarason, 1973). To reach this goal, Erikson's (1964, 1968) ideas about sex differences in adolescent personality and social development are presented first. Next, the ideas of social learning theorists like McCandless (1970) are reviewed. After this, some relevant research evidence is discussed.

ERIKSON'S THEORY OF INNER AND OUTER SPACE

Chapter 12 presented Erikson's views about the development of the ego. In that discussion it was noted that healthy or adaptive ego development requires a synthesis of the biological, psychological, and societal demands placed on the person. At each stage of ego development, the person is placed in a psychosocial crisis that can best be dealt with through such an integration.

In adolescence the identity crisis can only be resolved adequately through the attainment of a role. Such a role must involve an adoption of a set of behaviors and an ideology which allow the individual to contribute to society in a biologically appropriate way. Since males and females differ in terms of their physiological functions and reproductive organs, there will be different implications for role adoption. In other words, because of the basic biological differences between men and women, they necessarily will have to adopt different role-related behaviors and ideologies in order to be psychosocially "healthy." Thus, for Erikson (1964, 1968) the anatomical and physiological differences between the sexes relate directly to differences in personality:

> Many of the testable items on the long list of "inborn" differences between human males and females can be shown to have a meaningful function within an ecology which is built, as any mammalian ecology must be, around the fact that the human fetus must be carried inside the womb for a given number of months, and that the infant must be suckled or, at any rate, raised within a maternal world best staffed at first by the mother (and this for the sake of her own awakened motherliness, as well) with a gradual addition of other women. (Erikson, 1968, p. 281)

The inner-space orientation of females

Thus, Erikson sees women's reproductive role as the dominant force in shaping their personalities. However, his idea is more pervasive than this. He argues that because of their anatomical structure and the adaptive biological demand for carrying and nurturing the child of a man, a woman's whole sense of self is necessarily involved with motherhood and mothering. He says that:

> The stage of life crucial for the emergence of an integrated female identity is the step from youth to maturity, the state when the young woman, whatever her

work career, relinquishes the care received from the parental family in order to commit herself to the love of a stranger and to the care to be given to his and her offspring. (Erikson, 1968, p. 265)

To Erikson, identity development in females goes in the direction of being a wife and a mother. Accordingly, to fulfill her biologically based role appropriately, Erikson believes an adolescent female must be oriented to her *inner space*. To bear children in fulfillment of her biological directive, a female must be oriented toward *incorporation*, bringing a male's penis into her inner space, into her body. Only through such incorporation can the woman create a situation allowing adaptation. Only through incorporation can she create *within* herself the child that will fulfill her biological destiny. Because of this biologically based orientation to inner space, the female will undergo identity formation processes different than the male. The behaviors females will be committed to, or show fidelity toward, will be markedly different than those of males. Indeed, by asking some rhetorical questions, Erikson (1968) shows that despite whether a woman chooses a career outside of marriage, at her core the woman is always disposed to, dominated by, her orientation toward being a mother and mothering:

But how does the identity formation of women differ by dint of the fact that their somatic design harbors an "inner space" destined to bear the offspring of chosen men and, with it, a biological, psychological, and ethical commitment to take care of human infancy? Is not the disposition for this commitment (whether it be combined with a career, and even whether or not it be realized in actual motherhood) the core problem of female fidelity? (p. 266)

To become a mother and to engage in mothering, a female obviously needs a male. Thus, her inner-space–incorporative orientation leads to an *interpersonal* orientation. She needs to admit a male to her inner space so that her biologically invariant psychosocial role can be achieved. In short, because of her inner-space demands, a female becomes interpersonally oriented to search for a man to incorporate.

Although a female can prepare for this before she meets a particular male, she must keep her identity somewhat open in order to adjust herself to the specific characteristics of the particular male she attracts. Indeed, Erikson (1968) notes:

Young women often ask whether they can "have an identity" before they know whom they will marry and for whom they will make a home. Granted that something in the young woman's identity must keep itself open for the peculiarities of the man to be joined and of the children to be brought up, I think that much of a young woman's identity is already defined in her kind of attractiveness and in the selective nature of her search for the man (or men) by whom she wishes to be sought. (p. 283)

Hence, a female needs to attract a male to her in order that a biologically adaptive incorporation into inner space may occur. Thus, a female is dependent on a male for the attainment of her identity, since without a literal or at least symbolic incorporation of the penis, she cannot attain her requisite role. Indeed, all her psychosocial activities are directed toward this fulfillment of inner-space pressures. In fact, Erikson (1968) says: "But since a woman is never not-a-woman, she can see her long-range goals only in those modes of activity which include and integrate her natural dispositions" (p. 290). Moreover, he notes that identity can only be achieved, that "womanhood arrives when attractiveness and experience have succeeded in selecting what is to be admitted to the welcome of the inner space 'for keeps'" (1968, p. 283).

In sum, Erikson sees a female's inner-space, incorporative *mode of functioning* as making her committed to a role involving interpersonal orientations and dependency on others. Because of the invariant biological basis of these relations, Erikson appears to be taking a weak interactional, and hence nature-based, view of the basis of females' personality and social behavior. Indeed, he is quite explicit about this stance:

> *Am I saying, then, that "anatomy is destiny?" Yes, it is destiny, insofar as it determines not only the range and configuration of physiological functioning and its limitation but also, to an extent, personality configurations. The basic modalities of woman's commitment and involvement naturally also reflect the ground plan of her body. (Erikson, 1968, p. 285)*

If "anatomy is destiny" for females, it must also be so for males. Yet the different structure of male reproductive organs leads to quite different implications for them.

The outer-space orientation of males

Males must also use their reproductive organs in ways consistent with their biological roles, according to Erikson (1968). If they are to use their bodies appropriately, then they cannot be incorporative. Rather, they must seek to *intrude* upon, enter into, objects external to their own bodies. They must be oriented to *outer space* and develop an *intrusive mode* of dealing with the environment outside themselves in order to use their bodies for reproduction. Although we have seen that a female needs a male, either literally or symbolically, in order to attain an appropriate identity, the reverse is not the case for males. The outer-space orientation requires developing ego capabilities allowing for intrusion on target objects outside the body. Although such objects may be females, they need not be. As long as any object in the environment is being successfully intruded on—or in other words, *dominated, manipulated, or controlled*—then (at least symbolically) the male is conforming adaptively to his outer-space, intrusive mode of functioning.

Thus, as long as males are oriented toward, and effective in, gaining dominance over objects in their outer space, they are behaving in a biologically appropriate manner. Indeed, while the inner-space orientation of females leads to an inevitable press toward being a mother and mothering, males' outer-space orientation leads to quite distinct behaviors. Since appropriate use of the body involves intrusion upon any objects external to the self, the male does not need another person to show this orientation. Thus, the adaptive male should develop an independent, *individual* orientation. In fact, if the male depended on others in any way for his psychosocial functioning, then this would mean he was not dominating his outer space but instead was dependent on objects external to himself.

In contrast with a female, whose basic "unit" of reproduction—the ova—must passively wait for the male's sperm for impregnation and thus fulfillment of the inner space, the male must play an active role in life for meeting the demands of the outer space (Erikson, 1968). That is, if sperms are not active and mobile, then reproduction will not occur. Analogously, if males do not show behaviors which are effective, independent, and active manipulations of their environment, they cannot fulfill the demands of their outer space. Thus, roles allowing for these behaviors are appropriate ones for males.

In summary, the linkage between differences in reproductive anatomy and physiology and differences in the personality and social behavior of males and females is a nature-based, and hence invariant, one in Erikson's (1964, 1968) view. The biological basis of these differences *is construed to mean* that females' identities must, at their core, be oriented to being a mother and to mothering, while males' identities must, at their core, involve mastery of the external world. These sex differences not only reflect the different ways the genitals of the two sexes are structured, but also mirror the function of the reproductive cells of each sex. Additionally, they pervade each sex group's entire orientation to the world.

Furthermore, Erikson believes that play behaviors reflect the psychosocial preparation of the person for a role consistent with his or her anatomical and physiological characteristics. As evidence, Erikson (1968) reports that when he asked a group of 10- to 12-year-old males and females from the Berkeley Guidance Study to construct scenes with materials such as dolls and blocks, they portrayed scenes consistent with their respective genital structures. Although not instructed in any way about what sort of scene to construct, males built scenes figuratively related to an intrusive penis, or an organ attaining or losing its erect state. Females' scenes symbolically were related to their vaginal opening or to their internal genitalia. Erikson's report and interpretation of these data are instructive:

> Girls' enclosures consist of low walls, i.e., only one block high, except for an occasional elaborate doorway. These interiors of houses with or without walls were, for the most part, expressly peaceful. Often, a little girl was playing the piano. In a number of cases, however, the interior was intruded by animals or dangerous men. Yet the idea of an intruding creature did not necessarily lead to the defensive erection of walls or closing of doors. Rather the majority of these intrusions have an element of humor and pleasurable excitement.
>
> Boys' scenes are either houses with elaborate walls or facades with protrusions such as cones or cylinders representing ornaments or cannons. There are high towers, and there are entirely exterior scenes. . . .
>
> The male and female spaces, then, were dominated, respectively, by height and downfall and by strong motion and its channeling or arrest; and by static interiors which were open or simply enclosed, and peaceful or intruded upon. It may come as a surprise to some and seem a matter of course to others that here sexual differences in the organization of a play space seem to parallel the morphology of genital differentiation itself: in the male, an external organ, erectable and intrusive in character, serving the channelization of mobile sperm cells; in the female, internal organs, with vestibular access, leading to statically expectant ova. (Erikson, 1968, pp. 270–271)

Dimensions of sex differences predicted by Erikson's theory

In their play, in their behaviors, and in their ideologies, males and females show differences related to their respective biological status. The basis and nature of these differences converge to suggest three major domains of personality difference between males and females.

Body concept   If females use their bodies appropriately, they will incorporate a male into their inner space and fulfill their role regarding being a mother and mothering. Thus, they are oriented to use their bodies interpersonally, to attract a man to them and thus to fulfill the inner-space demands. In other words, the more a female uses her body as a vehicle for interpersonal attraction of males, the more likely she is to be in a position to play her incorporative role, and thus form a healthy, adaptive identity. The more a female views her body as physically attractive to others, the better sense of self, the better self-concept, she should have. The self-concept would be enhanced because of the greater likelihood of inner-space fulfillment.

An alternative set of relations should exist for males. If males use their bodies appropriately, they will use them individually, to intrude upon, show mastery over, or manipulate objects external to their bodies. To fulfill outer-space demands, the male must be effective in this intrusion. If he is not, he would be dependent on others for functioning in the environment, since he himself could not master it. And this reliance on others for survival is incompatible with male biological demands. Thus, the more a male uses his body as an instrument for individual physical effectiveness, the more likely he is to be playing an intrusive role, and thus forming a healthy, adaptive identity. The more a male views his body as physically effective, the better self-concept he should have.

In sum, different body concepts should develop in males and females, and these different body concepts should be related to self-concept and inner versus outer space orientation. Females should conceive of their bodies more in terms of physical attractiveness than physical effectiveness, while the reverse should be the case for males. This means that conceptions about body attractiveness should be related more highly to the self-concept of females than of males and that conceptions about body effectiveness should be more highly related to the self-concepts of males than of females. In addition, it may be predicted from Erikson's (1964, 1968) conceptions that females' body concepts and self-concepts should be related more highly to inner-space than to outer-space orientation, while males' body concepts and self-concepts should be related more highly to outer-space than to inner-space orientations. These predicted relations lead directly to the second domain of differences that can be predicted from Erikson's ideas.

Self-concept and self-esteem   Self-concept may be defined as the set of knowledge one maintains about oneself. Self-esteem is the level of positive or negative evaluation one associates with the self-concept. One person might know himself or herself as aggressive, intelligent, and calculating—and evaluate all the "traits" in this concept as positive. Thus, this person would have a high (positive) self-esteem. On the other hand, another person having an identical self-concept might have negative feelings about the first and the third trait; if this were the case, the person would be said to have lower (negative in this case) self-esteem.

Erikson's ideas have implications for the self-concepts and self-esteems of males and females. First, it is clear that the items or traits that make up the self-concept would show sex differences. Erikson depicts the female as dependent because of her incorporative, interpersonal orientation and as passive because of the nature of her reproductive functioning. Males, in turn, are independent because of their individual orientation and are active because of the nature of their reproductive functioning.

Thus, a female's self-concept should include the traits of dependency and passivity if she is playing her role appropriately. Moreover, since she is dependent on and passive to a male, she should be characterized as dominated, and as conforming to the suggestions of others. Furthermore, because she is oriented to using her body—and thus herself—in ways promoting interpersonal physical attractiveness, she should not focus on effectiveness or mastery endeavors. Thus, she should not be task-oriented, but rather person-oriented.

A male's self-concept, however, should include the items of independency, activity, and instrumental effectiveness, if he is playing his intrusive role appropriately. This would mean that he would not be conforming to the suggestions of others, but rather would attempt to assert himself to dominate the objects in his world, be they physical objects or people. This effectiveness, dominance, and activity style should lead to aggressive interaction with his physical and social world, and promote a task-mastery orientation rather than a person orientation.

Erikson (1964, 1968), then, predicts that males and females should define themselves differently. However, because the predictions characterizing the male self-concept (for example, independence, individuality, dominance, assertiveness, aggressiveness, activity, instrumental effectiveness, nonconformity, task orientation) tend to be ones very generally judged positively (Block, 1973; Broverman, Vogel, Broverman, Clarkson & Rosenkrantz, 1972), males should have a positive self-esteem. In turn, because the predictions characterizing the female self-concept (for example, dependence, submission, passivity, instrumental ineffectiveness, conformity) tend to be ones generally judged negatively (Block, 1973; Broverman et al., 1972), females should have a negative self-esteem, or certainly one less positive than that of males.

Accordingly, because they think about and regard themselves differently, males and females should not *do* the same things in their societal setting. They should play different roles. The understanding of such role differences is, of course, the central concern of Erikson's ideas about identity. The nature and direction of such role differences make up the third domain of differences that can be predicted on the basis of Erikson's ideas.

Vocational role orientation   It is obvious that men and women in the modern world do not always perform the same tasks. They tend to engage in different vocations, and thus are oriented to playing different roles in their lives. It is clear what Erikson's views are about the bases of these differences. Since "anatomy is destiny," there are biological reasons seen as *necessarily* fostering role adoption along particular paths. Thus, to Erikson, not only do men and women adopt different vocations, but it is biologically adaptive that they show an orientation to maintain these vocational role distinctions. If women denied the demands of their inner space, there would be no one to perpetuate and nurture society.

Accordingly, women should be oriented to adopt vocational roles consistent with their inner space. Obviously, the traditionally feminine roles—most notably of wife and mother—are those they should be oriented toward. Indeed, these roles are traditional because of their survival value for the species (Erikson, 1968). However, there are other traditionally feminine roles, endeavors that also have a component of nurturance associated with them, for example, nurse and elementary school teacher.

Moreover, because the commitment to interpersonal attractiveness exists to enhance the woman's chance to fulfill her inner space and thus reproductive function, no vocational orientations requiring a commitment of effort and time inconsistent with the mothering role would be appropriate. This orientation, coupled with the fact that the body concept of females promotes a self-concept denoting passivity and instrumental ineffectiveness and a negative self-esteem as well, suggests that only lower-status roles would be seen as appropriate for females. Such roles are those typically seen as feminine ones. Stated differently, roles which are traditionally feminine are also those which are traditionally lower status in society (O'Leary, 1974, 1977).

An alternative vocational role orientation would be expected for males. Because of their orientation toward individual intrusion and effectiveness, males should seek vocations allowing mastery, independence, dominance, and competent control over their world. This vocational role orientation is fostered by their body and self-concepts and their self-esteems. These attributes promote an orientation toward competence-effectiveness and/or high-status (for example, power, leadership, prestige) roles, which are of course conventionally those defined as traditional masculine endeavors. Thus, because of their outer-space body orientations, their self-concepts, and their self-esteems, males should be oriented to adopt vocational roles which are traditionally masculine ones (for example, ones requiring mastery or strength, such as engineer, truck driver, or farmer) and/or ones having high status in society (for example, doctor, lawyer, or banker).

In summary, Erikson's theory of sex differences in personal and social behavior leads to distinct predictions about the nature and direction of development in several domains of psychosocial functioning. The rather negative picture he draws of the types of behaviors developed by the female is made all the more disconcerting because Erikson sees these sex differences as biologically based; moreover, because he believes that a biological contribution is innate and hence stereotyped, fixed, and not amenable to basic alteration by the environment, by history, or by society, there is very little one can do to alter the basic character of these sex differences.

Although the particularities of a culture determine how, for instance, mothering may be expressed, and how it may relate to other components of a woman's role, the weak interactional view that Erikson takes does not allow for a shaping of that biological basis that he presumes innately disposes one to a mothering orientation. Although such a restricted view of nature contributions have been shown repeatedly in this book to be inappropriate, a nurture alternative to Erikson's ideas encounters the same problems. McCandless (1970) presents social learning ideas that lead to the same predictions regarding sex differences in personality that were associated with Erikson's views. We shall see that both views—in making the same predictions—encounter identical difficulties in attempts to integrate existing data.

McCANDLESS'S SOCIAL LEARNING INTERPRETATION OF SEX DIFFERENCES

Chapter 6 presented the nurture, social learning theory of development put forth by McCandless (1970). Although many different orientations exist that may be labeled social learning positions (Kuhn, 1978), all are unified by a common view that learning principles are the basic ones involved in development. We focus here on the social learning view of McCandless (1970) because his is a leading interpretation, and one specifically devised to be relevant to adolescence.

To restate McCandless's views, in his drive-based social learning theory there is a stress on the drives, such as hunger or sex, which energize behavior. Indeed, this stress is particularly important in adolescence, when for the first time in one's development a mature sex drive emerges. Since McCandless (1970) asserts that social learning involves organizing those behaviors which reduce the arousal created by our drives (for example, as in reducing our feelings of hunger), adolescence is a time when the person must learn to emit those behaviors which will reduce the sex drive. Since behaviors which reduce drives are therefore rewarding, while those that do not are punishing, the adolescent must come to show repeatedly those behaviors that are reward-producing. In short, the adolescent must form habits—sets of behavior which tend to be repeated by a person because they are rewarding and drive-reducing (McCandless, 1970).

The adolescent must learn what behaviors will effectively reduce the sex drive, as well as all other drive-states. That is, not only is there a new drive to form habits about (the sex drive), but also the habits formed in regard to the other drives may have to be revised. The adolescent is, for instance, at an age level different from a child, and age is one cue for differential reward of behavior in society. For example, a 2-year-old seated at the dinner table with his or her parents may learn that speaking out to ask for food, no matter who else is speaking, or reaching for food, no matter where it is located on the table (even on a parent's plate), is an effective behavior for acquiring food and causing hunger reduction. Parents of a 2-year-old are happy if their child can articulate a desire for specific foods and/or show the motor behavior necessary for self-feeding. However, if the behavior shown by the 2-year-old were shown by the 14-year-old, it would not be rewarded. Instead of being an effective habit, it would lead to punishment, because by 14 years of age, different social expectations regarding "table manners" typically are held by parents.

Furthermore, not only does one's age status play a differential role in determining what behaviors will be appropriately drive-reducing, but so too does one's sex status. McCandless (1970) indicates that society does not reward males and females for the same drive-reducing habits. Accordingly, just as people acquire those habits which are age-appropriate, they similarly are channeled into developing those habits which are socially prescribed as sex-appropriate. As a consequence, because of the sex drive and the differing social expectations regarding it, McCandless (1970) believes that adolescence is a period of defining oneself in terms of new and sex-specific habits.

Thus, like Erikson (1959, 1968), McCandless sees adolescence as a period of sex-differentiated identity formation. Indeed, McCandless (1970) believes that these sex differences involve differential male and female acquisitions of habits, if they are to show those behaviors which will lead to drive reduction and hence adaptation. It is these different sets of habits which compose the personality differences between males and females.

McCandless (1970), drawing on data from Douvan and Adelson (1966), Barry, Bacon, and Child (1957), and others, finds that males are being rewarded for a set of habits which form an individual competence-effectiveness cluster of behaviors. In describing the adolescent male's major social drive, McCandless (1970) says:

> His behavior is geared toward independence, self-sufficiency, and competence above all else; and his behavior—social and antisocial—can be understood only if it is viewed within such a framework. (pp. 32–33)

In turn, McCandless believes females are rewarded by society for a set of habits which form an interpersonal warmth-expressiveness cluster of behaviors. Thus, in indicating the adolescent female's major social drive, McCandless (1970) says:

> The American girl, in contrast to her male counterpart, strives principally to define herself as a woman and to achieve personal security. This includes finding and maintaining stable and intimate personal interrelationships. (p. 33)

Dimensions of sex differences predicted by McCandless's theory

McCandless believes that adolescent females are rewarded if they acquire behaviors allowing for stable and intimate interrelationships. Because these behaviors lead to a socially sanctioned reduction of the sex drive, these intimate relationships are typically heterosexual ones. Indeed, since McCandless also points out that females are oriented to find their definitions as "women," rewarding heterosexual intimacy is associated with females' search for their definition as women. Thus, not only are women interpersonally oriented in their reward-seeking behavior, but as such, this typically makes them dependent on others (usually men) for their self-definition as women.

Males, on the other hand, are rewarded if they acquire behaviors allowing for self-sufficiency, and hence individual competence and instrumental effectiveness. Thus, this orientation toward individual effectiveness makes males strive to be independent and autonomous in their social interactions. Indeed, McCandless (1970) says that "adolescent girls may continue to be feminine—to cling, to confide, to depend on others for decisions," but in regard to males he says "to be dependent is to be unmanly. It is not appropriate for an adolescent boy to ask openly for affection signs from adults, no matter how much he may want them" (p. 22). Hence, not only is it clear that McCandless is sex-biased in his characterization of feminine behavior—saying it is clinging and dependent in character—but it is also clear that that bias exists because of his belief in the differential types of behaviors typically rewarded in one sex group as opposed to the other. Simply, he says that:

> There is a sex difference in the urgency with which autonomy is sought. Obtaining it seems to be a major goal for boys, and a relatively minor goal for girls. (1970, p. 20)

Moreover, to be independent, autonomous, and hence effective in society, one typically must have some sort of vocational role. One would expect males to be more vocationally oriented than females, who should be more preoccupied with establishing intimate interpersonal relationships. Thus, in support of this expectation, McCandless cites the Douvan and Adelson (1966) findings that adolescent boys were highly vocationally oriented while adolescent girls were markedly unclear about career plans, even including marriage (remember here Erikson's, 1964, 1968, speculation that a female must keep her identity and vocational plans open in order to fit them to the specifics of the man she eventually admits to her inner space). However, Douvan and Adelson (1966) also found, as expected by McCandless (1970), that adolescent girls were more preoccupied with friendships, social relations, and self-definition concerns than were the boys they studied.

In summary, McCandless's conceptualization of the social situation of adolescent males and females becomes remarkably similar to that of Erikson. In fact, although to Erikson the adolescent behaves because of biological imperatives, while to McCandless the adolescent behaves because of social reward, the behavior itself is seen in the same way. Indeed, the same three sets of predictions may be derived.

Body concept   Females must be attractive to others, particularly men, in order to acquire the intimate (for example, warm, open, and expressive) relationships that will give them security and self-definition. Thus, the more they see their bodies as physically attractive, the more likely they are to conceive of themselves as possessing the characteristics that merit social rewards. Males, though, must be individually effective in order to obtain behaviors allowing independent competence. As such, the more they see their bodies as instruments of physical attractiveness, the more likely they are to conceive of themselves as possessing the characteristics that are socially rewarded. In sum, from McCandless's (1970) ideas, we may predict that body attitudes relating to physical attractiveness should be more important than those of physical effectiveness in the self-concept of females. But effectiveness rather than attractiveness attitudes should play the greater role for males.

Self-concept and self-esteem   The basis of the sex differences predicted for body attitudes lies, for McCandless, in the different behaviors that are socially rewarded for males and females. Because of these different patterns of reward, males should come to show habits, and also define themselves, according to behaviors indicating independence, competence, autonomy, and effectiveness, activity, and dominance. In turn, females should develop habits, and also define themselves, with behaviors such as dependency, passivity, intimacy, and expressiveness. Thus, not only would the different social systems of rewards and punishments associated with males and females promote sex differences in behaviors and self-concepts, but also because the alternative sets of behaviors have contrasting social evaluations, differences in self-esteem should develop. Like Erikson's (1968) ideas, those of McCandless (1970) lead to the idea that a male's self-esteem should be more positive than that of a female's.

Vocational role orientation   Because males can and must emit different behaviors than females in order to obtain social rewards, the sets of social behaviors—the roles—the two sexes engage in will be different. Because of their individual competence—effectiveness behavioral orientation, and the character of their self-concepts and self-esteems, males should strive to do those tasks, or in other words be oriented to engage in those roles, which allow for "male" rewards. Because of the social confounding that exists with regard to such roles, these traditionally male roles are those which are the higher-status ones in society, that is, the ones requiring activity, assertiveness, dominance, and/or high levels of instrumental effectiveness and competence. In turn, because of their interpersonal warmth—expressiveness behavioral orientation, and the character of their self-concepts and self-esteems, females should strive to engage in those roles which allow for "female rewards. This circular, social confounding accounts for pressures on females to seek those endeavors involving interpersonal security found through relationships with others (for example, mothering) and/or lower-status tasks stereotypically involving low degrees of instrumental effectiveness and autonomy.

To summarize, McCandless's (1970) social learning position leads to sets of predictions about sex differences in adolescent personality development that are quite compatible with those of Erikson (1964, 1968). The issue for science now becomes whether these predictions are useful in depicting actual, empirical differences between males and females. Does available research evidence show that male and female adolescents differ in regard to body concepts, self-concepts, self-esteems, and vocational role orientations in the ways Erikson and McCandless predict? Answering this question is a complex task for at least two reasons.

First, the research pertaining to this question is voluminous, and often contradictory. Second, despite the degree to which the available evidence *actually* shows sex differences consistent with the ideas of Erikson and McCandless, there is another, related body of research which shows that *people believe sex differences do exist*. Thus, because such social beliefs can indeed provide a basis for behavior development—through the creation of self-fulfilling prophecies (Anthony, 1969, Rosenthal, 1966)—we turn first to a consideration of research pertaining to the social expectations people maintain about sex differences in adolescent personality and social behavior.

SEX-ROLE STEREOTYPES

Not only do the nurture ideas of McCandless (1970) lead to the same predictions regarding sex differences in adolescent personality and social development as do the nature-oriented ideas of Erikson (1964, 1968), but both theorists describe males' and females' development in stereotypic and traditional ways. An earlier chapter defined a social *stereotype* as an over-generalized belief, that is, some combination of cognition and feeling—some *attitude*—which invariantly characterizes a stimulus object (for example, a person). A stereotype allows for little exception (Allport, 1954). Because of this rigidity, a social stereotype is relatively resistent to change, and as such, may become accepted as always true in a given society. The sex differences that Erikson and McCandless describe are consistent with traditional social stereotypes regarding males and females in American society. Such stereotypes are widely held in America today.

A *sex role* may be defined as a socially defined set of prescriptions for behavior for people of a particular sex group; *sex-role behavior* may be defined as behavioral functioning in accordance with the prescriptions; and *sex-role stereotypes* are the generalized beliefs that particular behaviors are characteristic of one sex group as opposed to the other (Worell, 1978). Broverman et al. (1972) report a series of studies they conducted using a questionnaire that assessed perceptions of "typical masculine and feminine behavior." In order to study sex-role stereotypes, Broverman et al. gave a group of college males and females a long (122-item) list, with each trait presented in a bipolar manner (for example, "not at all aggressive" to "very aggressive"). They conceptualized sex roles as "the degree to which men and women are perceived to possess any particular trait" (Broverman et al., 1972). They found 41 items with which at least 75 percent agreement existed among males and females as to which end of the bipolar dimension was more descriptive of the average man or the average woman. These were the items they concluded formed the sex-role stereotypes for these students. These items are presented in Exhibit 13.1.

From this exhibit, it can be noted that those item ends associated with males, as judged by *both* males and females, are markedly consistent with the expectations derived from Erikson and McCandless. For instance, we find males described as very

Exhibit 13.1
Stereotypic sex-role items

Competency cluster (masculine pole is more desirable)

Feminine	Masculine
Not at all aggressive	Very aggressive
Not at all independent	Very independent
Very emotional	Not at all emotional
Does not hide emotions at all	Almost always hides emotions
Very subjective	Very objective
Very easily influenced	Not at all easily influenced
Very submissive	Very dominant
Dislikes math and science very much	Likes math and science very much
Very excitable in a minor crisis	Not at all excitable in a minor crisis
Very passive	Very active
Not at all competitive	Very competitive
Very illogical	Very logical
Very home-oriented	Very worldly
Not at all skilled in business	Very skilled in business
Very sneaky	Very direct
Does not know the way of the world	Knows the way of the world
Feelings easily hurt	Feelings not easily hurt
Not at all adventurous	Very adventurous
Has difficulty making decisions	Can make decisions easily
Cries very easily	Never cries
Almost never acts as a leader	Almost always acts as a leader
Not at all self-confident	Very self-confident
Very uncomfortable about being aggressive	Not at all uncomfortable about being aggressive
Not at all ambitious	Very ambitious
Unable to separate feelings from ideas	Easily able to separate feelings from ideas
Very dependent	Not at all dependent
Very conceited about appearance	Never conceited about appearance
Thinks women are always superior to men	Thinks men are always superior to women
Does not talk freely about sex with men	Talks freely about sex with men

Warmth-expressiveness cluster (feminine pole is more desirable)

Feminine	Masculine
Doesn't use harsh language at all	Uses very harsh language
Very talkative	Not at all talkative
Very tactful	Very blunt
Very gentle	Very rough
Very aware of feelings of others	Not at all aware of feelings of others
Very religious	Not at all religious
Very interested in own appearance	Not at all interested in own appearance
Very neat in habits	Very sloppy in habits
Very quiet	Very loud
Very strong need for security	Very little need for security
Enjoys art and literature	Does not enjoy art and literature at all
Easily expresses tender feelings	Does not express tender feelings at all easily

Note: These results are based on the responses of seventy-four college men and eighty college women.
Source: Adapted from Broverman et al., 1972, p. 63.

aggressive, very independent, very dominant, very active, very skilled in business, and not at all dependent. These items form what Broverman et al. (1972) term a competency cluster; and this is indeed identical to the competency-effectiveness set of behaviors that McCandless and Erikson predict.

Moreover, not only are females judged by both males and females to be at the opposite (low) ends of these competency-effectiveness dimensions, but also they are judged to be high on the warmth-expressiveness items. For example, they are seen to be very gentle, to be very aware of feelings of others, to be very interested in appearance, and to have a very strong need for security.

Moreover, although Exhibit 13.1 shows that for competency items the masculine end of the trait dimension is more desirable, and for the warmth-expressiveness cluster the feminine end is more desirable, we see also that there are more competency items than warmth-expressiveness items. Thus, there are more positively evaluated traits stereotypically associated with males than with females. Broverman et al. (1972) found evidence that these attitudes are quite pervasive in society. They report that their questionnaire has been given to 599 men and 383 women, who vary in age (from 17 to 60 years), educational level (from elementary school completed to an advanced graduate degree), religious orientation, and marital status. Among all the respondents there was considerable consensus about the different characteristics of males and females; the degree of consensus was not dependent on one's age, sex, religion, educational level, or marital status (Broverman et al., 1972).

In fact, one of the most striking instances of the high consensus regarding sex-role stereotypes was derived from a special sample that the researchers studied. They administered the questionnaire to seventy-nine practicing mental health workers (clinical psychologists, psychiatrists, and psychiatric social workers). Of the forty-six men in this sample, thirty-one held a Ph.D. or M.D., while of the thirty-three women studied, eighteen held one of these degrees. The range of clinical experience in this group was from an internship to extensive professional practice. These professionals were asked to respond to the questionnaire three times, first to describe "a mature, healthy, socially competent adult male," second to give a corresponding description for an adult woman, and third for an adult (with no sex specified).

First, it was found that these male and female clinicians did not differ significantly from each other in their descriptions of men, women, and adults, respectively. Second, for each of these three categories there was high agreement about which end of the trait dimension reflected more healthy behavior. Thus, these clinicians had a generalized belief about what constituted good mental health. Third, it was found that these clinical judgments regarding mental health were highly consistent with college students' corresponding depictions.

Finally, and most importantly in terms of sex-role stereotypes, these professionals' judgments regarding what constituted the healthy male and the healthy female were consistent with sex-role stereotypes. The desirable "masculine" end of the competency cluster was attributed to the "healthy man" rather than to the "healthy woman" more than 90 percent of the time, while the desirable "feminine" end of the warmth-expressiveness cluster was attributed to the "healthy woman" rather than to the "healthy man" more than 60 percent of the time (Broverman et al., 1972, p. 70). Thus, if one considers the content of the items attributed by these mental health workers to males and females, respectively:

Clinicians are suggesting that healthy women differ from healthy men by being more submissive, less independent, less adventurous, less objective, more easily influenced, less aggressive, less competitive, more excitable in minor crises, more emotional, more conceited about their appearance, and having their feelings more easily hurt. (Broverman et al., 1972, p. 70)

Moreover, the mental health workers' judgments about what constitutes a "healthy adult" and what constitutes a "healthy man" did not differ. However, there was a difference when their view of the healthy adult was compared to their view of the "healthy woman." That is, among both the male and female professionals studied, the general idea of mental health for a sex-unspecified adult is:

. . . actually applied to men only, while healthy women are perceived as significantly less healthy by adult standards. (Broverman et al., 1972, p. 71)

Not only is there evidence that sex-role stereotypes are fairly consistent across the sex, age, and educational levels within society, but there is also evidence for considerable cross-cultural consistency in sex-role stereotypes. In fact, Block (1973), in a study of six different countries (Norway, Sweden, Denmark, Finland, England, and the United States), not only found marked cross-cultural consistency, but also found empirical verification of the differential emphases on competence-effectiveness and warmth-expressiveness for the two sexes that McCandless and Erikson predicted to exist and Broverman et al. (1970) found people to *believe* to exist.

Block's (1973) term for the type of behaviors we have labeled competence-effectiveness is *agency*. As seen Exhibits 13.2 and 13.3, the items she sees as characteristic of agency (for example, assertive, dominating, competitive, and independent) correspond to those in the Broverman et al. (1972) competency cluster. Block's (1973) term for the type of behaviors we label warmth-expressiveness is *communion*. The items she sees as constituting communion (for example, loving, affectionate, sympathetic, and considerate) correspond to those in the Broverman et al. warmth-expressiveness cluster.

Block (1973) had four psychologists classify all these items into either the agency or the communion category. Those items that showed high agreement among the judges are shown by classification in the first column of Exhibits 13.2 and 13.3. Exhibit 13.2 shows that among the university students in the samples there were sixteen items on which males were more stereotypically associated than were females. In this group, *all* items receiving a classification were agency (competence) ones. Moreover, although there are cross-cultural differences, the implications of which will be discussed below, we see that in at least four of the six cultural groups, both males and females within and across cultures agreed that males are higher than females in regard to being practical, shrewd, assertive, dominating, competitive, critical, and self-controlled.

Exhibit 13.3 shows that there were seventeen items on which females were more stereotypically associated than males. Of those eight items receiving a classification by the judges, seven were communion (warmth-expressiveness) ones. Moreover, in at least four of the six cultural groups, males and females within and across cultures agreed that females are higher than males in regard to being loving, affectionate, impulsive, sympathetic, and generous.

Exhibit 13.2
Adjective attributions among students in six countries: Items on which males are stereotypically associated

Agency-communion classification	Adjective	Country					
		United States	England	Sweden	Denmark	Finland	Norway
Agency	Practical, shrewd	X	X	X	X	X	X
Agency	Assertive	X	X		X	X	X
Agency	Dominating	X	X			X	X
Agency	Competitive	X	X				
Agency	Critical	X					X
	Self-controlled	X				X	
Agency	Rational, reasonable	X				X	
Agency	Ambitious						
	Feels guilty						X
	Moody		X				
Agency	Self-centered						
	Sense of humor				X		
	Responsible					X	
	Fair, just					X	
Agency	Independent						X
Agency	Adventurous						X

Note: X = significant difference found in number of attributions to males and females.
Source: Adapted from Block, 1973, p. 518.

In summary, across groups in American society and in comparisons among samples from different societies, there is clear evidence that stereotypes exist which specify that different sets of behaviors are expected from males and females. This evidence shows that the male role is associated with individual effectiveness, independent competence, or agency. On the other hand, the evidence shows that the female role is associated with interpersonal warmth and expressiveness, or communion. Although the existence of these stereotypes means that people believe males and females differ in these ways, the existence of the stereotype does not *necessarily* mean that males and females actually behave differently along these dimensions. Thus, although people's stereotypic beliefs do correspond to the theoretical expectations of Erikson and McCandless, this correspondence does not necessarily confirm their views, because as noted, stereotypic differences need not correspond to behavioral differences. Moreover, even if a correspondence between the stereotypes and behavior does exist, this relation would not provide unequivocal support for either Erikson or McCandless. Other processes, unspecified by these theorists, could be involved. Thus, before we evaluate data pertinent to the relations between sex-role stereotypes and sex differences in adolescent personality and social behavior, we consider some implications of the character of existing sex-role stereotypes.

Exhibit 13.3
Adjective attributions among students in six countries: Items on which females are stereotypically associated

Agency-communion classification	Adjective	Country					
		United States	England	Sweden	Denmark	Finland	Norway
Communion	Loving, affectionate	X	X		X	X	X
	Impulsive	X	X	X		X	X
Communion	Sympathetic		X			X	
Communion	Generous			X			
Agency	Vital, active	X		X			X
	Perceptive, aware						X
Communion	Sensitive	X	X				X
	Reserved, shy	X	X				
Communion	Artistic					X	
	Curious						X
	Uncertain, indecisive						
	Talkative					X	
Communion	Helpful		X			X	
	Sense of humor		X				
	Idealistic				X		
	Cheerful						X
Communion	Considerate						X

Note: X = significant difference found in number of attributions to males and females.
Source: Adapted from Block, 1973, p. 519.

Implications of sex-role stereotypes for socialization

Chapter 2 presented some ideas about the potential role that stereotypes could have for behavioral and social development. On the basis of initial stereotypic appraisals of people categorized in a particular group (for example, adolescents, endomorphs, Blacks, women), behavior is channeled in directions consistent with the stereotype. As a consequence, stereotype-consistent behavior often is developed. Once this self-fulfilling prophecy is created, behavior maintains the stereotype and a circular function is thus perpetuated. The self-fulfilling prophecy can be used to explain data pertinent to the implications of bodily changes in adolescence and to some cognitive developments in adolescence, as has been discussed already. Here we may note that there is evidence that a similar self-fulfilling prophecy process is involved in the creation of sex differences in adolescent personality and social behavior.

The socialization experiences of males and females differ in ways consistent with traditional sex-role stereotypes, and hence with the existence of a self-fulfilling prophecy process. Miller and Swanson (1958) found that a majority of urban,

Midwestern mothers who were studied channeled the behaviors of their children in accordance with traditional ideas about divisions of labor (for example, regarding "women's work" such as dishwashing). Brun-Gulbrandsen (1958) found in Norway results similar to those of Miller and Swanson (1958), and in addition, found that mothers put more pressure on girls than on boys to conform to societal norms.

In a series of investigations involving the mothers and fathers of boys and girls ranging in age level from early childhood through late adolescence, Block (1973) found further evidence pertaining to stereotype-related differences in the ways males and females are socialized. The parents were asked to describe their child-rearing attitudes and behaviors regarding one of their own children. Block assumed that parents of boys are not (at least beforehand) intrinsically different from parents of girls. Therefore, differences in the way parents socialize males or females should reflect sex-role stereotyping imposed by parents on the children.

In comparing the parents of boys with the parents of girls, Block (1973) reports that the socialization practices for boys across the age range studied reflected an emphasis on achievement, competition, an insistence on control of feelings, and a concern for rule conformity (for example, to parental authority). However, for girls of the age range studied, the socialization emphasis was placed—particularly by their fathers—on developing and maintaining close interpersonal relationships; the girls were encouraged to talk about their problems, and were given comfort, reassurance, protection, and support (Block, 1973, p. 517).

Thus, there appears to be evidence that parents strive to socialize their children in accordance with sex-role stereotypes. At least the *attempt* by parents to channel behavior, in a manner consistent with a self-fulfilling prophecy process, is apparent. But before data are reviewed pertaining to whether adolescents conform to these attempts, one must address the more basic issue of what is the source of behaviors that compose the definition of the role for each sex.

THE ADAPTIVE BASIS OF SEX DIFFERENCES IN ROLES

Why are there traditional, stereotypic sex-role prescriptions, and why does their content exist as it does? Chapter 12 discussed the adaptive significance of roles. The function of roles is to allow society to maintain and perpetuate itself. Indeed, in that discussion we speculated that the anatomical and physiological constitution of the sexes resulted in the first social roles being differentiated on the basis of sex. Although there is no way to test this idea directly, sex roles, like all other social roles, should have some basis in the functions of people and their society. Accordingly, from this reasoning, it follows that sex differences in role behavior, at least initially, arose from the different tasks males and females performed for survival, including reproduction.

However, although maintaining these sex differences—that is to say, making them traditional—could continue to serve this survival function (if the survival demands on people remained the same), it is also possible that sex roles could become traditionalized despite a change in the adaptive demands facing society. Indeed, not only is there cross-cultural empirical evidence consistent with our speculations about the basis of sex differences in roles, but there also is at least some indirect support for the possibility that sex roles may not be evolving apace with social changes promoting new adaptive demands.

Barry, Bacon, and Child (1957) reviewed anthropological (ethnographic) material which described patterns of socialization in mostly nonliterate cultures. They reported a general trend of greater socialization pressures toward nurturance, responsibility, and obedience for females, and greater socialization pressures toward self-reliance and achievement behaviors for males. In these relatively primitive societies, these different socialization pressures were seen to be associated with the contrasting biological and socioeconomic functions each sex had to assume when adult. Accordingly, as argued by Block (1973), such findings suggest that:

> When hunting or conquest is required for societal survival, the task naturally and functionally falls upon the male because of his intrinsically superior physical strength. So, boys more than girls receive training in self-reliance, achievement, and the agentic corollaries. Child-bearing is biologically assigned to women, and because, in marginally surviving societies, men must be out foraging for food, child rearing, with its requirement of continuous responsibility, is assigned to women. Thus, girls more than boys are socialized toward nurturance responsibility, and other qualities of communion. (p. 518)

Cultural-historical change and sex-role evolution.

In modern countries, the demands of day-to-day life are considerably different than those of primitive, marginally surviving societies. Accordingly, the meaning and function of these traditional sex roles may be different. As Block (1973) states the issue:

> The heritage and functional requiredness of sex typing in early or marginal cultures seem clear. The question for our times, however, is to what extent past socialization requirements must or should control current socialization emphases in our complex, technological, affluent society where, for example, physical strength is no longer especially important and where procreation is under some control. Under present conditions, and for the future, we might ask: What is necessary? What is "natural" in regard to sex typing? (p. 519)

One way of addressing this issue is to reconsider the data on cross-cultural analyses of sex-role stereotypes, presented in Exhibits 13.2 and 13.3. If sex roles do reflect to some extent the requirements placed on men and women in their particular societal setting, then differences in these settings should—to some extent—relate to differences in sex-role prescriptions in the different cultures. Thus, despite the fact that all countries studied by Block (1973) are Western societies, and despite the fact that we have seen general trends in all cultures toward agency stereotypes for males and communion stereotypes for females, there are nevertheless differences in the socioeconomic, political, and physical environmental pressures of people in the respective societal settings.

Bakan (1966) found a relationship to exist between socialization pressures for agency (competency-effectiveness) and the presence of a capitalistic social and economic system, which he believed required an intensification of the agency orientation. Consistent with this view, Block (1973) reported that in the two countries in her research that had long and widespread commitments to social welfare—Sweden and Denmark—there were fewer sex differences and less emphasis on agency than in the United States. In fact, Block (1973) found that American males were significantly different from the males of the other countries studied; they placed greater emphasis in their ratings on depictions of the male role as being adventurous, self-confident, assertive, restless, ambitious, self-centered, shrewd, and competitive. Their emphasis on these characteristics reflects their greater orientation to agency.

Moreover, also consistent with Bakan's (1966) idea of a relation between capitalism and agency, and our more general idea that behaviors associated with the roles of each sex necessarily reflect the sociocultural (for example, economic, political, and environmental) demands placed on people at a particular time in their society's history, are Block's findings regarding the females. Despite being more oriented to communion than to agency, American women nevertheless placed greater emphasis in their ratings on agency terms than did women in the other countries studied (Block, 1973). To a significantly greater extent than did the women from the other cultural settings, the American women gave higher ratings to traits such as practical, adventurous, assertive, ambitious, self-centered, shrewd, and self-confident in their responses about a woman's role (Block, 1973). These characteristics are also all agency ones.

The United States is the most capitalistic of the countries studied by Block (1973); and if we can assume that this characteristic is an important one differentiating the countries, then the differences between the sex-role stereotypes of males and females in the United States and those of the other countries may be understood better. Thus, differences in the behavior expected from males and females of a particular society are understandable on the basis of the sociocultural forces acting over time on the people. Moreover, not only should these different sociocultural-historical pressures influence behavioral expectations, but they should also influence child-rearing (socialization) practices. If the adaptive demands placed on people in a society are different, then the socialization of people to meet these demands should be different.

In support of this idea, Block (1973) reported that students' ratings of parental child-rearing practices differed between the United States sample and those of the five other countries. In the United States, it was found that significantly greater emphasis was placed on early and clear sex typing and on competitive achievement, and less importance was placed on the control of aggression in males (Block, 1973).

Thus, these differences between American and European child-rearing orientations and sex-role stereotypes show not only that there can be and are contrasts between different cultures (Block, 1973)—although they are highly similar, Western ones—but also that these contrasts are related to familial, sociocultural, and historical differences. Moreover, the character of the sex differences in some cultural settings shows that because of its long-term nature, a presumably adaptive narrowing of some of the agency-communion differences found traditionally in other cultural settings (for example, American ones) can occur, this suggests that humans can, insofar as sex-role stereotypes and socialization practices are concerned, overcome the divisions between the sexes that remain as perhaps less than optimal remnants from earlier times (Block, 1973).

Conclusions

The above evidence and arguments suggest that a biological theory, which stresses that anatomy is destiny, and a nurture theory, which emphasizes only social rewards and punishments, are limited views. Biology certainly does exert pressures on psychosocial development. However, this influence does not occur independently of the demands of the cultural and historical setting. The biological basis of one's psychosocial functioning relates to the adaptive orientation for survival. Hence, although it may be adaptive at some time in a given society to perform roles highly associated with anatomical and physiological differences, these same roles may not be adaptive in other societies or at other times in history. The agency-communion differences that were previously functional in primitive times may no longer be so in a modern society having greater leisure time, nearly equal opportunity for employment, and almost universal formal education. A similar argument has been advanced by Self (1975).

In fact, Block (1973) shows that at least one measure of more developed psychosocial functioning—the presence of a principled level of moral reasoning—is associated with American college-aged males and females who have less traditional sex-role definitions of themselves. In a series of studies by Bem (1974, 1975, 1977), it has been found that among men and women who have an orientation to *both* traditional male and traditional female behaviors, there is evidence for adaptive psychosocial functioning. Bem (1974, 1975) argued that internalization of the culturally stereotypic sex role inhibits the development of a fully adaptive and satisfying behavioral repertoire. Instead, a male or female who identifies with both desirable masculine and desirable feminine characteristics—an *androgynous* person—not only is free from the limitations of stereotypic sex roles, but should be able to engage more effectively in both traditional male and traditional female behaviors across a variety of social situations, presumably because of his or her flexibility, than should a nonandrogynous person (Jones, Chernovetz, & Hansson, 1978). Several studies (Bem, 1974, 1975, 1977; Spence & Helmreich, 1978; Worell, 1978) have provided data validating this general idea.

If one views individual development as reciprocally related to sociocultural change, then one may be led to predict that the current historical context presses males and females to forego the traditional vocational roles, perhaps adaptive in earlier times; instead, today's cohorts of males and females may be encouraged to adopt sex-role orientations showing flexibility and independence from traditional sex role prescriptions in order to be adaptive in the current social context. Thus, anatomy is not destiny. Rather, it is just one component of biology that *may be* of relevance for the adaptive roles in a particular sociocultural-historical setting (Self, 1975).

As such, a person's behavior in his or her cultural setting appears to involve much more than obtaining rewards for emitting behaviors that are drive-reducing. At any point in history, such behaviors involve (1) a coordination of the cultural, political, and economic values of one's society (2) as that society exists in a physical environmental setting that is placing changing survival demands on the people embedded within it and (3) in the context of family rearing pressures and psychological (for example, moral) developments.

We now consider the three major domains of functioning predicted to show sex differences by Erikson and McCandless in order to determine whether data directly relevant to these predictions support our conclusions.

BODY ATTITUDES IN ADOLESCENCE: ATTRACTIVENESS VERSUS EFFECTIVENESS

Predictions derived from both Erikson's and McCandless's respective theories coincide in suggesting that because females are incorporatively and interpersonally oriented they should be oriented to their inner body space and to seeing their body in terms of its physical attractiveness rather than its physical effectiveness. For instance, there should be a higher relation between inner-space orientation (or attractiveness attitudes) and self-concept than between outer-space orientation (or effectiveness attitudes) and self-concept. For males the opposite situation should exist. Because of their presumed intrusive and individual proneness, males should be oriented to their outer body space and to seeing their body in terms of its physical effectiveness rather than its physical attractiveness. For instance, there should be a higher relation between outer-space orientation (or effectiveness attitudes) and self-concept than between inner-space orientation (or attractiveness attitudes) and self-concept.

Some studies provide data relevant to these predictions. In a group of 118 male and 190 female late adolescent college students Lerner, Karabenick, and Stuart (1973) found a significant correlation between a measure of body satisfaction and self-esteem for males ($r = +.3$) and for females ($r = +.4$). The two groups did not differ significantly, and thus, for both, the more satisfied an individual was with his or her body, the higher was the self-esteem. However, people can differ about *why* they are satisfied with their bodies. One can be satisfied because one's body is physically attractive and/or because it is physically effective. The study did not question subjects about the bases of their body satisfaction, and was not directly relevant to a test of the male-female effectiveness-attractiveness predictions.

However, in a study of 70 male and 119 female late adolescent college students, correlations between a measure of self-esteem and one of how physically attractive one assumed one's body to be showed sex differences consistent with what Erikson and McCandless would predict (Lerner & Karabenick, 1974). The relation between the two scores for females was $r = +.4$, while for males it was $r = +.2$. Thus, more so for females than for males, the more attractive they viewed their bodies, the higher their self-esteem.

Data speaking to the converse of this relation, that is, pertaining to the relation between effectiveness and self-esteem for the two sexes, has also been reported (Lerner, Orlos, & Knapp, 1976). In addition to self-esteem and attractiveness measures, a measure of how physically effective one assumed one's body to be was included in this study. Using 124 male and 218 female college students as subjects, this study found sex differences that, at least in part, were consistent with the ideas derived from Erikson and McCandless. The combined (multiple) correlation *for females* between all items involved in the attractiveness ratings and self-esteem was higher ($R = +.52$) than was the combined correlation between the effectiveness ratings and self-esteem ($R = +.37$); with males the combined correlation between the effectiveness ratings and self-esteem was higher ($R = +.58$) than was the combined correlation between the attractiveness ratings and self-esteem ($R = +.50$). These data suggest that females' self-esteems are more strongly related to their attitudes about their body's physical attractiveness than its physical effectiveness. Conversely, males' self-esteems appear somewhat more related to their attitudes about body effectiveness than body attractiveness, despite the fact that these two types of body attitudes are highly related in males.

Although these findings are consistent with the ideas of Erikson and McCandless, the findings do not speak to all aspects of the two mens' views. All the measures of body attractiveness and effectiveness dealt only with ratings of *external* body parts. That is, in all the above studies subjects were asked to rate such parts as their face, eyes, or general appearance in terms of each one's attractiveness or effectiveness. As such, the findings may pertain more directly to the outer "world" of the body than to its inner domains and, in any event, do not directly show females to be more oriented to their inner space than are males, and that such contrasting orientations differentially relate to the self-esteems of the two sexes.

A test of whether this differential role exists was involved in a study by Lerner and Brackney (1978). Using 107 female and 72 male college students as subjects, these investigators measured self-esteem and, in addition, assessed the degree of emotion (affect) attached to inner and outer (external) body parts. They asked subjects to rate a list of body parts in terms of how important each was in making them attractive and effective. If the predictions being considered are correct, females should place more importance on their inner parts than their outer ones, while males should show the reverse.

In addition, if females show greater inner-space orientation, they should also have more knowledge about their inner space than should males. To test this, subjects were presented also with an asexual frontal outline of a human figure and asked to draw and label their internal organs inside the figure. It was found that females rated their outer (external) body parts as more important than did males, and that the sexes did not differ in regard to the importance placed on their internal common parts. However, females did place more importance on sex-specific internal parts than did males on theirs. Furthermore, females showed more knowledge of the parts inside their bodies than did males (for example, they drew more internal parts than did males).

These data provide only partial support for the idea that females are more oriented to inner space than are males. Although females had more knowledge about their inner bodies than did males about theirs, and although this knowledge was combined with more affect for sex-internal parts, the females did not show more affect than did males for most internal parts. Moreover, they showed more affect than did males for their external body parts, and this finding is counter to males' presumably greater outer-space orientation. Thus, it appears that females are just generally more attuned to their bodies—both internal and external—than are males.

However, the crucial issue for testing the inner-space–outer-space ideas pertains to the level of relation between inner-outer orientation and self-esteem. The relation between self-esteem scores and the affect and knowledge scores did differ for the sexes. But the correlation between measures of inner and outer body importance or inner body parts knowledge on the one hand and self-esteem on the other was *zero for females*. However, *for males* the correlation between the level of importance placed on internal body parts and self-esteem ($r = +.3$) was significant. Contrary to what would be expected if females had a greater inner-space orientation than males, and if males had a greater outer-space orientation than females, males and *not females* maintained affects about inner space which were positively related to self-esteem.

Together, the above studies suggest that the differing orientations to attractiveness and effectiveness shown by adolescents do not exist in relation to a greater inner-space orientation for females and a greater outer-space one for males. Indeed, if any conclusion can be drawn, it is that inner space is more important in the self-esteems of males than of females. Even the greater emphasis on attractiveness for females is uncertain since in two of the above three studies that measured attractiveness (Lerner & Brackney, 1978; Lerner et al., 1976), the correlation between self-rated physical attractiveness and self-esteem was as high for males as for females.

In essence then, neither the views of McCandless nor those of Erikson find great support in the above data, and as such, the first prediction drawn from their ideas is not a powerful one. Data relevant to the second prediction are reviewed in the next section.

BEHAVIOR, SELF-CONCEPT, AND SELF-ESTEEM IN ADOLESCENCE

Considerable data exist on the quality of the self-esteems of adolescents, and on sex differences in self-esteem (Block, 1973, 1976; Maccoby & Jacklin, 1974; O'Leary, 1977). However, important problems in integrating this literature are that researchers often do not distinguish between self-concept and self-esteem, they often define either of these terms in quite different ways, and they use different instruments to measure these constructs (Wylie, 1974). Because extensive information does not exist about how these different measures of self-esteem and/or self-concept relate to each other, important issues of interpretation are raised. For instance, one often does not know if when a study using a particular measure shows that groups of adolescents (for example, males and females) differ in their self-concepts, whether these differences reflect (1) true differences between the groups, (2) differences due to the fact that a particular measure was used, or (3) some combination of 1 and 2. These methodological problems make it difficult to assess unequivocally whether male and female adolescents differ in their self-concepts and self-esteems in the ways that McCandless and Erikson predict.

Moreover, this problem is complicated by a related one. Some data can be found to support their views that males' self-concepts are characterized by individual competency, independent effectiveness (that is, agency), and high, positive self-esteem, while females' self-concepts are characterized by warmth-expressiveness and dependency-passivity (that is, communion) and a lower, more negative self-esteem than that found with males. However, data can also be found to contradict these views.

For example, the longitudinal study reported by Kagan and Moss (1962) showed that males' scores relating to aggression and dominance (both agency characteristics) tended to be stable and continuous from the early years of life through young adulthood, but their scores relating to dependency and passivity (communion characteristics) tended to be unstable and discontinuous. In turn, communion-type characteristics were found to be stable and continuous for females during the age span, whereas agency-related characteristics tended to be unstable and discontinuous (Kagan & Moss, 1962). Similarly, in a study of the "self-images" of over 2,000 children and adolescents in the late 1960s, Rosenberg and Simmons (1975) report that adolescent females have images of themselves that are more "people-" oriented, while the view adolescent males have of themselves stresses achievement and competence. Indeed, more females than males view their own sex with displeasure, and this is related to females having a more negative self-image than is the case with males (Simmons & Rosenberg, 1975). Moreover, cross-sectional data derived from 139 male and 142 female high school students, reported by Hakstian and Cattell (1975), are consistent with the above data, in that males were shown to be more tough-minded and realistic, while females were seen to be more tender-minded, dependent, and sensitive.

Yet other data are not consistent with these findings. For instance, although as a consequence of their presumably greater dependency and domination by others, females should be more prone than males to conform to group pressures, studies of male and female 5- to 19-year-olds (Collins & Thomas, 1972) and of male and female

13- to 14-year-olds and 18- to 21-year-olds (Landsbaum & Willis, 1971) found no differences between the sexes in their incidence of conformity.

Thus, the issue is not whether there are absolute, nonoverlapping differences between males and females in regard to the agency and communion behaviors thought to differentiate them. Rather, the issue is the extent of overlap found between the sexes. Further, not only must one determine whether there are *behavioral* differences between the sexes relating to the incidence of agency-related and communion-related behaviors, but one also must see the correspondence between any such differences and self-concept and self-esteem.

Although the methodological problems identified above becloud the certainty of any interpretation, the range of findings existing in the literature shows that the predictions of Erikson and McCandless find some support, but are not without exception. As such, we shall see that the most important issue for science will become one of trying to learn what are the particular types of biological, psychological, sociocultural, and historical processes that promote what seems to be relatively changeable behaviors in members of each sex.

Differences in agency-related and communion-related behaviors

The first issue to address is whether the existing research literature indicates that males and females differ in agency-related and communion-related behaviors. If so, to what extent are these differences consistent with Erikson's and McCandless's views? As noted, although there are literally hundreds of studies that may be considered in order to address this issue, there have been several recent attempts to integrate these studies (Block, 1976; Maccoby & Jacklin, 1974; O'Leary, 1977). One of these (Maccoby & Jacklin, 1974) was sufficiently encompassing that it may serve as a basis for our presentation.

Maccoby and Jacklin (1974) evaluated the results of about 1,600 research reports, published for the most part between 1966 and 1973. Maccoby and Jacklin derived these studies from those professional research journals that frequently include information about psychological sex differences, as well as from other sources (for example, review chapters and theoretical papers). The studies they reviewed were classified into eight major topical areas (for example, perceptual abilities, intellectual abilities, and achievement motivation). Moreover, within each of these areas, studies were sorted on the basis of their relevance to particular behaviors or constructs, for example, aggression, dependency, helping, or anxiety. Although the number of studies dealing with the more than eighty behaviors or constructs evaluated by Maccoby and Jacklin differed from topic to topic, for each of these behaviors or constructs, tables were formed. These tables included information about the authors of the study, the ages and numbers of the people studied, and whether or not statistically significant differences between males and females had been found. Depending on the proportion of studies done on a topic for which significant sex differences occurred, Maccoby and Jacklin drew conclusions about whether sex differences were or were not well established.

However, there are some problems with the conclusions they drew. First, the proportion of findings used to decide whether a sex difference was well established varied for different domains of behavior. In addition, not all studies pertinent to a particular behavior were of the same quality. For example, some studies assessed very small samples. In such cases it is difficult for statistics to confidently confirm a difference between the sexes. At these times it is said that the statistic lacks *power*, and in deciding whether a sex difference was well established, Maccoby and Jacklin (1974) did not consider "how the poor statistical power of certain studies may have influenced adversely the trend of the findings they are attempting to integrate" (Block, 1976, p. 287).

Another problem with the conclusions that Maccoby and Jacklin (1974) drew was an unevenness in the representation of various age groups in the research they reviewed. Seventy-five percent of the studies on which Maccoby and Jacklin based their conclusions involved people 12 years of age or *younger*, and about forty percent studied preschool children (Block, 1976). Age is important because there is some evidence (Terman & Tyler, 1954) that sex differences increase in frequency during adolescence. Thus, Maccoby and Jacklin (1974) may have underestimated the proportion of sex differences that actually exist for a particular behavior by their review of studies of preadolescent samples.

Because of such problems with the conclusions that Maccoby and Jacklin reached, Block (1976) attempted to draw her own conclusions by tallying the number of studies reviewed by Maccoby and Jacklin which pertained to various domains of behavior. In other words, Block took those studies reviewed by Maccoby and Jacklin for each of several behaviors and calculated the ratio of significant differences favoring one or the other sex in each set of studies. Exhibit 13.4 is an adaptation of Block's (1976) tally. For each behavior, the number of studies in which females were significantly higher is reported in terms of both the ratio and the proportion of studies showing such a difference. The corresponding information for males is presented also. Finally, the present authors have classified each of the behaviors listed in the exhibit into either an agency or a communion category, based on the criteria for such behavior presented by Block (1973), Bakan (1966), and Broverman et al. (1972).

From Exhibit 13.4 we can see that for eight of the eleven behaviors classified into the communion category, females scored significantly higher than males in most studies. Moreover, on all five of the behaviors classified into the agency category, males scored significantly higher than females in most studies. This contrast shows that *when* sex differences are found in communion behaviors, the differences most often "favor" females, and in turn, *when* sex differences are found in agency behaviors, the differences most often favor males. However, just how often are these differences actually seen?

To answer this we must evaluate the magnitude of the proportion of studies showing sex differences for each of the behaviors listed. For communion behaviors, the total proportion of studies showing sex differences in either direction was greater than .50 for only four of the eleven behaviors. Thus, on most studies of most communion behaviors, females and males do not differ. Moreover, for seven of the eleven communion behaviors, the majority of studies did not report sex differences favoring females.

For agency behaviors, the total proportion of studies showing sex differences in either direction was greater than .50 for only two of the five behaviors. Thus, on most studies of most agency behaviors, males and females do not differ. Moreover, for three of the five agency behaviors, the majority of studies did not report sex differences favoring males.

It can be concluded that *most* studies of either agency or communion behaviors *do not* show that the sexes differ. However, when they do differ, females tend to score higher on communion behaviors, such as dependency, social desirability, compli-

Exhibit 13.4

A summary of Block's (1976) tally of studies reviewed by Maccoby and Jacklin (1974) showing significant sex differences

Behavior assessed	Classification of the behavior into agency or communion category†	Ratio of significant comparisons to total number of comparisons*			
		Number of studies in which girls and women were significantly higher		Number of studies in which boys and men were significantly higher	
		Ratio	Proportion	Ratio	Proportion
Dependency, undifferentiated with regard to other	Communion	13/13	1.00	0/13	.00
Social desirability	Communion	7/9	.78	0/9	.00
Compliance	Communion	13/24	.54	1/24	.04
Proximity to friends	Communion	10/23	.52	2/23	.09
Conformity, compliance with peers	Communion	19/59	.32	4/59	.07
Proximity to non-family adult	Communion	5/21	.24	2/21	.10
Empathy; sensitivity to social cues	Communion	7/31	.23	3/31	.10
Dependency (proximity to parent)	Communion	8/48	.17	7/48	.15
Helping	Communion	4/29	.14	4/29	.14
Positive sociability— peers	Communion	4/30	.13	10/30	.33
Positive sociability— adults	Communion	3/25	.12	3/25	.12
Competitiveness	Agency	3/26	.11	8/26	.31
Aggressiveness	Agency	5/94	.05	52/94	.55
Activity level	Agency	3/59	.05	24/59	.41
Dominance	Agency	2/47	.04	20/47	.42
Confidence in task performance	Agency	0/18	.00	14/18	.78

*When the number of studies showing a sex difference does not correspond to the total number of studies involved in a comparison, this means that in the remaining studies no sex difference occurred.
†Classifications by Lerner and Spanier.
Source: Adapted from Block, 1976, pp. 305–306.

ance, general anxiety, and staying in the proximity of friends (Block, 1976), and males tend to score higher on agency behaviors, such as aggression, confidence in task performance, dominance, and activity level (Block, 1976). Thus, only a minority of the studies are consistent with male and female agency and communion differences proposed by McCandless and by Erikson. As such, researchers must search for those biological-through-historical processes that produce such wide variation (such plasticity) in the presence and quality of communion and agency behaviors in *both* males and females.

In order to best discuss information about such interactive processes, data for the third prediction derived from the ideas of McCandless and Erikson will be evaluated. To consider this, however, we first ask: Do the self-concepts and self-esteems of males and females differ in the ways predicted by Erikson and McCandless?

Agency and communion
in self-concept and self-esteem of adolescents

As with predicted behavioral differences between males and females, self-concepts should reflect orientation toward agency for males and communion for females. Moreover, because agency is composed of more positively evaluated traits than is communion (Broverman et al., 1972), the self-esteems of males would be predicted as higher (more positive) than those of females.

Data relevant to these predicted self-concept/self-esteem differences are numerous, and have been integrated also by Maccoby and Jacklin (1974) and evaluated by Block (1976). A major methodological problem involved with these data, identified by Maccoby and Jacklin (1974), Block (1976), and Wylie (1974), however, serves to limit the usefulness of the data. Most studies assessing self-concept and/or self-esteem have used the person's own ratings of these constructs as the basis for measurement. Not only are such judgments obviously subjective, and probably considerably biased, but if only self-ratings are used, there is no way to check on the validity of the appraisals. In addition, Broverman et al. (1972) have shown that both males and females share the same sex-role stereotypes, and also tend to apply these stereotypes to themselves when characterizing their own behaviors. This stereotype-consistent appraisal may bias the self-concept and self-esteem scores in the direction of the predicted agency-communion differences.

Nevertheless, despite these biases, there is, *at best*, only partial support for these differences. Seven of the eight studies that Block (1976) tallied for levels of strength and potency (agency) of the self-concept showed males scoring higher than females. In the one remaining study, there was no sex difference. However, the more agency-oriented self-concepts of males do not appear to translate into the predicted higher self-esteems. In Block's assessment of those studies that looked at self-esteem sex differences, the majority (59 percent) of the forty-four studies showed no self-esteem differences between the sexes. Furthermore, females scored lower than males in eleven of the studies (25 percent), while males scored lower than females in seven (or 16 percent) of the studies.

Thus, although the sexes may differ in regard to the items that they use to define themselves (Maccoby & Jacklin, 1974; O'Leary, 1977), they do not evaluate the items differentially when applying them to themselves. This means that males and females are likely to have comparable levels of self-esteem. In fact, data pertaining to the relation of body attitudes and self-esteem reviewed earlier (Lerner et al., 1973, 1976; Lerner & Karabenick, 1974; Lerner & Brackney, 1978) showed virtually identical levels of self-esteem in four independent cohorts of male and female late adolescents. In summary, it is clear that agency and communion sex differences are not characteristic of most adolescents studied, and are not necessarily translated into the self-esteems of the sexes in any event. Accordingly, the question we are faced with is what are the conditions when such sex differences do occur? As noted above, aid in answering this question comes from a consideration of data relevant to the third prediction.

VOCATIONAL ROLE ORIENTATION
IN ADOLESCENCE

Both McCandless and Erikson predict that males and females should expect and aspire to play roles in society which are sex-role traditional ones. Such role orientations, it is held, are adaptive (for either biological or social reward reasons). The data to be reviewed provide both some support and some refutation for these ideas.

Sex differences in vocational role behavior

Independent of the expectations and aspirations of males and females, or of their implications for adaptive functioning, it is clear that the vocational roles of men and women in today's society are different. For instance, in the data reported in the 1970 United States Census, it was found that over 80 percent of the people engaged in the vocations of doctor, lawyer, dentist, truck driver, and farmer were males. Over 80 percent of the people engaged in the vocations of nurse, secretary, librarian, telephone operator, and elementary school teacher were females.

Moreover, in United States society, the primary role assigned to women is that of wife (O'Leary, 1977). In this country, only 5 percent of women never marry, and the average age of becoming a wife is 21 years (Spanier & Glick, 1979). In addition, the role of wife is associated with that of mother. Most people entering marriage expect to have children. Indeed, most do. The main reason for this is that men and women wish to have children. Another reason is that wives who are voluntarily childless are viewed negatively (Veevers, 1973), and are often characterized as neurotic or selfish (Bardwick, 1971). In fact, Russo (1976) notes that the number of children a woman has is sometimes used as a measure of her success in her mothering role. Although men are expected to marry and be fathers, there are role expectations for them outside of the marital union, and their success in these outside roles is of more importance than their success as husbands and fathers (Block, 1973, O'Leary, 1977).

However, it is not certain that these role behavior divisions are adaptive, despite their traditionality. There is a higher incidence of mental illness among married women than among single women (O'Leary, 1977), and Gove and Tudor (1973) suggest that this difference may reflect the difficulties involved in engaging in traditional female roles which are not highly valued.

Findings by Block (1973) support these ideas. Block notes that the traditional socialization process widens the sex-role definitions and behavioral options of men; we have just noted that in addition to being husbands and fathers, men are expected to (successfully) play roles outside of marriage. However, the traditional socialization process narrows the sex-role definitions and behavior options of women—wifing and mothering are the major roles some women play. Over half of married American women are not employed outside the home (U.S. Bureau of the Census, 1977a). Thus, in her research about sex differences in ego development, Block (1973) concluded that it is more difficult for women to achieve higher levels of ego functioning because it involves conflict with prevailing cultural norms. As a consequence, few women of the cohort she studied had sex-role definitions that combined agency and communion orientations. Block (1973) concludes that "it was simply too difficult and too lonely to oppose the cultural tide" (p. 26). Yet she notes that some balance of agency and communion was apparently necessary for advanced ego functioning. Highly socialized men had this adaptive status, but because of restricted socialization, highly socialized women did not (Block, 1973).

However, there is some evidence that adaptive behavior is associated with women who do engage in somewhat nontraditional role behavior. Although there are differences found in relation to socioeconomic status (Nye, 1974; Shappell, Hall, & Tarrier, 1971), employed women have been found to be more satisfied with their lives than are housewives (Hoffman & Nye, 1974). Similarly, Birnbaum (1975) reports that middle-aged career women, whether single or married, had higher self-esteems than housewives, and even felt that they were better mothers. Moreover, Traeldal (1973) found that Norwegian women who were housewives had stable feelings of life satisfaction across age, but that the life satisfaction of women who were employed increased with age.

Contrary to expectations derived from Erikson's and McCandless's theories then, traditional role behavior does not appear more adaptive for either males or females. Rather, the available evidence suggests that combinations of agency and communion behaviors can facilitate psychological and social processes related to ego development and life satisfaction (Block, 1973; O'Leary, 1974, 1977). However, Block (1973) suggests that most women do not achieve this. Instead, they remain oriented toward traditional female vocational patterns.

Sex differences in vocational role orientation

Most data indicate that men and women remain oriented to traditional sex differences in vocational roles, despite the fact that the complexion of the American work force continues to change (Block, 1976). From 1900 to 1978 the percentage of all adult women (aged 20 to 64) who were in the labor force rose from 20 percent to 58 percent. The percentage of married women who were employed rose from 5.5 percent in 1900 to 48 percent in 1978 (Bureau of Labor Statistics, 1978).

The female work force shows uneven representation in relation to education level and race. In 1977, 62.3 percent of women with college degrees and 71.5 percent of those with at least some graduate work were employed, while only 23 percent of women with eight or less years of education were employed. Black women are more likely than are White women to work outside the home, and this difference is maintained across various educational levels (Bureau of Labor Statistics, 1978).

Furthermore, since the number of women receiving college degrees and the proportion of women in professional graduate schools are increasing rapidly, the future complexion of the American work force will certainly be altered. In fact, Kreps (1976) estimates that the average woman's work life will be only about ten years shorter than that of the average man.

Yet despite the continuing changes in the proportion of women in the work force, the vocational role orientations of females—and of males—remain quite traditional. In fact, stereotypes of females as vocationally incompetent, emotional, and unable to handle high-level jobs persist (Huston-Stein & Higgins-Trenk, 1978). Indeed, in a review of the literature by Huston-Stein and Higgins-Trenk, it was concluded that most studies show that females accept this stereotyped view of themselves, particularly in vocations that are traditionally "male."

Given the apparent acceptance of these stereotypes by males and females, it might be expected that vocational aspirations and expectations will be traditional. Data support this inference.

Looft (1971) asked first and second grade males and females to indicate their *personal* vocational role orientations, that is, the vocations that they themselves expected to engage in as adults. The aspirations of both sexes were traditional. Boys commonly named football player and policeman as personal role orientations, while girls often named nurse or teacher. No girl mentioned vocations such as politician, lawyer, or scientist, although these were frequently noted by the boys.

In a related study, Bacon and Lerner (1975) interviewed second, fourth, and sixth grade females about their personal vocational role orientation and in addition assessed the females' *societal* vocational role orientation, that is, their conception of the roles in which the sexes could engage in society. At the higher two grade levels, females were more egalitarian (that is, nontraditional) in their societal responses than were females in the second grade. However, at all grade levels, most females had personal vocational orientations that were traditional. Thus, for most females, there was a self-other discrepancy between the nature of the vocational orientations associated with others (males *and* females) and the nature of the vocational orientation they associated with themselves. Others could have egalitarian vocations, but they aspired and expected to be traditional.

Lerner, Vincent, and Benson (1976) retested most of the second and fourth graders when they were in the third and fifth grades, respectively, and found the self-other discrepancy still evident. Furthermore, in an independent sample of fourth, fifth, and sixth grade females and males, the self-other discrepancy was confirmed (Lerner, Benson, & Vincent, 1976). Both males and females at all grade levels showed similar and high levels of societal egalitarianism, but insofar as personal vocational orientations were concerned, both groups were traditional. Thus, males associated themselves with the highly evaluated traditional male roles, while associating others with egalitarian possibilities; females had personal associations with the less favorable traditional female role, and associations of others (that is, females) with more favorable egalitarian opportunities.

In our view, however, the fact that the vocational role orientations of both sexes are, at least in part, egalitarian and nontraditional in character is both encouraging—if one favors social equality for the sexes—and, at the same time, a basis for suggesting that the third prediction derived from Erikson's and McCandless's writings is not supported.

Both theorists would hold that there should be comparability between personal and societal orientations, since for Erikson this relation would be necessary for biological adaption, while for McCandless it would be a product of learning and conforming to cultural norms for rewards. Moreover, not only would there be difficulty for these theorists' views when attempting to integrate the data about the dually directed personal-societal vocational orientations of both males and females, but also the fact that there is increasing evidence that some females, especially college-educated ones, are expecting to combine agency-type careers with marriage and family goals (and hence, communion), or in turn, are placing emphasis on the former not on the latter, would be problematic.

The percentage of college women who obtain graduate degrees, pursue careers, and yet engage in marriage has increased in recent years. Furthermore, fewer young women expect to be solely housewives and mothers. There has been a decrease in recent years in women's involvement in marriage and childbearing. Birthrates reached an all-time low in the 1970s, while female employment rates reached an all-time high. Only about 1 in 4 married women in the 18- to 24-year age range expect to have three or more children, although the proportion of young married women who desired to remain childless (1 in 20) has not changed much in recent years (U.S. Bureau of the Census, 1978c). In addition, it appears that there are the beginnings of some acceptance among males of this revised vocational role orientation among women. Although there are some data to indicate that middle-class males, especially those with high IQs, are the most traditional regarding vocational roles for males and females (Entwisle & Greenberger, 1972), other studies show that from 40 to 60 percent of college males would favor an interrupted career pattern for their wife; however, most define this pattern as meaning the wife should not work until children have completed school (Huston-Stein & Higgins-Trenk, 1978).

In conclusion, the third prediction of McCandless and Erikson does not appear very consistent with existing data. Nontraditional vocational role behavior appears to be adaptive for both sexes, and seems to involve a combination of agency and communion orientations. Moreover, the vocational role ideologies of males and females involve the perception—at least societally—of equal opportunity for males and females in endeavors traditionally defined as agency or communion. Not only may the self-other discrepancy in the personal vocational orientations of females facilitate social change, but there is also some tentative evidence that at least among adolescents in a college setting, some increasing orientation toward combining agency and communion behaviors is occurring.

Thus, in again rejecting the utility of either the McCandless or the Erikson position, we find evidence that complex alterations in personal development of males and females are occurring, and these developments involve changes associated with particular cohorts who are embedded in particular social settings (for example, college).

Some interactive bases of vocational role developments

What are the individual processes that may facilitate differences in vocational role orientations? As summarized by Huston-Stein and Higgins-Trenk (1978), it seems that:

> The most consistent and well-documented correlate of career orientation and departure from traditional feminine roles is maternal employment during childhood and adolescence. Daughters of employed mothers (i.e., mothers who were employed during some period of the daughter's childhood or adolescence) more often aspire to a career outside the home (Almquist & Angrist, 1971; Hoffman, 1974; Stein, 1973), get better grades in college (Nichols & Schauffer, 1975), and aspire to more advanced education (Hoffman, 1974; Stein, 1973). College women who have chosen a traditionally masculine occupation more often had employed mothers than those preparing for feminine occupations (Almquist, 1974; Tangri, 1972). (pp. 279–280)

Moreover, when females develop within a family in which their mother is employed, it has also been shown that (1) they have less stereotyped views of female roles than do daughters of nonworking mothers; (2) they have a broader definition of the female role, often including attributes that are traditionally male ones; and (3) they are more likely to emulate their mothers; that is, they more often name their mother as the person they aspire to be than is the case with daughters of nonworking mothers (Huston-Stein & Higgins-Trenk, 1978).

One possible basis for the apparent modeling influence of working mothers on their daughters is that there may be different family interactions in homes with working mothers. There are some data to suggest that mothers of achievement oriented-females take steps to promote independence rather than dependency in their daughters (Stein & Bailey, 1973), and since achievement orientations exist among daughters of working mothers, it may be that such interactions exist in these settings. Moreover, the father can promote the nontraditional vocational development of the daughter. Fathers having high occupational status more often promote such achievement in their daughters, especially when the daughter is the oldest child or when there are no sons (Huston-Stein & Higgins-Trenk, 1978). In summary, there are data to suggest that interaction in family settings having particular characteristics may promote the development of vocational role orientations and behaviors that are nontraditional.

INTERACTIVE BASES OF THE DEVELOPMENT OF INDIVIDUALITY

Because of the particular combination of forces acting on a person, the individual character of development stands out. Block (1973) notes that one's characterization of the attributes of the sexes "represents a synthesis of biological and cultural forces . . ." (p. 513). We have noted that variables associated with many processes play a role in the social and personality development of males and females, and one may conclude that few sex differences must necessarily apply across time, context, and age. Indeed, the major implication of the analysis in this chapter is that individual differences are dependent on the person's developmental context. One component of this context is composed of phenomena associated with time of testing. In support of this view, recall the Nesselroade and Baltes (1974) sequential longitudinal study, discussed in an earlier chapter. The basis of personality changes in adolescence was most related to the type of social change patterns which made up the environmental setting for *all* adolescents over time.

Perhaps the best example of how the changing social context provides a basis of individual development is derived from a study by Elder (1974), who presents longitudinal data about the development of people who were children and adolescents during the great economic depression in the United States (from 1929 to late 1941). Elder reports that among a group of eighty-four males and eighty-three females born in 1920–1921, characteristics of the historical era produced alterations in the influence that education had on achievement, affected later, adult health for youth from working-class families suffering deprivation during this era, and enhanced the importance of children in later, adult marriages for youth who suffered hardships during the Depression.

Other components of an adolescent's context are the physical and social characteristics of his or her school environment. Simmons, Rosenberg, and Rosenberg (1973) found that changes in the school context may influence adolescent personality. In a study of about 2,000 children and adolescents, they found that in comparison to 8- to 11-year-old children, early adolescents—and particularly those 12 to 13 years of age—showed more self-consciousness, greater instability of self-image, and slightly lower self-esteem. However, they discovered that contextual, rather than age-associated, effects seemed to account for these findings. Upon

INSIGHT INTO ADOLESCENCE

Simone de Beauvoir was born in Paris in 1908. She took a degree in philosophy at the Sorbonne in 1929, where she met Jean-Paul Sartre, who became her firm friend. During her very active life Simone de Beauvoir became a feminist, a philosopher and a writer. In addition to numerous novels and plays, she wrote a study of women, entitled *The Second Sex*. She tells us about her life in her several volumes of autobiography. This excerpt is from the first volume, *Memoirs of a Dutiful Daughter*.

I had always been sorry for the grown-ups' monotonous existence: when I realized that, within a short space of time, it would be my fate too, I was filled with panic. One afternoon I was helping Mama to wash up; she was washing the plates, and I was drying; through the window I could see the wall of the barracks, and other kitchens in which women were scrubbing out saucepans or peeling vegetables. Every day lunch and dinner; every day washing-up; all those hours, those endlessly recurring hours, all leading nowhere: could I live like that? An image was formed in my mind, an image of such desolate clarity that I can still remember it today: a row of grey squares, diminishing according to the laws of perspective, but all flat, all identical, extending away to the horizon; they were the days and weeks and years. Since the day I was born I had

gone to bed richer in the evening than I had been the day before; I was steadily improving myself, step by step; but if, when I got up there, I found a barren plateau, with no landmark to make for, what was the point in it all?

No, I told myself, arranging a pile of plates in the cupboard; my life is going to lead somewhere. Fortunately I was not dedicated to a life of toil at the kitchen sink. My father was no feminist; he admired the wisdom of the novels of Colette Yver in which the woman lawyer, or the woman doctor in the end sacrifice their careers in order to provide their children and husband with a happy home. But after all, necessity knows no law: 'You girls will never marry,' he often declared, 'you have no dowries; you'll have to work for a living.' I infinitely preferred the prospect of working for a living to that of marriage: at least it offered some hope. There *had* been people who had done things: I, too, would do things. I didn't quite know what; astronomy, archaeology, and palaeontology had in their turn appealed to me, and I was still toying vaguely with the idea of writing. But these projects were all in the air; I didn't believe enough in any of them to be able to face the future with confidence. Already I was in mourning for my past.

Source: Beauvoir, S. de, *Memoirs of a Dutiful Daughter*. Translated by James Kirkup. New York: The World Publishing Co., 1959, pp. 110–111.

---

completion of the sixth grade, one portion of the early adolescent group had moved to a *new* school (a local junior high school), while the remaining portion of the early adolescents stayed in the same schools (which offered seventh and eighth grade classes). The group of early adolescents who changed their school setting showed a much greater incidence of the personality changes than did the group that remained in elementary school. Thus, variables related to the school context seem to influence the personality of young adolescents. This idea finds further support in a study of 184 male and female Black early adolescents (Eato, 1979). It was found that perceptions of the social environment of the school had a significant influence on the females' self-esteems, and that perceptions of both the physical and social environment of the school setting significantly influenced the males' self-esteems.

Still another component of an adolescent's context is provided by his or her family setting. Just as family interaction differences seem to provide a basis of different vocational role orientations among females, there seems to be a role that such interactions play in other personality developments. For instance, Matteson (1974) found that adolescents with low self-esteems viewed communication with their parents as less facilitative than did adolescents with high self-esteems. Moreover, parents of low-self-esteem adolescents perceived their communication with spouses as less facilitative, and rated their marriages as less satisfactory, than did parents of high-self-esteem youth. Similarly, Scheck, Emerick, and El-Assal (1974) found that feelings of internal (personal) control over one's life, as opposed to believing that fate or luck was in control, were associated with adolescent males who perceived parental support for their actions. Furthermore, interactive differences associated with different types of families promote individual differences in personality development. Long, Henderson, and Platt (1973) found that among 11- to 13-year-old Israeli adolescents of both sexes, rearing in a kibbutzim, as compared to more traditional family rearing situations, was associated with higher self-esteem and social interest among both sexes.

The cultural context can also be influential. Evidence suggests that development in different cultures is related to the presence of sex differences. Offer and his colleagues (Offer & Howard, 1972; Offer, Ostrov, & Howard, 1977) report variation in sex differences from culture to culture. For example, the differences between the sexes in the United States are not as great as they are in Israeli and Irish cultural settings. However, there seem to be no differences in the types of sex differences found between American and Australian adolescent samples (Offer & Howard, 1972). Similarly, cultural context is related to the absence or presence of sex differences. Ramos (1974) found that among Brazilian adolescents of Japanese origin there are no sex differences in self-esteem.

In sum, it is our view that the nature of individual differences between the sexes is dependent on interactions among biological, psychological, sociocultural, and historical influences. In other words, we stress the implications of all aspects of the adolescent's context in attempts to understand his or her individual development.

CHAPTER SUMMARY

Many sex differences exist between male and female adolescents. Erikson theorizes that women's genitalia must be used for incorporation of the male's penis in order for women to function in their biologically appropriate (that is, reproductive) manner. Women must develop roles which allow this *inner space* to be fulfilled. Thus, to Erikson, women are oriented to roles as wives and mothers, and because this presumably adaptive role behavior is dependent on a man, women should develop self-concepts which are characterized by such traits as dependency, submissiveness, and passivity—all attributes which would lead to the presence of a negative self-esteem.

Males, on the other hand, need to use their genitalia to intrude on objects outside their bodies. Such "objects" may be women's bodies, or symbolically, any external environmental object. Oriented to this *outer space*, men must develop roles and self-conceptions which allow an independent, manipulative, active, and dominant mastery over their environment. Erikson argues that the attainment of such roles and self-concept traits would be associated with a positive self-esteem.

McCandless has similar ideas regarding sex differences in adolescent personality and social behavior. Drive-reducing, and hence rewarding, behaviors are associated with instrumentally effective and competent behaviors among males, and with interpersonal behaviors of warmth and expressiveness for females. As with Erikson's theory, McCandless's ideas lead to three sets of predictions: (1) males learn to use their bodies to be effective, and females use their bodies for attracting others; (2) males develop self-concepts characterized by instrumental effectiveness, activity, assertiveness, dominance, and competence—all favorable attributes that would lead to a positive self-esteem—while females develop self-concepts characterized by passivity, submissiveness, and instrumental ineffectiveness—all unfavorable attributes associated with a negative self-esteem; (3) because of contrasting body uses, self-concepts, and self-esteems, males would be oriented to adopt higher-status roles while females would be oriented to adopt lower-status ones.

Data show that male and female late adolescents have sex-role stereotypes that are consistent with the predictions of Erikson and McCandless. Males and females from American and Western European university settings share a common stereotype about the behaviors they believe associated with males and females. Males are believed to possess a group of behaviors characterized by competency and instrumental effectiveness, or an *agency* orientation; females are believed to possess a set of behaviors characterized by social warmth and interpersonal expressiveness, or a *communion* orientation.

Although it may have been the case that in earlier historical times (for example, in hunting and foraging societies) agency-communion distinctions may have served an adaptive function, recent data indicate that males and females who combine high levels of both agency and communion orientations are the most adaptive. Indeed, the weight of most recent evidence does not lend great support to the predictions of Erikson and McCandless.

In addition, although most men and women expect to marry, and most women expect to have children, recent data pertinent to the vocational development of male and female adolescents suggest that traditional vocational role distinctions between the sexes are diminishing. Many men and women still expect to engage in traditional vocations. However, the percentage of college women who obtain graduate degrees and who pursue careers in addition to marriage has increased in recent years. Indeed, such nontraditional role behavior for women has been found more adaptive, for example, in regard to feelings of life satisfaction and self-esteem, than traditional endeavors. Women who have careers both inside and outside the home thus are able to meet many needs in their lives.

Individual differences in adolescent personality and social behavior are influenced by one's social context. Differences in independence, superego control, achievement, importance placed on children, self-consciousness, and self-esteem exist in relation to one's context—factors associated with particular times in history, birth cohort membership, school environment, structure and function of the family unit, and cultural setting.

CHAPTER

OVERVIEW

Some adolescents are born with or develop characteristics that present problems for their individual adjustment and social interactions. This chapter discusses physical and behavioral problems in adolescent development. In addition, some intervention techniques useful for dealing with the problems are discussed.

INDIVIDUAL AND FAMILY THERAPY FOR ADOLESCENT PROBLEMS

Where to Turn for Help?
When Should Counseling Be Sought?
Some Basic Principles of Counseling
Behavior Therapy
Other Treatment Approaches

ISSUES
TO CONSIDER

What are the ways in which problems in adolescent development may be defined?

What are the major problems of adolescence associated with eating and weight control?

What is the magnitude of visual, hearing, and speech handicaps among adolescents in the United States?

What are the major forms of self-induced health and safety problems in adolescence?

What are the physical and behavioral problems associated with adolescent drug and alcohol abuse?

What are the major bases of adolescent morality?

What disturbances of growth occur in adolescence?

What are some examples of both biological and emotional components of menstrual disorders in adolescent females?

Why is it necessary to consider the implications of impairment for adaptive social functioning in order to understand mental retardation in adolescence?

What are the processes that differentiate learning disabled from nondisabled adolescents?

What are the implications of various types of temperament for the development of problem behavior in adolescence?

Which helping professionals might an adolescent and his or her family turn to for help with social-psychological problems?

What are some basic principles which counselors and therapists usually apply in their work?

ewspaper stories and television features have reported that the typical adolescent has watched several thousand hours of television during his or her life, spends hundreds of dollars during adolescence on cosmetics and toiletries, and will grow up to marry and have two children. But who is the typical adolescent? Could we ever meet him or her? Obviously not. Adolescence is for many reasons a period of individuality. There is no such thing as a perfectly "typical" adolescent. There is instead a range of interindividual variation within which adolescents usually develop.

No one would expect all adolescents to acquire the same height or weight. Indeed, individual differences are expected. However, it is also expected that most characteristics of adolescence will fall within a particular range. For example, not all females reach menarche at precisely the same age. Researchers have found that *almost all* girls will reach menarche between 9 and 18 years of age, but a small percentage will have this experience outside of this range. Thus, we could say that the *typical* or *normative* range is from 9 to 18 years. It is possible—but not likely—that the female will reach puberty either before age 9 or after age 18. Such a development would be considered *atypical*.

Atypical development refers to events, experiences, or characteristics which pertain only to a small proportion of the population. For example, deafness, schizophrenia, and an IQ of 200 are characteristics which apply to atypical adolescents. These individuals are atypical because they have traits which put them outside the range of usual experience. Something is considered atypical, then, if its timing or character is quite different from what would usually be expected, or if its existence at all is not very common. Sometimes, the presence of atypical development is associated with problems for the adolescent.

This chapter deals with problems of adolescence which for the most part are considered atypical. Deafness, mental retardation, and blindness are examples. However, we also examine some problems of adolescent development which are quite typical, for example, acne. Moreover, we shall discuss some problems which, although not necessarily typical, are common enough—obesity, for instance,

There are no clear-cut definitions of what is a problem and what is not, or of what is typical of adolescence and what is not. We can use statistical definitions, which specify that persons who are in extreme percentiles are atypical. Or we could use medical definitions of disease or impairment. We could even use a parent's judgment, or that of the adolescent, about whether there is anything atypical in the youth's development. Fortunately, one does not have to rely on any one particular definition, since many problems to merit attention.

Not very many adolescents possess even one serious atypical characteristic, let alone more than one. Yet despite their relatively small numbers, it is important to know about these individuals and about the problems that they have. The problem may present important hardships for adaptive psychosocial functioning; these problems pertain to the special adaptive challenges both that they face as individuals and that society faces in providing optimal contexts for their development. Furthermore, an understanding of these problems of development may provide some insight into normative development.

By learning about the problems of adolescent development, one is also in a better position to engage in *intervention*. Intervention is the general term which refers to enhancing the individual's personal, social, and physical development. Such knowledge may help to remedy the problems of those who are confronting atypical developments, and also may help to prevent these problems in the future. Knowledge of problematic development may also lead to ways of helping to optimize the development of adolescents falling within the normative range of experience.

Most of the problems in adolescent development have both biological and behavioral components. For example, deafness and blindness may be biological conditions, but they certainly have important behavioral consequences. Similarly, acne and obesity are physical conditions which are difficult to view separately from their social and psychological influences. On the other hand, disorders of mental retardation and temperament may seem overtly behavioral in nature, but in part may be caused by or subsequently may cause alterations in the biological state of the individual. Thus, in this chapter, we discuss a range of problems, most of which are complex in causes and consequences, and all of which undoubtedly bridge both the biological and behavioral domains of functioning.

EATING DISORDERS AND WEIGHT CONTROL

Although most American adolescents judge their own health to be very good to excellent (see Exhibit 14.1)—and, in fact, for most adolescents this is an accurate self-appraisal—many adolescents take actions which produce self-induced handicaps. A *biological handicap* may broadly be defined as any attribute to the person's physique or constitution which interferes with adaptive or optimal functioning. Although many different adolescent behaviors can induce biological (or physical) handicaps, those associated with *eating disorders* are especially prevalent among American adolescents. Eating disorders may take the form of either too great of an intake of calories or too little of an intake of them. In the former case a disorder termed *obesity* is a common occurrence. In the latter situation disorders such as *anorexia nervosa* occur.

Obesity

Obesity is the most prevalent eating disorder at all ages among Americans, and this of course includes adolescents (Katchadourian, 1977). About 10 percent of grade school children are obese; among adolescents, estimates of the frequency of obesity range from 10 to 30 percent (Paulsen, 1972, p. 215). Furthermore, people who were

Exhibit 14.1
Self-appraised health status of United States youths between 12 and 17 years of age. (*Source:* National Center for Health Statistics, *Vital Health Statistics*, Ser. 11, No. 147, 1975).

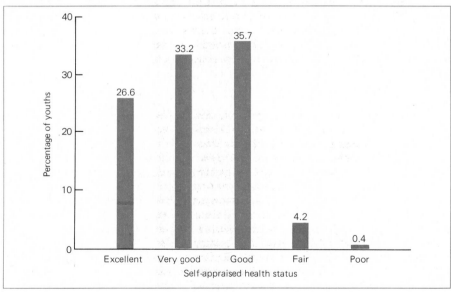

overweight as children or adolescents have an 80 percent chance of remaining this way as adults; in fact 50 percent of the markedly obese adult population is composed of people who were overweight children. Moreover, although between childhood and adulthood there is a general increase in the prevalence of obesity in the American population, between the ages of 20 and 50 years this increase is threefold (Moore, Stunkard, & Srole, 1962).

Criteria for obesity exist (Katchadourian, 1977). When a person is 10 percent above the average weight associated with others of his or her height, he or she can be classified as overweight. When a person is 20 percent above the average weight associated with others of his or her height, he or she can be classified as obese. However, it is important to make sure that this percentage of weight over the average is contributed to by an excess of body fat, and not body muscle or bone. Overweight per se refers to body weight in excess of some standard or average; however, only when this excess of weight is due to an excess of body fat (and not muscle or bone) is the overweight person obese (Dwyer & Mayer, 1968–1969). Thus, a weight lifter might be heavier than average, but if this excess weight is due to more body muscle than average, the weight lifter would not be considered obese.

Obesity is six times more frequent among males and females of low socioeconomic status than those of high socioeconomic status (Goldblatt, Moore & Stunkard, 1965); and there is some evidence (see Goodman, Dornbusch, Richardson, & Hastorf, 1963) that the obese are more likely to come from low socioeconomic backgrounds associated with particular ethnicities (for example, Jewish and Italian youth).

As noted earlier, obesity is a physical handicap which has well-established behavioral implications. Stunkard and Mendelson (1967) found that obese adolescents viewed their bodies as loathsome and grotesque, and that these views of their bodies persisted into later life, even if they lost weight. Moreover, Stunkard and Mendelson (1967) reported that others viewed the bodies of the obese with hostility and contempt. Such negative reactions seem to affect the obese. Monello and Mayer (1963) found that obese adolescent females had personality characteristics similar to people from social groups that are the victims of prejudice. Indeed, there is some evidence that there is social discrimination toward the obese. Canning and Mayer (1966) found that although neither application rates to high level colleges nor academic qualifications differed for obese and nonobese high school seniors, the obese students, and particularly the obese females, were not admitted as frequently as were the nonobese students.

Anorexia nervosa

Because of such negative implications of obesity, adolescents often make concerted efforts to reduce their caloric intakes. At times, this effort can be seriously overdone, and in these instances, undernutrition can result. While common causes of undernutrition—the ingestion of too few calories for optimal functioning—are poverty and drug or alcohol use, an overconcern with caloric intake due to the presence of body fat can lead to a sustained refusal to eat and/or a serious loss of appetite (Katchadourian, 1977).

In such cases an emotional disorder termed *anorexia nervosa* can occur. This condition predominantly affects adolescent females. Indeed, only 4 to 6 percent of those having this disorder are males. Estimates are that as many as 1 in 250 females, within the high-risk age range of from 12 to 18 years, may have this disease (Crisp,

1970, 1974; Sours, 1969; Vigersky, 1977). Although the onset of this disorder can occur in the prepubescent period (or rarely even in adulthood), females who are affected usually first develop this disorder in their early to late adolescence.

There are several distinct features of this disorder (Andersen, 1977; Bruch, 1973, 1977; Crisp, 1970, 1974; Sours, 1969; Vigersky, 1977):

1. *Behavior directed toward losing weight*—Anorectics make drastic reductions in their total food intake, especially of foods high in carbohydrate and fat content. There are daily intakes of as little as 80 to 100 calories, and anorectics often induce vomiting after ingestion of food and/or make extensive use of laxatives (Bruch, 1973; Crisp, 1970, 1974; Vigersky, 1977).

2. *Peculiar patterns of handling food*—Although limiting themselves to a few low-calorie foods, anorectics often prepare elaborate meals for others, collect recipes, and become preoccupied with thoughts of food and the calories contained in foods (Bruch, 1973, 1977; Sours, 1969). In addition, anorectics frequently have been known to hoard, conceal, and crumble food.

3. *Weight loss*—Anorectics are characterized by a loss of at least 25 percent of original body weight, but frequently as much as 50 percent of original body weight is lost (Bruch, 1973, 1977; Crisp, 1970, 1974; Sours, 1969; Vigersky, 1977).

4. *Intense fear of gaining weight*—Anorectics fear they will become obese. This fear does not lessen with increased weight loss; indeed, they become preoccupied with the size and appearance of their body, often spending long periods of time gazing in the mirror (Bruch, 1973, 1977; Vigersky, 1977).

5. *Disturbance of body image*—Although preoccupied with their body, anorectics do not perceive it accurately. They misjudge body size, often believing they are overweight—despite increasing thinness—or alternatively, that they look quite good, despite their poor physical state (Andersen, 1977; Bruch, 1973, 1977; Vigersky, 1977).

6. *Other medical and psychological problems*—Since anorexia nervosa predominately affects adolescent females, *amenorrhea* (failure to menstruate) is a common complication of this disorder. However, this is an outcome of the anorexia, and not a cause of it. Indeed, anorexia nervosa occurs when there are no known medical problems that would account for the weight loss (Bruch, 1973, 1977; Crisp, 1970, 1974; Sours, 1969; Vigersky, 1977). However, obesity often precedes anorexia nervosa, and some estimates are that about one-third of all anorectics have been at least slightly overweight prior to the onset of the disorder (Crisp, 1970, 1974; Sours, 1969; Vigersky, 1977).

It is generally believed that family problems and withdrawal from normal social relationships are the most common underlying causes of anorexia nervosa. For example, Bruch (1977) finds that two-thirds of anorectics come from families that only have daughters and/or that stress that "only outstanding is good enough." Treatment of the anorectics' psychosocial and medical problems is difficult, since most anorectics deny their problem and resist therapy (Bruch, 1973, 1977; Crisp, 1970, 1974).

With few calories ingested, and no body fat to use for calorie consumption, muscle tissue is soon metabolized. Hence, organ failures and heart attacks are frequently the "final" complications of anorexia nervosa. As such, there is a high mortality rate (15 to 21 percent) among those adolescents having this disorder (Crisp, 1970, 1974; Katchadourian, 1977; Vigersky, 1977). Literally, such adolescents starve themselves to death.

VISUAL IMPAIRMENTS

There are several handicapping conditions which arise most often not as a consequence of the adolescent's own actions, but rather in relation to events associated with in utero development, with the birth experience, or with genetically related anomalies. Blindness, deafness, speech defects, and the absence or incomplete presence of limbs are examples of such largely non-self-induced handicaps (Richardson, 1969, 1971; National Center for Health Statistics, 1975).

A continuing nationwide survey of households conducted by the National Center for Health Statistics of the Department of Health, Education, and Welfare reveals that there are about 11 million Americans with some form of visual impairment. About 1 in 7 of such impairments is considered severe. Examples of visual impairment are blindness in one or both eyes, cataracts, glaucoma, color

---

INSIGHT INTO ADOLESCENCE

At the age of 19 months, Helen Keller had an illness which left her deaf and blind. A few months before she was 7, Anne Mansfield Sullivan became her teacher. Helen Keller learned to read, write, and speak. She eventually graduated cum laude from Radcliffe College.

This excerpt is part of a letter which Helen Keller wrote to her mother on April 14, 1893, at the age of 13.

This was the surprise—I was to have the pleasure of taking my dear teacher to see Niagara Falls! . . .

The hotel was so near the river that I could feel it rushing past by putting my hand on the window. The next morning the sun rose bright and warm, and we got up quickly for our hearts were full of pleasant expectation. . . . You can never imagine how I felt when I stood in the presence of Niagara until you have the same mysterious sensations yourself. I could hardly realize that it was water that I felt rushing and plunging with impetuous fury at my feet. It seemed as if it were some living thing rushing on to some terrible fate. I wish I could describe the

cataract as it is, its beauty and awful grandeur, and the fearful and irresistible plunge of its waters over the brow of the precipice. One feels helpless and overwhelmed in the presence of such a vast force. I had the same feeling once before when I first stood by the great ocean and felt its waves beating against the shore. I suppose you feel so, too, when you gaze up to the stars in the stillness of the night, do you not? . . . We went down a hundred and twenty feet in an elevator that we might see the violent eddies and whirlpools in the deep gorge below the Falls. Within two miles of the Falls is a wonderful suspension bridge. It is thrown across the gorge at a height of two hundred and fifty-eight feet above the water and is supported on each bank by towers of solid rock, which are eight hundred feet apart. When we crossed over the Canadian side, I cried, "God save the Queen!" Teacher said I was a little traitor. But I do not think so. I was only doing as the Canadians do, while I was in their country, and besides I honor England's good queen. . . .

Source: Keller, H. The Story of My Life. New York: Grosset & Dunlop, 1905, pp. 217–218.

---

blindness, detached retina or other condition of the retina, or serious trouble seeing with one or both eyes even when wearing glasses. A serious visual impairment is one which results in blindness in both eyes, no useful vision in either eye, or inability to see regular newspaper print, even with glasses (National Center for Health Statistics, 1975; U.S. Bureau of the Census, 1977a).

Specific data on adolescents are scanty, but it can be estimated that there are about 300,000 adolescents with visual impairments, including about 15,000 to 20,000 who are blind (U.S. Bureau of the Census, 1977a). Such visually impaired adolescents are found throughout society, in all walks of life. The lack of research on visually impaired adolescents does not allow us to know with certainty what special problems they encounter in social and behavioral development, but it is likely that such handicaps make many of life's adjustments especially trying.

HEARING IMPAIRMENTS

Somewhat more is known about hearing impairments. These impairments are among the most widespread forms of handicap in the United States, with about 13 million persons reporting one of the conditions which qualify as a hearing impairment (National Center for Health Statistics, 1975). These conditions include *tinnitus*, or ringing in the ears, trouble hearing with one or both ears, need to wear a hearing aid, or deafness. It is estimated that about 2 percent of individuals with hearing impairments are totally deaf in both ears; in other words, they are unable to hear spoken words. About 700,000 adolescents have hearing impairments, including about 10,000 to 15,000 who at best can hear words only if shouted in their ear, and an additional 50,000 who can hear words shouted from across a room, but cannot hear words spoken in a normal voice (National Center for Health Statistics, 1975). These conditions often are described as *profound auditory loss*.

In addition to hearing loss, the deaf may be language-deficient. Researchers have been concerned with understanding the relation between language and cognition. This interest is related to the theory of Piaget (1950, 1970), who believes thought development precedes language development. Developmental specialists recently have emphasized the theoretical importance of studying deafness and the practical importance associated with optimizing the lives of people having this condition (Liben, 1978; Meadow, 1975). This theoretical interest, the research it has generated, and continuing research conducted at Gallaudet College in Washington, D.C., a federally supported school and college for adolescents and young adults, have led to some insight into deaf adolescents.

Magnitude of hearing loss

Most persons with hearing loss can have their hearing level improved with proper electronic amplification (Meadow, 1975). Hearing loss is measured in units of sound termed *decibels*. Sound waves travel at various cycles per second, and most speech sounds vary between 500 to 2,000 cycles per second (Meadow, 1975). A person whose hearing loss in this sound range is equal to 80 decibels would be labeled as profoundly deaf; however, very loud sounds would probably still be heard (Meadow, 1975). People who are termed either severely deaf or hard-of-hearing have a loss in the sound range of from 60 to 80 decibels. Despite such loss, the person may be able to identify some sounds and some vowels of speech (Silverman, 1966).

Bases of deafness

About 90 percent of deaf students are reported to be deaf between the time of birth and 1 year of age. Yet despite this early onset, in from one-third to one-half the occurrences of deafness, there is no known cause (Barton, Court & Walker, 1962; Meadow, 1975; Schein, 1968; Vernon, 1968). Some known bases of deafness involve hereditary factors—about 8 to 10 percent of all deaf children have at least one deaf parent (Meadow, 1975; Rainer, Altshuler, & Kallman, 1969)—and diseases, such as maternal rubella, and complications at birth are common (Meadow, 1975).

Language development in deaf adolescents

As noted earlier, there is little research about the deaf adolescent. However, there is some information regarding three domains of development: language, cognition, and personality.

About 75 percent of deaf American adults make use of *American Sign Language*, or *Ameslan* (Rainer et al., 1969). This language involves combinations of gestures having symbolic meaning, and such gesturing, or "signing," involves differentially shaping, moving, and locating the hands in relation to the body (Meadow, 1975). Some deaf children learn other forms of sign language instead of or in addition to Ameslan. Bellugi and Klima (1972) believe that the major ordering of language development is the same for deaf and hearing children, even though their languages are different. Moreover, Charrow and Fletcher (1974) found that if deaf adolescents had learned Ameslan as their primary language, they did better on a test of use of English as a foreign language than did deaf students who had not experienced Ameslan as their primary language.

Insofar as the use of written language is concerned, however, deaf adolescents do not seem to perform as do hearing adolescents. Myklebust (1960) analyzed stories written by 200 deaf children and adolescents, ranging in age from 7 to 15 years, and by 200 hearing children and adolescents of the same age range. At all age levels, the deaf used more nouns, and were more concrete in their stories. The deaf almost never used adverbs, while the hearing began using them by age 9 years. Similarly, Moores (1970) found that the written language of deaf adolescents, even when grammatically correct, was stereotyped and very repetitive.

In sum, deaf adolescents who learn sign language as a primary language develop their language skills in much the same way as do the hearing who learn orally communicated English. However, while the deafs' primary acquisition of Ameslan may facilitate their use of English as a second language, the written use of English by deaf adolescents reflects a more limited vocabulary and a simpler sentence structure (Meadow, 1975).

Cognitive development in deaf adolescents

The deaf typically score within the normal range on intelligence tests (when the tests are administered with nonverbal instructions and do not depend on spoken answers), although their average scores are somewhat lower than those of the hearing population (Meadow, 1975). However, despite this relatively close correspondence, studies of the general academic achievement of the deaf show them performing below levels that might be expected on the basis of their intelligence test scores.

of deaf students between the ages of 10.5 and 16.5 years. Using a score equivalent to performance at grade 4.9 to indicate a minimal level of literacy, Furth (1966) found that only about 1 percent of the deaf between the ages of 10.5 and 11.5 years scored at or beyond this level, only 7 percent of those 13.5 to 14.5 scored in this way, and only 12 percent of those 15.5 to 16.5 scored above this minimal level. Similarly, in a large study conducted in 1969 and 1971 by the Office of Demographic Studies of Gallaudet College, the average scores of early adolescents on a standardized achievement test were below normative expectations. The average age of those studied was 12.5 years, and thus a grade-level achievement of about 6.5 might be expected; however, both arithmetic and reading-related scores were below these levels (Meadow, 1975).

However, despite these levels of performance on achievement tests, other studies of cognitive ability—pertaining to the types of cognitive functions assessed by Piaget (1950, 1970)—show that the deaf perform equivalently to the hearing, at least during the earlier stages of cognitive development (Meadow, 1975). Rosenstein (1960) found no differences between 8-year-old to 12-year-old deaf and hearing groups on a concept classification task, and Kates, Yudin, and Tiffany (1962) found the same results with adolescent groups of hearing and deaf.

Personality development in deaf adolescents

Many studies show deaf adolescents to be less socially mature than hearing adolescents. For instance, Myklebust (1960) found that on a test of social maturity having an average expected score of 100, a group of deaf people ranging in age from 10 to 21 years scored only 85.8. Moreover, there were lower scores at older ages. Similar findings were reported by Burchard and Myklebust (1942).

Moreover, Craig (1965) found that deaf children and adolescents, aged 9.5 to 12 years old, had less accurate self-perception than did hearing children, and Levine (1956), in a study of thirty-one deaf adolescent females, aged 15 to 18 years, found a high incidence of immaturity and egocentricity in their responses to a personality test. However, there were few signs of emotional disturbance (for example, anxiety or depression). Similarly, in a study of deaf and normal hearing 15-year-olds, Bindon (1957) found the deaf adolescents' responses to a story completion test to be more immature than those of the hearing adolescents.

Conclusions

Although abundant information does not exist regarding the psychosocial implications of deafness in adolescence, we may conclude that deaf adolescents need not be cognitively or linguistically handicapped. Their progressions in the use of sign language correspond to language developments in the hearing, and their progressions in cognitive developments, such as those studied by Piaget, seem to correspond to progressions in hearing groups. Moreover, if administered in ways that take into account their hearing deficits, deaf adolescents score about the same as do hearing adolescents on intelligence tests.

Yet deaf adolescents do not speak or write English as well as hearing adolescents, they do not show comparable levels of achievement as do correspondingly aged hearing adolescents, and their personality reflects immature social behaviors and inaccurate self-appraisals. Thus, it seems that when the deaf are assessed in those domains of functioning which bring them into more direct social comparison with the hearing world, they do not do as well as might be expected from knowledge of their competencies. This suggests that a major basis of the deafs' deficits in comparison to the hearing may be different social interaction histories. Indeed, there is support for this interpretation.

Deaf children whose parents have interacted with them in the context of providing simultaneous combinations of signed and spoken English show better language development than deaf children whose parents use oral English only (Meadow, 1975). Moreover, the academic achievement of deaf children who come from families having deaf parents, as opposed to hearing parents, is better (Balow & Brill, 1972; Meadow, 1968; Stuckless & Birch, 1966). Similarly, deaf children of deaf parents show more mature and more independent personality responses than do deaf children of hearing parents (Meadow, 1968). This difference holds especially for deaf children who live in residential school settings (Schlesinger & Meadow, 1972).

Together these studies suggest that if the social interactional history of deaf adolescents involves socialization in family contexts and institutional settings wherein the primary mode of communication is *not* verbal, many of the deficits of deafness can be helped. If rules of behavior and the reasons for the rules are transmitted in ways appropriate for the deaf (for example, with Ameslan), then the deaf can better understand what is expected, and diminish their interactional disadvantage (Meadow, 1975). Improvement of other problem areas we discuss will be shown to also involve social interactions.

SPEECH DEFECTS

About 2 million Americans have some form of speech defect. Among the most common defects found in the National Center for Health Statistics (1975) survey of selected impairments were *cleft palate, harelip, stammering,* and *stuttering.* Speech impairments are sometimes due to *congenital* anomalies or disease, but particularly in cases of stammering and stuttering, the causes are thought to be social-psychological.

Unlike many other forms of handicaps, speech defects are particularly prevalent among children and adolescents. It can be estimated that about half a million adolescents have a speech defect, although unlike serious vision or hearing problems, speech handicaps are not as often reported by the individuals as a great limitation in day-to-day functioning. Furthermore, unlike conditions such as blindness and deafness, which become more prevalent in the population with age, speech defects such as stammering and stuttering tend to become less prevalent after adolescence.

Many school systems have speech therapists who work with adolescents who have speech defects. Speech therapy has a high degree of success, particularly when the student is motivated to improve the condition. When speech therapy is not available through the school system, it can often be obtained from clinics at nearby universities or hospitals. Speech defects caused by congenital anomalies or disease may often be averted by surgery early in life, or helped by a combination of surgery followed by speech therapy during childhood and adolescence.

SELF-INDUCED HEALTH AND SAFETY PROBLEMS

There are several health and safety problems that adolescents bring on themselves as a consequence of their own behaviors. These health hazards are caused by behaviors associated with adolescent drug and alcohol use, with adolescent tobacco use, and with adolescent accidents. The outcomes and/or symptoms associated with each of these instances of self-induced illnesses are discussed in this section. Another major example of largely self-induced diseases—venereal disease—has already been discussed in Chapter 11.

Adolescent drug and alcohol use

A drug is any substance (excluding food) that when taken into the living organism may alter one or more of its functions (Katchadourian, 1977). According to Katchadourian (1977) the major health problems among youth are self-inflicted, and drug use (including alcohol) is a prime example. To cite just one statistic, heroin use was the leading cause of death among adolescents in New York City in 1969 and 1970 (Katchadourian, 1977).

However, heroin is not the only drug taken by adolescents that can harm their health. Indeed, Exhibit 14.2 shows that within the six classes of drugs presented, there are several abused drugs. Also presented in this exhibit are the routes by which the drug is commonly taken into the body, the major behavioral and physical signs associated with drug abuse, and the medical complications resulting from drug use. It should be noted that for *all* drugs listed, excessive use has negative physical and behavioral consequences for a person's health. For some drugs, *any* use at all can be a dangerous health hazard.

Use of drugs like marijuana can increase the heart rate, increase blood pressure, and because of an increase in appetite, lead to weight gain. The single most common among the many complications of heroin use is *hepatitis* (Katchadourian, 1977). The health hazards introduced by adolescents' drug abuse are major problems confronting contemporary society. This statement is well-documented by research.

Prevalence of drug use   National data available on the adolescent population (ages 12 to 17) indicate that the majority of individuals in this age range have used alcohol and cigarettes. About one-third of adolescents are current users of alcohol, and about one-fourth currently smoke cigarettes (U.S. Bureau of the Census, 1977a). These proportions increase with age across adolescence.

More than 1 in 5 adolescents under 18 has ever used marijuana, and about 1 in 8 can be considered a current user. The use of marijuana has increased in recent years. By 1976, 40 percent of adolescents 16 to 17 years old had ever used marijuana, and 21 percent were current users. About 10 percent of adolescents have ever used hashish, 8 percent have used glue or other inhalants, and 5 percent have tried LSD and other hallucinogens. A small but significant proportion of adolescents have used *psychotherapeutic* drugs for nonmedical purposes (about 11 percent). Three percent of adolescents under 18 have used cocaine, and less than one percent have used heroin or methadone, although six percent have used other opiates.

Other surveys on more specialized populations showed roughly comparable levels of drug and alcohol use. Yancy, Nader, and Burnham (1972) studied 7,414 tenth, eleventh, and twelfth grade students in New York State. The most common drug ever used by these youth was alcohol (85 percent), followed by marijuana (27 percent), LSD (8.6 percent), and heroin (2.6 percent). Hartford (1975) also found that alcohol is currently the drug of choice among adolescents, followed in preference by marijuana. Indeed, Kandel and Faust (1975) found, in two longitudinal studies, that high school students show a progression of drug use which starts with alcohol use and moves toward marijuana use. They found four well-defined steps in drug use: (1)

Exhibit 14.2
Characteristics of drugs which may abuse the health of adolescents

Class of drug	Examples	Route by which taken into body
Opiates	Heroin, metha-done, morphine	Subcutaneous, intranasal, intravenous
Hypnotic sedatives	Barbiturates, glutethimide	Oral, intravenous
	Alcohol	Oral
Stimulants	Amphetamines	Oral, subcutaneous, intravenous
	Cocaine	Intravenous, intranasal
Hallucinogens	LSD, THC, PCP, STP (DOM), mescaline, DMT	Oral
Hydrocarbons, fluorocarbons	Glue (toluene)	Inhalant
	Cleaning fluid (trichloro-ethylene)	Inhalant
	Aerosol sprays (freon)	Inhalant
Cannibis	Marijuana, hashish, THC	Smoke, oral

Source: Adapted from Vaughn, V. C., & McKay, R. J. (Eds.). *Nelson textbook of pediatrics* (10th ed) Philadelphia: Saunders, 1975.

beer or wine, (2) hard liquor or cigarettes, (3) marijuana, and (4) other illicit drugs. They reported that few youths progress to step 4 without having been in step 3. Of course, this sequence does not prove a connection between one level of drug use and another, but it does demonstrate the progression of events which lead to any given level.

There seem to be sex differences in these general patterns of drug use. Krug and Henry (1974) report that female adolescents use amphetamines more than male adolescents. Also females tend to use a greater variety of drugs than do male adolescents. Hartford (1975) finds that although females still consume less alcohol than males, this difference has grown smaller in recent years. In fact, in one study (Wechsler & McFadden, 1976), involving 1,737 Massachusetts high school students,

Possible behavioral signs of drug's effect	Possible physical signs of drug's effect	Possible medical complication
Euphoria, lethargy to coma	Constricted pupils, respiratory depression, cyanosis, rales	Injection-site infection, bacterial endocarditis, amenorrhea, peptic ulcer, pulmonary edema, tetanus
Slurred speech, ataxia, short attention span, drowsiness, combative, violent	Constricted pupils, (barbiturates), dilated pupils (glutethimide), needle marks	Injection-site infection, endocarditis
As above	As above	Gastritis, central nervous system depression
Hyperactive, insomnia, anorexic paranoia, personality change, irritability	Hypertension, weight loss, dilated pupils	Injection-site infection, hepatitis, endocarditis, psychosis, depression
Restless, hyperactive, occasional depression or paranoia	Hypertension, tachycardia	Nausea, vomiting, inflammation or perforation of nasal septum
Euphoria, dysphoria, hallucinations, confusion, paranoia	Dilated pupils, occasional hypertension, hyperthermia, piloerection	Primarily psychiatric with high risk to individuals with unrecognized or previous psychiatric disorder
Euphoria, confusion, general intoxication	Nonspecific	Secondary trauma, asphyxiation fron plastic bag used to inhale fumes
Euphoria, confusion, general intoxication, vomiting, abdominal pain	Oliguria, jaundice	Hepatitis, renal injury
Euphoria, dysphoria, slurred speech, hallucinations	Nonspecific	Psychiatric
Mild intoxication and simple euphoria to hallucination (dose-related)	Occasional tachycardia, delayed response time, poor coordination	Occasional psychiatric, with depressive or anxiety reactions

females exceeded males in their use of alcohol. Moreover, females' tendency to use amphetamines more often than males was documented again in this study.

Reasons for drug use   The reasons that adolescents use drugs are both psychological and social in nature. Yancy et al. (1972), in their study of more than 7,000 senior high school students, found that curiosity was the main reason adolescents gave for beginning drug use. However, except for marijuana, most students viewed drugs as dangerous. They believed that "drug centers" are needed and would be used by youth if they were not staffed by parents or police.

Moreover, while adolescents believe curiosity is the major factor initiating drug use, other studies show the importance of the social context. In a survey of adolescents, Lawrence and Velleman (1974) found that while social institutions such as schools had little effect on a student's decision to use drugs, friends and family had a large effect. Although school drug programs and drug use laws seemed to suppress drug use, the behavior of parents and friends was more influential in suppressing or encouraging it. If peers and parents used drugs, the student was likely to do so as well. Kandel (1974) found that while peer marijuana use was more highly associated with adolescent marijuana use than was parental use, the highest rates of use were among adolescents whose parents *and* best friends were users.

Implications of drug use However, despite the reasons for drug use, there are well-documented implications for the individual's functioning. Although Exhibit 14.2 emphasizes the many behavioral implications of use of drugs like opiates, sedatives, stimulants, hallucinogens, and hydrocarbons, recent research has emphasized the implications of marijuana use because of its popularity among youth.

Victor, Grossman, and Eisenman (1973) found that in a study of 984 eighth to twelfth grade students, marijuana users were more likely to seek internal sensation and novelty. They tend to be more impulsive and adventuresome than nonusers. Moreover, although users did show more creativity and less authoritarianism than nonusers, and were less anxious than nonusers, users did earn lower grades than nonusers. Similarly, Lawrence and Velleman (1974) found that users tend to score below their academic potential.

These relations between marijuana use and personal functioning exist among college as well as high school students. Brill, Crumpton, and Grayson (1971) found that marijuana use among college freshmen and sophomores was associated with a higher stimulus-seeking orientation, higher responses on a psychopathic deviate scale, and more of an orientation to believe they always had, and continued to have, more emotional problems than other people. Similarly, Hogan, Mankin, Conway, and Fox (1970) found that although marijuana users were socially poised, concerned with others' feelings, and open to experience, they tended to be impulsive, pleasure-seeking, and rebellious. In addition, frequent use was associated with lower responses on a test of moral functioning.

Adolescent tobacco use

An estimated 360,000 people die annually in the United States because of tobacco use (Katchadourian, 1977). It has been estimated that every cigarette shortens the smoker's life by 14 minutes, and evidence of pulmonary damage can, for example, be detected even in high school students who have smoked for as little as one year (Katchadourian, 1977). Moreover, since smoking during pregnancy is associated with low birth weight, and with increased chances of prematurity, abortion, stillbirth, and neonatal death, smoking harms not only the smoker but the smoker's offspring as well.

Nevertheless, although most adolescents recognize the dangers of smoking, and say they disapprove of it, there is evidence that among older adolescents there is less negative feeling toward smoking, and more experimentation with it (Schneider & van Mastrigt, 1974). The National Center for Health Statistics estimates that by early adulthood, almost half of all males and almost one-third of all females have been regular smokers. Furthermore, 36 percent of the males 17 to 24 years old and 31 percent of the females 17 to 24 years old are active smokers. Recent trends suggest that the incidence of smoking among females is increasing at an unusually rapid pace.

That smoking is so prevalent is unfortunate given the known physical and even behavioral implications of tobacco use. The evidence for physical associations is better established than the evidence for behavioral associations. The general risk of death is 70 percent greater in males who smoke than in those who do not; the risk of death from chronic bronchitis and emphysema is 3 to 20 times greater among smokers than nonsmokers; the risk of death from coronary artery disease is 70 percent greater in smokers than nonsmokers; and life expectancy is 4 to 8 years shorter for smokers than nonsmokers (Katchadourian, 1977).

The psychosocial implications of smoking are not as well documented as the physical. What data do exist are as negative, however. The social context of the adolescent promotes smoking. Among a group of 453 fifth to twelfth graders it was found that having a cigarette-smoking best friend and being part of a group of friends that smoked were the best predictors of adolescent cigarette smoking. Yet despite the peer influence on smoking, the personality of adolescents who smoke, as rated by their peers, is not favorable. In two studies, involving over 2,000 junior high and high school students, it was found that the peers of smokers rated them to be less agreeable, to have less strength of character, and to be more crude than nonsmokers (Smith, 1969).

Although the negative health implications of tobacco use are quite pervasive, it is often true that many of these implications are not realized by the person until after adolescence. Most adolescent smokers do not die from tobacco-related illnesses while they are still adolescents. In fact, the leading cause of death in the adolescent period does not involve either drug or tobacco use. Accidents are the leading health hazard in adolescence.

Accidents in adolescence

Accidents are the fourth most frequent cause of death for all ages. More than 100,000 persons die in accidents each year. As seen in Exhibit 14.3, accidents are the *leading* cause of death in the adolescent years. Although the most frequent site for accidents is the home—80,000 people are injured there each week and 30,000 die yearly from home accidents (Johns, Sutton & Webster, 1975)—the most serious accidents occur more often in public places, such as buildings, parks, streets, and highways.

Motor vehicle accidents take the greatest toll, accounting for 65 percent of accidental deaths among older adolescents. The mortality rate for deaths by auto accidents is particularly high for White males, more than 70 percent higher than for non-White youths, and more than three times the rate for White females. An increasing proportion of motor vehicle–related deaths involve motorcycles. Deaths due to poisoning, drowning, and fire follow motor vehicle accidents (in the order presented) as leading accidental causes of death.

Homicide is the second leading cause of death after accidents among adolescents. The homicide rate among adolescents more than doubled between 1950 and 1975. It was the cause of death for 1 in 3 non-White adolescent males, but only 1 of every 15 White males. Suicide is the third leading cause of death among adolescents, with young men being four times more likely than young women to end their lives this way. The suicide rate among youth increased by more than 150 percent between

Exhibit 14.3
Death rates for the five leading causes of death for children and adolescents

Cause of death	Rates per 100,000	
	Ages 5 to 14 years	Ages 15 to 24 years
Accidents	18.1	60.3
Motor vehicle accidents	8.7	39.2
All other accidents	9.4	21.1
Drowning	3.2	2.9
Fire	1.5	1.3
Falls or poisoning	0.4	4.2
Malignant neoplasms (cancer)	4.8	6.8
Congenital anomalies	2.0	N.D.
Homicide	1.0	13.7
Suicide	N.D.	11.8
Total	35.7	118.9

Note: "N.D." means no data specified.
Source: Adapted from U.S. Bureau of the Census, Current Population Reports, 1978a.

1950 and 1975. Finally, *malignant neoplasms* (cancer) was the fourth leading cause of death, and has been declining slightly in recent years. But the death rate for cancer was only about half that of homicide, and about one-ninth that of accidents (U.S. Bureau of the Census, 1978a).

PROBLEMS OF PHYSICAL MATURATION

Some diseases in adolescence involve hormone imbalances associated with the bodily changes of adolescence. These hormonal irregularities take many forms, and vary in their incidence in the adolescent population. Three major instances of diseases involving hormonal irregularities that vary in this way are disturbances of growth, menstrual dysfunction, and acne. We consider each of these three diseases successively.

Disturbances of growth

According to Katchadourian (1977), most disturbances in adolescent growth can be detected before puberty. As such, while they are labeled more properly as problems of childhood, they are included in discussions of adolescent diseases since the effects persist beyond childhood. Two major types of these diseases involve insufficient and excessive growth. Criteria exist for determining if either of these types of growth occurs.

If a person's height differs by more than 20 percent from the norm for people of his or her age and sex group, the person may be labeled as either "short" or "tall," depending of course on the direction of deviation. However, if the deviation exceeds 40 percent, then the person is labeled a "dwarf" if below the norm, or a "giant" if above it (Katchadourian, 1977). Thus, given current adult height norms, men shorter than 4 feet 8 inches or taller than 6 feet 7 inches would be termed dwarfs and giants, respectively; the corresponding heights for women are 4 feet 5 inches and 6 feet 1 inch (Prader, 1974).

Short stature is typically caused by an insufficient production of hormones by the anterior pituitary gland. Sometimes, when this insufficiency is coupled with insufficient production of the sex hormone, a condition known as *delayed puberty* occurs. The person goes through the bodily changes associated with pubescence much later than usual.

In turn, a condition typically caused by the early production of sex hormones is termed *precocious puberty*. This condition exists when the changes of pubescence occur in females at age 8 years or earlier, and in males at age 9 years or earlier (Katchadourian, 1977). This disorder is twice as common in females as in males, but extreme cases of the disease have been reported for both sexes. For example, in females, menarche has been observed in the first year of life, and pregnancy has occurred as early as age 5.5 years; in males penis development has occurred in 5-month-olds, and spermatogenesis has been observed in 5-year-olds (Katchadourian, 1977).

Menstrual dysfunction

Menstruation is a natural, normal function which produces varying degrees of discomfort among adolescent females. It may also be accompanied by a brief period of depression, fatigue, or irritability. Painful menstruation (*dysmenorrhea*) may be the result of hypersensitivity of the lining of the uterus, a too tightly closed cervix, unusual flexion of the uterus backward or forward, atrophy of the uterus, tumors, inflammation of organs adjacent to the uterus, infection, congestion due to constant standing, disorders of the endocrine glands, allergies, constipation, and other similar contributing factors. It may also be due to subtle psychological factors (Bowman & Spanier, 1978).

Many cases of dysmenorrhea may be relieved by adequate medical treatment. In some instances, dysmenorrhea may be sufficiently disabling that the adolescent female will be unable to function at her usual levels for a day or two each menstrual cycle. With modern medical remedies, however, only a very small number of females are severely disabled during their menstrual periods. Many females, however, do experience sufficient discomfort during their menstrual periods that they restrict their activity and take medication to help relieve the symptoms.

Other problems that may be associated with the menstrual cycle are failure to menstruate (*amenorrhea*), excessive menstrual bleeding, and premenstrual tension. Some females begin their menstrual periods later than others, and much of the menstrual activity in early adolescence is erratic. However, some females who have experienced more or less regular menstruation cease having a period altogether. Amenorrhea may be caused by a number of medical conditions, and among adolescents especially, it often is caused by changes in emotions.

One common example of how amenorrhea is tied to the emotions relates to the fear of pregnancy. Some adolescent females who have had sexual intercourse without contraceptive protection fear that they may have become pregnant. They become very upset and anxious while they await their period. In extreme cases, this emotional upset interferes with the onset of the period. The delayed period continues to create anxiety, and a vicious circle of tension, anxiety, and delayed menstruation results. This phenomenon is why females who have a delayed period should always have a pregnancy test if pregnancy is suspected, rather than relying on the "missed" period itself as evidence of pregnancy.

Amenorrhea, then, may be characteristic of emotional disorders or temporary psychological distress among adolescent females, or it may be a symptom of underlying physical disorders or disease. In either case, medical and/or psychological treatment may be warranted.

For some young women there is a brief period during the menstrual cycle, usually just prior to the onset of menstruation, but sometimes earlier and at times persisting for a day or two after menstruation begins, when they exhibit one or more of a cluster of symptoms. These symptoms together are termed the *premenstrual syndrome*, sometimes referred to as *premenstrual tension*, although tension is only one of the possible symptoms (Bowman & Spanier, 1978). Perhaps 60 percent of women experience the premenstrual syndrome. There are many possible symptoms including headache, anxiety, inability to concentrate, depression, emotional outbursts, crying spells, hypersensitivity, unexplainable fears, and insomnia. Most women who experience premenstrual tension are able to control the expression of these symptoms, and thus the phenomenon is not a readily noticed problem for most adolescent females.

Acne

Acne is the most common disorder of medical significance in adolescence. Zeller (1970) reports that 85 percent of all adolescents have acne at least sometime during adolescence. The data presented in Exhibit 14.4 attest to this. Similar data have been reported by Burgoon (1975), who notes that female adolescents are most affected by acne in the age range from 14 to 17 years, while the corresponding age range for males is 16 to 19 years.

Because the presence of acne is enhanced by the presence of the hormone androgen, which is commonly present in greater concentrations in males, acne is more common among males than females, and infrequently occurs among prepubescent children of either sex (Katchadourian, 1977). The presence of acne represents a major concern for adolescents, despite its great prevalence. American adolescents spend more than $40 million a year for nonprescription acne "cures"; yet according to Katchadourian (1977), there is no convincing evidence that even medical treatment shortens the course of or cures acne.

MENTAL RETARDATION IN ADOLESCENCE

It has been estimated that 3 percent of the population is mentally retarded. However, estimates of *mental retardation* will vary in relation to the definition one uses. Nevertheless, despite varying definitions, research indicates that the incidence of mental retardation increases sharply at age 5 years, and that the highest proportion of cases exists at age 15 years (Gruenberg, 1966; Payne, 1971; Richardson, 1969). This same research shows that the incidence of mental retardation drops off considerably

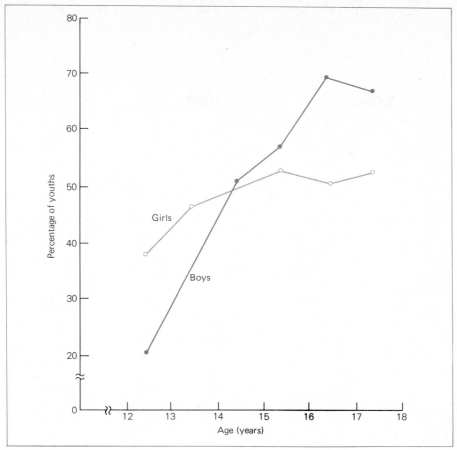

Exhibit 14.4
**Percentage of United State youths reporting acne, pimples, or black-
heads, by age and sex. (*Source:* Adapted from National Center for Health
Statistics, *Vital Health Statistics*, Series 11, No. 147, 1975.)**

after age 15 years. Thus, the early- to middle-adolescent period is the portion of the
life span most "at risk" for mental retardation.

In fact, Coleman (1972) suggests two reasons why adolescence and mental
retardation are so highly associated. First, the lower incidence of mental retardation
at age levels beyond adolescence may in part be accounted for by the short life
expectancy of mentally retarded individuals. Second, age-associated changes in
incidence reflect life-span changes in the adaptive demands placed on people. Most
people suffer only a mild degree of intellectual impairment, and in early childhood
there are not great differences between such children and nonimpaired ones.
However, as retarded children interact in school settings with other children, their
difficulties become diagnosed. Although the presence of their impairment may most

readily be detected in early adolescence, their relatively minimal inabilities allow them to leave school after adolescence in order to take a role in the community and thus lose their designation as mentally retarded (Coleman, 1972).

While this life-course alteration in the incidence of mental retardation promotes the view of retardation being an especially important problem for those concerned with adolescents, it also suggests that retardation involves more than a score on an intelligence test. Coleman (1972) suggests that the key to understanding mental retardation lies in appraising the limitations the person's functional capabilities place on adaptive psychosocial interactions. This suggestion is a key component of a definition of mental retardation.

A definition of mental retardation

The American Association on Mental Deficiency (AAMD) defines mental retardation as "subaverage intellectual functioning which originates during the developmental period and is associated with impairment in adaptive behavior" (Heber, 1959, 1961, p. 499). As pointed out by Matarazzo (1972), this conception stresses two major aspects of mental retardation.

First, there is an emphasis on the developmental nature of mental retardation. This means that mental retardation is not believed to "just be present." Rather, there are many possible categories of causes. These causative, or *etiological*, categories are (1) infection (for example, congenital syphilis); (2) intoxication (for example, maternal poisoning with lead); (3) physical trauma (for example, brain injury during labor); (4) poor nutrition; (5) new growths (for example, cancer); (6) congenital diseases having a prenatal influence (for example, hydrocephaly); (7) congenital diseases extending beyond the prenatal period (for example, sclerosis); and (8) psychological causes (for example, environmental deprivations or emotional disturbances). Although other categories of lesser importance are often used to give a more complete depiction of the bases of mental retardation in a specific case (see Matarazzo, 1972), this etiological component of the definition of mental retardation stresses that numerous physical, physiological, and behavioral processes may lead to subaverage intellectual functioning.

The second component of the definition of mental retardation stresses the crucial implication of subaverage intellectual functioning. Mental retardation impairs adaptive psychosocial functioning. If all that mental retardation implied was a low score on a standardized intelligence test, then its meaning would be less important. It is well known that there is at least some bias in any intelligence test (Lerner, 1976). However, when the person shows subaverage intellectual functioning, on the basis of a test score, *and* when this test score is related to impairment in general adaptive behavior, the person may appropriately be termed mentally retarded. Since test scores and real-world adaptive functioning are not perfectly correlated—especially in adolescence and beyond (Matarazzo, 1972)—both types of information are needed in order to judge a person mentally retarded.

Levels of mental retardation

This dual (test score plus adaptive behavior) conception of mental retardation recognizes that when one is mentally retarded, the impairment relates to *broad* aspects of social interactions—social adjustment, school learning, and vocational

Exhibit 14.5

Levels of mental retardation, suggested by the AAMD, and the corresponding IQ score range from two commonly used intelligence tests.

Word description of level of retardation	Level of deviation in measured intelligence	Corresponding IQ score range	
		Stanford-Binet test	Wechsler test
Borderline	−1	68–83	70–84
Mild	−2	52–67	55–69
Moderate	−3	36–51	40–54
Severe	−4	20–35	25–39
Profound	−5	Below 20	Below 25

Note: IQ score range for average intellectual functioning is *about* 85 to 115.
Source: Adapted from Heber, 1959, 1961.

trainability, for instance. Moreover, mentally retarded individuals also show interindividual variation. In fact, there are various levels of mental retardation, based on the degrees to which the person has subaverage test scores and shows maladaptive functioning.

Exhibit 14.5 shows five levels of mental retardation classified by the AAMD, and the associated range of IQ scores derived from two commonly used intelligence tests, the Stanford-Binet and the Wechsler tests. Someone who is "borderline" mentally retarded has an IQ score from 68 to 84 (depending on the test used), while someone who is at the next subaverage level scores between 52 and 69 (depending on the test used).

However, as we have noted, such scores tell us very little by themselves. To understand the psychosocial implications of mental retardation we need to know first if there is any significant deviation from typical adaptive functioning. We also need to note how the adaptive levels relate to the test score levels.

Sloan and Birch (1955) proposed that there are four levels or degrees of retardation in adaptive behavior. Exhibit 14.6 shows the adaptive limitations involved at each of these levels for three overlapping age periods: birth through early childhood, early childhood through late adolescence, and late adolescence through adulthood. Even given the fact that there is an imperfect correlation between test score categorizations of mental retardation and adaptive behavior categorizations—in one sample studied by Leland, Shellhaas, Nihira, and Foster (1967) the correlation was .58—the fact that over 90 percent of the instances of mental retardation fall into the borderline and mild categories (Coleman, 1972; Matarazzo, 1972) suggests that most mentally retarded people are likely to fall in the first two levels shown in Exhibit 14.6. This means that most mentally retarded people can, by the late adolescent years, acquire skills allowing them to hold jobs in the community as adults. In fact, even the adolescents and adults of level 3 can be trained to engage in their own adaptive behaviors, albeit under supervision.

Accordingly, as Coleman (1972) suggested, although deficient in adaptive

Exhibit 14.6
Levels of retardation in adaptive behavior in three age periods

	Age periods		
Level	Birth through early childhood	Early childhood through late adolescence	Late adolescence through adulthood
Level 1	Can develop social and communication skills; minimal retardation in sensorimotor areas; rarely distinguished from normal until later age.	Can learn academic skills to approximately sixth grade level by late teens; cannot learn general high school subjects; needs special education particularly at secondary school age levels. ("Educable.")	Capable of social and vocational adequacy with proper education and training; frequently needs supervision and guidance under serious social or economic stress.
Level 2	Can talk or learn to communicate; poor social awareness; fair motor development; may profit from some training in self-help; can be managed with moderate supervision.	Can learn functional academic skills to approximately fourth grade level by late teens if given special education. ("Educable.")	Capable of self-maintenance in unskilled or semiskilled occupations; needs supervision and guidance when under mild social or economic stress.
Level 3	Poor motor development; speech is minimal; generally unable to profit from training in self-help; little or no communication skills.	Can talk or learn to communicate; can be trained in elemental health habits; cannot learn functional academic skills; profits from systematic habit training. ("Trainable.")	Can contribute partially to self-support under complete supervision; can develop self-protection skills to a minimal useful level in controlled environment.
Level 4	Gross retardation; minimal capacity for functioning in sensorimotor areas; needs nursing care.	Some motor development present; cannot profit from training in self-help; needs total care.	Some motor and speech development; totally incapable of self-maintenance; needs complete care and supervision.

Source: Adapted from Sloan, W., and Birch, J. W. A rationale for degrees of retardation. *American Journal of Mental Deficiency*, 1955, *60*, 262.

capabilities, *most* mentally retarded youth are capable of progressing sufficiently during adolescence to make independent, adaptive contributions to society in adulthood. Indeed, in a proposal by the AAMD of levels of retardation associated with adaptive behavior, shown in Exhibit 14.7, the first four levels of such behavior involve people who are at least minimally capable of such performance. Since the vast majority of the mentally retarded, however, fall in the first two levels, this suggests that most mentally retarded adolescents can engage in responsible and effective social, interpersonal, and vocational endeavors. They can by adulthood engage in behaviors allowing them to avoid the label of mental retardate by most of those they encounter socially. In sum, although adolescent mental retardation involves below-average intellectual functioning, this characteristic acquires meaning

Exhibit 14.7
Levels of retardation in adaptive behavior proposed by the American Association on Mental Deficiency

Level 1	Individuals on this level are capable of effective social and economic functioning in a low-demand competitive environment, but need some support and supervision in the management of their personal affairs.
Level 2	Individuals of this level are capable of effective social and economic functioning in a partially competitive or noncompetitive environment, but need some continuing support and supervision in the management of their personal affairs.
Level 3	Individuals of this level are capable of limited social and economic functioning in a noncompetitive or sheltered environment, and are dependent upon continuing support and quasi-sheltered living.
Level 4	Individuals of this level are capable of responding to limited environmental stimuli and interpersonal relationships, and are dependent upon general supervision for their maintenance and help in following the routines of daily living.
Level 5	Individuals at this level are capable of responding to only the simplest environmental stimuli and interpersonal relationships, and are totally dependent upon nursing supervision for their maintenance and for the completion of daily living tasks.
Level 6	Individuals of this level are the grossly physically handicapped, or function in that manner, and require continuous medical-nursing care for their survival.

Source: Adapted from Nihira, K., Foster, R., Shellhaas, M., and Leland, H. *Adaptive behavior scales manual.* Washington, D.C.: American Association on Mental Deficiency, 1969, p. 35, as proposed by Leland on p. 11.

only when the implications for adaptive functioning in a variety of social contexts are considered.

LEARNING DISABILITIES IN ADOLESCENCE

Over the course of the last twenty years there has been a growing interest in youth of normal intelligence who do not progress normally in the classroom (Torgensen, 1975). This is a widespread problem. McCarthy and McCarthy (1969) estimate that as many as 20 percent of all American school students are performing below academic expectations. *Learning disabled* is the label given to youths who show a discrepancy between their estimated academic potential and their actual level of academic performance (Ross, 1974).

The study of learning disabilities currently is considered a specialty area within the field of education (Torgensen, 1975). Leaders in this field believe that their primary and most important problem is defining the term "learning disability" (see Torgensen, 1975). Workers in this area have come to recognize that failure to learn academically does not necessarily imply any general impairment in intellectual capacity that, like mental retardation, can seriously hamper broad adaptive functioning (Torgensen, 1975). In fact, learning-disabled youth seem to be people who show a largely selective deficit: despite apparently normative schooling experiences, seemingly normative family settings, appropriate "motivational" predispositions, intact sense organs, adequate physical status, and normal intelligence, they show a discrepancy between estimated and actual academic performance, and fail to learn with normal proficiency (Eisenberg, 1966; Ross, 1974).

Researchers predominantly focus on only one component of nonnormative academic proficiency in order to establish the presence of a learning disability. Over 70 percent of the recent research in studies of learning disabilities uses as a criterion for this disorder a *failure to learn to read* (Torgensen, 1975). This form of learning disability is known as *dyslexia*. Another learning disability, *dysgraphia*, refers to problems in writing, but is not as well studied as dyslexia. Reading disability is a problem of major proportions—especially during the adolescent period. For instance, for a national sample of children, Gates and MacGinitie (1965) found a two-year discrepancy from normal reading levels in 2 percent of third graders but 30 percent of ninth graders. Thus, in the study of disordered learning, most youth are selected as learning-disabled only by virtue of failure on reading tasks—tasks that involve a unique combination of abilities not necessarily common to all learning tasks (Torgensen, 1975). Eisenberg (1966) defines specific reading disability as "the failure to learn to read with normal proficiency despite conventional instruction, a culturally adequate home, proper motivation, intact senses, normal intelligence, and freedom from gross neurological defect" (p. 360). Thus, a learning disability means a failure to learn to read normatively.

Perception

Sometimes reading-disabled children have been shown to differ from those who learn to read normally in a broad variety of tasks. Yet often they also are found to perform identically, or at least very similarly, on these same tasks (Torgensen, 1975). This sort of finding exists in the first of several areas of reading disability research we examine—perception. A reason to focus on this topic has been that disorders in reading may occur because youth with reading disabilities may perceive the world differently than normal readers.

Owen, Adams, Forrest, Stolz, and Fisher (1971) studied a group of 304 elementary and high school students by use of a test designed to assess perceptual-motor development, the Bender Motor Gestalt Test (Bender, 1938). Although poor readers did not perform as well as normal readers on this test, they were just as accurate in recognizing their errors. Similarly, Whipple and Kodman (1969) found that fourth and fifth grade disabled readers were inferior to normal readers on a perceptual learning task, but Walters and Doan (1962) found no differences on this same task between disabled and normal seventh and eighth graders.

The above studies suggest that age-associated processes may be a factor leading to many differences seen between reading-disabled and normal adolescents on the same tasks. Another factor complicating the appraisal of the basis of difference between disabled and normal readers is raised in a study by Alexander and Money (1965). These researchers identified a group of preadolescent females who had an established biologically based problem in space-form perception and in directional orientation. Yet upon testing, all showed normal reading skills. These results suggest that if perceptual skills are involved in reading problems, they must be very specific ones. As such, a second area of research on reading disability involves the assessment of such a skill.

Intersensory integration

Intersensory integration involves the ability to equate stimulation derived from different sense modalities (for example, vision, touch, and hearing). If one hears the word "box" and can equate this stimulation with the sight of a box, then one is showing intersensory integration. Similarly, if one correctly can identify a coin by either touching it or seeing it, then one would be integrating visual and touch (tactile) stimulation. Several researchers have reasoned that reading may normatively involve the simultaneous use of several senses, for example, sight and hearing, and that disabled readers cannot simultaneously interrelate stimuli from two modalities as well as can normal readers.

Senf (1969) presented a set of intersensory integration learning tasks to a group of forty-eight males 8 to 15 years old, who were at least 1.5 years below grade level in language or reading skills, and a control group matched for age and IQ. Three pairs of visually and auditorily presented digits were presented simultaneously. For example, a youth could have been shown the number 3 at the same time as hearing the number 7. Youths were asked to recall which stimulus was presented to which sensory modality, or just to recall the pair of stimuli presented. Senf (1969) found that the reading-disabled children were less able to recall the stimuli in pairs than were the nondisabled. However, no significant differences were found in the recall of stimuli by modality between the normal and disabled *adolescent* readers in the sample. Again, this suggests the presence of different age-associated processes being involved in reading disability.

Further, support for this possibility comes from three other studies on a task requiring the ability to integrate information from the auditory and visual modes. Birch and Belmont (1965) found that task performance was closely related only to reading ability among the youngest subjects in a group having a child-to-early-adolescent age range (5 to 12 years old). Moreover, Rudnick, Sterritt, and Flax (1967) and Sterritt and Rudnick (1966) report that audiovisual integration shows an age-associated increase in importance in reading, while processes which are just visual decrease in such importance.

Moreover, while other studies also have found intersensory integration problems in the reading disabled, other non-age-related complications arise. For example, Beery (1967) found that a relation existed between reading ability and ability to match visual and auditory patterns, and Birch and Belmont (1964) found that performance on their audiovisual task related to reading achievement in 200 Scottish youth, aged 9.5 to 10.5 years. However, several other studies have found that the reading disabled also have problems equating two stimuli presented to the same sensory modality, that is, *intrasensory integration* (Vande Voort & Senf, 1973; Vande Voort, Senf, & Benton, 1972). For instance, when Estes and Huizinga (1974) asked 8- to 12.5-year-olds to learn stimulus pairs presented either aurally or visually, they found that learning was better in the visual mode. Thus, problems with age-associated changes in the role of specific intersensory integrations in reading, and issues relating to problems with intrasensory integration among the reading disabled, have led researchers to consider other bases of difference between normal and disabled readers.

Verbal and performance scores on intelligence tests

Heinicke (1972) notes that reading-disabled students often show lower verbal than performance scores on intelligence tests which include measures of both types of skills. Indeed, in his review of twenty studies of intellectual test performance of disabled readers, Huelsman (1970) found that in about 60 percent of the cases, the disabled readers had higher performance than verbal scores. However, the actual differences between scores tended to be small.

In his own study of this topic, Huelsman (1970) found that while only 38 percent of normal readers had higher performance than verbal scores, 61 percent of disabled readers showed such a difference. However, these findings also show that for 39 percent of the disabled readers, higher performance than verbal scores were not found, and this indicates a fairly large overlap in ability distributions between normal and disabled readers.

Memory

In a review of research on memory differences between normal and disabled readers, Johnson (1957) saw evidence for a relation between memory deficits and reading problems. Indeed, Kluever (1971) and Senf and Freundl (1972) found that in comparison to normal readers, disabled ones do progressively worse on memory tasks as the material to be remembered becomes more difficult.

However, Katz and Deutsch (1967) found that although poor readers did not do well on either visual or auditory memory tasks, memory accuracy in both modalities was influenced by the nature of the stimuli (digits, words, or pictures) to be remembered. Moreover, these authors report age-associated differences in the importance of processes linking (that is, integrating) this visual and auditory performance with reading. Such processes become particularly important in middle elementary school, while strictly visual processes decline in importance (Katz & Deutsch, 1967). Not only does this result agree with previously discussed findings (Rudnick et al., 1967; Sterritt & Rudnick, 1966), but other data on this topic (Beery, 1967) are also consistent. Moreover, once again the issue is raised of age-associated (developmental) differences in what processes are implicated in reading disability.

Developmental differences in reading disability processes

We have seen evidence that the processes involved in reading disabilities involve different variables at different portions of the life span. Indeed, research other than that reviewed suggests that poor reading tends to be related to different variables at different ages (Reed, 1968; Sabatino & Hayden, 1970). For instance, Benton (1962) notes that perceptual difficulties may be involved in some reading problems at younger ages, while older problem readers suffer from more complex conceptual and verbal difficulties.

However, because appropriate longitudinal research has not been done, it is not known whether the youth who have one process associated with their reading disability at one age come from the same population of youth who have another process associated with their reading disability at another age (Torgensen, 1975). If the same children are identified as disabled readers at different ages, and if these children seem to have different processes at work at different ages, then it may be that their problems relate to some basic developmental abnormality that they possess, one which affects performance on a variety of tasks at different developmental levels (see Blank & Bridger, 1966).

Attention

Noland and Schuldt (1971) found that reading-disabled children found it difficult to sustain attention to a task involving the detection of a light's flashing. Similarly, Katz and Deutsch (1967) found that poor readers had difficulty in switching their attention between auditory and visual modalities. Moreover, Lahaderne (1968) found that attention in school settings was *not* related to early adolescents' attitude about school, but it was related to their reading ability. Thus, the relation between poor attention and poor reading is not related to the adolescent's dislike of the school situation.

Furthermore, it is known that (1) reading-disabled youth do not show inappropriate attention in all situations (Bryan, 1974); and (2) through manipulation of the incentives and rewards for learning in a particular situation, the performance of the reading disabled can be improved (Walters & Doan, 1962; Walters & Kosowski, 1963). Thus, one has to look for what characteristics of what situations evoke those specific processes linked to reading disability at particular portions of the life span. Said more generally, one must consider individual characteristics of the person that, in interaction with a specific situation, lead to problem behaviors.

This general search—for attributes of the person that interact with the environment to create a basis of the person's own behavioral problems—has yet to develop in the area of learning disabilities. It has, however, in another area of problems we will discuss.

TEMPERAMENTAL PROBLEMS IN ADOLESCENCE

Throughout this book we have emphasized that individuals become unique as a consequence of their interactional history. The uniqueness may create a circular function in development. Youths differentially stimulate others with whom they interact, and others in return react differentially to the youth. These contrasting interactions, as part of the youths' experiences, will provide a source of further individuality in development.

Such circular functions are part of the life-span development of all processes for all people. For instance, we have discussed how children who differ in physical attractiveness promote different interactions with and evaluations from their school peers and teachers. These evaluations affect both academic and personal adjustments. With some of these children, this feedback is associated with developmental problems. Thus, circular functions between a youth and his or her social world can promote both normative and problem behavior development.

Physical characteristics are not the only traits possessed by youth which promote such circular functions. Due to the research of a group of psychiatrists and psychologists involved in what has come to be termed the New York Longitudinal Study (NYLS), social scientists have become aware that children and adolescents possess some characteristics that promote normative development and others which promote problem developments (Thomas & Chess, 1977; Thomas, Chess, & Birch, 1968, 1970; Thomas, Chess, Birch, Hertzig, & Korn, 1963). The NYLS group of researchers has especially studied temperament.

Temperament refers to the *style of behavior*. A focus on temperament concerns not *what* a person does (for example, eating, sleeping, or playing) or *why* a person does something (for example, because of being rewarded or not). A focus on temperament is a concern with *how* a person does whatever he or she does (for example, eating fast or slow, playing fast or slow, or playing with a *positive mood* or *a negative mood*). Thus, temperament is a term which describes the quality or style of any behavior.

In 1956, the NYLS research group began to study temperament in a group of over 130 children. They began to assess the child's temperament from his or her first days of life, and the researchers continue at this writing to follow the initial sample. Thus, although some children entered the study in different years, since most of the sample was born about 1956, most children are today young adults. As a consequence, the NYLS group has longitudinal data on the implications of characteristics of temperament for normative and problem development in infants, children, adolescents, and young adults. Their work represents the major study of this topic.

Dimensions of temperament

On the basis of lengthy interviews with parents, Thomas et al. (1963, 1968) were able to find that nine categories of temperament characterized the behaviors of their sample over the duration of the study. As shown in Exhibit 14.8, each of the nine categories of temperament is rated on a three-point scale. Also shown in Exhibit 14.8 are the definitions of each of the nine categories. Moreover, Thomas et al. (1963) found that there was no one combination of ratings from the nine categories that characterized the temperament of all the children.

Continuity in temperament from birth to adolescence

Not only were there differences between individuals in the group, but also a child's individual characteristics of temperament were found to continue to characterize his or her behavior through a major portion of the early life span. That is, Thomas et al. (1970) reported that a child's ratings for each of the various temperamental attributes were stable from infancy through early adolescence. The continuity in behavioral style for various ratings of each temperamental category is illustrated in Exhibit 14.9, which is adapted from the Thomas et al. (1970) report. In infancy, middle childhood, and late childhood–early adolescence periods, temperament tends to remain relatively the same, although specific activities change. Discontinuity in behavior is combined with continuity in behavior style or quality.

With temperament representing a stable and continuous characteristic of individual functioning, it is clear that it may serve to promote differential circular reactions in different children. An adaptable child with a positive mood and moderate intensity of reactions would differ in the ways he or she would stimulate parents when compared to an unadaptable child with a negative mood and high-intensity reactions. Because the former child would be relatively easy to interact with, while the latter would be difficult, the feedback the children receive would also vary as a consequence of their individual temperaments. We might expect that children like the latter one would be more "at risk" for developing behavior problems. Such implications of different temperamental types exist in the NYLS research.

Exhibit 14.8

The nine categories of temperament identified in the New York Longitudinal Study, and the definitions and ratings associated with each

Temperamental category	Definition	Type of ratings given
1. Activity level	The proportion of active periods to inactive ones	High, moderate, low
2. Rhythmicity	Regularity of hunger, excretion, sleep, and wakefulness	Regular, variable, irregular
3. Approach-withdrawal	The response to a new object or person	Approach, variable, withdraw
4. Adaptability	The ease with which a child adapts to changes in his or her environment	Adaptive, variable, nonadaptive
5. Intensity of reaction	The energy of response, regardless of its quality or direction	Intense, variable, mild
6. Threshold of responsiveness	The intensity of stimulation required to evoke a discernible response	High, moderate, low
7. Quality of mood	The amount of friendly, pleasant, joyful behavior as contrasted with unpleasant, unfriendly behavior	Positive, variable, negative
8. Distractibility	The degree to which extraneous stimuli alter behavior	Yes, variable, no
9. Attention span and persistence	The amount of time devoted to an activity, and the effect of distraction on the activity	High, variable, low

Source: Adapted from Thomas et al., 1963, 1970.

Temperamental types and behavior disorders

Although individual differences in temperament were the rule in the NYLS data, some temperamental attributes tended to go together consistently. Thomas et al. (1963, 1968, 1970) were able to identify three clusters of temperamental ratings, that is, a rating of one dimension typically being associated with ratings from several other dimensions. About 65 percent of the subjects in the NYLS were children who had such clusters of ratings. Three distinct clusters were found.

First, the *easy child* has a type of temperament composed of a positive mood, high rhythmicity, low- or moderate-intensity reactions, high adaptability, and an approach orientation to new situations and stimuli. About 40 percent of the children in the NYLS had this temperament type (Thomas et al., 1970). As infants and young children, such people slept and ate regularly, were generally happy, and readily adjusted to new people and events. Through later childhood and early adolescence such children also adjusted easily to changing school requirements and adapted and participated easily in games and other activities. Thomas et al. labeled such a child as

Exhibit 14.9
Illustrations of continuity in temperamental ratings between the infancy, middle childhood, and late childhood—early adolescent periods

Temperamental quality	Rating	Developmental period		
		Infancy	Middle childhood	Late childhood—early adolescence
Activity level	High	Tries to stand in tub and splashes. Bounces in crib. Crawls after dog.	Leaves table often during meals. Always runs.	Plays ball and engages in other sports. Cannot sit still long enough to do homework.
	Low	Passive in bath. Plays quietly in crib and falls asleep.	Takes a long time to dress. Sits quietly on long automobile rides.	Likes chess and reading. Eats very slowly.
Rhythmicity	Regular	Is asleep at 6:30 every night. Awakes at 7:00 A.M. Food intake is constant.	Falls asleep when put to bed. Bowel movement regular.	Eats only at meal-times. Sleeps the same amount of time each night.
	Irregular	Length of nap varies; so does food intake.	Food intake varies; so does time of bowel movement.	Food intake varies. Falls asleep at a different time each night.
Distract-ibility	Distract-ible	Stops crying when mother sings. Will remain still while clothing is changed if given a toy.	Can be coaxed out of forbidden activity by being led into something else.	Needs absolute silence for homework. Has a hard time choosing a shirt in a store because they all appeal to him or her.
	Not distract-ible	Stops crying only after dressing is finished. Cries until given bottle.	Seems not to hear if involved in favorite activity. Cries for long time when hurt.	Can read a book while television set is at high volume. Does chores on schedule.
Approach-withdrawal	Approach	Likes new foods. Enjoyed first bath in a large tub. Smiles and gurgles.	Entered school build-ing unhesitatingly. Tries new foods.	Went to camp happily. Loved to ski the first time.

		Example (infancy)	Example (childhood)	Example (adolescence)
Adaptability	Withdrawal	Cries and whimpers at strangers	Hid behind mother when entering school.	Severely homesick at camp during first days. Does not like new activities.
	Adaptive	Used to dislike new foods; now accepts them well.	Hesitated to go to nursery school at first; now goes eagerly. Slept well on camping trip.	Likes camp, although homesick during first days. Learns enthusiastically.
	Not adaptive	Does not cooperate with dressing. Fusses and cries when left with sitter.	Has to be hand-led into classroom each day. Bounces on bed in spite of spankings.	Does not adjust well to new school or new teacher; comes home late for dinner even when punished.
Attention span and persistence	Long	Watches toy mobile over crib intently. "Coos" frequently.	Practiced riding a two-wheeled bicycle for hours until he or she mastered it. Spent over an hour reading a book.	Reads for two hours before sleeping. Does homework carefully.
	Short	Sucks pacifier for only a few minutes and spits it out.	Still cannot tie his or her shoes because he gives up when he or she is not successful. Fidgets when parents read to him.	Gets up frequently from homework for a snack. Never finishes a book.
Intensity of reaction	Intense	Cries loudly at sound of thunder. Makes sucking movements when vitamins are administered.	Rushes to greet father. Gets hiccups from laughing hard.	Tears up an entire page of homework if one mistake is made. Slams door of room when teased by younger brother.
	Mild	Does not kick often in tub. Does not smile. Screams and kicks when temperature is taken.	Drops eyes and remains silent when given a firm parental "No." Does not laugh much.	When a mistake is made on a model airplane, corrects it quietly. Does not comment when reprimanded.

Exhibit 14.9 (continued)

Temperamental quality	Rating	Developmental period		
		Infancy	Middle childhood	Late childhood–early adolescence
Threshold of responsiveness	Low	Refuses fruit he or she likes when vitamins are added. Hides head from bright light.	Always notices when mother puts new dress on for first time. Refuses milk if it is not ice-cold.	Rejects fatty foods. Adjusts shower until water is at exactly the right temperature.
	High	Eats everything. Does not object to diapers being wet or soiled.	Does not hear loud, sudden noises when reading. Does not object to injections.	Never complains when sick. Eats all foods.
Quality of mood	Postive	Plays and splashes in bath. Smiles at everyone.	Laughs loudly while watching television cartoons. Smiles at everyone.	Enjoys new accomplishments. Laughs when reading a funny passage aloud.
	Negative	Cries when taken from tub. Cries when given food he or she does not like.	Objects to putting on boots. Cries when frustrated.	Cries when he or she cannot solve a homework problem. Very "weepy" if he or she does not get enough sleep.

Source: Adapted from Thomas et al., 1970, pp. 108–109.

easy because he or she presents few problems for parents, peers, or teachers. Such children would be expected to have adaptive, normative interactions.

A second temperamental type was labeled the *difficult child*. The child's temperamental style was characterized by five attributes (low rhythmicity, high-intensity reactions, a withdrawal orientation, slow adaptation, and a negative mood) which make for difficult social interactions. About 10 percent of the NYLS children had this temperament type. As infants and young children they ate and slept irregularly, took a long time to adjust to new situations, and were characterized by a great deal of crying. This pattern persisted into late childhood and early adolescence, and required parents, teachers, and peers to show both tolerance and patience in order to interact at all favorably with them.

A third temperamental type was labeled the *slow-to-warm-up child* and was characterized by a low activity level, a withdrawal orientation, slow adaptability, a somewhat negative mood, and relatively low-reaction intensities. About 15 percent of the NYLS children had this temperament. These children also presented interaction problems for parents and teachers; effort and time were required to get the child involved in new activities and situations, and this child's mood and adaptability characteristics created a barrier for positive interactions with parents and teachers.

Clearly, these groups of characteristics of temperament suggest different kinds of social interactions for youth of a particular type. In addition, because these interactions seem to vary along a positive-negative dimension, with the easy and difficult children being located on different ends, different incidences of behavior problems should be involved.

Indeed, of the total number of children studied in the Thomas et al. project (1963, 1968, 1970, 1977), 42 percent developed behavioral disorders (for example, neuroses or learning disabilities) at some time during their infancy to early adolescent years. Most of these problems occurred among children in the difficult child category. In fact, about 70 percent of these children developed behavior problems, while only 18 percent of the easy children did so. Similarly, in another analysis of some of the NYLS data, Thomas and Chess (1977) compared the temperamental attributes of forty-two children who were identified as having had a behavior problem from the study's beginning through 1966 with sixty-six children who had never had a problem during this time. Compared to the nonproblem group, those with a history of problems had temperaments characterized by high activity, irregularity, low threshold, nonadaptability, intensity, persistence, and distractibility.

Another study by Thomas and Chess (1977) further documents the contribution of the person's own temperament to interactions promoting his or her own problem behaviors. This sample was composed of mildly mentally retarded (IQ range was 50 to 75) children and early adolescents, and thus children who already were known to have one instance of a behavior problem. Yet other behavioral disorders (for example, emotional problems) were found mostly among those mentally retarded children who had several characteristics of the difficult child. Of the thirty-one of fifty-two children in the sample who had a behavioral disorder other than mental retardation, 61 percent had three or more of the five components of the difficult child temperament. In turn, of the twenty-one children without an additional behavior disorder, only three (14 percent) had three or more of these characteristics.

In summary, it appears that not only do youths possess characteristics of behavioral individuality which promote differential reactions in their socializing others (for example, parents), but that in relation to these different social interactional histories a youth can promote his or her own problem behavior development. Thus, here, and in fact throughout our discussion in this chapter of physical and behavioral problems in adolescent development, we have noted that adolescent-social interactions are often involved in the genesis of problems. Indeed, frequently we have seen that these adolescent-social interactions involve the family unit. As a consequence, although there are many levels and types of interventions one may use to modify or prevent problems in adolescent development, we will end this chapter by discussing intervention that emphasizes the adolescent-family relation.

INDIVIDUAL AND FAMILY THERAPY
FOR ADOLESCENT PROBLEMS

When problems during adolescence do arise, there are a variety of professionals to which the adolescent and his or her family may turn for help. Some of these professionals come to mind immediately. For example, medical and health problems may be helped by physicians, nurses, and other health professionals. Some persons are familiar with the help that can be given by nutritionists and dieticians, particularly problems associated with weight control. Clinicians in the fields of speech and hearing may be helpful in improving problems associated with speech pathology and audiology, for example, hearing loss, deafness, stuttering, and other speech defects.

There are many professionals who deal with problems of adolescence which are primarily social-psychological in nature. Most of the adjustment problems of adolescence, often involving the family, the school environment, and peers, can be helped by psychologists, social workers, and family counselors and therapists who are specially trained to work with adolescents and their families. Professional counselors are trained to deal with the psychological state of the adolescent, and the way in which social influences interact with each other to affect the social, behavioral, and personality development of the adolescent. This section focuses on those helping professionals who are concerned primarily with problems in these domains of adolescent development.

Where to turn for help?

Unlike some professions, counselors and therapists who deal with adolescents may come from many different academic disciplines or fields of training. There are several which are most readily identified, however. First, adolescents and their parents may turn to family counselors or therapists. Family counselors and therapists are trained to deal with the family environment and its influence on adolescent development. A family counselor will usually want to involve both the adolescent and the parents in the counseling, either in the same sessions or in different sessions.

Some family counselors use a format known as *family therapy*, which often requires that the entire family, including other children in the household, become involved in therapy. The central underlying theory in family therapy is that the entire family environment must be treated when problems show up with one child. Family therapy research has discovered that dysfunction in family relationships often leads to problems for just one person in the family—perhaps an adolescent—without leading to visible symptoms of dysfunction in other family members. Thus, it is assumed that to treat only the adolescent with the identified problem would be treating only the symptoms, but not eliminating the causes. Consequently, the family therapist seeks to eradicate the underlying causes by treating the entire family unit.

Other family counselors do not rely on the specific principles of family therapy, but use more traditional counseling approaches to solve problems of the adolescent period. Family counselors often will help the adolescent determine the sources of the problem, and will then help him or her to take the necessary steps to change the behaviors, circumstances, or relationships which are contributing to the problem. Family counselors will almost always require that the parents be involved in the treatment in some way, since they play such a central role in the adolescent's life, and may be a profound factor in the cause—and probably the solution—of the dysfunction.

Family counselors and therapists are located throughout the country. Qualified family counselors and therapists can be found by calling or writing the American Association for Marriage and Family Therapy, 924 W. Ninth Street, Upland, California 91786, telephone 714-981-0888. A referral will be made to an individual in the client's area. Counselors and therapists who qualify for membership in this organization have undergone several years of training, including an appropriate graduate degree, a minimum of 1,000 hours of supervised clinical experience in marriage and family therapy, and a thorough review of qualifications and competence by a national board.

Individuals may also turn to the school for help. Since many adolescent problems are school-related, it may be wise to consult with the school advisor or principal about whether there are professional counselors available in the school system. Many schools have social workers and/or school psychologists on the staff to help with the problems of adolescence. In most cases, access to a counselor will be provided even if the problem is not directly related to school or schoolwork. Unfortunately, many schools do not have such professionals on the staff, and other schools must share the services of a school psychologist or social worker with several other schools.

Social workers are trained to do individual and family counseling, and to help the adolescent to cope with the problems of the school, the family, and the larger social environment. The training of social workers and family counselors overlaps in many ways, but social workers often have more experience dealing with community agencies and the school system.

School psychologists have graduate degrees in psychology, and they usually specialize in diagnosing and testing children and adolescents for personality problems, learning disabilities, and adjustment problems. School psychologists are also trained in techniques of therapy, but the balance of testing and therapy in their jobs varies depending on the time demands they face in their particular communities.

Clinical psychologists, counseling psychologists, and psychiatrists also come into contact with adolescents, and are also appropriate professionals to whom adolescents can be referred. Psychiatrists are physicians who tend to deal with adolescent problems involving severe pathology, psychosis, and psychological problems which have significant health components, including drug dependency. When there is a profound medical component to the problem, or when medication may be required for treatment, a psychiatrist often will need to be consulted.

Clinical and counseling psychologists often specialize in the problems of child and adolescent development. These professionals are qualified to do testing, diagnosis, and therapy with adolescents, although as with other professionals, only some clinical and counseling psychologists have chosen to specialize in the problems of the adolescent population. Psychologists have advanced degrees and have had a supervised training experience. Most states license the practice of psychology, and thus an adolescent and his or her family should ascertain that the counselor is licensed and qualified to work with problems of adolescence.

In the event that a parent, teacher, or youth has consulted a professional for help who prefers not to deal with the problem at hand, most professionals readily will make a referral to someone who is trained appropriately for the problem. Sometimes an initial session will be arranged to assess the situation firsthand before a referral is made. A prospective client should never hesitate to inquire about the qualifications and training of the counselor or therapist or about his or her special interest in working with adolescents. Professionals who are reluctant to discuss such matters should be avoided.

When should counseling be sought?

Ordinarily, problems develop over a period of time. Hence, adolescents and their parents need not wait until their problems reach a crisis stage, until they are obviously insoluble, before counseling is sought. Unfortunately, many wait too long to seek help. They wait until a crisis point has been reached, making treatment of the problem all the more difficult. Counseling should be considered both a means of solving problems and a means of preventing them—or at least preventing them from reaching a critical stage. Counseling may also be thought of as a type of education as well as a type of therapy. In some instances, a discussion with a counselor about what is normal in adolescent development versus what is not can help relieve parental and adolescent anxiety about problems of development.

Some basic principles of counseling

Approaches to counseling are as numerous as there are counselors. Individuals go through extensive training, but then often develop their own style of treatment in which they integrate their training, new developments in the field over time, and their own ideas about what works best in given situations. However, there are some basic principles in counseling which almost always apply (Bowman & Spanier, 1978).

Rapport is one basic element of a counseling relationship. Rapport is necessary to establish an open line of communication between counselor and client(s). It also results in a more comfortable relationship between client and counselor, a very important requirement.

Ventilation is another basic principle. Individuals sometimes ask why they should have to pay somebody just to listen to their problems. It is true that counselors do a lot of listening, but there is a reason for this. The counselor needs to hear the problem in the words of the client. Furthermore, persons in distress usually have a need to ventilate their feelings—to get things off their chest. Ventilation may be in and of itself therapeutic.

A third important principle is *interpretation*. After hearing about the problem and evaluating it, the counselor may make certain interpretations of what dynamics may be involved in the problem. The counselor often strives to help the client understand the nature of the problem—something which may never have been pointed out to the client before.

Insight development has as its purpose encouraging the clients themselves to understand the source of the problem and what part they have in the dynamics of the situation. Insight development, then, is the hoped-for outcome of interpretation.

Support is another principle. Counselors often take a major role in providing support for their clients. Many clients are dejected or frustrated because of the problem at hand. They need to be told that the problem can be solved if they are motivated to do so. The counselor has a role, then, in providing the adolescent and his or her parents with the emotional and intellectual support they need to move toward solving their problem.

Finally, *motivation* is a very important ingredient in successful counseling. All persons involved must be willing to work at improving the situation and working toward a solution of the problem. Unmotivated clients are difficult to help because either they resist the efforts of the therapy at every turn or they are unwilling to change. Parents lack motivation in therapy at least as often as their adolescents. There are many situations in which a parent refuses to be involved in the treatment, or refuses to acknowledge that he, she, or they have a role in the problem.

Behavior therapy

There are several means by which properly trained professionals may intervene to modify or eliminate problematic behaviors. One type of treatment often used for individual disorders is known as *behavior therapy*. This form of therapy has been shown to be effective in dealing with a wide range of problems. Behavior therapy is a general term referring to a variety of approaches to treatment. However, what behavior therapy approaches have in common is their emphasis on changing actual problematic *behaviors* of the individual. *Behavior modification* is sometimes used as a synonym for behavior therapy, but is a less inclusive term.

Most forms of behavior therapy apply the principles of conditioning to clinical disorders (Kazdin & Wilson, 1978). That is, through the use of the rewards and punishments for behaviors that are involved in classical and operant conditioning, individual and social disorders are modified. There are a few basic assumptions of behavior therapy which can be cited (Rimm & Somervill, 1977):

1. Treatment emphasizes overt maladaptive behaviors, or internal activities or processes that are related to overt behavior, in a relatively straightforward manner.
2. Learning is assumed to play a vital role in the acquisition and modification of maladaptive behaviors.
3. Treatment is very much oriented to the present.
4. Treatment goals are very specific.
5. Behavior therapists place a great deal of emphasis on scientific validation of their techniques.

Behavior therapies have proved effective in the treatment of behavioral problems in adolescence such as delinquency, disorderly school conduct, distressful communication patterns in the family, and eating and drinking disorders. Not only does the application of principles of conditioning seem useful in the treatment of a variety of behavior problems that involve adolescents and youth, but the procedures involved in such behavior therapy seem to work better than many other types of "psychological" treatment.

Other treatment approaches

Counselors and therapists also use a number of other approaches, each with their own techniques, to treat the problems of adolescence. The choice of one approach over another is usually based on a combination of the professional's training, the theoretical approach the professional brings to his or her analysis of human development and social interaction, and the specific problem at hand. Some therapists mostly follow one particular approach, and others vary greatly in their treatment, depending on the individual being treated and the problem he or she has.

Psychoanalytic therapy has its roots in the work of Sigmund Freud. Freud developed psychological explanations for such daily events as dreams, emotions, sexual development, personality, and parent-child relationships. He also believed that when problems in these and other areas developed, the cause must lie in our psychological makeup. He developed *psychoanalytic psychotherapy*, a treatment approach which involves alteration of emotional and behavioral disturbances through the use of such methods as dream interpretation and free association and usually requires a long-range approach to therapy because the patient is asked to discuss his or her life in detail, in order to probe in depth the underlying causes of the disorder. Psychoanalysis assumes determinism in all human behavior, and the existence of unconscious mental processes. Although Freud's techniques are not as popular now as they were during the middle third of this century, many of his ideas and the techniques based on his theories are still used widely. The merits of psychoanalysis and Freudian theory are debated with vigor—and there is much that can be criticized—but Freud's contribution continues to be great nevertheless, since his theories have encouraged others to modify his approaches and to develop alternative theories.

Client-centered therapy is most closely associated with the name of Carl Rogers. His approach to psychotherapy emphasizes the individual's inherent capacity for self-understanding and self-direction. His technique is predominantly *nondirective* (the therapist avoids telling the client what to do) and *permissive* (the client is made to feel that what he or she believes or feels should be accepted as part of the individual's growth experience).

Client-centered therapy can be characterized by four basic principles (Rogers, 1970):

1. The therapy relies on the individual's drive toward growth, health, and adjustment. Therapy frees the client for normal growth and development.
2. Greater stress is placed upon the feeling aspects of the situation than upon the intellectual aspects.
3. Greater importance is placed on the immediate situation than on the past.
4. The therapeutic relationship itself is seen as a growth experience—a personal relationship which is a growth-promoting psychological climate.

Gestalt therapy is a humanistically oriented form of treatment which has become increasingly popular in the last two decades. Fritz Perls is the name most closely associated with gestalt therapy. The central thesis of gestalt therapy is that psychological difficulties arise when the individual loses touch with or avoids full awareness of himself or herself, the environment, and the activities which exist at the moment (Rimm & Somervill, 1977).

The goal of gestalt therapy is to restore the capacity to be aware and to help the individual learn *how* such awareness is lost. Gestalt therapy is based on several principles (Rimm & Somervill, 1977):

1. Staying with here-and-now events
2. Promoting direct experiencing
3. An experimental model that promotes self-discovery by the client
4. Focus on the client's awareness
5. Skillful frustration
6. Emphasis on responsibility and choice

The client is confronted with the ways he or she manipulates others and himself or herself, and the client learns to use and depend on his or her own resources. The creativity of the therapist is important in helping the client to gain the knowledge and skills needed to function optimally.

Finally, there is one form of intervention that relies on all others. *Community mental health* includes the spectrum of approaches available, but gains it uniqueness from its focus on *prevention* and *community-based* consultation and intervention. This approach, which has become increasingly popular in recent years, attempts to reach larger numbers of persons than traditional approaches. Moreover, it sees mental health as an important aspect of human functioning that should be attended to on a continuing basis. Community mental health programs range from crisis-intervention centers (phone-in and walk-in) to specialized training programs for public employees (such as police officers), to group training in communications for married couples.

CHAPTER SUMMARY

Few adolescents are typical in all respects, and some adolescents have characteristics which make them stand out noticeably from other adolescents. The individual problems which adolescents have may be biological in origin (such as blindness or deafness), but such problems certainly have important behavioral and social outcomes. Other problems are largely self-induced (drug abuse and some accidents, for example). And still others may be a special combination of biological, psychological, and social forces which act together (menstrual disorders, temperament, and learning disabilities, for instance).

Eating disorders can be especially problematic in adolescence. Obesity affects a significant minority of adolescents. Less frequent, but even more severe in its effects, however, is *anorexia nervosa*, a disorder found almost exclusively among adolescent females. This condition involves severe loss of weight and is a sign of an emotional problem requiring professional attention.

Visual, hearing, and speech impairments are found in hundreds of thousands of adolescents. These problems are not thought to be as widespread as they really are, since we tend to recognize only their extreme conditions (blindness, deafness, and muteness). However, many individuals have only partial vision, partial hearing loss, or a speech defect which can be corrected or improved.

Drug, alcohol, and tobacco use begins during adolescence for virtually all individuals who eventually become regular users. Many adolescents only experiment briefly with such substances, but others continue use into adulthood. Problems can develop when use of drugs, alcohol, or tobacco becomes habitual or abusive. Curiosity and peer and parent use of drugs are factors influencing adolescent drug use. Similarly, smoking usually begins as an experiment and as a "social" activity. There has been a dramatic increase in the incidence of smoking among females, a phenomenon undoubtedly related to the changing role of females in our society. Most adolescents recognize the dangers of drug, alcohol, and tobacco use, but social pressures can be powerful, and habits may be formed early.

Motor vehicle accidents rank first among the causes of death for adolescents, followed by homicide, suicide, and cancer. Motor vehicle deaths account for 65 percent of all accidental deaths among adolescents.

Some adolescents have developmental problems relating to physical growth. *Delayed puberty* and *precocious puberty* are related to the insufficient production or the early production of hormones, respectively. Some physical problems may be known only to the adolescent initially. Painful menstruation, known as *dysmenorrhea*, and the failure to menstruate, known as *amenorrhea*, affect females and may have both medical and emotional causes. Other physical disorders are noticeable to others. *Acne* is an example of a problem which causes great concern to adolescents, since it is visible to others and is the most common disorder of medical significance during this period of life. About 85 percent of adolescents have acne at least sometime during adolescence.

Mental retardation refers to subaverage intellectual functioning which originates during development and is associated with impairment in adaptive behavior. Mental retardation often is described in relation to IQ scores. *Learning disabilities* such as *dyslexia* (problems in reading) or *dysgraphia* (problems in writing) involve large numbers of adolescents. Learning disabled is the label given to youths who show a discrepancy between their estimated academic potential and their actual level of academic performance.

Temperament refers to the style of behavior. This topic is of interest in the study of individual problems in adolescence since temperament influences both what a person does and why he or she does something. It also helps us understand why some children are treated by parents and others in different ways. Some children and adolescents turn out to be more or less active, adaptable, moody, distractible, or responsive, for example, and these characteristics may serve as a basis for some individual differences and possibly problems which may develop.

Individuals with problems often need help, and the chapter concludes with a discussion of individual and family therapy and counseling for adolescent problems. A variety of trained professionals are available to help adolescents and their families. Although there are some common principles which most trained therapists use, there are many different approaches to treatment. *Behavior therapy*, *psychoanalysis*, *client-centered therapy*, *gestalt therapy*, and *community mental health* are some of the many approaches in use today.

SOCIAL PROBLEMS
AND SOCIAL CHANGE

CHAPTER

OVERVIEW

This chapter signals both an end of one venture—this book—and a beginning of another—the reader's future study of adolescent development. It focuses on many of the social problems of adolescence that have been mentioned throughout this book (for example, poverty, high school dropouts, pregnancy, parenthood, crime and delinquency), and thus provides a detailed picture of some of the real problems that might be encountered in working with or raising adolescents. It is a beginning, however, since it emphasizes social change, and thus forces us to think about the future of adolescence.

In what ways and to what extent are today's adolescents similar to and different from adolescents of earlier time periods?

Why is poverty a social problem of particular significance in adolescence?

What is the relationship between age at marriage and marital stability, and why are adolescent marriages so prone to failure?

How does adolescent parenthood compare to parenthood at other ages and in other countries?

What are the medical, social, and economic consequences of adolescent parenthood?

What are some of the proposals for dealing with the problems of adolescent parenthood, and which of these proposals are likely to be especially controversial?

How widespread are adolescent crime and delinquency compared to crime for adults?

How do crimes committed by adolescents tend to differ from those committed by adults?

What are some of the factors which may be related to juvenile delinquency, and how do they play a role in delinquent behavior?

Why do adolescents run away from home, and how big is the problem of runaways?

What social characteristics and circumstances are related to adolescents running away from home?

What might attract older adolescents to alternative life-styles?

In what ways do alternatives such as cohabitation, communes, and singleness differ from each other?

veryone moves through adolescence in his or her own way. For some, adolescence is a rather tranquil period of life. For others, it can be devastating. So far in this book, we have tried to point out some of what is known about the many factors which influence how one negotiates this period of life. Much is known, but much still remains to be discovered. It should be evident by now that the interrelationships between all the various influences are so complex that no simple explanation of how an adolescent turns out the way he or she does can be given. It is clear, however, that whatever the causes, the adolescent years are the focus of some of society's most profound social problems—drug and alcohol abuse, unwed motherhood, runaways and societal dropouts, crime and delinquency, and alienation from family, for example. This chapter discusses some of these social problems and considers how changes in society may play a role in such problems.

It is no wonder that many of our most troublesome social problems are rooted in adolescence. The movement from childhood to adulthood is perhaps the most difficult transition in our lives, requiring changes in virtually every domain of our day-to-day existence. Adolescents change in appearance, body size, and body proportions; they change in values, attitudes, and personality; they change in family behavior, peer-group interaction, and sexual behavior; and they change in self-concept, social maturity, and vocational ambitions. These and other aspects of life must all fall into place for millions of young people every year. In many ways, this metamorphosis can be thought of as an ambitious task for both the individual and the society. Is it any wonder, then, that for at least some of the adolescents involved, this transition is a breeding ground for many problems which impact profoundly on the society?

Those who study adolescence often ask what leads to some of the turmoil of this period. Whatever the answer, most realize that difficulties for some individuals are inevitable, and that society must expect and acknowledge these problems. Furthermore, questions about how to cope with the problems and how to help young people through adolescence are equally important questions for the society.

DIVERSITY AND CHANGE
IN THE PROBLEMS OF ADOLESCENCE

If we were to believe everything we hear in news reports or in casual conversation, we would believe that today's adolescent faces pressures that adolescents of earlier generations never had to contend with. Moreover, we might also conclude that adolescence today poses unheard of demands on parents and educators, due to some characteristics of the "youth subculture" which are virtually out of control. Although there is a little bit of truth to these ideas, they clearly are exaggerated. Most of the problems of adolescents today are no different than those of adolescents from earlier generations. And many deviant characteristics and social problems seen in the adolescent years apply only to a small minority of the population in question. Let us illustrate both how stable and how dynamic this period of life can be.

In the previous chapter, it was observed that today's typical adolescent probably has had some experience with drugs, alcohol, or tobacco. But this has been true for many decades, and undoubtedly some of the pressures which today's adolescent faces to experiment with drugs, alcohol, or tobacco are similar to the pressures which existed in earlier times. Thus, a picture of stability emerges. On the other hand, it was observed that females have become increasingly more likely to begin smoking. And it was noted that use of drugs, alcohol, and tobacco has increased for all adolescents. Thus, we see some aspects of change as well. The same observations can be made regarding adolescent sexual behavior. It has always existed, but perhaps not to the degree that we see today.

Actually, most of the features of adolescence remain constant over time. For example, in modern times, adolescence has been a period where the automobile has been of central interest. The earliest studies of dating (Waller, 1937) mentioned the automobile as something that enhanced a male's popularity and was often the focus of planning for dates. This interest in automobiles, especially among males, may be tied historically to one's ability to obtain a driver's license during adolescence, and to the symbolic value of the automobile in connoting independence, mobility, and maturity.

Dating itself has been a prominent feature of the adolescent years since the turn of the century. The more or less constant features of the dating period are the focus on recreational activities (movies, dances, parties, etc.), its definition as a casual social activity with no obligation to continue the relationship beyond the date, the role of dating in socialization for more lasting male-female relationships such as marriage, and the tendency for dating to be initiated by males.

Yet, as with other aspects of adolescence, dating has changed some. The automobile, the telephone, commercialized amusements, the growth of cities, the changing status of women, new expectations with regard to marriage, increased leisure time, the emancipation of youth from their parents, the greater freedom of association among young people, and a myriad of other factors are making dating somewhat different today. The expansion of the socialization function of the public school system and our social involvements within educational settings undoubtedly also have influenced the changing character of dating and courtship. Moreover, with less societal and parental control, a new responsibility is put on the shoulders of the young persons to make their own plans and choices.

The adolescent subculture has always been the focus of many other social phenomena such as the music industry, the movie industry, and the fashion industry. These are but three industries which have always given special attention to adolescents. Only the specific content of this attention has changed. For example, the 1940s, 1950s, and 1960s all had stars which became the heartthrobs of millions of adolescent females. Frank Sinatra, Elvis Presley, and the Beatles, respectively, are only names from the distant past to today's adolescents, but for females who went through their adolescence in those earlier times, these persons were the source of much attention. Over this same period, the adolescent's taste in music changed from the "big band sound" to rock and roll to folk songs and then to various syntheses of these forms. And fashions, hair lengths and styles, and forms of dancing all underwent shifts. The only thing we can predict with certainty about the 1980s in this regard is that interests such as music, movies, fashions, and the like will still be important. It is not easy to predict what specific tastes will develop in these areas.

Just as most of the nonproblematic aspects of adolescent development continue to be present from generation to generation, so do some of the more troublesome aspects. All the topics we shall discuss in this chapter could have been included in a text such as this a generation ago or even a century ago. Unwed motherhood, for example, has been known throughout recorded history. Juvenile delinquency also has a long history. Early marriage and its problems have been known since the earliest research on the topic.

This stability in the diversity of problems is superseded in attention, however, by the magnitude of some of these problems which we see in America today. Thus, it is appropriate that a discussion of the social problems of adolescence focuses on the severity and consequences as they apply in contemporary society. Our knowledge of the diversity of problems and the change which has occurred in recent years is helpful for understanding and coping with today's problems. Our knowledge of the stability of the problems from one generation to the next will assure us that such problems are not likely to go away, and should prompt us to be forward-thinking about solutions or coping mechanisms for these problems.

TYPES OF SOCIAL CHANGE

There can be different degrees or types of social change characteristic of society at any time in history. Bengtson (1970) suggests six different types of social change and defines each type in relation to the extent to which the behaviors, values, and attitudes of one generation are consistent with those of another. If, for example, there is great consistency between adolescents and their parents and other adults, then there is likely to be little social change. When there is little consistency between these generational groups, a greater degree of social change would be likely.

The *first* type of social change involves a relationship summarized by the term *social revolution*. Here adolescents are influenced vastly more by their peers than by the parental generation. Bengtson (1970) theorizes that such substantial age-group differences might result from such phenomena as great inequalities in status associated with age level. Such generational relationships would cause major and rapid social change because when youth become adults, they would remain influenced by the inequality they experienced.

Friedenberg (1969) believed such relationships characterized adolescents and their parents in the 1960s. He said that young people aren't rebelling from their parents; they're abandoning them. Yet more than 10 years after his observation a social revolution has not taken place in the United States. Many of the adolescents Friedenberg depicted are now adults and themselves parents; and at least anecdotal evidence suggests that these "new" adults are continuing in many of the traditions of their parents; thus, it is likely that the intergenerational relationships Friedenberg saw were of the second form Bengtson (1970) describes.

The *second* type of social change involves *normal rebellion*. Bengtson says that there may be major differences between generational groups, and as such, adolescents would be more influenced by peers than parents. However, this greater peer influence is only transitory in that the age-group differences are associated with developmental adaptational demands (such as those pertaining to identity). Thus, with the transition into adulthood roles, adolescent-specific attitudes, values, and behavior orientations would disappear. The person would adopt the adultlike attitudes, values, and behaviors, and as a consequence, social change would exist but it would be minimal.

A *third*, and related, type of change in intergenerational relationships is labeled *social evolution*. There are both important differences *and* similarities between the generations; whether continuity or discontinuity is seen depends on what social issue is focused on. Accordingly, although there will be social change, or what Bengtson terms a "selective generation gap," as a consequence of this type of relationship, change will be gradual, selective, and not abrupt or revolutionary.

A *fourth* type can be described as *"nothing really new."* There may be some generational differences, although presumably not of the scope or intensity existing in the first or second relationship types; however, like the normal rebellion type, any age-group differences would in any event disappear when the younger generation became older and assumed adult roles. But unlike normal rebellion, no social change would be expected.

However, social change may be influenced by factors other than interactions among generations. Bengtson (1970) notes that a *fifth* category of relationships involves social change, *but* does not necessarily involve generational interactions. There are major changes in society, for example revolutions, but they are not based on generational conflict alone. People may enter into conflict because of racial, sexual, religious, political, or economic differences. With this type of social change, neither peer- nor parent-generational relationships are the major source of influence.

Finally, a *sixth* form of relationship involves the significantly greater influence of the parents than the peers. *Intergenerational solidarity* will prevail over tangential differences. Although here there may be some differences between generations, these pertain only to minor issues. In the main, however, there would be continuous, unchanging and vast agreement, or solidarity, between the generations in their behavioral orientations, attitudes, and values.

It is possible to find historical times and/or societies where each of the above six types of social relationships were prominent. However, it appears that the third type of intergenerational relationship is most characteristic of the influences of peer and parent relationships on adolescents in contemporary society. Previous discussions of the topic of the alleged storm and stress of adolescence, and of the relative influences of parents and peers on adolescents, showed there was compatability in the influences of parents and peers on adolescents. While some differences existed between the generations, these differences were issue-dependent, tended not to be frequent, and in any event, were not relevant to all issues involved in adolescent-parent relationships (Bandura, 1964; Douvan & Adelson, 1966; Lerner, 1975; Lerner et al., 1975; Lerner & Knapp, 1975). Moreover, adolescents see themselves as having attitudes and values moderating between those of members of their own and their parents' generation (Lerner et al., 1975).

SOCIAL CHARACTERISTICS OF THE ADOLESCENT POPULATION

In order to understand the magnitude of some of the problems discussed in this book, it is useful to have a picture of the adolescent population as a whole, some of the social characteristics of this population, and how it is changing. Data which describe large populations usually are presented by age. Thus, for the present discussion, we must adopt an age definition of adolescence.

Changes in population growth and distribution

There are about 34 million persons ages 14 to 21 in the United States. The post-World War II baby boom, which occurred from 1945 to 1957, resulted in a record number of children reaching adolescence in the 1960s and 1970s. From 1980 to 1990, the number of individuals in the adolescent years is expected to decrease as a result of the lower birthrates which have existed since 1957. Between 1980 and 1990, the number of persons ages 14 to 17 years is expected to decrease 19 percent. The college-age population (18 to 21) is expected to decline from 17.1 million in 1980 to 14.5 million by 1990, a decrease of about 15 percent (U.S. Bureau of the Census, 1978b).

There are several other "social facts" of interest. More than two-thirds of America's youth (14 to 19) live in metropolitan areas, including 27 percent in central cities. Only one-third of adolescents ages 14 to 19 live outside of a metropolitan area. About 1 in 6 adolescents move each year, with about half of the moves to a residence within the same metropolitan area. About one-seventh of the American population of adolescents is non-White. Finally, due to the sex ratio at birth of 105 males for every 100 females, adolescent males outnumber females slightly; but this sex imbalance shifts in the other direction after adolescence, since males have higher mortality rates than do females (U.S. Bureau of the Census, 1978b).

Marital status and living arrangements

Almost 4 out of every 5 individuals ages 14 to 17 live with both of their parents. About 16 percent of adolescents not yet married live with their mother only, about 2 percent with their father only, and about 4 percent with neither parent. The percentages of persons living in "broken homes" has increased in recent years as a result of an increase in divorce rates and in the number of children in divorced families. These percentages are substantially higher for Black children, with only 50 percent of Black persons ages 14 to 17 living with both parents (U.S. Bureau of the Census, 1978b).

Only 3 percent of females 14 to 17 have married, and about ½ of 1 percent of the males in this age group have done so. But these percentages begin to change dramatically at age 18. By age 21, only 73 percent of the males are still single, and only 51 percent of the females have not yet married. These percentages are higher than they have been over most of the last two decades. In other words, a greater proportion of older adolescents are delaying marriage (U.S. Bureau of the Census, 1978b).

POVERTY

Poverty is one of society's most pressing social problems, and adolescents are often the group which brings to our attention the social and personal turmoil which can result from a culture of poverty. There has been much discussion about the role of poverty in contributing to civil disturbance, urban violence, juvenile delinquency, and social unrest (National Advisory Commission on Civil Disorders, 1968). The consequences of poverty can be very personal, resulting in poor nutrition, inadequate housing, overcrowding, a sense of normlessness and alienation, poor education, and a probability of unstable employment. The consequences for society can also be great. Poverty in communities often is viewed with despair. It hurts communities socially and economically, and is associated with many of the ills of both urban and rural life.

Adolescents bring poverty to our attention for many reasons. First, they are at the point in life where people first seek employment. In a community with high poverty rates, and among individuals who are raised in a poverty-stricken family, work is often hard to come by. Adolescent males from lower socioeconomic backgrounds have the highest unemployment rates of any group. That they tend to be less well educated than others competing for jobs makes it especially difficult for them to enter the job market (U.S. Bureau of the Census, 1978b).

Second, it is during adolescence when the individual begins to value independence. Yet one cannot easily become independent without some financial resources. The adolescent is caught between his or her aspirations for something better and the reality that it may be unattainable. Thus, poverty may create a sense of frustration for adolescents who grow up in a society which emphasizes glamour and materialism but which makes these things difficult to attain.

Third, although the adolescent living in poverty probably has the benefit of exposure to accepted laws, moral behavior, and the principle of respect for person and property, he or she undoubtedly finds it difficult to follow these teachings. Survival in the adolescent's subculture may require frequent departure from these teachings for several reasons. Crime may be an attractive alternative to the adolescent in poverty since it may provide rapid rewards for little effort. Robbery or burglary may lead to monetary rewards unmatched by employment, if it were available. Vandalism may be an outlet for frustration. And criminal behavior in general may lead to social approval and status within some peer groups or gangs. Similarly, drug use may be a coping mechanism for adolescents in poverty—a form of escape from the realities of the immediate environment. Thus, adolescents raised in conditions of poverty may sometimes find it difficult to follow accepted rules about proper behavior, because there is little reward in their environment for following these rules.

In 1975, 15 percent of persons ages 14 to 17 were considered to be living below the poverty level in the United States. Thirteen percent of individuals 18 to 21 were below the poverty level. The figures for Blacks are more than 2½ times as great as those for Whites, indicating the especially profound problem of poverty for Black adolescents. About 4.5 million persons ages 14 to 21 were living below the poverty

INSIGHT INTO ADOLESCENCE

James Baldwin is an American Black writer, essayist, and playwright. He was born in 1924 in New York City. His father was a minister, and he was himself a preacher for three years while in school. For many years James Baldwin lived in self-imposed exile in Europe. Presently he lives in New York.

On the 29th of July, in 1943, my father died. On the same day, a few hours later, his last child was born. Over a month before this, while all our energies were concentrated in waiting for these events, there had been in Detroit, one of the bloodiest race riots of the century. A few hours after my father's funeral, while he lay in state in the undertaker's chapel, a race riot broke out in Harlem. On the morning of the 3rd of August, we drove my father to the graveyard through a wilderness of smashed plate glass.

The day of my father's funeral had also been my nineteenth birthday. As we drove him to the graveyard, the spoils of injustice, anarchy, discontent, and hatred were all around us. It seemed to me that God himself had devised, to mark my father's end, the most sustained and brutally dissonant of codas. And it seemed to me, too, that the violence which rose all about us as my father left the world had been devised as a corrective for the pride of his eldest son. I had declined to believe in that apocalypse which had been central to my father's vision; very well, life seemed to be saying, here is something that will certainly pass for an apocalypse until the real thing comes along. I had inclined to be contemptuous of my father for the conditions of his life, for the conditions of our lives. When his life had ended I began to wonder about that life and also, in a new way, to be apprehensive about my own.

Source: Baldwin, J. *Notes of a Native Son.* New York: The Dial Press, 1963, pp. 76–77.

level in 1975, a figure which has remained fairly constant in recent years (U.S. Bureau of the Census, 1978b).

More than 2 million adolescent males and females are employed full-time in the United States. The median income for fully employed males was $5,657 in 1975, and for females it was $4,568. Of course, many other adolescents were employed part-time after school, weekends, or summers, and these persons are not included in the figures presented. Adolescents employed full-time usually are no longer in school and often are supporting themselves, sometimes with a spouse and children.

ADOLESCENT MARRIAGE AND DIVORCE

The median age at first marriage in the United States was 24.0 for males and 21.6 for females in 1977 (U.S. Bureau of the Census, 1978b). Whatever our definition of the age boundaries of adolescence, it is clear that Americans tend to marry young, and marriage is very much associated with the conclusion of adolescence and the beginning of adulthood. What special problems face the early-marrying individual or couple? Do persons who marry early—before the conclusion of adolescence— encounter marital adjustments which differ from those who marry later? The available evidence suggests that they do.

About one-fifth of the males and about two-fifths of the females in the United

States have married by their twentieth birthday. Early marriage is now more common than it was at the turn of the century, but the numbers and proportion of teenage marriages declined in the 1970s. Nevertheless, more than 800,000 males and females marry while still in their teens each year, more than 200,000 of them under age 18 (U.S. Bureau of the Census, 1978c; National Center for Health Statistics, 1973, 1978). Of course, there is nothing magical about a particular birthday, and many 18- or 19-year-olds are as well or better suited for marriage than some persons much older. But as mentioned earlier, analysis of social characteristics usually relies on age as an organizing variable, since it is the most readily available and easily categorized variable. Thus, let us examine more specifically what is known about marriages among persons in their teens.

Studies show that the younger people are when they marry, the greater the likelihood of both poor adjustment in marriage and subsequent divorce (Bumpass & Sweet, 1972; Lewis & Spanier, 1979; National Center for Health Statistics, 1973, 1978). Age is related to social and emotional development, and thus individuals marrying at especially early ages may find it difficult to cope with the adjustments to early marriage (Burchinal, 1959; deLissovoy, 1973; Eshleman, 1965; Martinson, 1955, 1959).

Persons who marry young are more likely than those marrying later to be confronted with the responsibilities of parenthood early in the marriage. Their educational attainment at the time of marriage is not likely to be as great, and consequently their occupational status and income may not be as high. These factors collectively may result in a poor economic situation for the couple, making marital adjustment more difficult.

Although many youthful marriages succeed, they appear to have some special challenges which predispose the couples to a greater likelihood of divorce. As noted, persons who marry when relatively young are significantly more likely to divorce than are persons who marry when they are older (National Center for Health Statistics, 1973, 1978). For example, the ages of first marriage of once-married individuals and individuals married two or more times can be compared using data from the U.S. Bureau of the Census (1978c). Males who marry in their teens are more than twice as likely to divorce as males married in their early twenties, and more than three times as likely to divorce as males married in their late twenties. Females married before their eighteenth birthday are more than twice as likely to divorce as females married at age 18 or 19, who in turn are twice as likely to divorce as females married in their early twenties. Thus, women married between ages 14 and 17 are more than four times as likely to divorce as women married in their late twenties. Furthermore, among those who remain married, evidence suggests that those marrying early are not as happy as those who married in their early to mid-twenties (Lewis & Spanier, 1979).

In a study of rural high school marriages, deLissovoy (1973) found low marital competence and satisfaction among young couples. Although some high school marriages were found to be satisfactory by objective research measures, most had serious problems. All except two of the forty-eight couples studied were expecting a child prior to marriage. The majority of both husbands and wives withdrew from high school before graduating. And only thirty-seven of the forty-eight couples remained legally married three years later. The variables associated with high risk of failure for these early marriages were premarital pregnancy, failure to complete high school, low socioeconomic status, limited dating experience, and lack of adequate income. The adolescents reported high marital tensions, poor marital adjustment, and high instability, despite a considerable amount of support for some from relatives and the church (deLissovoy, 1973).

There are several social trends which are conducive to early marriage (Davis, 1972). A century ago, men and women married at later ages than today because the male, usually engaged in agriculture, needed time to become economically independent. He needed to be able to support a family before he could marry, since childbirth to his wife usually followed marriage by only a year or two. The spread of contraceptive practice in America today allows young people the possibility of marrying at early ages without the responsibilities of parenthood. Furthermore, with graduation from high school or college, young Americans can obtain jobs which will allow them to support themselves immediately.

Of course, much teenage marriage is the result of poor planning and unwanted pregnancies, factors which in turn are conducive to divorce. But "forced" marriage aside, there are many other factors associated with early marriage today. The knowledge that a poor marriage can be ended by divorce may be a factor, even though individuals rarely enter a given marriage expecting it to fail. But the realization that divorce is a possibility may contribute in part to hasty marriage. The need for security in a male-female relationship that some adolescents often have can result in one partner pressuring the other to marry. Marriage may also be a form of escape from an unhappy parental home, or an opportunity to achieve independence with the establishment of one's own home.

Other factors such as liberal support of military dependents; educational and housing benefits for veterans; federal subsidization of home ownership; increased governmental assumption of educational, medical, and other costs of children; food stamps; college housing services for married students; unemployment compensation; and parental willingness to continue supporting offspring after they are married all may contribute to early marriage (Davis, 1972).

Despite these factors conducive to early marriage, there are others that encourage postponement of marriage. For an even greater proportion of the population these factors seem to be influential, since the age at first marriage is increasing and the number of teenage marriages is decreasing. The increase in premarital intercourse and the changes in sexual freedom which it signals undoubtedly make access to a sexual partner a less prominent reason for marriage. Knowledge that divorce rates are higher when marriage comes earlier may play a small part. Furthermore, for males and females entering college, adolescence may be "stretched," postponing the time when the adolescent becomes independent of parents and willing to marry. There is a large proportion of young men and women in college today, and there may be less pressure to marry when faced with the dual responsibilities of marriage and college work. The increase in the extent of unmarried cohabitation seen on college campuses may be a reflection of the contemporary college student's desire to postpone marriage but to experience some of the advantages of an intimate social and sexual relationship (Bower & Christopherson, 1977; Clayton & Voss, 1977; Spanier & Glick, 1979).

Finally, with a large field of eligible mates present in the college setting, the individual is less likely to feel that he or she may be unable to attract or find a mate in a few years. This impression of a narrow field of eligibles is more likely to be characteristic of men and women who do not go on to college or who have graduated from college and find themselves in communities or social settings in which the perceived or actual field of eligibles is small.

ADOLESCENT PARENTHOOD

The dramatic increase in sexual behavior among adolescent females and the lag in the adoption of effective contraception have resulted in great numbers of pregnancies to young females in the United States. As pointed out earlier, many young females terminate their pregnancies by abortion, but others continue their pregnancy to term. About 10 percent of United States teenagers get pregnant, and 6 percent give birth each year. This section examines the many problems associated with adolescent pregnancy and parenthood, both inside and outside of marriage.

Extent of teenage parenthood

The United States ranks fifth of all countries in the world in the proportion of adolescent females who give birth. Only East Germany, Bulgaria, New Zealand, and Romania have higher adolescent fertility rates (The Alan Guttmacher Institute, 1976). Nearly 600,000 births in 1975 were to mothers under 20 years of age. Births to teenagers accounted for about 1 in 5 of all births in that year. The birthrate in the United States decreased for women in most age groups during the 1960s and 1970s, but the rate of childbearing for adolescent females ages 15 to 17 actually increased by 22 percent during the period from 1966 to 1975. Although the decline in the birthrates seen in the population in general was also characteristic of older adolescent females, the 15- to 17-year-olds accounted for 227,000 births, a large share of the total for all women under 20 (National Center for Health Statistics, 1977b).

Most teenage mothers, both married and unmarried, keep their babies after the birth of the child. More than 9 in 10 of these babies stay with their mothers. One-third of births to teenagers are out of wedlock. The other two-thirds are to females who have married before the birth. And of the births that occur to married women in their teens, one-third of the children were conceived before the marriage (The Alan Guttmacher Institute, 1976). Exhibits 15.1 and 15.2 show that the percentage of out-of-wedlock births and the percentage of births that are conceived outside of marriage both are greatest for younger adolescents.

Socialization for parenthood

Parenthood, like marriage, tends to be romanticized in the United States. Parenthood is supposed to be a joyous experience, and for many couples—those who are most prepared and accepting of parenthood—it is (Russell, 1974). For many others, however, the joys of parenthood are at least partially overshadowed by the "crisis" it brings (LeMasters, 1974). No matter how well prepared they are, most couples will find many challenges in parenthood. It is also true, however, that this feeling of crisis usually subsides soon after the birth of the child, after the couple have adapted to their new life-style (Hobbs & Cole, 1976).

For adolescents, parenthood usually is unplanned, and even when planned, it

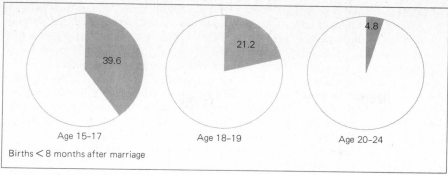

Exhibit 15.1
Percent of births to wives ages 15 to 17, 18 to 19, and 20 to 24 that were conceived before marriage. (*Source:* Adapted from The Alan Guttmacher Institute, 1976.). Reprinted with permission from *11 Million Teenagers: What Can Be Done About the Epidemic of Adolescent Pregnancies in the United States,* published by The Alan Guttmacher Institute, New York, 1976.

Exhibit 15.2
Percent of births to females aged 14 to 19 that were out of wedlock, by single years of age, United States 1970 to 1974. (*Source:* Adapted from The Alan Guttmacher Institute, 1976.). Reprinted with permission from *11 Million Teenagers: What Can Be Done About the Epidemic of Adolescent Pregnancies in the United States,* published by The Alan Guttmacher Institute, New York, 1976.

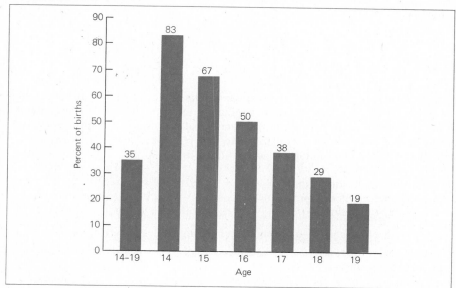

tends to coexist with poorer than desired economic and social conditions. And for single parents, of course, there are the additional burdens of raising the child without the help of a spouse. Thus, the "crisis" of parenthood tends to be felt most harshly by adolescent parents, and it tends to be more difficult for them to accept parenthood readily and happily as a desired event which will enhance their life-style.

Our society's romanticized notion of parenthood creates a belief in most adolescents that they will eventually marry and have children. In modern America, only a small portion of adolescents expect never to have children. Yet despite the nearly universal nature of parenthood, there is little preparation for it, either practical or emotional. Research has confirmed the existence of numerous adjustments required by parenthood, all of which are relevant to adolescent parenthood (Bowman & Spanier, 1978):

1. There tends to be a revised power structure, with the wife gaining more power in the marital relationship.
2. There is typically the loss of the wife's income from employment.
3. Extra expenses are created by the child, ranging from hospital and medical expenses to clothes, food, and furniture.
4. There tends to be a revision in the division of labor in the home.
5. Personal relationships usually are changed. For example, the amount of leisure time available decreases. Life-styles change, particularly since parental freedom and mobility are reduced.
6. There is a disruption of routines, since infants rarely conform to the parents' wishes about feeding, sleeping, and diapering.
7. There is an expansion of tasks, for example, more housekeeping.
8. Particularly with first children, parents often report anxiety about the child's welfare.

Medical and health consequences of teenage parenthood

Hundreds of research studies have documented the effects of early childbearing for both child and mother. The effects are numerous, and it is difficult not to conclude that the risks of having a child while young are great. Let us briefly highlight some of the findings of the research pertaining to the children (The Alan Guttmacher Institute, 1976; National Center for Health Statistics, 1978):

1. Children born to adolescents are more likely to be of low birth weight than children born to older women.
2. Pregnant adolescents are likely to have received inadequate prenatal care.
3. There are higher rates of infant mortality among babies born to young mothers.
4. Mental retardation and birth defects are more common among children of adolescent females.
5. All the tendencies cited above apply across different races.

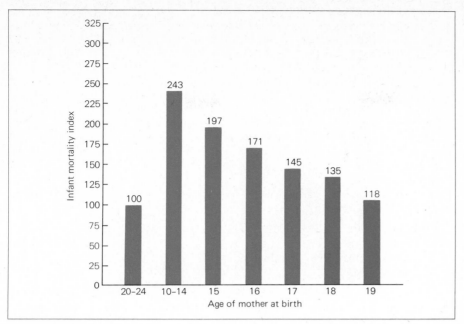

Exhibit 15.3
**Risk of death in first year of life, per 1,000 infants of mothers aged 19 and
younger and mothers aged 20 to 24. (Risk to babies of mothers 20 to 24 ×
100.) (*Source:* Adapted from The Alan Guttmacher Institute, 1976.).
Reprinted with permission from *11 Million Teenagers: What Can Be Done
About the Epidemic of Adolescent Pregnancies in the United States,*
published by The Alan Guttmacher Institute, New York, 1976.**

Exhibits 15.3 and 15.4 show the higher infant mortality and higher incidence of
low birth weight among infants of teens. Babies of young teens are two to three times
more likely to die in their first year of life than are the babies of older women, and the
incidence of low birth weight is about twice as high among teenagers. Low birth
weight is of importance because it is in turn related to a number of other possible
complications. Neurological defects, numerous childhood illnesses, and lifelong
mental retardation are often related to low birth weight (The Alan Guttmacher
Institute, 1976).

We may also examine some of the findings pertaining to consequences for the
adolescent who gives birth to a child:

1. The maternal death risk is higher for teenagers than for women in their
   twenties.

2. Pregnant adolescents are considerably more likely than women who are older to
   suffer from medical complications such as toxemia and anemia.

3. Teenage females who are pregnant are more likely than other females to suffer

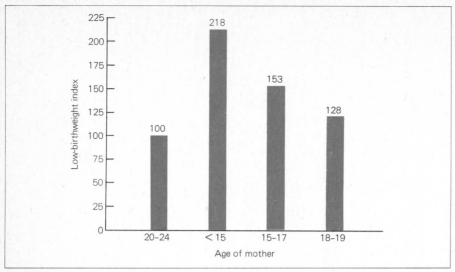

Exhibit 15.4
Risk of low birth weight (<2,500 grams) among babies born to teenage mothers and mothers aged 20 to 24. (Risk to babies of mothers 20 to 24 × 100.) (*Source:* Adapted from The Alan Guttmacher Institute, 1976.). Reprinted with permission from *11 Million Teenagers: What Can Be Done About the Epidemic of Adolescent Pregnancies in the United States,* published by The Alan Guttmacher Institute, New York, 1976.

Exhibit 15.5
Risk of fatal complications during pregnancy, labor, and childbirth to teenage mothers and mothers 20 to 24. (Risk to mothers 20 to 24 × 100.) (*Source:* Adapted from The Alan Guttmacher Institute, 1976.). Reprinted with permission from *11 Million Teenagers: What Can Be Done About the Epidemic of Adolescent Pregnancies in the United States,* published by The Alan Guttmacher Institute, New York, 1976.

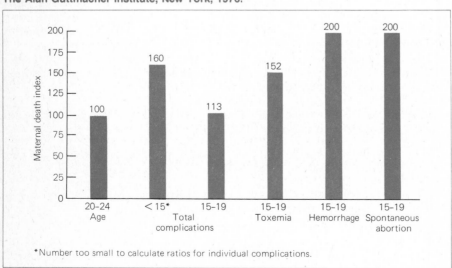

*Number too small to calculate ratios for individual complications.

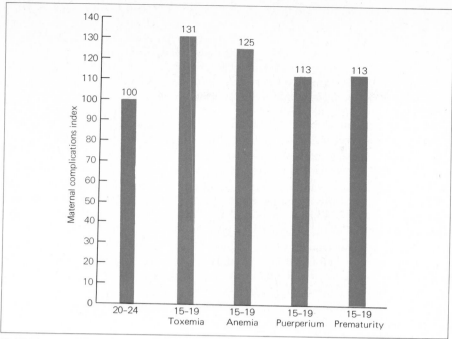

Exhibit 15.6
Risk of nonfatal complications of pregnancy, labor, and childbirth to previously nulliparous 15- to 19-year-old mothers. (Risk of complication to mothers 20 to 24 × 100.) (*Source:* Adapted from the Alan Guttmacher Institute, 1976.). Reprinted with permission from *11 Million Teenagers: What Can Be Done About the Epidemic of Adolescent Pregnancies in the United States,* published by The Alan Guttmacher Institute, New York, 1976.

from poor nutrition and inadequate prenatal care, thus increasing their chances of encountering threats to their health during and after pregnancy.

Exhibits 15.5 and 15.6 show the risks of both fatal and nonfatal complications which may occur during pregnancy, labor, or childbirth to women who are having their first child. *Toxemia* is a condition in which the blood contains poisonous products, sometimes resulting in *eclampsia* or *preeclampsia*, which cause convulsions and seizures during pregnancy. *Anemia* refers to a shortage of oxygen-carrying material in the red blood cells. *Hemorrhage* is a loss of blood. *Spontaneous abortion* is the medical term for a miscarriage. *Puerperium* refers to the period from labor to the time when the uterus has regained its normal size (about six weeks).

Social and economic consequences of teenage parenthood

In addition to the many possible medical and health consequences of parenthood for adolescent females, there are numerous documented social and economic consequences which seem to follow the female through her entire life span. Of course, there are exceptions to the rule, and we are presenting here only summary information from research studies. However, many social and economic consequences occur with such regularity that one can be reasonably certain that a great number of the females in question will encounter the problems discussed. Let us highlight some of the conclusions from the research literature (The Alan Guttmacher Institute, 1976; Furstenberg, 1976; National Center for Health Statistics, 1978):

1. Young mothers of all races are not likely to finish high school. Of adolescent females giving birth before age 18, less than 1 in 6 finishes high school.

2. As a result, teenage mothers, especially younger adolescents, lack key skills which would allow them to compete successfully for jobs.

3. Adolescent mothers experience higher rates of unemployment and dependence on welfare. In a study of young mothers in New York City, 91 percent of the females who first had babies at ages 15 to 17 had no employment whatsoever a year and a half after the birth, and 72 percent were receiving welfare.

4. Adolescent females who give birth before age 18 are more than twice as likely as women who have their first child in their twenties to be below the federal poverty line throughout their lives. Women who give birth at age 18 or 19 are almost 1½ times as likely to be below the poverty line.

5. Young mothers tend to have larger families than women who do not have their first child until they are at least 20 years old.

Furstenberg (1976a) conducted a longitudinal study of pregnant adolescent females which provides some insight into the consequences of the experience for them. He studied a predominately Black sample of 400 young women in the Baltimore area who became pregnant before age 18 and who decided to keep their babies. He was able to follow this low-income sample over a period of five years. He also conducted interviews with many of the mothers and classmates of the adolescent females, and with some of the fathers of the children who were born to these young women.

All the women studied had initiated sexual intercourse by their early or mid-teens. However, a substantial proportion of the pregnant adolescents and their mothers disapproved of premarital sex. Yet despite their belief that sex was wrong, they obviously were unable to follow their beliefs. Most of the females were vaguely aware of birth control. Most could mention some methods of contraception, and over half had used a condom at some time. However, contraceptive use was sporadic, and over half stated that they did not use contraception because the boyfriend was either unprepared or unwilling to use it most of the time (Furstenberg, 1976a).

Three-fourths of the females wished they had not become pregnant, and only one young woman among all those studied was unambivalently positive about becoming a parent. About 20 percent of these females married before the child was born, and most—but not all—of them married the father of the child. The economic situation of the male was a key factor in the decision of whether to marry. Most of the women who did not marry believed that they would eventually marry the father of the child, but less than half ever did. Among the females who eventually married, 3 out of 5 of the marriages were terminated within six years. Nearly a third were dissolved within two years (Furstenberg, 1976a).

Most of the children conceived by these women during adolescence were both unplanned and unwanted. When asked whether they wanted to become pregnant again soon, virtually all the respondents said no. Yet within five years after delivery of their first child, 70 percent of the females had become pregnant again at least once, and 30 percent had become pregnant again at least twice (Furstenberg, 1976a).

Finally, Furstenberg's sample of young mothers had little income, most had poor-paying jobs if they were employed at all, and they often had to rely on welfare for their support. Among couples who married after the pregnancy, more than three-fifths of the fathers of the children maintained some contact with their children, and many contributed to the support of the mother and child. However, among couples who never married, fathers rarely saw their children. It is evident from the national and selected sample data presented that adolescent parenthood has important implications for society. Moreover, it usually creates a set of social and economic circumstances that may pose significant burdens on the young men, women, and children involved.

What can be done?

The large number of adolescent pregnancies and childbirths and the potentially troublesome consequences of these events lead to a consideration of what can be done to change the magnitude of the problem. There are no recommendations on which all experts would agree, and some recommendations are actually somewhat controversial. One of the leading research organizations for problems concerning family planning is The Alan Guttmacher Institute, a division of the Planned Parenthood Federation of America. The institute has developed a set of recommendations to deal with the problem of adolescent pregnancies in the United States, and these are presented below (The Alan Guttmacher Institute, 1976):

1. Realistic sex education should be offered through school, churches, youth agencies and the media.
2. An expanded network of preventive family planning programs is needed, with particular emphasis on programs to reach adolescents.
3. Adequate pregnancy counseling services are needed so that teenagers can determine early if they are pregnant, and then receive complete information on the various options available to them.
4. Equal availability and accessibility of legal abortion is recommended so that adolescents can exercise their constitutional right to end an unwanted pregnancy.
5. Adequate prenatal, obstetrical and pediatric care is needed for those who carry their pregnancies to term.
6. Adolescents need social, educational, and employment services, and their children need day care facilities to allow for completion of education.
7. Finally, expansion of biomedical research is recommended to discover new, safe and effective techniques of fertility regulation.

CRIME AND DELINQUENCY

Adolescents commit a disproportionately large share of the crime in the United States and are also victims of an especially large share of the crimes committed. In

1975, 62 percent of all persons arrested in the United States for serious crimes were under 21 years of age. Forty-three percent of those arrested for serious crimes were under 18 years old, and 17 percent were under 15 years old (*Uniform Crime Reports*, 1976). Similarly, adolescents are about twice as likely to be victims both of crimes of violence and of crimes against property as are persons in the population as a whole (U.S. Bureau of the Census, 1978a).

Crime, then, is one of the most unsettling social problems of adolescence. Throughout the United States, there are two different legal systems—sometimes very different—for dealing with criminal behavior. There is one system for adults, usually defined to be 18 years of age and older, and there is the juvenile justice system. There are some jurisdictions in which a juvenile can be classified as an adult for legal purposes, but this happens rarely, and usually for the most serious crimes only. Adolescence straddles both legal systems, with younger adolescents usually having to contend with the juvenile justice system, and older adolescents having to face officials in the adult system. Thus, in law as in other aspects of the social system, adolescence can be seen as a transition from childhood to adulthood.

In technical terms, *juvenile delinquency* can be defined as the violation of a law committed by a person prior to his or her eighteenth birthday, which would have been a crime if committed by an adult (Law Enforcement Assistance Administration, 1974). Although we will use this definition in this section, it should be noted that the term has been defined in many different ways (Griffin & Griffin, 1978; Reed & Baali, 1972). In most general terms, juvenile delinquency has come to mean anything from persistent misbehavior to incorrigibility to conviction of a serious crime. Legal definitions of juvenile delinquency vary from state to state, and some of these definitions are rather vague. Historically, it was thought that the juvenile justice system existed mainly for corrective rather than punitive purposes. Thus, notions of delinquency could be used loosely, since children were not viewed as criminals, and only entered the court for "guidance."

It was also this concept of juveniles that led to the development of a justice system in the United States which historically did not provide for due process in juvenile court. The Supreme Court determined in 1967, however, that Gerald Gault, a 15-year-old boy who was imprisoned for making "lewd phone calls," deserved the same due process an adult deserves. Gault initially was not given the benefit of a lawyer and received an indeterminant disposition (which could have resulted in incarceration for up to six years) on the basis of an informal hearing with a juvenile judge. The Supreme Court concluded that the Constitution does not apply only to adults. Juveniles charged with serious crimes were to be given the same legal rights as adults (Griffin & Griffin, 1978).

Although juveniles are now entitled to due process when they face criminal charges, the juvenile justice system still deals with numerous problems which would never be considered in adult court. But although there are different procedures for dealing with juvenile and adult delinquency, many younger adolescents do find themselves incarcerated, since the crimes juveniles commit are often as severe as those committed by adults. Juveniles may be found in jails, detention homes, training schools, or other custodial facilities.

Most adolescents get into trouble at some point. Virtually all adults can recall as adolescents being guilty of underage drinking, speeding, driving while under the influence, shoplifting, violation of curfew, use of drugs, public intoxication, theft, vandalism, or one of many misdemeanors. However, only a minority of adolescents are actually arrested, charged, and adjudicated for one of these offenses or for an offense even more serious. Most parents are aware that their children may at some point commit a small act of vandalism, break into a house under construction, steal an inexpensive item from a store or from school, behave in an unruly way in public, or engage in fighting. Some of these activities are so characteristic of people that we would hardly think of someone who participated in one of these events as a criminal. But for some adolescents, many of these activities become a way of life. And others may commit a more serious crime (such as murder, rape, robbery, aggravated assault, arson, or carrying weapons). This section focuses attention on adolescents who actually are arrested and charged with crimes which are serious, and on adolescents who are victims of serious crimes.

Adolescents as offenders

Adolescent males and females under age 18 accounted for a total of more than 2 million arrests in 1975, and individuals 18 to 20 accounted for an additional 1.3 million arrests. Juvenile arrests increased substantially since 1960. The figures comparing males and females are particularly revealing. Although males currently are arrested more than three times as often as are females, the rates of female arrest are increasing much faster than the rates for males. Between 1960 and 1975, the number of arrests of adolescent females more than tripled, while the arrests of adolescent males doubled (*Uniform Crime Reports*, 1976). It is probable that increasing male-female equality in social relationships and the movement of females into traditionally male activities have had consequences even in the area of crime and delinquency. This trend is likely to continue in coming years, as social equality advances. The dramatic increase in arrests of adolescents was unique, in that the number of arrests for the adult population increased only 13 percent in the same time period.

Adolescent females increasingly have become attracted to certain types of crime in recent years. There was a sevenfold increase in adolescent female arrests for robbery between 1960 and 1975, a fivefold increase in the incidence of arrests for aggravated assault, and a ninefold increase in arrests for the purchase, receipt, or possession of stolen property. The general category of arrests for serious violent crime increased more than six times, and the general category of arrests for serious property crime increased more than five times during this period for female adolescents (*Uniform Crime Reports*, 1976). Even when corrected for the larger number of adolescents in the population during the 1960s and 1970s, the increase among females is startling.

To cite a few examples of the extent of adolescent crime, there were more than 2,500 arrests for criminal homicide in 1975, more than 9,000 arrests for forcible rape, about 75,000 arrests for robbery, and more than half a million arrests for larceny (theft). These statistics are just the tip of the iceberg of adolescent crime and delinquency, of course, since they represent only those who are caught, arrested, and reported to the FBI (*Uniform Crime Reports*, 1976).

There are significant racial differences in arrests of adolescents. Black adolescents account for more than one-fifth of all arrests, even though they constitute just over one-tenth of the population. In other words, their rates of criminal arrest are about twice what would be expected solely on the basis of their numbers in the population.

Adolescents as victims

Adolescents are responsible for much of the criminal activity in America, but data also reveal that they are the victims of a disproportionately large share of the crime (U.S. Bureau of the Census, 1978a). Adolescents 12 to 19 years old were the victims of about 1 in every 5 crimes committed in the United States in 1975, a number which is higher than would be expected on the basis of their numbers in the total population. The rate of victimization for adolescents is about double that for nonadolescents.

Adolescent males are more likely to be victims than are adolescent females. The crimes which are most prevalent among adolescents who become victims are simple assault and aggravated assault, both crimes of violence, and personal larceny without contact, a crime of theft.

Adolescents as inmates

Juveniles who commit crimes are not likely to find themselves in jail, even for some of the most serious crimes. The juvenile justice system in the United States favors rehabilitation through counseling, community programs, and supervision during probation as alternatives to incarceration. Indeed, in some jurisdictions, juvenile offenders may commit a series of crimes, some of them serious, and never be confined to a jail or institution for more than a brief time.

According to the Law Enforcement Assistance Administration (1974), the record of dealing with juveniles is not good. The *recidivism* (repeated offense) rate for youths who have been processed by the criminal justice system through the corrections phase exceeds 60 percent. In other words, 3 in 5 offenders who are found guilty of a crime and pass through the juvenile justice system are arrested again. In fact, the more involvement a juvenile has with the criminal justice system, the greater the chances that he or she will become involved again in the future.

There is agreement that some adolescent criminals ought to be incarcerated. Many would agree that those who pose great threat to the community, who have committed repeated offenses, and who may inflict harm on others probably ought to be confined in some way. But what about others? Forty percent of juveniles processed by the criminal justice system each year have committed offenses for which only juveniles can legally be detained. In other words, adults committing the same act could not be detained or arrested. Examples are violation of curfew and running away from home. It is possible that the stigma of encountering the juvenile justice system in some way predisposes an adolescent to running into trouble with the system again. Sometimes the adolescent who finds himself or herself in jail for a short period of time is confined with more "hardened" adult criminals. This may be a stigmatizing experience (Law Enforcement and Assistance Administration, 1974), isolating the youth from lawful society and making future contacts with agencies of training and employment potentially troublesome.

A survey of local jails in the United States found more than 50,000 adolescents confined (U.S. Bureau of the Census, 1978a). A jail is a locally administered institution that has the authority to retain adults for 48 hours or longer. The jail population includes those sentenced and those awaiting arraignment, transfer to other authorities, trial, or final sentencing. Persons under 18 years held by authorities are frequently incarcerated in special detention centers and training schools rather than in jails. In 1975, about 75,000 juveniles were found in such facilities. Almost half of the youth in jails are Black, indicating rates of incarceration which are substantially higher than those for Whites. Adolescents constitute about one-third of all persons in jails. About 10 percent of the adolescents in jail and more than 20 percent of those in other facilities are females (U.S. Bureau of the Census, 1978a). Adolescents are more likely than adults to be in jail for burglary, larceny, auto theft, and robbery. Black adolescents ages 14 to 17 are particularly more likely than Black adults to be in jail for murder or kidnapping (U.S. Bureau of the Census, 1978a).

Prisons in this country have been referred to as "crime schools," and adolescents are particularly susceptible to peer influence. According to the Law Enforcement Assistance Administration (1974), an adolescent may come away from an incarceration experience convinced that he or she has learned enough not to be caught the next time. Because of these concerns, officials in the criminal justice system have looked for alternatives to incarceration. The primary alternative has been community-based corrections programs, such as residential or nonresidential halfway houses, group homes, work release programs, or vocational and educational programs. These programs have the advantage of services in the community such as health, education, counseling, and employment services. Most juveniles are now handled through a community-based correctional program following adjudication for a criminal offense. Probation is widely used for juvenile offenses, often with minimal court supervision. Many believe that this system of rehabilitation may minimize the problems of readjustment that the offender might experience when released from supervision (Law Enforcement Assistance Administration, 1974).

Others, however, question the wisdom of the juvenile justice system that puts habitual youthful offenders back on the streets too quickly or without any confinement at all. There is some concern that crime can become a way of life for many youth because of the knowledge that they are unlikely to spend time in jail. Research on these issues is extensive, but the controversy is far from settled.

Factors contributing to adolescent crime and delinquency

There is very little agreement on what causes adolescents to commit a criminal act or to adopt a criminal life-style. One government survey asked Americans what they thought caused people to become criminals. More than twenty different reasons were cited often, but "lax parents" was the one cited most often—by more than half of all persons surveyed. Other reasons cited with high frequency were bad environments, poverty, unemployment, lack of education, lack of morals in young people, alcohol, drugs, and broken homes (Law Enforcement Assistance Administration, 1975).

Social scientists, however, are still uncertain about precisely what causes delinquency among adolescents. In fact, there have been hundreds of research studies which have addressed the issue, but very little agreement about the relative influences of factors contributing to delinquency, and how these factors interact with each other. The most comprehensive theory of the causes of delinquency would be one which included biological, psychological, sociological, and economic factors. But most theories of delinquency derive their explanations from one discipline only, thus providing us with only a partial understanding (Griffin & Griffin, 1978).

The earliest theories of criminal behavior assumed that persons were born criminals. *Demonology* was the belief that crime was caused by devils, evil spirits, or demons. *Physiognomy* was a method which purported to predict individual criminality by comparing the facial features of ordinary men with dead criminals. *Phrenology* attempted to explain the connection between criminal behavior and physical characteristics by the shape of the skull. These are but three examples of some early theories of the causes of delinquency which are no longer considered realistic (Griffin & Griffin, 1978).

Some modern theories of crime and delinquency focus on personality or character disorders, problems in social learning, and mental deficiency. These topics form the core of psychological and psychiatric theories of delinquency. Other theories focus on the socialization process, peer-group influence, social disorganization in society, and the impact of the social environment in the labeling of delinquent youth. These are the sociological theories of delinquency (Griffin & Griffin, 1978). Since there is no one comprehensive theory of delinquency which integrates the knowledge available in all the relevant scientific disciplines, we shall present some of the variables which research has indicated have some relevance to understanding delinquency. Perhaps a consideration of some of the most important contributing factors will give us some insight into the persistent problems of adolescent delinquency.

Labeling   Many social scientists believe that acts are not necessarily delinquent until they are defined as delinquent by society. What may be considered criminal in one society may be perfectly legal in another. Moreover, what may be illegal in a given country at one point in history may be acceptable at another time. And even within a given country at a given time, there may be variations in what is considered criminal or illegal from state to state or even city to city. Labeling theory suggests that an adolescent does not become delinquent until labeled by the society as delinquent. An adolescent who commits a minor deviant act without being caught, for example, will probably not think of himself or herself as a criminal or as delinquent. But if that person commits a more serious act, is caught, and is brought before the juvenile justice system, he or she may acquire the label of "delinquent," and a change in self-concept may result. The primary implication of labeling theory is the idea that labeling itself is a cause of delinquency. In other words, an adolescent who has acquired a delinquent label will think of himself or herself as a delinquent and will behave accordingly.

Family influences   There are numerous studies which trace part of the cause for adolescent delinquency to family life (Griffin & Griffin, 1978). Severe maladjustment and emotional problems among adolescents, which have been traced to childhood deprivations in the family, have been linked to delinquent behavior in adolescence. Hostility, rejection, harsh discipline, and other dysfunctions in the family also have been linked to delinquency. Adolescents who have no adequate role models or who adopt role models who encourage delinquency may be likely candidates for involvement in delinquent behavior. Since the family is the primary socialization agent in society, it has a great deal of influence in the social development of its members, including social and personality development which may lead an adolescent to or steer an adolescent away from crime.

Some of the specific dysfunctions which have been cited as causative agents in delinquency are broken homes, family tension, parental rejection, and problems in family finances and parental discipline (Griffin & Griffin, 1978). Delinquent adolescents are more likely to have come from broken homes (Glueck & Glueck, 1968), but many researchers have reported that it is not the broken home itself, but rather other factors associated with broken homes, which causes delinquency (McCord, McCord, & Thurber, 1962). Several studies found that family tension—constant bickering and turmoil—found in both broken and intact homes, is the more potent factor in contributing to delinquency. But since such tension is more apparent in broken homes, the dysfunctional aspects of these families tends to be emphasized (Griffin & Griffin, 1978). Nevertheless, Bachman (1970) reports, on the basis of data from the *Youth in Transition* project, that the single variable that most accurately predicts adolescent delinquency is the young person's relation with his or her parents. The better the relation is, the less likely the adolescent will become delinquent.

Some researchers believe that discipline which is overly harsh, erratic, and ineffective may contribute to delinquent behavior. Discrepancies between maternal and paternal discipline, as well as sporadic use of discipline, may create some confusion and anxiety for the adolescent which may make it difficult for the individual to establish for himself or herself values, self-control, and consistent behavior. Finally, as mentioned earlier, poverty breeds delinquency. Lack of adequate family finances poses special burdens on individuals and families, and makes crime as a way of life a more attractive alternative than it might be for persons in higher socioeconomic groups.

The educational system Most adolescents spend a great deal of their time in school. For most days of most months of the year, school is something from which an adolescent cannot escape. And for adolescents who dislike school, who do not do well, who would rather be somewhere else, and who do not see the value in their education, going to school may be considered oppressive. As noted earlier, the school is an important socializing agent. Much of the adolescent's life is spent within its confines, and our society has in many ways transferred to educational institutions responsibility for moral as well as academic education, and responsibility for providing the adolescent with the necessary skills to become a more or less responsible member of society. But when something goes wrong in the adolescent's development, the school may rightly or wrongly be placed at the center of the explanation for why problems developed.

The influence of the school in adolescent delinquency is indirect and subtle, and the school may in reality not be able to do much about the role it plays. All states have compulsory attendance laws requiring adolescents to attend school, usually until they are 16. Beyond that age, there may be strong parental or community pressures to continue. A lower-class youth who is not doing well in school, who sees little hope that additional education will enhance his or her socioeconomic status, and who is not eager to attend school each day may reach a point of frustration which partially may be relieved by delinquency. Furthermore, a lower-class youth may find school activities dominated by middle-class youth, or may encounter teachers who are not very supportive of his or her progress. Such experiences may further push the adolescent into other social settings and activities, sometimes leading to delinquency (Griffin & Griffin, 1978).

The school itself may serve as a location for delinquent behavior. Misbehavior in school is part of the problem. Misconduct such as discourtesy to teachers, assault, drug use, alcohol abuse, use of obscene language, cheating, lying, petty theft, fighting, and destroying and defacing property is common in some schools. However, these forms of misbehavior rarely lead to formal referral to the juvenile authorities. Serious acts which may lead the adolescent to the juvenile court are physical attacks on teachers, fighting, drug pushing, weapons possession, and vandalism (Griffin & Griffin, 1978).

The mass media The mass media may also have a role in juvenile delinquency. Adolescents spend a great deal of their time watching television, and they see movies often. Television has a profound impact on children and youth in America, and there are many who believe that its influence is negative. While the evidence presented earlier is too weak to suggest that viewing television *directly* leads to adolescent delinquency, a link between televised violence and adolescent aggression does exist, and it is likely that television and movies contribute in some way to acts of crime and violence. For example, there are instances in which television has given ideas to adolescents about how to commit a crime. There even have been court cases in which victims have tried to establish that adolescents who committed acts of violence get their ideas from television. As a result, some claim that a given television network should be held responsible for the misdeed, since it was negligent in showing the program or movie. So far, however, no victim has yet won such a case.

Many would argue that adolescents ought to be able to separate the fantasy of the media from the reality in their day-to-day lives. Acts of violence and aggression by adolescents may be related to media violence and aggression, but perhaps other influences, rather than the media, are really to blame. The media serve as the final catalyst, perhaps, but are not the real cause. Thus, like other possible factors relating to adolescent delinquency, media influence is controversial and not completely understood. Certainly the media do play an important role in giving the adolescent a view of the world around him or her, and television and movies in contemporary America give the impression of a violent and aggressive society.

Helping delinquent adolescents

Society has always attempted both to cope with problems of adolescent delinquency and to help those who have become delinquent. For the most part, such attempts have not been very successful. Of course, some delinquent acts, such as underage drinking, would by definition no longer be considered delinquent if the legal drinking age would be changed. But apart from a change in the legal definitions of delinquency, Americans have seen little success in dealing with adolescent criminal behavior.

There are several approaches which have been tried, each meeting with only partial degrees of success. One general approach involves *prevention*. Communities sometimes provide recreational, vocational, and social programs for adolescents in an attempt to help them avoid situations and associations which would encourage delinquency. After an adolescent gets in trouble, there are a number of alternative treatment approaches which have been used. These include various forms of institutional settings (reform schools, home-style family cottages, halfway houses, and outpatient community mental health programs). In addition, delinquents have been provided with the various forms of individual and family counseling described in Chapter 14.

For example, behavior therapy has been used in the treatment of adolescent delinquency—with some success. Fo and O'Donnell (1974, 1975) tried to modify the behavior and academic problems shown by a group of adolescent delinquents. On the basis of principles of conditioning involving the application of positive reinforcement for desired behaviors (that is, giving "rewards"), the researchers tried four different forms of treatment: (1) social reinforcement, (2) social reinforcement and monetary reinforcement, (3) a nonbehavior therapy type of treatment, and (4) no treatment to the delinquents. Those adolescents who received either of the two reinforcement treatments showed less truancy and less of other delinquent acts than those who received either conditions 3 or 4. Similarly, Alexander and Parsons (1973) and Klein, Alexander, and Parsons (1977) found that the positive social interactions of delinquent adolescents and their families were improved more as a consequence of reinforcement in behavior therapy than as a consequence of client-centered therapy, psychodynamic therapy, or no treatment. Thus, behavior therapy appears to be a promising intervention technique for the treatment of adolescent delinquency.

GANGS

Juveniles who commit delinquent acts often do not get into trouble alone. Much delinquency involves peer groups. At times, such peer groups are rather informal associations. Other times, the associations are more formal. Adolescents sometimes organize themselves into *gangs*, organized groups of youth usually from the same neighborhood who often engage in criminal behavior as a part of their peer-group activities. Gangs can be found in most large metropolitan areas in the United States today. However, gangs have existed for decades in America, and research on gang behavior has a long history (Cloward & Ohlin, 1960; Miller, 1937; Thrasher, 1936; Yablonsky, 1962).

Gangs are often formed during childhood. This is particularly evident in the slums of large cities, where children in elementary school begin to learn that the rigors of "survival" in their neighborhood are best met with some social and moral support from their peers (Spanier & Fishel, 1973). The child learns that there is strength in numbers, and that youth often develop a posture that an individual is either part of the group or not; those who are part of the group may gain security from such an affiliation, while those who are not part of the group may be viewed as potential adversaries or targets of group aggression.

Gangs come into existence because they meet certain needs for the individuals who affiliate. The gang may satisfy the wish for new experience, it may be a reaction to social pressure from peers, it may create a sense of security and belonging, and it may provide a way to pass one's idle time. Gang members often develop ties of loyalty which are quite strong, providing members with confidence to stand up to schools, parents, police, and rival gangs. Many individuals who are not able to become accomplished in school or elsewhere are able to obtain status in the gang. In some gangs, antisocial behavior such as violence and delinquency may be a way of achieving status. Consequently, gang behavior may be rewarding to individuals who have found little reward in other day-to-day activities.

Yablonsky (1962), who for several years directed a "gang control" program in New York City, has identified three types of gangs. There are *social gangs*. These are the informal gangs of the street corner society whose members gather around some local neighborhood store or landmark—a hangout—and by and large engage in socially acceptable activities.

The *delinquent gang* has a focus on illegal activities. Its members often engage in delinquent behaviors such as theft and robbery. Indeed, such behavior is a common tie that binds the gang together. Delinquent gangs tend to be interested in the products of theft, rather than the "thrills" that may accompany such delinquent behavior. Many delinquent gang members have been emotionally stable youth who have taken over delinquent patterns of behavior.

The *violent gang* is described as a moblike group which tends to attract antisocial, emotionally disturbed youths who have a strong conflict orientation.

Violent gangs develop strong claims to local territory. Their leaders are generally self-appointed. There is a widespread attitude of having to "get even" with people. There is constant talk of assault, and weapons such as knives and guns are standard equipment for members.

Gang membership seldom becomes a lifelong affiliation. There are, however, groups such as the Hell's Angels, based in California, which have members who are well past the adolescent years, yet who continue to be active. The Hell's Angels, which has received nationwide attention, has developed a public image of violence and criminal behavior—characterizations which are reinforced by news reports of the imprisonment of a number of gang members for a variety of crimes.

RUNAWAYS AND SOCIETAL DROPOUTS

Many adolescents find family life or school intolerable, and run away from home. Running away from one's environment, like some other social problems, is a form of escape from the alienation and oppression which some adolescents feel. Adolescents often feel that they are mature enough to be independent and to make important decisions about their own lives, but are confronted with the fact that they are unable to make a decision for themselves about one of the greatest freedoms adults have—where to live. Thus the problem of runaways is a symptom of alienation, perceived oppression, and turmoil in the home and school. In the most extreme form, a runaway becomes a societal dropout, not only leaving home, but breaking ties with most aspects of conventional society.

The extent of runaways as a social problem is not known, since accurate data on the phenomenon are not available. But there are some indirect indications that there are probably hundreds of thousands of cases each year in which adolescents run away from home for at least a short period of time. In 1975, for example, the FBI reported that 189,000 adolescents—all under 18—actually were arrested and reported to them as runaways (*Uniform Crime Reports*, 1976). Many adolescents who run away from home for a very short time, or who run away to stay with other relatives or friends, probably are not reported to police. Furthermore since many adolescents who are reported to police probably are not formally arrested, the number of adolescents arrested as runaways is undoubtedly a small portion of all cases.

There have been many studies of adolescent runaways, but most of this research has relied on small samples, and much of it is outdated. Perhaps the most ambitious study of runaways was conducted by a research team at the National Institute of Mental Health (NIMH). This study followed the cases of more than 1,000 adolescents who ran away and were reported to police (Shellow, Schamp, Liebow, & Unger, 1967). Data for the study were obtained from police reports, interviews with parents, classmates, and the runaways themselves, and from school, police, and court records. Our discussion will rely on the findings of this research and on official data reported for the country as a whole by the FBI (*Uniform Crime Reports*, 1976).

Running away is primarily a phenomenon of adolescence. Younger children sometimes think about leaving home, but rarely have the resources, knowledge, and courage to do it. Harsh discipline and the perception of lack of parental love are common reasons that enter into the minds of young children when they contemplate running away. By adolescence, however, many are able to muster the courage, resources, and skill to actually leave home for at least a short period of time. Most return (or are returned), and most find that they are not able after all to make it on their own, but the prospects often are not considered fully before a decision to leave is made. In fact, many persons who run away probably do not really want to leave, but do so as a sign to their parents. It is one of the strongest ways of letting parents know that something is wrong, that family or school life is intolerable. Those over 18, of course, cannot be considered runaways, since they are by law adults, and have the freedom to move about and live their life where they please.

Runaways span all the ages of adolescence. The data on runaway arrests show that more 15-year-olds are involved than adolescents of any other single age, but the numbers are almost as large for those at ages 13, 14, 16, and 17. Data on runaway arrests indicate males and females run away from home in about equal numbers (U.S. Bureau of the Census, 1977a), and the phenomenon is common at all socioeconomic levels. Runaways are not found just in urban society. Some adolescents leave farms, and there are great numbers of alienated youth in suburban environments. In fact, the National Institute of Mental Health study we shall discuss involves mostly suburban runaways.

When and why do they leave?

The NIMH study found little seasonal variation in runaway episodes, but there does appear to be some variation across the week. For example, 20 percent of all runaway episodes occur on Friday, and runaway episodes involving girls are particularly high on Friday and Saturday. It is possible that girls take advantage of the dating situation as a catalyst for running away. It is not unusual for a girl to run away with her boyfriend, who may be able to provide transportation, financial resources, and a reason for leaving. Thus, one cause for running away may be the dating relationship and some parent-peer problems which might be related to the relationship.

Most runaway episodes seem to be impulsive and poorly planned. In only one-third of the cases in the NIMH study did the children have more than a dollar with them when they left. Most parents act fairly promptly, with 60 percent reporting their children as missing within six hours. Thus, many parents may know immediately or soon after the episode that the child has left. A note may be left, friends may alert parents, or the departure may have been precipitated by an argument with the parent. Girls are not reported as missing any more quickly than boys. Thus, parents do not seem to be more concerned about the safety of their daughters than of their sons, if the data on reporting time are to be thought of as an indicator of such concern.

First-time runaways are reported most quickly. Perhaps the delay in reporting subsequent episodes of running away may reflect the parents' confidence or optimism—based on past experience—that the child will return on his or her own. Adolescents leave with another adolescent about as often as they take off alone. Females are more likely to run away with companions than are males, again suggesting that the dating relationship may play a role in the departure.

Runaways leave for many reasons. Problems at home, family discipline, and school difficulties were most frequently mentioned in one study (Hildebrand, 1963). Many studies have found various parent-child problems (for example, English, 1973; Matsumoto & Suzuki, 1974) and school problems (for example, Shellow et al., 1967) to be central to the decision to run away from home. Apparently then, it is difficulty in two of the influential social institutions affecting adolescents—family and school—which seems to underlie one's motivation to run away (Adams & Munro, 1978).

Who runs away?

There is no specific theory which would allow one to predict which adolescents will run away from home, and as mentioned earlier, this social problem cuts across society. Research does show, however, that certain social characteristics of the individual and the individual's environment are associated with the tendency to leave home. About half of runaways are oldest children, suggesting a possible relationship between ordinal position in the family and the likelihood of running away. Perhaps older children are subjected to more intense pressures. This tendency is not well established by the research, however, and so conclusions about ordinal ranking and likelihood of running away must be viewed cautiously.

Other relationships are clearer. The runaway is more likely to come from a broken home, or from one which has been reconstituted through remarriage. Runaways come from families which have moved more frequently, although it may not be the moving per se, but rather factors associated with the need to move, which predispose them to run away. Perhaps the most significant finding is that the homes of runaways are reported to be full of conflict and turmoil. More than 3 out of 4 of the parents of runaways reported conflict within the family, mostly over problems such as the child's school performance, choice of friends, and rejection of family rules and values. Parents of nonrunaways do not report such conflict—or at least they do not admit it.

Adolescents, however, whether runaways or not, almost always report conflict in the family. Over 80 percent of the respondents in the NIMH study—regardless of whether or not they had ever run away from home—reported family settings with a significant amount of conflict. Finally, contrary to what some might expect, runaways are no more likely to come from homes with mothers that work than are other adolescents.

Some have argued that running away may not be a pathological deviation, but rather a very rational alternative for youth given certain problems they face (Adams & Munro, 1978; Skinner & Nutt, 1944). Despite the problems that may have motivated the adolescent to leave home, many such individuals have been found to have positive self-concepts, got along well with siblings, had friends who would listen to them, and felt they could handle most of their problems (Adams & Munro, 1978).

The role of the school and police

As mentioned earlier, school can be troublesome for any adolescent. Research indicates that the school plays a role in the experience of runaways. First, most runaways do poorly in school. More than 4 out of 5 adolescents who run away have grade point averages of C or lower. Two-thirds of the parents of runaways report that their children were having problems in school. Second, nearly half of the runaways in the NIMH study had been held back a grade at some point in their schooling. Moreover, about 20 percent were more than two years older than the typical student in the corresponding year in school. School records show that runaways are absent more often than other adolescents. They have lower grades, and are more likely to have been retained.

Whereas early studies of runaways associated the phenomenon with delinquency, more recent studies lead to a somewhat mixed conclusion. Police files showed that about 1 out of every 6 runaways in the NIMH study had had a charge placed against him or her at some time before the runaway episode. This was four times more common than for nonrunaways. However, the researchers emphasize that most runaways did not have a history of delinquency before their reported departure. Thus, adolescents who leave home are more likely to have been in trouble with police, but most of them never have had such an experience. On the other hand, *after* running away the picture changes, with runaways becoming increasingly likely compared to other adolescents to encounter the juvenile justice system. Perhaps the most realistic explanation of the relationship between delinquency and running away from home is that they are both symptoms of other social problems (Hildebrand, 1968).

The problem does not go away

Many adolescents run away again and again. Only 28 percent of all adolescent runaways stay away from home for more than two days. Most, then, return before much time has passed. But after returning, some adolescents leave again. The repeaters tend to remain away longer, and are less likely to return on their own. More of the repeaters need to be located and caught, suggesting that the repeaters are more determined to leave home, and perhaps less likely to be running away as a symbol of protest as opposed to an actual desire to change environments. About 3 in 5 adolescents who run away for the first time return home voluntarily. But less than half of the repeaters return on their own. Considering all runaways, about half return voluntarily, and about half are caught and returned.

It has been estimated that only 1 in 6 runaways is reported, and some of those who run away and are returned to their homes run away again. The problem is an immense one. Further evidence of the intensity of the symptoms of the problem is the finding that 1 adolescent in 3 who has never run away has seriously considered doing so (Shellow et al., 1967). This social problem is certainly an awesome one for both parents and their children. It can be frustrating to parents because they may be trying very hard to be good parents and to provide a loving environment for their children. And it can be very frustrating to the adolescent because from his or her perspective—regardless of what the parents may be thinking or doing—there is little attraction to the home and family.

Runaways who are forced to leave

Although most of the attention given to runaways focuses on those who leave home against their parents' will, there is a small, but significant, proportion of runaways who leave home because they are forced to. These adolescents—who have been described as throwaways (Raskin & Males, 1978)—have been kicked out of the house by their parents for a variety of reasons. Many are caught in the middle of a divorce, separation, or remarriage. Single parents and stepparents, for example, may be unable to cope with the responsibilities of a developing adolescent. Older adolescents in poor families may be forced from home because of great economic stress, so there will be more food for younger children.

A recent estimate by the Department of Health, Education, and Welfare was that as many as 70,000 of the runaways in 1975 left home not because they chose to, but because they were forced to (Raskin & Males, 1978). It is likely, however, that many episodes of running away from home are the result of interactions between parents and adolescents in which all parties engage in behaviors which lead to the departure. Thus, both the high incidence of runaways and the high incidence of throwaways may be caused by problematic parent-child interactions in which everyone involved has played a contributing role.

Help for runaways

Runaways and their families usually can benefit from help in coping with the problem at hand. Local mental health associations, community agencies, psychologists, and family counselors may be helpful to runaways and their parents. However, of special interest are services designed especially for runaways. The U.S. Department of Health, Education, and Welfare runs a national toll-free switchboard for runaways (800-621-4000; 800-972-6004 in Illinois). They provide information on shelter, food, and counseling for youth, and they help young people to get in touch with their parents, if the service is desired.

Runaway houses are located throughout the country, particularly in large urban areas. They offer food and shelter for adolescents, and provide counseling services. They are legally obligated to make contact with parents or guardians soon after the adolescent arrives (Raskin & Males, 1978). Sometimes parents and adolescents are able to solve their conflicts with help from professionals. Other times they are unable to, and the youth ends up seeking a permanent alternative place of residence for the remainder of the adolescent years.

The societal dropout

Some adolescents who run away never return, and others who never run away become so removed from their environment emotionally and intellectually that they no longer identify with it in customary ways. The religious cults discussed earlier involve individuals who are societal dropouts of sorts. But there are many other instances of dropping out of the mainstream of society. Examples are affiliating with criminal gangs, adopting a life-style of prostitution, becoming involved with a subculture of drug addicts, joining extreme right-wing or left-wing political causes, affiliating with terrorist groups, or becoming a transient.

What all such individuals have in common is a rejection of at least some of the values which their parental generation holds, and thus a rejection of some of the most traditional values of the society in which they live. Sometimes, however, adolescents do not leave home for the purpose of joining these deviant groups or causes. In many instances, the adolescent first leaves home and later is seduced into the new life-style of the deviant group. Adolescent females who become prostitutes, for example, usually turn to prostitution out of necessity, not by plan or aspiration. Young men and women first experiment with hard drugs before becoming more closely affiliated with the subculture which promoted drug use. In fact, probably all societal dropouts go through a socialization process which prepares them for a closer affiliation with the deviant group and helps them establish a new identity. It should also be noted that while runaways are prime candidates for affiliation with individuals and groups that promote dropping out of the mainstream of society, one need not run away from home to become involved.

During the 1960s and 1970s Americans became very familiar with the phenomenon of societal dropouts. Increasing numbers of adolescents became disenchanted with the society in which they lived and began to reject the traditional values they had been taught. The large cohort of children born following World War II had now reached adolescence and young adulthood, and they were beginning to adopt new values which many believed were different from those of their parents and grandparents. Many observers in the country focused on the longer hair, greater outspokenness, and more liberal sexual behavior of this generation, but the adolescents of the 1960s were different in other ways.

Many new political causes were born, many new activist and terrorist groups were formed, and individuals with ideas different from those in the mainstream of the society sought to affiliate with others who shared the same values with regard to sex, religion, politics, drug use, war, and peace. The Vietnam war, changes in sexual behavior, enhanced equality of women, and increased independence among adolescents all contributed to the greatest surge in modern American history in the number of societal dropouts.

Much of the interest in affiliating with deviant social groups and causes waned during the late 1970s, but the cultural changes which occurred in the 1960s and early 1970s will continue to have an impact for some time. Society became more tolerant of—or at least more adjusted to—societal dropouts during those years. Of course, it is still upsetting for parents to contemplate the possibility that their son or daughter who has run away or who is living at home but has rejected many of the values of the family around him or her has become a societal dropout or affiliate with a deviant group. The problem for individual parents and for the society is to encourage adolescent development in ways that do not result in extreme departures from the values of the society, but also to be able to accept and deal with such extreme departures when they occur.

RELATIONSHIPS AND ALTERNATIVE LIFE-STYLES

When the older adolescent approaches the time when he or she becomes legally emancipated from parents, when the adolescent leaves home for college or for an apartment of his or her own, and when the adolescent begins to think of himself or herself as a potential marriage partner, decisions have to be made about the kind of life-style wanted. While growing up, most children assume they will marry and have families, just as their parents did. But the adolescent begins to realize that there are many options concerning living arrangements, life-style, and marriage which are available to the emancipated adolescent. This section examines some of the possible life-styles and living arrangements. It is perhaps fitting that we bring our discussion of adolescence to a close on this topic, since it is one of the most important considerations for the adolescent as he or she begins the transition to adulthood. Indeed, this discussion illustrates an important way that social change has influenced the adolescent of today. More so than ever before, today's adolescent may choose to establish a variety of different social relationships.

Marriage and its alternatives

Our need for close affectional ties traditionally has led Americans to marry. This is easy to understand, since marriage was the one clearly sanctioned relationship in which it was permissible to have sexual intercourse, live together, and have children. Americans no longer are uncompromisingly tied to the traditional system of dating, courtship, marriage, and childbearing. Although most of us eventually marry, the routes we take in getting there are considerably more varied than at any time in recent American history. The need for close affectional bonds with members of the opposite sex still seems to dominate much of our premarital, marital, and postmarital interaction. For example, despite suggestions from some parents to the cont[...] adolescents often prefer a succession of steady dating partners to "playing the fi[...] during their dating years. Couples who are not yet married often live together. [...] married persons develop affectional ties with persons other than their spouse. [...] couples who recently have been divorced are likely to remarry within surprisi[...] short periods following the final divorce decree.

Marriage is the most common type of lasting union between men and wor[...] But any treatment of marriage must acknowledge that not everyone marries, [...] among those who do, many divorce. Among those who do not marry, a rang[...] alternatives is available: cohabitation with persons of the same or opposite sex, communal living, or single living. Any of these alternatives might involve children. Among those who do marry, there is an option not to have children, although most couples do. And among those who marry and divorce, remarriage may follow. Marriage is not now and never was a simple institution. It involves many possibilities and options for its participants.

Singleness

There are many possible reasons why an individual may not marry. Some of the reasons involve involuntary factors over which the person really has no control. Many of these individuals might have married if circumstances had been different. Other persons voluntarily choose to remain single for a variety of reasons. A person who is single for his or her entire life may actually be involved in any number of different household arrangements. Single persons often share their households with

---

INSIGHT INTO ADOLESCENCE

Eleanor Roosevelt was born October 11, 1884. After spending her high school years in England, she returned to her traditional East Coast society, and married her distant cousin Franklin. She was at first a wife and mother, occupied with her five children and husband. Later she was a help and inspiration to her husband during the illness which crippled him. She served as his "eyes and ears" throughout the country and world. After President Roosevelt's death, she became a delegate to the United Nations, where she was the chairperson of the Commission on Human Rights for several years.

MY ENGAGEMENT

I had a great curiosity about life and a desire to participate in every experience that might be the lot of woman. There seemed to me to be a necessity for hurry; without rhyme or reason I felt the urge to be a part of the stream of life, and so in the autumn of 1903 when Franklin Roosevelt, my fifth cousin once removed, asked me to marry him, though I was only nineteen, it seemed an entirely natural thing and I never even thought that we were both rather young and inexperienced. I came back from Groton, where I had spent the week end, and asked Cousin Susie whether she thought I cared enough, and my grandmother, when I told her, asked me if I was sure I was really in love. I solemnly answered "yes," and yet I know now that it was years later before I understood what being in love was or what loving really meant.

I had very high standards as to what a wife and mother should be and not the faintest notion of what it meant to be either a wife or a mother, and none of my elders enlightened me.

Source: Roosevelt, E. Excerpt from p. 111 in *This Is My Story* by Eleanor Roosevelt. Copyright 1937 Anna Eleanor Roosevelt. Reprinted by permission of Harper & Row, Publishers, Inc.

unmarried persons of the same or opposite sex. Sharing living accommodations does not imply, although it does not rule out, sexual relations with a roommate or housemate. Single persons often have active sexual relationships, even though they may not be cohabiting or intending to marry. And of course, cohabiting couples who are not married to one another are generally single, but we shall discuss cohabitation separately.

Not everyone is suited for marriage. It takes a great deal of wisdom and courage for an individual to recognize that he or she would make a poor marriage partner or would simply find the confines of marriage too limiting. We live in a marriage-oriented society, and consequently we do not often realize that not everyone ought to marry. Some persons would take issue with such a statement. One could argue that *somewhere* there is a suitable mate for every person. Perhaps. But most marriage and family counselors are able to cite cases where, in their opinion, one or both spouses lack the personal qualities, preparation, motivation, or interest necessary to make marriage work. These characteristics sometimes apply only to the client's current marriage. But in other cases, counselors feel that they are able to cite individuals who would have been unsuitable marriage partners for anyone.

This observation does not imply that persons who are unsuited for or not interested in marriage are inferior in any way. Persons may choose a single life-style for very *positive* reasons, in contrast to others who avoid marriage for negative reasons. Our society is sufficiently heterogeneous that single persons choosing to remain single may be able to find satisfaction in this life-style. A man or woman who realizes that marriage is not for him or her and makes life-style decisions accordingly should be commended, rather than ridiculed, since that person is likely to make a better contribution to society than if he or she reluctantly entered into a marriage which ultimately failed. Let us now examine some other specific reasons for singleness.

Cohabitation outside of marriage

Cohabitation—most often defined as an unmarried male living together with an unmarried female—has become very common in the United States, and it now involves hundreds of thousands of young persons at any given time. Especially evident on college and university campuses, where most of the research on this phenomenon has been conducted, cohabitation is also becoming widespread in other than college and university settings throughout the country. A 1974 national study of a representative sample of American men between 20 and 30 years of age found that 18 percent of these young men reported having at some time lived with a woman for six months or more without being married to her (Clayton & Voss, 1977). On college campuses, studies have found that as many as half of the students have cohabited for some duration by the time they reach college graduation (Macklin, 1974; Peterman, Ridley, & Anderson, 1974).

Cohabitation, then, is a widespread phenomenon, particularly among late adolescents. Most persons who live together outside of marriage, however, eventually do marry, although data are not available about how often they marry the persons with whom they have cohabited. Some studies indicate more than half of the persons studied who have cohabited have done so more than once before marriage (Peterman, Ridley, & Anderson, 1974).

Cohabitation may take three distinct forms. First, it may be seen as a temporary matter of convenience or choice—an arrangement which appeals to the persons involved at the moment without any necessary commitment to marriage. Second, cohabitation may be defined as "trial marriage," in which the couple anticipate marriage and wish to "see if they are compatible," or simply live together until their own personal circumstances are more favorable to marriage. Third, and most rarely, cohabitation may be seen as a permanent and lasting alternative to marriage.

Cohabitation as a temporary matter of convenience or choice is the most common form of cohabitation. It is widespread at colleges and universities, both on and off campus. Many cohabiting relationships are very short-lived, some lasting only a matter of weeks and others lasting several months. It is rare to find a relationship which lasts for more than a year or two on college campuses (the relationship usually dissolves or results in marriage), although it is much more common to find long-term relationships away from universities. College campuses appear to have an insulating effect on students. It is possible to live together at college without much negative sanction, whereas such a relationship might be frowned upon and avoided in the student's home town. The majority of students who live together do not tell their parents about the relationship, although they readily tell friends (Macklin, 1974). The fact that students normally do not tell their parents indicates that as common as cohabitation is, it has not received widespread acceptance and may be considered deviant, wrong, or immoral by many Americans.

The evidence suggests that this form of cohabitation is likely to increase in the future. Young persons find that there is much to be gained by way of convenience, intimacy, and sharing. The primary rewards they report are the sexual, affectional, and companionship components that are found in many intimate personal relationships. The motivation to live together is essentially what might be expected as a normal extension of the courtship process—namely, the desire to spend increasing amounts of time with a person one wants to be with and/or loves. The reasons couples give for cohabiting, then, center on the intensity of their relationship, the possibility that they may marry, the added convenience of having their belongings together in the same place, or experimentation with a new life-style.

Many couples gradually drift into such a relationship. They find that they are spending more and more time with each other, sleeping together, eating together, and sharing expenses. They may "find" themselves living together, and one then gives up his or her former residence, or they may make a formal decision to live in the same household. Many cohabiting couples maintain two separate residences, even though they live in one, because of fear that parents or relatives might find that they are cohabiting. Some have special mailing addresses and separate phone numbers.

Many landlords will not rent to cohabiting couples, although the legal validity for such a decision is dubious. Nevertheless, some cohabiting couples find it difficult to rent an apartment or buy a house if their unmarried status is known. In university communities and urban areas, problems are not as great.

Cohabitation is characteristic mainly of the young—persons in their late teens and in their twenties. There are increasing numbers of individuals in their thirties and forties who are cohabiting, however, particularly after a divorce or separation (Glick & Spanier, 1980). Cohabitation has always been more common and better tolerated among persons of low socioeconomic standing. This can be explained by greater family instability, greater difficulty in being able to afford and obtain divorces, regulations cutting back aid for children when a woman with children remarries, and the more liberal acceptance of cohabitation as a life-style.

Cohabitation also exists among an often ignored group of individuals—the elderly. Perhaps because we are less inclined to think there is a sexual component to their relationship (a fact which should not always be assumed), there has been less concern about cohabitation among the aged.

The available evidence suggests that cohabitation as a temporary matter of convenience or choice is likely to be with us for some time. It appears to be a normal part of the premarriage process for some individuals and is gaining wider acceptance. It may be many years, however, before a majority of persons will be able to live together before marriage with full approval from parents and the community in which they live. Finally, it should be observed that many persons have no desire to cohabit before marriage. In this matter of choice, as with others, it is important to respect an individual's decision not to participate.

Some cohabiting couples have entered into what they consider to be a *trial marriage*. They intend to marry each other, but first want to make sure they are compatible. This type of relationship may also be considered a logical extension of the courtship process, since it is the couple's final test to determine whether or not they are suited to one another. The compatibility testing may involve sexual, emotional, and economic components, as well as test their ability to live in the same household with each other in a twenty-four-hour-a-day existence.

Although this form of relationship is conceptually meaningful, many of the same problems that may face other cohabiting couples may be present in a trial marriage. It is possible that the trial marriage truly will not be an adequate test of a marriage relationship, since the commitment to the partner may be different than it might be following marriage, and it has been demonstrated that commitment is a critical variable in the adjustment of both cohabiting and marital relationships (Dean & Spanier, 1974; Lewis, Spanier, Storm, & LeHecka, 1975; Spanier, 1976b). There may be parental, peer, or community sanctions against such an arrangement. A problem might emerge (for example, sexual adjustment, financial burden, pregnancy, conflict) which might be resolved following marriage but not during a trial marriage, thus prematurely terminating the relationship.

Only a small number of cohabitants report that they have rejected traditional marriage and intend always to live together without formally marrying. Couples have found that a *permanent* living-together relationship often presents legal problems, especially if there are children or if the relationship dissolves. Contrary to popular belief, a couple who live together do not have a "common-law marriage" unless some very special conditions exist—and even then only a few states allow for common-law relationships.

Communes

One of the alternative life-styles that has been given considerable attention in recent years is the *commune*, or *community*. It is difficult to generalize about communes because they represent such a broad spectrum of different types. Communal societies have been organized at various times throughout a good part of American history. Most of them have been short-lived. A few have continued in greatly altered form. Still fewer have persisted in approximately their original form for more than a few years.

Communes range in size from just a few individuals to several hundred. They have existed throughout the world (the Bruderhof of Germany, the kibbutz of Israel, the Shinkyo of Japan) and throughout history in the United States (the Shakers, the

Hutterites, the Moravians, the Oneida Community). They have never been the dominant family form in any society, nor have they existed for any sustained period of time through history. They are, nevertheless, fascinating entities.

Communes exist today throughout America, although it is probable that only a tiny fraction of the population is currently involved. There was a proliferation of interest in communes during the late 1960s and early 1970s, and much of this interest has since waned. Nevertheless, there are some young persons who would like to or intend to either experiment with communal living for a period of time in their lives or permanently join such a group. Communes of all varieties attempt to embody what social psychologists call a "sense of community" (Kanter, 1973).

There may be one or more persons in the commune representing authority or leadership either through being chosen for such a function or through having personal qualities and charisma that lead to the emergence of such a role. In other communes there is no one who has any more authority than anyone else. Decisions are made by vote of the entire group, a process that sometimes proves laborious and time-consuming, but is democratic. However, at other times it leads to inactivity when no decision can be reached.

In some communes there is a plan for work—for doing chores, for cooking, etc. Persons are assigned to jobs according to a schedule. In other communes there is no planning, no scheduling. Everyone is free to do as he or she wishes. There are no requirements, the assumption being that everyone will want to do one's share and the work will get done. In reality such an arrangement often results in work being left undone.

Some communes are productive and self-sustaining. They raise a good part of their own food, construct buildings, and repair equipment. Some members may be gainfully employed and contribute their earnings, or a portion of them, to the group. In some cases the commune or certain members manufacture salable products. In other communes attempts at productivity have been only partially successful or have failed completely, or the production of salable items has not been tried.

There is a variety of points of view and practices relative to sex and marriage. In some communes there are both married couples and single members. In some, sex is entirely free, and twosomes may pair up as they wish, whether or not one or both are married. In others there is "group marriage" by mutual understanding, although such an arrangement has no status within the law. Some communes are felt by their members to be large "families." In some communes children are cared for by their natural parents. In some, care of children is scheduled as other tasks are scheduled, while in others the assumption is made that all members of the group are responsible for all children.

Very few data are available to instruct us about the success of communes. What evidence there is (Berger, Hackett, & Millar, 1972; Kanter, 1973; Roberts, 1971) suggests that most communes tend to be very short-lived. Those that have the greatest chance of surviving are the ones based on a set of beliefs and the ones which have some organization and leadership.

CHAPTER SUMMARY

Throughout this book we have stressed the significance of the social context. This context includes our peers, our family, our community, and our society. The complexity of adolescent development and its interaction with this social context allow for the possibility of numerous social problems, many of which are described in this chapter.

Poverty is one of society's most pressing social problems, and is often brought to our attention by adolescents. Poverty is related to civil disturbances, urban violence, juvenile delinquency, social unrest, undernutrition, and other problems which often are seen in adolescence. About 1 in 7 adolescents live below the poverty level in the United States.

Only 3 percent of females 14 to 17 have married, and about one half of 1 percent of the males in this age group have done so; but these percentages change dramatically beginning at age 18. By age 21, only 73 percent of the males and 51 percent of the females have not yet married. Thus, marriage and divorce are important topics in the study of late adolescence in particular. Unfortunately, studies show that the younger people are when they marry, the greater the likelihood of both poor adjustment in marriage and subsequent divorce. Persons who marry young are more likely than those marrying later to be less socially and emotionally developed, and may find it difficult to cope with economic responsibilities and other adjustments to early marriage.

One common adjustment required in marriage follows from parenthood. Together, the dramatic increase in sexual behavior among adolescent females and the lag in the adoption of effective contraception have resulted in greater numbers of pregnancies to adolescent females, both married *and* unmarried, in the United States. About 10 percent of American teenagers get pregnant, and 6 percent give birth each year. Adolescents tend not to be well-prepared for parenthood, and there are a wide range of possible medical, health, social, and economic consequences which may result. Infant and maternal mortality is higher following adolescent pregnancy and childbirth, and complications such as low birth weight, birth defects, inadequate prenatal care, *toxemia*, *eclampsia*, *anemia*, *spontaneous abortion*, *hemorrhage*, dropping out of school, unemployment, and poverty are more common.

Adolescents commit a disproportionately large share of the crime in the United States, and are also victims of an especially large share of the crimes committed. *Juvenile delinquency* is defined as the violation of a law committed by a person prior to his or her eighteenth birthday, which would have been a crime if committed by an adult. However, the term has come to mean many different things to different people, and the complications of juvenile delinquency are among the greatest social problems of adolescence. It is not fully understood what causes delinquency, but there undoubtedly are influences from the family, the school, and the mass media.

Gangs are most often found in adolescents, and are an outgrowth of the importance of peer groups in the social behavior of adolescence. Gangs are organized groups of youth usually from the same neighborhood who often engage in criminal behavior as a part of their peer-group activity. Gangs probably came into existence because they meet certain needs for the individuals who participate. They may create security and belonging, a way to pass idle time, and a way to gain new experiences.

Running away from home technically is considered a delinquent act, but it is really more than that. There are probably hundreds of thousands of adolescents who run away from home each year in the United States. Runaways exist because of problems at home and at school. They are a sign of the youth's inability to tolerate the social setting in which he or she resides. Leaving home may also be a way of telling parents that the situation has become serious, or it may be a way of indicating one needs and wants help.

With the end of adolescence comes a partial emancipation from parents, and decisions must be made about future life-styles. Marriage and parenthood are alternatives which often are selected, but other possibilities also exist, either on a temporary or on a long-term basis. *Singleness* is, of course, an option which appeals to some. For others it is an alternative not chosen but dictated by circumstances. *Cohabitation*, an increasingly popular living status, may be a temporary matter of convenience, or it may be a more lasting arrangement chosen in place of marriage. *Communes* have always existed in America, but only a small portion of youth choose to live in one.

Finally, it should be noted that some individuals adopt different life-styles at different times in their lives. This should be expected for some individuals since we all change as the world around us changes. Social change is an ongoing process; it is the basis of progress, the reason for history, and one of the keys to understanding human development.

accommodation In Piaget's theory, the alteration of existing cognitive structure to fit new external stimulus objects.

achievement test A test designed to measure what has been learned in school either for many subjects or for just one subject.

active incidence The total amount of an activity which exists at one point in time.

adaptive Functional for survival, meeting demands of existence.

adolescere From the Latin, to grow into maturity.

affiliation Becoming a member of a group or belonging to a group, cause, or activity.

agency A set of behaviors involving instrumental effectiveness, competence, and mastery.

ahistorical When behavior is studied at one point in time with no regard as to how it came to be or what form it may take later.

altruism Unselfish regard for or devotion to the welfare of others.

amenorrhea Abnormal absence of menstruation.

androgens Male hormones secreted by the gonads.

anemia Shortage of oxygen-carrying material in the blood.

anomalies Irregularities or deviations from the common rules.

anorexia nervosa Emotionally based eating disorder resulting in being seriously underweight.

anterior Front part (for example, of the pituitary).

anterospective construction A method in which behavior is measured at or about the time that it occurs.

aptitude test A test, such as an intelligence test, which has been designed to measure one's capacity to learn.

area sampling See cluster sampling.

areola Elevated area surrounding the nipple of the breast.

assimilation In Piaget's theory, when an object, external to the person, is altered to fit the person's existing cognitive structure.

atypical development Events, experiences, or characteristics which pertain only to a small proportion of the population; not typical.

autonomous morality The second phase in Piaget's theory of moral reasoning, involving the child making subjective moral judgments.

availability sampling When the sample is obtained by using people who are most easily available for the research or who volunteer.

axillary hair Underarm hair.

behaviorism A theory derived from a mechanistic world view, which stresses that behavior may be understood by reference to external stimuli and responses.

behavior therapy A form of treatment, typically for individual-psychological disorders, that applies the principles of conditioning to clinical disorders.

biased sample When a sample is not representative of the population from which it is drawn.

biological handicap Any attribute of the person's physique or physiology which interferes with optimal functioning.

birth cohorts Persons born in a given year.

bisexual A person who is sexually attracted to both males and females.

breast bud Small conelike protuberance of the breast caused by the raising areola.

castration anxiety Male fear that father will punish him by removing his genitalia.

catholic Universal.

centration In Piaget's theory, a

focus on, or embeddedness in, a particular point of view (usually one's own).

clique Closely knit group of persons which tends to exclude others.

cluster sampling When a geographical area is repeatedly subdivided to obtain the many smaller sampling areas from which respondents are selected for study.

cognitive flexibility Ability to shift from one way of thinking to another.

cohabitation An unmarried male living together with an unmarried female.

cohort A group of persons experiencing some common event.

coitus Sexual intercourse.

communion A set of behaviors characterized by interpersonal warmth, expressiveness, and sensitivity.

concept An abstraction; a term used to represent or symbolize attributes of stimuli.

conditioning A process by which stimuli and responses become associated, as in classical or operant conditioning; learning.

confounding When a variable's influence on behavior cannot be separated from that of another variable that could be influencing behavior at the same time.

congenital Existing at or present since birth.

conscience In Freud's theory, the component of the superego which represents the internalization of society's demands.

conservation Ability to know that one aspect of a stimulus array has remained unchanged, although other aspects have changed.

contamination When data are influenced by variables extraneous to those which are central to the empirical study.

continuity When behavior and/or its explanations stay the same over time.

continuous growth Smooth and nonabrupt changes in behavior.

contraception Prevention of conception; use of birth control devices to prevent pregnancy.

controlled observation When the research situation is controlled by the researcher, but the behavior of the person is not directly manipulated.

conventional reasoning In Kohlberg's theory of moral reasoning development, the second level of reasoning, involving judgments based on conformity to or maintenance of societal rules and institutions.

correlation The degree of relationship between variables or measurements in a research study.

cosmology Philosophical concerns about the character of the universe.

counterfactual Not actually represented in the real world.

critical period A qualitatively discontinuous period of life which is fixed and universal, and involves the need for specific development in order for succeeding developments to proceed optimally.

cross-sectional design When differently aged individuals or groups are studied at one point in time.

crystall' d intelligence Knowledge ained through education and socialization.

cultural transmission The transmission of knowledge, skills, or values throughout a given society over time.

cumulative incidence The total amount of an activity that has occurred over time.

defense mechanisms In Freud's theory, techniques used by the ego to avoid dealing with emotional impulses (from the id).

delayed puberty When a person goes through the bodily changes associated with pubescence much later than usual.

demonology Belief that behavior is caused by evil spirits.

descriptive continuity When behavior at one point in the life span can be described in the same way as behavior at another point.

descriptive discontinuity When behavior at one point in the life span is not described in the same way as is behavior at another point.

developmental disturbance Imbalance in development resulting from new phenomena that come to influence a person powerfully.

developmental tasks In Havighurst's conception of development, the tasks people must master during specific portions of their lives in order for life satisfaction and future task success to occur.

dialectical A philosophical conception of reality (a world view) which stresses that constant, completely interrelated changes characterize humans and their contexts.

dimension An imaginary continuum (or line) existing between two bipolar endpoints.

discontinuity Changes in the descriptions and/or explanations involved in behavior over time.

dizygotic twins Siblings born of the same pregnancy but from two separate ova, thus having different genotypes (also termed fraternal twins).

drive An energizer of behavior.

dyad Two persons.

dynamic interaction An interrelation, among all levels of analysis involving humans and their contexts, which involves processes from each level being both a product and a producer of processes at all other levels.

dysgraphia A learning disability involving problems in writing.

dyslexia A learning disability involving problems in reading.

dysmenorrhea Difficult or painful menstruation.

early maturers People who go through their adolescent bodily changes faster than usual.

ecological milieu The naturally existing setting for an organism's development.

ecological validity A setting that corresponds to the naturally occurring one of an organism.

ectoderm The outermost of three primary germ layers of an embryo.

ectomorph Body type which is thin, has little muscle mass, and is frail-looking.

ego In Freud's theory, the personality structure whose sole function is to adapt to reality.

egocentrism Embeddedness in one's own point of view; failure to differentiate between subject and object.

ego ideal In Freud's theory, an internal representation of the perfect man or woman; component of superego.

ego strength The degree of capability of the ego to perform its function (to meet the demands of reality).

Electra complex In Freud's theory, the idea that all females experience incestuous love for their fathers and antagonism toward their mothers; corresponds to male's Oedipal complex.

emancipated Free (for example, from parental care) and independent enough to be responsible for one's own life.

embryology A branch of biology dealing with the development of embryos.

empathy The ability to take the perspective of another and feel what that person feels.

empirical Capable of observation; scientific; based on careful observation or research.

empiricism A view that knowledge is achieved through the systematic observation and analysis of data.

endocrine glands Glands which have no external ducts.

endoderm The innermost of the germ layers of the embryo.

endomorph Body type which is characterized by a plump build, fatness, and a rounded appearance.

entelechy In Aristotelian philosophy, a nonphysical, nonspatial, nontemporal force which brings life to matter.

epistemology Philosophy of knowledge.

equilibration In Piaget's theory, the balance between the activity of the person on the environment and the activity of the environment on the person.

estrogens Female hormones secreted by the gonads.

ethnographic A descriptive anthropological account (of a culture).

etiological Causative.

evolution History of biological changes characterizing a species.

exocrine glands Glands which have openings (ducts) to the world outside the body.

experimental observation A type of scientific observation involving maximum control over the setting of observations and direct manipulation of variables.

explanatory continuity When the same explanations are used to account for behavior across life.

explanatory discontinuity When different explanations are used to account for behavior across life.

explanatory studies Studies that attempt to find the bases or causes of social and behavioral development.

family A unit of related individuals in which children usually are produced and reared.

feral children Children separated from their families and supposedly raised by animals.

fidelity In Erikson's theory, an emotional orientation in which one is committed to a role and an ideology.

fixation In Freud's theory, an arrest of libidinal development.

fixity In development, the unchangeable character of a behavior.

follicle-stimulating hormone (FSH): Hormone which encourages ovulation in females and spermatogenesis in males.

functional When something contributes to maintenance and thus aids survival; contributing to, maintaining or furthering development optimally; aiding survival; adaptive.

gang Group which is selective about who may be considered a member and who may not, and which sometimes seeks unlawful or antisocial ends.

gastrula An embryo in an early stage of development.

gender identity A person's identification as male or female.

gender identity clinics Clinics which specialize in surgery which will alter genital structures and thus one's gender.

general developmental model Schaie's system for incorporating assessment of all sources of developmental change (age, cohort, and time) into one of several research designs.

generation Group of people born during one period of history or span of time; varies from several years to three or four decades.

generation gap Significant disparities in attitudes, behaviors, or values between generations.

genetics A branch of biology that deals with heredity and variations in organisms.

genotype invariancy Hereditary constancy.

genotypes The complement of genes transmitted to people at conception by the union of the sperm and ovum.

gestalt "Totality."

gestation (period) The time from fertilization until birth.

gonadotropic hormone Hormone which acts on those glands in males and females that are associated with each sex, respectively.

gonads Glands in males (the testes) and in females (the ovaries).

gratification In Freud's theory, tension reduction resulting from appropriate stimulation.

growth Change by tissue accretion.

growth spurt In adolescence, when the peak velocity of growth in height and weight occurs.

growth-stimulating hormone (GSH) Hormone which acts on all body tissues to stimulate their rate of growth and nourishment.

hedonism The idea that pleasure or happiness is the chief good in life.

hemorrhage Loss of blood.

hepatitis A disease involving inflammation of the liver.

heredity That which is genetically transmitted in one's genotype; the complement of genes received at conception.

hermaphrodite Person born with ambiguous, damaged, or both male and female genitals.

heteronomous morality In Piaget's theory of moral reasoning development, the first phase, involving the child being objective in moral judgments.

heterosexual When persons are attracted sexually to persons of the other sex.

hirsutism Excessive growth of hair.

holistic Emphasizing the whole; an approach which considers the relationship between the parts and the whole.

homosexual Person attracted sexually to persons of the same sex.

homunculus In medieval Christian theology, a full-grown but miniature adult, believed to be present from birth in the new-born's head, which contains sin and basic depravity.

hylomorphic doctrine In Aristotelian philosophy, the idea that spirit and matter are inseparable though distinct.

hypothalamus A structure of the brain which aids in initiation of bodily changes.

hypothesis A testable statement of the relation between two or more variables.

id In Freud's theory, the innate structure of personality which has all the person's libido.

identity crisis In Erikson's theory, the nuclear (core) crisis of adolescence, involving the need to attain a sense of self-definition.

ideology A set of rules, beliefs, attitudes, values, and behavioral prescriptions, usually for a particular role.

idiographic Of or about a single individual.

imaginary audience Component of adolescent egocentrism in which the individual believes others are as preoccupied with his or her appearance and behavior as he or she is.

imminent justice Belief that immediate punishment will be associated with any moral transgression.

imprinting Supposedly innately based predisposition for early social and emotional attachments to the first moving object seen.

individual life span One's development from birth to death (see ontogeny).

innate ideas Preexisting, preformed knowledge.

INRC group In Piaget's theory, the identity, negation, reciprocal, and correlative transformations (of cognitive problems) that characterize the structure of formal operational thought.

instability When a person's rate of change relative to the others in the group changes over time.

instincts Preformed, innate potentials for behavior.

instrumental ineffectiveness Inability to adequately or competently interact with or master objects in one's environment.

intellectualization Ego defense mechanism which allows a person to use highly abstract, intellectual reasons to justify his or her behavior.

interactionism A general term used in various theoretical contexts, to express the idea that two or more entities relate to each other in particular ways.

interdependent A relation between two or more elements, wherein the function of one element (for example, the behavior of one person) is both a product and producer of the function of the other elements in the relation.

intergenerational relationships Relationships between persons in different generations; parent-child and grandparent-child relations.

intergenerational solidarity When there is continuity of agreement between generations in behavioral orientations, attitudes, and values.

interindividual differences Differences between people.

intersensory integration Ability to equate stimulation derived from different sense modalities.

intervention Helping to enhance an individual's personal, social, and physical development; attempting to help persons to change.

intragenerational relationships Relationships among members of the same generation; peer relations.

intraindividual changes Within-person changes.

intrasensory integration Ability to relate two stimuli presented to the same modality.

judgmental sampling Choosing

subjects who fit a specific definition for the study.

juvenile delinquency Violation of a law committed by a person prior to his or her eighteenth birthday, which would have been a crime if committed by an adult.

late maturers People who go through phases of adolescent bodily change slower than usual.

libido In Freud's theory, human mental energy.

longitudinal design Research procedure in which the same persons are measured over time.

Luteinizing hormone (LH) Hormone which encourages ovulation in females and testicular development in males.

manipulative Varying stimuli to determine effects on responses.

marker variable Variable which helps monitor change, but which does not necessarily cause change.

masturbation Erotic stimulation of one's own genitals.

matrix A complex plan, array, or interrelation of elements.

maturation Change by tissue growth and differentiation at any time in life; in adolescence, the physical and physiological changes, involving reproductive capability, associated with the prepubescent through postpubescent phases.

maturational readiness In Gesell's theory, the belief that certain maturations must occur before experiential variables can exert any useful influence.

mature In a physiological sense, when an organism is capable of reproductive function.

mean Statistical average.

mechanistic Of or relating to a world view which stresses continuity and reductionism; a machine model of human functioning.

menarche The onset of menstruation in females.

mesoderm The middle of three primary germ layers of an embryo.

mesomorph A body type which is muscular, has strong bones, and is athletic-looking.

milieu Context; environmental setting.

minor A person who has not yet reached adult legal status; usually a person under 18 years old.

model In certain learning theories, the person who displays the behavior a subject observes.

moderate interaction theory A theory which places equal emphasis on nature and nurture but sees the two sources as independent of each other.

molecular level A subordinate level of analysis; a lower or the lowest level of analysis.

monozygotic twins Twins who arise from the same zygote which splits after conception (also termed identical twins).

moral rationality In Piaget's theory of moral reasoning development, moral judgments based on the intentions underlying an act.

moral realism In Piaget's theory of moral reasoning development, moral judgments based on the objective characteristics of an act.

moral relativism The idea that what is seen as moral behavior is defined in accordance with the cultural orientations of a particular society.

morphology Of or pertaining to the body.

multidisciplinary Involving many disciplines.

multivariate Many variables.

naïve egoistic In Kohlberg's theory of moral reasoning development, the second stage of this reasoning.

natural selection Evolutionary process in which the characteristics of the natural setting determine which organism characteristics will lead to survival and which ones will not.

naturalistic observation Observation of behavior as it occurs in its natural setting.

nature Pertaining to heredity, maturation, or genes.

nature-nurture issue Controversy over the source of human behavior and development.

negative identity formation In Erikson's theory, adoption of a role which is self-destructive or socially disapproved.

neurohormonal processes Mechanisms involved in the nervous system and endocrine system mechanisms.

nocturnal emission Discharge of semen during sleep.

nomothetic Of or pertaining to a group; group analysis.

nonobtrusive measures Any measure which naturally exists in the environment and which does not require direct collection of data from subjects.

nonprobability sampling When not everyone in the population of interest may have a chance of being sampled.

norm An average, typical, or modal characteristic of a group or population.

normative Pertaining to the average, typical, or modal characteristic.

normative studies Those which describe typical behavior of people of particular age levels and specific populations.

norm of reaction Range of potential outcomes that could result from a given genotype's potentially infinite interactions with environments.

nubility Endowed sexually; marriageable; ability to have sexual relations.

nurture Pertaining to environment, experience, or learning.

nurturance Affectionate care and attention.

obesity Eating disorder resulting in excess body fat; excessive overweight condition.

objective morality In Piaget's theory of moral reasoning development, judgment of an act in terms of its empirical consequences (associated with the first phase of such reasoning).

observational learning A type of learning stressing that behavior can be acquired through observation of a model's behavior. Reinforcement of the subject's behaviors is typically not seen as necessary from this viewpoint.

obtrusiveness Degree of visibility or presence.

Oedipus complex In Freud's theory, the idea that all males experience incestuous love for their mother and antagonism toward their father; corresponds to female's Electra complex.

ontogeny The life span of a single species from its conception to its death.

operation In Piaget's theory, an internalized action that is reversible.

operational definition A definition of a term which involves measurable statements.

optimize To provide maximum enhancement or to make as effective as possible.

orchialgia When unrelieved sexual tension results in pain in the region of the testes.

organism A living creature; a biological entity, such as a person.

organismic Of or pertaining to a philosophy of science (a world view) which stresses emergence, qualitative discontinuity, nonreductionism, and holism.

ova Mature female reproductive cells (a female gamete or egg).

ovulation The process of releasing an ovum or egg from the ovary.

panel design Longitudinal design; a design which follows the same individuals over time.

participant observation Where a researcher becomes part of the natural setting he or she is systematically observing.

peer Belonging to the same group in society; friend; person of a similar age.

penis envy In Freud's theory, when the female envies the male for his possession of a genital structure of which she has been deprived.

perinatal Occurring at about the time of birth.

period of the embryo From about the second week of life through the tenth to twelfth week of life in the human; period when all organ systems of the organism emerge.

period of the fetus From about the third through ninth month of gestation in humans, when organ systems continue to grow and functional characteristics appear.

period of the zygote Time from fertilization until the egg implants itself on the wall of the uterus (about 10 to 14 days after fertilization in humans).

personal fable Component of adolescent egocentrism wherein a person believes that he or she is a unique person having singular feelings and thoughts.

personological An orientation to understanding an individual's development and behavior through sole reference to variables and processes at the individual-psychological level of analysis.

petting To engage in kissing, embracing, and affectionate touching.

phenylketonuria (PKU) A disorder involving an inability to metabolize fatty substances because of the absence of a particular digestive enzyme.

phrenology Attempt to explain the connection between criminal behavior and physical characteristics by the shape of bumps on the skull.

phylogeny The evolutionary history of a species; phylogenetic; phyletic.

physiognomy Of or pertaining to the appearance of the face; method purported to predict individual criminality by comparing facial features of ordinary people with those of dead criminals.

pituitary Major endocrine gland, stimulated by the hypothalamus.

plasticity Ability or potential for change.

pleasure principle In Freud's theory, the id's striving for gratification of libidinal energy.

pluralism An orientation to science (for example, regarding theory or method) that stresses the need to use multiple approaches to a topic (instead of only one).

postnatal After birth.

postpubescent Period in adolescence after which most bodily changes have occurred.

precocial birds Birds that can walk upon hatching.

precocious puberty When a person goes through the bodily changes associated with pubescence much earlier than usual.

preconventional In Kohlberg's theory of moral reasoning development, the first level of such reasoning (involving the first two stages of moral reasoning).

premenstrual syndrome Cluster of symptoms which sometimes occurs just prior to the onset of menstruation.

prenatal Prior to birth.

prepubescent In adolescence, when changes in one or more bodily characteristics have begun, but the majority of changes that will take place have not yet been initiated.

primary graffian follicles A body which develops within the ovary and which later secretes hormones needed for reproduction.

primary process In Freud's theory, the fantasy or imaginary process associated with the id.

primary sexual characteristics Those which are present at birth and involve the internal and external genitalia.

principled reasoning In Kohlberg's theory of moral reasoning development, reasoning at the highest level of moral reasoning (involving stages 5 and 6).

probability sampling When all persons in the population have a known, nonzero chance of falling in the sample.

progesterone Primarily a female hormone which provides a basis for sexual maturation.

projection A defense mechanism in which one attributes one's own ideas, attitudes, or feelings to others.

projective personality test Test which assumes that the person's responses reflect his or her underlying personality dynamics.

promiscuity (promiscuous) Being sexually "free" or "loose"; having sexual relations with many partners or with little commitment or thought.

psychoanalytic Pertaining to psychoanalysis and the ideas of Sigmund Freud.

psychometric Measurement of mental or psychological functioning.

psychosexual Pertaining to the psychological aspects of sexual development.

psychosocial Pertaining to both psychological and social elements.

psychosocial crisis In Erikson's theory, a state of the ego wherein requisite societal demands within a stage are not yet met.

puberty The point at which the person is capable of reproduction; the event sometimes used to define the beginning of adolescence.

pubescent When most bodily changes that will eventually take place have been initiated.

puerperium Period of time from labor to when the uterus has regained its normal size.

purposive sampling See judgmental sampling.

qualitative change Alterations in the kind or type of phenomenon that exists.

quantitative change Alterations in how much or how many of a phenomenon exist.

quota sampling Selection of individuals on the basis of whether they can be used to fill a predetermined quota which is set up to represent the population in question.

rationalization A defense mechanism involving use of an untrue although plausible reason for conduct.

reactivity The tendency for a subject's responses or behavior to be influenced by the fact that he or she is participating in a research study.

reality principle In Freud's theory, the law governing the functioning of the ego; the ego requirement to adapt to reality.

recapitulation A repeating or mirroring.

reductionism Explanation by reference to the smaller elements involved in a whole.

reference group A group with which one identifies; a primary group to which one looks for guidance.

reinforcement Any stimulus which produces or maintains behavior; a stimulus which increases the probability of behavior.

reliability (reliable) When a measure gives consistent scores upon repeated administrations or when the parts of a measure are internally consistent.

religious cults Small groups of individuals who are together because they share a common set of beliefs, religious in nature; often small, off-beat groups.

representational ability Ability to represent internally an absent object; symbolic ability.

repression A defense mechanism involving the exclusion from consciousness of unacceptable impulses.

research methods The set of specific procedures by which a scientist makes observations and collects and examines data.

retrospection The process of reconstructing earlier, past events through remembering.

role A socially expected behavior pattern; a position or status someone accepts.

salience Importance; prominence; usefulness.

schemata A conceptual model for representing a phenomenon.

scheme An organized sensorimotor action sequence.

scientific method A set of empirically based techniques used by researchers to study the phenomena of the world.

scientific theory A system of statements about the ways in which variables are related to each other and from which hypotheses can be deduced.

scorer bias The degree to which the researcher gives a subjective and incorrect evaluation of a subject's behavior or characteristics.

secondary process In Freud's theory, the set of abilities possessed by the ego to adapt to reality (for example, cognition and perception).

secondary sexual characteristics Those physical and physiological characteristics which emerge during the prepubescent through postpubescent phases; the characteristics which are associated with reproductive capability and physical maturity.

secular trend The relation of adolescent bodily changes to historical time.

self-concept The set of knowledge one maintains about oneself.

self-esteem Level of positive or negative evaluation one associates with the self-concept.

self-fulfilling prophecy When attitudes about a target person's behaviors create a social climate which channels the target's behavior in a way consistent with the attitudes.

sequential method Studying a cross-sectional sample of people composed of various cohorts repeatedly over a fixed interval of time.

sequential research designs See sequential methods.

sex education Teaching the knowledge, skills, and values needed to function competently sexually.

sex role A socially defined set of prescriptions for behavior for people of a particular sex group.

sex-role behavior Behavioral functioning in accordance with sex-role behavioral prescriptions.

sex-role stereotypes Generalized beliefs that particular behaviors are characteristic of one sex group as opposed to the other.

sexual evolution When change regarding sexual values follows from or is compatible with other societal changes.

sexual revolution When changes regarding sexual values are rapid and abrupt, causing significant alteration of changes in sexuality and other aspects of social relations.

sexual socialization The process of becoming sexual, taking on a gender (sex) identity, learning sex roles, and acquiring the knowledge, skills, and values which allow one to function sexually.

simple random sampling When everyone in the population has an equal chance of being selected for the sample.

social evolution When the differences and similarities between generations result in gradual change.

social institutions Ongoing aspects of society around which many of life's most important activities revolve (the family, religion, the legal system, and the educational system are examples).

socialization Process by which members of one generation shape the behaviors and personalities of members of another generation; acquisition of knowledge, skills, and values which make us able members of our society.

socialized anxiety A learned anticipation of punishment for transgressing from society's rules, which involves an unpleasant feeling-state.

social learning theory A type of mechanistic theory wherein the principles of conditioning and learning are used to explain the acquisition of personality and social behaviors.

social relationships Ongoing interactions between two or more people.

social revolution When one generation is influenced vastly more by its peers than by the parental generation; a dramatic change in social structure and relationships.

sociopath Person who has no internalized morality and does not obey the rules of society.

somatotropin Growth-stimulating hormone.

somatotypes Body types.

spermatogenesis Sperm production.

stability When a person's rate of change relative to others in the group stays the same.

statistical significance The likelihood that a finding could not have been due to chance more than a small portion of the time.

status One's position in a group, community, or society relative to others.

stereotype An overgeneralized belief or standardized, invariant depiction of an object.

stimuli Changes in energy in the environment affecting a person's functioning.

stratified sampling When the population is proportionately divided according to categories of interest and then randomly sampled from within those categories.

strong interaction theory One which sees nature and nurture as inextricably and interdependently involved in all behavior development.

structure The pattern of organization of the elements of a phenomenon.

subjective morality In Piaget's theory of moral reasoning development, judging moral acts in regard to the intentions of the actor (a characteristic of the second phase of this reasoning).

substitution A defense mechanism involving the replacement of an unobtainable object with an obtainable one.

superego In Freud's theory, the structure of the personality composed of the conscience and the ego ideal.

surgent growth An abrupt spurt in growth.

survey research A method of data collection involving interviews or questionnaires, usually involving large samples.

survival of the fittest Idea that those organisms possessing characteristics fitting the adaptive requirements for a particular environmental setting will survive.

synthesis A meshing or blending of elements; in dialectics, a uniting of a thesis and an antithesis.

tabula rasa In Locke's empirical philosophy, the idea that the mind at birth is a blank slate and any knowledge attained is derived from experience.

tautological True by virtue of its logical form alone; needlessly repetitive; obviously true.

temperament A stylistic component of behavior, the way one performs a behavior of any content; how one does whatever one does.

testalgia When unrelieved sexual tension results in pain in the region of the testes.

testosterone Male hormone that provides a basis for sexual maturation.

thalidomide A drug prescribed to some pregnant women in the 1950s which was later discovered to cause serious birth defects in their offspring.

theory An interrelated set of propositions which integrates existing facts and leads to the generation of additional facts.

time-lag design When one age level is studied at different times in history.

tinnitus Ringing in the ears.

toxemia Condition in which the blood contains poisonous products; often associated with pregnancy.

transgression A violation of rules for conduct.

transsexual A person who believes he or she is trapped inside the wrong kind of body; one who has a gender identity incompatible with his or her genital, chromosomal, or hormonal gender (sex).

transvestism (transvestite) Person who enjoys dressing as a member of the opposite sex.

trophic hormone Hormone which stimulates other specific endocrine glands to produce their own specific hormones.

tumultuous growth Period of development characterized by crisis, stress, and problems.

umbilical cord The organ which is the attachment between mother and offspring during pregnancy and childbirth.

unconscious In Freud's theory, the area of the mind which contains material most difficult to bring into awareness.

universal sequences A series of changes that apply equally to all people of all cultures at all times of measurement.

validity The degree to which a measure assesses what it purports to assess.

variable Quantity or quality in which you are interested which

changes in the course of a research study.

vasocongestion Unrelieved sexual tension causing discomfort due to congestion (blood engorgement) in the pelvic region.

visualization Ability to organize and process visual information.

visual-motor flexibility Ability to shift in tasks requiring a coordination between vision and muscle movements.

vitalism In Aristotelian philosophy, the idea that a nonempirical entity present in all living organisms imparts life to that organism and directs its functioning.

weak interaction theory A theory which places primary stress on either nature or nurture (usually nature) as the source of the sequence and character of development.

world view The set of philosophical views a scientist holds that pertain to his or her ideas about human nature and/or about how the world is constructed.

zygote Fertilized egg.

Adams, G. R. Physical attractiveness research: Toward a developmental social psychology of beauty. *Human Development,* 1977, *20,* 217–239.

Adams, G. R., & Munro, G. The North American runaway: A critical review. Paper presented at the University of Arizona Symposium on Adolescents and Families, Tucson, March 1978.

Adams, G. R., Shea, J. A., & Fitch, S. A. An objective assessment of ego-identity status. *Journal of Youth and Adolescence,* in press.

Adelson, J. What generation gap? *New York Times Magazine,* 1970, Jan. 18 (Sec. 6), 10–45.

Adelson, J. The political imagination of the young adolescent. *Daedalus,* 1971, *100,* 1013–1050.

Adelson, J., & O'Neil, R. P. Growth of political ideas in adolescence: The sense of community. *Journal of Personality and Social Psychology,* 1966, 4, 295–306.

The Alan Guttmacher Institute, *11 million teenagers.* New York: The Alan Guttmacher Institute, Planned Parenthood Federation of America, 1976.

Alexander, D., & Money, J. Reading ability, object constancy, and Turner's syndrome. *Perceptual and Motor Skills,* 1965, *20,* 981–984.

Alexander, J. F., & Parsons, B. V. Short-term behavioral intervention with delinquent families: Impact on family process and recidivism. *Journal of Abnormal Psychology,* 1973, *81,* 219–225.

Allport, G. W. *The nature of prejudice.* Reading, Mass.: Addison-Wesley, 1954.

Allport, G. W., Gillespie, J. M., & Young, J. The religion of the post-war college student. *Journal of Psychology,* 1948, *25,* 3–33.

Almquist, E. M. Sex stereotype in occupational choice: The case for college women. *Journal of Vocational Behavior,* 1974, *5,* 13–21.

Almquist, E. M., & Angrist, S. S. Role model influences on college women's career aspirations. *Merrill-Palmer Quarterly,* 1971, *17,* 263–279.

American Social Health Association. *Today's VD control problem.* New York, 1971 and 1975.

Ames, R. Physical maturing among boys as related to adult social behavior: A longitudinal study. *California Journal of Educational Research,* 1957, *8,* 69–75.

Anastasi, A. Heredity, environ-ment, and the question "how?" *Psychological Review,* 1958, *65,* 197–208.

Anastasi, A. On the formation of psychological traits. *American Psychologist,* 1970, *25,* 899–910.

Andersen, A. E. Atypical anorexia nervosa. In R. A. Vigersky (Ed.), *Anorexia nervosa.* New York: Raven Press, 1977.

Anderson, J. E. The limitations of infant and pre-school tests in the measurement of intelligence. *Journal of Psychology,* 1939, *8,* 351–379.

Anthony, J. The reaction of adults to adolescents and their behavior. In G. Caplan & S. Lebovici (Eds.), *Adolescence.* New York: Basic Books, 1969.

Arbuthnot, J. Modification of moral judgment through role play. *Developmental Psychology,* 1975, *11,* 319–324.

Aries, P. *Centuries of childhood* (R. Baldick, trans.). New York: Knopf, 1962.

Arlin, P. K. Cognitive development in adulthood: A fifth stage? *Developmental Psychology,* 1975, *11,* 602–606.

Ausubel, D. P., Montemayor, R., & Svajian, P. *Theory and problems of adolescent development* (2d ed.). New York: Grune & Stratton, 1977.

Bachman, J. C. *Youth in transition: The impact of family background and intelligence on tenth-grade boys* (Vol. 2). Ann Arbor: University of Michigan Press, 1970.

Bachman, J. G., Green, S., & Wirtanen, I. D. *Youth in transition: Dropping out—problem or symptom?* (Vol. 3). Ann Arbor: University of Michigan Press, 1971.

Bachrach, R., Huesmann, L. R., & Peterson, R. A. The relation between locus of control and the development of moral judgment. *Child Development*, 1977, *48*, 1340–1352.

Bacon, C., & Lerner, R. M. Effects of maternal employment status on the development of vocational-role perception in females. *Journal of Genetic Psychology*, 1975, *126*, 187–193.

Baer, D. M. An age-irrelevant concept of development. *Merrill-Palmer Quarterly*, 1970, *16*, 238–246.

Bakan, D. *The duality of human existence*. Chicago: Rand McNally, 1966.

Bakwin, H., & McLaughlin, S. M. Secular increments in height: Is the end in sight? *Lancet*, 1964, *2*, 1195–1196.

Baldwin, A. H. Adolescent pregnancy and childbearing: Growing concerns for Americans. *Population Bulletin*, 1976, *31* (2).

Balow, I. H., & Brill, R. G. An evaluation study of reading and academic achievement levels of sixteen graduating classes of the California School for the Deaf, Riverside. Mimeographed report, Contract No. 4566, State of California, Department of Education, 1972.

Baltes, P. B. Longitudinal and cross-sectional sequences in the study of age and generation effects. *Human Development*, 1968, *11*, 145–171.

Baltes, P. B. Life-span models of psychological aging: A white ele-

phant? *Gerontologist*, 1973, *13*, 457–512.

Baltes, P. B. Life-span developmental psychology: Some converging observations on history and theory. In P. B. Baltes & O. G. Brim, Jr. (Eds.), *Life-span development and behavior* (Vol. 2). New York: Academic Press, 1979.

Baltes, P. B., Baltes, M. M., & Reinert, G. The relationship between time of measurement and age in cognitive development of children: An application of cross-sectional sequences. *Human Development*, 1970, *13*, 258–268.

Baltes, P. B., & Cornelius, S. W. The status of dialectics in developmental psychology: Theoretical orientation versus scientific method. In N. Datan & H. W. Reese (Eds.), *Life-span developmental psychology: Dialectical perspectives on experimental research*. New York: Academic Press, 1977.

Baltes, P. B., Cornelius, S. W., & Nesselroade, J. R. Cohort effects in behavioral development: Theoretical and methodological perspectives. In W. A. Collins (Ed.), *Minnesota symposium on child psychology* (Vol. 2). Hillsdale, N.J.: Erlbaum, 1978.

Baltes, P. B., & Goulet, L. R. Status and issues of a life-span developmental psychology. In L. R. Goulet & P. B. Baltes (Eds.), *Life-span developmental psychology: Research and theory*. New York: Academic Press, 1970.

Baltes, P. B., & Nesselroade, J. R. The developmental analysis of individual differences on multiple measures. In J. R. Nesselroade & H. W. Reese (Eds.), *Life-span developmental psychology: Methodological issues*. New York: Academic Press, 1973.

Baltes, P. B., Reese, H. W., & Nesselroade, J. R. *Life-span developmental psychology: Introduction to research methods*. Monterey, Calif.: Brooks/Cole, 1977.

Baltes, P. B., & Reinert, G. Cohort

effects in cognitive developmental research paradigms as revealed by cross-sectional sequences. *Developmental Psychology*, 1969, *1*, 169–177.

Baltes, P. B., & Schaie, K. W. (Eds.). *Life-span developmental psychology: Personality and socialization*. New York: Academic Press, 1973. (a)

Baltes, P. B., & Schaie, K. W. On life-span developmental research paradigms: Retrospects and prospects. In P. B. Baltes & K. W. Schaie (Eds.), *Life-span developmental psychology: Personality and socialization*. New York: Academic Press, 1973. (b)

Baltes, P. B., & Schaie, K. W. Aging and IQ: The myth of the twilight years. *Psychology Today*, 1974, *7*, 35–40.

Baltes, P. B., & Schaie, K. W. On the plasticity of intelligence in adulthood and old age: Where Horn and Donaldson fail. *American Psychologist*, 1976, *31*, 720–725.

Baltes, P. B., & Willis, S. L. Toward psychological theories of aging and development. In J. E. Birren & K. W. Schaie (Eds.), *Handbook of the psychology of aging*. New York: Van Nostrand Reinhold, 1977.

Bandura, A. The stormy decade: Fact or fiction? *Psychology in the School*, 1964, *1*, 224–231.

Bandura, A. *Principles of behavior modification*. New York: Holt, Rinehart and Winston, 1969.

Bandura, A., & Huston, A. C. Identification as a process of incidental learning. *Journal of Abnormal and Social Psychology*, 1961, *63*, 311–318.

Bandura, A., & McDonald, F. The influence of social reinforcement and the behavior of models in shaping children's moral judgment. *Journal of Abnormal and Social Psychology*, 1963, *67*, 274–281.

Bandura, A., & Walters, R. H. *Adolescent aggression*. New York: Ronald Press, 1959.

Bandura, A., & Walters, R. H. *Social learning and personality development.* New York: Holt, Rinehart and Winston, 1963.

Bardwick, J. M. *Psychology of women.* New York: Harper & Row, 1971.

Barnett, H. L., & Einhorn, A. H. (Eds.). *Pediatrics* (15th ed.). New York: Appleton Century Crofts, 1972.

Barry, H., Bacon, M. K., & Child, I. L. A cross-cultural survey of some sex differences in socialization. *Journal of Abnormal and Social Psychology,* 1957, *55,* 527–534.

Barton, M. E., Court, S. D., & Walker, W. Causes of severe deafness in school children in Northumberland and Durham. *British Medical Journal,* 1962, *1,* 351–355.

Bayley, N. Consistency and variability in the growth of intelligence from birth to eighteen years. *Journal of Genetic Psychology,* 1949, *75,* 165–196.

Bayley, N., & Oden, M. H. The maintenance of intellectual ability in gifted adults. *Journal of Gerontology,* 1955, *10,* 91–107.

Beach, F. A. The Snark was a Boojum. *American Psychologist,* 1950, *5,* 115–124.

Beery, J. W. Matching of auditory and visual stimuli by average and retarded readers. *Child Development,* 1967, *38,* 827–833.

Bell, H. M. *Youth tell their story.* Washington, D.C.: American Council on Education, 1938.

Bellugi, U., & Klima, E. S. The roots of language in the sign talk of the deaf. *Psychology Today,* 1972, *6,* 61–64, 76.

Bem, S. L. The measurement of psychological androgyny. *Journal of Consulting and Clinical Psychology,* 1974, *47,* 155–162.

Bem, S. L. Sex-role adaptability: One consequence of psychological androgyny. *Journal of Personality and Social Psychology,* 1975, *31,* 634–643.

Bem, S. L. On the utility of alternative procedures for assessing psychological androgyny. *Journal of Consulting and Clinical Psychology,* 1977, *45,* 196–205.

Bender, L. A. A visual motor gestalt test and its clinical use. *American Orthopsychiatric Association Research Monograph,* 1938, No. 3.

Benedict, R. Continuities and discontinuities on cultural conditioning. *Psychiatry,* 1938, *1,* 161–167.

Bengtson, V. L. The generation gap: A review and typology of social-psychological perspectives. *Youth and Society,* 1970, *2,* 7–32.

Bengtson, V. L., & Black, K. D. Intergenerational relations and continuities in socialization. In L. R. Goulet & P. B. Baltes (Eds.), *Life-span developmental psychology: Research and theory.* New York: Academic Press, 1970.

Bengston, V. L., & Kuypers, J. A. Generational differences and the developmental stake. *Aging and Human Development,* 1971, *2,* 249–260.

Bengtson, V. L., & Laufer, R. S. (Eds.). Youth, generations, and social changes: Part I and Part II. *Journal of Social Issues,* 1974, *30* (2 and 3).

Bengtson, V. L., & Troll, L. Youth and their parents: Feedback and intergenerational influence in socialization. In R. M. Lerner & G. B. Spanier (Eds.), *Child influences on marital and family interaction: A life-span perspective.* New York: Academic Press, 1978.

Benton, A. L. Dyslexia in relation to form perception and directional sense. In J. Money (Ed.), *Reading disability: Progress and research needs in dyslexia.* Baltimore: Johns Hopkins University Press, 1962.

Ber, A., & Brociner, C. Age of puberty in Israeli girls. *Fertility and Sterility,* 1964, *15,* 640–647.

Berger, B., Hackett, B., & Millar, R. M. The communal family.

Family Coordinator, 1972, *21,* 419–427.

Berscheid, E., & Walster, E. Physical attractiveness. In L. Berkowitz (Ed.), *Advances in experimental social psychology* (Vol. 7). New York: Academic Press, 1974.

Bertalanffy, von L. *Modern theories of development.* London: Oxford University Press, 1933.

Bijou, S. W. *Child development: The basic stage of early childhood.* Englewood Cliffs, N.J.: Prentice-Hall, 1976.

Bijou, S. W. Some clarifications on the meaning of a behavior analysis of child development. Paper presented at the Third Annual Midwestern Association of Behavior Analysis, Chicago, May 1977.

Bijou, S. W., & Baer, D. M. *Child development: A systematic and empirical theory.* New York: Appleton Century Crofts, 1961.

Bindon, D. M. Personality characteristics of rubella deaf children: Implications for teaching of the deaf in general. *American Annals of the Deaf,* 1957, *102,* 264–270.

Binet, A., & Simon, T. Sur la necéssité d'établir un diagnostic scientific des états inférieurs de l'intelligence. *L'Année Psychologique,* 1905, *11,* 162–190. (a)

Binet, A., & Simon, T. Méthodes nouvelles pour le diagnostic du niveau intellectual des anormaus. *L'Année Psychologique,* 1905, *11,* 191–244. (b)

Birch, H. G., & Belmont, L. Auditory-visual integration in normal and retarded readers. *American Journal of Orthopsychiatry,* 1964, *34,* 852–861.

Birch, H. G., & Belmont, L. Auditory-visual integration, intelligence and reading ability in school children. *Perceptual and Motor Skills,* 1965, *20,* 295–305.

Birnbaum, J. A. Life patterns and self-esteem in gifted family oriented and career committed women. In M. T. S. Mednick, S. S. Tangri, & L. W. Hoffman (Eds.),

Women and achievement. New York: Wiley, 1975.

Blank, M., & Bridger, W. H. Deficiencies in verbal labeling in retarded readers. *American Journal of Orthopsychiatry,* 1966, *36,* 840–847.

Block, J. H. Conceptions of sex roles: Some cross-cultural and longitudinal perspectives. *American Psychologist,* 1973, *28,* 512–526.

Block, J. H. Issues, problems, and pitfalls in assessing sex differences: A critical review of *The psychology of sex differences. Merrill-Palmer Quarterly,* 1976, *22,* 283–308.

Bloom, B. S. *Stability and change in human characteristics.* New York: Wiley, 1964.

The Boston Women's Health Book Collective. *Our bodies, ourselves: A book by and for women* (2d ed.). New York: Simon & Schuster, 1976.

Bower, D. W., & Christopherson, V. A. University student cohabitation: A regional comparison of selected attitudes and behavior. *Journal of Marriage and the Family,* 1977, *39,* 447–452.

Bowers, K. S. Situationalism in psychology. *Psychological Review,* 1973, *80,* 307–336.

Bowman, H. A., & Spanier, G. B. *Modern Marriage* (8th ed.). New York: McGraw-Hill, 1978.

Brainerd, C. J. The stage question in cognitive-developmental theory. *The Behavioral and Brain Sciences,* 1978, *2,* 173–182.

Brill, N., Crumpton, E., & Grayson, H. Personality factors in marijuana use. *Archives of General Psychiatry,* 1971, *24,* 163–165.

Brittain, C. V. Adolescent choices and parent-peer cross pressures. *American Sociological Review,* 1963, *28,* 385–391.

Brittain, C. V. A comparison of urban and rural adolescence with respect to peer versus parent compliance. *Adolescence,* 1969, *4,* 59–68.

Brody, E. B., & Brody, N. *Intelligence: Nature, determinants, and consequences.* New York: Academic Press, 1976.

Bronfenbrenner, U. Freudian theories of identification and their derivatives. *Child Development,* 1960, *31,* 15–40.

Bronfenbrenner, U. Developmental theory in transition. In H. W. Stevenson (Ed.), *Child psychology.* Sixty-second yearbook of the National Society for the Study of Education, Part 1. Chicago: University of Chicago Press, 1963.

Bronfenbrenner, U. Toward an experimental ecology of human development. *American Psychologist,* 1977, *32,* 513–531.

Broverman, I. K., Vogel, S. R., Broverman, D. M., Clarkson, F. E., & Rosenkrantz, P. S. Sex-role stereotypes: A current appraisal. *Journal of Social Issues,* 1972, *28,* 59–78.

Brown, L. B. Some attitudes underlying petitionary prayer. In A. Godin (Ed.), *From cry to word.* Brussels: Lumen Vitae Press, 1968.

Bruch, H. *Eating disorders: Obesity, anorexia nervosa and the person within.* New York: Basic Books, 1973.

Bruch, H. Psychological antecedents of anorexia nervosa. In R. A. Vigersky (Ed.), *Anorexia nervosa.* New York: Raven Press, 1977.

Brun-Gulbrandsen, S. Kjonnsrolle og ungdomskriminalitet. Oslo: Institute of Social Research, 1958 (Mimeographed).

Bryan, T. S. An observational analysis of classroom behaviors of children with learning disabilities. *Journal of Learning Disabilities,* 1974, *7,* 35–43.

Bumpass, L., & Sweet, J. A. Differentials in marital instability. *American Sociological Review,* 1972, *37,* 754–766.

Burchard, E. M., & Myklebust, H. R. A comparison of congenital and adventitious deafness with respect to its effects on intelligence, personality, and social maturity. *American Annals of the Deaf,* 1942, *87,* 140–154, 241–251, 342–360.

Burchinal, L. G. Adolescent role deprivation and high school age marriage. *Marriage and Family Living,* 1959, *21,* 378–384.

Bureau of Labor Statistics. *Handbook of labor statistics,* 1978, U.S. Department of Labor. Washington, D.C.: U.S. Government Printing Office.

Burgoon, C. F., Jr. Acne vulgaris. In V. C. Vaughan & R. J. McKay (Eds.), *Nelson textbook of pediatrics* (10th ed.). Philadelphia: Saunders, 1975.

Burt, C. The differentiation of intellectual abilities. *British Journal of Educational Psychology,* 1954, *24,* 76–90.

Burt, C. The evidence for the concept of intelligence. *British Journal of Educational Psychology,* 1955, *25,* 159–177.

Burt, C. The genetic determination of differences in intelligence: A study of monozygotic twins reared together and apart. *British Journal of Psychology,* 1966, *57,* 137–153.

Caldwell, B. M. The usefulness of the critical period hypothesis in the study of filiative behavior. *Merrill-Palmer Quarterly,* 1962, *8,* 229–242.

Canning, H., & Mayer, J. Obesity—its possible effect on college acceptance. *The New England Journal of Medicine,* 1966, *275,* 1172–1174.

Cannon, K. L., & Long, R. Premarital sexual behavior in the sixties. *Journal of Marriage and the Family,* 1971, *33,* 36–49.

Caplan, G., & Lebovici, S. (Eds.). *Adolescence: Psychosocial perspectives.* New York: Basic Books, 1969.

Carns, D. E. Talking about sex: Notes on first coitus and the double sexual standard. *Journal of Marriage and the Family,* 1973, *35,* 677–688.

Cattell, R. B. *Personality and mood by questionnaire.* San Francisco: Jossey-Bass, 1973.

Cauble, M. A. Formal operations, ego identity, and principled morality: Are they related? *Developmental Psychology,* 1976, *12,* 363–364.

Cawood, C. D. Petting and prostatic engorgement. *Medical Aspects of Human Sexuality,* 1971, *5,* 204–218.

Center for Disease Control, Department of Health, Education, and Welfare, *Abortion surveillance, annual summary 1975,* Atlanta, 1977.

Chand, I. P., Crider, D. M., & Willets, F. K. Parent-youth disagreement as perceived by youth: A longitudinal study. *Youth and Society,* 1975, *6,* 365–375.

Charles, D. C. Historical antecedents of life-span developmental psychology. In L. R. Goulet & P. B. Baltes (Eds.), *Life-span developmental psychology: Research and theory.* New York: Academic Press, 1970.

Charrow, V. R., & Fletcher, J. D. English as the second language of deaf children. *Developmental Psychology,* 1974, *10,* 463–470.

Child Study Association of America. *What to tell your child about sex* (rev. ed.). Des Moines: Meredith, 1968.

Ciaccio, N. V. A test of Erikson's theory of ego epigenesis. *Developmental Psychology,* 1971, *4,* 306–311.

Clark, G. H. *Thales to Dewey.* Boston: Houghton Mifflin, 1957.

Clayton, R. R., & Voss, H. L. Shacking up: Cohabitation in the 1970's. *Journal of Marriage and the Family,* 1977, *39,* 273–283.

Cloward, R. A., & Ohlin, L. E. *Delinquency and opportunity: A theory of delinquent gangs.* Glencoe, Ill.: Free Press, 1960.

Colby, A. Evolution of a moral-developmental theory. *New Directions for Child Development,* 1978, *2,* 89–104.

Coleman, J. S. *The adolescent society.* New York: Free Press, 1961.

Coleman, J. S. The adolescent culture. In I. J. Gordon (Ed.) *Human development.* Chicago: Scott, Foresman, 1965.

Coleman, J. S. How do the young become adults? *Review of Educational Research,* 1972, *42,* 431–439.

Collins, J. K., & Thomas, N. T. Age and susceptibility to same-sex peer pressure. *British Journal of Educational Psychology,* 1972, *42,* 83–85.

Collins, W. A. Effect of temporal separation between motivation, aggression, and consequences: A developmental study. *Developmental Psychology,* 1973, *8,* 215–221.

Combs, J., & Cooley, W. W. Dropouts in high school and after school. *American Educational Research Journal,* 1968, *5,* 343–363.

Constantinople, A. An Eriksonian measure of personality development in college students. *Developmental Psychology,* 1969, *1,* 357–372.

Costanzo, P. R., Coie, J. D., Grumet, J. F., & Farnill, D. A reexamination of the effects of intent and consequence on children's moral judgments. *Child Development,* 1973, *44,* 154–161.

Costanzo, P. R., & Shaw, M. E. Conformity as a function of age level. *Child Development,* 1966, *37,* 967–975.

Cottle, T. J. *Time's children.* Boston: Little, Brown, 1971.

Craig, H. B. A sociometric investigation of the self-concept of the deaf child. *American Annals of the Deaf,* 1965, *110,* 456–478.

Crans, W. D., Kenny, J., & Campbell, D. T. Does intelligence cause achievement? A cross-lagged panel analysis. *Journal of Educational Psychology,* 1972, *63,* 258–275.

Cronbach, L. J. *Essentials of psychological testing.* New York: Harper, 1960.

Crisp, A. H. Premorbid factors in adult disorders of weight, with particular reference to primary anorexia nervosa (weight phobia). *Journal of Psychosomatic Medicine,* 1970, *14,* 1–22.

Crisp, A. H. Primary anorexia nervosa or adolescent weight phobia. *Practitioner,* 1974, *212,* 525–535.

Cropper, D. A., Meck, D. S., & Ash, M. J. The relation between formal operations and a possible fifth stage of cognitive development. *Developmental Psychology,* 1977, *13,* 517–518.

D'Augelli, J. F. The relationship of moral reasoning, sex guilt, and interpersonal interaction to couple's premarital sexual experience. Unpublished doctoral dissertation, University of Connecticut, 1972.

D'Augelli, J. F., & Cross, H. J. Relationship of sex guilt and moral reasoning to premarital sex in college women and in couples. *Journal of Consulting and Clinical Psychology,* 1975, *43,* 40–47.

Dale, L. G. The growth of systematic thinking: Replication and analysis of Piaget's first chemical experiment. *Australian Journal of Psychology,* 1970, *22,* 277–286.

Darwin, C. *The origin of species by means of natural selection or the preservation of favoured races in the struggle for life.* London: J. Murray, 1859.

Darwin, C. *The expression of emotions in man and animals.* London: J. Murray, 1872.

Datan, N., & Ginsberg, L. H. (Eds.). *Life-span developmental psychology: Normative life crises.* New York: Academic Press, 1975.

Datan, N., & Reese, H. W. (Eds.). *Life-span developmental psychology: Dialectical perspectives on experimental research.* New York: Academic Press, 1977.

Davis, A. Socialization and the adolescent personality. *Forty-third yearbook of the national society for the study of education* (Vol. 43, Part 1). Chicago: University of Chicago Press, 1944.

Davis, K. The American family in relation to demographic change. In C. R. Westoff & R. Parke, Jr., (Eds.), *Demographic and social aspects of population growth.* Vol. I of U.S. Commission on Population Growth and the American Future. Washington, D.C.: U.S. Government Printing Office, 1972.

Davison, M. L., Robbins, S., & Swanson, D. B. Stage structure in objective moral judgments. *Developmental Psychology,* 1978, *14,* 137–146.

Dean, D. G., & Spanier, G. B. Commitment: An overlooked variable in marital adjustment. *Sociological Focus,* 1974, *7,* 113–118.

DeBord, L. W. Adolescent religious participation: An examination of sib-structure and church attendance. *Adolescence,* 1969, *4,* 557–570.

deLissovoy, V. High school marriages: A longitudinal study. *Journal of Marriage and the Family,* 1973, *35,* 245–255.

Del Solar, C. *Parent's answer book: What your child ought to know about sex.* New York: Grossett & Dunlap, 1971.

DeMause, L. (Ed.). *The history of childhood.* New York: Psychohistory Press, 1974.

Dennis, W. (Ed.). *Historical readings in developmental psychology.* New York: Appleton Century Crofts, 1972.

DeVries, R. Relationships among Piagetian, IQ, and achievement assessments. *Child Development,* 1974, *45,* 746–756.

Dollard, J., Doob, L. W., Miller, N. E., Mowrer, O. H., & Sears, R. R. *Frustration and aggression.* New Haven, Conn.: Yale University Press, 1939.

Dollard, J., & Miller, N. E. *Personality and psychotherapy.* New York: McGraw-Hill, 1950.

Dominick, J. R., & Greenberg, B. S. Attitudes toward violence: The interaction of television exposure, family attitudes, and social class. In G. A. Comstock & E. A. Rubinstein (Eds.), *Television and social behavior, Vol. 3. Television and adolescent aggressiveness.* Washington, D.C.: U.S. Government Printing Office, 1972.

Donovan, J. M. Identity status and interpersonal style. *Journal of Youth and Adolescence,* 1975, *4,* 37–55.

Doress, I., & Porter, J. N. Kids in cults. *Society,* 1978, *15,* 69–71.

Douglas, J. D., & Wong, A. C. Formal operations: Age and sex differences in Chinese and American children. *Child Development,* 1977, *48,* 689–692.

Douglas, J. W. B., & Ross, J. M. Age of puberty related to educational ability, attainment, and school leaving age. *Journal of Child Psychology and Psychiatry,* 1964, *5,* 185–196.

Douvan, E., & Adelson, J. *The adolescent experience.* New York: Wiley, 1966.

Douvan, E., & Gold, M. Modal patterns in American adolescence. In L. W. Hoffman & M. L. Hoffman (Eds.), *Review of child development research,* 1966, *2,* 469–528.

Droege, R. C. Sex differences in aptitude maturation during high school. *Journal of Counseling Psychology,* 1967, *14,* 407–411.

DuBois, C. *The people of Alor.* Minneapolis: University of Minnesota Press, 1944.

Dutt, N. K. Attitudes of the university students toward religion. *Journal of Psychological Research,* 1965, *9,* 127–130.

Duvall, E. M. Family dilemmas with teen-agers. *Family Life Coordinator,* 1965, *14,* 35–38.

Duvall, E. M. *Marriage and family development* (5th ed.). Philadelphia: Lippincott, 1977.

Dwyer, J., & Mayer, J. Psychological effects of variations in physical appearance during adolescence. *Adolescence,* 1968–1969, *3,* 353–380.

Eato, L. E. Perceptions of the physical and social environment in relation to self-esteem among male and female black adolescents. Unpublished master's thesis, The Pennsylvania State University, 1979.

Edwards, C. P. Society complexity and moral development: A Kenyan study. *Ethos,* 1975, *3,* 505–527.

Edwards, J. B. A developmental study of the acquisition of some moral concepts in children aged 7 to 15. *Educational Research,* 1974, *16,* 83–93.

Eisenberg, L. Reading retardation: Psychiatric and sociological aspects. *Pediatrics,* 1966, *37,* 352–365.

Eisenberg, L. The human nature of human nature. *Science,* 1976, *176,* 123–128.

Eisenberg-Berg, N. The relation of political attitudes to constraint-oriented and prosocial moral reasoning. *Developmental Psychology,* 1976, *12,* 552–553.

Eisenberg-Berg, N., & Mussen, P. Empathy and moral development in adolescence. *Developmental Psychology,* 1978, *14,* 185–186.

Elder, G. H. *Children of the great depression.* Chicago: University of Chicago Press, 1974.

Elkin, F., & Handel, G. *The child and society: The process of socialization.* New York: Random House, 1978.

Elkind, D. Quantity conceptions in college students. *Journal of Social Psychology,* 1962, *57,* 459–465.

Elkind, D. Egocentrism in adolescence. *Child Development,* 1967, *38,* 1025–1034.

Elkind, D. Combinatorial thinking in adolescents from graded and ungraded classrooms. *Perceptual and Motor Skills,* 1968, *27,* 1015–1018.

Ellis, A. *Sex without guilt.* New York: Lyle Stuart, 1958.

Emmerich, W. Personality development and concepts of structure. *Child Development*, 1968, *39*, 671–690.

English, C. Leaving home: A typology of runaways. *Society*, 1973, *10*, 22–24.

Entwisle, D. R., & Greenberger, E. Adolescents' views of women's work role. *American Journal of Orthopsychiatry*, 1972, *42*, 648–656.

Erikson, E. H. Identity and the life cycle. *Psychological Issues*, 1959, *1*, 18–164.

Erikson, E. H. *Childhood and society* (2d ed.). New York: Norton, 1963.

Erikson, E. H. Inner and outer space: Reflections on womanhood. In R. J. Lifton (Ed.), *The woman in America*. Boston: Beacon, 1964.

Erikson, E. H. *Identity, youth and crisis*. New York: Norton, 1968.

Erikson, E. H. *Gandhi's truth*. New York: Norton, 1969.

Eron, L. D., Lefkowitz, M. M., Huesmann, L. R., & Walder, L. O. Does television violence cause aggression? *American Psychologist*, 1972, *27*, 253–263.

Eshleman, J. R. Mental health and marital integration in young marriages. *Journal of Marriage and the Family*, 1965, *27*, 255–262.

Estes, R. E., & Huizinga, R. J. A comparison of visual and auditory presentations of a paired associated learning task with learning disabled children. *Journal of Learning Disabilities*, 1974, *7*, 44–51.

Fakouri, M. E. "Cognitive development in adulthood: A fifth stage?": A critique. *Developmental Psychology*, 1976, *12*, 472.

Falkner, F. Physical growth. In H. L. Bennett & A. H. Einhorn (Eds.), *Pediatrics*. New York: Appleton Century Crofts, 1972.

Family Planning Perspectives. Planned Parenthood Federation of America. The Alan Guttmacher Institute, New York.

Fass, P. S. *The damned and the beautiful: American youth in the 1920's*. New York: Oxford University Press, 1977.

Faust, D., & Arbuthnot, J. Relationship between moral and Piagetian reasoning and the effectiveness of moral education. *Developmental Psychology*, 1978, *14*, 435–436.

Faust, M. S. Developmental maturity as a determinant in prestige of adolescent girls. *Child Development*, 1960, *31*, 173–184.

Feshbach, S., & Singer, R. *Television and aggression*. San Francisco: Jossey-Bass, 1971.

Fitzgerald, J. M., Nesselroade, J. R., & Baltes, P. B. Emergence of adult intellectual structure. *Developmental Psychology*, 1973, *9*, 114–119.

Fiumara, N. J. Ineffectiveness of condoms in preventing venereal disease. *Medical Aspects of Human Sexuality*, 1972, *6*, 146–150.

Flavell, J. H. *The developmental psychology of Jean Piaget*. New York: Van Nostrand, 1963.

Flavell, J. H. Cognitive changes in adulthood. In L. R. Goulet & P. B. Baltes (Eds.), *Life-span developmental psychology: Research and theory*. New York: Academic Press, 1970.

Flavell, J. H., & Wholwill, J. F. Formal and functional aspects of cognitive development. In D. Elkind & J. H. Flavell (Eds.), *Studies in cognitive development*. New York: Oxford University Press, 1969.

Floyd, H. H., Jr., & South, D. R. Dilemma of youth: The choice of parents or peers as a frame of reference for behavior. *Journal of Marriage and the Family*, 1972, *34*, 627–634.

Fo, W. S. O., & O'Donnell, C. R. The buddy system: Relationship and contingency conditions in a community intervention program for youth with nonprofessionals as behavior change agents. *Journal*

of Consulting and Clinical Psychology, 1974, *42*, 163–169.

Fo, W. S. O., & O'Donnell, C. R. The buddy system: Effect of community intervention on delinquent offenses. *Behavior Therapy*, 1975, *6*, 522–524.

Freedle, R. Psychology, Thomian topologies, deviant logics, and human development. In N. Datan & H. W. Reese (Eds.), *Life-span developmental psychology: Dialectical perspectives on experimental research*. New York: Academic Press, 1977.

Freud, A. Adolescence as a developmental disturbance. In G. Caplan & S. Lebovici (Eds.), *Adolescence*. New York: Basic Books, 1969.

Freud, S. Psychopathology of everyday life. In *The basic writings of Sigmund Freud*. New York: Random House, 1938. (First German edition, 1904.)

Freud, S. Three essays on sexuality. In *Standard edition, Vol. VII*. London: Hogarth Press, 1953. (First German edition, 1905.)

Freud, S. *The ego and the id*. London: Hogarth, 1923.

Freud, S. *Outline of psychoanalysis*. New York: Norton, 1949.

Freud, S. Some psychological consequences of the anatomical distinction between the sexes. In *Collected papers* (Vol. 5). London: Hogarth, 1950.

Friedenberg, E. Z. *The vanishing adolescent*. New York: Dell, 1959.

Friedenberg, E. Z. The generation gap. *Annals of the American Academy of Political and Social Science*, 1969, *382*, 32–42.

Friedrich, L. K., & Stein, A. H. Aggressive and prosocial television programs and the natural behavior of preschool children. *Monographs of the Society for Research in Child Development*, 1973, *38* (4, Serial No. 151), 1–64.

Friesen, D. Academic-athletic-popularity syndrome in the Canadian high school society (1967). *Adolescence*, 1968, *3*, 39–52.

Furstenberg, F., Jr. The social consequences of teenage parenthood. *Family Planning Perspectives*, 1976, 8, 148–164. (a)

Furstenberg, F., Jr. *Unplanned parenthood: The social consequences of teenage parenthood.* New York: Free Press, 1976. (b)

Furth, H. G. A comparison of reading test norms of deaf and hearing children. *American Annals of the Deaf*, 1966, 111, 461–462.

Gagnon, J. H., & Simon, W. *Sexual conduct: The social sources of human sexuality.* Chicago: Adline, 1973.

Gallatin, J. E. The development of political thinking in urban adolescents. (Final Report, Office of Education Grant 0-0554) Washington, D.C.: National Institutes of Education, 1972.

Gallatin, J. E. *Adolescence and individuality.* New York: Harper & Row, 1975.

Gallatin, J. E. Theories of adolescence. In J. F. Adams (Ed.), *Understanding adolescence* (3d ed.). Boston: Allyn and Bacon, 1976.

Garrett, H. E. A developmental theory of intelligence. *American Psychologist*, 1946, 1, 372–378.

Garrity, F. D. A study of some secondary modern school pupils' attitudes towards religious education. *Religious Education*, 1961, 56, 141–143.

Gates, A. I., & MacGinitie, W. H. *Gates-MacGinitie reading tests (teacher's manual, levels A, B, C, & D).* New York: Teachers College Press, 1965.

Gengerelli, J. A. Graduate school reminiscence: Hull and Koffka. *American Psychologist*, 1976, 31, 685–688.

Gesell, A. L. Maturation and infant behavior pattern. *Psychological Review*, 1929, 36, 307–319.

Gesell, A. L. The individual in infancy. In C. Murchison (Ed.), *Handbook of child psychology.* Worcester, Mass.: Clark University Press, 1931.

Gesell, A. L. An *atlas of infant behavior.* New Haven, Conn.: Yale University Press, 1934.

Gesell, A. L. The ontogenesis of infant behavior. In L. Carmichael (Ed.), *Manual of child psychology.* New York: Wiley, 1946.

Gesell, A. L. The ontogenesis of infant behavior. In L. Carmichael (Ed.), *Manual of child psychology* (2d ed.). New York: Wiley, 1954.

Gewirtz, J. L., & Stingle, K. G. Learning of generalized imitation as the basis for identification. *Psychological Review*, 1968, 75, 374–397.

Gillis, J. R. *Youth and history.* New York: Academic Press, 1974.

Glick, P., & Spanier, G. B. Married and unmarried cohabitation in the United States. *Journal of Marriage and the Family*, 1980, in press.

Glueck, S., & Glueck, E. *Delinquents and nondelinquents in perspective.* Cambridge, Mass.: Harvard University Press, 1968.

Goddard, H. H. A measuring scale for intelligence. *Training School Bulletin*, 1910, 6, 146–154.

Goldblatt, P. B., Moore, M. E., & Stunkard, A. J. Social factors in obesity. *Journal of the American Medical Association*, 1965, 192, 1039–1044.

Goldfarb, W. Psychological privation in infancy and subsequent adjustment. *American Journal of Orthopsychiatry*, 1945, 15, 244–257.

Goldman, R. *Religious thinking from childhood to adolescence.* London: Routledge & Kegan Paul, 1964.

Goldsen, R. K., Rosenberg, M., Williams, R. M., Jr., & Suchman, E. A. *What college students think.* Princeton, N.J.: Van Nostrand, 1960.

Goldstein, B. *Human sexuality.* New York: McGraw-Hill, 1976.

Gollin, E. S. A developmental approach to learning and cognition. In L. P. Lipsitt & C. C. Spiker (Eds.), *Advances in child development and behavior* (Vol. 2). New York: Academic Press, 1965.

Goode, W. J. *World revolution and family patterns.* New York: Free Press, 1970.

Goodman, N., Dornbusch, S. M., Richardson, S. A., & Hastorf, A. H. Variant reactions to physical disabilities. *American Sociological Review*, 1963, 28, 429–435.

Goodnow, J. J. A test of milieu differences with some of Piaget's tasks. *Psychological Monographs*, 1962, 76, No. 36, Whole No. 555.

Goodnow, J. J., & Bethon, G. Piaget's tasks: The effects of schooling and intelligence. *Child Development*, 1966, 57, 573–582.

Gordon, E. M., & Thomas, A. Children's behavioral style and the teacher's appraisal of their intelligence. *Journal of School Psychology*, 1967, 5, 292–300.

Gordon, S. *The sexual adolescent: Communicating with teenagers about sex.* North Scituate, Mass.: Duxbury Press, 1973.

Gorsuch, R., & Barnes, M. Stages of ethical reasoning and moral norms of Carib youths. *Journal of Cross-cultural Psychology*, 1973, 4, 283–301.

Gottlieb, D. (Ed.). *Youth in contemporary society.* Beverly Hills, Calif.: Sage, 1973.

Goulet, L. R., & Baltes, P. B. (Eds.). *Life-span developmental psychology: Research and theory.* New York: Academic Press, 1970.

Gove, W. R., & Tudor, J. F. Adult sex roles and mental illness. *American Journal of Sociology*, 1973, 78, 812–835.

Grabill, W. H. Premarital fertility. U.S. Bureau of the Census, Current Population Reports, Series P-23, No. 63, August 1976.

Griffin, B. S., & Griffin, C. T. *Juvenile delinquency in perspective.* New York: Harper & Row, 1978.

Gross, L. The real world of television. *Today's Education*, 1974, 63, 86–92.

Gruenberg, E. M. Epidemiology of mental illness. *International Journal of Psychiatry*, 1966, *2*, 78–126.

Guerin, P. J., Jr. (Ed.). *Family therapy.* New York: Gardner, 1976.

Guerney, B. G., Jr. *Relationship enhancement: Skill training programs for therapy, problem prevention, and enrichment.* San Francisco: Jossey-Bass, 1977.

Guilford, J. P. *The nature of human intelligence.* New York: McGraw-Hill, 1967.

Gump, P. V. Ecological psychology and children. In E. M. Hetherington (Ed.), *Review of child development research.* Chicago: University of Chicago Press, 1975.

Haan, N. The adolescent antecedents of an ego model of coping and defense and comparisons with Q-sorted ideal personalities. *Genetic Psychology Monographs*, 1974, *89*, 273–306.

Haan, N. Two moralities in action contexts: Relationship to thought, ego regulation, and development. *Journal of Personality and Social Psychology*, 1978, *36*, 286–305.

Haan, N., Langer, J., & Kohlberg, L. Family patterns in moral reasoning. *Child Development*, 1976, *47*, 1204–1206.

Haan, N., Smith, M. B., & Block, J. Moral reasoning of young adults: Political-social behavior, family background, and personality correlates. *Journal of Personality and Social Psychology*, 1968, *10*, 183–201.

Hadden, J. K. The private generation. *Psychology Today*, 1969, *3*, 32–35.

Hafez, E. S. E., & Evans, T. N. (Eds.). *Human reproduction.* New York: Harper & Row, 1973.

Hakstian, A. R., & Cattell, R. B. An examination of adolescent sex differences in some ability and personality traits. *Canadian Journal of Behavioral Science*, 1975, *7*, 295–312.

Halbrecht, I., Sklorowski, E., & Tsafviv, J. Menarche and menstruation in various ethnic groups in Israel. *Acta Geneticae Medicae et Gemellologiae*, 1971, *20*, 384–391.

Haley, J. (Ed.). *Changing families: A family therapy reader.* New York: Grune & Stratton, 1971.

Hall, C. S. *A primer of Freudian psychology.* New York: World Publishing, 1954.

Hall, G. S. *Adolescence.* New York: Appleton, 1904.

Handlin, O., & Handlin, M. F. *Facing life: Youth and the family in American history.* Boston: Little, Brown, 1971.

Harlow, H. F., & Harlow, M. K. Social deprivation in monkeys. *Scientific American*, 1962, *207*, 137–146.

Harris, D. B. (Ed.). *The concept of development.* Minneapolis: University of Minnesota Press, 1957.

Harris, L. The Life poll. *Life*, 1969, *66*, 22–23.

Harris, L. Change, yes—upheaval, no. *Life*, 1971, *70*, 22–27.

Harris, S., Mussen, P., & Rutherford, E. Some cognitive, behavioral, and personality correlates of maturity of moral judgment. *Journal of Genetic Psychology*, 1976, *128*, 123–135.

Hart, G. Role of preventive methods in the control of venereal disease. *Clinical Obstetrics and Gynecology*, 1975, *18*, 243–253.

Hartford, T. C. Patterns of alcohol use among adolescents. *Psychiatric Opinion*, 1975, *12*, 17–21.

Hartmann, D. P. Influence of symbolically modeled instrumental aggression and pain cues on aggressive behavior. *Journal of Personality and Social Psychology*, 1969, *11*, 280–288.

Hartshorne, H., & May, M. A. *Studies in the nature of character* (Vols. 1–3). New York: Macmillan, 1928–1930.

Hartup, W. W. Perspectives on child and family interaction: Past, present, and future. In R. M. Lerner & G. B. Spanier (Eds.), *Child influences on marital and family interaction: A life-span perspective.* New York: Academic Press, 1978.

Hassenger, R. (Ed.). *The shape of Catholic higher education.* Chicago: University of Chicago Press, 1967.

Hatcher, R. A., Stewart, G. K., Guest, F., Finkelstein, R., & Goodwin, C. *Contraceptive technology: 1976–1977.* New York: Irvington Publishers, 1976.

Havighurst, R. J. *Developmental tasks and education.* New York: Longmans, 1951.

Havighurst, R. J. *Human development and education.* London: Longmans, 1953.

Havighurst, R. J. Research on the developmental task concept. *School Review*, 1956, *64*, 214–223.

Heber, R. A manual of terminology and classification in mental retardation. *American Journal of Mental Deficiency*, 1959, *64*, monograph supplement.

Heber, R. Modifications in the manual on terminology and classification in mental retardation. *American Journal of Mental Deficiency*, 1961, *65*, 499–500.

Heinicke, C. M. Learning disturbance in childhood. In B. J. Wolman (Ed.), *Manual of child psychopathology.* New York: McGraw-Hill, 1972.

Hempel, C. G. *Philosophy of natural science.* Englewood Cliffs, N.J.: Prentice-Hall, 1966.

Herrnstein, R. J. The evolution of behaviorism. *American Psychologist*, 1977, *32*, 593–603.

Hess, B. B., & Waring, J. M. Parent and child in later life: Rethinking the relationship. In R. M. Lerner & G. B. Spanier (Eds.), *Child influences on marital and family interaction: A life-span perspective.* New York: Academic Press, 1978.

Hess, R. D., & Torney, J. *The development of political attitudes in children.* New York: Aldine, 1967.

Hewitt, L. S. The effects of provocation, intentions, and consequences on children's moral judgments. *Child Development*, 1975, *46*, 540–544.

Hierneaux, J. La croissance des écoliers rwandais. *Royal Academy of Science* (Outre-Mer, Brussels), 1965.

Hiernaux, J. Ethnic differences in growth and development. *Eugenics Quarterly*, 1968, *15*, 12–21.

Hildebrand, J. A. Why runaways leave home. *Journal of Criminal Law, Criminology, and Police Science*, 1963, *54*, 211–216.

Hildebrand, J. A. Reasons for runaways. *Crime and Delinquency*, 1968, *5*, 42–48.

Hill, J. P., & Monks, F. J. *Adolescence and youth in prospect*. Surrey, England: IPC Science and Technology, 1977.

Hirsch, J. Behavior-genetic analysis and its biosocial consequences. *Seminars in Psychiatry*, 1970, *2*, 89–105.

Hite, S. *The Hite report*. New York: Macmillan, 1976.

Hobbs, D. F., & Cole, S. P. Transition to parenthood: A decade replication. *Journal of Marriage and the Family*, 1976, *38*, 723–732.

Hodos, W., & Campbell, C. B. G. Scala Naturae: Why there is no theory in comparative psychology. *Psychological Review*, 1969, *76*, 337–350.

Hoffman, L. W. The employment of women, education, and fertility. *Merrill-Palmer Quarterly*, 1974, 20 99–119.

Hoffman, L. W., & Manis, J. D. Influences of children on marital interaction and parental satisfactions and dissatisfactions. In R. M. Lerner & G. B. Spanier (Eds.), *Child influences on marital and family interaction: A life-span perspective*. New York: Academic Press, 1978.

Hoffman, L. W., & Nye, F. I. *Working mothers*. San Francisco: Jossey-Bass, 1974.

Hoffman, M. L. Sex differences in moral internalization and values. *Journal of Personality and Social Psychology*, 1975, *32*, 720–729.

Hogan, R., & Emler, R. H. Moral development. In M. E. Lamb (Ed.), *Social and personality development*. New York: Holt, Rinehart and Winston, 1978.

Hogan, R., Mankin, D., Conway, J., & Fox, S. Personality correlates of undergraduate marijuana use. *Journal of Consulting and Clinical Psychology*, 1970, *35*, 58–63.

Holstein, C. B. Irreversible, stepwise sequence in the development of moral judgment: A longitudinal study of males and females. *Child Development*, 1976, *47*, 57–61.

Homans, G. C. *Social behavior: Its elementary forms*. New York: Harcourt, Brace & World, 1961.

Horn, J. L. Intelligence—why it grows, why it declines. *Transaction*, 1967, *4*, 23–31.

Horn, J. L. Organization of abilities and the development of intelligence. *Psychological Review*, 1968, *75*, 242–259.

Horn, J. L. Organization of data on life-span development of human abilities. In L. R. Goulet & P. B. Baltes (Eds.), *Life-span developmental psychology: Research and theory*. New York: Academic Press, 1970.

Horn, J. L. Human ability systems. In P. B. Baltes (Ed.), *Life-span development and behavior* (Vol. 1). New York: Academic Press, 1978.

Horn, J. L., & Cattell, R. B. Age differences in primary mental ability factors. *Journal of Gerontology*, 1966, *21*, 210–220.

Horn, J. L. & Donaldson, G. On the myth of intellectual decline in adulthood. *American Psychologist*, 1976, *31*, 701–719.

Horn, J. L., & Knapp, J. R. On the subjective character of the empirical base of Guilford's structure-of-intellect model. *Psychological Bulletin*, 1973, *80*, 33–43.

Huelsman, C. B. The WISC subtest syndrome for disabled readers. *Perceptual and Motor Skills*, 1970, *30*, 535–550.

Hull, C. L. A functional interpretation of the conditioned reflex. *Psychological Review*, 1929, *36*, 498–511.

Hull, C. L. *A behavior system*. New Haven: Yale University Press, 1952.

Hultsch, D. F., & Hickey, T. External validity in the study of human development: Theoretical and methodological issues. *Human Development*, 1978, *21*, 76–91.

Hunt, M. *Sexual behavior in the 1970's*. Chicago: Playboy Press, 1974.

Hurlock, E. B. *Adolescent development*. New York: McGraw-Hill, 1973.

Huston, T. L., & Levinger, G. Interpersonal attraction and relationships. *Annual Review of Psychology*, 1978, *29*, 115–156.

Huston-Stein, A., & Higgins-Trenk, A. Development of females from childhood through adulthood: Career and feminine orientations. In P. B. Baltes (Ed.), *Life-span development and behavior* (Vol. 1). New York: Academic Press, 1978.

Inhelder, B., & Piaget, J. *The growth of logical thinking from childhood to adolescence*. New York: Basic Books, 1958.

Iwawaki, S., & Lerner, R. M. Cross-cultural analyses of body-behavior relations: I. A comparison of body build stereotypes of Japanese and American males and females. *Psychologia*, 1974, *17*, 75–81.

Iwawaki, S., & Lerner, R. M. Cross-cultural analyses of body-behavior relations: III. Developmental intra- and intercultural factor congruence in the body build stereotypes of Japanese and American males and females. *Psychologia*, 1976, *19*, 67–76.

Iwawaki, S., Lerner, R. M., & Chihara, T. Development of personal space schemata among Japanese in late childhood. *Psychologia*, 1977, *20*, 89–97.

Jackson, S. The growth of logical thinking in normal and subnormal children. *British Journal of Educational Psychology*, 1965, *35*, 255–258.

Jaffe, F. S., & Dryfoos, J. G. Fertility control services for adolescents: Access and utilization. *Family Planning Perspectives*, 1976, *8*, 167–175.

Jennings, M. K., & Niemi, R. G. The transmission of political values from parent to child. *American Political Science Review*, 1968, *62*, 169–184.

Jensen, A. R. How much can we boost IQ and scholastic achievement? *Harvard Educational Review*, 1969, *39*, 1–123.

Jensen, A. R. *Educability and group differences*. New York: Harper & Row, 1973.

Johns, E. B., Sutton, W. C., & Webster, L. E. *Health for effective living* (6th ed.). New York: McGraw-Hill, 1975.

Johnson, M. S. Factors relating to reading disability. *Journal of Experimental Education*, 1957, *26*, 1–26.

Johnston, L. D., & Bachman, J. G. Educational institutions. In J. F. Adams (Ed.), *Understanding adolescence* (3d ed.). Boston: Allyn and Bacon, 1976.

Jones, H. E. Adolescence in our society. In Anniversary Papers of the Community Service Society of New York. *The family in a democratic society*. New York: Columbia University Press, 1949, 70–82.

Jones, H. E. Intelligence and problem solving. In J. E. Birren (Ed.), *Handbook of aging and the individual*. Chicago: University of Chicago Press, 1959.

Jones, J. G., & Strowig, R. W. Adolescent identity and self-perception as predictors of scholastic achievement. *Journal of Ed-*

ucational Research, 1968, *62*, 78–82.

Jones, M. C. The later careers of boys who were early- or late-maturing. *Child Development*, 1957, *28*, 133–138.

Jones, M. C. Psychological correlates of somatic development. *Child Development*, 1965, *36*, 899–911.

Jones, M. C., & Bayley, N. Physical maturing among boys as related to behavior. *Journal of Educational Psychology*, 1950, *41*, 129–148.

Jones, M. C., & Mussen, P. H. Self-conceptions, motivations, and inter-personal attitudes of early and late-maturing girls. *Child Development*, 1958, *29*, 491–501.

Jones, W. H., Chernovetz, M. E. O'C., & Hansson, R. O. The enigma of androgyny: Differential implications for males and females. *Journal of Consulting and Clinical Psychology*, 1978, *46*, 298–313.

Kacerguis, M. A., & Adams, G. R. Erikson stage resolution: The relationship between identity and intimacy. *Journal of Youth and Adolescence*, in press.

Kagan, J. Inadequate evidence and illogical conclusions. *Harvard Educational Review*, 1969, *39*, 274–277.

Kagan, J., & Moss, H. A. *Birth to maturity: A study in psychological development*. New York: Wiley, 1962.

Kandel, D. B. Inter- and intragenerational influences on adolescent marijuana use. *Journal of Social Issues*, 1974, *30*, 107–135.

Kandel, D. B., & Faust, R. Sequence and stages in patterns of adolescent drug use. *Archives of General Psychiatry*, 1975, *32*, 923–932.

Kandel, D. B., & Lesser, G. S. Parental and peer influences on educational plans of adolescents. *American Sociological Review*, 1969, *34*, 213–223.

Kandel, D. B., & Lesser, G. S. *Youth in two worlds*. San Francisco: Jossey-Bass, 1972.

Kanin, E. J. Sex aggression by college men. *Medical Aspects of Human Sexuality*, 1970, 4, 25–40.

Kanter, R. M. *Communes: Creating and managing the collective life*. New York: Harper & Row, 1973.

Kantor, D., & Lehr, W. *Inside the family*. San Francisco: Jossey-Bass, 1975.

Katchadourian, H. *The biology of adolescence*. San Francisco: Freeman, 1977.

Katchadourian, H. A., & Lunde, D. T. *Fundamentals of human sexuality* (2d ed.). New York: Holt, Rinehart and Winston, 1975.

Kates, S. L., Yudin, L., & Tiffany, R. K. Concept attainment by deaf and hearing adolescents. *Journal of Educational Psychology*, 1962, *53*, 119–126.

Katz, P. A., & Deutsch, M. Auditory and visual functioning and reading achievement. In M. Deutsch (Ed.), *The disadvantaged child*. New York: Basic Books, 1967.

Kazdin, A. E., & Wilson, G. T. *Evaluation of behavior therapy: Issues, evidence, and research strategies*. Cambridge, Mass.: Ballinger, 1978.

Keasey, C. B. The influence of opinion agreement and quality of supportive reasoning in the evaluation of moral judgments. *Journal of Personality and Social Psychology*, 1974, *30*, 477–482.

Kelley, R. K. The premarital sexual revolution: Comments on research. *Family Coordinator*, 1972, *21*, 334–336.

Kendler, H. H., & Kendler, T. S. Vertical and horizontal processes in human concept learning. *Psychological Review*, 1962, *69*, 1–16.

Keniston, K. *Young radicals: Notes on committed youth*. New York: Harcourt Brace Jovanovich, 1968.

Keniston, K. Youth: A "new" stage of life. *American Scholar*, 1970, *39*, 631–641.

Kiell, N. *The adolescent through*

fiction. New York: International Universities Press, 1959.

Kinsey, A. C., Pomeroy, W. B., & Martin, C. E. *Sexual behavior in the human male*. Philadelphia: Saunders, 1948.

Kinsey, A. C., Pomeroy, W. B., Martin, C. E., & Gebhard, P. H. *Sexual behavior in the human female*. Philadelphia: Saunders, 1953.

Klein, N. C., Alexander, J. F., & Parsons, B. V. Impact of family systems intervention on recidivism and sibling delinquency: A model of primary prevention and program evaluation. *Journal of Consulting and Clinical Psychology*, 1977, *45*, 469–474.

Kluckhohn, C., & Murray, H. Personality formation: The determinants. In C. Kluckhohn & H. Murray (Eds.), *Personality in nature, society, and culture*. New York: Knopf, 1948.

Kluever, R. Mental abilities and disorders of learning. In H. R. Myklebust (Ed.), *Progress in learning disabilities* (Vol. 2). New York: Grune & Stratton, 1971.

Kohlberg, L. The development of modes of moral thinking and choice in the years ten to sixteen. Unpublished doctoral dissertation, University of Chicago, 1958.

Kohlberg, L. The development of children's orientations toward a moral order: 1. Sequence in the development of moral thought. *Vita Humana*, 1963, *6*, 11–33. (a)

Kohlberg, L. Moral development and identification. In H. Stevenson (Ed.), *Child psychology. 62nd Yearbook of the National Society for the Study of Education*. Chicago: University of Chicago Press, 1963. (b)

Kohlberg, L. A cognitive-developmental analysis of children's sex-role concepts and attitudes. In E. Maccoby (Ed.), *The development of sex differences*. Stanford, Calif.: Stanford University Press, 1966.

Kohlberg, L. Stage and sequence: The cognitive-developmental approach to socialization. In D. A. Goslin (Ed.), *Handbook of socialization theory and research*. Chicago: Rand McNally, 1969.

Kohlberg, L. From is to ought: How to commit the naturalistic fallacy and get away with it in the study of moral development. In W. Mischel (Ed.), *Cognitive development and epistemology*. New York: Academic Press, 1971.

Kohlberg, L. Continuities in childhood and adult moral development revisited. In P. B. Baltes & K. W. Schaie (Eds.), *Life-span developmental psychology: Personality and socialization*. New York: Academic Press, 1973.

Kohlberg, L. Moral stages and moralization: The cognitive-developmental approach. In T. Lickona (Ed.), *Moral development and behavior: Theory, research, and social issues*. New York: Holt, Rinehart and Winston, 1976.

Kohlberg, L. Revisions in the theory and practice of moral development. *New Directions for Child Development*, 1978, *2*, 83–88.

Kohlberg, L., & Kramer, R. B. Continuities and discontinuities in childhood and adult moral development. *Human Development*, 1969. *12*, 93–120.

Krause, H. D. Scientific evidence and the ascertainment of paternity. *Family Law Quarterly*, 1971, *5*, 252–281.

Kreps, J. M. (Ed.). *Women and the American economy: A look to the 1980's*. Englewood Cliffs, N.J.: Prentice-Hall, 1976.

Krout, M. A. *Introduction to social psychology*. New York: Harper & Row, 1942.

Krug, S. E., & Henry, T. J. Personality, motivation, and adolescent drug use patterns. *Journal of Counseling Psychology*, 1974, *21*, 440–445.

Kuhlen, R. G., & Arnold, M. Age differences in religious beliefs and problems during adolescence. *Journal of Genetic Psychology*, 1944, *65*, 291–300.

Kuhn, D. Short-term longitudinal evidence for the sequentiality of Kohlberg's early stages of moral development. *Developmental Psychology*, 1976, *12*, 162–166.

Kuhn, D. Mechanisms of cognitive and social development: One psychology or two? *Human Development*, 1978, *21*, 92–118.

Kuhn, D., & Angelev, J. An experimental study of the development of formal operational thought. *Child Development*, 1976, *47*, 697–706.

Kuhn, T. S. The structure of scientific revolutions. Chicago: University of Chicago Press, 1962.

Kurtines, W., & Greif, E. B. The development of moral thought: Review and evaluation of Kohlberg's approach. *Psychological Bulletin*, 1974, *81*, 453–469.

L'Abate, L. The status of adolescent psychology. *Developmental Psychology*, 1971, *4*, 201–205.

Lahaderne, H. M. Attitudinal and intellectual correlates of attention: A study of four sixth grade classrooms. *Journal of Educational Psychology*, 1968, *59*, 320–324.

Lamb, M. E. (Ed.). *Social and personality development*. New York: Holt, Rinehart and Winston, 1978.

Lamb, M. E., & Urberg, K. A. The development of gender role and gender identity. In M. E. Lamb (Ed.), *Social and personality development*. New York: Holt, Rinehart and Winston, 1978.

Landsbaum, J. B., & Willis, R. H. Conformity in early and late adolescence. *Developmental Psychology*, 1971, *4*, 334–337.

Langer, J. *Theories of development*. New York: Holt, Rinehart and Winston, 1969.

Langer, J. Werner's comparative organismic theory. In P. H. Mussen (Ed.), *Carmichael's manual of child psychology* (Vol. 1). New York: Wiley, 1970.

Langford, P. E., & George, S. Intellectual and moral development in adolescence. *British Jour-*

nal of Educational Psychology, 1975, 45, 330–332.

Langton, K. P., & Jennings, M. K. Political socialization and the high school civics curriculum in the United States. American Political Science Review, 1968, 52, 852–867.

Larson, L. E. The influence of parents and peers during adolescence: The situation hypothesis revisited. Journal of Marriage and the Family, 1972, 34, 67–74.

Lasagna, L. The VD epidemic. Philadelphia: Temple University Press, 1975.

Latham, A. J. The relationship between puberal status and leadership in junior high school boys. Journal of Genetic Psychology, 1951, 78, 185–194.

Lathey, J. W. Training effects and conservation of volume. Child Study Center Bulletin. Buffalo, N.Y.: State University College, 1970.

Lavin, D. E. The prediction of academic performance: A theoretical analysis and review of research. New York: Russell Sage Foundation, 1965.

LaVoie, J. C. Ego identity formation in middle adolescence. Journal of Youth and Adolescence, 1976, 5, 371–385.

LaVoie, J. C., & Adams, G. R. Erikson developmental stage resolution and attachment behavior in young adulthood. Adolescence, in press.

Law Enforcement Assistance Administration. Sixth annual report of LEAA. Washington, D.C.: U.S. Government Printing Office, 1974.

Law Enforcement Assistance Administration. Sourcebook of criminal justice statistics, 1974. Washington, D.C.: U.S. Government Printing Office, 1975.

Lawrence, T. S., & Velleman, J. D. Correlates of student drug use in a suburban high school. Psychiatry, 1974, 37, 129–136.

Lazorowitz, R., Stephen, W. G., & Friedman, S. T. Effects of moral justifications and moral reasoning on altruism. Developmental Psychology, 1976, 12, 353–354.

Lefkowitz, M. M., Eron, L. D., Walder, L. O., & Huesmann, L. R. Television violence and child aggression: A follow-up study. In G. A. Comstock & E. A. Rubinstein (Eds.), Television and social behavior, Vol. 3. Television and adolescent aggressiveness. Washington, D.C.: U.S. Government Printing Office, 1972.

Lehfeldt, H. Psychology of contraceptive failure. Medical Aspects of Human Sexuality, 1971, 5, 68–77.

Leifer, A. D., & Roberts, D. F. Children's responses to television violence. In J. P. Murray, E. A. Rubinstein, & G. A. Comstock (Eds.), Television and social behavior, Vol. 2. Television and social learning. Washington, D.C.: U.S. Government Printing Office, 1972.

Leland, H., Shellhaas, M., Nihira, K., & Foster, R. Adaptive behavior: A new dimension in the classification of the mentally retarded. Mental Retardation Abstracts, 1967, 4, 359–387.

LeMasters, E. E. Parents in modern America (rev. ed.). Homewood, Ill.: Dorsey, 1974.

Lerner, R. M. The development of stereotyped expectancies of body build-behavior relations. Child Development, 1969, 40, 137–141. (a)

Lerner, R. M. Some female stereotypes of male body build-behavior relations. Perceptual and Motor Skills, 1969. 28, 363–366. (b)

Lerner, R. M. Showdown at generation gap: Attitudes of adolescents and their parents toward contemporary issues. In H. D. Thornburg (Ed.), Contemporary adolescence (2d ed.). Belmont, Calif.: Brooks/Cole, 1975.

Lerner, R. M. Concepts and theories of human development. Reading, Mass.: Addison-Wesley, 1976.

Lerner, R. M. Nature, nurture, and dynamic interactionism. Human Development, 1978, 21, 1–20.

Lerner, R. M. The stage concept in developmental theory: A dialectical alternative. The Behavioral and Brain Sciences, 1979, 2, 144–145.

Lerner, R. M. A dynamic interaction concept of individual and social relationship development. In R. L. Burgess & T. L. Huston (Eds.), Social exchange in developing relationships. New York: Academic Press, 1979.

Lerner, R. M., Benson, P., & Vincent, S. Development of societal and personal vocational role perception in males and females. Journal of Genetic Psychology, 1976, 129, 167–168.

Lerner, R. M., & Brackney, B. E. The importance of inner and outer body parts attitudes in the self concept of late adolescents. Sex Roles, 1978, 4, 225–238.

Lerner, R. M., & Gellert, E. Body build identification, preference, and aversion in children. Developmental Psychology, 1969, 1, 456–462.

Lerner, R. M., & Iwawaki, S. Cross-cultural analyses of body-behavior relations: II. Factor structure of body build stereotypes of Japanese and American adolescents. Psychologia, 1975, 18, 83–91.

Lerner, R. M., Iwawaki, S., & Chihara, T. Development of personal space schemata among Japanese children. Developmental Psychology, 1976, 12, 466–467.

Lerner, R. M., & Karabenick, S. A. Physical attractiveness, body attitudes and self-concept in late adolescents. Journal of Youth and Adolescence, 1974, 3, 307–316.

Lerner, R. M., Karabenick, S. A., & Meisels, M. One-year stability of children's personal space schemata towards body build. Journal of Genetic Psychology, 1975, 127, 151–152.

Lerner, R. M., Karabenick, S. A., & Stuart, J. L. Relations among physical attractiveness, body attitudes, and self-concept in male and female college students. Journal of Psychology, 1973, 85, 119–129.

Lerner, R. M., Karson, M., Meisels, M., & Knapp, J. R. Actual and perceived attitudes of late adolescents and their parents: The phenomenon of the generation gaps. Journal of Genetic Psychology, 1975, 126, 195–207.

Lerner, R. M., & Knapp, J. R. Actual and perceived intrafamilial attitudes of late adolescents and their parents. Journal of Youth and Adolescence, 1975, 4, 17–36.

Lerner, R. M., & Knapp, J. R. Structure of racial attitudes in white middle adolescents. Journal of Youth and Adolescence, 1976, 5, 283–300.

Lerner, R. M., Knapp, J. R., & Pool, K. B. Structure of body-build stereotypes: A methodological analysis. Perceptual and Motor Skills, 1974, 39, 719–729.

Lerner, R. M., & Korn, S. J. The development of body build stereotypes in males. Child Development, 1972, 43, 912–920.

Lerner, R. M., & Lerner, J. V. Effects of age, sex, and physical attractiveness on child-peer relations, academic performance and elementary school adjustment. Developmental Psychology, 1977, 13, 585–590.

Lerner, R. M., & Miller, R. D. Relation of students' behavioral style to estimated and measured intelligence. Perceptual and Motor Skills, 1971, 33, 11–14.

Lerner, R. M., Orlos, J. B., & Knapp, J. R. Physical attractiveness, physical effectiveness, and self-concept in late adolescence. Adolescence, 1976, 11, 313–326.

Lerner, R. M., Pendorf, J., & Emery, A. Attitudes of adolescents and adults toward contemporary issues. Psychological Reports, 1971, 28, 139–145.

Lerner, R. M., & Pool, K. B. Body build stereotypes: A cross-cultural comparison. Psychological Reports, 1972, 31, 527–532.

Lerner, R. M., & Ryff, C. D. Implementation of the life-span view of human development: The sample case of attachment. In P. B. Baltes (Ed.), Life-span development and behavior (Vol. 1). New York: Academic Press, 1978.

Lerner, R. M., & Schroeder, C. Kindergarten children's active vocabulary about body build. Developmental Psychology, 1971, 5, 179.

Lerner, R. M., Schroeder, C., Rewitzer, M., & Weinstock, A. Attitudes of high school students and their parents toward contemporary issues. Psychological Reports, 1972, 31, 255–258.

Lerner, R. M., & Spanier, G. B. (Eds.). Child influences on marital and family interaction: A life-span perspective. New York: Academic Press, 1978. (a)

Lerner, R. M., & Spanier, G. B. A dynamic interactional view of child and family development. In R. M. Lerner & G. B. Spanier (Eds.), Child influences on marital and family interaction: A life-span perspective. New York: Academic Press, 1978. (b)

Lerner, R. M., Vincent, S., & Benson, P. One-year stability of societal and personal vocational role perceptions of females. Journal of Genetic Psychology, 1976, 129, 173–174.

Levine, E. S. Youth in a soundless world: A search for personality. New York: New York University Press, 1956.

Lewis, M., & Feiring, C. The child's social world. In R. M. Lerner & G. B. Spanier (Eds.), Child influences on marital and family interaction: A life-span perspective. New York: Academic Press, 1978.

Lewis, R. A., & Spanier, G. B. Theorizing about the quality and stability of marriage. In W. Burr, R. Hill, I. Nye, & I. Reiss (Eds.), Contemporary theories about the family. Glencoe, Ill.: Free Press, 1979.

Lewis, R. A., Spanier, G. B., Storm, V., & LeHecka, C. Commitment in married and unmarried cohabitation. Sociological Focus, 1977, 10, 367–374.

Lewontin, R. C. The fallacy of biological determinism. The Sciences, 1976, 16, 6–10.

Liben, L. S. (Ed.). Deaf children: Developmental perspectives. New York: Academic Press, 1978.

Lickona, T. (Ed.). Moral development and behavior: Theory, research, and social issues. New York: Holt, Rinehart and Winston, 1978.

Loehlin, J. C., Lindzey, G., & Spuhler, J. N. Race differences in intelligence. San Francisco: Freeman, 1975.

Loevinger, J. The meaning and measurement of ego development. American Psychologist, 1966, 21, 195–206.

Loevinger, J., & Wessler, R. Measuring ego development (Vol. 1). San Francisco: Jossey-Bass, 1970.

Long, B. H., Henderson, E. H., & Platt, L. Self-other orientations of Israeli adolescents reared in kibbutzim and moshavim. Developmental Psychology, 1973, 8, 300–308.

Looft, W. R. Egocentrism and social interaction in adolescence. Adolescence, 1971, 6, 487–494.

Looft, W. R. The evolution of developmental psychology. Human Development, 1972, 15, 187–201.

Looft, W. R. Socialization and personality throughout the life-span: An examination of contemporary psychological approaches. In P. B. Baltes & K. W. Schaie (Eds.), Life-span developmental psychology: Personality and sociali-

zation. New York: Academic Press, 1973.

Lorenz, K. Durch domestikation verusachte störungen arteigenen verhaltens. *Zeitschrift für Angewandte Psychologie und Charaterkunde,* 1940, *59,* 2–81.

Lorenz, K. *Evolution and modification of behavior.* Chicago: University of Chicago Press, 1965.

Lorenz, K. *On aggression.* New York: Harcourt, Brace & World, 1966.

Lovell, K. A follow-up study of Inhelder and Piaget's "The growth of logical thinking." *British Journal of Psychology,* 1961, *52,* 143–153.

Lyle, J. Television in daily life: Patterns of use (overview). In E. A. Rubinstein, G. A. Comstock, & J. P. Murray (Eds.), *Television and social behavior, Vol. 4. Television in day-to-day life: Patterns of use.* Washington, D.C.: U.S. Government Printing Office, 1972.

Lyle, J., & Hoffman, H. Children's use of television and other media. In E. A. Rubinstein, G. A. Comstock, & J. P. Murray (Eds.), *Television and social behavior, Vol. 4. Television in day-to-day life: Patterns of use.* Washington, D.C.: U.S. Government Printing Office, 1972.

Maccoby, E. E. (Ed.), *The development of sex differences.* Stanford, Calif.: Stanford University Press, 1966.

Maccoby, E. E., & Jacklin, C. N. *The psychology of sex differences.* Stanford, Calif.: Stanford University Press, 1974.

MacDonald, J. M. False accusations of rape. *Medical Aspects of Human Sexuality,* 1973, *7,* 170–194.

Macklin, E. D. Unmarried heterosexual cohabitation on the university campus. Unpublished manuscript, Cornell University, Ithaca, N.Y., 1974.

Marcia, J. E. Determination and construct validity of ego identity status. Unpublished doctoral dissertation, Ohio State University, 1964.

Marcia, J. E. Development and validation of ego-identity status. *Journal of Personality and Social Psychology,* 1966, *3,* 551–558.

Marcia, J. E. Ego identity status: Relationship to change in self-esteem, "general maladjustment," and authoritarianism. *Journal of Personality,* 1967, *1,* 118–133.

Marcia, J. E. Identity six years after: A follow-up study. *Journal of Youth and Adolescence,* 1976, *5,* 145–160.

Marcia, J. E., & Friedman, M. L. Ego identity status in college women. *Journal of Personality,* 1970, *38,* 249–263.

Maresh, M. M. A forty-five year investigation for secular changes in maturation. *American Journal of Physical Anthropology,* 1972, *36,* 103–110.

Martin, J., & Redmore, C. A longitudinal study of ego development. *Developmental Psychology,* 1978, *14,* 189–190.

Martineau, P. Adulthood in the adolescent perspective. *Adolescence,* 1966, *1,* 272–280.

Martinson, F. M. Ego deficiency as a factor in marriage. *American Sociological Review,* 1955, *20,* 161–164.

Martinson, F. M. Ego deficiency as a factor in marriage—a male sample. *Marriage and Family Living,* 1959, *21,* 48–52.

Martorano, S. C. A developmental analysis of performance on Piaget's formal operations tasks. *Developmental Psychology,* 1977, *13,* 666–672.

Masters, W. H., & Johnson, V. E. *Human sexual response.* Boston: Little, Brown, 1966.

Masters, W. H., & Johnson, V. E. *Human sexual inadequacy.* Boston: Little, Brown, 1970.

Matarazzo, J. D. *Wechsler's measurement and appraisal of adult intelligence* (5th ed.). Baltimore: Williams & Wilkins, 1972.

Matsumoto, I., & Suzuki, S. Parent-child relations and runaway behavior in first and repeated instances of running away from home. *Report of the National Research Institute of Police Science, Kagaku Keisatsu Kenkyusho Hokoku* (Text in Japanese; summaries in English), 1974, *15,* 99–104.

Matteson, D. R. Exploration and commitment: Sex differences and methodological problems in the use of identity status categories. *Journal of Youth and Adolescence,* 1977, *6,* 353–374.

Matteson, R. Adolescent self-esteem, family communication, and marital satisfaction. *Journal of Psychology,* 1974, *86,* 35–47.

Maulfair, V. A study of selected personality characteristics of non-runaway, delinquent non-runaway, and runaway youths in Missoula, Montana. Unpublished doctoral dissertation, University of Montana, 1974.

Mayo, C. C., Puryear, H. B., & Richey, H. G. MMPI correlates of religiousness in late adolescent college students. *Journal of Nervous and Mental Disease,* 1969, *149,* 381–385.

McCall, R. Challenges to a science of developmental psychology. *Child Development,* 1977, *48,* 333–344.

McCandless, B. R. *Children.* New York: Holt, Rinehart and Winston, 1967.

McCandless, B. R. *Adolescents.* Hinsdale, Ill.: Dryden Press, 1970.

McCarthy, J. J., & McCarthy, J. F. *Learning disabilities.* Boston: Allyn and Bacon, 1969.

McCary, J. L. *Human sexuality* (3d ed.). New York: Van Nostrand, 1978.

McClelland, D. C. Testing for competence rather than for "intelligence." *American Psychologist,* 1973, *28,* 1–14.

McCord, J., McCord, W., & Thurber, E. Some effects of parental absence on male children. *Journal* of *Abnormal and Social Psychology*, 1962, *64*, 361–369.

McGeorge, C. Situational variation in level of moral judgment. *British Journal of Educational Psychology*, 1974, 44, 116–122.

McIntyre, J. J., & Teevan, J. J. Television violence and deviant behavior. In G. A. Comstock & E. A. Rubinstein (Eds.), *Television and social behavior, Vol. 3. Television and adolescent aggressiveness*. Washington, D.C.: U.S. Government Printing Office, 1972.

McLeod, J. M., Atkin, C. K., & Chaffee, S. H. Adolescents, parents, and television use: Adolescent self-report measures from Maryland and Wisconsin sample. In G. A. Comstock & E. A. Rubinstein (Eds.), *Television and social behavior, Vol. 3. Television and adolescent aggressiveness*. Washington, D.C.: U.S. Government Printing Office, 1972. (a)

McLeod, J. M., Atkin, C. K., & Chaffee, S. H. Adolescents, parents, and television use: Self-report and other-report measures from the Wisconsin sample. In G. A. Comstock & E. A. Rubinstein (Eds.), *Television and social behavior, Vol. 3. Television and adolescent aggressiveness*. Washington, D.C.: U.S. Government Printing Office, 1972. (b)

Mead, M. *Coming of age in Samoa: A psychological study of primitive youth for Western civilization*. New York: Morrow, 1928.

Mead, M. *Growing up in New Guinea*. New York: Morrow, 1930.

Mead, M. *Sex and temperament in three primitive societies*. New York: Morrow, 1935.

Meadow, K. P. Early manual communication in relation to the deaf child's intellectual, social, and communicative functioning. *American Annals of the Deaf*, 1968, *113*, 29–41.

Meadow, K. P. The development of deaf children. In E. M. Hetherington (Ed.), *Review of child development research* (Vol. 5). Chicago: University of Chicago Press, 1975.

Miller, D. R., & Swanson, G. E. *The changing American parent*. New York: Wiley, 1958.

Miller, H. M. The gang boy in Texas. *Southern Methodist University Studies in Sociology*, 1937, *2*, 22–24.

Miller, N. E., & Dollard, J. *Social learning and imitation*. New Haven: Yale University Press, 1941.

Milson, F. *Youth in a changing society*. London: Routledge & Kegan Paul, 1972.

Mischel, W. A social learning view of sex differences in behavior. In E. Maccoby (Ed.), *The development of sex differences*. Stanford, Calif.: Stanford University Press, 1966.

Mischel, W. Sex typing and socialization. In P. H. Mussen (Ed.), *Carmichael's manual of child psychology* (Vol. 2). New York: Wiley, 1970.

Mischel, W. Toward a cognitive social learning reconceptualization of personality. *Psychological Review, 1973, 80*, 252–283.

Misiak, H., & Sexton, V. S. *History of psychology in overview*. New York: Grune & Stratton, 1966.

Misiak, H., & Staudt, V. M. *Catholics in psychology: A historical survey*. New York: McGraw-Hill, 1954.

Moir, D. J. Egocentrism and the emergence of conventional morality in adolescent girls. *Child Development, 1974, 45*, 299–304.

Moltz, H., & Stettner, L. J. The influence of patterned-light deprivation on the critical period for imprinting. *Journal of Comparative and Physiological Psychology, 1961, 54*, 279–283.

Monello, L. E., & Mayer, J. Obese adolescent girls: An unrecognized "minority group"? *American Journal of Clinical Nutrition, 1963, 13*, 35–39.

Money, J., & Ehrhardt, A. E. *Man and woman, boy and girl*. Baltimore: Johns Hopkins University Press, 1972.

Montagu, A. *Adolescent sterility*. Springfield, Ill.: Charles C Thomas, 1946.

Montemayor, R., & Eisen, M. The development of self-conceptions from childhood to adolescence. *Developmental Psychology, 1977, 13*, 314–319.

Moore, M. E., Stunkard, A. J., & Srole, L. Obesity, social class and mental illness. *Journal of the American Medical Association, 1962, 181*, 962–966.

Moores, D. F. An investigation of the psycholinguistic function of deaf adolescents. *Exceptional Children, 1970, 36*, 645–654.

Morrow, W. R., & Wilson, R. C. Family relations of bright high-achieving and under-achieving high school boys. *Child Development, 1961, 32*, 501–510.

Morse, S. J. Attacking youth crime. *New York Times*, Dec. 30, 1978, *19*, 5.

Moshman, D. Consolidation and stage formation in the emergence of formal operations. *Developmental Psychology, 1977, 13*, 95–100.

Munro, G., & Adams, G. R. Ego-identity formation in college students and working youth. *Developmental Psychology, 1977, 13*, 523–524.

Murchison, C. (Ed.). *Handbook of child psychology*. Worcester, Mass.: Clark University Press, 1931.

Mussen, P. H. (Ed.). *Handbook of research methods in child development*. New York: Wiley, 1960.

Mussen, P. H. (Ed.). *Carmichael's manual of child development*. New York: Wiley, 1970.

Mussen, P. H., & Bouterline-Young, H. Relationships between rate of physical maturing and personality among boys of Italian descent. *Vita Humana, 1964, 7*, 186–200.

Mussen, P. H., Conger, J. J., & Kagan, J. *Child development and personality* (4th ed.). New York: Harper & Row, 1974.

Mussen, P. H., & Jones, M. C. Self-conceptions, motivations, and interpersonal attitudes of late- and early-maturing boys. *Child Development*, 1957, *28*, 249–256.

Muuss, R. E. *Theories of adolescence.* New York: Random House, 1966.

Muuss, R. E. Puberty rites in primitive and modern societies. *Adolescence*, 1970, *5*, 109–128.

Muuss, R. E. The philosophical and historical roots of theories of adolescence. In R. E. Muuss (Ed.), *Adolescent behavior and society: A book of readings* (2d ed.). New York: Random House, 1975. (a)

Muuss, R. E. (Ed.). *Adolescent behavior and society: A book of readings* (2d ed.). New York: Random House, 1975. (b)

Muuss, R. E. *Theories of adolescence* (3d ed.). New York: Random House, 1975. (c)

Myers, E. D. *Christianity and reason: Seven essays.* New York: Oxford University Press, 1951.

Myklebust, H. R. *The psychology of deafness, sensory deprivation, learning and adjustment.* New York: Grune & Stratton, 1960.

Namenwirth, J. Z. Failing in New Haven: An analysis of high school graduates and dropouts. *Social Forces*, 1969, *48*, 23–36.

National Advisory Commission on Civil Disorders. *Report of the National Advisory Commission on Civil Disorders.* Washington, D.C.: U.S. Government Printing Office, 1968.

National Center for Health Statistics. Teenagers: Marriages, divorces, parenthood, and mortality. U.S. Department of Health, Education, and Welfare, Series 21, *23*, August 1973.

National Center for Health Statistics. *Vital health statistics,* Series 11, No. 147, 1975.

National Center for Health Statistics. Advance natality statistics 1975. *Monthly Vital Statistics Report*, *25*, Supplement (Feb. 13, 1976).

National Center for Health Statistics. Marriage and divorce. *Vital Statistics of the United States, 1974, 3.* U.S. Department of Health, Education, and Welfare, Hyattsville, Md., 1977. (a)

National Center for Health Statistics. Teenage childbearing: United States, 1966–1975. *Vital Statistics of the United States*, Sept. 8, 1977, *26*. U.S. Department of Health, Education, and Welfare, Hyattsville, Md. (b)

National Center for Health Statistics. Births, marriages, divorces, and deaths for 1977. Provisional statistics. *Monthly Vital Statistics Report, 26*, 1978.

Neimark, E. D. Intellectual development during adolescence. In F. D. Horowitz (Ed.), *Review of child development research* (Vol. 4). Chicago: University of Chicago Press, 1975.

Nelson, D. D. A study of personality adjustment among adolescent children with working and nonworking mothers. *Journal of Educational Research*, 1971, *64*, 328–330.

Nelson, E. Patterns of religious attitude shifts from college to fourteen years later. *Psychological Monographs*, 1956, *70*.

Niemi, R. G. Political socialization. In J. N. Knutson (Ed.), *Handbook of political psychology.* San Francisco: Jossey-Bass, 1973.

Nesselroade, J. R., & Baltes, P. B. Adolescent personality development and historical change: 1970–1972. *Monographs of the Society for Research in Child Development*, 1974, *39*, 1–80.

Nesselroade, J. R., & Reese, H. W. (Eds.). *Life-span developmental psychology: Methodological issues.* New York: Academic Press, 1973.

Neumann, H. H., & Baecker, J. M. Treatment of gonorrhea: Penicillin or tetratcyclines? *Journal of the American Medical Association*, 1972, *219*, 471–474.

Nichols, I. A., & Schauffer, C. B. Self-concept as a predictor of performance in college women. Paper presented at the 83rd Annual Convention of the American Psychological Association, Chicago, 1975.

Nihira, K., Foster, R., Shellhaas, M., & Leland, H. *Adaptive behavior scales manual.* Washington, D.C.: American Association on Mental Deficiency, 1969.

Nisbet, J. D., Illsley, R., Sutherland, A. E., & Douse, M. J. Puberty and test performance: A further report. *British Journal of Educational Psychology*, 1964, *34*, 202–203.

Noland, E. C., & Schuldt, W. J. Sustained attention and reading retardation. *Journal of Experimental Education*, 1971, *40*, 73–76.

Nye. F. I. Effects on mother. In L. W. Hoffman & F. I. Nye (Eds.), *Working mothers.* San Francisco: Jossey-Bass, 1974.

O'Donnell, W. J. Adolescent self-esteem related to feelings toward parents and friends. *Journal of Youth and Adolescence*, 1976, *5*, 179–185.

Offer, D. *The psychological world of the teen-ager.* New York: Basic Books, 1969.

Offer, D., & Howard, K. I. An empirical analysis of the Offer self-image questionnaire for adolescents. *Archives of General Psychiatry*, 1972, *27*, 529–533.

Offer, D., Ostrov, E., & Howard, K. I. The self-image of adolescents: A study of four cultures. *Journal of Youth and Adolescence*, 1977, *6*, 265–280.

Ogburn, W. F. The wolf boy of Agra. *American Journal of Sociology*, 1959, *64*, 449–454.

O'Leary, V. E. Some attitudinal barriers to occupational aspirations in women. *Psychological Bulletin*, 1974, *81*, 809–826.

O'Leary, V. E. *Toward understanding women*. Belmont, Calif.: Brooks/Cole, 1977.

Orlofsky, J. L., Marcia, J. E., & Lesser, I. M. Ego identity status and the intimacy versus isolation crisis of young adulthood. *Journal of Personality and Social Psychology*, 1973, *27*, 211–219.

Overton, W. F. On the assumptive base of the nature-nurture controversy: Additive versus interactive conceptions. *Human Development*, 1973, *16*, 74–89.

Overton, W. F., & Reese, H. W. Models of development: Methodological implications. In J. R. Nesselroade & H. W. Reese (Eds.), *Life-span developmental psychology: Methodological issues*. New York: Academic Press, 1973.

Owen, F. W., Adams, P. A., Forrest, T., Stolz, L. M., & Fischer, S. Learning disorders in children: Sibling studies. *Monographs of the Society for Research in Child Development*, 1971, *36*.

Palmer, F. Research reported at a colloquium at Harvard University, November 1968. (Cited in Kagan, J. Inadequate evidence and illogical conclusions.) *Harvard Educational Review*, 1969, *39*, 126–129.)

Pannor, R., Massarik, F., & Evans, B. *The unmarried father*. New York: Springer, 1971.

Papalia, D. E. The status of several conservation abilities across the life span. *Human Development*, 1972, *15*, 229–243.

Parke, R. D., Berkowitz, L., Leyens, J. P., West, S., & Sebastian, R. J. Film violence and aggression: A field experimental analysis. In L. Berkowitz (Ed.), *Advances in experimental social psychology* (Vol. 10). New York: Academic Press, 1977.

Parker, C. A. Changes in religious beliefs of college students. In M. P. Strommen (Ed.), *Research on religious development: A comprehensive handbook*. New York: Hawthorne Books, 1971.

Paul, E. W., Pilpel, H. F., & Wechsler, N. F. Pregnancy, teenagers, and the law, 1976. *Family Planning Perspectives*, 1976, *8*, 16–21.

Paulsen, E. P. Obesity in children and adolescents. In H. L. Barnett & A. H. Einhorn (Eds.), *Pediatrics*. New York: Appleton Century Crofts, 1972.

Payne, J. S. Prevalence survey of severely mentally retarded in Wyandotte County, Kansas. *Training School Bulletin*, 1971, *67*, 193–197.

Peluffo, N. The notions of conservation and causality in children of different physical and sociocultural environments. *Archives de Psychologie*, 1962, *38*, 275–291.

Peluffo, N. Culture and cognitive problems. *International Journal of Psychology*, 1967, *2*, 187–198.

Pepper, S. C. *World hypotheses*. Berkeley: University of California Press, 1942.

Peterman, D., Ridley, C. A., & Anderson, S. M. A comparison of cohabiting and non-cohabiting college students. *Journal of Marriage and the Family*, 1974, *36*, 344–354.

Piaget, J. La pensée symbolique et la pensée l'enfant. *Archives of Psychology*, Genève, 1923, *18*, 273–304.

Piaget, J. *The psychology of intelligence*. London: Routledge & Kegan Paul, 1950.

Piaget, J. *The origins of intelligence in children*. New York: International Universities Press, 1952.

Piaget, J. *The child's conceptions of numbers*. New York: Norton, 1965.

Piaget, J. *Six psychological studies*. New York: Random House, 1967.

Piaget, J. *The moral judgment of the child*. New York: Free Press, 1969.

Piaget, J. The intellectual development of the adolescent. In G. Caplan & S. Lebovici (Eds.), *Adolescence: Psychosocial perspective*. New York: Basic Books, 1969.

Piaget, J. Piaget's theory. In P. H. Mussen (Ed.), *Carmichael's manual of child psychology* (Vol. 1). New York: Wiley, 1970.

Piaget, J. Intellectual evolution from adolescence to adulthood. *Human Development*, 1972, *15*, 1–12.

Piaget, J., & Inhelder, B. *The psychology of the child*. New York: Basic Books, 1969.

Piersel, W. C., Brody, G. H., & Kratochwill, T. R. A further examination of motivational influences on disadvantaged minority group children's intelligence test performance. *Child Development*, 1977, *48*, 1142–1145.

Pixley, E., & Beckman, E. The faith of youth as shown by a survey in public schools of Los Angeles. *Religious Education*, 1949, *44*, 336–342.

Podd, M. H. Ego identity status and morality: The relationship between two developmental constructs. *Developmental Psychology*, 1972, *6*, 497–507.

Pomeroy, W. B. *Dr. Kinsey and the Institute for Sex Research*. New York: Harper & Row, 1972.

Pospisilova-Zuzakova, V., Stukousky, R., & Valsik, J. A. The menarche in Whites, Negresses, and Mulatto women of Havana. *Zeitschrift füer Äerztliche Fortbilding*, 1965, *59*, 500–516.

Prader, A. Growth and development. In A. Lobhart (Ed.), *Clinical endocrinology*. Springer-Verlag, 1974.

Rainer, J. D., Altshuler, K. Z., & Kallman, F. J. (Eds.). *Family and mental health problems in a deaf population* (2d ed.). Springfield, Ill.: Charles C Thomas, 1969.

Ramos, E. Imagen personal del adolescente nisei. *Revista Latinoamericana de Psicologia*, 1974, *6*, 229–234.

Raskin, J., & Males, C. Not all run

away—some are throwaways. *Parade Magazine*, Aug. 13., 1978, 4–5.

Reed, J. C. The ability deficits of good and poor readers. *Journal of Learning Disabilities*, 1968, *1*, 44–49.

Reed, J. P., & Baali, F. *Faces of delinquency*. Englewood Cliffs, N.J.: Prentice-Hall, 1972.

Reese, H. W., & Overton, W. F. Models of development and theories of development. In L. R. Goulet & P. B. Baltes (Eds.), *Life-span developmental psychology: Research and theory*. New York: Academic Press, 1970.

Rehberg, R. A., & Westby, D. L. Parental encouragement, occupation, education, and family size: Artifactual or independent determinants of adolescent educational expectations? *Social Forces*, 1967, *45*, 362–374.

Reinert, G. Comparative factor analytic studies of intelligence throughout the human life span. In L. R. Goulet & P. B. Baltes (Eds.), *Life-span developmental psychology: Research and theory*. New York: Academic Press, 1970.

Reiss, I. L. *Premarital sexual standards in America*. New York: Free Press of Glencoe, 1960.

Remmers, H. H., & Radler, D. H. *The American teen-ager*. Indianapolis: Bobbs-Merrill, 1957.

Rest, J. R. Longitudinal study of the defining issues test of moral judgment: A strategy for analyzing developmental change. *Developmental Psychology*, 1975, *11*, 738–748.

Rest, J. R., Cooper, D., Coder, R., Masanz, J., & Anderson, D. Judging the important issues in moral dilemmas—an objective measure of development. *Developmental Psychology*, 1974, *10*, 491–501.

Rice, F. P. *The adolescent: Development, relationships, and culture*. Boston: Allyn and Bacon, 1975.

Richardson, S. A. The effect of physical disability on the socialization of the child. In D. A. Goslin (Ed.), *Handbook of socialization: Theory and research*. New York: Rand McNally, 1969.

Richardson, S. A. Handicap, appearance and stigma. *Social Science and Medicine*, 1971, *5*, 621–628.

Riegel, K. F. Influence of economic and political ideologies on the development of developmental psychology. *Psychological Bulletin*, 1972, *78*, 129–141.

Riegel, K. F. Dialectical operations: The final period of cognitive development. *Human Development*, 1973, *16*, 346–370.

Riegel, K. F. Toward a dialectical theory of development. *Human Development*, 1975, *18*, 50–64.

Riegel, K. F. The dialectics of human development. *American Psychologist*, 1976, *31*, 689–700. (a)

Riegel, K. F. From traits and equilibrium toward developmental dialectics. In W. J. Arnold & J. K. Cole (Eds.), *Nebraska symposium on motivation*. Lincoln: University of Nebraska Press, 1976. (b)

Rigsby, L. C., & McDill, E. L. Adolescent peer influence processes: Conceptualization and measurement. *Social Science Research*, 1972, *37*, 189–207.

Rimm, D. C., & Somervill, J. W. *Abnormal psychology*. New York: Academic Press, 1977.

Robbins, T., & Anthony, D. New religions, families, and brainwashing. *Society*, 1978, *15*, 77–83.

Roberge, J. J. Developmental analyses of two formal operational structures: Combinatorial thinking and conditional reasoning. *Developmental Psychology*, 1976, *12*, 563–564.

Roberts, R. E. *The new communes*. Englewood Cliffs, N.J.: Prentice-Hall, 1971.

Robinson, J. P., & Bachman, J. G. Television viewing habits and aggression. In G. A. Comstock & E. A. Rubinstein (Eds.), *Television and social behavior, Vol. 3. Television and adolescent aggressiveness*. Washington, D.C.: U.S. Government Printing Office, 1972.

Rogers, C. R. Forward. In J. T. Hart & T. M. Tomlinson (Eds.), *New directions in client-centered therapy*. Boston: Houghton Mifflin, 1970.

Rogers, D. *The psychology of adolescence*. Englewood Cliffs, N.J.: Prentice-Hall, 1977.

Roof, W. C. Alienation and apostasy. *Society*, 1978, *15*, 41–45.

Roscoe, J. T. Religious beliefs of American college students. *College Student Survey*, 1968, *2*, 49–55.

Rosenberg, F. R., & Simmons, R. G. Sex differences in the self-concept in adolescence. *Sex Roles*, 1975, *1*, 147–159.

Rosenstein, J. Cognitive abilities of deaf children. *Journal of Speech and Hearing Research*, 1960, *3*, 108–119.

Rosenthal, P. *Experimenter effects in behavioral research*. New York: Appleton Century Crofts, 1966.

Ross, A. O. *Psychological disorders of children*. New York: McGraw-Hill, 1974.

Rubin, K. H., & Trotter, K. T. Kohlberg's moral judgment scale: Some methodological considerations. *Developmental Psychology*, 1977, *13*, 535–536.

Rudnick, M., Sterritt, G. M., & Flax, M. Auditory and visual rhythm perception and reading ability. *Child Development*, 1967, *38*, 581–587.

Rudolph, A. H. Control of gonorrhea: Guidelines for antibiotic treatment. *Journal of the American Medical Association*, 1972. *220*, 1587–1589.

Russell, C. S. Transition to parenthood: Problems and gratifications. *Journal of Marriage and the Family*, 1974, *36*, 294–303.

Russo, N. F. The motherhood mandate. *Journal of Social Issues*, 1976, *32*, 143–153.

Sabatino, D. A., & Hayden, D. L. Variation in information processing behaviors. *Journal of Learning Disabilities*, 1970, *4*, 404–412.

Salili, F., Maehr, M. L., & Gillmore, G. Achievement and morality: A cross-cultural analysis of causal attribution and evaluation. *Journal of Personality and Social Psychology*, 1976, *33*, 327–337.

Sameroff, A. Transactional models in early social relations. *Human Development*, 1975, *18*, 65–79.

Sampson, E. E. Psychology and the American ideal. *Journal of Personality and Social Psychology*, 1977, *35*, 767–782.

Sandberg, E. C., & Jacobs, R. I. Psychology of the misuse and rejection of contraception. *Medical Aspects of Human Sexuality*, 1972, *6*, 34–70.

Sanford, N. Developmental status of the entering freshman. In N. Sanford (Ed.), *The American College*. New York: Wiley, 1962.

Santrock, J. W. Influence of onset and type of paternal absence on the first four Eriksonian developmental crises. *Developmental Psychology*, 1970, *3*, 273–274.

Santrock, J. W. Father absence, perceived maternal behavior, and moral development in boys. *Child Development*, 1975, *46*, 753–757.

Sarason, S. B. Jewishness, Blackishness, and the nature-nurture controversy. *American Psychologist*, 1973, *28*, 962–971.

Schacter, B. Identity crisis and occupational processes: An intensive exploratory study of emotionally disturbed male adolescents. *Child Welfare*, 1968, *47*, 26–37.

Schaie, K. W. Cross-sectional methods in the study of psychological aspects of aging. *Journal of Gerontology*, 1959, *14*, 208–215.

Schaie, K. W. A general model for the study of developmental problems. *Psychological Bulletin*, 1965, *64*, 92–107.

Schaie, K. W., & Baltes, P. B. Some faith helps to see the forest: A final comment on the Horn and Donaldson myth of the Baltes-Schaie position on adult intelligence. *American Psychologist*, 1977, *32*, 1118–1120.

Schaie, K. W., & Gribbin, K. J. Adult development and aging. *Annual Review of Psychology*, 1975, *26*, 65–96.

Schaie, K. W., Labouvie, G. V., & Buech, B. U. Generational and cohort-specific differences in adult cognitive functioning: A fourteen-year study of independent samples. *Developmental Psychology*, 1973, *9*, 151–166.

Schaie, K. W., & Strother, C. R. The effects of time and cohort differences on the interpretation of age changes in cognitive behavior. *Multivariate Behavioral Research*, 1968, *3*, 259–294.

Scheck, D. C., Emerick, R., & El-Assal, M. M. Adolescents' perceptions of parent-child external control orientation. *Journal of Marriage and the Family*, 1974, *35*, 643–654.

Schein, J. D. The deaf community: Studies in the social psychology of deafness. Washington, D.C.: Gallaudet College Press, 1968.

Schenkel, S. Relationship among ego identity status, field-independence, and traditional femininity. *Journal of Youth and Adolescence*, 1975, *4*, 73–82.

Schlesinger, H. S., & Meadow, K. P. *Sound and sign: Childhood deafness and mental health*. Berkeley: University of California Press, 1972.

Schneider, F. W., & van Mastrigt, L. A. Adolescent-preadolescent differences in beliefs and attitudes about cigarette smoking. *Journal of Psychology*, 1974, *87*, 71–81.

Schneirla, T. C. The concept of development in comparative psychology. In D. B. Harris (Ed.), *The concept of development*. Minneapolis: University of Minnesota Press, 1957.

Schneirla, T. C. Instinct and aggression: Reviews of Konrad Lorenz, *Evolution and modification of behavior* (Chicago: The University of Chicago Press, 1965), and *On aggression* (New York: Harcourt, Brace & World, 1966). *Natural History*, 1966, *75*, 16.

Schneirla, T. C., & Rosenblatt, J. S. Behavioral organization and genesis of the social bond in insects and mammals. *American Journal of Orthopsychiatry*, 1961, *31*, 223–253.

Schneirla, T. C., & Rosenblatt, J. S. Critical periods in behavioral development. *Science*, 1963, *139*, 1110–1114.

Schonfeld, W. A. The body and the body image in adolescents. In G. Caplan & S. Lebovici (Eds.), *Adolescence: Psychosocial perspectives*. New York: Basic Books, 1969.

Schroeter, A. L., & Lucas, J. B. Gonorrhea diagnosis and treatment. *Obstetrics and Gynecology*, 1972, *39*, 274–285.

Schwebel, M. Logical thinking in college freshman. Final report, Project No. O-B-105, Grant No. OEG-2-7-0039(509), April 1972.

Sears, R. R. Identification as a form of behavioral development. In D. B. Harris (Ed.), *The concept of development*. Minneapolis: University of Minnesota Press, 1957.

Sears, R. R. Your ancients revisited. In E. M. Hetherington, J. W. Hagen, R. Kron, & A. H. Stein (Eds.), *Review of child development research* (Vol. 5). Chicago: University of Chicago Press, 1975.

Sebald, H. *Adolescence: A sociological analysis*. New York: Appleton Century Crofts, 1968.

Self, P. A. The further evolution of the parental imperative. In N. Datan & L. H. Ginsberg (Eds.), *Life-span developmental psychology: Normative life crises*. New York: Academic Press, 1975.

Senf, G. M. Development of immediate memory for bisensory stimuli in normal children and children with learning disorders. *De-*

velopmental *Psychology Monographs*, 1969, *1* (6, Pt. 2).

Senf, G. M., & Freundl, P. C. Sequential auditory and visual memory in learning disabled children. Paper presented at the meeting of the American Psychological Association, Honolulu, 1972.

Sewell, W. H., & Shah, V. P. Parents' education and children's educational aspirations and achievements. *American Sociological Review*, 1968, *33*, 191–209. (a)

Sewell, W. H., & Shah, V. P. Social class, parental encouragement, and educational aspirations. *American Journal of Sociology*, 1968, *73*, 559–572. (b)

Shah, F., Zelnik, M., & Kantner, J. F. Unprotected intercourse among unwed teenagers. *Family Planning Perspectives*, 1975, *7*, 39–43.

Shappell, D. L., Hall, L. G., & Tarrier, R. B. Perceptions of the world of work: Inner-city versus suburbia. *Journal of Counseling Psychology*, 1971, *18*, 55–59.

Shaw, M. E., & White, D. L. The relationship between child-parent identification and academic underachievement. *Journal of Clinical Psychology*, 1965, *21*, 10–13.

Sheldon, W. H. *The varieties of human physique.* New York: Harper & Row, 1940.

Sheldon, W. H. *The varieties of temperament.* New York: Harper & Row, 1942.

Shellow, R., Schamp, J., Liebow, E., & Unger, E. Suburban runaways of the 1960's. *Monographs of the Society for Research in Child Development*, 1967, *32* (Serial No. 111).

Shipman, W. G. Age of menarche and adult personality. *Archives of General Psychiatry*, 1964, *10*, 155–159.

Shuttleworth, F. H. The adolescent period: A pictorial atlas. *Monographs of the Society for Research in Child Development*, 1951, *14* (Serial No. 50).

Siegel, L. S., & Brainerd, C. J. (Eds.). *Alternatives to Piaget: Critical essays on the theory.* New York: Academic Press, 1977.

Silverman, S. R. Rehabilitation for irreversible deafness. *Journal of the American Medical Association*, 1966, *196*, 843–846.

Simmons, R. G., & Rosenberg, F. Sex, sex roles, and self-image. *Journal of Youth and Adolescence*, 1975, 4, 229–258.

Simmons, R. G., Rosenberg, F. R., & Rosenberg, M. Disturbances in the self-image in adolescence. *American Sociological Review*, 1973, *38*, 553–568.

Simpson, E. L. Moral development research: A case study of scientific cultural bias. *Human Development*, 1974, *17*, 81–106.

Singer, R. D., & Kaplan, R. M. (Eds.). Television and social behavior. *Journal of Social Issues*, 1976, *32*, 1–247.

Singh, J. A. L., & Zingg, R. M. *Wolf-children and feral men.* New York: Harper & Row, 1942.

Skinner, B. F. *The behavior of organisms.* New York: Appleton, 1938.

Skinner, B. F. Are theories of learning necessary? *Psychological Review*, 1950, *57*, 211–220.

Skinner, M., & Nutt, A. Adolescents away from home. *Annals of the American Academy of Political and Social Science*, 1944, *236*, 51–59.

Sloan, W., & Birch, J. W. A rationale for degrees of retardation. *American Journal of Mental Deficiency*, 1955, *60*, 262.

Sluckin, W. *Imprinting and early experience.* Chicago: Aldine, 1965.

Smith, G. M. Relations between personality and smoking behavior in preadult subjects. *Journal of Consulting and Clinical Psychology*, 1969, *33*, 710–715.

Smith. T. E. Push versus pull: Intra-family versus peer-group

variables as possible determinants of adolescent orientations toward parents. *Youth and Society*, 1976, *8*, 5–26.

Snyder, E. E. High school student perceptions of prestige criteria. *Adolescence*, 1972, *6*, 129–136.

Sorensen, R. C. *Adolescent sexuality in contemporary America.* New York: World Publishing, 1973.

Sours, J. A. Anorexia nervosa: Nosology, diagnosis, developmental patterns, and power-control dynamics. In G. Caplan & S. Lebovici (Eds.), *Adolescence: Psychosocial perspectives.* New York: Basic Books, 1969.

Spanier, G. B. Sexual socialization and premarital sexual behavior: An empirical investigation of the impact of formal and informal sex education. Unpublished doctoral dissertation, Northwestern University, 1973.

Spanier, G. B. Formal and informal sex education as determinants of premarital sexual behavior. *Archives of Sexual Behavior*, 1976, *5*, 39–67. (a)

Spanier, G. B. Measuring dyadic adjustment: New scales for assessing the quality of marriage and similar dyads. *Journal of Marriage and the Family*, 1976, *38*, 15–28. (b)

Spanier, G. B. Perceived sex knowledge, exposure to eroticism and premarital sexual behavior: The impact of dating. *Sociological Quarterly*, 1976, *17*, 247–261. (c)

Spanier, G. B. Use of recall data in survey research on human sexual behavior. *Social Biology*, 1976, *23*, 244–253. (d)

Spanier, G. B. Sexual socialization: A conceptual review. *International Journal of Sociology of the Family*, 1977, *6*, 121–146.

Spanier, G. B. *Human sexuality in a changing society.* Minneapolis: Burgess, 1979.

Spanier, G. B., & Fishel, C. The housing project and familial functions: Consequences for low income, urban families. *Family Coordinator*, 1973, *22*, 235–240.

Spanier, G. B., & Glick, P. C. The life cycle of American families: An expanded analysis. *Journal of Family History*, 1980, *5*, in press.

Spearman, C. *The abilities of man.* New York: Macmillan, 1927.

Spelt, D. K. The conditioning of the human fetus in utero. *Journal of Experimental Psychology*, 1948, *38*, 375–376.

Spence, J. T., & Helmreich, R. *Masculinity and femininity: Their psychological dimensions, correlates and antecedents.* Austin: University of Texas Press, 1978.

Spitz, R. A. Hospitalism: An inquiry into the genesis of psychiatric conditions in early childhood. *Psychoanalytic Study of the Child*, 1945, *1*, 53–74, 113–117.

Staffieri, J. R. Body build and behavioral expectancies in young females. *Developmental Psychology*, 1972, *6*, 125–127.

Stein, A. H. The effects of maternal employment and educational attainment on the sex-typed attributes of college females. *Social Behavior and Personality*, 1973, *1*, 111–114.

Stein, A. H. Sex role development. In J. F. Adams (Ed.), *Understanding adolescence* (3d ed.). Boston: Allyn and Bacon, 1976.

Stein, A. H., & Bailey, M. M. The socialization of achievement orientation in females. *Psychological Bulletin*, 1973, *80*, 345–366.

Stein, A. H., & Friedrich, L. K. Television content and young children's behavior. In J. P. Murray, E. A. Rubinstein, & G. A. Comstock (Eds.), *Television and social behavior, Vol. 2. Television and social learning.* Washington, D.C.: U.S. Government Printing Office, 1972.

Stein, A. H., & Friedrich, L. K. Impact of television on children and youth. In E. M. Hetherington (Ed.), *Review of Child Development Research* (Vol. 5). Chicago: University of Chicago Press, 1975.

Stern, W. L. Über die psychologischen methoden der Intelligenzprüfung. *Ber. V. Kongress Exp., Psychol.*, 1912, *16*, 1–160. American translation by G. M. Whipple, The psychological methods of testing intelligence. *Educational Psychology Monographs*, No. 13. Baltimore: Warwick & York, 1914.

Sterritt, G. M., & Rudnick, M. Auditory and visual rhythm perception in relation to reading ability in fourth grade boys. *Perceptual and Motor Skills*, 1966, *22*, 859–864.

Stoller, R. J. *Sex and gender: On the development of masculinity and femininity.* New York: Science House, 1968.

Stolz, H. R., & Stolz, L. M. Adolescence related to somatic variation. In *Adolescence: 43rd yearbook of the National Committee for the Study of Education.* Chicago: University of Chicago Press, 1944.

Straus, M. A., & Steinmetz, S. K. *Violence in the family.* New York: Dodd, Mead, 1974.

Strauss, S., Danziger, J., & Ramati, T. University students' understanding of nonconservation: Implications for structural reversion. *Developmental Psychology*, 1977, *13*, 359–363.

Stuckless, E. R., & Birch, J. W. The influence of early manual communication on the linguistic development of deaf children. *American Annals of the Deaf*, 1966, *111*, 452–460, 499–504.

Stunkard, A. J. Obesity. In A. M. Freman, H. I. Kaplan, & B. J. Sadock (Eds.), *Comprehensive textbook of psychiatry.* Baltimore: Williams & Wilkins, 1975.

Stunkard, A. J., & Mendelson, M. Obesity and the body image: I. Characteristics of disturbances in the body image of some obese persons. *American Journal of Psychiatry*, 1967, *123*, 1296–1300.

Sugar, M. (Ed.). *The adolescent in group and family therapy.* New York: Brunner/Mazel, 1975.

Sullivan, E., Tietze, C., & Dryfoos, J. G. Legal abortion in the United States, 1975–1976. *Family Planning Perspectives*, 1977, *9*, 116–129.

Surber, C. F. Developmental processes in social inference: Averaging of intentions and consequences in moral judgment. *Developmental Psychology*, 1977, *13*, 654–665.

Survey of college freshman. *Intellect*, 1974, *102*, 482.

Sutton-Smith, B. *Child psychology.* New York: Appleton Century Crofts, 1973.

Sutton-Smith, B., & Rosenberg, B. G. *The sibling.* New York: Holt, Rinehart and Winston, 1970.

Swift, D. F. Family environment and 11+ success: Some basic predictions. *British Journal of Educational Psychology*, 1967, *37*, 10–21.

Tangri, S. S. Determinants of occupational role innovation in college women. *Journal of Social Issues*, 1972, *28*, 177–199.

Tanner, J. M. *Growth at adolescence* (2d ed.). Oxford: Blackwell, 1962.

Tanner, J. M. The secular trend towards earlier physical maturation. *Trans. Soc. Geneeskd.*, 1966, *44*, 524–538.

Tanner, J. M. Physical growth. In P. H. Mussen (Ed.), *Carmichael's manual of child psychology* (Vol. 1, 3d ed.). New York: Wiley, 1970.

Tanner, J. M. Growing up. *Scientific American*, 1973, *229*, 34–43.

Tanner, J. M., Whitehouse, R. H., & Takaishi, M. Standards from birth to maturity for height, weight, height velocity and weight velocity: British children, 1965. *Archives of Diseases in*

Childhood, 1966, *41*, 457–471, 613–635.

Terman, L. M. *The measurement of intelligence.* Boston: Houghton, 1916.

Terman, L. M. (Ed.). *Genetic studies of genius, I: Mental and physical traits of a thousand gifted children.* Stanford, Calif.: Stanford University Press, 1925.

Terman, L. M., & Oden, M. H. *Genetic studies of genius, V: The gifted group at mid-life.* Palo Alto, Calif.: Stanford University Press, 1959.

Terman, L. M., & Tyler, L. E. Psychological sex differences. In L. Carmichael (Ed.), *Manual of child psychology.* New York: Wiley, 1954.

Thomas, A., & Chess, S. *Temperament and development.* New York: Brunner/Mazel, 1977.

Thomas, A., Chess, S., & Birch, H. G. *Temperament and behavior disorders in children.* New York: New York University Press, 1968.

Thomas, A., Chess, S., & Birch, H. G. The origin of personality. *Scientific American*, 1970, *223*, 102–109.

Thomas, A., Chess, S., Birch, H. G., Hertzig, M. E., & Korn, S. *Behavioral individuality in early childhood.* New York: New York University Press, 1963.

Thompson, L., & Spanier, G. B. Influence of parents, peers, and partners on the contraceptive use of college men and women. *Journal of Marriage and the Family*, 1978, *40*, 481–492.

Thornburg, H. Adolescence: A reinterpretation. *Adolescence*, 1970, *5*, 463–484.

Thornburg, H. D. Student assessment of contemporary issues. *College Student Survey*, 1969, *3*, 1–5, 22.

Thornburg, H. D. Student assessment of contemporary issues. In H. D. Thornburg (Ed.), *Contempo-* *rary adolescence: Readings.* Monterey, Calif.: Brooks/Cole, 1971.

Thorndike, E. L. The newest psychology. *Educational Review*, 1904, *28*, 217–227.

Thrasher, F. M. *The gang* (rev. ed.). Chicago: University of Chicago Press, 1936.

Thurstone, L. L., & Thurstone, T. G. *SRA primary mental abilities.* Chicago: Science Research Associates, 1962.

Tobach, E., & Schneirla, T. C. The biopsychology of social behavior of animals. In R. E. Cooke & S. Levin (Eds.), *Biologic basis of pediatric practice.* New York: McGraw-Hill, 1968.

Toder, N. L., & Marcia, J. E. Ego identity status and response to conformity pressure in college women. *Journal of Personality and Social Psychology*, 1973, *26*, 287–294.

Tomlinson-Keasey, C. Formal operation in females from eleven to fifty-four years of age. *Developmental Psychology*, 1972, *6*, 364.

Tomlinson-Keasey, C., & Keasey, C. B. The mediating role of cognitive development in moral judgment. *Child Development*, 1974, *45*, 291–298.

Torgensen, J. Problems and prospects in the study of learning disabilities. In E. M. Hetherington (Ed.), *Review of child development research* (Vol. 5). Chicago: University of Chicago Press, 1975.

Towler, J. O., & Wheatley, G. Conservation concepts in college students: A replication and critique. *Journal of Genetic Psychology*, 1971, *118*, 265–270.

Traeldal, A. The work role and life satisfaction over the life-span. Paper presented at the Biennial Meeting of the International Society for the Study of Behavioral Development, Ann Arbor, Mich., August 1973.

Turiel, E. Developmental processes in the child's moral thinking. In P. H. Mussen, J. Langer, & M. Covington (Eds.), *Trends and issues in developmental psychology.* New York: Holt, Rinehart and Winston, 1969.

Turiel, E. Conflict and transition in adolescent moral development. *Child Development*, 1974, *45*, 14–29.

Turiel, E., & Rothman, G. The influence of reasoning on behavioral choices at different stages of moral development. *Child Development*, 1972, *43*, 741–756.

Uniform Crime Reports for the United States, 1975. Federal Bureau of Investigation, Washington, D.C.: U.S. Government Printing Office, 1976.

U.S. Bureau of the Census. *Characteristics of American youth: 1974.* Current Population Reports, Series P-23, No. 51, April 1975. Washington, D.C.: U.S. Government Printing Office.

U.S. Bureau of the Census. *Number, timing, and duration of marriages and divorces in the United States: June, 1975.* Current Population Reports, Series P-20, No. 297, October 1976. Washington, D.C.: U.S. Government Printing Office.

U.S. Bureau of the Census. *Statistical abstract of the United States, 1977* (98th ed.), 1977. Washington, D.C.: U.S. Government Printing Office. (a)

U.S. Bureau of the Census. *Educational attainment in the United States: March 1977 and 1976.* Current Population Reports, Series P-20, No. 314, December 1977. Washington, D.C.: U.S. Government Printing Office. (b)

U.S. Bureau of the Census. *Characteristics of American children and youth: 1976.* Current Population Reports, Series P-23, No. 66, January 1978. Washington, D.C.: U.S. Government Printing Office. (a)

U.S. Bureau of the Census. *School enrollment—social and economic* characteristics of students: October 1976. Current Population Reports, Series P-20, No. 319, February 1978. Washington, D.C.: U.S. Government Printing Office. (b)

U.S. Bureau of the Census. *Perspectives on American husbands and wives.* Current Population Reports, Series P-23, No. 77, December 1978. Washington, D.C.: U.S. Government Printing Office. (c)

U.S. Bureau of the Census. Unpublished data analyzed by Graham Spanier and Paul Glick, 1979.

Vande Voort, L., & Senf, G. M. Audiovisual integration in retarded readers. *Journal of Learning Disabilities,* 1973, *6,* 49–58.

Vande Voort, L., Senf, G. M., & Benton, A. L. Development of audiovisual integration in normal and retarded readers. *Child Development,* 1972, *4,* 1260–1272.

Vaughan, V. C., & McKay, R. J. (Eds.). *Nelson textbook of pediatrics* (10th ed.). Philadelphia: Saunders, 1975.

Veevers, J. E. Voluntarily childless wives: An exploratory study. *Sociology and Social Research,* 1973, *57,* 356–366.

Vernon, M. Current etiological factors in deafness. *American Annals of the Deaf,* 1968, *113,* 1–12.

Victor, H. R., Grossman, J. C., & Eisenman, R. Openness to experience and marijuana use in high school students. *Journal of Consulting and Clinical Psychology,* 1973, *41,* 78–85.

Vigersky, R. A. (Ed.). *Anorexia nervosa.* New York: Raven Press, 1977.

Vincent, C. E. *Unmarried mothers.* New York: Free Press, 1961.

Voss, H. L., Wendling, A., & Elliott, D. S. Some types of high-school dropouts. *Journal of Educational Research,* 1966, *59,* 363–368.

Waber, D. P. Sex differences in mental abilities, hemispheric lateralization, and rate of physical growth in adolescence. *Developmental Psychology,* 1977, *13,* 29–38.

Wadsworth, B. J. *Piaget's theory of cognitive development.* New York: McKay, 1971.

Walker, R. N. Body build and behavior in young children: I. Body build and nursery school teacher's ratings. *Monographs of the Society for Research in Child Development,* 1962 (Serial No. 3), 27.

Waller, W. The rating and dating complex. *American Sociological Review,* 1937, *2,* 727–734.

Walters, R. H., & Doan, H. Perceptual and cognitive functioning of retarded readers. *Journal of Consulting Psychology,* 1962, *26,* 355–361.

Walters, R. H., & Kosowski, I. Symbolic learning and reading retardation. *Journal of Consulting Psychology,* 1963, *27,* 75–82.

Walters, R. H., & Thomas, E. L. Enhancement of punitiveness by visual and audio-visual displays. *Canadian Journal of Psychology,* 1963, *17,* 244–255.

Waterman, A. S., & Goldman, J. A. A longitudinal study of ego identity development at a liberal arts college. *Journal of Youth and Adolescence,* 1976, *5,* 361–370.

Waterman, A. S., Kohutis, E., & Pulone, J. The role of expressive writing in ego identity formation. *Developmental Psychology,* 1977, *13,* 286–287.

Waterman, A. S., & Waterman, C. K. A longitudinal study of changes in ego identity status during the freshman year at college. *Developmental Psychology,* 1971, *5,* 167–173.

Waterman, C. K., Beubel, M. E., & Waterman, A. S. Relationship between resolution of the identity crisis and outcomes of previous psychosocial crises. *Proceedings of the 78th Annual Convention of the American Psychological Association,* 1970, *5,* 467–468.

Waterman, G., Geary, P., & Waterman, C. Longitudinal study of changes in ego identity status from the freshman to the senior year at college. *Developmental Psychology,* 1974, *10,* 387–392.

Watson, J. B. Psychology as the behaviorist views it. *Psychological Review,* 1913, *20,* 158–177.

Watson, J. B. *Psychology from the standpoint of a behaviorist.* Philadelphia: Lippincott, 1918.

Watson, J. B. *Psychological care of infant and child.* New York: Norton, 1928.

Watson, J. B., & Raynor, R. Conditional emotional reactions. *Journal of Experimental Psychology,* 1920, *3,* 1–14.

Weatherly, D. Self-perceived rate of physical maturation and personality in late adolescence. *Child Development,* 1964, *35,* 1197–1210.

Webb, E. J., Campbell, D. T., Schwartz, R. D., & Sechrest, L. *Unobtrusive measures: Nonreactive research in the social sciences.* Chicago: Rand McNally, 1966.

Wechsler, H., & McFadden, M. Sex differences in adolescent alcohol and drug use: A disappearing phenomenon. *Journal of Studies on Alcohol,* 1976, *37,* 1291–1301.

Weiner, B., & Peter, N. A cognitive-developmental analysis of achievement and moral judgment. *Developmental Psychology,* 1973, *9,* 290–309.

Weinstock, A., & Lerner, R. M. Attitudes of late adolescents and their parents toward contemporary issues. *Psychological Reports,* 1972, *30,* 239–244.

Wells, W. D. Television and aggression: Replication of an experimental field study. Unpublished manuscript, University of Chicago Graduate School of Business, 1973.

Werner, H. *Comparative psycholo-*

gy *of mental development.* New York: International Universities Press, 1948.

Werner, H. The concept of development from a comparative and organismic point of view. In D. B. Harris (Ed.), *The concept of development.* Minneapolis: University of Minnesota Press, 1957.

Whipple, C. I., & Kodman, F. A study of discrimination and perceptual learning with retarded readers. *Journal of Educational Psychology,* 1969, *60,* 1–5.

White, C. B. Moral development in Bahamian school children: A cross-cultural examination of Kohlberg's stages of moral reasoning. *Developmental Psychology,* 1975, *11,* 535–536.

White, C. B., Bushnell, N., & Regnemer, J. L. Moral development in Bahamian school children: A 3-year examination of Kohlberg's stages of moral development. *Developmental Psychology,* 1978, *14,* 58–65.

White, S. H. The learning-maturation controversy: Hall to Hull. *Merrill-Palmer Quarterly,* 1968, *14,* 187–196.

White, S. H. The learning theory tradition and child psychology. In P. H. Mussen (Ed.), *Carmichael's manual of child psychology* (3d ed.). New York: Wiley, 1970.

Wiggins, J. S. Personality structure. In P. R. Farnsworth, M. R. Rosenzweig, & J. T. Polepka (Eds.), *Annual review of psychology* (Vol. 19). Palo Alto, Calif.: Annual Reviews, 1968.

Wilkins, L. *The diagnosis and treatment of endocrine disorders in childhood and adolescence,* (3d ed.). Springfield, Ill.: Charles C Thomas, 1965.

Willems, E. P. Behavioral ecology and experimental analysis: Courtship is not enough. In J. R. Nessel-roade & H. W. Reese (Eds.), *Lifespan development psychology: Methodological issues.* New York: Academic Press, 1973.

Winch, R. F. *The modern family* (3d ed.). New York: Holt, Rinehart and Winston, 1971.

Winch, R. F., & Gordon, M. T. *Family structure and function as influence.* Lexington, Mass.: Heath, 1974.

Winch, R. F., & Spanier, G. B. Scientific method in the study of the family. In R. F. Winch & G. B. Spanier (Eds.), *Selected studies in marriage and the family* (4th ed.). New York: Holt, Rinehart and Winston, 1974.

Winter, G. D., & Nuss, E. M. *The young adult.* Glenview, Ill.: Scott, Foresman, 1969.

Wohlwill, J. F. *The study of behavioral development.* New York: Academic Press, 1973.

Wolf, R. M. The identification and measurement of environmental process variables related to intelligence. Unpublished doctoral dissertation, University of Chicago, 1964.

Worell, J. Sex roles and psychological well-being: Perspectives on methodology. *Journal of Consulting and Clinical Psychology,* 1978, *46,* 777–791.

Wuthnow, R., & Glock, C. Y. Religious loyalty, defection, and experimentation among college youth. *Journal for the Scientific Study of Religion,* 1973, *12,* 157–180.

Wylie, R. C. *The self-concept* (Vol. 1). Lincoln: University of Nebraska Press, 1974.

Yablonsky, L. *The violent gang.* New York: Macmillan, 1962.

Yancy, W. S., Nader, P. R., & Burnham, K. L. Drug use and attitudes of high school students. *Pediatrics,* 1972, *50,* 739–745.

Yankelovich, D. *Youth in turmoil.* New York: Time-Life Books, 1969.

Yankelovich, D. *The changing values on campus.* New York: Pocket Books, 1972.

Young, R. K., Dustin, D. S., & Holtzman, W. H. Change in attitude toward religion in a Southern university. *Psychological Reports,* 1966, *18,* 39–46.

Youniss, J., & Dean, A. Judgment and imagery aspects of operations: A Piagetian study with Korean and Costa Rican children. *Child Development,* 1974, *45,* 1020–1031.

Yussen, S. R. Moral reasoning from the perspective of others. *Child Development,* 1976, *47,* 551–555.

Zajonc, R. B., & Marcus, G. B. Birth order and intellectual development. *Psychological Review,* 1975, *82,* 74–88.

Zeller, W. W. Adolescent attitudes and cutaneous health. *Journal of School Health,* 1970, *40,* 115–120.

Zelnik, M., & Kantner, J. F. Sexual and contraceptive experience of young unmarried women in the United States, 1976 and 1971. *Family Planning Perspective,* 1977, *9,* 55–71.

Zelnik, M., & Kantner, J. F. First pregnancies to women aged 15–19: 1976 and 1971. *Family Planning Perspectives,* 1978, *10,* 11–20. (a)

Zelnik, M., & Kantner, J. F. Contraceptive patterns and premarital pregnancy among women aged 15–19 in 1976. *Family Planning Perspectives,* 1978, *10,* 135–142. (b)

Zubin, J., & Money, J. (Eds.). *Contemporary sexual behavior: Critical issues in the 1970's.* Baltimore: Johns Hopkins University Press, 1973.

Name Index

Name Index

Adams, G. R., 11, 331, 345, 351, 463, 464
Adams, P. A., 418
Adelson, J., 52, 54, 58, 66, 79, 135, 136, 138, 156, 257, 345, 365, 366, 441
Alexander, D., 418
Alexander, J. F., 461
Allport, G. W., 66, 368
Almquist, E. M., 388
Altshuler, K. Z., 402
Ames, R., 210
Anastasi, A., 110, 111, 225, 232
Anderson, A. E., 399
Anderson, D., 271, 274, 275, 277
Anderson, J. E., 229
Anderson, S. M., 469
Angelev, J., 250
Angrist, S. S., 388
Anthony, D., 69, 70
Anthony, J., 36, 38, 39, 368
Arbuthnot, J., 276, 277
Aristotle, 90–92, 97
Arlin, P. K., 252
Arnold, M., 67, 68
Ash, M. J., 252
Atkin, C. K., 82
Ausubel, D. P., 59, 60, 66

Baali, F., 454
Bachman, J. G., 60, 61, 63–65, 82, 459
Bachrach, R., 279
Bacon, C., 387
Bacon, M. K., 365, 374
Baecker, J. M., 319
Baer, D. M., 24, 93, 141, 259, 328
Bailey, M. M., 389
Bain, A., 93
Bakan, D., 375, 376, 382
Bakwin, H., 202
Baldwin, A. H., 314, 315
Baldwin, J., 443
Balow, I. H., 404
Baltes, M. M., 180, 227
Baltes, P. B., 6, 7, 10, 24, 29, 30, 87, 106, 129, 172, 176, 179, 180, 215, 224, 225, 227, 229, 230, 232, 235, 237, 389
Bandura, A., 38, 52, 54, 66, 135–138, 142, 156, 257, 259, 274, 441
Bardwick, J. M., 385
Barnes, M., 273
Barnett, H. L., 163
Barry, H., 365, 374
Barton, M. E., 402
Bayley, N., 18, 175, 206, 208, 209, 227, 228

Russell, C. S., 446
Russo, N. F., 385
Rutherford, E., 280
Ryff, C. D., 224

Sabatino, D. A., 420
Salili, F., 273
Salinger, J. D., 303
Sameroff, A., 145
Sampson, E. E., 158
Sandberg, E. C., 307
Sanford, N., 353
Santrock, J. W., 284, 351
Sarason, S. B., 358
Sartre, J. P., 280, 390
Schacter, B., 348
Schaie, K. W., 5, 6, 22, 29, 106, 172,
    174–176, 180, 224, 225, 227,
    229–232
Schamp, J., 462, 463, 465
Schauffer, C. B., 388
Scheck, D. C., 391
Schein, J. D., 402
Schenkel, S., 331, 350
Schlesinger, H. S., 404
Schneider, F. W., 408
Schneirla, T. C., 44, 131, 139–141
Schonfeld, W. A., 26, 190, 192–194,
    197, 198, 200–202
Schroeder, C., 53, 58, 213, 217
Schroeter, A. L., 319
Schuldt, W. J., 421
Schwartz, R. D., 169
Schwebel, M., 250
Sears, R. R., 102–104, 259
Sebastian, R. J., 81
Sechrest, L., 169
Self, P. A., 377
Senf, G. M., 419, 420
Sewell, W. H., 61
Sexton, V. S., 91, 92, 98, 104
Shah, F., 307
Shah, V. P., 61
Shappell, D. L., 386
Shaw, G. B., 39
Shaw, M. E., 52, 62
Shea, J. A., 351
Sheldon, W. H., 181, 214, 215, 220,
    328, 329
Shellhaas, M., 415, 417

Shellow, R., 462, 463, 465
Shipman, W. G., 213
Shuttleworth, F. H., 206, 207
Siegel, L. S., 105
Silverman, S. R., 401
Simmons, R. G., 380, 389
Simon, T., 101, 224, 225
Simpson, E. L., 264, 269, 270, 273
Sinatra, F., 439
Singer, R., 81
Singh, J. A. L., 44
Skinner, B. F., 15, 93, 96, 103, 142
Skinner, M., 464
Sklorowski, E., 200
Sloan, W., 415, 416
Smith, G. M., 409
Smith, M. B., 54, 268, 280–284
Smith, T. E., 52
Snyder, E. E., 60
Socrates, 234
Somervill, J. W., 431–433
Sorensen, R. C., 290, 297
Sours, J. A., 399
South, D. R., 52, 53
Spanier, G. B., 11, 16, 65, 106, 145,
    162, 289, 295, 296, 299, 300, 304,
    305, 308, 320, 383, 385, 411, 412,
    430, 444, 445, 448, 461, 470, 471
Spearman, C., 232
Spelt, D. K., 98
Spence, J. T., 377
Spitz, R. A., 44
Spuhler, J. N., 164
Srole, L., 398
Staffieri, J. R., 211, 213
Staudt, V. M., 91
Stein, A. H., 80–83, 388, 389
Stephen, W. G., 272
Stern, W. L., 226
Sterritt, G. M., 419, 420
Stettner, L. J., 131, 139
Stewart, G. K., 305
Stingle, K. G., 142
Stoller, R. J., 291
Stolz, H. R., 212, 213
Stolz, L. M., 212, 213, 418
Storm, V., 471
Strauss, S., 248
Strother, C. R., 174, 175
Strowig, R. W., 350

Subject Index

Subject Index

Erikson's theory:
    of psychosocial development: stages of:
        anal-musculature (second), 336
        genital-locomotor (third), 336
        latency, (fourth) 337
        maturity (seventh), 342
        oral sensory (first), 335–336
        puberty and adolescence (fifth),
          337–339
        young adulthood (sixth), 340–341
      trust versus mistrust, 335
      universality, 330
Erogenous zone, 148
Estrogens, 193
Exocrine glands, 192
Explanatory studies, defined, 164–165

Family:
    characteristics of, 49
    defined, 49
    importance of parental influences,
      52–53
    nonparent influences, 50–52
Father identification, 149
Fertilization, 192
Fixation, 148
Follicles, primary graffian, 194
Fraternal twins, 118
Freud's belief about personality
    structures, 152–153
Freud's ideas, critique of, 151–152
Freud's theory:
    of moral development, 258–259
    of psychosexual stage development,
      147–152
      stages: anal (second), 148–149
        genital (fifth), 151
        latency (fourth), 151
        oral (first), 148
        phallic (third), 149–151
Friends, parent-adolescent
    conflicts over, 137

Gangs, 47, 461–462
    and delinquency, 461
    delinquent, 461
    duration of membership in, 462
    reasons for, 461

Gangs:
    social, 461
    violent, 461–462
Gender identity clinics, 291
Generation, defined, 45
Generation gap, 54
Genetic material, 114
Genotype, 114
Genotype-phenotype relationships, 119
Genotypic invariancy, 114
Gestation, 98, 357
Gonadotropic hormones, 193
Gonads, 193
Growth:
    continuous, 138
    defined, 204
    disturbances of, 410–411
    surgent, 138
    tumultuous, 138
Growth spurt, 26, 195

Habits, 143
Hall's influence in shaping develop-
    mental psychology, 98
Hall's personal accomplishments,
    97–98
Hall's recapitulationist theory,
    99–100
Handicaps:
    biological, 397
    non-self-induced, 400–404
Harelips, 404
Hearing loss, 401–404
    causes of, 402
    and cognitive development, 402–403
    and effects of social interaction
      histories, 404
    and language development, 402
    magnitude of, 401–402
    and personality development, 403
Hemorrhage, 451
Hepatitis, 405
Hermaphrodites, 290–291
Heterosexual, 290
Homosexual, 290
Homunculus idea of creation, 92
Hormonal changes, 26

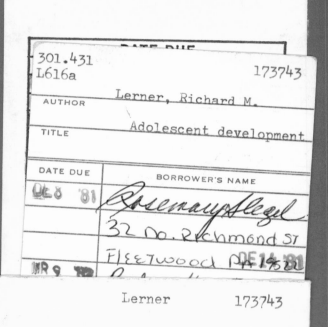